Lecture Notes in Compute

Lecture Notes in Artificial Intelligence 14979

Founding Editor

Jörg Siekmann

Series Editors

Randy Goebel, *University of Alberta, Edmonton, Canada*
Wolfgang Wahlster, *DFKI, Berlin, Germany*
Zhi-Hua Zhou, *Nanjing University, Nanjing, China*

The series Lecture Notes in Artificial Intelligence (LNAI) was established in 1988 as a topical subseries of LNCS devoted to artificial intelligence.

The series publishes state-of-the-art research results at a high level. As with the LNCS mother series, the mission of the series is to serve the international R & D community by providing an invaluable service, mainly focused on the publication of conference and workshop proceedings and postproceedings.

Tarek R. Besold · Artur d'Avila Garcez ·
Ernesto Jimenez-Ruiz · Roberto Confalonieri ·
Pranava Madhyastha · Benedikt Wagner
Editors

Neural-Symbolic Learning and Reasoning

18th International Conference, NeSy 2024
Barcelona, Spain, September 9–12, 2024
Proceedings, Part I

Editors
Tarek R. Besold
Sony AI
Barcelona, Spain

Artur d'Avila Garcez
City, University of London
London, UK

Ernesto Jimenez-Ruiz
City, University of London
London, UK

Roberto Confalonieri
University of Padova
Padua, Italy

Pranava Madhyastha
City, University of London
London, UK

Benedikt Wagner
City, University of London
London, UK

ISSN 0302-9743　　　　　　ISSN 1611-3349　(electronic)
Lecture Notes in Artificial Intelligence
ISBN 978-3-031-71166-4　　　ISBN 978-3-031-71167-1　(eBook)
https://doi.org/10.1007/978-3-031-71167-1

LNCS Sublibrary: SL7 – Artificial Intelligence

© The Editor(s) (if applicable) and The Author(s), under exclusive license
to Springer Nature Switzerland AG 2024

This work is subject to copyright. All rights are solely and exclusively licensed by the Publisher, whether the whole or part of the material is concerned, specifically the rights of translation, reprinting, reuse of illustrations, recitation, broadcasting, reproduction on microfilms or in any other physical way, and transmission or information storage and retrieval, electronic adaptation, computer software, or by similar or dissimilar methodology now known or hereafter developed.
The use of general descriptive names, registered names, trademarks, service marks, etc. in this publication does not imply, even in the absence of a specific statement, that such names are exempt from the relevant protective laws and regulations and therefore free for general use.
The publisher, the authors and the editors are safe to assume that the advice and information in this book are believed to be true and accurate at the date of publication. Neither the publisher nor the authors or the editors give a warranty, expressed or implied, with respect to the material contained herein or for any errors or omissions that may have been made. The publisher remains neutral with regard to jurisdictional claims in published maps and institutional affiliations.

This Springer imprint is published by the registered company Springer Nature Switzerland AG
The registered company address is: Gewerbestrasse 11, 6330 Cham, Switzerland

If disposing of this product, please recycle the paper.

Preface

NeSy is the annual meeting of the Neural-Symbolic Learning and Reasoning Association[1] and the premier venue for the presentation and discussion of the theory and practice of neuro-symbolic AI systems.[2] Since 2005, NeSy has provided an atmosphere for the free exchange of ideas, bringing together the community of scientists and practitioners that straddle the line between deep learning and symbolic AI.

Neural networks and statistical Machine Learning have obtained industrial relevance in a number of areas from commerce to healthcare, achieving state-of-the-art performance at language translation, speech recognition, graph analytics, image, video and sensor data analysis. Symbolic AI, on the other hand, is challenged by such unstructured data, but is recognised as being transparent, in that reasoned facts from knowledge bases can be inspected to interpret how decisions follow from input. Neural and symbolic methods also contrast in the problems that they excel at: scene recognition from images appears to be a problem still outside the capabilities of symbolic systems, for example, while neural networks are not yet sufficient for industrial-strength complex planning scenarios and deductive reasoning tasks.

Neuro-symbolic AI aims to build rich computational models and systems by combining neural and symbolic learning and reasoning paradigms. This combination hopes to form synergies among their strengths while overcoming their complementary weaknesses.

Following the great success of NeSy 2023, which was held in La Certosa di Pontignano, Siena, Italy, 3–5 July 2023,[3] NeSy 2024 took place in Barcelona, Spain from 9 to 12 September 2024.[4] NeSy 2024 welcomed submissions of the latest and ongoing research work on neuro-symbolic AI for presentation at the conference. Topics of interest included, but were not limited to:

- Knowledge representation and reasoning using deep neural networks;
- Symbolic knowledge extraction from neural networks and statistical learning systems;
- Explainable AI methods, systems and techniques integrating connectionist and symbolic AI;
- Enhancing deep learning systems with structured background knowledge;
- Neural-symbolic cognitive agents;
- Biologically-inspired neuro-symbolic integration;
- Integration of logics and probabilities in neural networks;
- Neural-symbolic methods for structure learning, transfer learning, meta-learning, multi-task and continual learning, relational learning;
- Novel connectionist systems able to perform traditionally symbolic AI tasks (e.g. abduction, deduction, out-of-distribution learning);

---

[1] https://www.city-data-science-institute.com/nesy.
[2] http://www.neural-symbolic.org/.
[3] https://sites.google.com/view/nesy2023.
[4] https://sites.google.com/view/nesy2024.

- Novel symbolic systems able to perform traditionally connectionist tasks (e.g. learning from unstructured data, distributed learning);
- Embedding methods for structured information, such as knowledge graphs, mathematical expressions, grammars, knowledge bases and logical theories, into neural nets;
- Applications of neuro-symbolic and hybrid systems, including in simulation, finance, healthcare, robotics, Semantic Web, software engineering, systems engineering, bioinformatics and visual intelligence.

NeSy 2024 received 89 submissions (including the special session papers) for peer-review; out of these, 48 papers were accepted for presentation at the conference and inclusion in these proceedings (30 as full papers and 18 as short papers).

NeSy 2025 is planned to take place at UC Santa Cruz, California, from 8 to 10 September 2025. For more information, please visit https://sites.google.com/view/nesy2025.

Keynote and Invited Talks

NeSy 2024 featured the following keynote speakers:

- Catia Pesquita (University of Lisbon, Portugal)
- Kristian Kersting (TU Darmstadt, Germany)
- Willem (Jelle) Zuidema (University of Amsterdam, The Netherlands)

Special Sessions

Explainable AI: The NeSy 2024 XAI special track received 9 submissions, of which 6 were accepted (3 as full papers and 3 as short papers). The papers accepted refer to various proposed solutions for neuro-symbolic Explainable AI, including deriving concept-based explanations, creating interpretable vector spaces with human-understandable dimensions, interpreting hidden layers of deep neural networks, leveraging domain knowledge and the capabilities of Large Language Models (LLMs) to generate high-level, meaningful concepts as explanations for humans, assessing whether explanations are perceived as understandable by humans, and applying logic-explained networks to the predictions of the quality of life for people with disabilities.

Generative AI: The NeSy 2024 special track on Generative AI received 12 submissions, of which 8 were selected (5 as long papers and 3 as short papers). The papers highlight a growing trend towards enhancing the reasoning and analytical capabilities of LLMs and exploring their integration with structured knowledge representations. The dominant areas of focus in the submitted papers include research that improves logical reasoning and planning capabilities in LLMs, enhancing arithmetic and domain-specific problem-solving skills, integrating LLMs with knowledge graphs and symbolic systems, and methods for explainable AI using natural language prompts.

From the neuro-symbolic learning and reasoning perspective, the main conclusions from the papers highlight the usefulness of combining LLMs with external symbolic executors to perform complex reasoning tasks, such as theory of mind reasoning. They also demonstrate effective ways of integrating declarative knowledge into neuro-symbolic models using natural language prompts. These papers collectively contribute to advancing the field of generative AI by exploring new approaches to enhancing reasoning, analytical and knowledge representation capabilities of AI systems, with a particular emphasis on improving LLMs and investigating their potential in specialised applications.

Recently Published Papers Track

Authors of highly relevant papers in neuro-symbolic AI published recently in leading AI and Machine Learning journals and conferences were invited to submit proposals to present their work at NeSy 2024. This includes papers published recently at venues such as JAIR, MLJ, AIJ, JMLR, IEEE TNNLS, AAAI, IJCAI, NeurIPS, ICLR and ICML. We accepted the following proposals:

Cristina Cornelio and Mohammed Diab	Recover: A Neuro-Symbolic Framework for Failure Detection and Recovery
Nicolas Menet, Michael Hersche, Geethan Karunaratne, Abu Sebastian and Abbas Rahimi	Exploiting Computation in Superposition via Multiple-Input-Multiple-Output Neural Networks
Tommaso Carraro, Alessandro Daniele, Fabio Aiolli and Luciano Serafini	Mitigating Data Sparsity via Neuro-Symbolic Knowledge Transfer
Pedro Zuidberg Dos Martires	Autoregressive Connections in Probabilistic Circuits
Emile van Krieken, Pasquale Minervini, Edoardo M. Ponti and Antonio Vergari	On the Independence Assumption in Neurosymbolic Learning
Nicholas Rossetti, Massimiliano Tummolo, Alfonso Emilio Gerevini, Luca Putelli, Ivan Serina, Mattia Chiari and Matteo Olivato	Learning General Policies for Planning through GPT Models
Jaron Maene and Luc De Raedt	Soft-Unification in Deep Probabilistic Logic (Extended Abstract)
Jaron Maene, Vincent Derkinderen and Luc De Raedt	On the Hardness of Probabilistic Neurosymbolic Learning (Extended Abstract)
Lauren Nicole DeLong and Jacques D. Fleuriot	Neurosymbolic AI on Knowledge Graphs: Characterization, Payoff, and Pitfalls
Eleonora Giunchiglia, Alex Tatomir, Mihaela Cătălina Stoian and Thomas Lukasiewicz	CCN+: A neuro-symbolic framework for deep learning with requirements
Mihaela C. Stoian, Salijona Dyrmishi, Maxime Cordy, Thomas Lukasiewicz and Eleonora Giunchiglia	How Realistic Is Your Synthetic Data? Constraining Deep Generative Models For Tabular Data
Jared Strader, Nathan Hughes, William Chen, Alberto Speranzon and Luca Carlone	Indoor and Outdoor 3D Scene Graph Generation via Language-Enabled Spatial Ontologies
Charles Dickens, Connor Pryor and Lise Getoor	Modeling Patterns for Neural-Symbolic Reasoning Using Energy-based Models

Acknowledgements

We thank all members of the program committee, additional reviewers, the keynote speakers, authors and local organizers for their time and contributions to the success of NeSy 2024. We would also like to acknowledge that the work of the conference organisers was greatly simplified by the use of the EasyChair conference management system.

July 2024

Tarek R. Besold
Artur d'Avila Garcez
Ernesto Jimenez-Ruiz
Pranava Madhyastha
Benedikt Wagner
Roberto Confalonieri

Organization

Programme Chairs

Tarek R. Besold	Sony AI, Spain
Artur d'Avila Garcez	City, University of London, UK
Ernesto Jiménez Ruiz	City, University of London, UK
Roberto Confalonieri	University of Padova, Italy
Benedikt Wagner	City, University of London, UK
Pranava Madhyastha	City, University of London, UK

Steering Committee

Artur d'Avila Garcez	City, University of London, UK
Danny Silver	Acadia University, Canada
Pascal Hitzler	Kansas State University, USA
Kai-Uwe Kühnberger	Osnabrück University, Germany
Luis Lamb	University of Rio Grande do Sul, Brazil
Luc de Raedt	KU Leuven, Belgium
Tarek R. Besold	Sony AI, Spain
Marco Gori	University of Siena, Italy
Kristian Kersting	TU Darmstadt, Germany
Francesca Rossi	IBM Research, USA

NeSy Advisory Board

Leslie Valiant	Harvard University, USA
Josh Tenenbaum	MIT, USA

NeSy History and Past Proceedings

Please visit the Data Science Institute's webpage for the links: https://www.city-data-science-institute.com/nesy

The proceedings of earlier editions of NeSy are indexed by DBLP at: https://dblp.uni-trier.de/db/conf/nesy/index.html

Senior Program Committee

Bernardo Cuenca Grau	University of Oxford, UK
Luc De Raedt	KU Leuven, Belgium
Pascal Hitzler	Kansas State University, USA
Kristian Kersting	TU Darmstadt, Germany
Kai-Uwe Kühnberger	Osnabrück University, Germany
Luis Lamb	Federal University of Rio Grande do Sul, Brazil
Alessio Lomuscio	Imperial College London, UK
Thomas Lukasiewicz	Vienna University of Technology, Austria; University of Oxford, UK
Francesca Rossi	IBM, USA
Alessandra Russo	Imperial College London, UK
Ute Schmid	University of Bamberg, Germany
Luciano Serafini	Fondazione Bruno Kessler, Italy
Alberto Speranzon	Lockheed Martin Advanced Technology Labs, USA
Francesca Toni	Imperial College London, UK
Frank Van Harmelen	Vrije Universiteit Amsterdam, Netherlands

Program Committee

Hanna Abi Akl	Data ScienceTech Institute, Paris, France
Rebecca Adam	German Research Center for Artificial Intelligence (DFKI), Germany
Sudhir Agarwal	Intuit Inc., USA
Mehwish Alam	Télécom Paris, France
Jose M. Alonso-Moral	CiTIUS, Universidade de Santiago de Compostela, Spain
Elvira Amador-Domínguez	Universidad Politécnica de Madrid, Spain
Vito Walter Anelli	Politecnico di Bari, Italy
Octavio Arriaga	University of Bremen, Germany
Samy Badreddine	Sony AI, Spain
Vaishak Belle	University of Edinburgh, UK
Rafael Berlanga	Universitat Jaume I, Spain
Alice Bizzarri	University of Ferrara, Italy
Justin Brody	Franklin and Marshall College, USA
Matthew Brown	University of California Los Angeles, USA
Damir Cavar	Indiana University at Bloomington, USA
Jiaoyan Chen	University of Manchester, UK
Michele Collevati	Vienna University of Technology, Austria

Roberto Confalonieri	University of Padua, Italy
Cristina Cornelio	Samsung AI, UK
Fabio G. Cozman	University of São Paulo, Brazil
Claudia d'Amato	University of Bari, Italy
Wang-Zhou Dai	Nanjing University, China
Alessandro Daniele	Fondazione Bruno Kessler, Italy
Brandon Dave	Wright State University, USA
Paulo Vitor de Campos Souza	Fondazione Bruno Kessler, Italy
Hugo Cesar de Castro Carneiro	Universität Hamburg, Germany
Luke Dickens	University College London, UK
Ivan Donadello	Free University of Bozen-Bolzano, Italy
Mauro Dragoni	Fondazione Bruno Kessler, Italy
Rim El Cheikh	University of Clermont Auvergne, LIMOS, France
Zoe Falomir	Umeå University, Sweden
Eric Ferreira dos Santos	Dublin City University, Ireland
Vijay Ganesh	Georgia Tech, USA
Leilani Gilpin	University of California, Santa Cruz, USA
Eleonora Giunchiglia	Imperial College London, UK
Martin Glauer	Otto-von-Guericke-Universität Magdeburg, Germany
Riccardo Guidotti	University of Pisa, Italy
Jichen Guo	University of Bremen, Germany
Oktie Hassanzadeh	IBM Research, USA
Janna Hastings	University of Zurich and University of St. Gallen, Switzerland
Dave Herron	City, University of London, UK
Michael Hersche	IBM Research Zurich, Switzerland
Nelson Higuera Ruiz	TU Wien, Austria
Robert Hoehndorf	King Abdullah University of Science and Technology, Saudi Arabia
Andreas Holzinger	Medical University and Graz University of Technology, Austria
Céline Hudelot	CentraleSupélec, Paris-Saclay University, France
Neymika Jain	Barnstorm Research, USA
Ying Jiao	KU Leuven, Belgium
Azanzi Jiomekong	University of Yaounde I, Cameroon
Moa Johansson	Chalmers University of Technology, Sweden
Burak Can Kaplan	University of Hamburg, Germany
Irfan Kareem	University of Calabria, Italy
M. Jaleed Khan	University of Oxford, UK
Mostepha Khouadjia	IRT SystemX, France

Egor V. Kostylev	University of Oslo, Norway
Krzysztof Krawiec	Poznań University of Technology, Poland
Sofoklis Kyriakopoulos	City, University of London, UK
Yannick Le Nir	CY Tech, CY Cergy Paris University, France
Arthur Ledaguenel	IRT SystemX, Paris
Majlinda Llugiqi	Vienna University of Economics and Business, Austria
Sagar Malhotra	TU Wien, Austria
Robin Manhaeve	KU Leuven, Belgium
Lissangel Martinez	Barnstorm Research Corporation, USA
Olga Mashkova	King Abdullah University of Science and Technology, Saudi Arabia
Stefano Melacci	University of Siena, Italy
Daniele Meli	University of Verona, Italy
André Meyer-Vitali	Deutsches Forschungszentrum für Künstliche Intelligenz, Germany
Alessandra Mileo	Dublin City University, INSIGHT Centre for Data Analytics, Ireland
Lia Morra	Politecnico di Torino, Italy
Till Mossakowski	Otto-von-Guericke-Universität Magdeburg, Germany
Raghava Mutharaju	IIIT-Delhi, India
Alessandro Oltramari	Bosch Research and Technology Center, USA
Roko Parać	Imperial College London, UK
Alan Perotti	CENTAI Institute, Italy
Catia Pesquita	Universidade de Lisboa, Portugal
Alina Petrova	Thomson Reuters Lab, UK
Yin Jun Phua	Tokyo Institute of Technology, Japan
Paulo Pirozelli	University of São Paulo, Brazil
Irina Rabkina	Barnstorm Research, USA
Balaji Rao	Stevens Institute of Technology, USA
Sanaz Saki Norouzi	Kansas State University, USA
Md Kamruzzaman Sarker	Bowie State University, USA
David Sekora	University of Maryland, USA
Mattia Setzu	University of Pisa, Italy
Paulo Shakarian	Arizona State University, USA
Cogan Shimizu	Wright State University, USA
Mihaela Stoian	University of Oxford, UK
Patrick Takenaka	Hochschule der Medien, Germany
Tanel Tammet	Tallinn University of Technology, Estonia
David Tena Cucala	University of Oxford, UK
Aleksandar Terzic	IBM Research Zurich, ETH Zurich, Switzerland

Jonathan Thomm	IBM Research Zurich, ETH Zurich, Switzerland
Ilaria Tiddi	Vrije Universiteit Amsterdam, Netherlands
Son Tran	Deakin University, Australia
Elena Umili	Sapienza University of Rome, Italy
Emile van Krieken	University of Edinburgh, UK
Hua Wei	Arizona State University, USA
Tillman Weyde	City, University of London, UK
Siyu Wu	Penn State University, USA
Binxia Xu	University College London, UK
Gerson Zaverucha	Federal University of Rio de Janeiro (UFRJ), Brazil
Weihao Zeng	Carnegie Mellon University, USA
Fernando Zhapa-Camacho	King Abdullah University of Science and Technology, Saudi Arabia
Agnieszka Ławrynowicz	Poznań University of Technology, Poland
Gustav Šír	Czech Technical University in Prague, Czech Republic

Additional Reviewers

Aisha Aijaz	IIIT-Delhi, India
Mohammad Albinhassan	Imperial College London, UK
Leo Ardon	Imperial College London, UK
Francesco Argenziano	Sapienza University of Rome, Italy
Antrea Christou	Wright State University, USA
Alessandro De Bellis	Politecnico di Bari, Italy
Dario Di Palma	Politecnico di Bari, Italy
Andrea Fedele	University of Pisa, Italy
En-Hao Gao	Nanjing University, China
Wen-Chao Hu	Nanjing University, China
Yu-Xuan Huang	Nanjing University, China
Marco Huber	University of Stuttgart and Fraunhofer IPA, Germany
Navdeep Kaur	Alan Turing Institute, London, UK
John Lu	University of Waterloo, Canada
Francesco Manigrasso	Politecnico di Torino, Italy
Rakhilya Mekhtieva	Imperial College London, UK
Kaustuv Mukherji	Arizona State University, USA
Philipp Rader	Imperial College London, UK
Kaushik Roy	University of South Carolina, USA
Giovanni Servedio	Politecnico di Bari, Italy

Andrea Silvi	Chalmers University of Technology, Sweden
Gunjan Singh	IIIT-Delhi, India
Francesco Spinnato	University of Pisa, Italy
Maarten C. Stol	BrainCreators, Netherlands
Yijin Yang	Arizona State University, USA

Contents – Part I

NeSy 2024 Papers (Part 1)

Context Helps: Integrating Context Information with Videos
in a Graph-Based HAR Framework 3
  *Binxia Xu, Antonis Bikakis, Daniel Onah, Andreas Vlachidis,
  and Luke Dickens*

Assessing Logical Reasoning Capabilities of Encoder-Only Transformer
Models 29
  *Paulo Pirozelli, Marcos M. José, Paulo de Tarso P. Filho,
  Anarosa A. F. Brandão, and Fabio G. Cozman*

Variable Assignment Invariant Neural Networks for Learning Logic
Programs 47
  Yin Jun Phua and Katsumi Inoue

ViPro: Enabling and Controlling Video Prediction for Complex Dynamical
Scenarios Using Procedural Knowledge 62
  Patrick Takenaka, Johannes Maucher, and Marco F. Huber

The Role of Foundation Models in Neuro-Symbolic Learning
and Reasoning 84
  Daniel Cunnington, Mark Law, Jorge Lobo, and Alessandra Russo

A Fuzzy Loss for Ontology Classification 101
  Simon Flügel, Martin Glauer, Till Mossakowski, and Fabian Neuhaus

On the Use of Neurosymbolic AI for Defending Against Cyber Attacks 119
  *Gudmund Grov, Jonas Halvorsen, Magnus Wiik Eckhoff,
  Bjørn Jervell Hansen, Martin Eian, and Vasileios Mavroeidis*

Bayesian Inverse Graphics for Few-Shot Concept Learning 141
  *Octavio Arriaga, Jichen Guo, Rebecca Adam, Sebastian Houben,
  and Frank Kirchner*

Simple and Effective Transfer Learning for Neuro-Symbolic Integration 166
  *Alessandro Daniele, Tommaso Campari, Sagar Malhotra,
  and Luciano Serafini*

Ethical Reward Machine 180
   Jessica Ciupa and Vaishak Belle

Embed2Rule Scalable Neuro-Symbolic Learning via Latent Space
Weak-Labelling 195
   Yaniv Aspis, Mohammad Albinhassan, Jorge Lobo, and Alessandra Russo

ULLER: A Unified Language for Learning and Reasoning 219
   *Emile van Krieken, Samy Badreddine, Robin Manhaeve,
   and Eleonora Giunchiglia*

Disentangling Visual Priors: Unsupervised Learning of Scene
Interpretations with Compositional Autoencoder 240
   Krzysztof Krawiec and Antoni Nowinowski

Probing LLMs for Logical Reasoning 257
   Francesco Manigrasso, Stefan Schouten, Lia Morra, and Peter Bloem

Enhancing Machine Learning Predictions Through Knowledge Graph
Embeddings 279
   Majlinda Llugiqi, Fajar J. Ekaputra, and Marta Sabou

Terminating Differentiable Tree Experts 296
   *Jonathan Thomm, Michael Hersche, Giacomo Camposampiero,
   Aleksandar Terzić, Bernhard Schölkopf, and Abbas Rahimi*

Valid Text-to-SQL Generation with Unification-Based DeepStochLog 312
   Ying Jiao, Luc De Raedt, and Giuseppe Marra

Enhancing Geometric Ontology Embeddings for $\mathcal{EL}^{++}$ with Negative
Sampling and Deductive Closure Filtering 331
   Olga Mashkova, Fernando Zhapa-Camacho, and Robert Hoehndorf

Lattice-Preserving $\mathcal{ALC}$ Ontology Embeddings 355
   Fernando Zhapa-Camacho and Robert Hoehndorf

Towards Learning Abductive Reasoning Using VSA Distributed
Representations 370
   *Giacomo Camposampiero, Michael Hersche, Aleksandar Terzić,
   Roger Wattenhofer, Abu Sebastian, and Abbas Rahimi*

Learning to Solve Abstract Reasoning Problems with Neurosymbolic
Program Synthesis and Task Generation 386
   Jakub Bednarek and Krzysztof Krawiec

Leveraging Neurosymbolic AI for Slice Discovery 403
  Michele Collevati, Thomas Eiter, and Nelson Higuera

Author Index 419

Contents – Part II

NeSy 2024 Papers

IID Relaxation by Logical Expressivity: A Research Agenda for Fitting Logics to Neurosymbolic Requirements 3
Maarten C. Stol and Alessandra Mileo

Enhancing Neuro-Symbolic Integration with Focal Loss: A Study on Logic Tensor Networks 14
Luca Piano, Francesco Manigrasso, Alessandro Russo, and Lia Morra

WineGraph: A Graph Representation for Food-Wine Pairing 24
Zuzanna Gawrysiak, Agata Żywot, and Agnieszka Ławrynowicz

Logic Supervised Learning for Time Series - Continual Learning for Appliance Detection 32
Benjamin Duppe

Towards Understanding the Impact of Graph Structure on Knowledge Graph Embeddings 41
Brandon Dave, Antrea Christou, and Cogan Shimizu

Commonsense Ontology Micropatterns 51
Andrew Eells, Brandon Dave, Pascal Hitzler, and Cogan Shimizu

Metacognitive AI: Framework and the Case for a Neurosymbolic Approach 60
Hua Wei, Paulo Shakarian, Christian Lebiere, Bruce Draper, Nikhil Krishnaswamy, and Sergei Nirenburg

Enhancing Logical Tensor Networks: Integrating Uninorm-Based Fuzzy Operators for Complex Reasoning 68
Paulo Vitor de Campos Souza, Gianluca Apriceno, and Mauro Dragoni

Parameter Learning Using Approximate Model Counting 80
Lucile Dierckx, Alexandre Dubray, and Siegfried Nijssen

Large-Scale Knowledge Integration for Enhanced Molecular Property Prediction 89
Yasir Ghunaim and Robert Hoehndorf

Towards Understanding Graph Neural Networks: Functional-Semantic
Activation Mapping 98
   Kislay Raj and Alessandra Mileo

NeSy 2024 XAI Special Track

On the Value of Labeled Data and Symbolic Methods for Hidden Neuron
Activation Analysis 109
   Abhilekha Dalal, Rushrukh Rayan, Adrita Barua,
   Eugene Y. Vasserman, Md Kamruzzaman Sarker, and Pascal Hitzler

Concept Induction Using LLMs: A User Experiment for Assessment 132
   Adrita Barua, Cara Widmer, and Pascal Hitzler

Error-Margin Analysis for Hidden Neuron Activation Labels 149
   Abhilekha Dalal, Rushrukh Rayan, and Pascal Hitzler

LENs for Analyzing the Quality of Life of People with Intellectual
Disability 165
   Diego Fraile-Parra, Vicent Costa, and Pilar Dellunde

ECATS: Explainable-by-Design Concept-Based Anomaly Detection
for Time Series 175
   Irene Ferfoglia, Gaia Saveri, Laura Nenzi, and Luca Bortolussi

Bringing Back Semantics to Knowledge Graph Embeddings:
An Interpretability Approach 192
   Antoine Domingues, Nitisha Jain, Albert Meroño Peñuela,
   and Elena Simperl

NeSy 2024 GenAI Special Track

Reasoning in Transformers – Mitigating Spurious Correlations
and Reasoning Shortcuts 207
   Daniel Enström, Viktor Kjellberg, and Moa Johansson

TIC: Translate-Infer-Compile for Accurate "Text to Plan" Using LLMs
and Logical Representations 222
   Sudhir Agarwal and Anu Sreepathy

ToM-LM: Delegating Theory of Mind Reasoning to External Symbolic
Executors in Large Language Models 245
   Weizhi Tang and Vaishak Belle

Can Large Language Models Put 2 and 2 Together? Probing for Entailed
Arithmetical Relationships 258
    Dagmara Panas, Sohan Seth, and Vaishak Belle

Assessing LLMs Suitability for Knowledge Graph Completion 277
    Vasile Ionut Remus Iga and Gheorghe Cosmin Silaghi

ProSLM: A Prolog Synergized Language Model for explainable Domain
Specific Knowledge Based Question Answering 291
    Priyesh Vakharia, Abigail Kufeldt, Max Meyers, Ian Lane,
    and Leilani H. Gilpin

Experiments with LLMs for Converting Language to Logic 305
    Tanel Tammet, Priit Järv, Martin Verrev, and Dirk Draheim

Prompt2DeModel: Declarative Neuro-Symbolic Modeling with Natural
Language 315
    Hossein Rajaby Faghihi, Aliakbar Nafar, Andrzej Uszok,
    Hamid Karimian, and Parisa Kordjamshidi

Enhancing GPT-Based Planning Policies by Model-Based Plan Validation 328
    Nicholas Rossetti, Massimiliano Tummolo, Alfonso Emilio Gerevini,
    Matteo Olivato, Luca Putelli, and Ivan Serina

Author Index 339

NeSy 2024 Papers (Part 1)

Context Helps: Integrating Context Information with Videos in a Graph-Based HAR Framework

Binxia Xu, Antonis Bikakis, Daniel Onah, Andreas Vlachidis, and Luke Dickens(✉)

Department of Information Studies, University College London, London, England
{b.xu,l.dickens}@ucl.ac.uk

Abstract. Human Activity Recognition (HAR) from videos is a challenging, data intensive task. There have been significant strides in recent years, but even state-of-the-art (SoTA) models rely heavily on domain specific supervised fine-tuning of visual features, and even with this data- and compute-intensive fine-tuning, overall performance can still be limited. We argue that the next generation of HAR models could benefit from explicit neuro-symbolic mechanisms in order to flexibly exploit rich contextual information available in, and for, videos. With a view to this, we propose a Human Activity Recognition with Context Prompt (HARCP) task to investigate the value of contextual information for video-based HAR. We also present a neuro-symbolic graph neural network-based framework that integrates zero-shot object localisation to address the HARCP task. This captures the human activity as a sequence of graph-based scene representations relating parts of the human body to key objects, supporting the targeted injection of external contextual knowledge in symbolic form. We evaluate existing HAR baselines alongside our graph-based methods to demonstrate the advantage of being able to accommodate this additional channel of information. Our evaluations show that not only does context information from key objects boost accuracy beyond that provided by SoTA HAR models alone, there is also a greater semantic similarity between our model's errors and the target class. We argue that this represents an improved model alignment with human-like errors and quantify this with a novel measure we call *Semantic Prediction Dispersion*.

Keywords: context · human activity recognition · neuro-symbolic integration · graph neural network · human alignment

1 Introduction

Video-based Human Activity Recognition (HAR) captures spatial and temporal information in videos to identify human activities [6]. It is being widely used in ambient intelligent systems like public security surveillance and virtual assistants [13,41,46]. Compared to the recognition of objects, recognising human

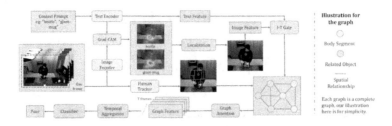

Fig. 1. The architecture of our proposed framework for the HARCP task.

activities has proven difficult to achieve, and we focus here on two possible reasons that have been identified in the literature [32,34,51]. First, in HAR, there is a high intra-class variability, meaning different videos of the same activity class can be visually very different, and this difference can be large relative to the typical difference between videos from two closely related activity classes. Second, recognition of an activity is influenced by the context in which it is happening, like its location and held objects. For example, a person crouching can be interpreted in different ways depending on whether they are picking up an object or dodging a blow. Accordingly, HAR systems must utilise all this information, e.g. human pose, movement, class-class relationships, and relative positions of key objects and body parts to support robust and accurate predictions.

State-of-the-art (SoTA) video-based HAR models include Two-stream ConvNet [8,42], 3D ConvNet [16,20,47] and video Transformer [4,7]. All achieve excellent performance in certain datasets, but are computationally intensive to fine-tune on downstream tasks. Moreover, these backbone models for video classification may be insufficient for activities that are visually similar in terms of body gesture movements and require contextual cues - specifically, key objects related to the activities-to help disambiguate them. For instance, when observing a person holding a glass and moving it toward their mouth, it is sometimes the liquid in the glass that helps distinguish between drinking water and drinking beer. Some efforts have been made to incorporate additional knowledge for fine-tuning in specific domains [12,32], but this still involves retraining and provides no mechanism to directly inject such contextual information. Instead, we argue that an HAR system should be sensitive to context and capable of incorporating contextual information as external input without the need for retraining.

Additional concerns for these HAR models arise from their black-box nature. Predictions from these models cannot be readily interpreted in order to be verified and ultimately trusted, and this limits their use in domains such as healthcare and security. We take the viewpoint from [38] that an interpretable model should have an interpretable decision-making process rather than providing post-hoc explanations for the decision, and see structured representations, namely graphs, as a natural way to achieve this for HAR models (see also [15,44,49,54]). The use of spatio-temporal graph representation can be linked to the hypothesis in cognitive science that people may recognise an activity by decomposing it into a hierarchical structure [26,53]. More precisely, a human-centric activity can often be recognised by reasoning from a sequence of spatial relations between involved body parts or between those parts and related objects, and a neuro-symbolic integration between low-level neural perception and high-level reasoning capability is an effective way to formulate this problem [3]. Some works have demonstrated the success of the graph representation for the boost of performance in HAR [19,21,33,43,49,50]. However, all of these rely on annotated bounding boxes for objects in the videos, or similar human-labor-intensive annotations, which makes the framework less generalisable. Moreover, the importance of context to HAR, as well as an effective way to build and evaluate interpretable HAR models, are still under-investigated.

Why the HARCP Task? To begin to address these concerns, we introduce a new human activity recognition with context prompt HAR (HARCP) task as part of an evaluation framework for context-sensitive HAR. Here, we would like to first differentiate our framework from SoTA video-question-answering (Video-QA) models such as LlaVA [29] and VideoBLIP [52]. Although prompts are used in both cases to query the videos, our task addresses different challenges compared to those faced by Video-QA models. Our framework is specifically designed to investigate how contextual information regarding key objects can enhance both the performance and interpretability of activity recognition in videos, which is achieved by injecting the names of key objects as prompts. Our framework could be conceivably embedded within a Video-QA system to support the solving of questions involving recognition of activities such as "What is that person doing with the spoon?" This type of question can be transformed into a task where the machine knows the name of a certain related object and aims to recognise the activity involving this specified object. Previously mentioned Video-QA models use questions as prompts directly and do not facilitate the decomposition of humans and context or the construction of their interaction. We demonstrate here that there are benefits to such decomposition and representation, both in terms of granular interpretability of model predictions (via the nodes and edge weights within the graph), the targeted injection of additional sources of information (here contextual objects) and controlled evaluation of the impact of such knowledge injection (exemplified by our context evaluations). Put simply, in our task, a video is presented alongside the names of key objects observable in the video and we aim to explore how this simple, high-level, additional input can boost recognition within suitable models. As presented in Fig. 1, our proposed framework for this task comprises three main components: zero-shot context localisation, a human tracker, and a graph attention model to represent spatial relationships between pairs of elements in the scene. Compared to previous graph-based models with detectors trained on a specific set of objects, our model supports zero-shot object detection using Grad-CAM and pretrained large image-language models. Like other recent graph-based HAR approaches, e.g. STRG [49], we construct spatio-temporal graph-based representations that capture key regions of interest within videos and relate these to one another. Note that our framework is highly modular and various components can be swapped out for alternative approaches. For instance, the components for context detection (here a CLIP based segmenter) can be replaced with any future approaches that serve the same functions but achieve more advanced performance. A key difference to previous approaches, is that our model uses a human tracker to detect the key points of the human body before converting these to image regions corresponding to body segments. These regions for body segments are integrated with the context prompt (as text) and detected objects (as image regions) within a spatial relational graph for each video frame, before temporally aggregating them. Previous models, such as STRG [49], SRNN [18] and LSTGN [51], regard the human body as a whole entity and locate it with a unified object detector, treating humans and related object equally. Separating the detection of human body segments from objects allows us, for the first time, to systematically evaluate the contribution of contextual objects to model performance and interpretability.

Building and Evaluating Interpretable Models. Here, we address our concern regarding the black-box issue: how to build and evaluate interpretable HAR models. Our graph-based HAR model is designed to expose the state of, and key interactions between, objects and body parts. We then describe how to interpret these model features to understand their relevance to the final prediction. The attention mechanism is used to specify which pair of interactions contribute most to the final predictions. Put another way, it determines which pair of interactions should receive the most focus throughout the entire sequence of frames. In addition, we propose a new way to measure one aspect of a model's interpretability, we call Semantic Prediction Dispersion (SPD). Our SPD measure is based on three underlying ideas. First that, given all else is equal, humans are more likely to confuse two semantically similar classes than those that are semantically distinct. For instance, the actions of slicing an onion and dicing an onion are very similar in terms of objects used and how the body operates to perform them, but are both distinct from opening a fridge door. These similarities and differences relate directly to the underlying meaning of these actions – their semantics. The second idea is to utilise measures of semantic similarities constructed by recent large language models to capture the semantic difference between classes. The intuition is supported by [10], which demonstrates that the representation space for action concepts in a large language model is similar to that of the human mind to a certain degree. Therefore, in this work, we employ CLIP Language [36] to construct the vector embeddings, although any reliable proxy encoder of human concepts could be used as a replacement. The final idea associates the interpretability of a model with how similar its errors are to those of a human–a form of human-AI alignment [9,39]. This doesn't mean a model cannot outperform a human, but that the error profile of the machine should be dominated by mistakes that are also more common for humans. This is informed by recent work that argues that the level of consistency between a model's errors with those of humans can indicate to what degree the model constructs its predictions using similar analogous processes to humans [14].

The main contributions of this work are three-fold: 1) our HARCP task, and associated evaluation framework, designed to investigate how simple information about the context (key objects) can be exploited to improve HAR predictions; 2) an interpretable graph attention framework integrating zero-shot context localisation using Grad-CAM to address the HARCP task alongside a comprehensive series of experiments to evaluate our proposed framework; and 3) a novel evaluation metric named SPD to evaluate a key aspect of interpretability relating to human-machine error alignment. Key findings are that our graph model for human activities with a context prompt substantially outperforms fine-tuned large backbone models without context prompt, and that our model with context information has a lower (better) SPD than a baseline graph model without context, and ViViT, our SoTA video-transformer baseline.

2 A Graph-Based Interpretable Framework for HARCP

This section presents the relational graph-based neuro-symbolic framework for context-sensitive HAR with the proposed HARCP task, and a novel evaluation metric to interrogate the model's error alignment with humans named *Semantic Prediction Dispersion (SPD)* . A **HARCP task** is to identify a human activity, given a video and context: thus, the input consists of a video, $\mathcal{V}$ – a sequence of image frames showing one human activity from a set of possible activity classes, $\mathcal{A}$, alongside a context prompt, $\mathcal{S}_J$ – a collection of strings each describing an object which plays a key role in that activity. Our framework is said to localise those context objects in a **zero-shot manner** if it does so without domain-specific object detection training. Within the framework, for each video frame, once the key elements, including both body segments and contextual objects, are enclosed by bounding boxes, existing pre-trained feature extractors, such as ResNet [16] and ViT [11], are employed to capture the visual features from these regions of interest. A graph attention model, a method argued to be an effective way to conduct relational learning [27], is then utilised to capture the information flow between the visual features for those key elements and construct the spatial relationships between each pair of them. We wish to emphasise that the information passed in messages along edges in the graph capture all relevant information from one node to the other, so attention weights on these edges inform us about the general relatedness of one node to another, at a given layer of graph processing, and do not isolate specific named relationships between entities. Hence some care is required when interpreting the attention weights between nodes. Nonetheless, these attention weights provide key information about the strength of connections between pairs of elements (objects or body parts) at a given point in the video.

More formally, a video $\mathcal{V}$, corresponds to an activity class $\hat{a} \in \mathcal{A}$. Given video sequence, $\mathcal{V}$, and context prompt, $\mathcal{S}_J$, we aim to learn a scoring function $F(.)$ that returns the correct activity with:

$$\hat{a} = \arg\max_{a \in \mathcal{A}} F(a|\mathcal{V}, \mathcal{S}_J). \tag{1}$$

Video $\mathcal{V}$ is represented as a set of T video frames (or images) $\mathcal{V} = \{i_t\}_{t=0}^{T-1}$. Each frame i_t (width X, height Y) gives pixel information, i_{txy}, at locations $(x,y) \in \{1,\ldots,X\} \times \{1,\ldots,Y\}$. Context prompt, $\mathcal{S}_J$, is a collection of one or more strings describing key objects related to the activity shown in the video, denoted $s \in \mathcal{S}_J$. For each frame i_t, we specify two families of regions of interest: human body parts $\mathcal{R}_B[i_t]$ and object contexts $\mathcal{R}_J[i_t]$, where i_t is clear we denote these as $\mathcal{R}_B$ and $\mathcal{R}_J$ respectively. For a given frame, $r_B \in \mathcal{R}_B$ is a region containing a body segment of the person performing the activity, and $r_J \in \mathcal{R}_J$ is a region containing a context object.

Our approach uses $\mathcal{V}$ and $\mathcal{S}_J$ to determine $\mathcal{R}_B$ and $\mathcal{R}_J$ in each frame, then combines this textual, visual and spatial information within a graph representation. Temporal aggregation is then applied to integrate these spatio-visual representations over time. This allows the model to capture the activity as a higher-level abstraction of the spatial and temporal relationships among various related components, such as body segments and related objects. The overall architecture of our method is presented in Fig. 1.

2.1 Zero-Shot Context Localisation

Although some previous graph-based methods for HAR have used context information [49,51], these methods involve training object-detectors on the object classes, and this limits their applicability. More recently, large image-language models pretrained on very large datasets, such as CLIP [36], have demonstrated excellent performance on downstream zero-shot object detection tasks. We therefore propose using these joint image-language foundation models to implement zero-shot localisation for arbitrary context prompts as part of our framework.

A Class Activation Map (CAM) [55], which is commonly employed to investigate the retrospective explainability of a model, reveals the distinctive regions in an image that a model relies on to recognise a specific category. The Gradient-weighted CAM (Grad-CAM) [40] generates a localisation map by leveraging gradients from a target concept that flows into the final feature map. This map highlights crucial regions in the image for predicting the given concept and has been adopted in some Weakly-Supervised Localisation tasks [1,2,28], showing promising results. Different from the vanilla Grad-CAM which is applied to CNN-based models, we apply Grad-CAM to the ViT model because of its SoTA performance. The details of the implementation of Grad-CAM on ViT are illustrated in Appendix C.1. Based on the top K most activated regions in the frame, we apply semantic segmentation [24] to get the bounding box for the target context. We denote the whole process as a context object detector D_o.

2.2 Graph Representation for Human Activities

Reasoning with spatial relations is common in everyday life [31]. When identifying a human activity, the spatial relations between the involved parts are arguably one of the decisive factors. As hypothesised in cognitive science, people can recognise an activity by decomposing it into a hierarchical structure [26,53].

To be more specific, a human-centric activity can often be represented as a sequence of spatial relations between the involved body parts or between the body parts and related objects. To facilitate the identification of arbitrary activities, we utilise a graph representation for all the spatial relationships between arbitary pairs of elements at each time-step simultaneously and perform relational learning using GNN. An attention mechanism is employed to identify spatial relationships most relevant to the recognition of an activity.

At each time step, we construct a graph $\mathcal{G}(i_t) = \langle \mathcal{N}_t, \mathcal{E}_t \rangle$ with the number of nodes $|\mathcal{N}_t| = |\mathcal{R}_J[i_t]| + |\mathcal{R}_B[i_t]|$ for a video frame i_t (each node corresponds to a different object or body parts in the frame), the edges of which represent the spatial relationships between each component. Again, for simplicity, we drop explicit reference to frame i_t in our sets of regions following descriptions.

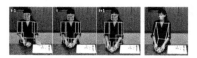

Fig. 2. The detected key points of a human body (right) and the drawn bounding boxes for the corresponding body segment (left).

Since a Graph $\mathcal{G}$ represents the pairwise spatial relationships among all elements in one frame, the nodes $\mathcal{N}$ in the graph correspond to the RoIs of those elements. In our approach, there are two types of node $\mathcal{N}_B$ and $\mathcal{N}_C$, which correspond to sets of regions $\mathcal{R}_B$ and $\mathcal{R}_J$, respectively. Each node $v \in \mathcal{N}_B \cup \mathcal{N}_C$ is then converted into a set of features f_v as described below.

Body Segments ($\mathcal{N}_B$): To get each $r_B \in \mathcal{R}_B$, we first apply a human tracker D_H to detect the key points for human and enclose the key points by bounding boxes, as shown in Fig. 2. For each r_B, an image encoder E_B is applied to generate an appearance feature: $f_B = E_B(r_B)$ for each $v_B \in \mathcal{N}_B$.

Contexts ($\mathcal{N}_C$): For each frame i_t, based on objects $s \in \mathcal{S}_J$, a set of RoIs $r_J \in \mathcal{R}_J$ is localised by D_o. An image encoder E_J is applied to each r_J to generate the appearance feature: $f_J = E_J(r_J)$. Additionally, for each s, a text encoder is employed to generate the text feature $f_S = E_S(s)$. We construct an I-T Gate for the combination of image and text features for each object, which is a mixing weight w_j for the two features:

$$f_C = w_j f_J + (1 - w_j) f_S \qquad (2)$$

where f_C is the node feature for each $v_C \in \mathcal{N}_C$.

2.3 Graph Attention

Given the graph structure introduced in the previous section, we are now focusing on the propagation of the message through the graphs. Here, we use a graph neural network with an attention mechanism to learn the relations between nodes. In this graph architecture, the information held by one node will be passed to its neighbors through the edges, which represents the interaction between the pair of elements. In our current setting, the f_B and f_C have the same dimension and the information flow for v_B and v_C are identical. Thus we use $v \in \mathcal{N}$ to denote all the nodes in the graph and f_v to represent the node features for all nodes.

The whole learning process for graphs includes a Message Function Msg(.), an Attention Mechanism with parameters and an Aggregation Function Agg(.) as described in [23,48]. For each iteration $l = 1, \ldots, L$, $h_v^l \in \mathcal{R}^d$ indicates the updated hidden state of node $v \in \mathcal{N}$, with the initial hidden state $h_v^0 = f_v$. To evaluate layer l, first, a Message Function Msg($\cdot$) is applied to each node $u \in \mathcal{N}$:

$$m_u^l = \text{Msg}(h_u^{l-1}) = W_m h_u^{l-1} \qquad (3)$$

in which matrix $W_m \in \mathcal{R}^{d \times d}$ is a learnable parameter.

For each node $v \in \mathcal{N}$, we next calculate the attention weights, α_{uv} for each edge $u \in \mathcal{N}(v)$ (neighbours of v).

$$e_{uv}^l = w_a^T [m_u^l; m_v^l], \qquad \alpha_{uv}^l = \frac{\exp(e_{uv}^l)}{\sum_{k \in \mathcal{N}(v)} \exp(e_{kv}^l)}. \qquad (4)$$

where vector $w_a \in \mathcal{R}^{2d}$ is a learnable parameter, and edge weights e_{uv}^l form softmax activations for attention weights α_{uv}^l.

For each node v, we then aggregate the messages passed from v's neighbours using attention weights α_{uv}^l and non-linearity σ:

$$h_v^l = \text{Agg}\left(\{m_u^l, \alpha_{uv}^l\}_{u \in \mathcal{N}(v)}\right) = \sigma\left(\frac{\sum_{u \in \mathcal{N}(v)} \alpha_{uv}^l m_u^l}{|\mathcal{N}(v)|} + m_v^l\right). \qquad (5)$$

Note that the weighted message components, $\alpha_{uv}^l m_u^l$, carry information about the appearance of node u and are used to update the hidden representation for node v. Since these update functions form part of an end-to-end differentiable architecture, the model training will seek to optimise the throughput of relevant information across the edges of these graphs. As such, we interpret the repeated aggregation of messages from a node's neighbours as capturing the (potentially asymmetric) informational relationship of each element with its spatially neighbouring elements in the video.

2.4 Temporal Aggregation

The output hidden state for each node in the graph (after L iterations) is then temporally aggregated over all graphs. One graph represents the state of a scene at a time step. We use a sequence model to aggregate those graph components (here we use an LSTM model). In the temporal sequence, one graph component is represented by the sum of the hidden states for each node:

$$g_t = \sum_{v \in \mathcal{N}} h_{tv}^L. \tag{6}$$

where h_{tv}^L is the Lth layer of node v for graph a time-point t. The sequential representation for those graph components is:

$$H_t^g = Seq(g_t, H_{t-1}^g, c_{t-1}^g), \tag{7}$$

in which H_t^g is the hidden state for time point t, and c_{t-1}^g is the memory cell vector in the previous time step. We use the last hidden state of the sequence, H_T^g as the input of the activity classifier.

2.5 Semantic Prediction Dispersion

As argued in the introduction, we identify a key desideratum for interpretable models that their error profiles align with those of humans, and argue that two classes being *semantically very similar* is equivalent to them being *easily confused*. This builds on extensive work on classification tasks from the neuro- and cognitive sciences which represent the internal states of the brain in terms of pairwise dissimilarities between classes, see [25, 45]. Given this, we posit that a model is more interpretable if false positive predictions for a given class are typically semantically close to the target class. For example, in the cooking domain, a person tends to more easily confuse the activity "cut apart" with "cut dice" than with activities like "open" or "clean". Therefore, false positive predictions for "cut apart" of a more human-aligned HAR model should include classes like "chop" and "cut dice" more frequently than "clean".

To quantify this, we utilise the representation space of large language models as a proxy for that of the human concept. As demonstrated in [10], pairwise dissimilarities between action concepts in the human mind correlate, to some degree, with representational dissimilarities in large language models such as CLIP Language and GPT. Based on the vectors of action concepts in the embedding space, we then define a measure of semantic prediction dispersion (SPD) which estimates the average semantic difference between predicted and target classes, both in a class-wise (classwise-SPD) and aggregate (overall-SPD) manner. We say that models with smaller SPD are more *semantically aligned* .

More precisely, we define v_c as the semantic vector for class c derived from a large language model, and the semantic similarity between true class c_T and predicted class c_P is $\text{Sim}(v_{c_T}, v_{c_P})$. We use cosine similarity between two vectors as the Sim function in our experiments. The semantic prediction similarity for class c is defined, respectively with and without correct classifications, as

$$sps_c = \frac{1}{|\mathcal{D}_c|} \sum_{x_i \in \mathcal{D}_c} \text{Sim}(v_c, v_{y(x_i)}), \quad sps_c^- = \frac{1}{|\mathcal{D}_c^-|} \sum_{x_i \in \mathcal{D}_c^-} \text{Sim}(v_c, v_{y(x_i)}) \quad (8)$$

where $\mathcal{D}_c$ are all data samples where the predicted class is c and $\mathcal{D}_c^-$ is the set $\mathcal{D}_c$ with correct predictions removed. sps_c is sensitive to accuracy, and relative differences in accuracy can swamp the error alignment signal. We therefore focus on sps_c^- rather than sps_c. Although, sps_c^- can be used to compare the degree of semantic alignment, it cannot be directly used to facilitate the training of human-aligned HAR models. In future work, we aim to explore the use semantic alignment to construct an auxiliary loss that has the potential to be directly used in the training of future human-aligned HAR models. In contrast, SPD measures for class c, with and without correct classifications respectively, are defined as

$$spd_c = \frac{1}{sps_c} - 1 \quad \text{and} \quad spd_c^- = \frac{1}{sps_c^-} - 1 \quad (9)$$

We define Overall SPD as the average classwise-SPD over the whole dataset:

$$spd = \sum_c \frac{|\mathcal{D}_c|}{\sum_{c'} |\mathcal{D}_{c'}|} spd_c \quad \text{and} \quad spd^- = \sum_c \frac{|\mathcal{D}_c^-|}{\sum_{c'} |\mathcal{D}_{c'}^-|} spd_c^-$$

and lower spd^- means better semantic alignment.

3 Experiment

The aims of these experiments are threefold: 1) to investigate the importance of contextual information for HAR, how this information contributes to different types of activities and how context facilitates both performance and interpretability compared to the conventional HAR models; 2) to analyse how the information flow across edges in the graphs can be used to interpret the role that each element in a video plays in the activity recognition; and 3) validate our proposed SPD measurement for a model by showing how it relates to the semantic alignment of a model, a measure of interpretability.

We validate our framework using the MPII-Cooking 2 dataset [37], a video dataset recording human subjects cooking a diverse set of dishes. We chose this as it is a challenging dataset, with one person (the subject) in each clip, making human poses easier to capture, and annotations for key objects are provided. See Appendix A for more details on this dataset and our preprocessing pipeline.

Table 1. Performance for the recognition in MPII-Cooking dataset. The first two rows of the table show the results of baseline models. The subsequent rows display all the results from our framework, both with and without context information. Models that incorporate global paths are those in which plain global features are combined alongside the graph.

Graph	Global	Accuracy(%)	Macro F-1(%)
-	Conv+Seq	40.22	19.02
-	ViViT	51.01	25.00
$\mathcal{R}_B$	-	42.70	21.21
$\mathcal{R}_B$	Conv+Seq	44.94	23.81
$\mathcal{R}_B$	ViViT(Frozen)	44.49	24.21
$\mathcal{R}_B \cup \mathcal{R}_J$	-	50.56	27.94
$\mathcal{R}_B \cup \mathcal{S}_J$	-	67.64	46.22
$\mathcal{R}_B \cup \mathcal{R}_J \cup \mathcal{S}_J$	-	**68.53**	**50.87**
$\mathcal{R}_B \cup \mathcal{R}_J \cup \mathcal{S}_J$	Conv+Seq	67.19	48.54
$\mathcal{R}_B \cup \mathcal{R}_J \cup \mathcal{S}_J$	ViViT(Frozen)	67.86	48.80

Table 2. The performance of the model (without context) with different pre-trained feature extractors. CLIP as a feature extractor is slightly better than ResNet.

$\mathcal{R}_B$	Conv+Seq	Accuracy(%)	Macro F-1(%)
-	CLIP + S	40.22	19.02
-	ResNet + S	39.55	18.33
CLIP	-	42.70	21.21
ResNet	-	40.0	19.76
CLIP	CLIP + S	44.94	23.81
ResNet	ResNet + S	43.82	23.38

3.1 Conventional HAR

Here we present the performance of SoTA baselines and our body segment-only GNN baseline on the conventional HAR task (without a context prompt). Table 1 (rows 1–5) shows classification performance for different representational choices. The first two rows show the results of two baselines: a large Video Transformer model (ViViT) trained end-to-end, and a lightweight model, Conv+Seq – a LSTM with a CNN feature extractor per time step. The following three rows show the results of the body segment-only graph with or without a global path. We use the CLIP Vision as our visual feature extractor according to the results in Table 2. From pilot observations, the performance of the human tracker is not perfect, which means that body segments are not precisely detected for some samples, when using $\mathcal{R}_B$. Despite this, Table 1 shows that this context free graph model (row 3) outperforms Conv+Seq (row 1). The graph models (for body segments only) are improved when combined with a plain global path. This enhancement may result from context information introduced by the global features. We note that our GNN model, built as it is on a number of pretrained foundational models, has a finetuning cost far below the end-to-end training cost of the best performing SoTA method, ViViT (see Appendix B for details).

3.2 Predictions with Context Prompts

One key motivation for our HARCP task is to show the effectiveness of the context in the recognised activities. The results in Table 1 (rows 3–5 versus rows 6–10) demonstrate that introducing contextual information can dramatically improve the classification, and the fusion of visual and text features attain the optimal performance, with 68.53% in accuracy and 50.87% in macro f-1. This macro f-1 is two times more than all of the other models without using context prompts, including our graph with body segments only and two baseline models. We are not claiming an architectural advantage over the baseline models such as ViViT, instead, we are demonstrating the informational advantage provided by the appropriate inclusion of context information via the identity of key objects (elements). We also examined whether context prompts alone can achieve good results for classification using only text features. We extracted the features of the object strings for each video using CLIP Language and trained the concatenation of those features using an MLP classifier. We achieved a 38% accuracy with only 8.9% macro F1 score, indicating the limitation of using context texts alone and emphasising the importance of combining context information with human pose. The recognition performs best when combining the two features with the visual weight (w_j) set at 0.4. Further investigations on the relative importance of image versus text information can be found in Appendix D.

To investigate in more detail how context information affects performance, we calculate the boost of average precision (AP) for each class (see Appendix E). We find that the recognition of activities that are strongly related to certain types of objects benefits more. For example, the AP boost of "stir" is +0.98 (stir is highly associated with a spatula). A reader may challenge this set up by saying that it is unfair to pre-existing models, such as ViViT, since they do not have access to the additional context prompt input, nor are they designed to exploit it if they were. However, rather than simply comparing accuracy between our approach and other SoTA models, we aim to demonstrate that this simple additional input provides an unexpected boost to model performance, and given that the objects themselves are already visible in the image, it is the contextual information that they are relevant to the activity that fuels the improved accuracy.

3.3 Relational Attention Weights and Interpretability

Fig. 3. Example frames for activities: "peel", "cut apart", and their corresponding spatial relational graph. Nodes 0 to 7 represent 8 body segments. For "peel", node 8 and node 9 represent the orange and the knife, respectively; for "cut apart", nodes 8, 9, and 10 correspond to the cutting board, broccoli, and knife. (Color figure online)

In our framework, we use an attention mechanism in graphs to capture those relationships between elements key to recognising the activity. Intuitively, key spatial relations between elements will correspond to high attention weight.

Figure 3 shows the spatial relational graph for two activities: peel and cut apart. For the activity "peel", node 9 (knife) receives the most information from those nodes representing body segments, showing that the interaction of the knife and body segment contributes more to the prediction of this activity. For the activity "cut apart", the interaction between the cutting board and broccoli and the interaction between the body segment and knife are more important than other pairwise interactions of existing elements. These results are consistent with the hypothesis of hierarchical attributes (mentioned in Sect. 2.2) of human activities and facilitate the interpretability of HAR. (See Appendix H for more.)

3.4 Semantic Alignment, Interpretability and SPD

Fig. 4. An example treemap indicating proportion of incorrect predictions by class for "cut apart" for graph models without context (left) and with context (right).

Figure 4 illustrates the incorrectly predicted class distribution on videos with ground truth "cut apart" for graph models without context and those with. On first appearance, the names of these falsely predicted classes appear to be semantically closer to the predicted class when context is included (right image). For example, all classes on the right map are related to humans using knives, as is "cut apart" (the ground truth class), while the left map contains activities such as "move" "pull apart" and "add" which do not involve a knife (See Appendix F for more examples). Note also that the number of unique falsely predicted classes falls when context is included. Darker shading on the image indicates greater semantic similarity between predicted and target class, Sim with CLIP Language vectors, and the right hand image is a little darker overall as we would expect. In some cases, shading may not correspond to human judgment of class similarity though, as Sim is an imperfect proxy for human judgments of class similarity.

The overall SPD for the models and the class-level SPD for some example activities are presented in Table 3 and this quantifies the changes in semantic similarity illustrated in Fig. 6. Note that the overall SPD with the correctly predicted samples is lower than that without those samples, which confirms our analysis for the implication of accuracy in Sect. 2.5. For both SPD scores with correct prediction samples (spd) and those without (spd^-), the same trend is seen for almost all activities, that ViViT reduces SPD compared to graph without context, while the graph with context reduces the SPD further. We read this as graph with context improving this aspect of interpretability over ViViT and ViViT improving over body segment only graphs. This reduction in SPD

Table 3. Example results for class-level SPD^- and SPD. A higher value means a larger semantic dispersion of the prediction for a certain activity.

Activities	SPD^-			SPD		
	$\mathcal{R}_B$	$\mathcal{R}_B \cup \mathcal{R}_J \cup \mathcal{S}_J$	ViViT	$\mathcal{R}_B$	$\mathcal{R}_B \cup \mathcal{R}_J \cup \mathcal{S}_J$	ViViT
add	0.233	**0.082**	0.120	0.192	**0.027**	0.044
change temperature	0.369	**0.032**	0.275	0.283	**0.011**	0.162
cut apart	0.392	**0.270**	0.402	0.304	**0.198**	0.313
move	0.310	**0.205**	0.249	0.213	**0.046**	0.107
slice	**0.370**	0.572	0.379	0.047	**0.036**	0.299
shake	0.226	**0.138**	0.263	0.154	**0.053**	0.099
screw close	0.122	**0.085**	0.332	0.169	**0.034**	0.151
wash	0.138	0.177	**0.126**	0.047	**0.036**	0.045
overall (weighted)	0.322	**0.258**	0.283	0.191	**0.088**	0.135

corresponds to the qualitative results seen in Fig. 6: for "cut apart", "move", and "change temperature", all the SPD values become smaller under the contextual setting. The SPD differences between ViViT and graph without context suggests that ViViT is incorporating additional information from video regions beyond those showing the body segments, and we argue that this is precisely where the contextual information is. We argue further that the additional improvement seen by graph with context is achieved by using the context prompt to guide the incorporation of contextual information. Note that the differences in SPD scores with correct predictions (right of table) are dominated by differences in the accuracy of the predictions. Therefore, the more significant result appears to be that this trend is also seen for SPD scores excluding correct predictions (left of table). This trend is in spite of the fact that the spd^- for ViViT includes 17% more of the "easier" instances – those predicted correctly by the graph with context model and thus excluded from the corresponding SPD calculation. An illustration of SPD performance of each class is given in Appendix G.

4 Related Work

For HAR tasks, Convolutional Neural Networks (CNNs) are powerful backbone models (feature extractors) primarily applied to 2D images. Karpathy et al. propose an approach [22] to extend CNN connectivity in the temporal domain. Two-Stream CNNs [42] capture appearance features from still frames and motion features between frames using spatial and temporal streams. Another track of methods extend the architecture of CNNs from 2D to 3D for the video-based HAR tasks [8,20,47]. In general, 2D CNNs only encode the spatial information from images, while 3D CNNs are able to capture both the spatial and temporal information from videos. Most recently, transformer-based models have emerged as a dominant trend in current vision tasks, as they outperform conventional

CNNs in various computer vision applications. Video transformer architecture such as ViViT [4], TimeSformer [7] extract spatiotemporal tokens from input videos, employing transformer layers for encoding. These video transformer models present SoTA results on many video classification tasks.

Due to the computational intensity and the black-box nature of backbone models, some studies aim to leverage structural representations to enhance their performance [15,30,50,54]. Graphs are a popular structural representation for human activities, which can be integrated into a neuro-symbolic learning process. Qualitative Spatio-temporal Graphs represent activities as interactions between scene elements, decomposing prolonged activities into events represented by event graphs [44]. STAG uses spatial and temporal hierarchies to model inter-object relations, capturing activity representations [17]. STRG employs a similarity graph and a spatio-temporal graph to capture the appearance of both humans and related objects and their changes over time [49].

Some graph-based HAR method is based on a common presumption about hierarchy, which posits that higher-level activities can be seen as some composition of lower-level activities. Prior work [19,21,33,43] all predefine these compositions in some way. For instance, *getting up* is defined as a change from *lying on (the bed)* to *sitting on (the bed)* in [19]. In comparison, we capture higher level activities as spatio-temporal graph representations, where nodes are key regions of interest with latent visio-semantic features, and relate to human body parts and objects from the context prompt. Directed edges govern the passing of messages between nodes, which are latent representations of the relationship of one node to another, and edge weights indicate the relevance of this relationship to the final prediction. We argue that our approach is more flexible and does not rely on predefined (and fairly rigid) assumptions about which actions composed to form others, while still supporting action compositionally.

5 Conclusion

In this paper, we introduce a graph-based neuro-symbolic framework to investigate the role of context in human activity recognition with the HARCP task and its impact on interpretability. We also show that the attention mechanism can enhance interpretability by effectively capturing the most important interactions between the key elements of the activities. To quantitatively assess interpretability, we propose a novel metric, SPD, to measure how the prediction errors align with human norms. Our results show that our graph model for human activities with a context prompt substantially outperforms fine-tuned large backbone models without a context prompt. We also demonstrate that our model with context information has a lower (better) SPD indicating closer semantic alignment, and hence better interpretability, compared to other models.

A Dataset and Preprocessing Pipeline

A.1 Dataset

We validate our framework using the MPII-Cooking 2 dataset [37], a video dataset recording human subjects cooking a diverse set of dishes. In total, there are 30 subjects performing 87 different types of fine-grained activities, across more than 14000 clips (our data points). We chose this dataset for the following reasons: the videos are stable; there is one person (the subject) in each clip, making human poses easier to capture; and the related objects are provided alongside the videos. All these attributes align with our needs for investigating context.

A.2 Preprocessing Pipeline

We sample the videos so that each video contains 16 frames. The whole framework was built on PyTorch [35]. We split the train, test and validation set the same as [37]. We extracted the body key points from the video using the MediaPipe framework [5]. Considering that the activities in the cooking domain usually involve the upper body, to reduce redundancy, we only keep the key points for the upper body resulting in 8 body segments. For those RoIs, we tried both ImageNet pre-trained ResNet18 [16] and CLIP image encoder [36] as the feature extractor in each video frame. More details of our implementation of the framework are presented in the appendix.

B Memory and Computational Costs

The two-path setting without context outperforms the graph only setting without context. It is not clear why, but may be due to the global path compensating for some missing context information in the body segment based graph. ViViT is a SOTA large backbone model for video classification, and while it outperforms other visual-only models (e.g. graph without context), fine-tuning it requires a significant amount of computational resources. Table 4 shows the number of parameters trained and the FLOP values for different models. The results indicate that the parameters in ViViT are almost 400 times those of the graph model, and the FLOPs are more than 30K times those of the graph comparison.

Table 4. The comparison of computational resources consumed for different architectures. (L is the lightweight two-path model.)

	ViViT	Conv+Seq	Graph	Two-Path(L)
Params ($\times 10^6$)	114	6.167	0.298	0.440
FLOPs ($\times 10^9$)	284.4	0.012	0.008	0.008

C Details of Implementation

C.1 Grad-CAM for ViT

Considering a ViT model for a classification task. An input image is separated into $N = n \times n$ tokens, and the output of the encoder is a $(1+N) \times d$ dimension matrix A (there is one classification token and N image tokens; d is the dimension of the output features for each token). In this matrix, the first token carries the classification information and it is used to perform the classification through a fully connected layer. The logit for each category is noted as y^c. For the matrix A, we remove the classification token, remaining the dimensions $N \times d$ to calculate the gradients to y^c. For each token k in A, the conventional calculation of class feature weight for each token α_k^c is

$$\alpha_k^c = \frac{1}{d} \sum_j \frac{\partial y^c}{\partial A_{kj}} \tag{10}$$

where α^c is a N dimensional vector.

However, since the pertaining of CLIP model is based on sentence instead of labels for specific categories, the generated CAM contains a lot of noise. We utilise the denoising method proposed in [28] to alleviate the category confusion problem, which replace the logit y^c with the softmax value s^c:

$$s^c = \frac{exp(y^c)}{\sum_{\hat{c}=1}^{C} exp(y^{\hat{c}})} \tag{11}$$

and the refined class feature weights can be calculated as:

$$\alpha_k^c = \frac{1}{d} \sum_j \sum_{\hat{c}} \frac{\partial y^{\hat{c}}}{\partial A_{kj}} * \frac{\partial s^c}{\partial y^{\hat{c}}} \tag{12}$$

The weight is then applied back to the feature matrix A,

$$z_k^c = ReLU(\sum_j \alpha_k^c A_{kj}) \tag{13}$$

where z^c is an N-dimensional vector and each element represents the contribution of a token k to a certain class c. ReLU is employed to remove the negative values. The z^c is then reshaped into an $n \times n$ CAM, each element of which represents the contribution of each separated grid of an original input image to the class.

C.2 Framework Implementation

We sample the videos so that each video contains 16 frames. In the training process, we use Adam Optimiser with a 0.0005 learning rate for the body-segment only graph, 0.0001 for the graph with context, and 0.001 for the Conv + LSTM global path.

For the training of Graph Attention Network. For each RoI (body segments and objects), the dimension of the extracted features from the corresponding region is 500 when using ResNet18 backbone model and 512 when using CLIP VIT-B backbone model. The node embedding size during the training process is 250. For the temporal aggregation of each graph, we used a 3-layer LSTM model with 200-dimensional hidden state size.

For the training of the global path, the dimension of the input feature is 1000 when using ResNet18 as the feature extractor and 512 when using CLIP as the feature extractor. We aggregated the features for each frame by a 3-layer LSTM, the hidden state size of which is 200.

D Weighting Image versus Text Information

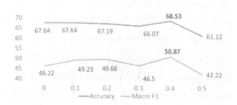

Fig. 5. The change of the performance according to the weight (w_j in Eq. 2) on the I-T gate.

Figure 5 illustrates the relationship between the weight in the I-T gate and the model's performance. The recognition performs best when combining the two features with the visual weight (w_j) set at 0.4. Introducing only text features can significantly improve accuracy compared to using image features alone. The main reason for this improvement could be the noise caused by the imperfect localisation of regions for objects. Specifically, the bounding boxes assigned may be either too small, too large, or not precisely positioned for the objects, while text features remain consistent and stable across the entire dataset. Since there is a 4.6% performance gain on Macro-f1 based on the fusion of the two features, the contribution of image features to the recognition cannot be ignored. Although text features are more stable, the variability in representing different states of an object is sometimes limited. For example, in a "washing" activity, an apple would be represented as a whole apple, while in a "cutting" activity, the status of an apple changes from a whole apple to slices, which cannot be represented by using only text features.

E Investigating the Impact of the Context Prompt

Table 5 shows the performance boost for each class in the validation set.

Table 5. The class-level Average Precision(AP) for the validation set (those classes not in the validation set are removed). The performance gain is the boost of AP in the graph with context setting compared to the body segment-only graph.

Activity	$\mathcal{R}_B$(%)	$\mathcal{R}_B \cup \mathcal{R}_J \cup \mathcal{S}_J$(%)	Gain(%)
taste	0.39	100.00	+99.61
clean	0.48	100.00	+99.52
pour	0.83	100.00	+99.17
fill	0.87	100.00	+99.13
stir	1.57	100.00	+98.43
squeeze	1.61	100.00	+98.39
spice	1.73	100.00	+98.27
remove from package	1.08	95.00	+93.92
dry	7.14	100.00	+92.86
scratch off	2.66	86.67	+84.00
put lid	3.52	86.99	+83.47
pull apart	3.73	80.06	+76.34
take lid	5.97	70.88	+64.91
change temperature	17.31	75.24	+57.94
move	24.64	81.64	+57.00
peel	22.97	79.34	+56.37
add	12.40	68.31	+55.91
plug	0.54	50.00	+49.46
screw open	1.85	46.30	+44.45
enter	72.63	100.00	+27.37
wash	67.67	89.66	+21.99
cut apart	24.05	43.55	+19.50
shake	60.03	77.41	+17.38
slice	5.20	18.44	+13.24
throw in garbage	75.87	86.74	+10.87
wring out	1.21	9.35	+8.14
screw close	46.49	51.23	+4.74
pull up	0.45	4.17	+3.72
rip off	0.61	1.67	+1.06
turn off	1.14	1.84	+0.70
unplug	1.96	2.22	+0.26
open egg	0.24	0.37	+0.13
package	0.29	0.36	+0.07
push down	0.51	0.52	+0.01
open	1.80	1.75	-0.06
test temperature	0.75	0.65	-0.10
cut off ends	2.29	2.10	-0.19
turn on	2.03	1.84	-0.20
read	1.23	0.94	-0.29
put on	1.16	0.59	-0.57
chop	1.23	0.40	-0.84
cut dice	7.02	5.73	-1.28
cut	3.02	1.45	-1.57
purge	2.78	0.86	-1.92
cut out inside	3.26	0.44	-2.82
pull	6.53	3.46	-3.07
open close	16.04	1.23	-14.81
take out	80.48	63.56	-16.92
put in	34.94	2.40	-32.54
close	58.86	2.49	-56.37

F Qualitative Semantic Errors

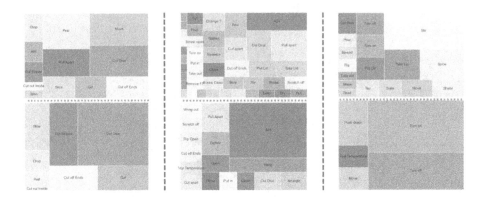

Fig. 6. Treemap indicating proportion of incorrect predictions by class for "cut apart" (left), "move" (middle) and "change temperature" (right), for graph models without context (top) and with context (bottom). Darker shades indicate greater semantic similarity with target class.

Figure 6 illustrates the proportion of incorrectly predicted activity classes for three predicted activities: cut apart, move, and change temperature, considering both graph models without context and those with. This shows that when introducing context information (bottom row), the number of falsely predicted classes falls in all cases. From first impressions, the names of these falsely predicted class are semantically closer to the predicted class when context is included. For instance, all classes presented in the bottom-left map are related to humans using knives, which is similar to "cut apart" (the predicted class), while the top-left map contains activities such as "move," "pull apart," and "add," which are not scenes involving knife usage. For "change temperature," compared to the body-segment-only model, which confuses it with "stir" and "spice" more, the context-aware model confuses it with "turn on" and "turn off" more, which is much more semantically similar to the activity.

G Class-Level SPD

Table 6 presents the SPD value for each class.

H Relational Attention Weight

Figure 7 shows the spatial relational graph for three activities.

Table 6. The class-level SPD^- and SPD (combining validation and testing set; - denotes that no sample is classified into this class).

	SPD^-			SPD		
Activities	$\mathcal{R}_B$	$\mathcal{R}_B \cup \mathcal{R}_J \cup \mathcal{S}_J$	ViViT	$\mathcal{R}_B$	$\mathcal{R}_B \cup \mathcal{R}_J \cup \mathcal{S}_J$	ViViT
stir	-	**0.033**	0.231	-	**0.008**	0.122
spice	-	**0.005**	0.398	-	**0.000**	0.178
turn on	-	-	0.134	-	-	0.101
shake	0.226	**0.138**	0.263	0.154	**0.053**	0.099
move	0.310	**0.206**	0.249	0.213	**0.046**	0.107
press	-	-	-	-	-	-
grate	-	-	0.204	-	**0.000**	0.204
cut apart	0.392	**0.270**	0.402	0.304	**0.198**	0.313
test temperature	-	-	-	-	-	-
rip off	-	-	-	-	-	-
pull up	-	**0.000**	0.018	-	**0.000**	0.006
mix	-	-	-	-	-	-
enter	0.490	-	**0.380**	0.077	**0.000**	0.019
pour	-	**0.012**	0.100	-	**0.001**	0.068
taste	-	**0.233**	0.889	-	**0.147**	0.186
smell	-	0.897	**0.259**	-	**0.117**	0.159
slice	**0.370**	0.572	0.379	0.308	0.449	**0.299**
cut stripes	-	-	0.000	-	-	0.000
wash	0.138	0.177	**0.126**	0.047	**0.036**	0.045
remove label	-	-	-	-	-	-
turn off	-	-	0.138	-	-	0.109
fill	-	0.131	**0.090**	-	0.026	**0.025**
cut off ends	-	-	0.959	-	-	0.774
tap	-	-	0.174	-	-	0.174
gather	-	-	0.190	-	-	0.160
cut	-	-	0.469	-	-	0.396
open close	0.376	-	**0.233**	0.286	-	**0.125**
spread	-	-	0.104	-	-	0.072
take lid	-	**0.089**	0.445	-	**0.027**	0.275
rip open	-	-	-	-	-	-
strew	-	-	-	-	-	-
put rubber band	-	-	-	-	-	-
screw close	0.247	**0.108**	0.332	0.169	**0.034**	0.151

continued

Table 6. continued

Activities	SPD^-			SPD		
	$\mathcal{R}_B$	$\mathcal{R}_B \cup \mathcal{R}_J \cup \mathcal{S}_J$	ViViT	$\mathcal{R}_B$	$\mathcal{R}_B \cup \mathcal{R}_J \cup \mathcal{S}_J$	ViViT
unplug	-	-	0.619	-	-	0.236
put lid	-	**0.000**	0.228	-	**0.000**	0.130
cut dice	-	-	0.264	-	-	0.162
flip	-	-	-	-	-	-
take apart	-	-	0.761	-	-	0.529
hang	-	-	0.142	-	-	0.110
poke	-	-	-	-	-	-
squeeze	-	-	0.557	-	-	0.189
put on	**0.495**	0.963	-	**0.495**	0.963	-
scratch off	-	0.591	**0.328**	-	0.329	**0.219**
take out	0.352	0.239	**0.167**	0.108	0.080	**0.031**
read	-	-	0.388	-	-	0.388
add	0.233	**0.082**	0.200	0.192	**0.027**	0.158
wring out	-	-	0.981	-	-	0.656
change temperature	0.369	**0.032**	0.275	0.283	**0.011**	0.162
close	**0.267**	-	0.337	0.133	-	**0.079**
arrange	-	-	-	-	-	-
open egg	-	-	0.856	-	-	0.300
open	-	0.483	-	-	0.341	**0.000**
pull	-	-	-	-	-	-
remove from package	-	**0.710**	0.858	-	**0.206**	0.445
remove rubber band	-	-	-	-	-	-
throw in garbage	0.757	0.808	**0.466**	0.196	0.082	**0.062**
purge	-	-	-	-	-	-
dry	0.351	**0.198**	0.230	0.240	**0.017**	0.128
pull apart	0.846	0.729	**0.325**	0.846	**0.105**	0.230
plug	0.706	0.507	**0.197**	0.706	0.253	**0.090**
push down	-	0.942	**0.584**	-	0.320	**0.267**
put in	0.232	-	**0.117**	0.145	-	**0.060**
chop	-	-	0.428	-	-	0.402
screw open	-	0.128	**0.125**	-	**0.039**	0.052
clean	-	**0.000**	0.221	-	**0.000**	0.115
assemble	-	-	-	-	-	-
cut out inside	-	-	-	-	-	-
package	-	-	-	-	-	-
peel	0.397	0.643	**0.373**	0.283	**0.124**	0.219

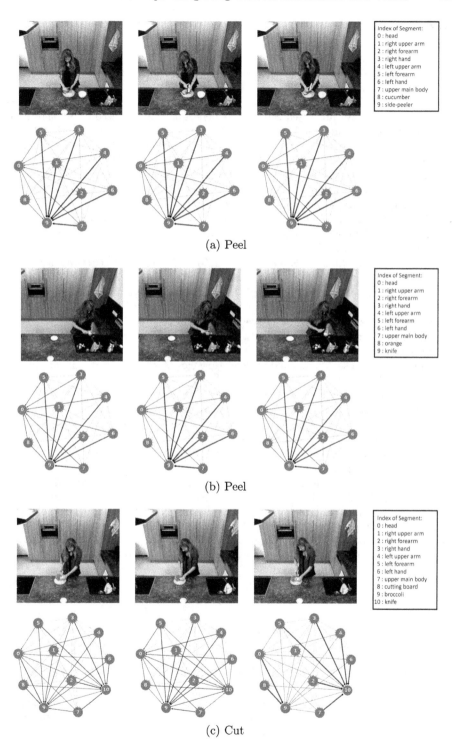

Fig. 7. Example frames for activities and their corresponding spatial relational graph. For each activity, we provide three frames in chronological order.

References

1. Ahn, J., Cho, S., Kwak, S.: Weakly supervised learning of instance segmentation with inter-pixel relations. In: Proceedings of the IEEE/CVF Conference on Computer Vision and Pattern Recognition, pp. 2209–2218 (2019)
2. Ahn, J., Kwak, S.: Learning pixel-level semantic affinity with image-level supervision for weakly supervised semantic segmentation. In: Proceedings of the IEEE Conference on Computer Vision and Pattern Recognition, pp. 4981–4990 (2018)
3. Apriceno, G., Passerini, A., Serafini, L., et al.: A neuro-symbolic approach to structured event recognition. Leibniz Int. Proc. Inf. **206**, 1101–1114 (2021)
4. Arnab, A., Dehghani, M., Heigold, G., Sun, C., Lučić, M., Schmid, C.: ViViT: a video vision transformer. In: Proceedings of the IEEE/CVF International Conference on Computer Vision, pp. 6836–6846 (2021)
5. Bazarevsky, V., Grishchenko, I., Raveendran, K., Zhu, T., Zhang, F., Grundmann, M.: BlazePose: on-device real-time body pose tracking. arXiv preprint arXiv:2006.10204 (2020)
6. Beddiar, D.R., Nini, B., Sabokrou, M., Hadid, A.: Vision-based human activity recognition: a survey. Multimedia Tools Appl. **79**(41), 30509–30555 (2020)
7. Bertasius, G., Wang, H., Torresani, L.: Is space-time attention all you need for video understanding? In: ICML. vol. 2, p. 4 (2021)
8. Carreira, J., Zisserman, A.: Quo Vadis, action recognition? A new model and the kinetics dataset. In: Proceedings of the IEEE Conference on Computer Vision and Pattern Recognition, pp. 6299–6308 (2017)
9. Christian, B.: The Alignment Problem: How can Machines Learn Human Values? Atlantic Books (2021)
10. Dima, D.C., Janarthanan, S., Culham, J.C., Mohsenzadeh, Y.: Shared representations of human actions across vision and language. bioRxiv (2023)
11. Dosovitskiy, A., et al.: An image is worth 16x16 words: transformers for image recognition at scale. arXiv preprint arXiv:2010.11929 (2020)
12. Gao, J., Zhang, T., Xu, C.: I know the relationships: zero-shot action recognition via two-stream graph convolutional networks and knowledge graphs. In: Proceedings of the AAAI Conference on Artificial Intelligence, vol. 33, pp. 8303–8311 (2019)
13. Geetha, M.K., Arunnehru, J., Geetha, A.: Early recognition of suspicious activity for crime prevention. In: Computer Vision: Concepts, Methodologies, Tools, and Applications, pp. 2139–2165. IGI Global (2018)
14. Geirhos, R., Meding, K., Wichmann, F.A.: Beyond accuracy: quantifying trial-by-trial behaviour of CNNs and humans by measuring error consistency. Adv. Neural. Inf. Process. Syst. **33**, 13890–13902 (2020)
15. Gkioxari, G., Girshick, R., Malik, J.: Contextual action recognition with R* CNN. In: Proceedings of the IEEE International Conference on Computer Vision, pp. 1080–1088 (2015)
16. He, K., Zhang, X., Ren, S., Sun, J.: Deep residual learning for image recognition. In: Proceedings of the IEEE Conference on Computer Vision and Pattern Recognition, pp. 770–778 (2016)
17. Herzig, R., et al.: Spatio-temporal action graph networks. In: Proceedings of the IEEE/CVF International Conference on Computer Vision Workshops (2019)
18. Jain, A., Zamir, A.R., Savarese, S., Saxena, A.: Structural-RNN: deep learning on spatio-temporal graphs. In: Proceedings of the IEEE Conference on Computer Vision and Pattern Recognition, pp. 5308–5317 (2016)

19. Ji, J., Krishna, R., Fei-Fei, L., Niebles, J.C.: Action genome: actions as compositions of spatio-temporal scene graphs. In: Proceedings of the IEEE/CVF Conference on Computer Vision and Pattern Recognition, pp. 10236–10247 (2020)
20. Ji, S., Xu, W., Yang, M., Yu, K.: 3D convolutional neural networks for human action recognition. IEEE Trans. Pattern Anal. Mach. Intell. **35**(1), 221–231 (2012)
21. Jin, Y., Zhu, L., Mu, Y.: Complex video action reasoning via learnable Markov logic network. In: Proceedings of the IEEE/CVF Conference on Computer Vision and Pattern Recognition, pp. 3242–3251 (2022)
22. Karpathy, A., Toderici, G., Shetty, S., Leung, T., Sukthankar, R., Fei-Fei, L.: Large-scale video classification with convolutional neural networks. In: Proceedings of the IEEE Conference on Computer Vision and Pattern Recognition, pp. 1725–1732 (2014)
23. Kipf, T.N., Welling, M.: Semi-supervised classification with graph convolutional networks. In: International Conference on Learning Representations (2017). https://openreview.net/forum?id=SJU4ayYgl
24. Kirillov, A., et al.: Segment anything. arXiv preprint arXiv:2304.02643 (2023)
25. Kriegeskorte, N., Mur, M., Bandettini, P.A.: Representational similarity analysis-connecting the branches of systems neuroscience. Front. Syst. Neurosci. **2**, 249 (2008)
26. Kurby, C.A., Zacks, J.M.: Segmentation in the perception and memory of events. Trends Cogn. Sci. **12**(2), 72–79 (2008)
27. Lamb, L.C., Garcez, A., Gori, M., Prates, M., Avelar, P., Vardi, M.: Graph neural networks meet neural-symbolic computing: a survey and perspective. arXiv preprint arXiv:2003.00330 (2020)
28. Lin, Y., et al.: Clip is also an efficient segmenter: a text-driven approach for weakly supervised semantic segmentation. In: Proceedings of the IEEE/CVF Conference on Computer Vision and Pattern Recognition, pp. 15305–15314 (2023)
29. Liu, H., Li, C., Li, Y., Lee, Y.J.: Improved baselines with visual instruction tuning. In: Proceedings of the IEEE/CVF Conference on Computer Vision and Pattern Recognition, pp. 26296–26306 (2024)
30. Ma, C.Y., Kadav, A., Melvin, I., Kira, Z., AlRegib, G., Graf, H.P.: Attend and interact: higher-order object interactions for video understanding. In: Proceedings of the IEEE Conference on Computer Vision and Pattern Recognition, pp. 6790–6800 (2018)
31. Newcombe, N., Huttenlocher, J.: Making Space: The Development of Spatial Representation and Reasoning. MIT Press (2000)
32. Onofri, L., Soda, P., Pechenizkiy, M., Iannello, G.: A survey on using domain and contextual knowledge for human activity recognition in video streams. Expert Syst. Appl. **63**, 97–111 (2016)
33. Ou, Y., Mi, L., Chen, Z.: Object-relation reasoning graph for action recognition. In: Proceedings of the IEEE/CVF Conference on Computer Vision and Pattern Recognition, pp. 20133–20142 (2022)
34. Pareek, P., Thakkar, A.: A survey on video-based human action recognition: recent updates, datasets, challenges, and applications. Artif. Intell. Rev. **54**(3), 2259–2322 (2021)
35. Paszke, A., et al.: PyTorch: an imperative style, high-performance deep learning library. Adv. Neural Inf. Process. Syst. **32** (2019)
36. Radford, A., et al.: Learning transferable visual models from natural language supervision. In: International Conference on Machine Learning, pp. 8748–8763. PMLR (2021)

37. Rohrbach, M., et al.: Recognizing fine-grained and composite activities using hand-centric features and script data. Int. J. Comput. Vision **119**, 346–373 (2016)
38. Rudin, C.: Stop explaining black box machine learning models for high stakes decisions and use interpretable models instead. Nat. Mach. Intell. **1**(5), 206–215 (2019)
39. Russell, S.: Human Compatible: AI and the Problem of Control. Penguin UK (2019)
40. Selvaraju, R.R., Cogswell, M., Das, A., Vedantam, R., Parikh, D., Batra, D.: Grad-CAM: visual explanations from deep networks via gradient-based localization. Int. J. Comput. Vision **128**(2), 336–359 (2019). https://doi.org/10.1007/s11263-019-01228-7
41. Shao, J., Kang, K., Change Loy, C., Wang, X.: Deeply learned attributes for crowded scene understanding. In: Proceedings of the IEEE Conference on Computer Vision and Pattern Recognition, pp. 4657–4666 (2015)
42. Simonyan, K., Zisserman, A.: Two-stream convolutional networks for action recognition in videos. Adv. Neural Inf. Process. Syst. **27** (2014)
43. de Souza, F.D., Sarkar, S., Srivastava, A., Su, J.: Spatially coherent interpretations of videos using pattern theory. Int. J. Comput. Vision **121**, 5–25 (2017)
44. Sridhar, M., Cohn, A.G., Hogg, D.C.: Unsupervised learning of event classes from video. In: Twenty-Fourth AAAI Conference on Artificial Intelligence (2010)
45. Sucholutsky, I., et al.: Getting aligned on representational alignment. arXiv Preprint arXiv:2310.13018 (2023)
46. Sujith, B.: Crime detection and avoidance in ATM: a new framework. Int. J. Comput. Sci. Inf. Technol. **5**, 6068–6071 (2014)
47. Tran, D., Bourdev, L., Fergus, R., Torresani, L., Paluri, M.: Learning spatiotemporal features with 3D convolutional networks. In: Proceedings of the IEEE International Conference on Computer Vision, pp. 4489–4497 (2015)
48. Velickovic, P., Cucurull, G., Casanova, A., Romero, A., Lio, P., Bengio, Y., et al.: Graph attention networks. stat **1050**(20), 10–48550 (2017)
49. Wang, X., Gupta, A.: Videos as space-time region graphs. In: Proceedings of the European Conference on Computer Vision (ECCV), pp. 399–417 (2018)
50. Wu, C.Y., Feichtenhofer, C., Fan, H., He, K., Krahenbuhl, P., Girshick, R.: Long-term feature banks for detailed video understanding. In: Proceedings of the IEEE/CVF Conference on Computer Vision and Pattern Recognition, pp. 284–293 (2019)
51. Wu, X., Wang, R., Hou, J., Lin, H., Luo, J.: Spatial-temporal relation reasoning for action prediction in videos. Int. J. Comput. Vision **129**, 1484–1505 (2021)
52. Yu, K.P., Zhang, Z., Hu, F., Chai, J.: Efficient in-context learning in vision-language models for egocentric videos. arXiv preprint arXiv:2311.17041 (2023)
53. Zacks, J.M., Tversky, B., Iyer, G.: Perceiving, remembering, and communicating structure in events. J. Exp. Psychol. Gen. **130**(1), 29 (2001)
54. Zhou, B., Andonian, A., Oliva, A., Torralba, A.: Temporal relational reasoning in videos. In: Proceedings of the European Conference on Computer Vision (ECCV), pp. 803–818 (2018)
55. Zhou, B., Khosla, A., Lapedriza, A., Oliva, A., Torralba, A.: Learning deep features for discriminative localization. In: Proceedings of the IEEE Conference on Computer Vision and Pattern Recognition, pp. 2921–2929 (2016)

Assessing Logical Reasoning Capabilities of Encoder-Only Transformer Models

Paulo Pirozelli[1]([✉]), Marcos M. José[3], Paulo de Tarso P. Filho[2],
Anarosa A. F. Brandão[2], and Fabio G. Cozman[2]

[1] Instituto Mauá de Tecnologia, São Caetano do Sul, Brazil
paulo.silva@maua.br
[2] Universidade de São Paulo, São Paulo, Brazil
[3] University of Alberta, Edmonton, Canada

Abstract. Transformer models have shown impressive abilities in natural language tasks such as text generation and question answering. Still, it is not clear whether these models can successfully conduct a rule-guided task such as logical reasoning. In this paper, we investigate the extent to which encoder-only transformer language models (LMs) can reason according to logical rules. We ask whether these LMs can deduce theorems in propositional calculus and first-order logic, if their relative success in these problems reflects general logical capabilities, and which layers contribute the most to the task. First, we show for several encoder-only LMs that they can be trained, to a reasonable degree, to determine logical validity on various datasets. Next, by cross-probing fine-tuned models on these datasets, we show that LMs have difficulty in transferring their putative logical reasoning ability, which suggests that they may have learned dataset-specific features instead of a general capability. Finally, we conduct a layerwise probing experiment, which shows that the hypothesis classification task is mostly solved through higher layers.

Keywords: Logical reasoning · Language models · Transformer · Probing

1 Introduction

Transformer models are remarkably effective at a wide range of natural language processing (NLP) tasks, such as question answering, summarization, and text generation. By and large, these abilities are the result of specific training processes, where a language model is fine-tuned on a task-specific dataset. Curiously, encoder-only transformer models (LMs) also exhibit *implicit* linguistic and cognitive abilities for which they were not directly supervised. Such LMs have been shown to encode information on tense and number [7], anaphora and determiner-noun agreement [49], semantic roles [46], syntactic dependencies [32], relational knowledge [8], and spatiotemporal representation [15].

Given that logical reasoning is a core component of intelligence, human or otherwise [38], it is worth investigating the capabilities of encoder-only transformer models in executing tasks that necessitate such reasoning. Understanding whether LMs can solve logical problems, and the manner in which they tackle these problems, may enable us to understand the extent to which their inferences arise from reasoning rather than purely associative memory. This understanding is crucial for developing mechanisms that facilitate the generation of consistent outputs, whether in a neural-symbolic fashion or through the improvement of model architectures.

The goal of this paper is, thus, to assess the ability of encoder-only transformer models to reason according to the rules of logic—understood here as deductive arguments expressable in propositional calculus or first-order logic. We examine three main questions throughout this paper: i) Can encoder-only transformer models perform logical reasoning tasks?; ii) How general is this ability?; and iii) What layers better contribute to solving these tasks?

Section 2 reviews the work on transformers' logical reasoning abilities, as well as the function of probing in uncovering latent knowledge. Next, we gather and describe four datasets grounded on logical deduction (Sect. 3). In a first batch of experiments, we conduct a systematic comparison of encoder-only transformer models on these datasets (Sect. 4). Section 5 then investigates whether the performance in the previous task could be attributed to some general ability and whether the reasoning learned from one dataset could be transferred to a similar dataset. Finally, we perform a layerwise probing to understand which layers are responsible for solving logical deduction problems (Sect. 6).[1]

2 Related Work

Logical Reasoning in Transformer Models Transformer models are powerful enough to solve logical reasoning tasks expressed in natural language [4,17,47,55]. Yet, it is not clear if these models have actually mastered logical reasoning. LMs seem to inevitably rely on statistical artifacts to deduce theorems, rather than on general, rule-based relationships [55]. They use shortcuts to solve hypothesis classification problems, leading to vulnerabilities in reasoning (e.g., LMs are fooled when hypotheses appear within rules), and making them susceptible to irrelevant (logically consistent) perturbations [14].

Studies focused on functional words close to logical operators have identified similar shortcomings in LMs' reasoning capabilities. Transformers struggle to deal with negation, predicting similar probabilities to a sentence and its negation [22,25]. [24] extend these findings to conjunction, disjunction, and existential and universal quantification, showing that expressions associated with these operations are frequently dominated by semantically rich words. Transformers also fail in modeling semi-functional-semi-content words in general, such as quantifiers and modals [41]. Tangentially to logic, [9] show that transformer models do not always properly handle compositionality: sometimes a translation is more local than desired (treating idioms as regular constructions), sometimes it is excessively global (paying attention to irrelevant parts of the sentence). Moreover, there is evidence that the way LMs compose sentences does not align well with human judgment [28].

---

[1] Data, code, and complete results are available at github.com/paulopirozelli/logicalreasoning.

Large LMs have also been assessed for their logical reasoning capabilities. Despite their impressive achievements in numerous tasks, these models still struggle with multi-step and compositional problems [12,36]. Although good at individual deductions, large LMs struggle with proof planing: when many valid proof steps are available, they often take the wrong path [40]. Large LMs also appear to suffer from human-like biases in logical tasks: they perform significantly worse when the semantic content is too abstract or conflicts with prior knowledge [10,44].

Probing Tasks. Probing is a technique used to discover if a model has acquired certain type of knowledge. In probing, a dataset that encodes a particular property (e.g., part-of-speech) is used to train a classifier (the probe), taking the representations produced by the original model as inputs for the classification [1]. As the LM is not further trained on the task, as it would be in fine-tuning, the probe's performance depends on whether the information about that property had already been encoded by the model. Thus, success in the task provides some evidence that the model has stored such knowledge in its parameters. Probing can be used to examine several components of LMs, such as embeddings, attention heads, and feedforward computations.

Transformer models have been extensively studied through probing [1]. Most attention has been given to BERT, which gave rise to a large literature on the properties encoded by this model [37]. RoBERTa has also been studied in some detail through probing; e.g., what abilities that model learns during training [30,56] and its knowledge of semantic structural information [51].

Facts: St Johnstone is a Scottish team. St Johnstone is part of the Scottish Premiership.
Rules: If a team is part of the league, it has joined the league. St Johnstone and Minsk are different teams. For two different teams, either one team wins or the other team wins. Minsk won against St Johnstone.
Hypothesis: At least one Scottish team has joined the Scottish Premiership.
Label: TRUE

Facts: Bob is young. Bob is red. Bob is nice. Charlie is young. Charlie is rough. Charlie is big. Dave is red. Dave is cold. Dave is blue. Fred is kind. Fred is green. Fred is cold.
Rules: If someone is rough and kind and round then they are big. If someone is round and red then they are kind. If someone is nice and round and cold then they are young. If someone is cold and kind then they are nice. If someone is cold and blue then they are round.
Hypothesis: Fred is rough.
Label: FALSE

Fig. 1. Examples of logical reasoning arguments. The argument at the top is from FOLIO, a manually-written dataset; the one at the bottom is from RuleTaker, a dataset that uses a semi-synthetic approach.

Table 1. Main features of the logical reasoning datasets. FOL stands for first-order logic, PC for propositional calculus, and CI for conjunctive implication. The labels in the datasets are as follows: **FOLIO** (False, True, Unknown), **LogicNLI** (Contradiction, Entailment, Neutral, Paradox), **RuleTaker** (False, True), **SimpleLogic** (False, True). The average number of premises and the average number of words per argument refer to the training set statistics. Appendix B shows the full dataset label distribution.

Dataset	Size (train/val/test)	Scope	Type	Label	Avg. Premises	Avg. Words
FOLIO	1003 / 204 / -	FOL	Manual	3	5.23	64.01
LogicNLI	16000 / 2000 / 2000	FOL	Semi-synt.	4	24	211.86
RuleTaker	27363 / 3899 / 7793	FOL (CI)	Semi-synt.	2	16.30	100.06
SimpleLogic	11341 / 1418 / 1417	PC (CI)	Synthetic	2	60.76	467.45

3 Logical Reasoning Datasets

In assessing logical reasoning, we restricted our analysis to datasets related to propositional calculus (PC) and first-order logic (FOL), with FOL being an extension of PC that includes predicates and quantifiers. These logical systems offer a powerful formalism that balances simplicity and expressivity in representing and reasoning about statements and relationships. They are suitable for capturing a wide range of knowledge and formalizing a large number of domains.

In addition to being expressible in PC or FOL, we selected datasets that satisfied three other properties: i) observations had to be as self-contained as possible; ii) sentences needed to have corresponding translations in both logical formalism and natural language; and iii) hypotheses had to be declarative sentences. The first property aims to decouple logic from background knowledge in order to assess pure reasoning capabilities. While using natural language examples means implicit knowledge can never be completely erased, we opted for datasets that minimized this by explicitly stating prior knowledge or by using inference patterns where resorting to prior knowledge is unnecessary. For this reason, we only considered pure logical datasets and did not include other forms of reasoning such as scientific reasoning [3,26,54], mathematical reasoning [5,20,34], counterfactual reasoning [33,35,52], planning [48], inductive reasoning [42,44], and abductive reasoning [44]. The second property, the translation into logical formalism, allows one to determine unambiguously the logical relationship between premises and hypotheses, while the natural language counterpart allows us to probe the LMs. Hence, we excluded datasets that lacked natural language translations, such as LTL [16]. The last property excluded QA datasets [29,43], as they required the understanding of several types of questions (e.g., who, where) that are entangled with semantic and contextual knowledge (e.g., that "Alice" is the name of a person).

In the end, four logical reasoning datasets were selected: FOLIO [17], LogicNLI [47], RuleTaker [4], and SimpleLogic [55]. Examples of arguments can be seen in Fig. 1. These datasets cover a wide range of variations in terms of construction (manual, semi-synthetic, synthetic), alignment with common sense, linguistic variability, and scope (PC, full or partial FOL). For instance, FOLIO is human-written; LogicNLI and RuleTaker both use a template which is then manually edited; and SimpleLogic is fully synthetic. FOLIO and LogicNLI encompass the full spectrum of FOL; RuleTaker is expressible in FOL but only covers negation and conjunctive implications,[2] and SimpleLogic is restricted to conjunctive implications in PC. Regarding the number of labels, RuleTaker and SimpleLogic have True and False labels; FOLIO includes an Unknown label; and LogicNLI admits a fourth possibility, Paradox, where both a hypothesis and its negation can be deduced from the premises. Table 1 summarizes the main statistics of the datasets. Appendix A provides a detailed description of the four datasets.

For all datasets, inputs are formatted as "fact$_1$. fact$_2$. ... fact$_n$. rule$_1$. rule$_2$. ... rule$_m$ <SEP> shypothesis.", for which a label must be predicted. The output is simply a probability distribution over the possible labels, which varies from dataset to dataset.

4 Testing LMs for Hypothesis Classification

The performance of LMs in logical reasoning, including in the datasets described in the previous section, has been studied in scattered experiments without a clear unified context that allows direct comparison. Due to this, we decided to fine-tune a wide range of pretrained encoder-only transformer models on those datasets.[3] We modeled this problem as a *hypothesis classification task*, where the goal is to determine the logical relationship between a set of premises and a conclusion. To ensure comprehensive coverage, eight families of LMs were assessed: DistilBERT [39], BERT [11], RoBERTa [31], Longformer [2], DeBERTa [19], AlBERT [27], XLM-RoBERTa [6], and XLNet [53]. The full list of models is displayed in the left column of Table 2.

To fine-tune our models, we used a classification head with a single linear layer of dimension (embedding-length, labels), and applied a dropout of 0.5 to the linear operation. As input for the classification head, we used the last hidden embedding of the [CLS] token, as is customary for classification tasks in NLP. Sequences were padded and truncated to the maximum length allowed by each LM. Models were trained for up to 50 epochs, using early stopping with a patience of 5 epochs. We used Adam as our optimizer (with β = [0.9, 0.999] and no weight decay) and experimented with two different learning rates (1e-5 and 1e-6). Models were selected based on the loss for the validation set, with results reported for the test set. The only exception is FOLIO, where only the validation set is publicly available; results are thus reported for this set. We report accuracy as the standard metric, as classes in the datasets are balanced. Table 2 displays the best result achieved in each case. The best and worst scores for each dataset are highlighted in blue and red, respectively. We also provide a largest class baseline for comparison.

Results show that the LMs were able to classify hypotheses with reasonable success. Almost all models came close to solving RuleTaker and achieved an accuracy above 90% in SimpleLogic. Results were comparatively lower for FOLIO and LogicNLI, but

---

[2] Conjunctive implications are arguments of the form $(fact.[\wedge fact.]^* rule.[\wedge rule.]^* \Rightarrow hypothesis)$.

[3] We opted to explore encoder-only models because this type of architecture is well-suited for classification tasks. These models have access to the whole input sequence and are typically trained on discriminative tasks, such as masked language modeling.

Table 2. Accuracy comparison among several encoder-only transformer models for the hypothesis classification task across four datasets: FOLIO, LogicNLI, RuleTaker, and SimpleLogic. The models are listed in the left column of the table. The best and worst scores for each dataset are highlighted in blue and red, respectively. "Largest class" refers to the accuracy achieved by always selecting the class with the highest frequency in the training set. Results for RoBERTa-large, selected for subsequent analyses, are in bold.

	FOLIO	LogicNLI	RuleTaker	SimpleLogic
DistilBERT	50.98	36.20	86.55	93.58
BERT base	52.45	48.75	98.91	92.31
BERT large	61.76	42.50	99.94	91.88
RoBERTa base	58.82	62.90	98.04	92.87
RoBERTa large	**64.71**	**72.70**	**99.78**	**90.83**
Longformer base	62.75	58.05	99.92	94.21
Longformer large	62.25	74.15	99.94	92.37
DeBERTa xsmall	54.41	65.30	99.81	91.67
DeBERTa small	53.43	59.65	95.23	93.23
DeBERTa base	60.78	66.70	99.81	93.72
DeBERTa large	64.71	84.70	99.97	93.72
DeBERTa xlarge	62.25	25.00	99.99	49.96
DeBERTa xxlarge	71.57	25.00	50.02	50.04
ALBERT base	57.35	66.80	99.91	92.17
ALBERT large	56.37	66.20	99.88	91.53
ALBERT xlarge	38.73	65.10	99.97	90.05
ALBERT xxlarge	56.86	93.90	99.94	92.24
XLM-RoBERTa base	55.88	45.20	97.64	91.74
XLM-RoBERTa large	62.75	65.45	99.95	91.74
XLNet base	58.33	55.00	99.19	94.28
XLNet large	58.33	71.40	99.86	92.94
Largest class	35.29	25.00	50.02	50.03

the LMs generally surpassed the largest class baselines by a considerable margin. A weaker performance observed in these two datasets was expected, given their greater language variability and broader logical scope; and in the case of FOLIO, its smaller size as well. Overall, the encoder-only transformer models worked relatively well as *soft reasoners* [4], being able to successfully deduce theorems from premises expressed in natural language. Noteworthy exceptions were the performances of AlBERT-XL in FOLIO, DeBERTa-XL and -XXL in LogicNLI and SimpleLogic, DeBERTa-XXL in RuleTaker, and the overall lower performance of DistilBERT.

5 Cross-Probing Fine-Tuned LMs

The encoder-only transformer models showed reasonable performance on the hypothesis classification task, where they were fine-tuned on the logical reasoning datasets. This, however, raises some questions: has the ability to solve this task, whatever it is, been acquired during the fine-tuning stage, or was it present from the start (i.e., from

Table 3. Results for the cross-probing task. On the left, we present the best fine-tuned RoBERTa-large models for each dataset. The datasets used in the probes are listed at the top. We report only the best result for each probe. Blue cells indicate the probe of a fine-tuned model on the same dataset. In parentheses, we denote the percentage difference from the pretrained model. "Largest class" refers to the accuracy achieved by always selecting the class with the highest frequency in the training set.

	FOLIO	LogicNLI	RuleTaker	SimpleLogic
Pretrained	32.88	25.54	50.01	61.19
FOLIO	55.05 (+67.42)	27.28 (+6.81)	60.74 (+21.45)	62.82 (+2.66)
LogicNLI	36.60 (+11.31)	67.95 (+166.05)	69.37 (+38.70)	62.06 (+1.42)
RuleTaker	40.32 (+22.62)	36.01 (+40.99)	99.44 (+98.84)	62.89 (+2.77)
SimpleLogic	32.88 (0)	25.44 (-0.39)	51.02 (+2.01)	92.35 (+50.92)
Largest class	35.29	25.00	50.02	50.03

pretraining)? Most importantly, have LMs truly developed a generalized logical reasoning capability? To examine these questions, we run a *cross-probing* task: we take the LMs previously fine-tuned on our logical datasets, as well as a pretrained LM, and probe them on these same datasets. Given the large number of possible tests, we restricted our investigation to a single model, RoBERTa-large, so as to dig deeper on it. This LM demonstrated a suitable balance between performance, consistency among datasets, and training time in the previous tests.

To start, we took the best fine-tuned RoBERTa-large model for each dataset and removed their classification heads, leaving just the transformer blocks, as in a pretrained model. Then, we attached a new classification head to it; i.e., the probe. As in the fine-tuning stage, we passed the formatted inputs in natural language to the LMs and tried to predict the correct label for a set of premises. However, unlike the fine-tuning stage, only the probe is updated now, while the model's body is kept frozen during the backward pass. The goal is to assess if some logical reasoning ability was learned by the LM without letting the model adapt to the task.

The same training policies from the fine-tuning step were followed in this stage: models were trained with early stopping for up to 50 epochs (patience of 5 epochs) based on the validation loss, using two learning rates (1e-5 and 1e-6). Also, two different classifiers were tested as probes:

- **1-layer** A single affine transformation is applied to the embedding of the [CLS] token. The classification head has shape (1024, labels); 1024 being the dimensionality of RoBERTa-large hidden states. We used a dropout of 0.5 before the classifier.
- **3-layer** The [CLS] embedding passes through three consecutive layers of shape (1024, 256), (256, 64), and (256, labels), respectively. We used a dropout of 0.5 in between linear layers and ReLU as the activation function.

In the tests, the two probes led to similar results. We take this as strong evidence that the knowledge used in the logical reasoning tasks, whatever it is, can be linearly recovered from the internal representations of RoBERTa-large.

Table 3 displays the best results attained in the cross-probing task. The left column lists the RoBERTa-large fine-tuned models from the previous experiment, while the remaining columns represent the datasets they were probed against. The blue cells along the diagonal indicate instances where models were probed on the same datasets they were initially fine-tuned on. Percentage differences in accuracy relative to the pretrained case are reported in parentheses. As expected, the fine-tuned model for a specific dataset performed better in that same dataset, albeit less than in the fine-tuning scenario. This makes sense, since in fine-tuning, both the model's body and head are optimized, whereas in a probe the head is in charge of all the learning. These results serve as a sanity check that our probing is working.

The first row in Table 3 contains the scores for the probes with pretrained RoBERTa. Accuracy levels for LogicNLI and RuleTaker closely resemble the largest class baseline, while the result for FOLIO falls below its corresponding baseline. Pretrained RoBERTa only helped to solve SimpleLogic, a dataset constrained to conjunctive implication with minimal language variation. Its pretraining scheme, dynamic masked language modeling, did not equip it with adequate logic-like knowledge to solve complex reasoning problems without specific training.

We can see from this that pretrained RoBERTa appears to have no proper logical reasoning skills. But has it acquired such an ability through fine-tuning on logical datasets? After all, RoBERTa-large was able to solve the hypothesis classification tasks reasonably well after specific training. When analyzing the results of the cross-probing task, however, we may doubt whether a general logical reasoning ability in fact emerged from fine-tuning.

In general, the fine-tuned LMs showed limited transferability when probed on different datasets. Although some gain was achieved compared to the pretrained model, they remained well below what an LM fine-tuned on the same dataset could obtain. SimpleLogic presents an interesting case. The LMs fine-tuned on the other datasets performed similarly to the pretrained model on this dataset. This is despite SimpleLogic covering only a subset of propositional calculus, a domain included in those datasets. One would expect that a model capable of solving more complex problems would be able to reason on this simpler dataset (in terms of logical scope and linguistic variability). At the same time, the LM fine-tuned on SimpleLogic did not exhibit improved performance on the other datasets, indicating a lack of acquired general logical reasoning ability during its training.

Two main conclusions can be drawn from this experiment:

1. If the difference in accuracy between pretrained RoBERTa and the largest class baseline indicates the amount of logical reasoning contained in this LM, then pretrained RoBERTa seems to have very limited or no logical reasoning abilities.
2. If the difference in accuracy between fine-tuned LMs (when applied to different datasets) and the pretrained RoBERTa model indicates the amount of logical reasoning they acquired in the fine-tuning process, then these LMs have acquired little or no general logical reasoning capability as well, suggesting that they mostly learned statistical features of the datasets. This aligns with other findings for transformer models [12,55].

6 Inspecting Fine-Tuned Models Layerwise

We now address another question: which parts of the LMs are more capable of solving logical reasoning tasks? To answer this, we probe the different layers of the fine-tuned

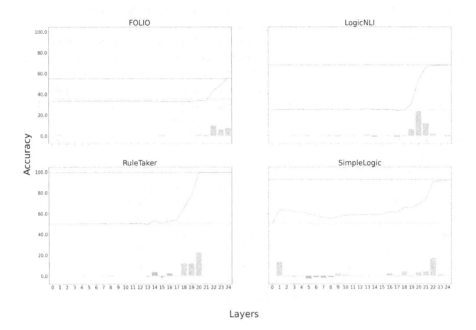

Fig. 2. RoBERTa-large models fine-tuned on FOLIO, LogicNLI, RuleTaker, and SimpleLogic, and probed for the same datasets layerwise. The pretrained baselines are indicated by gray lines, while the values achieved in the cross-probing task are represented by black lines. The colored bars indicate the change in accuracy from the previous layers. Probing was performed with a 1-layer classifier and a learning rate of 1e-6. (Color figure online)

RoBERTa-large models using the same datasets they were trained on. Our goal is to identify which layers are more effective in deducing hypotheses. We expect this to provide further evidence of what sort of knowledge LMs are using to solve the hypothesis classification task. Similar to the previous experiment, the fine-tuned LMs were frozen, the older classification head was removed, and a probe was trained on top of the layers. More concretely, for each layer i in the model, we passed the premises through the model up to layer i, and used the outputted embedding of the [CLS] token at that layer as the input to the probe. As in the previous experiment, only the probe was trained. The same two classifiers from the last experiment were tested. They were positioned on top of the [CLS] token of each layer, with 25 layers in total (24 transformer blocks plus the initial embedding layer). We adopted the same configurations from the previous tests: models were trained with early stopping for up to 50 epochs (with a patience of 5 epochs) based on the validation loss, using two learning rates (1e-5 and 1e-6).

Figure 2 shows the accuracy for the probes stacked on the various layers of the fine-tuned LMs, using a 1-layer classifier and a learning rate of 1e-6 (Appendix C presents graphs for the other configurations). The blue line plots the accuracy on the task for each layer, while the bars display the differential score for layer$_i$; i.e., the change in accuracy from layer$_i$ to layer$_{i-1}$ [45]. The gray line marks the pretrained model baseline, and the black line indicates the score achieved in the cross-probing task.

A similar behavior is exhibited by all models. They remain close to the pretrained baseline in the low and mid layers. Accuracy then grows rapidly in the final layers, achieving a performance equal to the cross-probing baseline. How does this compare to other types of knowledge found in transformer models? Literature on transformers shows that surface information, such as sentence length [23], is mostly captured by lower layers. Middle layers are responsible for processing syntactic knowledge, like syntax trees [21]. Finally, higher layers are responsible for task-specific functions [18] and contextual representations [13].

In our layerwise probing, higher layers were the only ones able to solve the hypothesis classification task better than a pretrained model. This suggests that the knowledge acquired during fine-tuning was connected to dataset-specific features rather than general representations. It also explains why the information was not transferable among datasets. Although indirect, this experiment provides further evidence that encoder-only transformer models do not possess robust logical reasoning capabilities. SimpleLogic was the only case that presented a growth in the initial layers. This behavior may indicate that the dataset is solvable through the use of some heuristics based on shallow statistical features, such as the number of premises, as discussed by [55].

7 Conclusion

Logical reasoning is a valuable ability that humans use in thinking, arguing, and planning, as well as a core component of many AI systems. Here, we investigated the role of logical reasoning in encoder-only transformer models. By gathering a number of logical reasoning datasets, we observed that language models can be trained to perform complex logical tasks with relative success. However, upon closer inspection, doubts arose regarding whether these models have truly learned to reason according to logical rules. First, by probing a pretrained RoBERTa-large model with logical reasoning datasets, it became apparent that this language model did not possess intrinsic logical reasoning abilities. Second, models fine-tuned on one dataset struggled to generalize well to other datasets, even within the same domain. This observation suggests that these language models did not acquire robust logical reasoning capabilities even after specific training. Third, the knowledge necessary to solve logical reasoning tasks seems to emerge primarily at higher, more contextual layers, probably linked to statistical features of the datasets rather than deeper representations.

8 Limitations

We run experiments for a large variety of encoder-only transformer models in Sect. 4. However, due to space and time constraints, we focused on RoBERTa-large for the analysis in Sects. 5–6. While we expect the same behavior to appear in the other encode-only models, further tests are needed to verify whether conclusions can be reliably extended to them. We have not explored decoder nor encoder-decoder models either, which could widely extend the number of models to be tested. We cannot rule out the possibility that robust logical reasoning is an emergent ability only manifested in large language models [50]. Additionally, other types of representations, such as attentions and feedforward computations, could be analyzed in relation to logical reasoning. Further work should also focus on other types of logical formalism beyond PC and FOL.

Acknowledgements. This work was supported by the Center for Artificial Intelligence USP/IBM/FAPESP (C4AI), jointly funded by the São Paulo Research Foundation (FAPESP grant 2019/07665-4) and by the IBM Corporation. Research by Marcos José has been carried out with support by *Itaú Unibanco S.A.* through the scholarship program *Programa de Bolsas Itaú* (PBI); Fabio Cozman was partially supported by CNPq grants 312180/2018-7 and 305753/2022-3. We acknowledge support also by CAPES - Finance Code 001.

A Datasets

In this appendix, we describe the four logical reasoning datasets in more detail. Table 4 indicates the sources from where they were obtained.

FOLIO. [17] is a human-annotated dataset for FOL reasoning problems. Logically-sound contexts were generated in two ways: in the first, annotators created contexts from scratch, based on random Wikipedia pages; in the second, a template of nested syllogisms was used, from which annotators then replaced the abstract entities and categories by nouns, phrases or clauses, as to make the text to reflect real-life scenarios. Next, the authors verified the alignment between natural language sentences and FOL formulas and added implicit commonsense knowledge as premises. After that, they verified the syntactic validity and label consistency of FOL formula annotations with a FOL prover. Finally, sentences were reviewed for grammar issues and language fluency. Only train and validation tests are available, so we used the latter for reporting tests. Hypotheses can be *True*, *False*, or *Unknown*.

LogicNLI. [47] is a FOL dataset created through a semi-automatic method. A set of logical templates was defined and then filled by subjects and predicates sampled from predefined sets. Next, manual edits were made to correct grammatical errors and resolve semantic ambiguities. Hypothesis are classified as *Entailment*, *Contradiction*, *Neutral*, and *Paradox*. A paradox is defined as a situation where both a sentence and its contrary can be inferred from the premises. We used the standard version of the dataset, which encompasses all labels.

RuleTaker. [4] is a logical reasoning dataset in which rules are conjunctive implications. Predicates may be negated and facts may be either attributes (which assign properties to entities) or relations (which relate two entities). We used the ParaRules version, where rules and facts were paraphrased by crowdworkers into more natural language; paraphrased constructions were then combined to form new templates. We also used the updated version of RuleTaker (problog), which eliminated some world model inconsistencies. Hypothesis can be *True*, when a hypothesis follows from the premises, and *False* otherwise (closed-world assumption, CWA).

SimpleLogic. [55] is similar to RuleTaker, only supporting conjunctive implication (facts are simply conjunctive implications with empty antecedents). Language variance is virtually removed by using a fixed template for translating FOL into natural language and by the use of a small random list of words as predicates. Argumentative complexity is limited by setting thresholds for input length, number of predicates, and reasoning depth. We reconstructed the original template based on the examples given in the paper. For our tests, we used the RP Balanced version. We undersampled the largest class (True) to obtain the same number of observations as for the False class. Labels can be *True* and *False* (CWA).

Table 4. Sources for the datasets.

Dataset	Source
FOLIO	https://github.com/Yale-LILY/FOLIO
LogicNLI	https://github.com/omnilabNL/LogicNLI
RuleTaker	https://allenai.org/data/ruletaker
SimpleLogic	https://github.com/joshuacnf/paradox-learning2reason

B Label distribution

Table 5 shows the label distribution for the datasets used in the paper. The row above provides the number of observations per label, and the row below shows their relative percentage. Labels: **FOLIO**: False, True, Unknown. **LogicNLI**: Contradiction, Entailment, Neutral, Paradox. **RuleTaker**: False, True. **SimpleLogic**: False, True.

Table 5. Label distribution for logical reasoning datasets.

	Train	Validation	Test
FOLIO	286 / 388 / 329	-	63 / 72 / 69
	(28.51% / 38.68% / 32.80%)	-	(30.88% / 35.29% / 33.82%)
LogicNLI	4000 / 4000 / 4000 / 4000	500 / 500 / 500 / 500	500 / 500 / 500 / 500
	(25% each)	(25% each)	(25% each)
RuleTaker	13666 / 13697	1946 / 1953	3895 / 3898
	(49.94% / 50.05%)	(49.91% / 50.09%)	(49.98% / 50.02%)
SimpleLogic	5696 / 5645	683 / 735	709 / 708
	(50.22% / 49.77%)	(48.16% / 51.83%)	(50.03% / 49.96%)

C Laywerwise probing

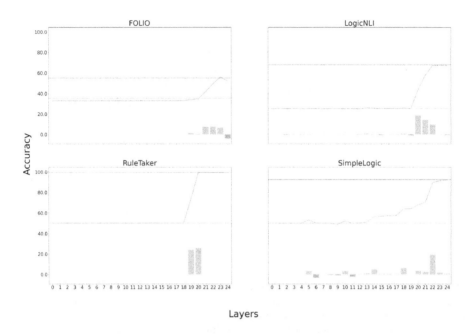

Fig. 3. RoBERTa-large models fine-tuned on FOLIO, LogicNLI, RuleTaker, and SimpleLogic, and probed for the same datasets layerwise. The pretrained baselines are indicated by gray lines, while the values achieved in the cross-probing task are represented by black lines. The colored bars indicate the change in accuracy from the previous layers. Probing was performed with a 3-layer classifier and a learning rate of 1e-6. (Color figure online)

For the layerwise probing (Sect. 6), we tested two different classifiers (1-layer and 3-layer) and two learning rates (1e-6 and 1e-5). Figure 2 above displayed the results for the 1-linear classifier and 1e-6 learning rate. The figures below display the results for the other probes. Figure 3 provides the graphs for the 3-layer classifier and learning rate of 1e-6; Fig. 4 provides the graphs for the 1-layer classifier and learning rate of 1e-5; and Fig. 5 provides the graphs for the 3-layer classifier and learning rate of 1e-5.

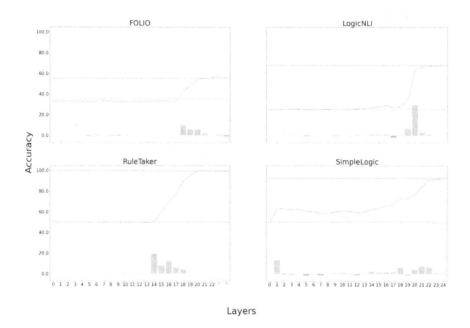

Fig. 4. RoBERTa-large models fine-tuned on FOLIO, LogicNLI, RuleTaker, and SimpleLogic, and probed for the same datasets layerwise. The pretrained baselines are indicated by gray lines, while the values achieved in the cross-probing task are represented by black lines. The colored bars indicate the change in accuracy from the previous layers. Probing was performed with a 1-layer classifier and a learning rate of 1e-5. (Color figure online)

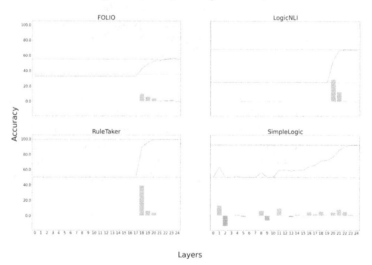

Fig. 5. RoBERTa-large models fine-tuned on FOLIO, LogicNLI, RuleTaker, and SimpleLogic, and probed for the same datasets layerwise. The pretrained baselines are indicated by gray lines, while the values achieved in the cross-probing task are represented by black lines. The colored bars indicate the change in accuracy from the previous layers. Probing was performed with a 3-layer classifier and a learning rate of 1e-5. (Color figure online)

References

1. Belinkov, Y.: Probing classifiers: promises, shortcomings, and advances. Comput. Linguist. **48**(1), 207–219 (2022). https://doi.org/10.1162/coli_a_00422, https://aclanthology.org/2022.cl-1.7
2. Beltagy, I., Peters, M.E., Cohan, A.: Longformer: The Long-Document Transformer. CoRR **abs/2004.05150** (2020). https://arxiv.org/abs/2004.05150
3. Clark, P., et al.: Think you have Solved Question Answering? Try ARC, the AI2 Reasoning Challenge. arXiv preprint arXiv:1803.05457 (2018)
4. Clark, P., Tafjord, O., Richardson, K.: Transformers as Soft Reasoners over Language. arXiv preprint arXiv:2002.05867 (2020)
5. Cobbe, K., et al.: Training Verifiers to Solve Math Word Problems (2021). https://doi.org/10.48550/ARXIV.2110.14168. https://arxiv.org/abs/2110.14168
6. Conneau, A., et al.: Unsupervised cross-lingual representation learning at scale (2020)
7. Conneau, A., Kruszewski, G., Lample, G., Barrault, L., Baroni, M.: What you Can Cram into a Single $&!#* Vector: Probing Sentence Embeddings for Linguistic Properties. In: Proceedings of the 56th Annual Meeting of the Association for Computational Linguistics (Volume 1: Long Papers), pp. 2126–2136. Association for Computational Linguistics, Melbourne, Australia (Jul 2018). https://doi.org/10.18653/v1/P18-1198, https://aclanthology.org/P18-1198
8. Dai, D., Dong, L., Hao, Y., Sui, Z., Wei, F.: Knowledge Neurons in Pretrained Transformers. CoRR abs/2104.08696 (2021). https://arxiv.org/abs/2104.08696
9. Dankers, V., Bruni, E., Hupkes, D.: The paradox of the compositionality of natural language: a neural machine translation case study. In: Proceedings of the 60th Annual Meeting of the Association for Computational Linguistics (Volume 1: Long Papers), pp. 4154–4175. Association for Computational Linguistics, Dublin, Ireland, May 2022. https://doi.org/10.18653/v1/2022.acl-long.286, https://aclanthology.org/2022.acl-long.286
10. Dasgupta, I., et al.: Language Models Show Human-Like Content Effects on Reasoning (2022). https://doi.org/10.48550/ARXIV.2207.07051, https://arxiv.org/abs/2207.07051
11. Devlin, J., Chang, M., Lee, K., Toutanova, K.: BERT: pre-training of Deep Bidirectional Transformers for Language Understanding. CoRR abs/1810.04805 (2018). http://arxiv.org/abs/1810.04805
12. Dziri, N., et al.: Faith and Fate: Limits of Transformers on Compositionality (2023)
13. Ethayarajh, K.: How Contextual are Contextualized Word Representations? Comparing the Geometry of BERT, ELMo, and GPT-2 Embeddings. CoRR abs/1909.00512 (2019). http://arxiv.org/abs/1909.00512
14. Gaskell, A., Miao, Y., Specia, L., Toni, F.: Logically consistent adversarial attacks for soft theorem provers (2022)
15. Gurnee, W., Tegmark, M.: Language models represent space and time (2023)
16. Hahn, C., Schmitt, F., Kreber, J.U., Rabe, M.N., Finkbeiner, B.: Teaching Temporal Logics to Neural Networks (2020). https://doi.org/10.48550/ARXIV.2003.04218, https://arxiv.org/abs/2003.04218
17. Han, S., et al.: FOLIO: Natural Language Reasoning with First-Order Logic. arXiv preprint arXiv:2209.00840 (2022)
18. Hao, Y., Dong, L., Wei, F., Xu, K.: Visualizing and Understanding the Effectiveness of BERT. CoRR abs/1908.05620 (2019). http://arxiv.org/abs/1908.05620
19. He, P., Liu, X., Gao, J., Chen, W.: DeBERTa: Decoding-enhanced BERT with Disentangled Attention. CoRR abs/2006.03654 (2020). https://arxiv.org/abs/2006.03654
20. Hendrycks, D., et al.: Measuring Mathematical Problem Solving with the Math Dataset. arXiv preprint arXiv:2103.03874 (2021)

21. Hewitt, J., Manning, C.D.: A structural probe for finding syntax in word representations. In: Proceedings of the 2019 Conference of the North American Chapter of the Association for Computational Linguistics: Human Language Technologies, Volume 1 (Long and Short Papers). pp. 4129–4138. Association for Computational Linguistics, Minneapolis, Minnesota (Jun 2019). https://doi.org/10.18653/v1/N19-1419, https://aclanthology.org/N19-1419
22. Hossain, M.M., Kovatchev, V., Dutta, P., Kao, T., Wei, E., Blanco, E.: An Analysis of Natural Language Inference Benchmarks through the Lens of Negation. In: Proceedings of the 2020 Conference on Empirical Methods in Natural Language Processing (EMNLP), pp. 9106–9118. Association for Computational Linguistics, Online, November 2020. https://doi.org/10.18653/v1/2020.emnlp-main.732, https://aclanthology.org/2020.emnlp-main.732
23. Jawahar, G., Sagot, B., Seddah, D.: What Does BERT Learn about the Structure of Language? In: Proceedings of the 57th Annual Meeting of the Association for Computational Linguistics. pp. 3651–3657. Association for Computational Linguistics, Florence, Italy, July 2019. https://doi.org/10.18653/v1/P19-1356, https://aclanthology.org/P19-1356
24. Kalouli, A.L., Sevastjanova, R., Beck, C., Romero, M.: Negation, coordination, and quantifiers in contextualized language models. In: Proceedings of the 29th International Conference on Computational Linguistics. pp. 3074–3085. International Committee on Computational Linguistics, Gyeongju, Republic of Korea. October 2022. https://aclanthology.org/2022.coling-1.272
25. Kassner, N., Schütze, H.: Negated and misprimed probes for pretrained language models: birds can talk, but cannot fly. In: Proceedings of the 58th Annual Meeting of the Association for Computational Linguistics, pp. 7811–7818. Association for Computational Linguistics, Online, July 2020. https://doi.org/10.18653/v1/2020.acl-main.698, https://aclanthology.org/2020.acl-main.698
26. Lai, G., Xie, Q., Liu, H., Yang, Y., Hovy, E.: RACE: large-scale ReAding Comprehension Dataset From Examinations (2017). https://doi.org/10.48550/ARXIV.1704.04683, https://arxiv.org/abs/1704.04683
27. Lan, Z., Chen, M., Goodman, S., Gimpel, K., Sharma, P., Soricut, R.: Albert: A lite bert for self-supervised learning of language representations. arXiv preprint arXiv:1909.11942 (2019)
28. Liu, E., Neubig, G.: Are representations built from the ground up? an empirical examination of local composition in language models (2022). https://doi.org/10.48550/ARXIV.2210.03575, https://arxiv.org/abs/2210.03575
29. Liu, J., Cui, L., Liu, H., Huang, D., Wang, Y., Zhang, Y.: LogiQA: a challenge dataset for machine reading comprehension with logical reasoning (2020). https://doi.org/10.48550/ARXIV.2007.08124, https://arxiv.org/abs/2007.08124
30. Liu, L.Z., Wang, Y., Kasai, J., Hajishirzi, H., Smith, N.A.: Probing Across Time: What Does RoBERTa Know and When? CoRR **abs/2104.07885** (2021). https://arxiv.org/abs/2104.07885
31. Liu, Y., et al.: Roberta: A Robustly Optimized BERT Pretraining Approach. arXiv preprint arXiv:1907.11692 (2019)
32. Manning, C.D., Clark, K., Hewitt, J., Khandelwal, U., Levy, O.: Emergent Linguistic Structure in Artificial Neural Networks Trained by Self-Supervision. Proc. Natl. Acad. Sci. **117**(48), 30046–30054 (2020). https://doi.org/10.1073/pnas.1907367117, https://www.pnas.org/doi/abs/10.1073/pnas.1907367117
33. O'Neill, J., Rozenshtein, P., Kiryo, R., Kubota, M., Bollegala, D.: I Wish I Would Have Loved This One, But I Didn't–A Multilingual Dataset for Counterfactual Detection in Product Reviews. arXiv preprint arXiv:2104.06893 (2021)
34. Patel, A., Bhattamishra, S., Goyal, N.: Are NLP Models Really Able to Solve Simple Math Word Problems? (2021). https://doi.org/10.48550/ARXIV.2103.07191, https://arxiv.org/abs/2103.07191

35. Qin, L., Bosselut, A., Holtzman, A., Bhagavatula, C., Clark, E., Choi, Y.: Counterfactual Story Reasoning and Generation (2019). https://doi.org/10.48550/ARXIV.1909.04076, https://arxiv.org/abs/1909.04076
36. Rae, J.W., et al.: Scaling Language Models: Methods, Analysis & Insights from Training Gopher. CoRR **abs/2112.11446** (2021). https://arxiv.org/abs/2112.11446
37. Rogers, A., Kovaleva, O., Rumshisky, A.: A primer in BERTology: what we know about how BERT works. Trans. Assoc. Comput. Linguist. **8**, 842–866 (2020). https://doi.org/10.1162/tacl_a_00349, https://aclanthology.org/2020.tacl-1.54
38. Russell, S., Norvig, P.: Artificial Intelligence: A Modern Approach. Prentice Hall, 3 edn. (2010)
39. Sanh, V., Debut, L., Chaumond, J., Wolf, T.: Distilbert, a distilled version of bert: smaller, faster, cheaper and lighter (2020)
40. Saparov, A., He, H.: Language Models Are Greedy Reasoners: A Systematic Formal Analysis of Chain-of-Thought (2023)
41. Sevastjanova, R., Kalouli, A.L., Beck, C., Schäfer, H., El-Assady, M.: Explaining contextualization in language models using visual analytics. In: Proceedings of the 59th Annual Meeting of the Association for Computational Linguistics and the 11th International Joint Conference on Natural Language Processing (Volume 1: Long Papers), pp. 464–476. Association for Computational Linguistics, Online (Aug 2021). https://doi.org/10.18653/v1/2021.acl-long.39, https://aclanthology.org/2021.acl-long.39
42. Sinha, K., Sodhani, S., Dong, J., Pineau, J., Hamilton, W.L.: CLUTRR: A Diagnostic Benchmark for Inductive Reasoning from Text. In: Proceedings of the 2019 Conference on Empirical Methods in Natural Language Processing and the 9th International Joint Conference on Natural Language Processing (EMNLP-IJCNLP), pp. 4506–4515. Association for Computational Linguistics, Hong Kong, China, November 2019. https://doi.org/10.18653/v1/D19-1458, https://aclanthology.org/D19-1458
43. Talmor, A., Herzig, J., Lourie, N., Berant, J.: CommonsenseQA: a question answering challenge targeting commonsense knowledge. In: Proceedings of the 2019 Conference of the North American Chapter of the Association for Computational Linguistics: Human Language Technologies, Volume 1 (Long and Short Papers), pp. 4149–4158. Association for Computational Linguistics, Minneapolis, Minnesota, June 2019. https://doi.org/10.18653/v1/N19-1421, https://aclanthology.org/N19-1421
44. Tang, X., et al.: Large Language Models are In-Context Semantic Reasoners rather than Symbolic Reasoners (2023)
45. Tenney, I., Das, D., Pavlick, E.: BERT Rediscovers the Classical NLP Pipeline. CoRR abs/1905.05950 (2019). http://arxiv.org/abs/1905.05950
46. Tenney, I., et al.: What do you Learn from Context? Probing for Sentence Structure in Contextualized Word Representations. CoRR abs/1905.06316 (2019). http://arxiv.org/abs/1905.06316
47. Tian, J., Li, Y., Chen, W., Xiao, L., He, H., Jin, Y.: Diagnosing the first-order logical reasoning ability through LogicNLI. In: Proceedings of the 2021 Conference on Empirical Methods in Natural Language Processing, pp. 3738–3747. Association for Computational Linguistics, Online and Punta Cana, Dominican Republic, November 2021. https://doi.org/10.18653/v1/2021.emnlp-main.303, https://aclanthology.org/2021.emnlp-main.303
48. Valmeekam, K., Olmo, A., Sreedharan, S., Kambhampati, S.: Large Language Models Still Can't Plan (A Benchmark for LLMs on Planning and Reasoning about Change) (2023)
49. Warstadt, A., et al.: BLiMP: the benchmark of linguistic minimal pairs for English. Trans. Assoc. Comput. Linguist. **8**, 377–392 (2020). https://doi.org/10.1162/tacl_a_00321, https://aclanthology.org/2020.tacl-1.25
50. Wei, J., et al.: Emergent Abilities of Large Language Models (2022). https://doi.org/10.48550/ARXIV.2206.07682, https://arxiv.org/abs/2206.07682

51. Wu, Z., Peng, H., Smith, N.A.: Infusing finetuning with semantic dependencies. Trans. Assoc. Comput. Linguist. **9**, 226–242 (2021). https://doi.org/10.1162/tacl_a_00363
52. Yang, X., Obadinma, S., Zhao, H., Zhang, Q., Matwin, S., Zhu, X.: SemEval-2020 Task 5: Counterfactual Recognition. arXiv preprint arXiv:2008.00563 (2020)
53. Yang, Z., Dai, Z., Yang, Y., Carbonell, J., Salakhutdinov, R., Le, Q.V.: Xlnet: generalized autoregressive pretraining for language understanding (2020)
54. Yu, W., Jiang, Z., Dong, Y., Feng, J.: ReClor: A Reading Comprehension Dataset Requiring Logical Reasoning (2020). https://doi.org/10.48550/ARXIV.2002.04326, https://arxiv.org/abs/2002.04326
55. Zhang, H., Li, L.H., Meng, T., Chang, K., den Broeck, G.V.: On the Paradox of Learning to Reason from Data. CoRR abs/2205.11502 (2022). https://doi.org/10.48550/arXiv.2205.11502, https://doi.org/10.48550/arXiv.2205.11502
56. Zhang, Y., Warstadt, A., Li, X., Bowman, S.R.: When do you need billions of words of pretraining data? In: Proceedings of the 59th Annual Meeting of the Association for Computational Linguistics and the 11th International Joint Conference on Natural Language Processing (Volume 1: Long Papers), pp. 1112–1125. Association for Computational Linguistics, Online, August 2021. https://doi.org/10.18653/v1/2021.acl-long.90, https://aclanthology.org/2021.acl-long.90

Variable Assignment Invariant Neural Networks for Learning Logic Programs

Yin Jun Phua[1(✉)] and Katsumi Inoue[1,2]

[1] Tokyo Institute of Technology, Tokyo, Japan
phua@c.citech.ac.jp, inoue@nii.ac.jp
[2] National Institute of Technology, Tokyo, Japan

Abstract. Learning from interpretation transition (LFIT) is a framework for learning rules from observed state transitions. LFIT has been implemented in purely symbolic algorithms, but they are unable to deal with noise or generalize to unobserved transitions. Rule extraction based neural network methods suffer from overfitting, while more general implementation that categorize rules suffer from combinatorial explosion. In this paper, we introduce a technique to leverage variable permutation invariance inherent in symbolic domains. Our technique ensures that the permutation and the naming of the variables would not affect the results. We demonstrate the effectiveness and the scalability of this method with various experiments. Our code is publicly available at https://github.com/phuayj/delta-lfit-2.

Keywords: Logic Program · Dynamic Systems · Symbolic Invariance

1 Introduction

Dynamic systems exist in every aspect of our world. Understanding and being able to model such dynamic systems allow us to predict and even control the outcomes of such systems. Learning from Interpretation Transition (LFIT) [10] is a framework that allows automatic construction of a model in the form of logic programs, based solely on the state transitions observed from dynamic systems. LFIT has been largely implemented with symbolic algorithms [20] that utilize logic operations. These algorithms are therefore interpretable and independently verifiable. The resulting model, a logic program that describes the dynamics of the system, is also interpretable. However, these symbolic algorithms treat all data as equally valid and thus are vulnerable to ambiguous, conflicting or noisy data. Symbolic LFIT algorithms also require all state transitions to be observable, and thus cannot generalize to or predict unobserved data.

Recent advances in deep learning and neural network represent a good opportunity to address the above issues. The field of combining neural network and symbolic algorithms, dubbed Neural-Symbolic AI (NSAI) provides an interesting avenue for addressing the issues above, while retaining the advantages of being interpretable and verifiable. With the advent of large language models

(LLM), there have been renewed interests [13] in combining symbolic reasoning with LLMs [17]. While these are promising directions for increasing reliability in LLMs, they are still far from being able to tackle the issue of being able to understand and verify the output of a neural network model.

In the field of understanding dynamic systems, NN-LFIT [8] proposes an extraction-based method that trains a neural network and extracts a logic program. DFOL [5] learns first-order rules also extracting symbolic knowledge from trained neural network. An advantage of these methods is the ability to retain interpretability while also capturing statistical characteristics of the dataset. However, these methods place limitations on the architecture of the neural network, making it difficult to utilize advancements in the deep learning field. For instance, application of these methods to the infamous attention mechanism is not straightforward.

δLFIT+ [19] has been proposed to take advantage of the strengths of neural network, while producing a model that is interpretable and verifiable. Based on the LFIT framework, δLFIT+ takes as input a set of state transitions and outputs the logic program that describes the state transitions. By not performing extractions and not placing any constraints on the neural network, δLFIT+ can utilize Set Transformer [16] to exploit the invariance in the permutation of the inputs. Instead of using gradient descent as an equivalence of the learning in symbolic algorithms, δLFIT+ trains a model that learns to perform the learning. In a sense, it is a meta-learning model that produces a symbolic model as an output.

However, there are several limitations to δLFIT+. First, while δLFIT+ is invariant to the order of state transitions in the input, it is not invariant to the permutation of the variables within each state. Next, δLFIT+ employs an "output node reuse" strategy to address scalability issues in the model architecture, but it also leads to a loss function that is difficult to optimize.

This paper proposes δLFIT2, shown in Fig. 1, that addresses the above limitations. δLFIT2 introduces a variable assignment invariant technique that addresses the issue of variable permutation within states. δLFIT2 also utilizes multiple different output heads instead of reusing the same node for different purposes, leading to a smoother loss function.

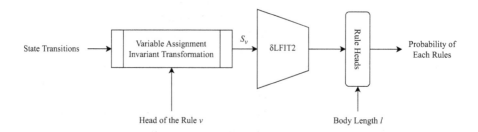

Fig. 1. Overview of the δLFIT2 Framework.

2 Related Work

Recent advancements in deep learning models have renewed interests in NSAI. In particular, as LLMs gain attention and are used widely, the lack of reasoning ability [25] starts to become critical.

Extraction-Based Methods. CIL^2-P [7] introduced the foundation for extracting symbolic knowledge from neural networks. While simple, the algorithm placed heavy constraints on the architecture of the neural network. Related to LFIT, NN-LFIT [8] proposed a method that trains a minimal neural network to model the dynamic system, then extracts symbolic rules based on the weights of the neural network.

Differentiable Programming-Based Methods. The Apperception Engine [3], δILP [2] and Logic Tensor Network [1] proposed methods that leverage gradient descent to learn a matrix that can later be transformed into symbolic knowledge. These methods can be integrated with CNN or other neural network modules to further process continuous data. D-LFIT [6] uses gradient descent to optimize a learnable matrix that semantically mirrors the T_P operator. Compared to δLFIT2, these methods require optimization for every problem instance. Scalability issues also remain, as the size of the learnable matrix scales together with the problem size.

Integration-Based Methods. NeurASP [28], Deepstochlog [26] and other similar works propose methods that either uses symbolic reasoning engines to drive neural network models or vice versa. Recent works that combine LLMs and reasoning such as [17] work similarly.

Invariance in Deep Learning. An increasing amount of work have started to focus on the permutation invariance inherent in the problem domain, leading to an increase in performance [14] [12] [23]. While most works focus on spatial invariance, this work focuses primarily on the invariance within the semantics.

In contrast to the above works, the neural network in δLFIT2 performs the semantic equivalent of learning in the symbolic algorithm. Symbolic knowledge is produced directly by the output of the neural network, instead of extraction from the results of the gradient descent optimization.

3 Background

Normal Logic Program for State Transitions. A normal logic program for state transitions (NLP) P is a set of logical state transition rules R that are of the following form:

$$R : A(t+1) \leftarrow A_1(t) \wedge \cdots \wedge A_m(t) \wedge \neg A_{m+1}(t) \wedge \cdots \wedge \neg A_n(t) \qquad (1)$$

where $A(t+1)$ is the head of the rule $h(R)$ and everything to the right of $\leftarrow$ is known as the body $b(R)$. This represents a rule where $A(t+1)$ is true if and only if $b^+(R) = \{A_1(t), \ldots, A_m(t)\}$ are true and $b^-(R) = \{A_{m+1}(t), \ldots, A_n(t)\}$ are false. If we consider a system with a set of variables $\{A, A_1, \ldots, A_m, A_{m+1}, \ldots, A_n\}$, and $A(t)$ represents the state of the atom A at time t, then the above is also a dynamic rule. Thus, the above rule can be described in plain English as, the state of the variable A at time $t+1$ is true if and only if the state of $A_1, \ldots, A_m$ is true and $A_{m+1}, \ldots, A_n$ is false at time t.

Note however, that even though the rule has time arguments for each atom, $t+1$ only appears in the head while t only appears in the body. Therefore, we can also equally express it with the following propositional rule:

$$A \leftarrow A_1 \wedge \cdots \wedge A_m \wedge \neg A_{m+1} \wedge \cdots \wedge \neg A_n$$

In this case, A can be any of $A_1, \ldots, A_n$ and will not be considered as a cyclic rule because of the implicit time parameter attached to the atom.

LFIT. Given an NLP P of such propositional rules, we can simulate the state transition of a dynamical system with the T_P operator.

An Herbrand base $\mathcal{B}$ represents all variables involved within a dynamic system. An Herbrand interpretation I is a subset of the $\mathcal{B}$ representing a snapshot of the state of the dynamic system. For an NLP P and an Herbrand interpretation I, the immediate consequence operator (or T_P operator) is the mapping $T_P : 2^\mathcal{B} \to 2^\mathcal{B}$:

$$T_P(I) = \{h(R) \mid R \in P, b^+(R) \subseteq I, b^-(R) \cap I = \emptyset\}. \tag{2}$$

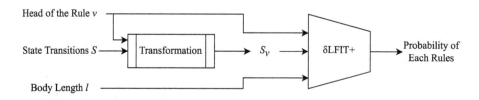

Fig. 2. Overview of the δLFIT+ Framework.

which represents the prediction of the next state of the dynamic system given the model of it P. Given a set of Herbrand interpretations E and $\{T_P(I) \mid I \in E\}$, the LFIT framework outputs a logic program P which completely represents the dynamics of E.

The LFIT framework can be described as an algorithm that takes a set of state transitions $S = \{(I, T_P(I)) \mid I \in E\}$ and an initial NLP P_0 which is usually empty as inputs, then outputs an NLP P such that P is consistent with the input S. Various symbolic algorithms have been proposed to implement the

LFIT framework. However, purely symbolic methods are unable to learn general rules where state transitions might be noisy or missing, thus NSAI methods have also been proposed.

δLFIT+ is a neural network implementation of the LFIT framework. Contrasting to many NSAI extraction based methods that extract symbolic knowledge from neural networks, δLFIT+ leverages neural networks to directly output symbolic knowledge, as depicted in Fig. 2.

δLFIT+ relies on the insight that the state transitions of a particular variable in a dynamic system can be uniquely described by a set of minimal rules. This means that a 1-to-1 mapping of state transitions to rules can be constructed. Indeed, this is the function approximated by the neural network.

δLFIT+ uses Set Transformer [16] to process the state transitions in a permutation invariant manner. In the LFIT framework, state transitions are expressed as $S = \{(I, T_P(I)) \mid I \in E\}$ where E is every observable state. In δLFIT+, the rules are generated for a single variable at a time. Therefore, for a variable $v \in \mathcal{B}$ that we are generating the rules for, the set of state transitions are transformed to $S_v = \{(I, v \in T_P(I)) \mid I \in E\}$ where the second element of the tuple is 1 if v is in the next state and 0 otherwise. The elements are tokenized and fed into the Set Transformer.

To be able to output rules, all possible rules have to be enumerable. The number of possible rules can scale very quickly if no restrictions are applied. To make it feasible, only minimal rules according to the definition of [19], which removes trivial rules and standardizes the order of the rule body, is considered. For every Herbrand base $\mathcal{B}$, a finite ordered set $\tau(\mathcal{B})$ that contains all minimal rules within $\mathcal{B}$ can be defined. δLFIT+ outputs rules by the head of the rule v and by the length of the body l one at a time. Since the output nodes of the neural network are fixed, v and l are provided as input which changes the interpretation of the outputs. Consider the Herbrand base $\mathcal{B} = \{p, q, r\}$. The rule for the output node at the first position can mean $p \wedge q$ if l is 2 or $p \wedge q \wedge r$ if l is 3. The head of the rule is also determined by the input v. Therefore, if the input for v is given as p and l is 2, the rule for the output node at the first position is $p \leftarrow p \wedge q$.

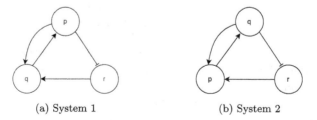

(a) System 1   (b) System 2

Fig. 3. Two identical systems with the labels of the top nodes swapped. Arrows signify activation, whereas flat-edged symbols signify inhibition.

4 Proposed Method

The loss function for δLFIT+ is not sufficiently smooth and thus very difficult to optimize. This is mainly caused by the non-continuous inputs of l and v that change the meaning of the output nodes. In particular, with the same set of state transitions, the neural network model needs to learn different sets of rules depending on l and v. Another issue was the permutation of the variables in the dynamic system. While δLFIT+ utilized Set Transformer to ensure the invariance in the ordering of the input of state transitions, the ordering of the variables within the state itself still causes the model to output different results.

In this section, we describe our proposed method δLFIT2 which addresses the issues mentioned above.

4.1 Variable Assignment Invariance

In δLFIT+, the state transitions are tokenized based on the lexicographical ordering of the variable names. However, while variable names in real world systems are mostly based on their functions, names are ultimately arbitrary and unrelated to the actual dynamics. This means 2 topologically identical systems, with only variables being assigned differently, produce 2 different sets of state transitions. Having to learn both sets of transitions increases the complexity of the problem space. If instead, we can abstract the variable names (and thus the ordering of the variables), leading to just one set of state transitions, we can simplify the learning problem for the neural network model.

Table 1. Logic programs representing the two identical systems.

System 1	System 2
$p \leftarrow q.$	$q \leftarrow p.$
$q \leftarrow p \wedge r.$	$p \leftarrow q \wedge r.$
$r \leftarrow \neg p.$	$r \leftarrow \neg q.$

Consider the identical systems shown in Fig. 3. These are boolean networks but can be represented by the logic programs in Table 1 respectively. Looking at the node on the top, which is variable p in Fig. 3a but variable q in Fig. 3b, they should result in the same identical set of rules, which is that they are activated by the variable in the bottom left. This is best achieved if the inputs into the model are the same.

The state transition that can be obtained for p in System 1 and q in System 2 respectively, based on the encoding described in Sect. 3, is as follows:

$$S_p^1 = \{(pqr, 1), (pq, 1), (p, 0), (\epsilon, 0), (r, 0), (qr, 1), (pr, 0), (q, 1)\} \quad (3)$$

$$S_q^2 = \{(pqr, 1), (pq, 1), (q, 0), (\epsilon, 0), (r, 0), (pr, 1), (qr, 0), (p, 1)\} \quad (4)$$

here we denote S^1 as state transitions obtained from System 1. Note that S_p^1 and S_q^2 are different.

To overcome this, we propose to use a permutation function Ω which reorders the variables, such that the variable that we are currently concerned about is in the first position.

As an example, consider the system in Fig. 3a again. Since the variable that we are currently concerned is p, we can define the permutation function such that $\Omega_1 : \{p, q, r\} \rightarrow \{v_0, v_1, v_2\}$ which maps p to v_0, and so on. In System 2 on the other hand, when we are concerned with q, we can define a permutation function $\Omega_2 : \{q, p, r\} \rightarrow \{v_0, v_1, v_2\}$ which maps q to v_0 and so on. S_q^2 in equation (4). With both permutations, the transitions in equation (4) is transformed to:

$$S_p^1 = \{(v_0v_1v_2, 1), (v_0v_1, 1), (v_0, 0), (\epsilon, 0), (v_2, 0), (v_1v_2, 1), (v_0v_2, 0), (v_1, 1)\} \quad (5)$$
$$S_q^2 = \{(v_0v_1v_2, 1), (v_0v_1, 1), (v_0, 0), (\epsilon, 0), (v_2, 0), (v_1v_2, 1), (v_0v_2, 0), (v_1, 1)\} \quad (6)$$

Notice that both transitions are now equivalent.

Both of these transitions lead to the same rule:

$$v_0 \leftarrow v_1.$$

Incidentally, this rule corresponds to the first output node when $l = 1$, according to the rule indexing in δLFIT+ [19]. This means that given the same input of (6), the neural network model only has to learn 1 output.

By applying the inverse permutation function Ω_1^{-1} and Ω_2^{-1} respectively, we can recover the following rules for System 1 and System 2 respectively:

$$\text{System 1: } p \leftarrow q.$$
$$\text{System 2: } q \leftarrow p.$$

In the example and in our implementation, we've used a rotating permutation, which rotates the variables in order. In practice, any permutation function can be used as long as it can be consistently applied to all variables and the inverse is as easily computable.

4.2 Dynamic Rule Heads

In δLFIT+, an "output node reuse" technique was employed to address the scalability issue. The naive way is to assign an output node for all possible minimal rules, which leads to 3^n number of nodes. This grows very quickly as n gets larger. To address this, the rules are partitioned by body length and the neural network is constructed such that it covers the body length that consists of the most number of rules. For example, for Herbrand base with 3 variables, the body length that consists of the most number of rules is 2 with 12 such rules. The corresponding rules and the position of output nodes assigned is shown in table 2. Some output nodes utilized more (node 0 is used 4 times) and some less (nodes 8–11 are only used once), leading to an imbalance in the training data.

In δLFIT2, we construct separate output layers for each of the body lengths and dynamically load them into memory when required. This means that while the other layers are shared between each body length, the final layer is constructed separately. By dynamically loading and unloading the final layer, the memory usage of the model will not increase, even compared to that of δLFIT+.

In addition to each of the rules, the final layer also includes one extra output node, which indicates that there is no rule applicable for that body length. This is to combat the sparsity issue when there are no rules applicable for a specific body length. For example, the systems in Fig. 3 has no applicable rules for $l = 3$. This sparsity issue makes optimization particularly difficult. In δLFIT+, this was countered by defining a subsumption matrix, where all subsumed rules are also given a small value. However, this subsumption matrix is expensive to compute and can grow very quickly as the number of variables increase.

Table 2. Mapping of output nodes to rule bodies with various lengths.

Nodes	0	1	2	3	4	5
$l = 0$	$\bot$	-	-	-	-	-
$l = 1$	v_0	v_1	v_2	$\neg v_0$	$\neg v_1$	$\neg v_2$
$l = 2$	$v_0 \wedge v_1$	$v_0 \wedge v_2$	$v_1 \wedge v_2$	$\neg v_0 \wedge v_1$	$\neg v_0 \wedge v_2$	$v_0 \wedge \neg v_1$
$l = 3$	$v_0 \wedge v_1 \wedge v_2$	$\neg v_0 \wedge v_1 \wedge v_2$	$v_0 \wedge \neg v_1 \wedge v_2$	$\neg v_0 \wedge \neg v_1 \wedge v_2$	$v_0 \wedge v_1 \wedge \neg v_2$	$\neg v_0 \wedge v_1 \wedge \neg v_2$
Nodes	6	7	8	9	10	11
$l = 0$	-	-	-	-	-	-
$l = 1$	-	-	-	-	-	-
$l = 2$	$\neg v_1 \wedge v_2$	$v_0 \wedge \neg v_2$	$v_1 \wedge \neg v_2$	$\neg v_0 \wedge \neg v_1$	$\neg v_0 \wedge \neg v_2$	$\neg v_1 \wedge \neg v_2$
$l = 3$	$v_0 \wedge \neg v_1 \wedge \neg v_2$	$\neg v_0 \wedge \neg v_1 \wedge \neg v_2$	-	-	-	-

4.3 Overview of δLFIT2

The overall of δLFIT2 from the input of state transitions to the output of the probability of each rule is depicted in Fig. 1. Contrasting to δLFIT+ in Fig. 2, we can see that the core neural network model now only has to be concerned with 1 input, which is the transformed set of state transitions S_v.

The model architecture of δLFIT2 consists of an embedding layer, which converts the tokens of the elements of S_v, into a sequence of embedding vectors. The sequence of embedding vectors is then fed into the Set Transformer, which produces a latent vector. We utilize both the encoder and the decoder part of the Set Transformer. The latent vector is then fed through several feed forward layers and finally, the result is fed to the final layer which then produces the probability of each rule being present or not.

In summary, δLFIT2 takes as input the head of the rule v, the body length l and the observed state transitions S, then outputs a set of rules R of body length l and has v as the head that partly explains S. So do we have to decide v and l? The answer is that we do not. We would iterate v over the entire Herbrand base and l from 0 to the maximum body length, which is the number of variables in the Herbrand base. The rules predicted for each v and l are then specialized if they subsume each other and then combined into a final set of rules P which is then the logic program that explains S.

To train δLFIT2, random state transitions are generated and rules that explain them are produced by the symbolic LFIT algorithm. We consider the synchronous semantic [21] of the LFIT framework, where in a specific dynamic system, each state can only transition to another state deterministically. This means that we can generate many different systems by randomly generating pairs of interpretations. Once we enumerate every possible state and their random transitions, we can apply the symbolic LFIT algorithm [22] and generate the corresponding rules. We can then split them up for every variable and for different rule body lengths to construct the training dataset.

4.4 Scaling to Larger Systems

Due to having to enumerate all possible rules at the output, δLFIT2 suffers from scalability issues in the architecture and the spatial dimension. This is in contrast to symbolic methods, where the scalability issue is in the time dimension.

A δLFIT2 model is trained for a fixed number of variables. This means that a model trained on 3 variables cannot be directly applied to learn a system with 5 variables that may have a rule with a body length of 5. However, especially in real world scenarios, rules that involve a large number of variables are incredibly rare. This is because a rule that involves many variables will remain inactive for most of the time. In the PyBoolNet repository [15], even a large system such as grieco_mapk, a real world system from [9], that has 53 variables, the longest rule only involves 10 variables.

To apply δLFIT2 to a larger system, consider the subsets of the Herbrand base of size n, where n is the number of variables that the δLFIT2 model is trained for. For each of these subsets, we can define a mapping function from the subset to an index. This index is then used as the variable name for the δLFIT2 model. Once we obtain the rules, we can use the inverse of the mapping function to map from the index to the original variables.

By using the assumptions of the synchronous semantics, where every state deterministically only transitions to one state, it is possible to discard subsets of variables that produce transitions to different states. If all subsets for a particular variable are discarded, we know that the body length must be larger than the length of the subset. This can be used to determine whether a δLFIT2 model trained on a larger system is required when the maximum body length is unknown.

Table 3. MSE between state transitions generated by predicted logic programs for each method and state transitions from the original boolean network. n denotes number of variables in the system, b denotes the maximum rule body length.

Boolean Network	n	b	NN-LFIT	δLFIT	δLFIT+	δLFIT2^3	δLFIT2^4
3-node a	3	2	**0.000**	0.095	0.271	**0.000**	0.054
3-node b	3	2	0.042	0.188	0.083	**0.000**	**0.000**
Raf	3	2	0.333	0.253	0.188	**0.000**	0.025
5-node	5	4	0.514	**0.142**	0.278	0.238	0.214
7-node	7	3	0.299	-	0.223	**0.035**	0.152
WNT5A [27]	7	2	0.063	-	0.194	**0.009**	0.073
Circadian [4]	10	4	0.260	-	-	**0.033**	0.136
Gene Network [24]	12	3	0.029	-	-	**0.005**	0.159
Budding Yeast [11]	18	4	-	-	-	**0.121**	0.307

5 Experiments

To verify the effectiveness of the above proposed improvements, we report the results of the experiments on various dynamic systems in this section.

Datasets. The boolean networks used in the experiments are taken from the PyBoolNet repository [15]. The boolean networks in the repository contain both synthetic systems and real world systems. The boolean networks are converted into logic programs, and state transitions are obtained by applying the T_P operator on all possible states 2^B. The training dataset is randomly generated as described in Sect. 4.3.

Experimental Methods. We use the Mean Squared Error (MSE) as the evaluation metric. Given the original program P and the predicted program P', every possible interpretation of the Herbrand base 2^B, the MSE is calculated by the difference between the next states provided by the original program $\{T_P(I) \mid I \in 2^B\}$ and the next states provided by the predicted program $\{T_{P'}(I) \mid I \in 2^B\}$. This metric is chosen because 2 different programs can generate the same exact state transitions. Therefore, a direct comparison of the rules will not reflect that both programs are equally valid semantically. All results presented are averaged across 3 runs.

We compare our proposed method δLFIT2 with NN-LFIT [8], δLFIT [18] and δLFIT+ [19]. We denote the number of variables n that δLFIT2 is trained on by a superscript δLFIT2^n.

Results. The experimental results are shown in Table 3. We trained a 3-variable model noted as δLFIT2^3. We have also performed experiments with a model

Table 4. Comparison of results when only partial state transitions is given.

Given	3-node (a)			3-node (b)			Raf		
	NN-LFIT	δLFIT+	δLFIT2³	NN-LFIT	δLFIT+	δLFIT2³	NN-LFIT	δLFIT+	δLFIT2³
3/8	0.542	0.319	**0.308**	**0.292**	0.472	0.362	0.458	**0.319**	0.358
4/8	0.500	**0.264**	0.296	0.403	0.403	**0.321**	0.417	**0.264**	0.287
5/8	0.333	0.389	**0.188**	0.292	0.389	**0.267**	0.458	0.306	**0.242**
6/8	0.375	0.236	**0.183**	0.167	0.222	**0.154**	0.333	0.278	**0.150**
7/8	0.083	0.292	**0.071**	0.083	0.195	**0.079**	0.250	0.236	**0.063**

trained on 4 variables noted as δLFIT2⁴, however due to time and resource constraints we were not able to fully train the model, leading to lower performance overall. In particular, while the entire input space for the 3-variable model is $(2^3)^{(2^3)} \approx 1.6 \times 10^7$ which can be generated in a trivial amount of time, the input space for the 4-variable model is $(2^4)^{(2^4)} \approx 1.8 \times 10^{19}$, which is difficult to generate. Nevertheless, we report the results in Table 3.

δLFIT2³ achieved the best results in most cases. In particular, Raf which transitions to the same exact state from various states, NN-LFIT has a tendency to overfit and thus unable to produce the proper rules. In contrast, δLFIT2 is resistant to overfitting and thus able to recover the rules without issues. This highlights the advantage of our approach compared to extraction-based approaches.

Even for boolean networks that have a larger number of variables than what the δLFIT2 model were trained for, δLFIT2 can still recover a good amount of the rules. In particular, in WNT5A and Gene Network which only has rules with a maximum body length of 3, δLFIT2³ is able to almost recover all the rules. For the 5-node network, a 4-body rule is included and therefore δLFIT2³ was not able to recover the rules. δLFIT2⁴ achieved better results than δLFIT2³, but still fell short of δLFIT. We speculate that a fully trained δLFIT2⁴ model would achieve better performance. Notably, we've demonstrated that δLFIT2 is able to scale to systems as large as 18 variables, which has $2^{18} = 262,144$ state transitions.

δLFIT2 was also able to produce rules that are more succinct and minimal than NN-LFIT. This is because δLFIT2 is trained specifically on training data that is produced by a symbolic algorithm that learns minimal rules. This is particularly evident for larger systems where NN-LFIT would produce large amount of rules, whereas δLFIT2 almost reconstructed the original minimal rules.

In terms of run time, once a δLFIT2 model is trained, the process of obtaining the rules only consists of forward inference. While the training process can take longer, it opens the avenue for a foundational model. In contrast, NN-LFIT has to perform the train, inference, and extraction process for every new system. And the extraction process in particular, can take a long period of time. For Budding Yeast, although NN-LFIT was able to train in a short amount of time, the production of the learned rules took more than a month, and thus we were not able to obtain a result.

We also performed experiments where a certain number of transitions is held out from the model. The results are shown in Table 4. At less than 50% of the transitions provided, it is difficult for δLFIT2 to determine the correct rules. However, once exceeding 50%, δLFIT2 can recover the rules better than other compared methods.

6 Conclusion

In this paper, we proposed a technique that leverages another invariance in the symbolic domain, namely the variable assignment invariance, and showed its effectiveness. We have also improved the architecture of the neural network model to make it easier to optimize. We combined these improvements and proposed a new method named δLFIT2 which greatly improves upon prior methods. We also showed that it is possible to apply δLFIT2 to a larger dynamic system. Future work can consider extending δLFIT2 to various asynchronous semantics and dynamic systems with delay or memory. Extending the δLFIT2 model to first order logic also represents an interesting avenue to explore. We hope this work will inspire more Neuro-Symbolic works that employ techniques to exploit variable name invariance in semantics.

Acknowledgements. This work was supported by JSPS KAKENHI Grant Number JP22K21302, JP21H04905, the JST CREST Grant Number JPMJCR22D3. This research was also supported by ROIS NII Open Collaborative Research 2024-24S1203.

A Implementation Details

The model was implemented in PyTorch 2.1 with Python 3.10. The model architectures are as follows. All models include 3 components, i.e., the Set Transformer encoder, the Set Transformer decoder and a feed-forward layer. The activation function used is ReLU.

A.1 δLFIT2[3]

We did not do any grid search for the following hyperparameters because we were happy with the performance. A smaller model can possibly be constructed.

- Set Transformer Encoder
  - Input dimensions: 256
  - Output dimensions: 256
  - Layers: 3
  - Number of heads: 8
  - Number of indices: 64
- Set Transformer Decoder

- Input dimensions: 256
  - Hidden dimensions: 256
  - Output dimensions: 256
  - Layers: 1
  - Number of heads: 8
- Feed-forward Layer
  - Hidden dimensions: 1024
  - Layers: 3
- Learning rate: 1×10^{-4}
- Weight decay: 1×10^{-4}
- Optimizer: SGD
- Dropout: 0.2
- Layer normalization: yes
- Training data percentage: 95%
- Test data percentage: 0.5%
- Validation data percentage: 4.5%

A.2 δLFIT2[4]

We did not do any grid search for the following hyperparameters due to the training time required. A more optimized hyperparameter possibly still exists.

- Set Transformer Encoder
  - Input dimensions: 1024
  - Output dimensions: 1024
  - Layers: 5
  - Number of heads: 8
  - Number of indices: 64
- Set Transformer Decoder
  - Input dimensions: 1024
  - Hidden dimensions: 1024
  - Output dimensions: 1024
  - Layers: 3
  - Number of heads: 8
- Feed-forward Layer
  - Hidden dimensions: 2048
  - Layers: 4
- Learning rate: 1×10^{-5}
- Weight decay: 1×10^{-6}
- Optimizer: SGD
- Dropout: 0.2
- Layer normalization: yes
- Training data percentage: 75%
- Test data percentage: 15%
- Validation data percentage: 5%

B Algorithm for Applying to Larger Systems

Algorithm 1 Algorithm for Applying to Larger Systems

Inputs: State transitions S, Herbrand base $\mathcal{B}$, Trained model δLFIT2^n
Output: Logic program P
    $\mathcal{T}$ = All subsets of $2^{\mathcal{B}}$ with elements equal to n
    for each $v \in \mathcal{B}$ **do**
        for each $s \in \mathcal{T}$ **do**
            $\mathcal{V} = \Omega(s)$
            $S_v = \Omega(S)$
            if S_v is not consistent **then**
                continue   ▷ // if the states are not consistent after mapping, skip it
            end if
            $P_v = \delta\text{LFIT2}^n(S_v)$
            $P_v = \Omega^{-1}(P_v)$
            $P = P \cup P_v$
        end for
    end for

Ω is the mapping function that maps variables into a new assignment of n variables.

References

1. Badreddine, S., Garcez, A.d., Serafini, L., Spranger, M.: Logic tensor networks. Artif. Intell. **303**, 103649 (2022)
2. Evans, R., Grefenstette, E.: Learning explanatory rules from noisy data. J. Artif. Intell. Res. **61**, 1–64 (2018)
3. Evans, R., Hernández-Orallo, J., Welbl, J., Kohli, P., Sergot, M.: Making sense of sensory input. Artif. Intell. **293**, 103438 (2021)
4. Fauré, A., Naldi, A., Chaouiya, C., Thieffry, D.: Dynamical analysis of a generic Boolean model for the control of the mammalian cell cycle. Bioinformatics **22**(14), e124–e131 (2006)
5. Gao, K., Inoue, K., Cao, Y., Wang, H.: Learning first-order rules with differentiable logic program semantics. In: Proceedings of the Thirty-First International Joint Conference on Artificial Intelligence, IJCAI 2022, Vienna, Austria, 23-29 July 2022, pp. 3008–3014 (2022)
6. Gao, K., Wang, H., Cao, Y., Inoue, K.: Learning from interpretation transition using differentiable logic programming semantics. Mach. Learn. **111**(1), 123–145 (2022)
7. Garcez, A.d., Broda, K., Gabbay, D.M.: Symbolic knowledge extraction from trained neural networks: a sound approach. Artif. Intell. **125**(1-2), 155–207 (2001)
8. Gentet, E., Tourret, S., Inoue, K.: Learning from interpretation transition using feed-forward neural network. In: Proceedings of ILP 2016, CEUR Proceedings 1865, pp. 27–33 (2016)
9. Grieco, L., Calzone, L., Bernard-Pierrot, I., Radvanyi, F., Kahn-Perles, B., Thieffry, D.: Integrative modelling of the influence of MAPK network on cancer cell fate decision. PLoS Comput. Biol. **9**(10), e1003286 (2013)

10. Inoue, K., Ribeiro, T., Sakama, C.: Learning from interpretation transition. Mach. Learn. **94**(1), 51–79 (2014)
11. Irons, D.J.: Logical analysis of the budding yeast cell cycle. J. Theor. Biol. **257**(4), 543–559 (2009)
12. Jaegle, A., Gimeno, F., Brock, A., Vinyals, O., Zisserman, A., Carreira, J.: Perceiver: general perception with iterative attention. In: International Conference on Machine Learning, pp. 4651–4664. PMLR (2021)
13. Ji, Z., et al.: Survey of hallucination in natural language generation. ACM Comput. Surv. **55**(12), 1–38 (2023)
14. Jumper, J., et al.: Highly accurate protein structure prediction with AlphaFold. Nature **596**(7873), 583–589 (2021)
15. Klarner, H., Streck, A., Siebert, H.: PyBoolNet: a python package for the generation, analysis and visualization of Boolean networks. Bioinformatics **33**(5), 770–772 (2016). https://doi.org/10.1093/bioinformatics/btw682
16. Lee, J., Lee, Y., Kim, J., Kosiorek, A.R., Choi, S., Teh, Y.W.: Set transformer. arXiv preprint arXiv:1810.00825 (2018)
17. Messina, N., Falchi, F., Esuli, A., Amato, G.: Transformer reasoning network for image-text matching and retrieval. In: 2020 25th International Conference on Pattern Recognition (ICPR), pp. 5222–5229. IEEE (2021)
18. Phua, Y.J., Inoue, K.: Learning logic programs from noisy state transition data. In: Kazakov, D., Erten, C. (eds.) ILP 2019. LNCS (LNAI), vol. 11770, pp. 72–80. Springer, Cham (2020). https://doi.org/10.1007/978-3-030-49210-6_7
19. Phua, Y.J., Inoue, K.: Learning logic programs using neural networks by exploiting symbolic invariance. In: Katzouris, N., Artikis, A. (eds.) Inductive Logic Programming, pp. 203–218. Springer, Cham (2022). https://doi.org/10.1007/978-3-030-97454-1_15
20. Ribeiro, T., Folschette, M., Magnin, M., Inoue, K.: Polynomial algorithm for learning from interpretation transition. In: 1st International Joint Conference on Learning and Reasoning (2021)
21. Ribeiro, T., Folschette, M., Magnin, M., Inoue, K.: Learning any memory-less discrete semantics for dynamical systems represented by logic programs. Mach. Learn. **111**, 3593–3670 (2022). https://doi.org/10.1007/s10994-021-06105-4
22. Ribeiro, T., Inoue, K.: Learning prime implicant conditions from interpretation transition. In: Davis, J., Ramon, J. (eds.) ILP 2014. LNCS (LNAI), vol. 9046, pp. 108–125. Springer, Cham (2015). https://doi.org/10.1007/978-3-319-23708-4_8
23. Su, J., Ahmed, M., Lu, Y., Pan, S., Bo, W., Liu, Y.: RoFormer: enhanced transformer with rotary position embedding. Neurocomputing **568**, 127063 (2024). https://doi.org/10.1016/j.neucom.2023.127063
24. Tournier, L., Chaves, M.: Uncovering operational interactions in genetic networks using asynchronous Boolean dynamics. J. Theor. Biol. **260**(2), 196–209 (2009)
25. Valmeekam, K., Olmo, A., Sreedharan, S., Kambhampati, S.: Large language models still can't plan (a benchmark for LLMs on planning and reasoning about change). arXiv preprint arXiv:2206.10498 (2022)
26. Winters, T., Marra, G., Manhaeve, R., De Raedt, L.: Deepstochlog: neural stochastic logic programming. In: Proceedings of the AAAI Conference on Artificial Intelligence, vol. 36, pp. 10090–10100 (2022)
27. Xiao, Y., Dougherty, E.R.: The impact of function perturbations in Boolean networks. Bioinformatics **23**(10), 1265–1273 (2007)
28. Yang, Z., Ishay, A., Lee, J.: Neurasp: embracing neural networks into answer set programming. In: Proceedings of the Twenty-Ninth International Joint Conference on Artificial Intelligence, IJCAI 2020, pp. 1755–1762. ijcai.org (2020)

ViPro: Enabling and Controlling Video Prediction for Complex Dynamical Scenarios Using Procedural Knowledge

Patrick Takenaka[1,2]((✉)), Johannes Maucher[1], and Marco F. Huber[2,3]

[1] Institute for Applied AI, Hochschule der Medien Stuttgart, Stuttgart, Germany
{takenaka,maucher}@hdm-stuttgart.de
[2] Institute of Industrial Manufacturing and Management IFF, University of Stuttgart, Stuttgart, Germany
marco.huber@ieee.org
[3] Fraunhofer Institute for Manufacturing Engineering and Automation IPA, Stuttgart, Germany

Abstract. We propose a novel architecture design for video prediction in order to utilize procedural domain knowledge directly as part of the computational graph of data-driven models. On the basis of new challenging scenarios we show that state-of-the-art video predictors struggle in complex dynamical settings, and highlight that the introduction of prior process knowledge makes their learning problem feasible. Our approach results in the learning of a symbolically addressable interface between data-driven aspects in the model and our dedicated procedural knowledge module, which we utilize in downstream control tasks.

Keywords: Informed Machine Learning · Procedural Knowledge · Video Prediction

1 Introduction

Current advances in deep learning research [2,8,19] have shown the tremendous potential of data-driven approaches. However, upon taking a closer look, oftentimes domain-specific inductive biases in the training process or the architecture [8] play a critical role in making the most of the available data. While an end-to-end generalized architecture that is able to tackle a wide range of problems is elegant, we argue that this often leads to models that require large amounts of data to be feasible while still being unable to generalize well outside of the training distribution [16], leading to limited applicability for more specialized use cases where data are often scarce, such as, for instance, in the medical domain. Transfer of deep learning research into applications usually requires further fine-tuning of the model for the given use case, and this often corresponds to collecting specialized data. We believe that providing additional means for domain experts—who may or may not be experts in machine learning—to represent their knowledge besides data in deep learning models is crucial for driving

AI adaption in more areas. Ideally, specializing the model to a domain should reduce the complexity of the learning task and thus, lead to leaner architectures that require less data than a domain agnostic variant, while providing better predictions for sparsely observed situations. Furthermore, as we show with our approach, such grey box modelling approaches also inherently increase the controllability of the model. Thus, developing a model that benefits from both domain knowledge and data samples together is our objective.

There are various types of domain knowledge that can be integrated, and ways how they can be integrated [24], ranging from using logic rules or differential equations to structure and expand both the loss function and the learning process [20,32], to architectural considerations that take into account the structure of the underlying problem, such as Graph Neural Networks (GNNs) [28] to model interactions, or more famously to use Convolutional Neural Networks (CNNs) for spatial data.

We propose to view the knowledge integration types from a different perspective and group them in either procedural or declarative knowledge. While the latter encompasses domain facts or rules ("Knowing-That"), procedural knowledge represents a more abstract level of information by describing a domain process irrespective of any concrete observation ("Knowing-How"). A straightforward representative of this paradigm would be a mathematical formula, which can describe a certain relation between variables in a concise manner without risk of running into a long-tail problem for less frequently observed variable assignments as would be the case in data-driven approaches. Without a doubt, however, data-driven function approximators are immensely successful in the real world because we are often not able—or it is impossible—to describe the problem in such a precise way. However, we argue that currently data-driven approaches are often used without considering whether the underlying mechanisms of the domain could be described in a more efficient manner without resorting to arduous data collection.

In this work, we propose a novel architecture design that integrates such procedural knowledge as an independent module into the overall architecture. We apply it to video prediction, a task where state-of-the-art models often still struggle due to the high spatio-temporal complexity involved in scenes. Its environments often involve understanding complex domain processes that are hard to robustly learn from observations only and thus are likely to benefit from domain inductive biases. At the same time, this field is the foundation for many possible downstream tasks such as Visual Question Answering (VQA) [30], Model Predictive Control (MPC) [7], or system identification [7]. We create several scenarios which feature complex dynamics, and integrate the knowledge about these dynamics. We show that current deep learning models struggle on their own, but can thrive once enhanced with procedural domain knowledge. We verify that this is still possible even with very limited data, and further highlight that such an interface enables control in the target domain w.r.t. the integrated function parameters at test time, providing a potential basis for downstream control tasks and allowing flexibility in adjusting the model for novel scene dynamics.

In summary, our contributions are:

- Specification and analysis of an architectural design for interfacing procedural knowledge with a data-driven model.
- Introduction of novel challenging scenarios with complex dynamics for video prediction.
- Application to a downstream control task by relying on the inherently achieved disentanglement w.r.t. the function parameters.

The paper is structured as follows: First, relevant related work is shown in Sect. 2, after which our proposed procedural knowledge integration scheme is introduced in Sect. 3, followed by a description of our datasets in Sect. 4. In Sect. 5, we first describe our used setup including implementation details in Sect. 5.1 and continue by establishing baseline results in Sect. 5.2. We then analyze the latent state of the model and the resulting controllability in Sect. 5.3. We conclude by discussing limitations and potential directions for future work in Sect. 6. Our datasets and code are available at https://github.com/P-Takenaka/nesy2024-vipro.

2 Related Work

Predicting future video frames is a challenging task that requires certain inductive biases in the training process or model architecture in order to lead to acceptable prediction outcomes. The most commonly integrated bias is the modelling of the temporal dependency between individual frames, which assumes that future frames are dependent on past frames [3,25,26]. Some methods also exploit the fact that the scene is composed of objects by structuring the latent space accordingly [12,14,22,30], which improved scene reconstruction performance further compared to approaches that rely on a single global latent scene representation for predictions.

Since many dynamics in video scenes are of a physical nature, there are also works that explore the learning of the underlying Partial Differential Equations (PDEs) to facilitate video reconstruction [4,13,29,33]. Another line of work—most similar to our approach—considers a more explicit representation of dynamics knowledge in the model [7,9]. Here, discretized PDEs are integrated to calculate a physical state for each frame, which is decoded back into an image representation. These approaches were, however, limited to 2D dynamics of sprites, which allowed the dynamics model to operate directly in the screen space, making the learning problem much easier, while limiting applicability to more realistic settings. These methods also relied on the Spatial Transformer Network [6] for decoding purposes. Dynamical properties of the scene besides the object positions—such as for instance changing lighting conditions or object orientations—are not modelled with this approach, since it is based on sampling pixel predictions directly from the input reference frames. More recently, an architecture was proposed in a preliminary workshop publication [21] that could in theory handle such dynamic properties. It was, however, only applied

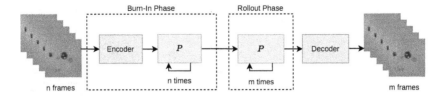

Fig. 1. Overview of our auto-regressive video prediction process. The first n frames are used as reference and are encoded by the model in order to obtain an initial latent representation of the scene. After this burn-in phase the model has to rollout future m frames on its own.

to semantic segmentation in visually simple settings and we show that it fails at video reconstruction in our datasets. Our work continues in this line of research and increases the complexity of video scenarios that can be handled, while broadening the applicability by bridging the gap to control-based downstream tasks such as MPC.

3 Proposed Architecture

Our objective is to allow domain experts to integrate their knowledge of underlying domain processes in a data-driven architecture in a domain-independent way. As such, we embed this knowledge represented as a *programmatic function* F within a distinct *procedural knowledge module* P inside the overall architecture. Instead of learning the domain dynamics itself, we thus provide the means for the model to learn the interface between F and its data-driven components. This is possible since we can directly execute the program code that is F—as opposed to for instance natural language instructions that would need some kind of encoding first—and make it part of the computational graph.

We opt for an auto-regressive frame prediction scheme in which the model is exposed to the initial n video frames in order to learn the data sample dynamics, before it auto-regressively predicts the next m frames on its own. Learning is guided by the reconstruction loss

$$\mathcal{L}_{\text{rec}} = \frac{1}{N} \sum_{i=0}^{N} (\hat{V}_i - V_i)^2 \tag{1}$$

of all $N = m + n$ predicted RGB frames $\hat{V}$ and the ground-truth V.

Our architecture is thus composed of three main components: 1) An initial video frame encoder, which embeds the n observed frames into a suitable latent representation, 2) our *procedural knowledge module P* that transforms the frame's latent representation to the next time step, and 3) a final video frame decoder that transforms the latent representations back into an image representation, as depicted in Fig. 1.

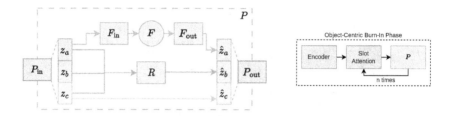

Fig. 2. Left: Structure of our proposed *procedural knowledge module* P. **Right:** Abstract view of the burn-in phase for the object-centric variant of our architecture.

The core of our contribution resides in P (see Fig. 2): It combines the integrated *programmatic function* F with a deep *spatio-temporal prediction model* R to obtain the latent frame representation $\hat{z}$ of the next time step based on the latent representation z of the current step. We implement this by transforming the latent vector z into a representation that is separable into three components z_a, z_b, and z_c via a latent encoder P_{in} and a decoder P_{out}. Each part a, b, c is responsible for encoding different aspects of the frame that are learned implicitly through our architectural design, which we now describe and also later verify in our experiments.

z_a represents features that are relevant for F—i.e. which correspond to its input and output parameters—in latent space. Since F is a programmatic function, we can directly integrate it into the computational graph as an individual layer. However, since its input space is usually symbolic and not in a latent representation, z_a is translated into and from its symbolic pendant s through dedicated mapping layers F_{in} and F_{out}, respectively. We further facilitate the transformation between latent and symbolic representation of the state by introducing a regularization loss $\mathcal{L}_s$ that is based on the symbolic state s and its auto-encoded version for all N predicted frames:

$$\mathcal{L}_s = \frac{1}{N} \sum_{i=0}^{N}(s_i - F_{\text{in}}(F_{\text{out}}(s_i)))^2 \quad (2)$$

The final loss is thus $\mathcal{L} = \mathcal{L}_{\text{rec}} + \lambda \mathcal{L}_s$, with λ being a constant weighting coefficient.

The second part z_b contains residual scene dynamics that are not covered by F. It corresponds to the output of R, which is a typical auto-regressive frame predictor model [30] with the goal of modelling spatio-temporal scene properties. It takes into account the whole latent representation consisting of z_a, z_b, and z_c. Instead of predicting the full future latent state on its own, we show that when combined with F, this model R focuses on residual scene dynamics only and does not interfere with dynamics handled by F. This property allows us to exert a certain level of control when predicting frames w.r.t. the inputs and outputs of F, as shown in Sect. 5.3.

Finally, z_c contains static scene features that do not change frame-to-frame, such as for instance parts of the background or object colors. It is thus realized as a residual connection directly mapping from z_c to $\hat{z}_c$. Auto-regressive approaches often suffer from accumulating errors, as future predictions build on top of past prediction mistakes. We were able to alleviate this issue by allowing the model to store scene statics in z_c.

Thus, our model has three different pathways available to pass latent features from one video time step to the next. Each contains meaningful inductive biases that encourage the model to follow our interpretation of the latent vectors. z_a contains only the encoded state required for F and is limited by an information bottleneck induced by the symbolic state transformation for F. z_c is a direct shortcut from the first encoded frame, and thus offers an easy to learn path for time-invariant features. Finally, z_b offers the only unrestricted pathway that allows encoding time-variant features. Keeping representations intact over many frames in auto-regressive models such as R is a challenging learning objective however, which 1) makes it less likely that the model will try to encode static scene features that are better handled by z_c, and 2) encourages the model to rely on z_a for dynamics that are handled by F.

Object-centric representations have shown to further improve video prediction performance over methods that work with a single latent state for the whole scene [30]. Since some of our datasets are object based, we also introduce a variant of our proposed architecture that operates on slot-based object representations. For our module P the main difference is that the latent state of a single frame is now separated into multiple object representations. In practice, this amounts to an additional dimension in the tensors which can be handled in parallel by all components of P. During the burn-in phase, our module P takes turns with a slot attention [15] module to assemble these frame object representations. For each frame, the latter refines slot-based object representations w.r.t. the encoded video frame of the current time step and the object representation prediction of our module P from the last time step (cf. Figure 2). Afterwards, P uses this refined representation to predict the next time step.

With our architecture we aim to concentrate the domain inductive biases within P, and keep the image encoder and decoder parts domain agnostic and in line with current state-of-the-art models in video prediction. As opposed to models that use domain-specific decoders such as neural renderers [17], we thus do not need to obtain a full symbolic representation of the scene and can keep parts not relevant for F in the latent space of the model. At the same time, the architecture's modularity facilitates the integration of and interfacing with future developments in video prediction, such as better image encoder or decoders but also better predictors in place of R.

4 Data

We designed and introduce three new datasets which consist of videos of rendered 3D scenes using Kubric [5]. They feature complex, nonlinear physical dynamics and aim to provide suitable testing grounds for our approach. Other video dynamics datasets in the literature often either happened in 2D screen space only

[4,7], or involved only short-term dynamics for which linear approximations of the underlying dynamics were sufficient [11,30]. As we also show in our experiments, such models fail once the underlying dynamics increase in complexity as in our datasets. Thus, our settings are an ideal candidate for which the introduction of domain knowledge can supplement—or even enable—purely data-driven approaches. We integrate the dynamics equations of each dataset as F within the *procedural knowledge module P* of our model.

Our main and most challenging dataset "Orbits" is based on the three body problem [18], in which multiple objects attract each other, resulting in chaotic movements once three or more objects are involved. A similar dataset was introduced in previous related work [21], albeit with no background and only sphere object shapes.

Our second dataset is a rendering of an Acrobot environment, a setting which is commonly used for benchmarking physics and control models [1]. It features a double pendulum where one end is fixed in space, resulting in dynamics that are inherently complex with chaotic movements without further actuation. As we show in our experiments these environments are easier to predict in pixel-space for data-driven models compared to our Orbits dataset, however stabilizing the pole by actuating the joint between the pendulums is a common control objective that we want to work with as a downstream task.

Our third dataset features a non object-centric variant of the Acrobot setting. Instead of observing the double pendulum directly we mount the camera on it, while orienting it towards a static, texturized background, whose texture is the same for all data samples. We let the double pendulum move according to the dynamics defined in the Acrobot setting, and the now also moving camera observes different parts of the background texture in each frame. The prediction of future frames is thus only successful if the model is able to correctly estimate and utlize the indirectly observed pendulum dynamics. The overall dataset setup is otherwise the same as in the Acrobot setting. This dataset is related to visual Simultaneous Localization And Mapping (SLAM), in which models establish a map of the environment based on video input, since an internal representation of the whole—always only partially observed—scene is necessary. By applying our approach to this dataset we also show its potential for visual robotics navigation tasks as future work, for which we could exchange the pendulum dynamics for a robot dynamics model in F.

We use our object-centric architecture variant for the Orbits and Acrobot dataset, and the non object-centric variant for the Pendulum Camera dataset. We describe further details of these datasets in Appendix C and their underlying dynamics equations in Appendix E.

5 Experiments

In the following we first describe our experimental setup and continue by analyzing our proposed approach w.r.t. its performance in contrast to existing methods. Afterwards we study the feasibility of using our model for downstream control tasks.

5.1 Setup

All models observe the initial six video frames and—where applicable—the symbolic input for F for the very first frame. We evaluate the performance based on the prediction performance of the next 24 frames, however during training only the next twelve frames contribute to the loss in order to observe generalization performance for more rollouts.

We compare the performance with two groups of relevant state-of-the-art work in video prediction: 1) Purely data-driven approaches that do not rely on physical inductive biases in the architecture such as Slot Diffusion [31], Slot-Former [30] and PredRNN-V2 [26] and 2) approaches that include general physical inductive biases such as PhyDNet [13], Dona et al. [4], and Takenaka et al. [21]. We describe the details of the configurations of these models in Appendix B.

We measure the averaged reconstruction performance for three different random seeds with the Learned Perceptual Image Patch Similarity (LPIPS), which has shown better alignment with human perception than other metrics by relying on a pretrained image encoder. However, for completeness we also report the standard metrics Structural Similarity (SSIM) and Peak Signal-to-Noise Ratio (PSNR).

Implementation Details. Our used video frame encoder is a standard CNN with a subsequent position embedding. The modules P_{in} and P_{out} within P are implemented as fully-connected networks including a single hidden layer with the ReLU activation function, whose non-linearity enables the model to learn the separable latent space that we require without relying on the learning capacity of the video frame encoder. We linearly transform z_a from the symbolic to the latent space and back by implementing F_{in} and F_{out} as fully-connected layers without bias neurons. This enables easy auto-encoding between both spaces while within P, and forces the model to learn the complex transformation between the symbolic state for F and its latent version that can be used by the video frame decoder in P_{in} and P_{out}. The *spatio-temporal prediction model* R within P is implemented as a transformer [23] with temporal position embedding. Finally, we use a Spatial Broadcast Decoder [27] as our video frame decoder.

For the object-centric variant of our model we use Slot Attention [15] to obtain object representations in the latent space. For a scene with M objects and N rollout frames, we thus obtain $N \times M$ latent representations, which are decoded individually into the image space by the video frame decoder. The final frame prediction is assembled by combining the M object representations as in Slot Attention for Video (SAVi) [11], which predicts an auxiliary masking channel in addition to the RGB channels to weigh the individual object frame decodings.

More implementation details can be found in Appendix A, and details about the integrated functions in Appendix E.

Table 1. Performance comparison of our proposed complete architecture (Base) with ablations and relevant related work for the Orbits dataset.

	LPIPS↓	SSIM↑	PSNR↑
Ours	**4.0**±1	**97.2**±0	**34.7**±0
Limited Data	19.5±2	87.1±0	27.7±0
Learned Parameters in F	**3.9**±1	**97.1**±0	**34.7**±1
Architecture Ablations			
1) No z_c	5.2±0	96.4±0	33.8±0
2) No z_b, R	5.7±0	95.8±0	33.0±0
3) F as Identity	35.5±5	77.9±1	24.2±1
4) Only R instead of P	41.8±0	76.8±0	23.5±0
Related Work			
Slot Diffusion	26.7±1	68.7±1	21.9±0
Takenaka et al.	36.8±0	78.1±0	24.8±0
Slotformer	34.2±0	75.3±0	23.2±0
PhyDNet	35.7±1	77.6±0	24.0±0
PredRNN-V2	34.4±0	78.5±0	24.3±0
Dona et al.	41.1±0	76.7±0	23.5±0

5.2 Video Prediction

Here we establish and discuss the video prediction performance of our proposed architecture and compare it with related work.

Orbits. For the Orbits dataset we are able to significantly outperform other approaches (cf. Table 1 and Fig. 3). Our model is able to follow the correct object trajectories and render the objects accordingly. When comparing the symbolic state s used by F with its auto-encoded version $F_{in}(F_{out}(s))$ we observe a low Mean Absolute Error (MAE) of 0.005. This indicates that frame-to-frame object states can be accurately recovered from the latent representation without too much error accumulation.

In order to verify the impact of the integrated procedural knowledge, we train two variants of our model which replace the integrated function F with an identity function, and use only the residual model R in place of our procedural knowledge module P (ablations 3) and 4) in Table 1, respectively). In both cases the performance decreases substantially and converges to the same performance as the related work, giving clear evidence that F has a large positive impact on the performance.

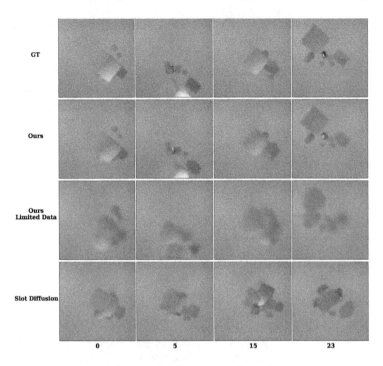

Fig. 3. Qualitative performance of different model configurations compared to the ground-truth (GT). Predictions of selected frame iterations are shown from left to right. Our model is able to position objects correctly in future frames, while keeping object shading and overall appearance intact.

Since we expect that the integration of procedural knowledge should decrease the complexity of the learning problem, and as such require less data than a completely uninformed model, we also train our model with a very small dataset consisting of only 300 training samples instead of 10K to test this hypothesis. As can be seen in Table 1 the performance significantly decreases, but stays well above variants that do not include F. When looking at the predictions in Fig. 3, the reason for this is a quality loss in object appearance prediction, however the objects are still rendered at the correct positions. As we will further show in Sect. 5.3, the latent vectors z_b and z_c contain such appearance features, both of which are purely based on the data-driven aspects of our model. These results indicate that while our data-driven parts suffer equally to regular data-driven models when trained with small amounts of data, the inclusion of a procedural knowledge path z_a can enable the model to still provide meaningful predictions. Through this experiment we thus highlight that our model not only benefits from the integrated knowledge, but also still benefits from additional data, which conforms to our goal of providing domain experts with additional avenues to improve their models without removing options.

Table 2. Performance comparison for the Acrobot and the Pendulum Camera dataset. Purely object-centric models such as SlotFormer cannot be applied to the Pendulum Camera dataset as no objects are visible in the scene.

	Acrobot			Pendulum Camera		
	LPIPS↓	SSIM↑	PSNR↑	LPIPS↓	SSIM↑	PSNR↑
Ours	**3.1**±0	**97.9**±0	**37.2**±2	**26.9**±1	**65.4**±1	**31.7**±0
Slot Diffusion	18.2±0	84.0±1	26.6±1	N/A	N/A	N/A
Takenaka et al.	4.4±0	96.9±0	34.9±0	N/A	N/A	N/A
Slotformer	13.2±0	88.0±0	28.3±0	N/A	N/A	N/A
PhyDNet	14.2±2	90.2±1	29.8±0	50.9±0	39.7±1	21.7±1
Dona et al.	31.4±9	85.7±4	23.7±8	50.8±0	41.6±2	21.7±0
PredRNN-V2	17.5±2	88.3±0	28.9±0	50.4±0	39.8±0	21.8±0

We also test our approach in the face of uncertainties in the integrated function. For this we let the model learn the environment constants `object mass` and `gravitational constant` present within F in an unsupervised manner. We used a modified learning rate of $1e^{-2}$ instead of the regular $2e^{-4}$ for these parameters to improve and speed up convergence due to the larger magnitudes compared to regular network weights. The performance is comparable to our model without any learned parameters (see "Learned Parameters in F" in Table 1). In fact, the model converges on the ground-truth values of the learned parameters without ever supplying these as a supervision signal, highlighting the potential of our approach for system and parameter identification tasks as well.

Finally, we analyze the impact of individual components of our approach. We train variants of our architecture that do not use the residual path z_c and do not use a residual model R and thus z_b (see ablations 1) and 2) in Table 1). Removing either only has a slight negative influence on performance, which aligns with the finding earlier that using F has the largest performance impact in the model. It shows however that predictions can further be improved by using a suitable model R, especially when there are environment processes not covered by F, such as dynamic lighting conditions.

Acrobot and Pendulum Camera. The Acrobot dataset features a smaller performance gap between our approach and purely data-driven methods such as SlotFormer (cf. Table 2 and Fig. 4), indicating that this scenario is easier when relying on data alone. This is probably due to the restricted movements in the scene, whereas in the Orbits setting objects are able to move freely in space, making predictions more difficult. Still, the integration of procedural knowledge was beneficial and lead to improved performance across the board even when compared to Takenaka et al. with a similarly informed model. The challenging nature of modelling indirectly observed dynamics in the Pendulum Camera dataset is reflected in both the quantitative and qualitative performance observed

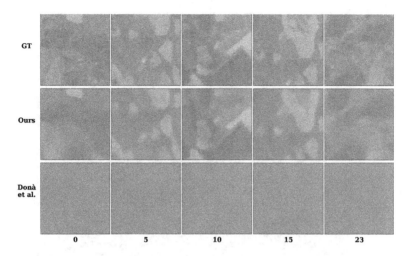

Fig. 4. Frame predictions of different time steps (left-to-right) for the Pendulum Camera dataset, with the ground-truth being in the top row (GT).

in Table 2 and Fig. 4. While our model is able to reconstruct the overall patterns present in each frame, all comparison models were unable to model the pendulum trajectory correctly and instead produced uniform blurry predictions.

5.3 Control Interface

The model appears to have used the integrated function F correctly in order to obtain better frame predictions. Since F is based on symbolic inputs and outputs, the question arises whether we can use these to control the predictions in an interpretable manner. To evaluate this, we consider two scenarios: (1) We modify z_b and z_c—i.e. the appearance features—and observe whether the dynamics do not change; (2) we directly adjust z_a and observe whether the rendered outputs correlate with our modifications of the symbolic state.

For (1), we leverage the object-centric representations in the Orbits scenario and simply swap z_b and z_c between different objects. Figure 5 shows the qualitative results. First, as we expected in Sect. 3 we can observe that z_c contains static object properties, such as their size, color, and overall shape. At the same time, when modifying z_b we can see changes in time variant features in the image such as object shading, occlusions, and shape changes due to the cameras perspective projection. Finally, all changes to z_b and z_c did not change the scene dynamics, as the objects simply continue their trajectory, albeit with new appearances.

For (2), we interface our model with MPC and by doing this show that our model not only renders objects at intended locations, but also inherently enables the integration of downstream tasks that operate in symbolic space. We use an off-the-shelf MPC controller that interacts with our model through F. We build on top of the Acrobot scenario and define a control task to swing up the double pendulum by allowing a torque to be applied to the joint between the poles. We

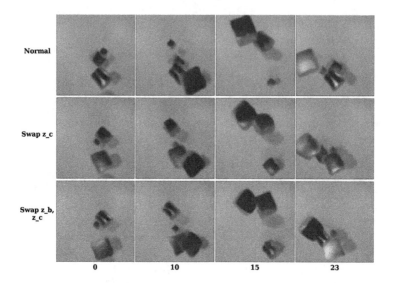

Fig. 5. Frame predictions of our model for different time steps (left-to-right) in the case of no changes to the latent vector (**Normal**), swapping z_c between the object latent vectors (**Swap z_c**) before decoding, and swapping both latent vectors z_b and z_c with the same permutation (**Swap z_b, z_c**). Object appearances are swapped, but the dynamics stay unchanged.

encode the initial six frames with our model as usual and use the sixth predicted physical state as initialization for the MPC task. We store the predicted torque action sequence for the next 75 frames and apply the corresponding torque for each frame prediction in F before decoding. We show the qualitative results in Fig. 6, and more in Appendix F.

We can observe that the model is able to correctly decode predicted object states into a rendered scene. We conclude that the downstream integration of symbolic methods into our method is possible and a large benefit over purely black-box predictors that have no way of interacting in such a manner with existing symbolic tools. We further verified the controllability for the Orbits setting in Appendix D and show that the model can adapt to new dynamics simply by exchanging F.

6 Limitations and Future Work

Our work puts a spotlight on the benefit of procedural knowledge represented as programmatic functions and aims to answer some fundamental questions on how it could be utilized in data-driven video predictors. As such, there are still many follow-up questions and directions that can be the topic of future research.

One assumption that we made was to let the model observe the correct function input of the very first frame in order to give the model a hint of the magnitude and distribution of possible symbolic states. The prediction of initial

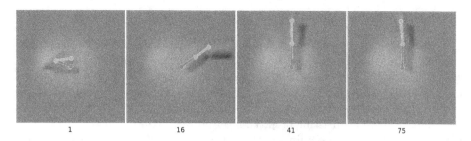

Fig. 6. Frame predictions of our model for the Acrobot swing-up control task. We overlay a direct plot of the predicted physics states on the rendered frames. Our model renders the states with only slight divergences from the direct plot.

values—especially in physics—is a known problem with a large body of research behind it. As our focus was on establishing our procedural knowledge module P in the architecture in a domain-independent way, we excluded this aspect as it is part of the encoder module of the underlying model, which should be domain-specific. Still, the integration of a suitable encoder for predicting initial state values is interesting for future work.

It would also be interesting to combine the given integrated knowledge with synthesis approaches which might dynamically extend or repair the integrated function. Neural program synthesis is an active field of research which might give many insights in this regard. It could also be used to move towards having a dynamically extending library of domain functions available instead of only a single procedural knowledge function, greatly increasing the utility.

7 Conclusion

We have introduced a novel architectural scheme to join procedural knowledge in the form of programmatic functions with data-driven models. By applying it to video prediction, we show that our approach can enable models to handle tasks for which data-driven models alone would struggle. While our approach also works with very limited data, we highlight that it still benefits from more data, leaving it open for domain experts whether they want to refine their integrated knowledge, or to collect more data, essentially broadening the means by which performance improvements can be made. Furthermore, our grey-box modelling approach increases the transparency of the overall model and allows direct control of the model predictions through the learned interface to the integrated procedural knowledge, enabling easy interfacing with downstream tasks such as MPC.

A Further Implementation Details

In the following we describe the core components of our architecture in more detail.

A.1 Video Frame Encoder

The used video frame encoder is a standard CNN. The input video frames are encoded in parallel by merging the temporal dimension T with the batch dimension B. The CNN consists of four convolutional layers, each with a filter size of 64, kernel size of 5, and a stride of 1. In the non object-centric variant of our architecture, the output features are flattened and transformed by a final fully connected network, consisting of initial layer normalization, a single hidden layer with ReLU activation and a final output linear layer with $C = 768$ neurons each. The result is a latent vector of size $B \times T \times C$ that serves as input to P.

In the object-centric variant, a position embedding is additionally applied after the CNN, and only the spatial dimensions H and W are flattened before the transformation of the fully connected network, with C reduced to 128. The result is a latent vector of size $B \times T \times C \times H \times W$. In each burn-in iteration of the object-centric variant, we use the Slot Attention mechanism [15] to obtain updated object latent vectors before applying P.

A.2 Procedural Knowledge Module

P is responsible for predicting the latent vector of the next frame. It consists of the following submodules:

P_{in}. Responsible for transforming the latent vector obtained from the image frame encoder into a separable latent vector z. It is implemented as a fully connected network with a single hidden layer using the ReLU activation function. All layers have a subsequent ReLU activation function. The number of neurons in all layers corresponds to C.

P_{out}. Responsible for transforming z back into the latent image space. It has the same structure as P_{in}.

F_{in}. Responsible for transforming z_a within z into the symbolic space required for F. It is a single linear layer without bias neurons. In the object-centric case, its output size directly corresponds to the number of parameters required for F N_{param} for a single object. In the non object-centric case when there is no separate object dimension available, it instead corresponds to $N_{\text{param}} \times N_{\text{objects}}$, where N_{objects} corresponds to the (fixed) number of objects (if present in the dataset).

F. Contains the integrated function directly as part of the computational graph. Details about F for the individual data scenarios can be found in Appendix E.

F_{out}. Same structure as F_{in}, with the input and output sizes reversed.

R. Responsible for modelling residual dynamics not handled by F. We implement it as a transformer [23] with two layers and four heads. We set the latent size to C and the dimension of its feed-forward network to 512. It takes into account the most recent 6 frame encodings. Its output corresponds to z_b. A temporal position embedding is applied before the transformer.

We first transform the latent image vector into a separable latent vector z by transforming it with P_{in}. We then split z of size C into the three equally sized components z_a, z_b, and z_c. We continue by obtaining their respective next frame predictions $\hat{z}_a$, $\hat{z}_b$, and $\hat{z}_c$ as follows: $\hat{z}_a$ by F, z_b by transforming z with R, and $\hat{z}_c$ directly corresponds to z_c. All three components are merged back together and transformed into the image latent space with P_{out} before decoding.

A.3 Video Frame Decoder

We implement the video frame decoder as a Spatial Broadcast Decoder [27]. We set the resolution for the spatial broadcast to 8, and first apply positional embedding on the expanded latent vector. We then transform the output by four deconvolutional layers, each with filter size 64. We add a final convolutional layer with filter size of 3 to obtain the decoded image. We set the strides to 2 in each layer until we arrive at the desired output resolution of 64, after which we use a stride of 1. In the object-centric variant, we set the output filter size to 4 and use the first channel as weights w. We then reduce the object dimension after the decoding as in [15] by normalizing the object dimension of w via softmax, and using it to calculate a weighted sum with the object dimensions of the RGB output channels.

A.4 Training Details

We train all models for at maximum 500k iterations each or until convergence is observed by early stopping. We clip gradients to a maximum norm of 0.05 and train using the Adam Optimizer [10] with an initial learning rate of $2e^{-4}$. We set the loss weighting factor λ to 1. We set the batch size according to the available GPU memory, which was 32 in our case. We performed the experiments on four NVIDIA TITAN Xp with 12GB of VRAM, taking—on average—one to two days per run.

B Details for Comparison Models

Takenaka et al. [21]. We apply the training process and configuration as described in their paper, and instead use RGB reconstruction loss to fit into our training framework. We integrate the same procedural function here as in our model.

Slot Diffusion. [31]. We use the three-stage training process as described in the paper with all hyperparameters being set as recommended.

SlotFormer. [30]. We use their proposed training and architecture configuration for the CLEVRER [34] dataset, as its makeup is the most similar to our datasets and follow their proposed training regimen.

PhyDNet. We use their recommended training and architecture configuration without changes.

PredRNN-V2. We use their recommended configuration for the Moving MNIST dataset.

Dona et al. [4]. We report the performance for their recommended configuration for the Sea Surface Temperature (SST) dataset, as it resulted in the best performance on our datasets.

C Further Dataset Details

In Table 3 we show further statistics of our introduced datasets.

Table 3. Detailed statistics of our introduced datasets.

	Orbits	Acrobot	Pendulum Camera
Number of			
training samples	10K	2K	2K
evaluation samples	256	256	256
burn-in frames	6	6	6
training rollout frames	12	12	12
validation rollout frames	24	24	24
Spatial size	64 × 64	64 × 64	64 × 64
Video FPS	4	10	10
Physics FPS	40	40	40
Symbolic State	Position and velocity of each object	Pole angles and their angular velocities	As in Acrobot, and also the camera position

D Orbits Control Validation Dataset Details

In the Orbits setting the object positions are part of the symbolic state, which are an integral factor of correctly rendering the output frame. However, it is not trivial to measure how well our model is able to decode "hand-controlled" 3D object positions into a 2D frame in a generalizable manner. Therefore we chose to setup an empirical evaluation framework by assembling variations of the Orbits dataset, ranging from different simulation parameters, over completely novel dynamics, up to non-physics settings such as trajectory following. For each validation set, we replace F of a model trained on the default Orbits dataset with the respective version that handles these new dynamics, and then validate the model without any retraining.

Table 4. LPIPS↓ Performance on the default Orbits dataset and the validation settings **A-H**. **A**: Increased frame rate; **B**: Increased gravitational constant; **C**: Tripled force; **D**: Repulsion instead of attraction; **E**: No forces; **F**: No forces and zero velocities; **G**: Objects follow set trajectories; **H**: Objects appear at random locations in each frame.

Default	A	B	C	D	E	F	G	H
5.6	5.9	5.8	5.8	5.1	2.4	5.4	4.5	4.7

As can be seen in Table 4, the performance across all validation settings is comparable to the default dataset and thus, shows that the outputs of F work as a reliable control interface at test time. We note that the much lower LPIPS for test setting E is due to the objects quickly leaving the scene, resulting in mostly background scenes. Table 5 describes each setting in more detail.

Table 5. Detailed description of the Orbits dataset variants that are used to verify generative control over the integrated function parameters.

Setting	Description
Original Dynamics	
A	Increased frame rate from 4 to 10 frames per second
B	Increased gravitational constant for the physical simulation from 7.0 to 20.0
C	Tripled the force applied to objects
Novel Dynamics	
D	Objects are repulsed instead of attracted to each other by inverting the force. However, they are still attracted to the camera focal point in order to stay in view longer
E	No force is applied to the objects, however initial velocities are kept
F	No force is applied to the objects. In addition, all objects have zero velocity, i.e. no object moves
Non-Physical Dynamics	
G	Objects move along a predefined 6 point trajectory
H	Objects are at a randomly sampled location in each frame

E   Integrated Function Details

This section shows the functions integrated in our model. All functions first calculate the appropriate acceleration a before applying it in a semi-implicit euler integration step with a step size of Δt.

For the Orbits dataset each objects state consists of position p and velocity v. The environmental constants correspond to the gravitational constant g and object mass m. Given N objects in the scene at video frame t, the object state of the next time step $t+1$ for any object n is obtained as follows:

$$F_{t,n} = \sum_{\substack{i=0 \\ i \neq n}}^{N} \frac{(p_{t,i} - p_{t,n})}{|(p_{t,i} - p_{t,n})|} \frac{gm}{|(p_{t,i} - p_{t,n})|^2} \tag{3}$$

$$a_{t,n} = \frac{F_{t,n}}{m} \tag{4}$$

$$v_{t+1,n} = v_{t,n} + \Delta t a_{t,n} \tag{5}$$

$$p_{t+1,n} = p_{t,n} + \Delta t v_{t+1,n} \tag{6}$$

For the Acrobot dataset the per-frame state consists of the pendulum angles θ_1 and θ_2 and their angular velocities $\dot{\theta}_1$ and $\dot{\theta}_2$. The environmental constants consist of the pendulum masses m_1 and m_2, the pendulum lengths l_1 and l_2, the link center of mass c_1 and c_2, the inertias I_1 and I_2, and the gravitational constant G. The pendulum state of the next time step $t+1$ is calculated as follows:

$$\delta_{1_t} = m_1 c_1^2 + m_2(l_1^2 + c_2^2 + 2l_1 c_2 \cos(\theta_{2_t})) + I_1 + I_2 \tag{7}$$

$$\delta_{2_t} = m_2(c_2^2 + l_1 c_2 \cos(\theta_{2_t})) + I_2 \tag{8}$$

$$\phi_{2_t} = m_2 c_2 G \cos\left(\theta_{1_t} + \theta_{2_t} - \frac{\pi}{2}\right) \tag{9}$$

$$\phi_{1_t} = -m_2 l_1 c_2 \dot{\theta}_{2_t}^2 \sin(\theta_{2_t}) - 2m_2 l_1 c_2 \dot{\theta}_{2_t} \dot{\theta}_{1_t} \sin(\theta_{2_t}) \tag{10}$$

$$+ (m_1 c_1 + m_2 l_1) G \cos\left(\theta_{1_t} - \frac{\pi}{2}\right) + \phi_{2_t} \tag{11}$$

$$\ddot{\theta}_{2_t} = \frac{\frac{\delta_{2_t}}{\delta_{1_t}} \phi_{1,t} - m_2 l_1 c_2 \dot{\theta}_{1,t}^2 \sin(\theta_{2,t}) - \phi_{2,t}}{m_2 c_2^2 + I_2 - \frac{\delta_{2_t}^2}{\delta_{1_t}}} \tag{12}$$

$$\ddot{\theta}_{1_t} = -\frac{\delta_{2_t} \ddot{\theta}_{2_t} + \phi_{1_t}}{\delta_{1_t}} \tag{13}$$

$$\dot{\theta}_{1_{t+1}} = \dot{\theta}_{1_t} + \Delta t \ddot{\theta}_{1_t} \tag{14}$$

$$\dot{\theta}_{2_{t+1}} = \dot{\theta}_{2_t} + \Delta t \ddot{\theta}_{2_t} \tag{15}$$

$$\theta_{1_{t+1}} = \theta_{1_t} + \Delta t \dot{\theta}_{1_{t+1}} \tag{16}$$

$$\theta_{2_{t+1}} = \theta_{2_t} + \Delta t \dot{\theta}_{2_{t+1}} \tag{17}$$

The Pendulum Camera dataset follows the same equations of the Acrobot dataset to obtain an updated pendulum state. Afterwards, this state is used to obtain the new camera position $p_{c_{t+1}}$:

$$p_{c_{t+1}} = \begin{bmatrix} p_x \\ p_y \\ p_z \end{bmatrix} = \begin{bmatrix} -2l_1 \sin(\theta_{1_{t+1}}) - l_2 \sin(\theta_{1_{t+1}} + \theta_{2_{t+1}}) \\ 2l_1 \cos(\theta_{1_{t+1}}) + l_2 \cos(\theta_{1_{t+1}} + \theta_{2_{t+1}}) \\ 10 \end{bmatrix} \tag{18}$$

F MPC Details

We set the control objective as the maximization of the potential energy—i.e. both pendulums oriented upwards—and the minimization of the kinetic energy—i.e. resting pendulums. The system model corresponds to our integrated function F and due to already being discretized does not require further processing. We use a controller with a prediction horizon of 150 steps and store the predicted torque action sequence for the next 75 frames.

F.1 Qualitative Results

This section shows additional qualitative results for the MPC task.

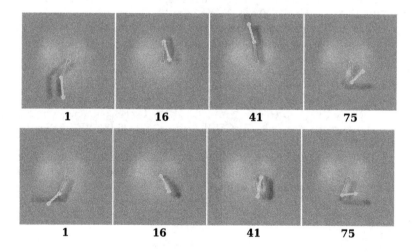

Fig. 7. Qualitative results for the MPC task.

References

1. Brockman, G., et al.: OpenAI gym. arXiv preprint arXiv:1606.01540 (2016)
2. Brown, T.B., et al.: Language models are few-shot learners. arXiv preprint arXiv:2005.14165 (2020)

3. Denton, E., Fergus, R.: Stochastic video generation with a learned prior. In: Proceedings of the 35th International Conference on Machine Learning, pp. 1174–1183. PMLR (2018)
4. Donà, J., Franceschi, J.Y., Lamprier, S., Gallinari, P.: PDE-driven spatiotemporal disentanglement. In: International Conference on Learning Representations (2021)
5. Greff, K., et al.: Kubric: a scalable dataset generator. In: 2022 IEEE/CVF Conference on Computer Vision and Pattern Recognition (CVPR), pp. 3739–3751 (2022). https://doi.org/10.1109/CVPR52688.2022.00373
6. Jaderberg, M., Simonyan, K., Zisserman, A., Kavukcuoglu, K.: Spatial transformer networks. In: Cortes, C., Lawrence, N., Lee, D., Sugiyama, M., Garnett, R. (eds.) Advances in Neural Information Processing Systems, vol. 28. Curran Associates, Inc. (2015)
7. Jaques, M., Burke, M., Hospedales, T.: Physics-as-inverse-graphics: unsupervised physical parameter estimation from video. In: International Conference on Learning Representations (2019)
8. Jumper, J., et al.: Highly accurate protein structure prediction with AlphaFold. Nature **596**(7873), 583–589 (2021). https://doi.org/10.1038/s41586-021-03819-2
9. Kandukuri, R.K., Achterhold, J., Moeller, M., Stueckler, J.: Physical representation learning and parameter identification from video using differentiable physics. Int. J. Comput. Vision **130**(1), 3–16 (2022). https://doi.org/10.1007/s11263-021-01493-5
10. Kingma, D.P., Ba, J.: Adam: a method for stochastic optimization. In: 3rd International Conference on Learning Representations, ICLR 2015, San Diego, CA, USA, May 7–9, 2015, Conference Track Proceedings (2015)
11. Kipf, T., et al.: Conditional object-centric learning from video. In: International Conference on Learning Representations (2022)
12. Kosiorek, A., Kim, H., Teh, Y.W., Posner, I.: Sequential attend, infer, repeat: generative modelling of moving objects. In: Advances in Neural Information Processing Systems, vol. 31. Curran Associates, Inc. (2018)
13. Le Guen, V., Thome, N.: Disentangling physical dynamics from unknown factors for unsupervised video prediction. In: 2020 IEEE/CVF Conference on Computer Vision and Pattern Recognition (CVPR), pp. 11471–11481. IEEE, Seattle, WA, USA (2020). https://doi.org/10.1109/CVPR42600.2020.01149
14. Lin, Z., Wu, Y.F., Peri, S., Fu, B., Jiang, J., Ahn, S.: Improving generative imagination in object-centric world models. In: Proceedings of the 37th International Conference on Machine Learning, pp. 6140–6149. PMLR (2020)
15. Locatello, F., et al.: Object-centric learning with slot attention. In: Advances in Neural Information Processing Systems, vol. 33, pp. 11525–11538. Curran Associates, Inc. (2020)
16. Marcus, G., Davis, E.: Rebooting AI: Building Artificial Intelligence We Can Trust. Pantheon Books, USA (2019)
17. Murthy, J.K., et al.: gradSim: differentiable simulation for system identification and visuomotor control. In: International Conference on Learning Representations (2020)
18. Musielak, Z.E., Quarles, B.: The three-body problem. Rep. Prog. Phys. **77**(6), 065901 (2014). https://doi.org/10.1088/0034-4885/77/6/065901
19. Ouyang, L., et al.: Training language models to follow instructions with human feedback. Adv. Neural. Inf. Process. Syst. **35**, 27730–27744 (2022)
20. Raissi, M., Perdikaris, P., Karniadakis, G.E.: Physics-informed neural networks: a deep learning framework for solving forward and inverse problems involving nonlinear partial differential equations. J. Comput. Phys. **378**, 686–707 (2019). https://doi.org/10.1016/j.jcp.2018.10.045

21. Takenaka, P., Maucher, J., Huber, M.F.: Guiding video prediction with explicit procedural knowledge. In: Proceedings of the IEEE/CVF International Conference on Computer Vision (ICCV) Workshops, pp. 1084–1092 (2023)
22. Traub, M., Otte, S., Menge, T., Karlbauer, M., Thuemmel, J., Butz, M.V.: Learning what and where: disentangling location and identity tracking without supervision. In: The Eleventh International Conference on Learning Representations (2023)
23. Vaswani, A., et al.: Attention is all you need. arXiv preprint arXiv:1706.03762 (2017)
24. von Rueden, L., et al.: Informed machine learning - a taxonomy and survey of integrating prior knowledge into learning systems. IEEE Trans. Knowl. Data Eng. **35**(1), 614–633 (2023). https://doi.org/10.1109/TKDE.2021.3079836
25. Wang, Y., Long, M., Wang, J., Gao, Z., Yu, P.S.: PredRNN: recurrent neural networks for predictive learning using spatiotemporal LSTMs. In: Proceedings of the 31st International Conference on Neural Information Processing Systems, pp. 879–888. NIPS'17, Curran Associates Inc., Red Hook, NY, USA (2017)
26. Wang, Y., et al.: PredRNN: a recurrent neural network for spatiotemporal predictive learning. IEEE Trans. Pattern Anal. Mach. Intell. **45**(2), 2208–2225 (2023). https://doi.org/10.1109/TPAMI.2022.3165153
27. Watters, N., Matthey, L., Burgess, C.P., Lerchner, A.: Spatial broadcast decoder: a simple architecture for learning disentangled representations in VAEs. arXiv preprint arXiv:1901.07017 (2019)
28. Watters, N., Zoran, D., Weber, T., Battaglia, P., Pascanu, R., Tacchetti, A.: Visual interaction networks: learning a physics simulator from video. In: Advances in Neural Information Processing Systems, vol. 30. Curran Associates, Inc. (2017)
29. Wu, X., Lu, J., Yan, Z., Zhang, G.: Disentangling stochastic PDE dynamics for unsupervised video prediction. In: IEEE Transactions on Neural Networks and Learning Systems, pp. 1–15 (2023). https://doi.org/10.1109/TNNLS.2023.3286890
30. Wu, Z., Dvornik, N., Greff, K., Kipf, T., Garg, A.: SlotFormer: unsupervised visual dynamics simulation with object-centric models. In: The Eleventh International Conference on Learning Representations (2023)
31. Wu, Z., Hu, J., Lu, W., Gilitschenski, I., Garg, A.: SlotDiffusion: object-centric generative modeling with diffusion models (2023). https://openreview.net/forum?id=ETk6cfS3vk
32. Xu, J., Zhang, Z., Friedman, T., Liang, Y., Broeck, G.: A semantic loss function for deep learning with symbolic knowledge. In: Proceedings of the 35th International Conference on Machine Learning, pp. 5502–5511. PMLR (2018)
33. Yang, T.Y., Rosca, J.P., Narasimhan, K.R., Ramadge, P.: Learning physics constrained dynamics using autoencoders. In: Advances in Neural Information Processing Systems (2022)
34. Yi, K., et al.: CLEVRER: collision events for video representation and reasoning. In: International Conference on Learning Representations (2019)

The Role of Foundation Models in Neuro-Symbolic Learning and Reasoning

Daniel Cunnington[1,2](✉), Mark Law[3], Jorge Lobo[4], and Alessandra Russo[2]

[1] Durable.ai, Louisville, CO, USA
[2] Imperial College London, London, UK
dtc20@imperial.ac.uk
[3] ILASP Limited, Grantham, UK
[4] Universitat Pompeu Fabra, Barcelona, Spain

Abstract. Neuro-Symbolic AI (NeSy) holds promise to ensure the safe deployment of AI systems, as interpretable symbolic techniques provide formal behaviour guarantees. The challenge is how to effectively integrate neural and symbolic computation, to enable learning and reasoning from raw data. Existing pipelines that train the neural and symbolic components sequentially require extensive labelling, whereas end-to-end approaches are limited in terms of scalability, due to the combinatorial explosion in the symbol grounding problem. In this paper, we leverage the implicit knowledge within foundation models to enhance the performance in NeSy tasks, whilst reducing the amount of data labelling and manual engineering. We introduce a new architecture, called NeSyGPT, which fine-tunes a vision-language foundation model to extract symbolic features from raw data, before learning a highly expressive answer set program to solve a downstream task. Our comprehensive evaluation demonstrates that NeSyGPT has superior accuracy over various baselines, and can scale to complex NeSy tasks. Finally, we highlight the effective use of a large language model to generate the programmatic interface between the neural and symbolic components, significantly reducing the amount of manual engineering required. The Appendix is presented in the longer version of this paper, which contains additional results and analysis [8].

Keywords: Neuro-Symbolic Learning · Foundation Models · Answer Set Programming

1 Introduction

Ensuring the safe deployment of AI systems is a top-priority. Neuro-Symbolic AI (NeSy) [15] is well-suited to help achieve this goal, as interpretable symbolic components enable manual inspection, whilst providing formal guarantees of

Daniel was previously employed at IBM Research, when this work was performed.

their behaviour. However, integrating neural components to enable learning and reasoning from raw data remains an open challenge. Existing approaches either require extensive data labelling and manual engineering of symbolic rules [13], or, when neural and symbolic components are trained end-to-end [9], they encounter difficulties scaling to complex tasks. This is due to the combinatorial explosion in learning the correct assignment of symbolic features to the raw input (i.e., the symbol grounding problem [17]). End-to-end approaches are also difficult to control, causing unintended concepts to be learned, thus posing a challenge to AI safety [28]. Pre-trained foundation models on the other hand, have a large amount of implicit knowledge embedded within their latent space, which could be leveraged during the training of a NeSy system. The question we address in this paper is: *How can we use this knowledge to reduce the amount of data labelling and engineering required, whilst solving complex neuro-symbolic tasks that have many possible values for the symbolic features?*

We introduce a new architecture, called NeSyGPT, that fine-tunes the BLIP vision-language foundation model [26] to extract symbolic features from raw data, before learning a set of logical rules to solve a downstream task. The architecture utilises the implicit knowledge of BLIP, and therefore, we only require a few labelled data points to fine-tune for a specific task. Logical rules are learned as Answer Set Programming (ASP) programs, since ASP is suited for efficiently representing solutions to computationally complex problems [16]. The rules are learned using a state-of-the-art Learning from Answer Sets (LAS) symbolic learner robust to noise. We evaluate NeSyGPT in four problem domains, each with specific challenges, and demonstrate that we out-perform a variety of neural and NeSy baselines. The main contribution of this paper is a novel architecture that integrates a vision-language foundation model, and a symbolic learner, for solving complex neuro-symbolic tasks, offering the following advantages: (1) It requires a reduced amount of labelled data points to extract symbolic features from raw data, and learn the rules of the downstream task. (2) It scales to complex tasks that have a large number of possible symbolic feature values. (3) It does not require the symbolic rules to be manually engineered. (4) It can solve tasks that require detecting multiple objects and their properties within a single image, e.g., the CLEVR-Hans3 dataset [36]. (5) It can utilise a Large Language Model (LLM) to generate questions and answers for fine-tuning BLIP, and to construct the interface between the neural and symbolic components.

2 Related Work

There are various NeSy systems proposed in the literature [3]. Some inject neural architectures with symbolic rules [2,32], whereas others perform neural and symbolic computation in separate modules [1,7,27,31,39]. Whilst various architectures, types of logic, and computation techniques have been explored, many systems lack the expressivity required to learn or reason with general and complex rules, and are either restricted to definite clauses [9,10,27,33], graphical models with cost matrices [12], or look-up tables [11]. In this paper, we focus on ASP-based NeSy systems, as they are able to express general and complex rules.

Current NeSy approaches still suffer drawbacks. Some rely on pre-trained pipelines that require extensive data labelling and manual engineering [6,13], whereas others are limited in terms of scalability, in the case of end-to-end training [1,5,7,14,35,39]. This is due to the aforementioned symbol grounding problem. Furthermore, only [5–7,14] are able to perform rule learning from raw data in ASP for NeSy tasks, whereas other approaches assume the symbolic rules are manually specified. Our approach is able to seamlessly integrate rule learning and reasoning in ASP, and scales to tasks with a large amount of choice for the values of the symbolic features, thus avoiding the combinatorial explosion that end-to-end methods suffer. Also, we require very few labelled data points, and a reduced amount of manual engineering, thus gaining an advantage over existing pipeline approaches. Finally, it is difficult to integrate object detection within current NeSy architectures, as many approaches rely upon a CNN to classify an entire image. Our approach is more general, and can extract various objects and their properties from a single image through Visual Question Answering (VQA) (see CLEVR-Hans results in Sect. 5).

Integrating foundation models with symbolic computation has also been studied previously. [19,40] leverage LLMs to generate ASP programs to solve complex reasoning problems, and [29] use a LLM to iteratively generate candidate solutions, accepting a solution if it satisfies some given background knowledge. In contrast to our approach, these focus purely on language models, and are unable to support visual input. Also, none of these approaches learn symbolic rules, as they are either specified symbolically, or in textual form.

There are cases where rules are generated automatically. [38] uses a language model to perform inductive reasoning, by generating multiple candidate hypotheses and having a human-oracle or another language model select a subset for validation. This technique does not support visual input, and crucially, the final hypothesis is chosen as the candidate that covers the most training examples, during a post-processing stage.[1] In contrast, our approach takes advantage of a symbolic learner that includes a more advanced optimisation algorithm, which maximises example coverage as part of the hypothesis search, and provides a formal guarantee of the optimality and consistency of the learned rules. Finally, [37] achieves VQA, by using a LLM to generate python programs that call external modules for image processing. However, as evidenced in our results, it is difficult to generate solutions to complex problems that require negation, choice, and constraints using current LLMs [21]. Our approach can learn and efficiently express such rules using ASP.

3 Background

BLIP. BLIP uses a multi-modal mixture of encoder-decoder transformer modules. The image encoder is a Vision Transformer, and the text encoder is a BERT model. BLIP is pre-trained to jointly optimise three objectives; (1) *Image-Text*

---

[1] A hypothesis is said to *cover* an example, if the target label is deduced given the input features.

Contrastive Loss, which aligns the embedding space of the vision transformer and BERT by encouraging positive image-text pairs to have similar latent representations in contrast to negative pairs. (2) *Image-Text Matching Loss*, which is a binary classification task that trains BLIP to predict whether an image-text pair is matched (positive) or unmatched (negative). (3) *Language Modelling Loss* which aims to generate a textual description given an image. This is achieved using the cross-entropy loss with a ground-truth description. In this paper, we use the "VQA" mode to perform fine-tuning. The pre-trained BLIP model is rearranged by encoding an image-question pair into multi-modal embeddings, before passing the embeddings to a text decoder to obtain the answer. The VQA architecture is then trained end-to-end using the Language Modelling Loss with ground-truth answers. For more details, please refer to [26].

LAS. A LAS symbolic learner learns a set of rules, called a *hypothesis*. The symbolic learner accepts as input a set of training examples $E = \{\langle e_{\text{id}}, e_{\text{pos}}, e_{\text{pen}}, e_{\text{inc}}, e_{\text{exc}}, e_{\text{ctx}} \rangle, \ldots\}$, where e_{id} is an identifier, e_{pos} denotes whether the example is either positive or negative, e_{pen} is a weight penalty, which is paid if the example is not *covered* by the learned rules, e_{inc} and e_{exc} contain inclusion and exclusion atoms respectively, and e_{ctx} contains a set of contextual facts. Alongside E, the symbolic learner also requires a domain knowledge B that contains relations used to construct a search space $\mathcal{H}$, and any (optional) background knowledge. The output is a hypothesis $H \in \mathcal{H}$ in the form of an ASP program. H minimises a scoring function based on its length, and its example coverage. Let us assume the set of examples uncovered by H is denoted by $UNCOV(H, (B, E))$. The score of H is given by $score(H, (B, E)) = |H| + \sum_{e \in UNCOV(H,(B,E))} e_{\text{pen}}$. A LAS symbolic learner computes the optimal solution H^* that satisfies:

$$H^* = \arg\min_{H \in \mathcal{H}} [score(H, (B, E))] \tag{1}$$

This can be interpreted as jointly maximising the generality of H (i.e., a concise ASP program), and example coverage. For more details, please refer to [23].

4 Method

4.1 Problem Formulation

We assume a perception function $f : \langle \mathcal{X}, \mathcal{Q} \rangle \to \mathcal{A}$ that performs VQA. $\mathcal{X}$, $\mathcal{Q}$, and $\mathcal{A}$ are the spaces of raw image inputs, natural language questions, and answers, respectively. The answers represent symbolic features related to an image. We also assume a reasoning function $h : \langle \mathcal{A}^u, \mathcal{M} \rangle^n \to \mathcal{Y}$ that maps n-length sequences of answers and meta-data pairs to a target value. Note that there could be u questions asked of each image, and therefore, u answers for each pair. The meta-data in the space $\mathcal{M}$ is used to encode any extra information associated with the raw input. $\mathcal{Y}$ is the space of the target values.

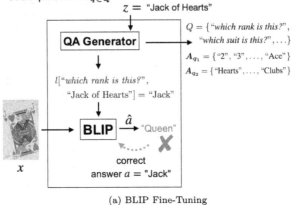

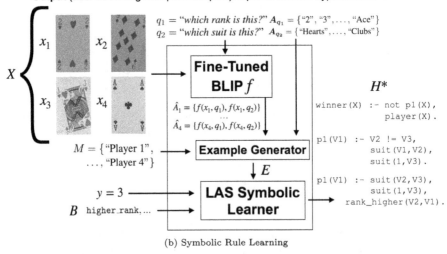

Fig. 1. NeSyGPT architecture with one data point in the Follow Suit task. The goal is to learn the rules of the game: The winner is the player with the highest ranked card with the same suit as Player 1. (a) BLIP is fine-tuned using playing card images and natural language questions and answers. (b) A hypothesis is learned from BLIP predictions. Note in (a), fine-tuning occurs with both suit and rank answers.

During training, we use two datasets: (1) $D_{\text{image}} = \{\langle x, z \rangle, \ldots\}$, where $x \in \mathcal{X}$ is an image, and $z \in \mathcal{Z}$ is an image label, and (2) $D_{\text{task}} = \{\langle X, M, y \rangle, \ldots\}$ where X is a sequence of images $x \in \mathcal{X}$, $M \subseteq \mathcal{M}$ is a (possibly empty) set of meta-data associated with X, and $y \in \mathcal{Y}$ is a downstream task label. We learn f and h sequentially,[2] as our experiments demonstrate this outperforms an end-to-end approach (see Sect. 5). To learn f, we require, in addition to the raw input, sets of questions and answers. These are generated automatically, and are assumed constant for a given task. We denote the set of questions as $Q \subseteq \mathcal{Q}$ and the set of possible answers for a given question $q \in Q$ as $\boldsymbol{A_q} \subseteq \mathcal{A}$. For example, in the Follow Suit task (see Fig. 1), the question $q =$ "which rank is this?" has the set of possible answers $\boldsymbol{A_q} = \{$"2", "3", \ldots, "Ace"$\}$. We also require a look-up table $l : \langle \mathcal{Q}, \mathcal{Z} \rangle \to \mathcal{A}$ which is used to map question and image label pairs to the correct answer. For example, given an image label $z =$ "Jack of Hearts", the look-up table returns the answer "Jack" for the question $q =$ "which rank is this?", and the answer "Hearts" for $q =$ "which suit is this?".

The first goal is to learn f s.t. $\forall \langle x, z \rangle \in D_{\text{image}}$, and $\forall q \in Q$, $f(x, q) = l(q, z)$, i.e., f returns the correct answer for all images and all questions. Once f is learned, the next objective is to learn h. Let us define the set of predicted answers for an image $x_i \in X$ as $\hat{A}_i = [f(x_i, q_1), \ldots, f(x_i, q_u)]$, where $q_j \in Q$. The goal is to learn h, s.t. $\forall \langle X, M, y \rangle \in D_{\text{task}}$, $h([\langle \hat{A}_i, m_i \rangle : x_i \in X]) = y$, where $m_i \in M$. Intuitively, this means that each data point in D_{task} has a correct downstream prediction. For example, in Fig. 1, assuming correct predictions, the answers are $\hat{A}_1 = [$"2","Hearts"$]$, $\hat{A}_2 = [$"9","Diamonds"$]$, $\hat{A}_3 = [$"Jack","Hearts"$]$, and $\hat{A}_4 = [$"Ace","Clubs"$]$, and the meta-data M indicates which player each card corresponds to, e.g., $m_1 =$ "Player 1". The target label is $y = 3$, as Player 3 is the winner. We propose the NeSyGPT architecture which consists of the BLIP Fine-Tuning phase for learning f, and the Symbolic Rule Learning phase for learning h (see Fig. 1).

4.2 BLIP Fine-Tuning

Given an image data point $\langle x_i, z_i \rangle \in D_{\text{image}}$, and a question $q \in Q$, the answer returned from the look-up table $l(q, z_i)$ is used to fine-tune BLIP, alongside the image x_i. The question-answer generator is specific to each task, and can be manually engineered or obtained automatically using a LLM. Our experiments show that the LLM output is below the level of accuracy achieved with manual engineering. However, we expect this to improve as LLMs themselves continue to improve. To fine-tune BLIP with the generated questions and answers, we use the "VQA" mode as presented in Sect. 3.

4.3 Symbolic Rule Learning

Example Generator. Given a task data point $\langle X, M, y \rangle \in D_{\text{task}}$, and a sequence of answer meta-data pairs $[\langle \hat{A}_i, m_i \rangle : x_i \in X]$ from the BLIP Fine-Tuning phase, the goal is to generate a LAS training example $e \in E$ for

---

[2] where h is learned using predictions from f, once f is learned.

the symbolic learner. The inclusion and exclusion sets of e encode the downstream label. Formally, $e_{\text{inc}} = \{y\}$, and $e_{\text{exc}} = \{y' : y' \in \mathcal{Y}, y' \neq y\}$. The answers and meta-data are encoded into the example's context e_{ctx}. In the case of feature classification questions (e.g., $q =$ "which rank is this?"), there is no guarantee that BLIP predicts a valid answer for a given question. To tackle this problem, we use the Levenshtein string distance to return the answer $a \in A_q$ with the lowest edit distance compared to the predicted answer $\hat{a}$ [41]. The answers and meta-data are then encoded into e_{ctx} in ASP form, which is task specific. For example, in Fig. 1b, assuming correct BLIP predictions, $e_{\text{ctx}} = \{\texttt{card}(1,2,\texttt{h})., \texttt{card}(2,9,\texttt{d})., \texttt{card}(3,\texttt{j},\texttt{h})., \texttt{card}(4,\texttt{a},\texttt{c}).\}$, representing the "*Two of Hearts*", "*Nine of Diamonds*", "*Jack of Hearts*", and "*Ace of Clubs*" for each player's card, respectively. The Example Generator can be manually engineered, or obtained using a LLM, which generates Python code that encodes the ASP representation of a full training example e. We use the string distance method to obtain valid answers before using the LLM to encode e. In the Appendix, we demonstrate that with small syntactic fixes, the LLM can encode the training examples with competitive accuracy compared to a manual specification.

LAS Symbolic Learner. Given a set of training examples E, and a domain knowledge B, the symbolic learner learns an optimal hypothesis H^*, satisfying the scoring function in Eq. 1. H^*, together with B, forms the reasoning function $h = H^* \cup B$. Let us now present our experimental results.

5 Evaluation

Our evaluation investigates whether the implicit knowledge embedded within BLIP can improve the accuracy of NeSy learning and reasoning, whilst reducing the amount of labelled data required. We compare NeSyGPT against the following types of architectures: *NeSy Reasoning*, where the symbolic rules are given, *NeSy Learning*, where the symbolic rules are learned, and *Fully Neural Methods* including deep learning, and generative models.

We choose four problem domains; MNIST Arithmetic, Follow Suit, Plant Disease Hitting Sets, and CLEVR-Hans, each with their own characteristics. The MNIST Arithmetic domain includes the standard NeSy benchmark from [27], and the E9P task from [7], where we demonstrate learning negation as failure. The Follow Suit domain tests scalability w.r.t. the number of choices for the symbolic features [6]. A given data point has $\sim$ 6.5m choices in the 4-player variant, and $\sim 5.74 \times 10^{16}$ choices in the 10-player variant. For reference, the 2-digit MNIST Addition task has 100 choices per data point. This domain also requires learning predicates that are not directly observed in the examples (i.e., predicate invention). The Plant Hitting Sets domain includes real-world images, and requires learning complex rules including constraints and choice, as well as reasoning over multiple models (answer sets). Finally, the CLEVR-Hans domain tests object detection, as up to 10 objects and their properties need to be extracted from a single image.

The results show that NeSyGPT: (1) Achieves better performance than any of the other approaches. (2) Requires very few labelled data points. (3) Can scale to complex tasks with a large number of choices for the symbolic features. (4) Can easily integrate symbolic learning of ASP programs to learn complex and interpretable rules. (5) Can achieve state-of-the-art performance on CLEVR-Hans. We also demonstrate that the amount of manual engineering can be reduced using GPT-4 [30]. The results indicate GPT-4 can generate reasonable questions and answers for feature extraction. We present these results in the Appendix.

Baselines. Our baselines have symbolic components that are either fully neural, or are capable of learning or representing complex rules expressed in ASP. This is in order to show that the proposed benefits of NeSyGPT are due to the implicit knowledge embedded within BLIP, and our novel method of integrating BLIP with the symbolic component, as opposed to the symbolic representation used. For NeSy Reasoning, we compare our approach to **NeurASP** [39], **SLASH** [35], and two variants of Embed2Sym [1]: One trained end-to-end as usual (**Embed2Sym**), and another where clustering is performed on an embedding space resulting from fine-tuning a perception model with ground-truth image labels (**Embed2Sym***). We also use a modified version of ABL [10] as an additional baseline, which uses the same perception component as in our approach (**BLIP+ABL**). Note that BLIP can't directly be used in NeurASP, SLASH, and Embed2Sym because these methods require back-propagating gradients to a softmax layer for training the perception model. BLIP on the other hand, is fine-tuned with natural language questions and answers. For NeurASP, SLASH, and Embed2Sym, we use the best pre-trained model available; the Vision Transformer *ViT-B-32* from PyTorch, which is pre-trained on ImageNet.

For NeSy Learning, we compare to **FF-NSL** [6] and **NSIL** [7], using the pre-trained ViT-B-32 as the perception model. Note FF-NSL essentially implements a standard neural network (which is fine-tuned), and connected to a LAS symbolic learner, to highlight the impact of using BLIP. For Fully Neural Methods, we compare to: (1) The ViT-B-32 connected to a fully differentiable reasoning network (**ViT+ReasoningNet**), which is an MLP in the MNIST Arithmetic and Follow Suit domains, and a Recurrent Transformer in the Plant Hitting Sets domain, since longer sequences are observed [18]. (2) BLIP connected to GPT-4 for rule learning (**BLIP+GPT4**). We prompt GPT-4 to generate Python programs for the MNIST Arithmetic and Follow Suit domains, since it is easy to express solutions to these tasks in Python, and GPT-4 has likely seen many Python examples during its pre-training. For Plant Hitting Sets, we prompt GPT-4 to generate ASP programs, given it is more natural to express the solution to this problem in a declarative manner. (3) BLIP solving the downstream task with all images contained within a single image (**BLIP Single Image**). Finally, in the CLEVR-Hans domain, we consider α**ILP** [33] as our baseline, since αILP has achieved state-of-the-art performance.

Experiment Setup. In the MNIST Arithmetic, Follow Suit, and Plant Hitting Sets tasks, we generate questions and answers for fine-tuning BLIP using a varying number of image labels: $\{0, 1, 2, 5, 10, 20, 50, 100\} \times$ the number of feature values for each image. This represents zero-shot, one-shot, two-shot, etc. To learn the symbolic rules, we use $\{10, 20, 50, 100\}$ labelled examples for the symbolic learner. In all datasets, we use an even distribution of labels. For the baselines, we use the same total number of labels, distributed as follows. For NeurASP, SLASH, Embed2Sym, BLIP+ABL, NSIL, and BLIP Single Image, we train these models end-to-end with the same total number of labels as required for our approach, with no supervision on the symbolic features. For Embed2Sym*, FF-NSL, ViT+ReasoningNet, and BLIP+GPT4, we follow a similar approach to ours: We first fine-tune the perception component using ground-truth image labels, and then train the reasoning component using the same number of task labels.

In the MNIST Arithmetic and CLEVR-Hans domains, we use FastLAS for the symbolic learner due to FastLAS' increased efficiency in larger search spaces [22]. We use ILASP in the Follow Suit and Plant Hitting Sets domains, as ILASP supports predicate invention (required in the Follow Suit domain), and the ability to learn choice rules and constraints (required in the Plant Hitting Sets domain) [24]. We set the LAS example weight penalty to 10 in all experiments except CLEVR-Hans, where a penalty of 1 is used. 10 and 1 are chosen because they provide adequate balance against the length of the hypothesis. In CLEVR-Hans, there are more symbolic examples given, so a lower weight penalty is required to learn a shorter, more general hypothesis.

Each experiment is repeated 5 times using 5 randomly generated seeds and datasets. We use the "vqav2" BLIP model from the LAVIS library [25], which is pre-trained on the Visual Genome, Conceptual Captions, Conceptual 12M, SBU captions, LAION, and the VQA v2.0 datasets. In our paper, BLIP is fine-tuned using a distinct set of training images, and the images in the training examples for the symbolic learner are not used for BLIP fine-tuning. We use 5 held-out test sets (not seen in any training stage) to evaluate task accuracy, and report the mean and standard error. For all models, we train with the most performant number of epochs we can achieve within a 24 h time limit. For NeSyGPT, we train for 10 epochs on MNIST Arithmetic and Follow Suit, and 20 epochs on Plant Hitting Sets and CLEVR. For all baselines, we train for 50 epochs unless otherwise stated. All hyper-parameters are left as default, and we use the SGD optimiser with a learning rate of 0.01 for all models, unless specified in a methods codebase. All experiments are run on a shared cluster with the following specification: RHEL 8.5 × 86 64 with Intel Xeon E5-2667 CPUs (10 cores total), and 1 NVIDIA A100 GPU, 150GB RAM. The domain knowledge and search spaces are given in the Appendix.

5.1 MNIST Arithmetic

This includes 2-digit Addition from [27], and E9P, where the input is 2 MNIST images, and the label is equal to the digit value of the second image, if the digit value of the first image is even, or 9 plus the digit value in the second image otherwise. The symbolic search space follows [7], and includes the relations even, not even, plus_nine, '=', and the function '+'. We fine-tune BLIP using the question *"which digit is this?"*, and the digit value as the answer. Image accuracies are reported over the standard MNIST test set of 10,000 images, and task accuracies are reported over held-out test sets of 1000 examples.

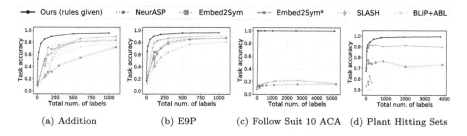

Fig. 2. Task accuracy when the symbolic rules are given.

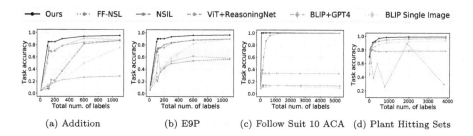

Fig. 3. Task accuracy when the symbolic rules are learned.

The results are shown in Figs. 2a-2b when the symbolic rules are given, and Figs. 3a-3b when the rules are learned. NeSyGPT outperforms all baselines, and learns the correct rules (see Fig. 4a). The rules represent the Addition and E9P functions over two input digits, where the definitions of even and plus_nine predicates are given in the background knowledge (see Appendix). In both cases, BLIP is fine-tuned to a mean image accuracy of 0.9216 with 100 labels, increasing to 0.9753 with 1000 labels. This is within 2.34% of the state-of-the-art result of 0.9987 [4], whilst using only 1.67% of the 60,000 labels available. NeSyGPT is able to learn the correct rules in all 5 repeats when BLIP is fine-tuned using only 10 image labels. To do so, the symbolic learner requires 50 task labels for the Addition task, and 20 for the E9P task. Note that the NeSyGPT curves in Figs. 2a-2b are shifted to the left because no task examples are required as the rules are given. All baselines use the same total number of examples as NeSyGPT does when learning the rules (Fig. 3).

```
result(V0,V1,V2) :- V2 = V0 + V1.

result(V0,V1,V2) :- even(V0),V2 = V1.
result(V0,V1,V2) :- not even(V0),
                    plus_nine(V1,V2).
```

(a) MNIST Arithmetic

```
winner(X) :- not p1(X), player(X).
p1(V1) :- V2 != V3, suit(V1,V2), suit(1,V3).
p1(V1) :- suit(V2,V3), suit(1,V3),
          rank_higher(V2,V1).
```

(b) Follow Suit

```
0 {hs(V1,V2) } 1.
hit(V1) :- hs(V3,V2),
           ss_element(V1,V2).
:- ss_element(V1,V2), not hit(V1).
:- hs(V3,V1), hs(V3,V2), V1 != V2.
:- hs(V1,V2), healthy(V2).
```

(c) Plant Hitting Sets

```
label(0) :- size(V0,large), shape(V0,cube),
            size(V1,large), shape(V1,cylinder).
label(1) :- size(V0,small), material(V0,metal),
            shape(V0,cube), size(V1,small),
            shape(V1,sphere).
label(2) :- size(V0,large), color(V0,blue),
            shape(V0,sphere), size(V1,small),
            color(V1,yellow), shape(V1,sphere).
```

(d) CLEVR-Hans

Fig. 4. NeSyGPT learned rules.

In terms of the baselines in Fig. 2, all methods except SLASH perform better on the E9P task than Addition. This is expected as the downstream label is more informative in E9P: There is a reduced number of possible digit choices for certain examples, which gives a stronger signal for training the perception model. NeSyGPT is unaffected by this, given it is fine-tuned directly with answers generated from image labels. With fewer labels, the end-to-end variant of Embed2Sym struggles to achieve a good clustering in the embedding space of the perception model in Addition, again because it's more difficult to distinguish the individual digits in these examples. In Fig. 3, a similar pattern occurs, with the notable exception of BLIP+GPT4. It performs well in Addition, but fails to generate the correct rules in the E9P task. The E9P task is less common than Addition, and it is unlikely GPT4 has seen many examples of this during pre-training. The fully neural ViT+ReasoningNet struggles in such low-label settings, whereas the NeSy approaches perform better. NSIL has to explore more of the search space in Addition before converging to the correct rules, and FF-NSL follows a similar curve to NeSyGPT, but has lower performance due to an inferior perception component.

5.2 Follow Suit

The Follow Suit domain requires learning the rules of a playing card game, called Follow Suit Winner. Each player plays a card from a standard deck of 52 cards, and the winner is the player with the highest ranked card with the same suit as the first player. This domain involves a large amount of choice for the symbolic features, and therefore presents a challenge for end-to-end methods. To investigate this, we introduce a new 10-player variant, which significantly increases the number of choices compared to the 4-player variant. Assuming a single deck of cards, the 4-player variant has $\sim$ 6.5m choices for the symbolic features, whereas the 10-player variant has $\sim 5.74 \times 10^{16}$ choices. The search space for the symbolic learner follows [6] and includes the relations `higher_rank` of arity 2 which denotes a certain player having a higher ranked card than another player, and the '!=' relation to denote two suit values are not equal. The search space also includes an instruction to perform predicate invention, to enable the definition of a winning player to be learned.

For images, we use the *Standard* and *Adversarial Captain America (ACA)* decks from [6], where the ACA deck contains card images from a Captain America card deck placed on a background of standard card images. BLIP is fine-tuned with the questions *"which rank is this?"*, and *"which suit is this?"*. Image accuracies are reported over a test set of 1040 card images, and task accuracies are reported over held-out test sets of 1000 examples. The results for the most challenging 10-player ACA variant are shown in Figs. 2c and 3c for reasoning and learning respectively. The results for the other variants are shown in the Appendix. Note that all of the methods in Fig. 3c have low standard error across 5 repeats. In both reasoning and learning, NeSyGPT achieves perfect performance on all variants, and significantly outperforms the baselines. When the symbolic rules are given, NeurASP, SLASH, and BLIP+ABL all reach the 24-hour time limit, even with the 4-player standard variant. NeurASP struggles with the large number of choices, and we had to limit the number of answer sets calculated during each example to 5000, so it is not able to update gradients based on all the answer sets. We also had to limit NeurASP to 10 epochs. SLASH became stuck in the ASP grounding stage, and therefore we are unable to obtain any results. For BLIP+ABL, the 10-player variant takes longer because there are more images in each example to calculate pseudo-labels for. Embed2Sym* is able to learn a good playing card clustering in the embedding space, but the ASP Optimisation used to label the clusters struggles, and we had to limit the ASP solver to return the best cluster labelling discovered within a 60 s timeout. The end-to-end variant of Embed2Sym also struggles with cluster labelling, and is unable to learn a good clustering in the embedding space.

When learning the rules, FF-NSL requires more labels to fine-tune the perception component to the same level of accuracy. As NSIL is based upon NeurASP, it suffers similar timeout issues. The fully neural VIT+ReasoningNet struggles in such low-label settings. BLIP+GPT4 and BLIP Single Image perform well in the 4-player variants, with BLIP Single Image achieving perfect accuracy given enough labels in the 4-player standard case. However, both of these approaches fail to solve the 10-player variant. For NeSyGPT, BLIP is fine-tuned to an image accuracy of 0.9832 and 0.9988 for standard and ACA decks respectively, with only 52 image labels (single-shot). This increases to 1.0 in all 5 repeats for both standard and ACA variants, given 520 and 2600 labels respectively. In all variants the correct rules are learned with only 10 task labels, (see Fig. 4b). The rules define whether a given player is a winner. `winner(X)` is true if neither of the `p1` rules hold. `p1` is the invented predicate, and is true if the suit of the given player is different from the suit of Player 1, or if there is another player with the same suit as Player 1 with a higher ranked card than the given player.

5.3 Plant Hitting Sets

The goal is to learn a variation of the Hitting Set problem [20] from images of plant leaves of various crops [34]. Let us assume a collection of crop fields, where each field contains a set of crops that can be diseased or healthy. In this context, a "hitting set" represents a set of diseased crops that intersects with each crop field. This enables a prioritisation in terms of which diseases should be eradicated first, as one may wish to eradicate diseases that occur in each crop field. The size of the hitting set can be viewed as the budget for how many crops are able to be eradicated. The standard rules of the Hitting Set problem apply, and we also require the constraint that no healthy crops should appear in the hitting set, since we are not interested in eradicating those. To solve this task, complex rules are required involving constraints, choice rules, and, to generate *all* the hitting sets with a certain budget, the solution requires multiple models.

The input consists of a collection of plant disease images arranged into various subsets. We generate the examples randomly, where each example contains at most 5 subsets, and each subset contains at most 5 elements. In the image dataset [34], each element can take an integer value in $\{1..38\}$ to denote a particular plant species and disease. We remove the "background" class. We assume the budget is 2, and the label is binary, indicating whether the collection contains a hitting set with no healthy images of size ≤ 2. The search space for the symbolic learner contains the relation '!=' and the relation hs, which defines an element of the hitting set. The budget 2, as well as the integer values which correspond to healthy plant images, are given as background knowledge. To fine-tune BLIP, we use the questions "*which plant species is this?*", and "*which disease is this?*". If the plant image is not diseased, we use the answer "*healthy*". Image accuracies are reported over a test set of 5000 plant images, and task accuracies are reported over held-out test sets of 1000 examples. The results are shown in Figs. 2d and 3d, for reasoning and learning respectively. With > 10 labels, NeSyGPT is able to match or out-perform all the baseline methods. BLIP is fine-tuned to an accuracy of 0.8826 with 380 image labels, and 0.9871 with 3800 labels. The correct rules are learned using the BLIP model fine-tuned with 380 image labels, when 100 examples are given to the symbolic learner (see Fig. 4c). The first rule is a choice rule that generates all possible hitting sets, where V1 is the index and V2 is the element. The second rule defines whether a subset is "hit", i.e., if it contains an element in the hitting set. The remaining rules are constraints that ensure all subsets are hit, the hitting set must not contain different elements at a given index, and there are no "healthy" elements in the hitting set.

In terms of the baselines, when the rules are given, NeurASP and BLIP+ABL suffer timeout issues, and the implementation of SLASH does not support variable length sequences in the examples, so results can't be obtained. Both variants of Embed2Sym are fairly constant, regardless of the number of labels. Inspecting the perception model's embedding space, it appears the pre-trained vision transformer model is able to return a reasonably good image clustering without any fine-tuning. However, labelling the clusters accurately is very difficult, since there are many possible choices of symbolic features that satisfy the downstream label. When learning the rules, FF-NSL performs similarly to NeSyGPT, as does BLIP Single Image. The ViT+ReasoningNet is unable to solve the task, although when the reasoning network (a Recurrent Transformer) is given 5000 downstream examples (50× more than shown in Fig. 3d), the task accuracy approaches 90%. The results for BLIP+GPT4 are very variable. We note that this method requires extensive prompt tuning, although is able to learn the correct rules on some repeats. We had to limit the number of downstream examples to a maximum of 20 as otherwise the token limit in the prompt is exceeded.

Table 1. CLEVR-Hans Results.

	Num Im.	Task Acc. (250 Ex.)	Task Acc. (500 Ex.)
αILP	70k	0.9505 (0.0024)	0.9752 (0.0081)
	9k	0.4992 (0.0116)	0.4808 (0.0160)
NeSyGPT	70k	**0.9853** (0.0012)	**0.9853** (0.0012)
	9k	**0.8629** (0.0090)	**0.8691** (0.0085)

5.4 CLEVR-Hans

To demonstrate NeSyGPT can solve tasks that require detecting multiple objects within an image, we evaluate the CLEVR-Hans3 task [36]. The input is a single image containing up to 10 objects, and the downstream label is one of three classes, which groups images with certain objects and properties together. To solve this task, BLIP must detect the properties of the various objects, namely, their *size, material, color,* and *shape*. The learned rules then classify a set of objects and their properties. The search space for the symbolic learner contains all possible properties and their values. BLIP is fine-tuned using the question "*what does the image contain?*" and the answer contains the list of object properties, e.g., "*The image contains a large gray cube made of metal, a large yellow cylinder made of rubber, ...*". Image and task accuracies are reported over the CLEVR-Hans test set, where we count an image prediction as correct if *all* ground truth objects and their properties are correctly identified. For training, we fine-tune BLIP firstly using the 70k-example CLEVR dataset, as performed in [33], and secondly, using the 9000-example CLEVR-Hans training set. For rule learning, we use 250 and 500 task examples. In all cases, we run 5 repeats with different randomly generated seeds. For αILP, we use the 5 seeds specified in their implementation. The results are shown in Table 1. NeSyGPT outperforms αILP in all cases, achieving state-of-the-art performance using 50% of the downstream labels. BLIP is fine-tuned to an image accuracy of 0.410 and 0.934, and the average rule accuracy with 250 task examples is 0.831 and 1.0, for the 9000 and 70k cases respectively. With 500 task examples, the average rule accuracy increases to 0.833 in the 9000 case.

6 Conclusion

In this paper, we have introduced a new architecture called NeSyGPT, that integrates a vision-language foundation model with symbolic learning and reasoning in ASP. Our evaluation demonstrates NeSyGPT provides many benefits over existing ASP-based NeSy systems, including strong performance, reduced labelling, advanced perception, and symbolic learning. The results in the appendix show that LLMs can be used to reduce the manual engineering effort, generating questions and answers to fine-tune the perception model, and also the programmatic interface between the neural and symbolic components.

References

1. Aspis, Y., Broda, K., Lobo, J., Russo, A.: Embed2sym-scalable neuro-symbolic reasoning via clustered embeddings. In: Proceedings of the International Conference on Principles of Knowledge Representation and Reasoning, vol. 19, pp. 421–431 (2022)
2. Badreddine, S., d'Avila Garcez, A., Serafini, L., Spranger, M.: Logic tensor networks. Artif. Intell. **303**, 103649 (2022). https://doi.org/10.1016/j.artint.2021.103649
3. Besold, T.R., et al.: Neural-symbolic learning and reasoning: a survey and interpretation. In: Neuro-Symbolic Artificial Intelligence: The State of the Art. IOS Press (2022)
4. Byerly, A., Kalganova, T., Dear, I.: No routing needed between capsules. Neurocomputing **463**, 545–553 (2021)
5. Charalambous, T., Aspis, Y., Russo, A.: NeuralFastLAS: fast logic-based learning from raw data. arXiv preprint arXiv:2310.05145 (2023)
6. Cunnington, D., Law, M., Lobo, J., Russo, A.: FFNSL: feed-forward neural-symbolic learner. Mach. Learn. **112**(2), 515–569 (2023)
7. Cunnington, D., Law, M., Lobo, J., Russo, A.: Neuro-symbolic learning of answer set programs from raw data. In: Proceedings of the Thirty-Second International Joint Conference on Artificial Intelligence, pp. 3586–3596 (2023)
8. Cunnington, D., Law, M., Lobo, J., Russo, A.: The role of foundation models in neuro-symbolic learning and reasoning. arXiv preprint arXiv:2402.01889 (2024)
9. Dai, W.Z., Muggleton, S.: Abductive knowledge induction from raw data. In: Zhou, Z.H. (ed.) Proceedings of the Thirtieth International Joint Conference on Artificial Intelligence, IJCAI-21, pp. 1845–1851. International Joint Conferences on Artificial Intelligence Organization (2021). https://doi.org/10.24963/ijcai.2021/254
10. Dai, W.Z., Xu, Q., Yu, Y., Zhou, Z.H.: Bridging machine learning and logical reasoning by abductive learning. Adv. Neural Inf. Process. Syst. **32** (2019)
11. Daniele, A., Campari, T., Malhotra, S., Serafini, L.: Deep symbolic learning: discovering symbols and rules from perceptions. In: Elkind, E. (ed.) Proceedings of the Thirty-Second International Joint Conference on Artificial Intelligence, IJCAI-23, pp. 3597–3605. International Joint Conferences on Artificial Intelligence Organization (2023). https://doi.org/10.24963/ijcai.2023/400
12. Defresne, M., Barbe, S., Schiex, T.: Scalable coupling of deep learning with logical reasoning. In: Elkind, E. (ed.) Proceedings of the Thirty-Second International Joint Conference on Artificial Intelligence, IJCAI-23, pp. 3615–3623. International Joint Conferences on Artificial Intelligence Organization (2023). https://doi.org/10.24963/ijcai.2023/402

13. Eiter, T., Higuera, N., Oetsch, J., Pritz, M.: A neuro-symbolic ASP pipeline for visual question answering. Theory Pract. Logic Program. **22**(5), 739–754 (2022)
14. Evans, R., et al.: Making sense of raw input. Artif. Intell. **299**, 103521 (2021). https://doi.org/10.1016/j.artint.2021.103521
15. d'Avila Garcez, A., Gori, M., Lamb, L.C., Serafini, L., Spranger, M., Tran, S.N.: Neural-symbolic computing: an effective methodology for principled integration of machine learning and reasoning. FLAP **6**(4), 611–632 (2019)
16. Gelfond, M., Kahl, Y.: Knowledge Representation, Reasoning, and the Design of Intelligent Agents: The Answer-set Programming Approach. Cambridge University Press, Cambridge, UK (2014)
17. Harnad, S.: The symbol grounding problem. Phys. D **42**(1–3), 335–346 (1990)
18. Hutchins, D., Schlag, I., Wu, Y., Dyer, E., Neyshabur, B.: Block-recurrent transformers. Adv. Neural. Inf. Process. Syst. **35**, 33248–33261 (2022)
19. Ishay, A., Yang, Z., Lee, J.: Leveraging large language models to generate answer set programs. In: Proceedings of the 20th International Conference on Principles of Knowledge Representation and Reasoning, pp. 374–383 (2023). https://doi.org/10.24963/kr.2023/37
20. Karp, R.M.: Reducibility among combinatorial problems. In: Miller, R.E., Thatcher, J.W., Bohlinger, J.D. (eds.) Complexity of Computer Computations, pp. 85–103. Springer, Boston, MA, US (1972). https://doi.org/10.1007/978-1-4684-2001-2_9
21. Kassner, N., Schütze, H.: Negated and misprimed probes for pretrained language models: birds can talk, but cannot fly. arXiv preprint arXiv:1911.03343 (2019)
22. Law, M., Russo, A., Bertino, E., Broda, K., Lobo, J.: FastLAS: scalable inductive logic programming incorporating domain-specific optimisation criteria. In: Proceedings of the AAAI Conference on Artificial Intelligence, vol. 34, pp. 2877–2885 (2020)
23. Law, M., Russo, A., Broda, K.: Logic-based learning of answer set programs. In: Reasoning Web, Explainable Artificial Intelligence - 15th International Summer School 2019, Bolzano, Italy, September 20-24, 2019, Tutorial Lectures, pp. 196–231 (2019)
24. Law, M., Russo, A., Broda, K.: The ilasp system for inductive learning of answer set programs. arXiv preprint arXiv:2005.00904 (2020)
25. Li, D., Li, J., Le, H., Wang, G., Savarese, S., Hoi, S.C.: Lavis: a library for language-vision intelligence. arXiv preprint arXiv:2209.09019 (2022)
26. Li, J., Li, D., Xiong, C., Hoi, S.: BLIP: bootstrapping language-image pre-training for unified vision-language understanding and generation. In: International Conference on Machine Learning, pp. 12888–12900. PMLR (2022)
27. Manhaeve, R., Dumancic, S., Kimmig, A., Demeester, T., De Raedt, L.: Deepproblog: neural probabilistic logic programming. Adv. Neural Inf. Process. Syst. **31** (2018)
28. Marconato, E., Teso, S., Vergari, A., Passerini, A.: Not all neuro-symbolic concepts are created equal: analysis and mitigation of reasoning shortcuts. Adv. Neural Inf. Process. Syst. **36** (2024)
29. Nye, M., Tessler, M., Tenenbaum, J., Lake, B.M.: Improving coherence and consistency in neural sequence models with dual-system, neuro-symbolic reasoning. Adv. Neural. Inf. Process. Syst. **34**, 25192–25204 (2021)
30. OpenAI, et al.: GPT-4 technical report (2023)

31. Pryor, C., Dickens, C., Augustine, E., Albalak, A., Wang, W.Y., Getoor, L.: NeuPSL: neural probabilistic soft logic. In: Elkind, E. (ed.) Proceedings of the Thirty-Second International Joint Conference on Artificial Intelligence, IJCAI-23, pp. 4145–4153. International Joint Conferences on Artificial Intelligence Organization (2023). https://doi.org/10.24963/ijcai.2023/461
32. Riegel, R., et al.: Logical neural networks. arXiv preprint arXiv:2006.13155 (2020)
33. Shindo, H., Pfanschilling, V., Dhami, D.S., Kersting, K.: α ILP: thinking visual scenes as differentiable logic programs. Mach. Learn. **112**(5), 1465–1497 (2023)
34. Singh, D., Jain, N., Jain, P., Kayal, P., Kumawat, S., Batra, N.: PlantDoc: a dataset for visual plant disease detection. In: Proceedings of the 7th ACM IKDD CoDS and 25th COMAD, pp. 249–253 (2020)
35. Skryagin, A., Ochs, D., Dhami, D.S., Kersting, K.: Scalable neural-probabilistic answer set programming. arXiv preprint arXiv:2306.08397 (2023)
36. Stammer, W., Schramowski, P., Kersting, K.: Right for the right concept: revising neuro-symbolic concepts by interacting with their explanations. In: Proceedings of the IEEE/CVF Conference on Computer Vision and Pattern Recognition, pp. 3619–3629 (2021)
37. Surís, D., Menon, S., Vondrick, C.: ViperGPT: visual inference via python execution for reasoning. arXiv preprint arXiv:2303.08128 (2023)
38. Wang, R., Zelikman, E., Poesia, G., Pu, Y., Haber, N., Goodman, N.D.: Hypothesis search: inductive reasoning with language models. arXiv preprint arXiv:2309.05660 (2023)
39. Yang, Z., Ishay, A., Lee, J.: NeurASP: embracing neural networks into answer set programming. In: Bessiere, C. (ed.) Proceedings of the Twenty-Ninth International Joint Conference on Artificial Intelligence, IJCAI-20, pp. 1755–1762. International Joint Conferences on Artificial Intelligence Organization (2020). https://doi.org/10.24963/ijcai.2020/243
40. Yang, Z., Ishay, A., Lee, J.: Coupling large language models with logic programming for robust and general reasoning from text. arXiv preprint arXiv:2307.07696 (2023)
41. Yujian, L., Bo, L.: A normalized Levenshtein distance metric. IEEE Trans. Pattern Anal. Mach. Intell. **29**(6), 1091–1095 (2007)

A Fuzzy Loss for Ontology Classification

Simon Flügel[✉][iD], Martin Glauer[iD], Till Mossakowski[iD], and Fabian Neuhaus[iD]

Otto von Guericke University Magdeburg, Magdeburg, Germany
{sfluegel,martin.glauer,till.mossakowski,fneuhaus}@ovgu.de

Abstract. Deep learning models are often unaware of the inherent constraints of the task they are applied to. However, many downstream tasks require logical consistency. For ontology classification tasks, such constraints include subsumption and disjointness relations between classes. In order to increase the consistency of deep learning models, we propose a fuzzy loss that combines label-based loss with terms penalising subsumption- or disjointness-violations. Our evaluation on the ChEBI ontology shows that the fuzzy loss is able to decrease the number of consistency violations by several orders of magnitude without decreasing the classification performance. In addition, we use the fuzzy loss for unsupervised learning. We show that this can further improve consistency on data from a distribution outside the scope of the supervised training.

Keywords: fuzzy loss · ontology classification · ChEBI

1 Introduction

Deep learning models have been successfully applied to a wide range of classification tasks over the past years, often replacing hand-crafted features with end-to-end feature learning [3,8]. This approach is based on the assumption that all the knowledge required to solve a specific classification task is available in the data used. These systems are often built for a specific use case. In the case of a classification problem, emphasis is placed on the correct classification of the input data and the success of a system is measured in its ability to correctly perform this task. However, this approach disregards that there are often domain-specific logical constraints between different classification targets.

These logical constraints can be of great importance, as applications, especially those leading to further development, are often based on the assumption that inputs are logically consistent. Imagine a system consisting of two components in an autonomous vehicle. The first component recognises and labels objects using a deep learning model. Based on this output, a rule-based system built by experts determines the direction of travel. A contradictory classification of the first system, e.g. a traffic light as both red and green, or a road user as a pedestrian and as a car, can have fatal consequences, as the control system may not cover such a scenario.

It is therefore important to prime systems towards logical consistency. Learning concepts by example is not optimally suited to adhere to domain-specific constraints out of the box. Instead, reliance is placed on the fact that the corresponding constraints are represented in the data and that the model can approximate them accordingly during training. However, this approach has significant disadvantages. Firstly, it assumes that there is a sufficiently large amount of data so that the corresponding constraints are well represented. Secondly, the system is deprived of important information that is readily available in the domain. Thirdly, it creates an additional, implicit learning task that is not adequately represented by the loss function.

For many research domains, ontologies exist that define important concepts and their relations via logical constraints [2,4,19]. Ontologies therefore provide a necessary logical axiomatisation that can be used to check the consistency of models and to prime them for consistency. For instance, the subsumption relation A *is-a* B requires that every entity classified as A is also classified as B. Usually, this knowledge is not explicitly given to machine learning models trained on concepts from an ontology. Instead, it can only be derived implicitly from seeing a large enough number of A samples that are also B samples.

The aim of this paper is to integrate symbolic knowledge from ontologies into the learning process of a machine learning model. To this end, in Sect. 3, we present a *fuzzy loss* that extends regular loss functions by additional terms that ensure the model's coherence with ontological constraints. In Sect. 4, we introduce a classification task on the ChEBI ontology and appropriate evaluation metrics. These are used in Sect. 5, where we evaluate different fuzzy loss variants. The results are discussed in Sect. 6 and a conclusion is drawn in Sect. 7.

2 Related Work

A well-studied field within Machine Learning are hierarchical multi-label classification tasks, in which labels are structured in a hierarchy, similar to subsumption relations in an ontology. However, it is usually assumed that each class only has one superclass, which allows the assigning of hierarchy levels. Many models use these levels directly in their architecture [5,27]. In ontologies such as ChEBI, many classes have multiple superclasses, which makes the assignment of hierarchy levels non-trivial. In addition, ontologies include different kinds of logical relations between classes, such as disjointness or parthood relations. Therefore, our task requires a more general approach towards ensuring logical consistency.

Neural networks are, in particular during training, prone to making mistakes that may result in logically inconsistent predictions. An image recognition system may, for example, classify the same picture as a cat and a dog, although the classes "cat" and "dog" are known to be disjoint. Neuro-symbolic systems [20] integrate deep learning systems which such background knowledge, pushing the classification towards results that are consistent with this knowledge. This allows the priming of a learning system with prior knowledge.

The training process of neural networks is usually based on a form of gradient descent. Consequently, in order to allow answers as truth values $\{0, 1\}$, one must allow arbitrary predictions from [0, 1] in order to remain differentiable. This naturally leads to an interpretation of these values as values from a many-valued logic such as fuzzy logic or probabilistic logic.

The probabilistic interpretation has been used e.g. in DeepProbLog [24], and in the semantic loss of Xu et al. [29]. Semantic loss in based on weighted model counting (WMC) [6], a technique to efficiently support Bayesian inference. Xu et al. apply this technique to neural networks. They interpret outputs of a neural network (once normalised into [0,1]) as probabilities of Boolean variables. The semantic loss integrates propositional constraints over these Boolean variables into the loss function. However, Xu et al. make the simplifying assumption that these variables are all independent of each other, which means that neither a more complex Bayesian inference, nor a more complex encoding of random variables into logical propositions that also cover conditional probabilities (as done in [6]) are necessary.

We do not follow this probabilistic approach here, mainly because in our case, neural outputs are better interpreted as confidence values than as probabilities. Also, the independence assumption is not realistic—after all, we want to use background knowledge to express certain dependencies. Hence, we employ fuzzy logic. Indeed, there have been many approaches that aim to combine fuzzy systems and neural networks [23, 30]. These systems are particularly useful when training data is limited. In a recent work [15, 18], we applied an ontology-based neuro-fuzzy controller. The approach in this paper is inspired by this work, in which we also apply a semantic penalty system to ensure logically sound rules.

Most prominently, a form of fuzzy loss has been employed by Logic Tensor Networks (LTNs, [1]). They use such a loss to train neural predicates to maximise satisfiability of a background theory. Also Logical Neural Networks (LNNs, [26]) employ fuzzy logic. Using upper and lower bounds instead of exact truth values, they model uncertainty. Their fuzzy loss measures a fuzzy form of inconsistency, pushing the network to avoid logical inconsistencies between the classification and the background theory.

[22] consider different fuzzy operators and examine their suitability for a fuzzy loss. Here, we mainly follow their findings, especially the good suitability of fuzzy logic based on the product t-norm. That said, we also exploit the flexibility of a fuzzy approach, especially when considering variants of fuzzy implication below.

Given a class subsumption $A \sqsubseteq B$ in the ontology, it can be violated by classifying an entity as A but not B. Consequently, using the product t-norm, our loss for such a subsumption for a given prediction $\hat{y}$ (for an input instance $x \in X$) is defined as

$$L_{prod}(A \sqsubseteq B, \hat{y}) = \hat{y}_A \cdot (1 - \hat{y}_B) \tag{1}$$

where for any class $A \in O$ of the ontology O, $\hat{y}_A$ is the component of $\hat{y}$ predicting membership of the input instance in class A.

Interestingly, a fuzzy loss based on the product t-norm bears a certain similarity to Xu et al.'s semantic loss. The reason is that fuzzy conjunction is a product in this case, and probabilistic conjunction is product as well, at least for independent variables. In more detail, Xu et al. [29] propose a more general definition of a semantic loss for arbitrary propositional sentences over propositions $V_1, \cdots, V_n$. Given a prediction $\hat{y}$ and a sentence φ, Xu et al. define their loss using a variant of weighted model counting. Herein, a model v is weighted by its probability w.r.t. $\hat{y}$, meaning that for each proposition V_i, the prediction of the neural network $\hat{y}_i$ is construed to be a probability. This loss can therefore be expressed as

$$L'_{Xu}(\varphi, \hat{y}) \propto -\log \sum_{v \models \varphi} \prod_{i \in \{1,\ldots,n\}, v \models V_i} \hat{y}_i \prod_{i \in \{1,\ldots,n\}, v \models \neg V_i} (1 - \hat{y}_i). \quad (2)$$

We can apply the loss defined by Xu et al. to a subsumption relation $A \sqsubseteq B$ by interpreting it as an implication $V_A \to V_B$, where for any class $C \in O$, V_C is a proposition expressing membership in class C. Moreover, we construe (crisp) ground truth label vectors y as propositional models $y : \{V_C \mid C \in O\} \to \{0, 1\}$. Because the satisfaction relation $y \models V_C$ is defined under propositional semantics, $y \models A \to B$ holds iff $y \models \neg V_A$ or $y \models V_B$ for the corresponding propositions V_A and V_B. Therefore, given a prediction vector $\hat{y}$, the loss is calculated as $L_{Xu}(A \sqsubseteq B, \hat{y}) := L'_{Xu}(V_A \to V_B, \hat{y})$ and

$$\begin{aligned} L'_{Xu}(V_A \to V_B, \hat{y}) &\propto -\log \sum_{y \models V_A \to V_B} \prod_{C \in O, y \models V_C} \hat{y}_C \prod_{C \in O, y \models \neg V_C} (1 - \hat{y}_C) \\ (*) &= -\log \sum_{y \models V_A \to V_B} \prod_{C \in \{A,B\}, y \models V_C} \hat{y}_C \prod_{C \in \{A,B\}, y \models \neg V_C} (1 - \hat{y}_C) \\ (**) &= -\log((1 - \hat{y}_A) \cdot (1 - \hat{y}_B) + (1 - \hat{y}_A) \cdot \hat{y}_B + \hat{y}_A \cdot \hat{y}_B) \\ &= -\log(\hat{y}_A \cdot \hat{y}_B - \hat{y}_A + 1) \\ &= -\log(1 - \hat{y}_A \cdot (1 - \hat{y}_B)) \end{aligned}$$

(3)

Here, (*) holds because we only need to consider variables occurring in the implication $V_A \to V_B$: for any other variable V_C, make a case split—both cases $V_C = 0$ and $V_C = 1$ are included, and $\hat{y}_C + (1 - \hat{y}_C) = 1$. Moreover, (**) just sums up the three probabilities of different possibilities for Boolean variables V_A and V_B to satisfy $V_A \to V_B$.

Compared to Eq. 1, Eq. 3 negates the term (using $N(t) = 1 - t$) and applies a negative logarithm. Xu et al. introduce the logarithm to achieve a closer correspondence to cross-entropy loss functions, while we use the result of the logical evaluation directly. For comparison, we include the semantic loss defined by Xu et al. in our evaluation in Sect. 5.

3 Fuzzy Loss

Predictions made by a neural network may contradict a logical theory that underlies the predicted labels. In this work, we aim to incentivise a model to produce logically more consistent predictions by adding an additional term to its loss function. While many types of ontology axioms exist, here, we focus on two types that are widely used and domain independent: subsumption relations, i.e., $A \sqsubseteq B$, and disjointness, i.e., $C \sqcap D \equiv \bot$. While these axioms are usually interpreted in binary semantics, we need differentiable terms that can be used for training a neural network. We achieve differentiability by applying a fuzzy-logic interpretation [16] to our output values. Let $h_C : X \to [0, 1]$ be a fuzzy membership function for a given class C (leading to predictions $\hat{y}_C = h_C(x)$) and T a fuzzy t-norm. Our fuzzy loss term for implications is then defined as Reichenbach implication [22]:

$$L_T(A \sqsubseteq B, x) := \hat{h}(\neg(A \to B), x) = \hat{h}(\neg(\neg A \vee B), x) = \hat{h}(A \wedge \neg B, x) \\ = T(h_A(x), 1 - h_B(x)). \quad (4)$$

This assumes that the fuzzy negation used is a strong negation $N(t) = 1 - t$. [22] also discuss other fuzzy implications, but their finding is that the product t-norm for conjunction together with Reichenbach implication are among the best-working fuzzy connectives in a machine learning context. (Another good candidate is Łukasiewicz implication that we consider below.)

Accordingly, the fuzzy loss term for disjointness is defined as

$$L_T(C \sqcap D \equiv \bot, x) := \hat{h}(\neg\neg(C \wedge D), x) = \hat{h}(C \wedge D, x) = T(h_C(x), h_D(x)). \quad (5)$$

Intuitively, the fuzzy loss can be interpreted as the degree to which a given prediction violates an ontological constraint.

In Sect. 5, we evaluate loss functions derived from two commonly used t-norms, the product t-norm $T_{prod}(a, b) = a \cdot b$ and the Łukasiewicz t-norm $T_{luka}(a, b) = \max(a + b - 1, 0)$.

Let $x \in X$ be a sample vector, y the corresponding label vector and $\hat{y} = [h_C(x)]_{C \in O}$ the vector of predicted labels. Based on the loss terms given in Eqs. 4 and 5, we define our loss function as follows:

$$L_T(x, y) = L_{base}(y, \hat{y}) \\ + w_{impl} \sum_{A \sqsubseteq B} T(\hat{y}_A, 1 - \hat{y}_B) \\ + w_{disj} \sum_{C \sqcap D \equiv \bot} T(\hat{y}_C, \hat{y}_D) \quad (6)$$

The L_{base} term refers to the supervised loss used to train the model on the classification task. The weights w_{impl} and w_{disj} are intended to adjust the importance of the fuzzy loss terms in relation to the base loss and to compensate for the different prevalences of the axiom types in the ontology. In general, we expect the number of subsumption and disjointness relations in an ontology to vary based on the hierarchy depth and number of disjointness axioms available. Therefore, these weights have to be adjusted based on the task at hand.

3.1 Balanced Implication Loss

The loss terms for implication face an imbalance issue: Since the classes on the left-hand side of each implication are subclasses of the right-hand side classes, they necessarily have fewer members in the ontology and therefore fewer labels in a given dataset. Since we include transitive subsumption relations as well, the difference may be drastic, with some left-hand side classes representing only a small fraction of the right-hand side class. Therefore, in case of violations, it might be relatively inexpensive for the model to predict non-membership for classes further down in the hierarchy entirely. This strategy results in a low number of implication violations, since such classes appear mostly on the left-hand side of implications, and a low supervised loss, due to the lack of positive samples.

However, this behaviour is clearly not in our interest. If class membership in smaller classes is not predicted correctly, the most important information is lost. After all, membership in classes higher up in the hierarchy is more common and therefore less interesting. To counter-balance this effect, the *balanced implication loss* has a lower gradient for the left-hand class and a higher gradient for the right-hand class instead of applying the same gradient to both classes. Practically, this is achieved with two additional parameters $k > 1$ and $\epsilon > 0$:

$$L_T^B(A \sqsubseteq B, x; k, \epsilon) = T\left(\frac{((h_A(x) + \epsilon)^{1/k} - \epsilon^{1/k})}{((1+\epsilon)^{1/k} - \epsilon^{1/k})}, (1 - h_B(x))^k\right) \quad (7)$$

ϵ is a small constant that is added to $h_A(x)$ to avoid an infinite gradient at $h_A(x) = 0$. The additional ϵ-terms adjust the loss so that $L_T^B = 0$ if $h_A(x) = 0$ and $L_T^B = 1$ if $h_A(x) = 1$ and $h_B(x) = 0$. In our evaluation, we will use $\epsilon = 0.01$. The parameter k modifies the loss term such that, in the maximal violation case of $h_A(x) = 1$ and $h_B(x) = 0$, the gradient is larger for h_B than for h_A. For instance, for the product T-norm, $\frac{\partial L_{prod}^B}{\partial h_A(x)}\big|_1 = \frac{1}{k}$ and $\frac{\partial L_{prod}^B}{\partial h_B(x)}\big|_0 = -k$.

The regular implication loss can be seen as a specialised version of this balanced implication loss where $k = 1$ and $\epsilon = 0$.

4 Experimental Setup

We evaluate the fuzzy loss for a classification task in the ChEBI ontology. This task has been studied in our previous work and a deep learning-based approach for the ChEBI classification task has been developed [11,12,17]. In all evaluations, we train an ELECTRA model [7] for a hierarchical multi-label classification task in which ChEBI classes act as labels and molecules as instances. For a detailed description of the approach, we refer to [13]. Here, we just provide an overview. The source code for our implementation is available on GitHub[1].

4.1 Datasets

Our setup draws data from two sources. Labelled data is taken from the ChEBI ontology [10,19], while additional unlabelled data is sourced from the PubChem database [21]. All datasets are available on Kaggle[2].

---
[1] https://github.com/ChEB-AI/python-chebai.
[2] https://www.kaggle.com/datasets/sfluegel/chebai-semantic-loss.

In all datasets, we use the SMILES (Simplified Molecular Input Line Entry System) [28], a common string representation for chemical structures. It encodes molecules as sequences in which characters represent atoms and bonds, with additional notation for branches, rings and stereoisomerism.

For the labelled data, we use version 231 of ChEBI, which contains 185 thousand SMILES-annotated classes. Out of these classes, we form the ChEBI_{100} dataset by attaching all superclasses as labels which have at least 100 SMILES-annotated subclasses. The transitive closure of subsumption relations between the labels is used for the fuzzy loss. Disjointness axioms for ChEBI are provided by an additional ontology module[3]. Here as well, we take the subsumption closure of all disjointness relations between label-classes. I.e., for each pair of disjoint classes $C \sqcap D \equiv \bot$ and their subclasses $A \sqsubseteq C$ and $B \sqsubseteq D$, we also use $A \sqcap B \equiv \bot$ for the loss function. In total, this provides us with 997 labels, 19,308 implication loss terms and 31,416 disjointness loss terms.

From PubChem, we have sourced two distinct unlabelled datasets. The first is used during training while the second one, *PubChem Hazardous*, is only used in the evaluation. The Hazardous dataset includes SMILES strings for chemicals that are annotated with a class from the Globally Harmonized System of Classification and Labelling of Chemicals (GHS) [25]. The GHS covers different kinds of health, physical and environmental hazards and has been developed by the United Nations as a standard for labelling hazardous chemicals and providing related safety instructions. From this, we have removed all SMILES strings that also appear in the labelled dataset. In our evaluation, we use this dataset to test model performance for a data distribution outside the learning distribution.

For the unlabelled training dataset, we have randomly selected 1 million SMILES strings from PubChem. This set has been split into groups of 10,000. From each group, we have selected the 2,000 SMILES strings with the lowest similarity score, resulting in 200,000 instances. The similarity score used is the sum of pairwise Tanimoto similarities between the RDKit fingerprints of a given SMILES string and all other SMILES strings in the group. This way, we ensure with limited computational expense that our dataset covers a broad range of chemicals.

The overall training set (consisting of labelled and unlabelled data) is used for two tasks: Firstly, a pretraining step prior to the training on the ChEBI_{100} dataset which is shared by all models in our evaluation. And secondly, a semi-supervised training, in which we train a model simultaneously on labelled and unlabelled data. While labelled data contributes to both prediction loss and fuzzy loss, unlabelled data contributes to the fuzzy loss only, that is, only the consistency of the prediction with the ontology is measured.

In our evaluation, we will compare semi-supervised training to training on only labelled data.

---

[3] https://ftp.ebi.ac.uk/pub/databases/chebi/ontology/chebi-disjoints.owl.

4.2 Loss Function

In order to apply the fuzzy loss function from Eq. 6, we need to choose a classification loss L_{base} and assign the weights w_{impl} and w_{disj}.

For the classification loss, we have chosen a weighted binary cross-entropy loss:

$$L_{base}(x, y) = \sum_{C \in O} w_C y_C \cdot \log h_C(x) + (1 - y_C) \cdot \log(1 - h_C(x)) \qquad (8)$$

Here, w_C is a weight assigned to positive entries based on the class c. These weights are used to increase the importance of classes with fewer members in an imbalanced dataset. We apply the scheme introduced by [9] with $\beta = 0.99$ and normalize the weights:

$$w_C = \frac{w'_C \cdot |O|}{\sum_{C' \in O} w'_{C'}} \quad \text{where} \quad w'_C = \frac{1 - \beta}{1 - \beta^{|O|}} \qquad (9)$$

For the fuzzy loss terms, although the number of disjointness terms (31,416) is larger than the number of implication terms (19,308), we have chosen the weights $w_{impl} = 0.01$ and $w_{disj} = 100$. This is motivated by preliminary experiments in which the implication loss was larger than the disjointness loss by several orders of magnitude.

4.3 Violation Metrics

In order to quantify the consistency of model predictions with the ontology, we introduce a notion of true positives (TPs) and false negatives (FNs) for consistency violations. In this context, all pairs of $ChEBI_{100}$-labels are considered as violation-labels. These labels are positive if an explicit subsumption/disjointness relation between both classes exists in ChEBI. Individual predictions are converted into truth values according to a threshold of 0.5 and the resulting truth values are compared against the label-pairs.

Given a sample x, we define the number of TPs as

$$\#TP_{impl}(x) = |\{(A, B) : A \sqsubseteq B \wedge h_A(x) > 0.5 \wedge h_B(x) > 0.5\}| \qquad (10)$$

and the number of FNs as

$$\#FN_{impl}(x) = |\{(A, B) : A \sqsubseteq B \wedge h_A(x) > 0.5 \wedge h_B(x) \leq 0.5\}|. \qquad (11)$$

For disjointness, the definition is analogous:

$$\#TP_{disj}(x) = |\{(C, D) : C \sqcap D \equiv \bot \wedge h_C(x) > 0.5 \wedge h_D(x) \leq 0.5\}| \qquad (12)$$

$$\#FN_{disj}(x) = |\{(C, D) : C \sqcap D \equiv \bot \wedge h_C(x) > 0.5 \wedge h_D(x) > 0.5\}|. \qquad (13)$$

This definition does not take the cases $h_A(x) \leq 0.5$ or $h_C(x) \leq 0.5$ into account which could be considered as true positives as well since they do not contradict the ontology axioms. However, since these cases do not require an active prediction, we consider them as "consistent by default" and as less relevant for our evaluation. Note that, although disjointness axioms are symmetric, this non-symmetric metric requires that we consider both "directions" of the axiom: If $C \sqcap D \equiv \bot$, $h_C(x) \leq 0.5$ and $h_D(x) > 0.5$, we do not count (C, D) as a true positive, but instead count (D, C). This also means that $\#FN_{disj}(x)$ will necessarily be even since for every false negative (C, D), there is another false negative (D, C).

Given the numbers of TPs and FNs, we use the false negative rate (FNR), defined as

$$FNR_t(x) = \frac{\#FN_t(x)}{\#FN_t(x) + \#TP_t(x)}, \qquad (14)$$

in our evaluation, t being either $impl$ or $disj$.

Table 1. Hyperparameters used during training

Vocabulary size	1,400
Hidden size	256
# attention heads	8
# hidden layers	6
# max. epochs	200
learning rate	10^{-3}
Optimizer	Adamax
w_{impl}	0.01
w_{disj}	100
β	0.99

Table 2. Average FNR for binary implication violations on the ChEBI$_{100}$ and PubChem Hazardous datasets. The FNR has been calculated separately for each run before averaging. In addition, the table shows the standard deviation between the runs.

	ChEBI$_{100}$	PubChem Hazardous
baseline	0.0031 ± 0.0002	0.0067 ± 0.005
T_{Luka}	$\mathbf{2.09 \times 10^{-5} \pm 3.3 \times 10^{-6}}$	$1.49 \times 10^{-5} \pm 2.6 \times 10^{-5}$
T_{prod}	$3.18 \times 10^{-5} \pm 1.2 \times 10^{-5}$	$5.54 \times 10^{-5} \pm 4.6 \times 10^{-5}$
T_{prod} (k=2)	$3.74 \times 10^{-5} \pm 1.5 \times 10^{-5}$	$7.29 \times 10^{-5} \pm 8.8 \times 10^{-5}$
T_{prod} (mixed data)	$5.91 \times 10^{-5} \pm 3.2 \times 10^{-5}$	$\mathbf{1.05 \times 10^{-5} \pm 9.8 \times 10^{-6}}$
Xu et al.	$3.62 \times 10^{-5} \pm 1.2 \times 10^{-5}$	$3.93 \times 10^{-5} \pm 2.8 \times 10^{-5}$

5 Results

We evaluate four configurations of the fuzzy loss, one using the Łukasiewicz T-norm $T_{Luka}(x,y) = \max(0, a+b-1)$ and three using the product T-norm $T_{prod}(x,y) = x \cdot y$. For the product T-norm, we include, besides the "standard" variant, one which uses the balanced implication loss L^B described in Sect. 3.1 with $k=2$ and the semi-supervised variant trained on a mixed ChEBI$_{100}$ and PubChem dataset (see Sect. 4.1). For comparison, we also include a configuration using the semantic loss described by Xu et al. [29] and a baseline configuration trained without fuzzy nor semantic loss.

We have conducted a pretraining run on our PubChem dataset and subsequently, 3 fine-tuning runs for each variant. In the following, we will only report averages for the 3 runs, the results for individual runs can be found in Appendix A.

The hyperparameters shared by all models are given in Table 1. We have split the ChEBI$_{100}$ dataset into a training, validation and test set with a 340/9/51 ratio. The evaluation has been conducted on the test set using the models with the highest micro-F1 score from each training run.

Table 2 and Fig. 1a show the false negative rate (FNR) for implication and disjointness violations on the ChEBI$_{100}$ and the PubChem Hazardous datasets. It can be seen that all models outperform the baseline by a margin of about two orders of magnitude. In absolute terms, this corresponds to 1.3×10^4 false negatives for the baseline and between 81 FNs (for T_{Luka}) and 247 FNs (T_{prod}

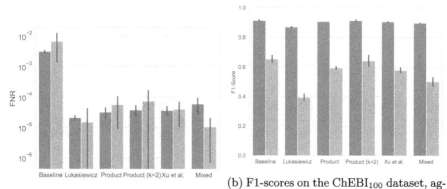

(a) FNR for implication violations on the ChEBI$_{100}$ (left) and PubChem Hazardous datasets. A lower FNR corresponds to more consistent predictions.

(b) F1-scores on the ChEBI$_{100}$ dataset, aggregated on the micro- (left) and macro-level using a threshold of $t = 0.5$. A higher F1-score corresponds to better classification performance.

Fig. 1. Performance of the evaluated models regarding implication violations classification performance. In both figures, the standard deviation is indicated by a black line for each bar.

with mixed data) for the fuzzy loss models. The number of true positives is similar for all models (between 3.85×10^6 and 4.29×10^6).

For the Łukasiewicz t-norm models, we observe the lowest FNR on $ChEBI_{100}$. The models trained with a product t-norm based loss and the semantic loss of Xu et al. have slightly higher FNRs on $ChEBI_{100}$. Regarding the PubChem Hazardous dataset, it is remarkable that, while most models have a similar or slightly higher FNR compared to $ChEBI_{100}$, the models trained with additional PubChem data perform significantly better on PubChem Hazardous.

Regarding the disjointness violations, we have not observed any violations for any model except the baseline models. There, we have averages of 171 FNs on $ChEBI_{100}$ and 4 FNs on PubChem Hazardous. While these numbers are far below the numbers of TPs (1.07×10^7 for $ChEBI_{100}$ and 1.12×10^8 for PubChem Hazardous), they show that the fuzzy loss had a consistency-improving effect. For all fuzzy loss variants, the models were able to produce inconsistency-free results regarding disjointness.

In addition, we also evaluated the predictive performance of all configurations. As can be seen in Table 3 and Fig. 1b, the F1-score for the models that were trained with fuzzy loss, with exception of the balanced version, is slightly lower than for the baseline models. This is particularly true for the models that were trained on mixed data or with the Łukasiewicz loss.

The lower performance of the Łukasiewicz models is linked to an unsuccessful training. While the performance of all other models continuously increased during training and converged to the level reported here near the end of allotted 200 epochs, for all 3 Łukasiewicz models, the performance started to drop at approximately 50 epochs into the training. Further analysis suggests that the drop during training has been caused by exploding gradients. Here, we report the results for the best-performing models near the 50 epoch-mark. At that point, the performance of the other fuzzy loss models was similar to the Łukasiewicz models.

Table 3. F1-scores calculated on labelled data. The micro-F1 aggregates predictions over all classes before calculation the score, while the macro-F1 is the average of the class-wise scores. t refers to the prediction threshold used. t_{max} is the optimal threshold for each model, calculated based on the micro-F1 of the training set for different thresholds. The exact threshold values used are reported in Appendix A.

	$t = 0.5$		$t = t_{max}$	
	Micro-F1	Macro-F1	Micro-F1	Macro-F1
baseline	**0.913 ± 0.004**	**0.653 ± 0.02**	**0.913 ± 0.003**	**0.654 ± 0.02**
T_{Luka}	0.869 ± 0.003	0.395 ± 0.02	0.870 ± 0.003	0.405 ± 0.02
T_{prod}	0.907 ± 0.0003	0.593 ± 0.009	0.908 ± 0.0004	0.576 ± 0.009
T_{prod} (k=2)	**0.913 ± 0.004**	0.643 ± 0.04	**0.913 ± 0.005**	0.636 ± 0.04
T_{prod} (mixed data)	0.898 ± 0.002	0.501 ± 0.03	0.898 ± 0.002	0.479 ± 0.02
Xu et al.	0.906 ± 0.002	0.579 ± 0.02	0.906 ± 0.002	0.559 ± 0.02

Table 4. ROC-AUC calculated on labelled data. The micro-ROC-AUC aggregates predictions over all classes before calculation the score, while the macro-ROC-AUC is the average of the class-wise scores.

	Micro-ROC-AUC	Macro-ROC-AUC
baseline	0.9969 ± 0.0003	0.9838 ± 0.002
T_{Luka}	**0.9974 ± 0.0001**	**0.9842 ± 0.0007**
T_{prod}	0.9957 ± 0.0002	$0.9821 \pm 8.5 \times 10^{-5}$
T_{prod} (k=2)	0.9936 ± 0.0008	0.9813 ± 0.001
T_{prod} (mixed data)	0.9947 ± 0.0002	0.9754 ± 0.0007
Xu et al.	0.9958 ± 0.0002	0.9818 ± 0.0009

Table 4 depicts the ROC-AUC metric for all models. All models show very high performance under this metric. Notably, the Łukasiewicz-based model marginally outperforms all models when considering this metric.

6 Discussion

Our results indicate that the introduction of a fuzzy loss during training increases the overall logical consistency of predictions significantly. However, since the number of consistency violations is relatively low even for the baseline model, one might consider a posteriori processing step that transforms the model output into consistent predictions (e.g., by setting all but the highest output value to 0 for disjointness axioms). This can expectedly lead to little or no loss in predictive performance since most predictions are already non-violating and some corrections might even turn wrong predictions into correct ones. However, we have only considered the unprocessed predictions in our evaluation. We justify this by the intended use cases: A model trained on the classification task may further be used in downstream tasks (e.g., prediction of chemical properties [14]). Those require that the model has actually learned the ontology's structure. This can only be achieved by giving the model direct feedback during training (as we did with the fuzzy loss) instead of superficially correcting the results.

For most fuzzy loss variants, their increase of consistency comes to the detriment of the actual predictive quality. This result seems contradictory at first, as one would assume more consistent results to be better overall. One possible explanation lies in the imbalanced character of ontology-based datasets. The hierarchical relations between labels create a dataset in which a significant imbalance is inevitable and cannot be overcome by sampling procedures in any significant way. A class will always have less members than its parents as long as there is an ontological distinction between them that is also represented in the dataset. Consequently, classes that reside further down in the hierarchy are often significantly smaller than those higher up. For ChEBI in particular, more specialised classes also require the model to learn relatively complex patterns from a limited amount of samples. The corresponding labels receive a relatively small training signal that is then counteracted by the additional loss due to violations. This may render the model unable to learn some smaller classes.

This view is supported by the differences between micro- and macro-F1. For all models, the macro-F1 is far lower than the micro-F1. This means that many small classes that contribute little to the micro-F1, but receive a stronger weighting in the macro-F1, perform badly. For the fuzzy loss variants, with the exception of the balanced fuzzy loss, this gap widens (from 26% for the baseline to 31% for T_{prod} or 47% for T_{luka}). This shows that, when the predictive performance decreases, it mostly affects classes with fewer members.

However, a general tendency to make less predictions cannot be observed. While all models make a similar amount of predictions on the $ChEBI_{100}$ dataset, the fuzzy loss models make more predictions on average for the PubChem dataset (9.4 with product loss, 8.1 for the baseline). This shows that the lower F1-score in the final models is not due to a generally more "cautious" behaviour. Instead, only some classes may get left out while additional (consistent, but wrong) predictions are made for other classes. Also, the lower performance may be attributed to differences in the learning process, e.g., a less explorative model behaviour or a slower convergence.

In addition, the results confirm our hypothesis regarding the balanced fuzzy loss. Without losing consistency compared to the unbalanced variant, it is able to reach a predictive performance similar to the baseline. Recall that the main difference between the balanced and unbalanced fuzzy loss is the gradient in cases where for a subsumption relation $A \sqsubseteq B$, the model predicts $h_A(x)$ close to 1 and $h_B(x)$ close to 0 (cf. Figure 2). There, without the balancing, both classes get the same gradient. With balancing, the gradient is stronger for $h_B(x)$ than for $h_A(x)$ (in our experiment, by a factor of approximately 4).

The balanced fuzzy loss has been successful in pushing the model towards more consistent predictions without pushing it towards predictions that contradict the labels of the classification task.

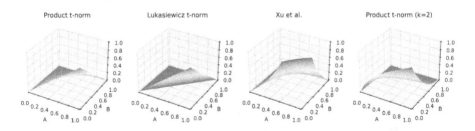

Fig. 2. Value of the fuzzy loss variants L_{prod}, L_{luka}, L_{Xu} and L_{prod}^B with $k = 2$ for a subsumption relation $A \sqsubseteq B$ with different values of $h_A(x)$ and $h_B(x)$. L_{Xu} has been cut off at $L_{Xu} = 1$ since $\lim_{p_a \to 0, p_b \to 1} L_{Xu}(A \sqsubseteq B, p) = \infty$

Notably, the Łukasiewicz-based model marginally outperforms all models when considering the ROC-AUC metric. However, it should be noted that the standard method used to calculate ROC-AUC is based on an analysis of all threshold values on the test data. We see this approach as problematic. The goal of evaluating a machine learning model is to determine whether the model can be used to make accurate predictions. However, we see the threshold as part of this prediction system. The test set should therefore only be used in the final evaluation and no parameters should be chosen to fit a particular test set particularly well. The way in which the ROC-AUC curves are computed dilutes this approach as different thresholds are evaluated using the test data. It is not clear how this analysis can be used to generate a threshold for a good predictive model that is test data agnostic. We conclude, that the threshold should either be fixed for all models or individually determined based on the training set. The performance analysis based on those individual thresholds shows that using those threshold for which each model performed best on the training leads to results that are consistent with those produced by fixed thresholds of 0.5.

The results also indicate that the inclusion of unlabelled data into the training process does hedge the system against inconsistencies on unseen data. This result can be particularly useful in scenarios in which the distribution of features in the dataset is limited. Deep learning systems are prone to suffer from out-of-distribution errors, e.g., unpredictable behaviour on data that has not been sampled from the same distribution as the training data. Lifting this limitation is often not easy because additional labelling is required. The semi-supervised training method presented here can help to alleviate this problem.

7 Conclusion

In this work, we have introduced a fuzzy loss function for the task of ontology classification. Our fuzzy loss is based on a fuzzy logic interpretation of the ontology subsumption and disjointness relations. To counteract the loss function's tendency to disincentivise predictions of low-level ontology classes, we have proposed a balanced fuzzy loss variant as well. In our evaluation, we have compared different versions of our fuzzy loss (based on either the Łukasiewicz t-norm or the product t-norm) to a baseline model and the semantic loss function proposed by [29]. We have shown that all fuzzy loss variants were able to reduce the number of consistency violations by approximately two orders of magnitude.

Regarding performance on the classification task, we have seen greater differences between the loss functions. Most variants have both a slightly lower micro- and a significantly macro-F1 than the baseline (especially the Łukasiewicz-based variant). This indicates that especially the predictive performance of small classes is affected by the fuzzy loss. Only the balanced fuzzy loss was able to perform on a par with our baseline.

In addition, we have used the fuzzy loss for an additional training task on unlabelled data. This allows us to generalise beyond the original data distribution used for supervised training. Our evaluation on the Hazardous subset of

PubChem shows that this form of training can further improve the consistency of predictions for out-of-distribution data.

Future work will include an improved normalisation to avoid performance issues like we reported for the Łukasiewicz fuzzy loss. Also, it is possible to extend our approach to other types of ontology axioms, e.g., parthood relations. Finally, it would be interesting to incorporate our finding of a balanced implication loss into more general frameworks like LTNs or LNNs.

Acknowledgements. This work has been funded by the Deutsche Forschungsgesellschaft (DFG, German Research Foundation) - 522907718.

A Result for individual runs

In Sect. 5, we have presented results as the average and standard deviation out of 3 runs for every configuration.

Table 5. FNRs for implication violations on the $ChEBI_{100}$ and PubChem datasets.

	Dataset	Run1	Run2	Run3
Baseline	$ChEBI_{100}$	0.0034	0.0031	**0.0029**
	Hazardous	0.0066	0.012	**0.0015**
T_{Luka}	$ChEBI_{100}$	2.32×10^{-5}	$\mathbf{1.72 \times 10^{-5}}$	2.23×10^{-5}
	Hazardous	4.45×10^{-5}	**0**	1.79×10^{-7}
T_{prod}	$ChEBI_{100}$	$\mathbf{1.94 \times 10^{-5}}$	3.36×10^{-5}	4.24×10^{-5}
	Hazardous	6.26×10^{-5}	$\mathbf{5.72 \times 10^{-6}}$	9.78×10^{-5}
T_{prod} (k=2)	$ChEBI_{100}$	$\mathbf{2.41 \times 10^{-5}}$	3.46×10^{-5}	5.35×10^{-5}
	Hazardous	$\mathbf{2.22 \times 10^{-5}}$	0.00017	2.25×10^{-5}
Xu et al.	$ChEBI_{100}$	4.44×10^{-5}	$\mathbf{2.30 \times 10^{-5}}$	4.12×10^{-5}
	Hazardous	$\mathbf{6.68 \times 10^{-6}}$	5.58×10^{-5}	5.56×10^{-5}
T_{prod} (mixed data)	$ChEBI_{100}$	4.78×10^{-5}	$\mathbf{3.46 \times 10^{-5}}$	9.48×10^{-5}
	Hazardous	$\mathbf{2.98 \times 10^{-7}}$	1.98×10^{-5}	1.14×10^{-5}

Tables 5, 6 and 7 show the FNR and F1-scores for the individual runs. For the FNR, it can be observed that the results vary significantly between runs, especially on the Hazardous datasets. This is likely due to the small scale we are considering: On the $ChEBI_{100}$, a FNR of 2.5×10^{-5} roughly corresponds to about 100 observed false negatives over the whole test set. I.e., out of 19 thousand samples, each of which had 19 thousand subsumption relations that could have resulted in a false negative, only 100 actually are false negatives. Therefore, slight changes in the predictive performance can have a significant impact on the false negative rate.

The F1-scores are more stable overall, with a range of less than one percent for the micro aggregation and up to six percent for the macro aggregation.

Table 6. F1-scores with micro and macro aggregation, using the threshold $t = 0.5$.

	Aggregation	Run1	Run2	Run3
Baseline	micro	0.909	**0.915**	0.915
	macro	0.625	**0.669**	0.665
T_{Luka}	micro	0.870	0.866	**0.873**
	macro	0.399	0.369	**0.415**
T_{prod}	micro	0.907	**0.907**	0.907
	macro	0.584	**0.600**	0.597
T_{prod} (k=2)	micro	0.915	**0.916**	0.908
	macro	0.661	**0.666**	0.601
Xu et al.	micro	0.904	**0.908**	0.905
	macro	0.570	**0.597**	0.569
T_{prod} (mixed data)	micro	0.895	**0.899**	0.899
	macro	0.471	0.502	**0.529**

Table 7. F1-scores with micro and macro aggregation, using the threshold t_{max}. t_{max} is the threshold for which the maximum micro-F1 was reached on the training set.

	Value	Run1	Run2	Run3
Baseline	t_{max}	0.5	0.5	0.45
	Micro-F1	0.909	**0.915**	0.915
	Macro-F1	0.625	**0.669**	0.668
T_{Luka}	t_{max}	0.5	0.45	0.45
	Micro-F1	0.870	0.866	**0.873**
	Macro-F1	0.399	0.386	**0.429**
T_{prod}	t_{max}	0.65	0.65	0.65
	Micro-F1	0.908	**0.908**	0.908
	Macro-F1	0.566	**0.582**	0.580
T_{prod} (k=2)	t_{max}	0.55	0.6	0.55
	Micro-F1	0.915	**0.917**	0.908
	Macro-F1	**0.657**	0.656	0.595
Xu et al.	t_{max}	0.7	0.65	0.65
	Micro-F1	0.905	**0.909**	0.905
	Macro-F1	0.547	**0.580**	0.551
T_{prod} (mixed data)	t_{max}	0.6	0.6	0.7
	Micro-F1	0.896	**0.899**	0.899
	Macro-F1	0.457	0.487	**0.495**

References

1. Badreddine, S., d'Avila Garcez, A.S., Serafini, L., Spranger, M.: Logic tensor networks. Artif. Intell. **303**, 103649 (2022) https://doi.org/10.1016/J.ARTINT.2021.103649
2. Bayerlein, B., et al.: PMD core ontology: achieving semantic interoperability in materials science. Mater. Des. **237**, 112603 (2024)
3. Bojarski, M., et al.: End to end learning for self-driving cars (2016). arXiv preprint arXiv:1604.07316
4. Booshehri, M., et al.: Introducing the open energy ontology: enhancing data interpretation and interfacing in energy systems analysis. Energy AI **5**, 100074 (2021)
5. Cerri, R., Barros, R.C., De Carvalho, A.C.: Hierarchical multi-label classification using local neural networks. J. Comput. Syst. Sci. **80**(1), 39–56 (2014)
6. Chavira, M., Darwiche, A.: On probabilistic inference by weighted model counting. Artif. Intell. **172**(6–7), 772–799 (2008) https://doi.org/10.1016/J.ARTINT.2007.11.002
7. Clark, K., Luong, M.T., Le, Q.V., Manning, C.D.: ELECTRA: Pre-training text encoders as discriminators rather than generators (2020). arXiv preprint arXiv:2003.10555
8. Collobert, R., Weston, J., Bottou, L., Karlen, M., Kavukcuoglu, K., Kuksa, P.: Natural language processing (almost) from scratch. J. Mach. Learn. Res. **12**, 2493–2537 (2011)
9. Cui, Y., Jia, M., Lin, T.Y., Song, Y., Belongie, S.: Class-balanced loss based on effective number of samples. In: Proceedings of the IEEE/CVF Conference on Computer Vision and Pattern Recognition, pp. 9268–9277 (2019)
10. Degtyarenko, K., et al.: ChEBI: a database and ontology for chemical entities of biological interest. Nucleic Acids Res. **36**(Database issue), D344–D350 (2008). https://doi.org/10.1093/nar/gkm791, http://dx.doi.org/10.1093/nar/gkm791, publisher: European Bioinformatics Institute, Wellcome Trust Genome Campus, Hinxton, Cambridge, UK
11. Glauer, M., Memariani, A., Neuhaus, F., Mossakowski, T., Hastings, J.: Interpretable ontology extension in chemistry. Semantic Web **Preprint**(Preprint), 1–22 (2023)
12. Glauer, M., et al.: Neuro-symbolic semantic learning for chemistry. In: Compendium of Neurosymbolic Artificial Intelligence. Frontiers in Artificial Intelligence and Applications, pp. 460–484 (2023)
13. Glauer, M., et al.: Chebifier: Automating semantic classification in ChEBI to accelerate data-driven discovery. Digital Discovery, p. to appear (2024)
14. Glauer, M., Neuhaus, F., Mossakowski, T., Hastings, J.: Ontology pre-training for poison prediction. In: Seipel, D., Steen, A. (eds.) KI 2023: Advances in Artificial Intelligence. KI 2023. LNCS(), vol. 14236. Springer, Cham (2023). https://doi.org/10.1007/978-3-031-42608-7_4
15. Glauer, M., West, R., Michie, S., Hastings, J.: Esc-rules: Explainable, semantically constrained rule sets (2022). arXiv preprint arXiv:2208.12523
16. Hájek, P.: Metamathematics of fuzzy logic, vol. 4. Springer Science & Business Media (2013). https://doi.org/10.1007/978-94-011-5300-3
17. Hastings, J., Glauer, M., Memariani, A., Neuhaus, F., Mossakowski, T.: Learning chemistry: exploring the suitability of machine learning for the task of structure-based chemical ontology classification. J. Cheminformatics **13**, 1–20 (2021)

18. Hastings, J., Glauer, M., West, R., Thomas, J., Wright, A.J., Michie, S.: Predicting outcomes of smoking cessation interventions in novel scenarios using ontology-informed, interpretable machine learning. Wellcome Open Res. **8**(503), 503 (2023)
19. Hastings, J., et al.: ChEBI in 2016: improved services and an expanding collection of metabolites. Nucleic Acids Res. **44**(D1), D1214–D1219 (2016). https://doi.org/10.1093/nar/gkv1031
20. Hitzler, P., Sarker, M.K., Eberhart, A. (eds.): Compendium of Neurosymbolic Artificial Intelligence, Frontiers in Artificial Intelligence and Applications, vol. 369. IOS Press (2023). https://doi.org/10.3233/FAIA369
21. Kim, S., et al.: Pubchem 2023 update. Nucleic Acids Res. **51**(D1), D1373–D1380 (2023)
22. van Krieken, E., Acar, E., van Harmelen, F.: Analyzing differentiable fuzzy logic operators. Artif. Intell. **302**, 103602 (2022). https://doi.org/10.1016/J.ARTINT.2021.103602
23. Kruse, R., Nauck, D.: Neuro-fuzzy systems. In: Kaynak, O., Zadeh, L.A., Türkşen, B., Rudas, I.J. (eds.) Computational Intelligence: Soft Computing and Fuzzy-Neuro Integration with Applications. NATO ASI Series, vol. 162, pp. 230–259. Springer, Berlin, Heidelberg (1998). https://doi.org/10.1007/978-3-642-58930-0_12
24. n Manhaeve, R., Dumancic, S., Kimmig, A., Demeester, T., De Raedt, L.: DeepProbLog: neural probabilistic logic programming. In: Advances in Neural Information Processing Systems, vol. 31 (2018)
25. Nations, U.: Globally harmonized system of classification and labelling of chemicals, rev. 10. Tech. rep., United Nations (2023)
26. Riegel, R., et al.: Logical neural networks (2020). arXiv preprint arXiv:2006.13155
27. Wehrmann, J., Cerri, R., Barros, R.: Hierarchical multi-label classification networks. In: International Conference on Machine Learning, pp. 5075–5084. PMLR (2018)
28. Weininger, D.: Smiles, a chemical language and information system. 1. introduction to methodology and encoding rules. J. Chem. Inf. Comput. Sci. **28**(1), 31–36 (1988)
29. Xu, J., Zhang, Z., Friedman, T., Liang, Y., Broeck, G.: A semantic loss function for deep learning with symbolic knowledge. In: International Conference on Machine Learning, pp. 5502–5511. PMLR (2018)
30. Zhang, D., Bai, X.L., Cai, K.Y.: Extended neuro-fuzzy models of multilayer perceptrons. Fuzzy Sets Syst. **142**(2), 221–242 (2004)

On the Use of Neurosymbolic AI for Defending Against Cyber Attacks

Gudmund Grov[1,2(✉)], Jonas Halvorsen[1], Magnus Wiik Eckhoff[1,2], Bjørn Jervell Hansen[1], Martin Eian[3], and Vasileios Mavroeidis[2]

[1] Norwegian Defence Research Establishment (FFI), Kjeller, Norway
{Gudmund.Grov,Jonas.Halvorsen,Magnus-Wiik.Eckhoff,
Bjorn-Jervell.Hansen}@ffi.no
[2] University of Oslo, Oslo, Norway
vasileim@ifi.uio.no
[3] mnemonic, Oslo, Norway
meian@mnemonic.no

Abstract. It is generally accepted that all cyber attacks cannot be prevented, creating a need for the ability to detect and respond to cyber attacks. Both connectionist and symbolic AI are currently being used to support such detection and response. In this paper, we make the case for combining them using neurosymbolic AI. We identify a set of challenges when using AI today and propose a set of neurosymbolic use cases we believe are both interesting research directions for the neurosymbolic AI community and can have an impact on the cyber security field. We demonstrate feasibility through two proof-of-concept experiments.

Keywords: AI · neurosymbolic AI · cyber security · incident detection and response

1 Introduction

Protecting assets in the cyber domain requires a combination of *preventive measures*, such as access control and firewalls, and the ability to *defend* against cyber operations when the preventive measures were not sufficient.[1]

Our focus in this paper is on defending against offensive cyber operations, and before going into details, some concepts and terminology need to be in place:

Terminology & concepts The focus of this paper is to defend *assets* against *threats* in cyberspace. An *asset* can be anything from information or physical infrastructure to the internal processes of an enterprise. *Threats* manifest themselves in the form of *cyber operations* (or *cyber attacks*) conducted by an *adversary* (or *threat actor*). In our context of defending, the term *incident* is used for a potential attack that is deemed to have an impact

---

[1] It is generally accepted that preventive measures are not sufficient in cyberspace. An analogy is that we still need smoke detectors and a fire brigade, even if we take all possible preventive measures to reduce the risk of a fire.

on assets, and the process of defending comes under the area of *incident management* [19]. This is typically conducted in a *security operations centre* (SOC), which consists of people, processes and tools. One of the objectives of a SOC is to detect and respond to threats and attacks, where *security analysts* play a key role. Knowledge/intelligence of threats and threat actors in the cyber domain is called *cyber threat intelligence* (CTI). Networks and systems to be protected are monitored and *events* – e.g., network traffic, file changes, or processes executing on a host – are forwarded and typically stored in a *security information and event management* (SIEM) system, where events can be searched and queried. We will use the term *obseverations* for these events resulting from monitoring. Suspicious activity that is observed may raise *alerts*, which may indicate an incident that has to be analysed and responded to in the SOC. *Neurosymbolic AI* [34], which aims to combine connectionist and symbolic AI, will be abbreviated *NeSy*.

Why is a SOC relevant for NeSy? A SOC essentially conducts abductive reasoning by observing traces and identifying and analysing their cause in order to respond. This involves sifting through masses of events for suspicious behaviour, an area in which there has been extensive research for several decades using statistics and machine learning. Identifying the cause of observed suspicious behaviour requires situational awareness, achieved by combining and reasoning about different types of knowledge. There are various ways knowledge is represented, such as structured events and alerts, unstructured reports, and semantic knowledge [60,88]. In a SOC, the ability to *learn* models to detect suspicious activities, and the ability to *reason* about identified activity from such models to understand their cause and respond, is thus required. These abilities are at the core of NeSy and our hypothesis is that '*a SOC provides an ideal environment to study NeSy with great potential for both scientific and financial impact*'. Some early work has explored NeSy in the cyber security domain [25,43,46,74,79] and our goal with this paper is to showcase the possibilities and encourage the NeSy community to conduct research in the SOC field. The contributions of the paper are threefold: (1) we outline how AI is used today in a SOC and identify and structure a set of challenges practitioners using AI are faced with; (2) we create a set of promising use cases for NeSy in a SOC and review current NeSy approaches in light of them; (3) we conduct two proof-of-concept NeSy experiments to showcase feasibility. The focus here is to demonstrate NeSy possibilities and not on realistic conditions or performance.

Methodology: The identified challenges are derived from a combination of existing published studies of SOCs, the experience and expertise of the authors and discussions with SOC practitioners. The use cases are a result of reviewing NeSy literature in the context of the identified challenges, and the experiments follows from the use cases.

Paper Structure: In Sect. 2, we describe the typical use of AI in a SOC and the identified challenges. In Sect. 3, we make the case for NeSy and outline the NeSy use cases. In Sect. 4, we describe the proof-of-concept experiments, before we conclude in Sect. 5.

2 Challenges Faced When Using AI in a SOC

MAPE-K (Monitor-Analyse-Plan-Execute over a shared Knowledge) [51] is a common reference model to structure the different phases when managing an incident.[2] For each phase of MAPE-K, we below discuss the common use of AI, including underlying representations, and identify key challenges security practitioners face when using AI.[3]

Monitor. In the *monitor* phase, systems and networks are monitored and the telemetry is represented as sequences of *events*. An *event* could, for instance, be a network packet, a file update, a user that logs on to a service, or a process being executed. Events are typically structured as key-value pairs. For a large enterprise, there may be tens of thousands of events generated per second. In this phase, a key objective is to detect suspicious behaviours from the events and generate *alerts*, which are analysed and handled in the later phases of MAKE-K.

This is a topic where machine learning (ML) has been extensively studied by training ML models on the vast amount of captured event data (see e.g. [5]). A challenge with such data is the lack of *ground truth*, in the sense that for the vast majority of events we do not know if they are benign or malicious. As most events will be benign (albeit we do not know which ones), one can exploit this assumption and use unsupervised methods to train anomaly detectors. This is a common approach. For at least research purposes, synthetic datasets from simulated attacks are also commonly used [53]. However, synthetic datasets suffer from several issues [9,50] and promising results in research papers using synthetic data tend not to be recreated in real-world settings – whilst anomaly detectors often create a high number of false alerts[4] [16,89]. Our first challenge, which follows from the *European Union Agency for Cybersecurity* (ENISA) [30], addresses this performance issue for ML models for real-world conditions:

Challenge 1 *Achieve optimal accuracy of ML models under real-world conditions.*

As both normal software and malware are continuously updated, the notion of *concept drift* is prevalent, and ML models must thus be retrained regularly. Moreover, in addition to the large amount of data, requiring scalability, real-world conditions will have a large amount of noise (i.e. aleatoric uncertainty) in the data, which is not well reflected in synthetic data.

---

[2] Other common reference models are the OODA (Observe-Orient-Decide-Act) loop [14] and IACD (Integrated Adaptive Cyber Defense) [26].

[3] There has recently been a vast number of proposals for using *large language models* (LLMs) across MAPE-K. Here, we include what we currently consider the most promising uses of LLMs, and refer to [13,69] for a more complete discussion.

[4] As most events are benign, the base rate fallacy is important in this domain.

For previous incidents that have been handled, we know the ground truth of the associated alerts and events. Compared with the full set of events, this dataset will, however, be tiny. Still, it is important as it is labelled and contains data we know are relevant – either in terms of actual attacks experienced or false alerts that should be filtered out. One important challenge, also identified by ENISA [30], is the ability to exploit such labelled "incident datasets" and train ML models based on them:

Challenge 2 *Learning with small (labelled) datasets (from cyber incidents).*

New knowledge, e.g. about certain threats, attacks, malware or vulnerability exploits, is frequently published (in e.g. threat reports). The traditional, and still most common, method of threat detection is so-called *signature-based* detection, where such knowledge is (often manually) encoded as specific patterns (called signatures). Detection is achieved by matching events with these signatures, and generating alerts when they match. While signature-based methods have their limitations, such knowledge could improve the performance of ML-based detection models trained on event data, requiring the ability to extract relevant knowledge and including it in the ML models:

Challenge 3 *Extract knowledge (including about threats, malware and vulnerabilities) and enrich ML-based detection models with it.*

In addition to reports, there are many knowledge bases and formal ontologies that can be used to enrich ML models with such knowledge. There are also attempts to extend the coverage domain for such ontologies: one example is the *unified cybersecurity ontology* (UCO) [91] and another is the SEPSES knowledge graph [52]. To represent cyber threat intelligence (CTI), a commonly used schema is *Structured Threat Information Expression* (STIX) [72], with the associated *Threat Actor Context* (TAC) ontology [64]. A widely used knowledge base for threat actors and attacks is the MITRE ATT&CK [68]. ML, and in particular *natural language processing* (NLP), is being explored for extracting CTI into symbolic forms (e.g. STIX) [63] or to map with MITRE ATT&CK [58]. *Large language models* (LLMs) are also explored for this topic [41,59], with limitations identified [95]. However, we are not familiar with approaches to combine and integrate such knowledge with ML models for detection trained on events.

A different approach to identify malicious behaviour is *cyber threat hunting*. This is a *hypothesis-driven* approach where hypotheses are iteratively formulated (typically using CTI) and validated using event logs, as well as other knowledge [87]. Automating this process is our final challenge for the monitor phase:

Challenge 4 *Automated generation of hypotheses from CTI and validation of hypotheses using observations for threat hunting.*

There are AI-based approaches to facilitate threat hunting [70]. Most have focused on supporting hypothesis generation by extracting relevant CTI, and using both ML/NLP [33] and symbolic AI [82]. Symbolic AI has been used to support validation [18].

Analyse. The goal of the analysis phase is to understand the nature of the observed alerts, determine possible business impact and create sufficient situational awareness to support the subsequent pland and execute phases.

Both malware and benign software continuously evolve. This makes it difficult to separate malicious from benign behaviour [30], despite continuous detection engineering efforts improving the capabilities. For example, an update to benign software may cause a match with an existing malware signature, and may also show up as an anomaly in the network traffic. As a result, most of the alerts are either false or not sufficiently important for further investigation [16]. The analysis phase is, therefore, labour-intensive, where security analysts must plough through and analyse a large number of alerts – most of them false – to decide their nature and importance. This could lead to so-called *alert fatigue* among security analysts:

Challenge 5 *The volume of alerts leads to alert flooding and alert fatigue in SOCs.*

Understanding the nature of alerts is important, and studies have shown that a lack of understanding of the underlying scores, or reasoning, behind the alerts have led to misuse and mistrust of ML systems [73]. Both studies [16] and guidance from ENISA [30] have highlighted the need for alerts to be reliable, explainable and possible to analyse. The use of explainable AI to support this has shown some promise [27], and both knowledge graphs [16] and LLMs[5] have been identified as promising approaches.

An alert is just one observation and needs to be put into a larger context to identify an *incident* and provide necessary *situational awareness* as a result of the analysis [31]. Such contextualisation includes enriching alerts with relevant knowledge from previous incidents, common systems behaviour, infrastructure details, threats, assets, etc. The same attack – or the same phase of a larger attack – is likely to trigger many different alerts. Different ML techniques, particularly clustering, have been studied to fuse or aggregate related alerts [55,92]. In addition to understanding an incident and achieving situational awareness, contextualisation will also help a security analyst understand individual alerts. Similar to challenge 3, contextualization of alerts will necessarily involve extracting symbolic representation from a vast amount of available (and typically unstructured) information. A cyber attack conducted by an advanced adversary will, in most cases, manifest itself over several phases, creating a need to discover the relationships (between the alerts) across the different phases of an attack. A common reference model to relate such phases is the *cyber kill chain*, originally developed by Lockheed Martin and later refined into the *unified cyber kill chain* [80]. Other formalisms that enable modelling different phases of attacks include *MITRE Attack Flow* [67] and the *Meta Attack Language* (MAL) [47]. Different approaches have been studied to relate the different phases, including symbolic approaches [76], AI planning [7,66], knowledge graphs [18,56], state machines [93], clustering [39] and statistics [41]. However, this research topic is

---

[5] E.g. Microsoft security co-pilot and an Elastic/LongChain initiative [1] .

considerably less mature compared with ML models for detection in the monitor phase. We summarise the challenges of combining, understanding and explaining observations in the following challenge:

Challenge 6 *Combine observation with knowledge to analyse, develop and communicate situational awareness.*

Developing cyber situational awareness requires connecting a plethora of different sources, such as alerts and details about infrastructure and threats. There have been proposals to use knowledge graphs to combine these different sources to support analysis [60,88], including explanation [16].

When an incident is understood and sufficient situational awareness is achieved, a suitable amount of resources have to be allocated to handle the incident. There may be multiple incidents, requiring some prioritisation between them. This involves understanding the risks and potential impacts of the incident, including the risks and impacts of any mitigating actions that may be taken in subsequent MAPE-K phases:

Challenge 7 *Understanding the risk, impact, importance and priority of incidents.*

Plan & Execute. The last two phases of MAPE-K, plan and execute, focus on responding to detected incidents. This involves finding suitable responses in the plan phase, and prepare and execute the response(s) in the execute phase. From an AI perspective, research in these phases is not as mature as in the monitor and analyse phases. We will here only focus on the plan phase, which we currently consider to have the more interesting AI-related challenges. To plan a suitable response, two promising AI techniques are *AI planning* (e.g. [36]) and *reinforcement learning* (RL – e.g. [45,71]). Each of them have their pros and cons: AI planning requires considerable knowledge and formulation of the underlying environment, whilst reinforcement learning requires a considerable amount of interactions/simulations (often in the millions). In certain cases, a quick response time is necessary, which means this level of interaction would be too time-consuming. When generating response actions, their risk and impact must be taken into account (including the risk and impact of doing nothing), which is an unsolved problem when using AI. Moreover, when proposing a response action, an AI-generated solution must be able to explain both what the response action will do and why it is suitable for the given problem:

Challenge 8 *Generate and recommend suitable response actions in a timely manner that take into account both risk and impact and are understandable for a security analyst.*

To support such generation, there are several frameworks and formal ontologies that can be used, such as MITRE *D3FEND* [49], *RE&CT* [2] and *CACAO playbooks* [65].

Shared Knowledge. The 'K' in MAPE-K stands for *knowledge* shared across the phases, and we have, for instance, seen knowledge about threats and the infrastructure being protected used across different phases. Moreover, this knowledge takes different forms and representations (structured and unstructured) and is analysed using different techniques (symbolic and sub-symbolic). In addition to consuming knowledge, it is also important to share knowledge with key stakeholders, both technical and non-technical [29]. This may be a report about an incident for internal use (e.g. to board members) or sharing of discovered threat intelligence with a wider community:

Challenge 9 *Generating suitable incident and CTI reports for the target audience.*

To summarise, we have shown the need to learn and reason across MAPE-K and that both symbolic and connectionist AI are being used across the phases. We have identified several challenges, and next, we make the case for NeSy to address them.

3 The Case for Neurosymbolic AI

Kahneman's [48] distinction between (fast) instinctive and unconscious '*system 1*' processes from (slow) more reasoned '*system 2*' processes, has often been used to illustrate the NeSy integration of neural networks (system 1) and logical reasoning (system 2). Building on this analogy, system 1 can, in a SOC, be seen as the ML-based AI used to identify potentially malicious behaviour in the monitor phase. Here, a large amount of noise needs to be filtered out from the large amount of events (thus a need for speed and scalability). System 2 is the reasoning conducted in the analysis phase, which requires deeper insight with the need for scalability less significant.

This dichotomy of requirements entails that neither end-to-end pure statistical nor pure logical approaches will be sufficient, and a NeSy combination seems ideal. Three commonly used reasons for pursuing NeSy are to design systems that are *human auditable and augmentable*, can *learn with less* and provide *out-of-distribution generalisation* [37]. We have seen examples of each of these in the challenges described in Sect. 2: the use of knowledge to both contextualise, analyse and explain alerts, and to generate and explain and response actions; to learn from (relatively few) incidents; and to handle concept drifts and noise in order to achieve high accuracy of ML models under real-world conditions. From the challenges in Sect. 2, we will here outline a set of NeSy use cases we believe are promising and identify some promising NeSy tools and techniques for each of them. This work is not complete and should be seen as a start (see Sect. 5). Moreover, this section is speculative by nature, but we provide some evidence in terms of existing work and experiments conducted in Sect. 4.

Monitor. The ability to integrate relevant knowledge into ML-based detection models (challenge 3) falls directly under the NeSy paradigm, and could both improve performance under real-world conditions (challenge 1) and help to reduce the number of false alerts (challenge 5):

Use case 1 *Use (symbolic) knowledge of threats and assets to guide or constrain ML-based detection engines.*

A similar case for such a NeSy use case is made in [79]. *Logical Neural Networks (LNN)* [85] are designed to simultaneously provide key properties of both neural nets (learning) and symbolic logic (knowledge and reasoning), enabling both logic inference and injecting desired knowledge (e.g. about threats and infrastructure) into the neural architecture. In *Logic Tensor Networks (LTN)* [12], a membership function for concepts are learned based on both labelled examples and abstract (logical) rules. LTN introduces a fully differentiable logical language, called *real logic*, where elements of first-order logic can be used to encode the necessary knowledge. LTN has been studied to detect suspicious behaviour [74] and is the topic of one of our experiments in §4.

In challenge 2, we highlighted the need to learn from (relatively small) datasets, which is one of the key features of NeSy [37]:

Use case 2 *Learn detection models from a limited number of (labelled) incidents*

Additional embedded knowledge in an LNN or LTN may help to reduce training time. *NS-CL* [62], which builds models to learn visual perception including semantic interpretation of the images, has shown it can be trained on a fraction of the data required by comparable methods – albeit in a different domain with different data sources. NeSy-based inductive logic programming variants, such as ∂ILP [28], would also be able to learn from small datasets. The learned logic program will also be inherently explainable (see challenge 6).

Threat hunting involves generating suitable hypotheses, applying and validating them, then update and iterate (challenge 4). Work has started investigating LLMs for this challenge [78]. It has been argued for symbolism in LLMs [40], and based on that we define an LLM-based NeSy threat hunting use case:

Use case 3 *LLM-driven threat hunting using symbolic knowledge and reasoning capabilities.*

LLMs have been used for hypothesis generation in other domains [83], which can be further investigated for threat hunting. Hypothesis generation is typically driven by CTI, which can be captured in a knowledge graph. The integration of LLMs and knowledge graphs is an active research field [77]. In addition, symbolic or computational methods could be used for other steps in the hunting process, including: planning how to answer the hypothesis; reasoning about available data sources to execute this plan; ensuring correct translation to required query language[6] to validate the hypothesis using the observations; and finally, reason about the results from the execution and provide input for any refinement of the hypothesis for a new hunting iteration.

---

[6] Events are stored in a SIEM system, which will have a query language.

Analyse. A prominent characteristic of NeSy is its capacity to combine learning and reasoning. Such a combination is desirable in a SOC, and our next use case, which cuts across the monitor and analyse phases, addresses several of the challenges from Sect. 2:

Use case 4 *Incorporate learning of detection models with the ability to reason about their outcomes to understand and explain their nature and impact.*

In [79], the case for such integration of detection and analysis using NeSy is also made. One way to achieve this is to simultaneously train a neural network (for detection) with related symbolic rules that can be used for contextualization, analysis and explanation (challenge 6). Two NeSy techniques that can accomplish this are *Deep Symbolic Learning (DSL)* [23] and *Neuro-Symbolic Inductive Learner (NSIL)* [22]. *dPASP* [35] and *NeurASP* [96] are techniques based on Answer Set Programming (ASP) [15], which seems promising for this use case. *dPASP* is based on furnishing ASP with neural predicates as interface to both deep learning components and probabilistic features in order to afford differentiable neurosymbolic reasoning. dPASP is suitable for detecting under incomplete information, abductive reasoning, analysis of competing hypotheses (ACH) [42], and what-if reasoning.[7] *NeurASP* improves the results from neural classifiers by applying knowledge-driven symbolic reasoning to them. This is achieved by treating the output from the neural classifier as a probability distribution over the atomic facts, which are then treated in ASP. The ASP rules can also be used to improve the training of the neural networks (use case 1). *DeepProbLog* [61] and *DeepStochLog* [94] incorporate reasoning, probability and deep learning, by extending probabilistic logic programs with neural predicates created from a neural classifier, and may thus provide the necessary combination of learning and reasoning for this use case.

Breaking use case 4 into smaller sub-cases, the first being extracting symbolic alerts, in order to support alert contextualization, analysis and explanation:

Use case 5 *Extracting alerts in a symbolic form.*

In [43], symbolic alerts are extracted from a *graph neural network* (GNN) based detection engine. A combination of *GNNExplainer* [97] and DL-Learner [57] is used to extract the symbolic alerts. The symbolic rules learnt by both DSL and NSIL may also provide such symbolic alert representation, and the use of e.g. ∂ILP for detection will learn symbolic alerts by design. *Embed2Sym* [10] extracts latent concepts from a neural network architecture, and assigns symbolic meanings to these concepts. These symbolic meanings can then be used to encode symbolic alerts.

A SOC typically receives a large volume of threat intelligence, which is too large to thoroughly analyse manually. Such intelligence is used to contextualise alerts, and it is thus desirable to enrich the SOCs knowledge bases with relevant intelligence reports:

---

[7] dPASP can leverage existing LLM-ASP integrations [84] to facilitate use case 3.

Use case 6 *Use statistical AI to enrich or extract symbolic knowledge.*

This use case addresses challenge 6. In Sect. 2, we discussed several approaches to extract knowledge in a suitable symbolic form from reports [58,59,63]. *STAR* [84] is a possible NeSy technique that can be used. It combines LLMs with ASP, where ASP can be employed to reason over the extracted knowledge, in addition to just extracting it.

This ability to reason is crucial as the intelligence report may be incorrect or superseded for different reasons, including underlying (aleatoric) uncertainty, deterioration over time, or from sources one does not fully trust. It may also simply not be relevant for our purposes, or more importantly, intelligence reports may conflict with our existing knowledge or our observations. It would therefore be desirable to quantify and reason about knowledge, including the level of trust, from both own observations and existing knowledge:

Use case 7 *Reason about and quantify knowledge.*

This use case is aimed at addressing challenge 7. It may play a role in implementing a technique known as *risk-based alerting* [90], which involves using data analysis to determine the potential severity and impact of alerts and incidents. *Probabilistic attack graphs* [38] has been used to add probabilities to CTI. One potential NeSy approach for this use case is *Recurrent Reasoning Networks* (RRNs) [44]. RRNs could be used to train a ML model from observations to reason about our existing knowledge graph, e.g. to quantify or identify inconsistencies. Another NeSy example is *Neural Probabilistic Soft Logic* (NeuPSL) [81], where the output from the trained neural networks is in (symbolic) *Probabilistic Soft Logic* (PSL) [11], which can be treated by probabilistic graphical models. NeurASP, dPASP, DeepProbLog and DeepStochLog may also be applicable here.

As discussed in Sect. 2, a cyber attack conducted by an advanced adversary will consist of multiple phases and the ability to relate these phases is essential when developing cyber situational awareness (challenge 6):

Use case 8 *Relate the different phases of cyber incidents.*

One concrete NeSy use case would be to merge the statistics- and semantics-driven approaches outlined in [8]. Further, *PyReason* [4] enables temporal reasoning over graphical structures, such as knowledge graphs. This can be used to exploit the temporal aspect of relating the different phases. The second experiment in Sect. 4 addresses this use case by exploring temporal reasoning using a combination of LLMs, temporal logic, ASP and plan recognition. The ontological reasoning supported by RRNs also seems promising for this type of problem.

Plan & Execute. Neurosymbolic reinforcement learning (NeuroRL) [3] combines the respective advantages of reinforcement learning and AI planning. NeuroRL can learn with fewer interactions compared with traditional RL by using inherent knowledge, thus making it more applicable than both RL and AI planning when (near) real-time response is required and a complete model of the environment is infeasible. Moreover, it has the promise of more explainable response actions, whilst a reasoning engine could, in principle, help to take into account both risk and impact[8]. Thus, this seems like promising approach for challenge 8:

Use case 9 *Generating impact and risk aware explainable response actions in a timely fashion using neurosymbolic reinforcement learning,*

Neurosymbolic reinforcement learning has been used in offensive cyber security settings for penetration testing[9] [25]. Whilst there are some commonalities with our challenges, defending has their own peculiarities. For example, speed, risk, impact and explainability are more prominent when defending against attacks.

Shared Knowledge. Our final use case directly addresses challenge 9. LLMs are extensively studied for generating reports and this is also the case for cyber defence [69]. The generation process is likely to use symbolism (e.g. knowledge graphs [77]). The reports need to be correct, which is one area symbolic AI can help [40]. We, therefore, rephrase challenge 9 as a NeSy use case:

Use case 10 *Generation of incident reports and CTI reports tailored for a given audience and/or formal requirements, using (symbolic) knowledge and LLMs.*

4 Proof-of-Concept Experiments

To showcase the feasibility of using NeSy for our use cases, we have conducted two initial experiments: 1) using LTN to show how knowledge in symbolic form can be used to improve an ML-based detection engine (use case 1); and 2) using LLMs and ASP to elicit and reason with adversary attack patterns and observed alerts for situational awareness (use case 6). Both experiments are deliberately simplified and are not conducted in realistic conditions. They do, however, demonstrate the potential of NeSy in a SOC setting. Additional technical details can be found in appendix A and all source code can be found on GitHub: https://github.com/FFI-no/Paper-NeSy24.

Experiment 1: LTN for knowledge-aware intrusion detection The first experiment addresses use case 1 and is in the monitor phase of MAPE-K. Here, the goal is to detect malicious traffic by training a classifier that can separate benign traffic from two different classes of malicious traffic: brute force attacks and cross-site scripting (XSS) attacks. The classifier will produce an alert if malicious traffic is seen. The input data are *NetFlow* entries [20], which provide aggregated information on traffic between two distinct ports on distinct IP addresses for a given protocol. The data is a subset of the CICIDS2017 dataset [86], which is

---

[8] We note that there are additional challenges when generating risk and impact-aware responses, such as both deriving the requirements in the first place and representing them in a suitable way.

[9] Penetration tests are simulated attacks against the infrastructure and assets being protected, for instance, to identify vulnerabilities.

a labelled dataset containing simulated attacks on a network, with additional details in Appendix A.

The experiment consists of two parts: In the first part, a simple 3-layered fully connected neural network is trained and used as a baseline. In the second part, this neural network is extended using an LTN [12], where additional domain knowledge is encoded. In both cases, 70% of the data is used for training and 30% for testing. The experiment is inspired by [74], where LTN is used in a similar, but more limited, way.

The LTN consists of one predicate for class membership, $P(x, class)$, and is configured as a neural network with the same structure as the baseline neural network. We define the following axioms (expressed in Real Logic [12]):

$$\forall x \in B : P(x, Benign) \quad \forall x \in BF : P(x, Brute\_force) \quad \forall x \in X : P(x, XSS)$$

These axioms describe how all flows in the training set labelled as a given class are a member of the class. This encodes the information of the baseline neural network with no additional knowledge. From the dataset network topology, we define NWS to be the set of all NetFlows that do not communicate with a web server. We know that if a NetFlow is in this NWS-set, then it cannot be a web attack (that we are interested in). We add this domain knowledge as a fourth axiom used by the LTN:

$$\forall x \in NWS : \neg(P(x, Brute\_force) \vee P(x, XSS))$$

Training consists of updating the neural network P to maximize the accumulated truth value of the axioms [12]. The following table shows the results on the test data:

Labels	Baseline Neural Network			Logic Tensor Network		
	Precision	Recall	F1	Precision	Recall	F1
Benign	0.999	0.916	0.956	0.998	0.963	0.981
Brute Force	0.090	0.686	0.159	0.155	0.622	0.248
XSS	0.088	0.628	0.155	0.213	0.648	0.321

This was a very simple extension, yet precision was almost doubled, illustrating the potential for using NeSy to embed additional knowledge in ML models. Recall was largely the same. This was expected since the additional axiom was related to removing false alerts and not to find missed attacks. Further knowledge could be additional details of our infrastructure or assets (including known vulnerabilities) as well as information about the attacker (e.g., from threat intelligence). Furthermore, state-of-the-art detectors are not as simple as the neural network used here and will typically combine related NetFlows before detecting (see, e.g., [21]). Still, this simplified version shows promise for the use of NeSy to enrich ML-based models with (symbolic) knowledge.

Experiment 2: LLMs and ASP for Situational Awareness. The second experiment illustrates the use of NeSy to relate different phases of an attack (use case 8). Here, alerts that are sequenced by time, are mapped to adversary attack patterns, gleaned from textual CTI reports into symbolic form using statistical methods (use case 6). The experiment is inspired by existing work such as: neurosymbolic plan recognition [6], attack plan recognition [7], and the use of LLMs to extract both LTL [32] and CTI (in the form of MITRE ATT&CK *tactics* or *techniques*)[10] [41,75,98]. An LLM (GPT4) is first used to elicit formal representations of attack patterns described in CTI reports, affording us a rapid way of converting CTI to symbolic knowledge. Here, we use the NL2LTL Python library [32] to extract representations of attack patterns in LTL_f [24], a temporal logic for finite traces. The following visualises a conceptual adversary attack pattern, sequencing MITRE ATT&CK techniques:

$$\{t1556\} \quad \ldots \quad \{t1059\} \quad \ldots \quad \{t1548\} \quad \ldots \quad \{t1059\}$$
$$\longrightarrow \bullet \longrightarrow \ldots \longrightarrow \bullet \longrightarrow \ldots \longrightarrow \bullet \longrightarrow \ldots \longrightarrow \bullet$$
$$t_i \quad \ldots \quad t_j \quad \ldots \quad t_k \quad \ldots \quad t_l$$
$$LTL_f : \Box(\mathbf{I} \to \circ\Diamond(t1556 \land \circ\Diamond(t1059 \land \circ\Diamond(t1548 \land \circ\Diamond t1059))))$$

Each '*txxx*', where x is a number, is a unique technique from the MITRE ATT&CK framework [68], $\mathbf{I}$ is the initial state, and $\Box$, $\circ$ and $\Diamond$ are the 'always', 'next' and 'eventually' operators in LTL. Next, telingo [17], an ASP solver for temporal programs, is used to postdict possible attacks. It is given: (i) LTL_f representations of known attack patterns; (ii) sequences of observed alerts; and (iii) knowledge linking alerts to techniques. The attack patterns outlined in (i) are acquired by the elicitation step described above, and the sequences of observed alerts outlined in (ii) are assumed to come from a SIEM system. That is, alerts produced are in a structured form amenable to be represented as Prolog/ASP terms. We assume that this conversion of alerts to symbolic form (use case 5) exists (see e.g. [43]). Furthermore, they are temporally ordered inducing a sequence of alerts (where a_x is an alert in symbolic form):

$$\{a_{addGrpMem}\} \quad \{a_{benign}\} \quad \{a_{execIam}\} \quad \ldots \quad \{a_{latMvmSaml}\} \quad \{a_{benign}\} \quad \{a_{execWinPsh}\}$$
$$\bullet \longrightarrow \bullet \longrightarrow \bullet \longrightarrow \ldots \longrightarrow \bullet \longrightarrow \bullet \longrightarrow \bullet$$
$$t_1 \quad t_2 \quad t_3 \quad \ldots \quad t_{n-2} \quad t_{n-1} \quad t_n$$

Finally, we assume that all the alerts produced can be associated with MITRE ATT&CK techniques, which is common for many signature-based alerts. Note, however, that it is a many-to-many relationship: an alert can be an indicator for several techniques, and a technique can have several alert indicators. This knowledge[11] can be represented in ASP with choice rules:

$$1\ \{t1556; t1548\}\ 1 \leftarrow a_{addGrpMem}$$
$$1\ \{t1059\} \leftarrow a_{execIam}$$
$$1\ \{t1548\} \leftarrow a_{latMvmSaml}$$
$$1\ \{t1059\} \leftarrow a_{execWinPsh}$$

---

[10] A MITRE ATT&CK *tactic* describes why an adversary performs an action, while a MITRE ATT&CK *technique* describes how the action is performed [68].

[11] Extracted from alert rules found at https://github.com/SigmaHQ/sigma.

We encode the problem in a `telingo` program where the adversary attack plan from (i) is formulated as a model constraint, the trace in (ii) is encoded as a temporal fact, and the rules in (iii) are encoded as dynamic rules. A stable model produced by the `telingo` solver tells us that it is plausible that the trace is an instance of the attack plan, while the absence of a model will rule it out, thus achieving the goal set out in the experiment. The `telingo` program and LTL extraction are detailed in Appendix A.

5 Conclusion

Our main goal with this paper has been to showcase the possibilities for NeSy in cyber security, focusing on problems within SOCs, which we hope will help stimulate a concerted effort in studying NeSy in this domain. The use of NeSy in cyber security is in its infancy, with some work having appeared over the last few years, including using for detection [74], generating symbolic alerts [43] and extracting semantic knowledge from reports [63].

We have demonstrated that a considerable amount of symbolic and statistics-based AI is studied in SOC settings, and using it in real-world settings presents several challenges. We believe NeSy can address many of these challenges. Others have made some of the same points [46,79], but not to the extent as we do here. We have contributed by defining a set of NeSy use cases and identifying promising NeSy approaches that serve as a starting point—two of them demonstrated in our proof-of-concept experiments. This work is just a start, and we both hope and expect that many new use cases and promising NeSy approaches that we have not covered here will appear in the not-too-distant future. The use cases and experiments provide a starting point for such future work. A challenge with AI in the cyber security domain is available datasets. Due to issues such as privacy, confidentiality and lack of ground truth, researchers tend to use synthetic data, which has their limitations [9,50]. Furthermore, such datasets tend to focus only on detection (monitor phase), containing only events and lack the additional (symbolic) knowledge which is important in SOCs and for our use cases. This is also one of the reasons that our experiments lack realistic conditions. An important first step will be to develop synthetic datasets containing both events for detection and necessary knowledge in order to address the use cases. This can either be achieved by extending existing "detection datasets" [53] with the necessary knowledge or by developing new "NeSy datasets" from scratch.

Acknowledgements. This work was partly funded by the European Union as part of the European Defence Fund (EDF) project AInception (GA No. 101103385). Views and opinions expressed are however those of the authors only and do not necessarily reflect those of the European Union (EU). The EU cannot be held responsible for them.

A Further Details of Experiments

A.1 Experiment 1

The recorded NetFlows are an aggregation of metadata of the IP traffic in the network. All traffic where a specific subset of features are the same is believed to be regarding the same activity is recorded as the one flow [20].

The dataset is a subset of the CICIDS2017 dataset [86], specifically looking at the "Tursday Morning" part. For simplicity we have chosen a selection of flow features and attack classes. The datasets contain labelled flows categorized into the categories: Web Attack - Benign, Web Attack - Brute Force, and Web Attack - XSS. The classes are greatly imbalanced, with 168 000 flows in the benign class and 2 159 flows in the remaining classes. Such imbalance is common for this type of cyber security dataset where most traffic (by far) will be benign. The dataset is partitioned into a 30%/70%-split between the training set and the test set. Each flow is encoded as a tensor.

The NetFlow features extracted in this experiment are:

- Source Port
- Destination Port
- Protocol
- Flow Duration
- Total Length of Fwd Packets
- Total Length of Bwd Packets
- Fwd Header Length
- Bwd Header Length
- Fwd PSH Flags
- FIN Flag Count
- Bwd Packet Length Min
- Init Win bytes forward
- Init Win bytes backward
- Subflow Fwd Bytes
- Total Length of Fwd Packets

The baseline neural network is encoded as a fully connected multi-layer perceptron with dimensions (16,16,8). This represents the predicate for class membership $P(x, class)$. The samples are assigned to the class with the highest confidence.

The weights of the network are updated using the Adam optimization algorithm [54] with the aggregated truth of axioms used to define the loss. The network is trained over 200 epochs.

A.2 Experiment 2

telingo program The following code listing shows the telingo program from the first experiment:

```
#program initial.
1 { plan(plan1;plan2) } 1 .

%Trace of alerts
&tel{&true
    ;> o(alert(addGrpMem))
    ;> o(alert(benign))
    ;> o(alert(execIam))
```

```
;> o(alert(latMvmSaml))
;> o(alert(benign))
;> o(alert(execWinPsh))}.
```

```
% Adversary attack plans
:- plan(plan1), not &tel{
    >? (h(techn(t1556))
    & > (>? h(techn(t1059))
    & > (>? h(techn(t1548))
    & > (>? h(techn(t1059))))))}.

:- plan(plan2), not &tel{
    >? (h(techn(t1556))
    & > (>? (h(techn(t1059)) | h(techn(t1548))))))}.
```

```
#program dynamic.
```

```
% abduce technique based on alert
1 {hyp(techn(t1556)); hyp(techn(t1548))} 1 :- o(alert(addGrpMem)) .
1 {hyp(techn(t1059))} 1 :- o(alert(execIam)) .
1 {hyp(techn(t1548))} 1 :- o(alert(latMvmSaml)) .
1 {hyp(techn(t1059))} 1 :- o(alert(execWinPsh)) .
```

```
%hypothesized -> happened
h(X) :- hyp(X).
```

CTI Transformed to LTL. This subsection explains how CTI reports of previous attacks are transformed into LTL temporal representations of the attack patterns. The CTI reports are in natural language and we utilize the NL2LTL [32] Python package for the translation. We define a custom pattern template *ExistenceEventuallyOther* to express the LTL property $\Diamond a \land \circ \Diamond b$. Additionally, we create a custom prompt tailored for our domain. The prompt contains the allowed pattern (*ExistenceEventuallyOther*), allowed symbols (MITRE ATT&CK technique IDs), and multiple examples. The LTL representation is a chain of MITRE ATT&CK techniques. However, CTI descriptions of an attack might not reference any specific techniques. In those cases, we let the LLM deduce which MITRE ATT&CK technique is referenced from the general description in natural language. This is a minimal implementation, and extraction of MITRE ATT&CK *tactics* from CTI reports have been investigated before [75,98].

```
Translate natural language sentences into patterns:
ALLOWED_PATTERNS: ExistenceEventuallyOther
ALLOWED_SYMBOLS: T1548 (Abuse Elevation Control Mechanism),
T1530 (Data From Cloud Storage), [...]

NL: The adversary logs into the Kubernetes console.
This leads to: The adversary can view plaintext AWS keys
in the Kubernetes console.
PATTERN: ExistenceEventuallyOther
```

SYMBOLS: T1133, T1552
[...]

Listing 1.1. Prompt

A previous attack is described in natural language, where it is assumed that the first sentence describes an action that happened before the second sentence. The sentences in Listing 1.2 correspond to the MITRE ATT&CK tactics T1566, T1548 and T1048, respectively. This description is based on the procedure examples of techniques in MITRE ATT&CK [68].

```
Attackers leveraged spearphishing emails with malicious links
to gain access to the system. Attackers modifies the tty_tickets
line in the sudoers file to gain root access. Exfiltration over
standard encrypted web protocols to disguise the exchanges as
normal network traffic.
```

Listing 1.2. attack description

We combine each sentence with the next sentence by adding *"This leads to:"*. The sentences are given to NL2LTL. As a result, we get a sequence of LTL statements that can be combined into one statement. In this example, the three sentences are transformed into the following LTL formula:

$$\Box(\mathbf{I} \rightarrow \circ\Diamond(t1566 \land \circ\Diamond(t1548 \land \circ\Diamond t1048)))$$

References

1. Elastic AI assistant. https://github.com/elastic/kibana/tree/main/x-pack/plugins/elastic_assistant
2. RE&CT. https://atc-project.github.io/atc-react/
3. Acharya, K., Raza, W., Dourado, C., Velasquez, A., Song, H.H.: Neurosymbolic reinforcement learning and planning: a survey. IEEE Trans. Artif. Intell. **5**, 1939–1953 (2023)
4. Aditya, D., Mukherji, K., Balasubramanian, S., Chaudhary, A., Shakarian, P.: PyReason: software for open world temporal logic. In: Proceedings of 2023 Spring Symposium on Challenges Requiring the Combination of Machine Learning and Knowledge Engineering (AAAI-MAKE 2023). arXiv:2302.13482 (2023)
5. Ahmad, Z., Shahid Khan, A., Wai Shiang, C., Abdullah, J., Ahmad, F.: Network intrusion detection system: a systematic study of machine learning and deep learning approaches. Trans. Emerg. Telecommun. Technol. **32**(1), e4150 (2021)
6. Amado, L., Pereira, R.F., Meneguzzi, F.: Robust neuro-symbolic goal and plan recognition. In: Proceedings of the AAAI Conference on Artificial Intelligence, vol. 37, pp. 11937–11944 (2023)
7. Amos-Binks, A., Clark, J., Weston, K., Winters, M., Harfoush, K.: Efficient attack plan recognition using automated planning. In: 2017 IEEE Symposium on Computers and Communications (ISCC), pp. 1001–1006. IEEE (2017)
8. Applebaum, A.: Finding dependencies between adversary techniques. In: Presented at the FIRST 2019 Conference (2019). https://www.first.org/resources/papers/conf2019/1100-Applebaum.pdf

9. Apruzzese, G., Laskov, P., Schneider, J.: Sok: pragmatic assessment of machine learning for network intrusion detection. In: 2023 IEEE 8th European Symposium on Security and Privacy (EuroS&P), pp. 592–614. IEEE (2023)
10. Aspis, Y., Broda, K., Lobo, J., Russo, A.: Embed2Sym-scalable neuro-symbolic reasoning via clustered embeddings. In: Proceedings of the International Conference on Principles of Knowledge Representation and Reasoning, vol. 19, pp. 421–431 (2022)
11. Bach, S.H., Broecheler, M., Huang, B., Getoor, L.: Hinge-loss markov random fields and probabilistic soft logic. J. Mach. Learn. Res. **18**(109), 1–67 (2017)
12. Badreddine, S., Garcez, A.D.A., Serafini, L., Spranger, M.: Logic tensor networks. Artif. Intell. **303**, 103649 (2022)
13. Bodungen, C.: ChatGPT for Cybersecurity Cookbook. Packt Publishing (2024)
14. Boyd, J.R.: The essence of winning and losing. Unpubl. Lect. Notes **12**(23), 123–125 (1996)
15. Brewka, G., Eiter, T., Truszczyński, M.: Answer set programming at a glance. Commun. ACM **54**(12), 92–103 (2011)
16. Alahmadi, B.A., Axon, L.: 99% false positives: a qualitative study of SOC analysts' perspectives on security alarms. In: Proceedings of the 31st USENIX Security Symposium (2022)
17. Cabalar, P., Kaminski, R., Schaub, T., Schuhmann, A.: Temporal answer set programming on finite traces. Theory Pract. Logic Program. **18**(3–4), 406–420 (2018)
18. Chetwin, R., Eian, M., Jøsang, A.: Modelling indicators of behaviour for cyber threat hunting via sysmon. In: To appear in Proceedings of European Interdisciplinary Cybersecurity Conference (EICC 2024), pp. 327–352 (2024)
19. Cichonski, P., Millar, T., Grance, T., Scarfone, K., et al.: Computer security incident handling guide - revision 2. NIST Spec. Publ. **800**(61), 1–147 (2012)
20. Cisco. Overview of netflow. Accessed 03 Apr 2024
21. Clausen, H., Grov, G., Aspinall, D.: Cbam: a contextual model for network anomaly detection. Computers **10**(6) (2021)
22. Cunnington, D., Law, M., Lobo, J., Russo, A.: Neuro-symbolic learning of answer set programs from raw data. In: International Joint Conference on Artificial Intelligence (2023)
23. Daniele, A., Campari, T., Malhotra, S., Serafini, L.: Deep symbolic learning: discovering symbols and rules from perceptions. In: Proceedings of the Thirty-Second International Joint Conference on Artificial Intelligence (IJCAI-23), Main Track, pp. 3597–3605 (2023)
24. De Giacomo, G., Vardi, M.Y., et al.: Linear temporal logic and linear dynamic logic on finite traces. In: IJCAI, vol. 13, pp. 854–860 (2013)
25. Ding, R.K.S., Taylor, L.L.A.: Accelerating autonomous cyber operations: a symbolic logic planner guided reinforcement learning approach. In: Proceedings of the International Conference on Computing, Networking and Communications (ICNC 2024), pp. 641–647 (2024)
26. Done, B.K., Willett, K.D., Viel, D.W., Tally, G.W., Sterne, D.F., Benjamin, B.: Towards a capability-based architecture for cyberspace defense. In: 2016, Concept Paper Approved for Public Release, US Department of Homeland Security, US National Security Agency Information Assurance Directorate, and the Johns Hopkins University Applied Physics Laboratory, AOS-16-0099 (2016)
27. Eriksson, H.S., Grov, G.: Towards XAI in the SOC - a user centric study of explainable alerts with SHAP and LIME. In: 2022 IEEE International Conference on Big Data (Big Data), pp. 2595–2600 (2022)

28. Evans, R., Grefenstette, E.: Learning explanatory rules from noisy data. J. Artif. Intell. Res. **61**, 1–64 (2018)
29. Bruggink, G.J., Toelen, M., Carrillo, S., Mavroeidis, V.: ENISA Threat Landscape Methodology. European Union Agency for Cybersecurity (2023). https://doi.org/10.2824/339396
30. Ntalampiras, S., Pascu, C., Barros Lourenco, M., Misuraca, G., Rossel, P.: Artificial intelligence and cybersecurity research – ENISA research and innovation Brief. European Union Agency for Cybersecurity (2023). https://doi.org/10.2824/808362
31. Franke, U., Andreasson, A., Artman, H., Brynielsson, J., Varga, S., Vilhelm, N.: Cyber situational awareness issues and challenges. In: Cybersecurity and Cognitive Science, pp. 235–265. Elsevier (2022)
32. Fuggitti, F., Chakraborti, T.: Nl2ltl-a python package for converting natural language (nl) instructions to linear temporal logic (ltl) formulas. In: Proceedings of the AAAI Conference on Artificial Intelligence, vol. 37, pp. 16428–16430 (2023)
33. Gao, P., et al.: Enabling efficient cyber threat hunting with cyber threat intelligence. In: 2021 IEEE 37th International Conference on Data Engineering (ICDE), pp. 193–204. IEEE (2021)
34. d'Avila Garcez, A., Lamb, L.C.: Neurosymbolic AI: the 3rd wave. Artif. Intell. Rev. **56**(11), 12387–12406 (2023)
35. Geh, R.L., Gonçalves, J., Silveira, I.C., Mauá, D.D., Cozman, F.G.: dPASP: a comprehensive differentiable probabilistic answer set programming environment for neurosymbolic learning and reasoning. arXiv preprint arXiv:2308.02944 (2023)
36. Ghosh, N., Ghosh, S.K.: A planner-based approach to generate and analyze minimal attack graph. Appl. Intell. **36**, 369–390 (2012)
37. Gray, A.: IBM Neuro-Symbolic AI Workshop 23–27 Jan 2023. https://ibm.github.io/neuro-symbolic-ai/blog/nsai-wkshp-2023-blog/
38. Gylling, A., Ekstedt, M., Afzal, Z., Eliasson, P.: Mapping cyber threat intelligence to probabilistic attack graphs. In: 2021 IEEE International Conference on Cyber Security and Resilience (CSR), pp. 304–311. IEEE (2021)
39. Haas, S., Fischer, M.: Gac: graph-based alert correlation for the detection of distributed multi-step attacks. In: Proceedings of the 33rd Annual ACM Symposium on Applied Computing, SAC 2018, pp. 979–988. Association for Computing Machinery, New York (2018)
40. Hammond, K., Leake, D.: Large language models need symbolic ai. In: Proceedings of the 17th International Workshop on Neural-Symbolic Learning and Reasoning, La Certosa di Pontignano, Siena, Italy, vol. 3432, pp. 204–209 (2023)
41. Haque, M.A., Shetty, S., Kamhoua, C.A., Gold, K.: Adversarial technique validation & defense selection using attack graph & att&ck matrix. In: 2023 International Conference on Computing, Networking and Communications (ICNC), pp. 181–187. IEEE (2023)
42. Heuer Jr, R.J.: Analysis of competing hypotheses. In: Psychology of Intelligence Analysis, pp. 95–110 (1999)
43. Himmelhuber, A., Dold, D., Grimm, S., Zillner, S., Runkler, T.: Detection, explanation and filtering of cyber attacks combining symbolic and sub-symbolic methods. In: 2022 IEEE Symposium Series on Computational Intelligence (SSCI), pp. 381–388. IEEE (2022)
44. Hohenecker, P., Lukasiewicz, T.: Ontology reasoning with deep neural networks. J. Artif. Intell. Res. **68**, 503–540 (2020)
45. Zhisheng, H., Zhu, M., Liu, P.: Adaptive cyber defense against multi-stage attacks using learning-based pomdp. ACM Trans. Priv. Secur. (TOPS) **24**(1), 1–25 (2020)

46. Jalaian, B., Bastian, N.D.: Neurosymbolic AI in cybersecurity: bridging pattern recognition and symbolic reasoning. In: MILCOM 2023 - 2023 IEEE Military Communications Conference (MILCOM), pp. 268–273 (2023)
47. Johnson, P., Lagerström, R., Ekstedt, M.: A meta language for threat modeling and attack simulations. In: Proceedings of the 13th International Conference on Availability, Reliability and Security, pp. 1–8 (2018)
48. Kahneman, D.: Thinking, Fast and Slow. Farrar, Straus and Giroux, New York (2011)
49. Kaloroumakis, P.E., Smith, M.J.: Toward a knowledge graph of cybersecurity countermeasures. In: The MITRE Corporation (2021)
50. Kenyon, A., Deka, L., Elizondo, D.: Are public intrusion datasets fit for purpose characterising the state of the art in intrusion event datasets. Comput. Secur. **99**, 102022 (2020)
51. Kephart, J.O., Chess, D.M.: The vision of autonomic computing. Computer **36**(1), 41–50 (2003)
52. Kiesling, E., Ekelhart, A., Kurniawan, K., Ekaputra, F.: The SEPSES knowledge graph: an integrated resource for cybersecurity. In: Ghidini, C., et al. (eds.) ISWC 2019. LNCS, vol. 11779, pp. 198–214. Springer, Cham (2019). https://doi.org/10.1007/978-3-030-30796-7_13
53. Kilincer, I.F., Ertam, F., Sengur, A.: Machine learning methods for cyber security intrusion detection: datasets and comparative study. Comput. Netw. **188**, 107840 (2021)
54. Kingma, D.P., Ba, J.: Adam: a method for stochastic optimization. arXiv preprint arXiv:1412.6980 (2014)
55. Kotenko, I., Gaifulina, D., Zelichenok, I.: Systematic literature review of security event correlation methods. IEEE Access **10**, 43387–43420 (2022)
56. Kurniawan, K., Ekelhart, A., Kiesling, E.: An att&ck-kg for linking cybersecurity attacks to adversary tactics and techniques. In: International Semantic Web Conference (ISWC) - Posters and Demos (2021)
57. Lehmann, J.: Dl-learner: learning concepts in description logics. J. Mach. Learn. Res. **10**, 2639–2642 (2009)
58. Li, Z., Zeng, J., Chen, Y., Liang, Z.: AttacKG: constructing technique knowledge graph from cyber threat intelligence reports. In: Atluri, V., Di Pietro, R., Jensen, C.D., Meng, W. (eds.) Computer Security – ESORICS 2022, pp. 589–609. Springer, Heidelberg (2022). https://doi.org/10.1007/978-3-031-17140-6_29
59. Liu, J., Zhan, J.: Constructing knowledge graph from cyber threat intelligence using large language model. In: 2023 IEEE International Conference on Big Data (BigData), pp. 516–521. IEEE (2023)
60. Liu, K., Wang, F., Ding, Z., Liang, S., Yu, Z., Zhou, Y.: A review of knowledge graph application scenarios in cyber security. arXiv preprint arXiv:2204.04769 (2022)
61. Manhaeve, R., Dumancic, S., Kimmig, A., Demeester, T., De Raedt, L.: DeepProbLog: neural probabilistic logic programming. Adv. Neural Inf. Process. Syst. **31** (2018)
62. Mao, J., Gan, C., Kohli, P., Tenenbaum, J.B., Wu, J.: The neuro-symbolic concept learner: interpreting scenes, words, and sentences from natural supervision. In: International Conference on Learning Representations. International Conference on Learning Representations, ICLR (2019)
63. Marchiori, F., Conti, M., Verde, N.V.: Stixnet: a novel and modular solution for extracting all stix objects in cti reports. In: Proceedings of the 18th International Conference on Availability, Reliability and Security, pp. 1–11 (2023)

64. Mavroeidis, V., Hohimer, R., Casey, T., Jøsang, A.: Threat actor type inference and characterization within cyber threat intelligence. In: 2021 13th International Conference on Cyber Conflict (CyCon), pp. 327–352 (2021)
65. Mavroeidis, V., Zych, M.: Cybersecurity playbook sharing with stix 2.1. arXiv preprint arXiv:2203.04136 (2022)
66. Miller, D., Alford, R., Applebaum, A., Foster, H., Little, C., Strom, B.: Automated adversary emulation: a case for planning and acting with unknowns. MITRE CORP MCLEAN VA MCLEAN (2018)
67. MITRE. Attack flow. https://github.com/center-for-threat-informed-defense/attack-flow.html
68. Mitre. Mitre ATT&CK. https://attack.mitre.org/
69. Motlagh, E.N., Hajizadeh, M., Majd, M., Najafi, P., Cheng, F., Meinel, C.: Large language models in cybersecurity: state-of-the-art. arXiv preprint arXiv:2402.00891 (2024)
70. Nour, B., Pourzandi, M., Debbabi, M.: A survey on threat hunting in enterprise networks. IEEE Commun. Surv. Tutor. (2023)
71. Nyberg, J., Johnson, P., Méhes, A.: Cyber threat response using reinforcement learning in graph-based attack simulations. In: NOMS 2022-2022 IEEE/IFIP Network Operations and Management Symposium, pp. 1–4. IEEE (2022)
72. OASIS. Introduction to STIX. https://oasis-open.github.io/cti-documentation/stix/intro.html
73. Oesch, S., et al.: An assessment of the usability of machine learning based tools for the security operations center. In: 2020 International Conferences on Internet of Things (iThings) and IEEE Green Computing and Communications (GreenCom) and IEEE Cyber, Physical and Social Computing (CPSCom) and IEEE Smart Data (SmartData) and IEEE Congress on Cybermatics (Cybermatics), pp. 634–641 (2020)
74. Onchis, D.M., Istin, C., Eduard-Florin, H.: Advantages of a neuro-symbolic solution for monitoring IT infrastructures alerts. In: 2022 24th International Symposium on Symbolic and Numeric Algorithms for Scientific Computing (SYNASC), pp. 189–194. IEEE (2022)
75. Orbinato, V., Barbaraci, M., Natella, R., Cotroneo, D.: Automatic mapping of unstructured cyber threat intelligence: an experimental study: (practical experience report). In: 2022 IEEE 33rd International Symposium on Software Reliability Engineering (ISSRE), pp. 181–192. IEEE (2022)
76. Ou, X., Govindavajhala, S., Appel, A.W., et al.: Mulval: a logic-based network security analyzer. In: USENIX Security Symposium, Baltimore, MD, vol. 8, pp. 113–128 (2005)
77. Pan, S., Luo, L., Wang, Y., Chen, C., Wang, J., Wu, X.: Unifying large language models and knowledge graphs: a roadmap. IEEE Trans. Knowl. Data Eng. **36**, 3580–3599 (2024)
78. Perrina, F., Marchiori, F., Conti, M., Verde, N.V.: Agir: automating cyber threat intelligence reporting with natural language generation. In: 2023 IEEE International Conference on Big Data (BigData), pp. 3053–3062. IEEE (2023)
79. Piplai, A., Kotal, A., Mohseni, S., Gaur, M., Mittal, S., Joshi, A.: Knowledge-enhanced neurosymbolic artificial intelligence for cybersecurity and privacy. IEEE Internet Comput. **27**(5), 43–48 (2023)
80. Pols, P., van den Berg, J.: The unified kill chain. CSA Thesis, Hague, pp. 1–104 (2017)

81. Pryor, C., Dickens, C., Augustine, E., Albalak, A., Wang, W.Y., Getoor, L.: Neupsl: neural probabilistic soft logic. In: Elkind, E., (eds.) Proceedings of the Thirty-Second International Joint Conference on Artificial Intelligence, IJCAI-2023, pp. 4145–4153. International Joint Conferences on Artificial Intelligence Organization (2023)
82. Qamar, S., Anwar, Z., Rahman, M.A., Al-Shaer, E., Chu, B.T.: Data-driven analytics for cyber-threat intelligence and information sharing. Comput. Secur. **67**, 35–58 (2017)
83. Qiu, L., et al.: Phenomenal yet puzzling: testing inductive reasoning capabilities of language models with hypothesis refinement. arXiv preprint arXiv:2310.08559 (2023)
84. Rajasekharan, A., Zeng, Y., Padalkar, P., Gupta, G.: Reliable natural language understanding with large language models and answer set programming (2023)
85. Riegel, R., et al.: Logical neural networks. arXiv preprint arXiv:2006.13155 (2020)
86. Sharafaldin, I., Lashkari, A.H., Ghorbani, A.A., et al.: Toward generating a new intrusion detection dataset and intrusion traffic characterization. ICISSp **1**, 108–116 (2018)
87. Shu, X., et al.: Threat intelligence computing. In: Proceedings of the 2018 ACM SIGSAC Conference on Computer and Communications Security, pp. 1883–1898 (2018)
88. Sikos, L.F.: Cybersecurity knowledge graphs. Knowl. Inf. Syst. **65**(9), 3511–3531 (2023)
89. Sommer, R., Paxson, V.: Outside the closed world: on using machine learning for network intrusion detection. In: 2010 IEEE Symposium on Security and Privacy, pp. 305–316. IEEE (2010)
90. Splunk. Splunk RBA. https://splunk.github.io/rba/
91. Syed, Z., Padia, A., Finin, T., Mathews, L., Joshi, A.: Uco: a unified cybersecurity ontology. In: Workshops at the Thirtieth AAAI Conference on Artificial Intelligence (2016)
92. Syvertsen, T.: A comparison of machine learning based approaches for alert aggregation. Master thesis, University of Oslo (2023). https://www.duo.uio.no/handle/10852/104437
93. Wilkens, F., Ortmann, F., Haas, S., Vallentin, M., Fischer, M.: Multi-stage attack detection via kill chain state machines. In: Proceedings of the 3rd Workshop on Cyber-Security Arms Race, pp. 13–24 (2021)
94. Winters, T., Marra, G., Manhaeve, R., De Raedt, L.: DeepStochLog: neural stochastic logic programming. In: Proceedings of the AAAI Conference on Artificial Intelligence, vol. 36, pp. 10090–10100 (2022)
95. Würsch, M., Kucharavy, A., David, D.P., Mermoud, A.: Llms perform poorly at concept extraction in cyber-security research literature. arXiv preprint arXiv:2312.07110 (2023)
96. Yang, Z., Ishay, A., Lee, J.: NeurASP: embracing neural networks into answer set programming. arXiv preprint arXiv:2307.07700 (2023)
97. Ying, Z., Bourgeois, D., You, J., Zitnik, M., Leskovec, J.: Gnnexplainer: generating explanations for graph neural networks. Adv. Neural Inf. Process. Syst. **32** (2019)
98. You, Y., et al.: Tim: threat context-enhanced TTP intelligence mining on unstructured threat data. Cybersecurity **5**(1), 3 (2022)

Bayesian Inverse Graphics for Few-Shot Concept Learning

Octavio Arriaga[1(✉)], Jichen Guo[1], Rebecca Adam[3], Sebastian Houben[2], and Frank Kirchner[1,3]

[1] Robotics Research Group, University of Bremen, Bremen, Germany
arriagac@uni-bremen.de
[2] University of Applied Sciences, Bonn-Rhein-Sieg, Sankt Augustin, Germany
[3] Robotics Innovation Center, DFKI GmbH, Bremen, Germany

Abstract. Humans excel at building generalizations of new concepts from just one single example. Contrary to this, current computer vision models typically require large amount of training samples to achieve a comparable accuracy. In this work we present a Bayesian model of perception that learns using only minimal data, a prototypical probabilistic program of an object. Specifically, we propose a generative inverse graphics model of primitive shapes, to infer posterior distributions over physically consistent parameters from one or several images. We show how this representation can be used for downstream tasks such as few-shot classification and pose estimation. Our model outperforms existing few-shot neural-only classification algorithms and demonstrates generalization across varying lighting conditions, backgrounds, and out-of-distribution shapes. By design, our model is uncertainty-aware and uses our new differentiable renderer for optimizing global scene parameters through gradient descent, sampling posterior distributions over object parameters with Markov Chain Monte Carlo (MCMC), and using a neural based likelihood function. The code and datasets are available at github.com/oarriaga/bayesian-inverse-graphics.

1 Introduction

Children have the remarkable ability to learn new concepts from only a small set of examples [13,27,54]. Replicating this human capacity has been a long standing challenge within the few-shot learning research community, and has been considered a milestone for building machines capable of having the same flexibility and learning capacity of humans [30,49]. Current deep learning models hold state of the art results in many few-shot learning tasks, owning great part of their success to the unprecedented availability of large datasets and computational resources [19,32]. This has resulted in large language models (LLMs) and vision transformers (ViT) [8] showing realistic generative capabilities [41], as well as zero-shot task generalization. These new deep learning paradigm contains architectures with billions of parameters, which are optimized over billions of data samples. For instance, a generic vision model like SAM [25] contains

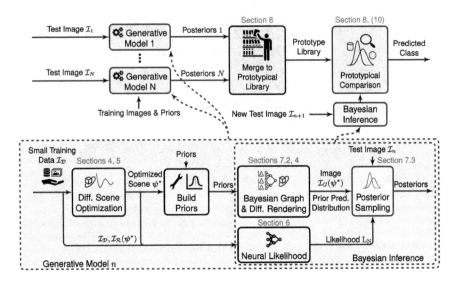

Fig. 1. Neuro-symbolic inverse graphics model for few-shot learning

more than half a billion parameters, which were optimized using more than one billion segmentation masks.

Despite the striking results of these models, this high sample complexity still remains exceptionally large when compared to the learning ability of humans [30]. Few-shot learning methods aim to reduce this sample and model complexity by extending learning algorithms with meta-learning, composition and intuitive physics [28]. However, DL models rarely use composable structures that are physically consistent. Rather, they are often justified by meta design choices, such as optimization ease through residual connections [16], or prevention of feature information loss through densely connected layers [20] or multiple feature map resolutions [42,52]. Moreover, these design choices are often validated only through predictive accuracy which disregards any form of uncertainty quantification, eventually leading into uncalibrated predictions [50]. Although these issues are discussed within some of the few-shot learning literature [28,29], few-shot learning datasets continue to favour large parametric models by having large training datasets; thus, defying the purpose of learning from only few data points.

In order to address the open challenges within the current paradigm of computing large point estimates using billions of samples, we propose exploring an opposite question: How can we build the smallest uncertainty aware vision model that can generalize from only few training images? We approach this question using an inverse graphics framework based on probabilistic cognitive models [11,12,15,43]. Specifically, we apply the *Bayesian workflow* [10] to build a probabilistic generative model (PGM) to simulate the data generative process of images [26]. We test our model through prior and posterior predictive checks, which aim to mitigate any possible bias, or incorrect model assumption [34].

By explicitly using a physics-based model, we reduce the model complexity to a short parametric description that allows us to estimate the full posterior of our parameters. Figure 1 shows an overview of our neuro-symbolic architecture for few-shot learning with minimal data. Our main contributions include:

- A probabilistic generative model that allows us to infer distributions over the properties and poses of new unseen objects from a single image.
- A few-shot classification algorithm that uses posterior distributions to build prototypical probabilistic programs with an embedded distance function.
- A set of benchmarks that test generalization in a low training sample regime, under different lighting conditions, backgrounds, and novel unseen objects.
- A new differentiable renderer that is compatible with probabilistic programming languages, deep learning models and optimization libraries.
- Finally, the application of a probabilistic physics-based model does not remove the possibility of using data-driven methods; rather, we show that one can combine neural architectures with probabilistic symbolic representations through a neural color likelihood function, which outperforms each of these elements separately.

2 Related Work

Few-shot learning models have been classified into metric learning, meta-learning, memory-augmented networks and generative models [53]. One of the most relevant models under the metric learning classification is the prototypical network model [46]. This model is trained using meta learning episodes that build new classification problems at every optimization step. The model learns to embed images into a latent vector space that is reused to classify new samples based on their distance to the projected mean of the support classes. Other meta-learning neural algorithms perform a double optimization loop that updates the model weights within episodes and training samples [9,35]. The method most similar to our approach is the influential Bayesian program learning (BPL) model [28]. This method builds a meta generative model of characters by building stochastic programs that are optimized under a Bayesian criterion. In a revision of the state-of-the-art few-shot algorithms, the BPL model still

Table 1. Few-shot classification datasets with their number of samples

Classification	samples	Pose estimation	samples
mini-imagenet [51]	60K	Latent fusion [37]	480M
CIFAR-FS [3]	60K	OnePose [48]	128K
FGVCAircraft [33]	10K	ShapeNet6D [17]	800K
FGVCFungi [2]	89K	**CLEVR-FS (ours)**	300
Omniglot [28]	32K	**CLEVR-FS dark (ours)**	300
Omniglot small [28]	2.7K	**CLEVR-FS room (ours)**	300

outperformed neural variants in the Omniglot dataset [29]. However, the original BPL algorithm was created as a generative meta-program of characters, and is not directly applicable to 3D geometric objects under realistic lighting conditions. Analogously to few-shot classification algorithms, neural few-shot pose estimation methods also rely to a greater extend in large training datasets. Moreover, in contrast to the few-shot classification task, there is no clear benchmark dataset for few-shot pose estimation. As a consequence, they are often tested on different datasets precluding a fair evaluation. Some of the most relevant models are FS6D [17], OnePose [48] and LatentFusion [37]. The corresponding number of images used for training these few-shot learning methods are listed in Table 1.

3 Minimal-Data Benchmarks

As indicated in Table 1, current few-shot datasets contain a large amount of training samples; thus, undermining the ability of current few-shot models to learn from only few data points. Under this consideration, we adapted the ubiquitously employed CLEVR dataset [23] for few-shot learning and few-shot pose estimation. Specifically, we present the following 4 benchmarks FS-CLVR, FS-CLVR-room, FS-CLVR-dark and YCB-OOD. These benchmarks assess in a controllable environment the generalization of few-shot learning models when using only minimal data. All samples include their respective 6D poses making it a suitable benchmark for few-shot pose estimation models. The FS-CLVR-room, FS-CLVR-dark and YCB-OOD validate respectively the model generalization to new backgrounds, darker lighting conditions, and to out-of-distribution (OOD) complex shapes. These FS-CLVR datasets were rendered using the same shape, materials and colors employed in CLEVR, as well as a vertical field of view (VFOV) of 42.5° present in most commercial depth cameras. Each of these benchmarks contain 300 images separated into 30 training classes and 20 test classes, each class having 6 shot images. The YCB-OOD has no training samples and it contains 10 test classes with 6 shots each. This dataset is meant to validate the OOD generalization of few-shot models to unseen classes, and consists of the following 10 classes from the YCB dataset [6]: power-drill, tomato-soup, airplane-A, foam brick, softball, apple, cracker box, mustard bottle, tuna fish can and mug. Furthermore, while these datasets mostly consist of primitive shapes, they still remain challenging to generic perception algorithms and deep learning models. Specifically, they pose the following open problems: finite and infinite symmetries, textureless objects, reflective materials, changing lighting conditions and ultimately few number of training samples. Finally, as shown in Fig. 2a these few shot tasks can remain challenging for humans.

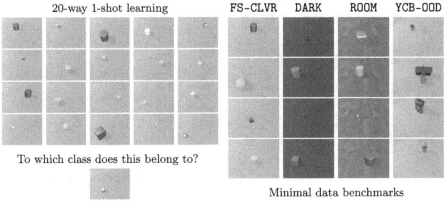

Fig. 2. Samples of our few-shot training datasets. Answer to the left image: 2nd row, 1st column. The absence of additional samples (shots) prevents us from understanding the relationship between the object size and the scene's depth.

4 Merging Bayesian Inference, Graphics and DL

Our inverse graphics model uses elements from three different fields: Bayesian inference, computer graphics, and deep learning. This allows us to reduce the weaknesses of each model by using their complementary strengths. For example, most DL architectures ignore the best known physical descriptions of the problems they aim to solve [30]. Specifically, most computer vision tasks take as input a set of color images from different viewpoints and lighting conditions, and aim to extract information about the physical world. However, most DL vision models don't use any physical simulation between light and matter [47]. In contrast to DL, our model does incorporate this explicit physical knowledge by using a computer graphics pipeline that also encodes known physical limits as prior distributions. Furthermore, many physical phenomena can be described using different models that compromise between accurate predictions and computational complexity. Fortunately, the computer graphics community has been developing the right abstractions, algorithms, and hardware, to efficiently simulate and optimize these models in a physically consistent manner [21,39,56]. Our model uses a common physical approximation known as ray-tracing [5,38], in which an image is rendered by simulating the intersection of light rays with the properties of a given scene, such as the geometry of the objects, or the location of different light sources. Finally, our renderer does not consider all nuances that real images could have. Those can include complex material models (metallic-roughness), soft shadows, and smooth cornered shapes. To address this gap between simulation and reality we propose a neural likelihood function that measures image similarity in features space.

Moreover, we would like to emphasize that our approach is not limited to computer vision, and that the same framework can be applied to many machine

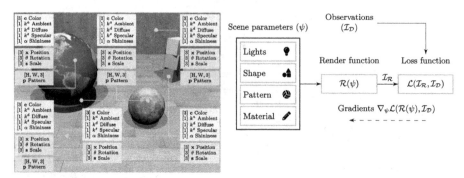

(a) Differentiable scene parameters (b) Differentiable rendering pipeline

Fig. 3. Model based scene optimization

learning problems. This approach can be understood more broadly under the term *Bayesian workflow* [10,34]. In which a general recipe starts by collecting all the known information about the system of study, then encoding information and known physical limitations of the variables of such system through prior distributions. Then, validating all encoded elements by simulating forward the system and confirming that the outputted samples show what one expects to observe before any new evidence is presented. Subsequently, one performs Bayesian inference by conditioning the model on new observations. Finally, one validates that the outputted posterior distributions correspond to a plausible solution.

In this work we introduce a new differentiable ray tracer built entirely using JAX primitives [4]; thus, allowing it to render images using CPUs and GPUs while simultaneously retaining compatibility with modern optimization libraries [1], deep learning frameworks [24], probabilistic programming languages [7] and posterior sampling libraries [31]. Moreover, we can auto-vectorize our renderer to render multiple images in batches. This is a useful feature when sampling multiple MCMC chains or when training deep neural networks with stochastic gradient descent (SGD). Our renderer uses the Phong reflection model [40] and can render a simple scene with a sphere and a single light source with an image size of 480 × 640 in 2.8ms using a low end GPU (GTX 1650 Ti), and in 12ms under the CPU backend (i7-10750H). Finally, we can use the automatic differentiation system to compute gradients and Hessians for gradient descent optimization or Hamiltonian Monte Carlo (HMC). Figure 3 shows an image rendered with our ray tracer as well as the available differentiable parameters. We opted to build a flexible system rather than relying on more realistic renderers that use global illumination [36]. This flexibility allowed us to directly use within our few-shot learning algorithm, gradient descent optimization followed by posterior sampling with a deep neural network in our likelihood function.

5 Scene Optimization

To maximize realism between our generative model and the training dataset, we optimize the scene parametrization $\psi = \{\psi_\mathcal{G}, \psi_\mathcal{O}\}$, including global $\psi_\mathcal{G}$ and object parameters $\psi_\mathcal{O}$. The global parameters $\psi_\mathcal{G} = \{\mathbf{x}_k, \mathbf{l}_k, \mathbf{c}_F, \mathbf{p}_F, k_F^a, k_F^d,\}$ include the kth light position, light intensities, floor color, floor pattern, floor ambient, floor diffuse variable. The object parameters $\psi_\mathcal{O} = \{\mathbf{c}_j, k_j^a, k_j^d, k_j^s, \alpha_j\}$ include the jth training objects' color, ambient, diffuse, specular, and shininess property. Specifically $\mathbf{x}_k, \mathbf{l}_k, \mathbf{c}_F, \mathbf{c}_F, \mathbf{c}_j \in \mathbb{R}^3, \mathbf{p}_f \in \mathbb{R}^{H \times W \times 3}$ and all remaining variables are scalars. To match real and rendered images, for all N_c channels and all N_p pixels we minimize the L_2 loss over ψ using gradient descent through the differentiable renderer $\mathcal{R}(\psi)$:

$$\psi^* = \arg\min_{\psi} L_2(\mathcal{I}_\mathcal{D}, \mathcal{R}(\psi)). \tag{1}$$

Moreover, the reflected colors from a realistic material depend on the lighting conditions. This implies that color reflections contain information about light location and intensity. Thus, we optimized the scene parameters by alternating gradient updates between $\psi_\mathcal{G}$ and $\psi_\mathcal{O}$ with $N = 7$ epochs, $k = 5$, and a pattern image of shape $200 \times 200 \times 3$. We used ADAM with a learning rate of 0.01. Figure 4 shows some results of our optimization problem at different epochs. In total we optimized 120K physically interpretable parameters. All material point estimates optimized on the FS-CLVR training set are displayed in Fig. 4b.

6 Neural Likelihood

While maximizing realism does close the simulation-reality gap, there are still elements for which our differentiable renderer is unable to match perfectly with the true images. These elements are related to soft shadows, material reflections and different shape topologies. Thus, we propose a neural metric that measures image discrepancy in feature space. We apply this neural metric as a likelihood function when fitting a probabilistic graphical model using MCMC. Using a neural network within MCMC implies performing a forward pass for every sample; moreover, not all feature maps are relevant for all tasks. Thus, we opted to use only those feature maps $\mathbf{F}_m$, where each channel m remains invariant between our rendered images $\mathcal{I}_\mathcal{R}$ and the true images $\mathcal{I}_\mathcal{D}$

$$\mathbf{F}_m(\mathcal{I}_\mathcal{R}) \approx \mathbf{F}_m(\mathcal{I}_\mathcal{D}). \tag{2}$$

This implies that we use only those neural features that map similar images to similar feature values. To construct this invariant transformation we compute the mean square error (MSE) across all feature maps channels M of VGG16 [45]. We choose this network due to both its fast inference time, and its widespread application as a feature extraction model [55]. Moreover, our methodology is generic and can be applied to any deep learning model. Specifically, we used

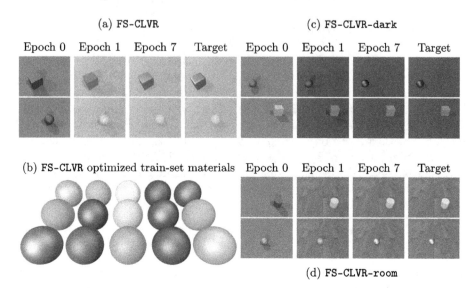

Fig. 4. Model based scene optimization: Subfigure 4b displays in each sphere one extracted material obtained from our optimization process. Moreover, one can observe how each material behaves differently under the same lighting conditions.

the training pairs of true images and the previously optimized image scenes $(\mathcal{I}_\mathcal{D}, \mathcal{I}_\mathcal{R}^*) \in P$ to compute the accumulated loss $\mathcal{L}(m)$, the channel specific MSE, for each feature map channel M:

$$\mathcal{L}(m) = \frac{1}{N(m)} \sum_{(\mathcal{I}_\mathcal{D}, \mathcal{I}_\mathcal{R}^*) \in P} |\mathrm{F}_m(\mathcal{I}_\mathcal{R}^*) - \mathrm{F}_m(\mathcal{I}_\mathcal{D})|^2. \quad (3)$$

where $N(m)$ indicates the number of pixel features in channel m. We select the feature channels M^* that accumulate the least amount of loss across the training image pairs P. For the FS-CLVR training the top 3 channels correspond to the 25th, 51th and 2nd of the 1st convolution layer. This result is computationally favorable since we can extract the first layer of our model and use it during sampling.

During posterior sampling the neural likelihood takes as input samples from our prior distributions. The variables associated with those distributions include the object's position $\mathbf{x} \in \mathbb{R}^{3\times 1}$, its angle alongside the z-axis θ, its scales $\mathbf{s} \in \mathbb{R}^{3\times 1}$, its class $\kappa \in \{\text{sphere,cube,cylinder}\}$ and its set of material properties $\psi_\mathcal{M} = \{\mathbf{c}, k^a, k^d, k^s, \alpha\}$. With these parameters we build the parameterization $\Omega = \{\mathbf{x}, \theta, \mathbf{s}, \psi_\mathcal{M}, \kappa\}$ and formulate the neural likelihood function $\mathrm{L}_\mathrm{N}(\Omega, \mathcal{I}_D)$ as:

$$\mathrm{L}_\mathrm{N}(\mathcal{I}|\Omega) \propto \prod_{m=1}^{M^*} \prod_{n=1}^{N(m)} \exp(\mathrm{F}_m^n(\mathcal{I}_D)) - \mathrm{F}_m^n(\mathcal{I}_\mathcal{R}(\Omega)). \quad (4)$$

7 Probabilistic Inverse Graphics Models

7.1 Building Priors

We provide our inverse graphical model with physically consistent priors for Ω by considering the following elements:

- The object translation prior $p(\mathbf{x})$ is a truncated Gaussian distribution (Tr$\mathcal{N}$) with its limits determined such that the translation of an object has the highest probability mass in the middle of the image plane and 0 mass outside.
- The angle prior $p(\theta)$ across the object's the z-axis was selected using a von Mises distribution which assigns equal probability to all angles.
- The object scales' prior $p(\mathbf{s})$ are modelled as a Log-normal (Log$\mathcal{N}$) distribution excluding negative scales, or extremely small or large objects.
- The prior distribution $p(\kappa)$ for the shape classes {sphere, cube, cylinder} is a Gumbel-Softmax distribution (Gmb) [22], which locates most of the probability mass as one-hot vectors instead of uniformly distributed classes, modelling that objects should not be simultaneously multiple classes at once.
- We used the optimized parameters from our scene optimization pipeline to build priors for our material variables $\psi_\mathcal{M}$. Specifically, we fitted a Gaussian Mixture Model (GMM) to each variable using expectation maximization (EM). We used 2 mixture components for each variable, and a diagonal covariance matrix.

The parameters and distributions of all our priors are shown in the supplementary Sect. 11. All GMM prior models are shown in the supplementary Sect. 12.

7.2 Probabilistic Generative Model

Having defined our prior distributions, we proceed to build a probabilistic generative model of images. Figure 5a shows our model in plate notation and Fig. 5b shows its prior predictive samples. These prior predictive samples reflect what the model expects to see before making any observation. Moreover, our model outputs a probability for each sample. This all being referred as the prior predictive distribution (PPD). We now proceed to explain in detail the probability density functions (PDFs) and the deterministic functions applied to our model.

We define the (PDF) over possible materials $\mathcal{M}$ by considering each material property in $\psi_\mathcal{O}$ as independent:

$$p(\mathcal{M}|\psi_\mathcal{M}) = \prod_{m \in \psi_\mathcal{M}} \left[\sum_{k=0}^{K} \pi_k^m \mathcal{N}(m|\mu_k^m, \Sigma_k^m) \right]. \tag{5}$$

As shown in Fig. 5a the PDF over possible affine transformations $\mathcal{A}$ includes a Tr$\mathcal{N}$, von Mises, and a Log$\mathcal{N}$ distribution, and considers the translation, angle and scale as independent events:

$$p(\mathcal{A}|\mathbf{x}, \theta, \mathbf{s}) = \prod_{t \in T} \left[\frac{\text{Tr}\mathcal{N}(\mathbf{x}|\mu_t, \sigma_t)}{2\pi I_0(0)} \right] \prod_{s \in S} \frac{\exp(-\frac{(\ln(s) - \mu_s)^2}{2\sigma_s^2})}{s\sigma_s \sqrt{2\pi}}. \tag{6}$$

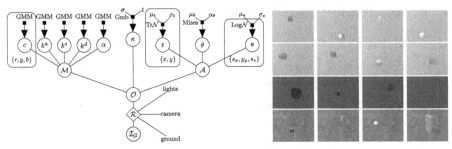

(a) Probabilistic inverse graphics model (b) Prior predictive samples

Fig. 5. Inverse graphics model and prior predictive samples for `FS-CLVR`, `FS-CLVR-dark`, and the `FS-CLVR-room` datasets

where $T = \{x, y\}$, $S = \{s_x, s_y, s_z\}$ and I_0 is the Bessel function of order zero. Finally, we compute the probability density function over objects $p(\mathcal{O}|\mathcal{M}, \mathcal{S}, \mathcal{A})$ using the previously defined PDFs for materials 5 and transforms 6, as well as $p(\kappa|\sigma, t)$ corresponding to the Gumbel-Softmax probability with a class probability σ and a temperature t

$$p(\kappa|\sigma, t)p(\mathcal{M}|\psi_\mathcal{M})p(\mathcal{A}|\mathbf{x}, \theta, \mathbf{s}). \tag{7}$$

Furthermore, the object variable $\mathcal{O}$ is passed through our deterministic differentiable rendering function $\mathcal{R}$ outputting image samples, and similarly to [14] we build an affine transform that enforces objects to not collide with the floor. Having defined a forward generative model of images, we now perform Bayesian inference in order to obtain the posterior distributions over the variables Ω given an observation $\mathcal{I}$, here denoting a test image.

$$p(\Omega|\mathcal{I}) \sim p(\mathcal{I}|\Omega)p(\Omega). \tag{8}$$

We define a color likelihood function L_C using a truncated normal distribution over each pixel argument (u, v, c) of an image $\mathcal{I}$ with shape [H, W, 3]:

$$\xi(u, v, c) = \mathcal{I}_\mathcal{R}(u, v, c|\Omega) - \mathcal{I}_\mathcal{D}(u, v, c) \tag{9}$$

$$L(u, v|\Omega)_C = \prod_{u=0}^{W} \prod_{v=0}^{H} \prod_{c=0}^{3} \text{Tr}\mathcal{N}(\xi(u, v, c), \sigma_I). \tag{10}$$

All parameters of our PGM are displayed in the supplementary Sect. 11. Given our target probability function, and an observation $\mathcal{I}$, we can now sample from a conditioned posterior distribution using MCMC.

7.3 Posterior Sampling

For each of the test images we sampled from the target distribution using the Rosenbluth-Metropolis Hastings (RMH) MCMC method. We used 20 chains

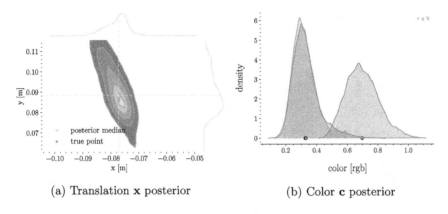

(a) Translation **x** posterior (b) Color **c** posterior

Fig. 6. Posteriors from a single test image. Each contour in a) indicates the highest density intervals with 5%, 10%, 20%, 40%, 60%, 80% probability

sampling 30K posterior samples per chain with a burn-in of 1K samples. We used a diagonal Gaussian kernel as our proposal generator which we initialized with all diagonal elements being 0.05. Before sampling we performed automatic tuning of our chains to have an acceptance rate between 20% and 50%. In order to speed-up sampling we reparametrized our prior distributions and resized each test image to a shape of [160, 120, 3], and removed all shadows from our ray-tracing pipeline. Details of the prior reparametrization are show in the supplementary Sect. 13. In total we approximated 420 13-dimensional integrals using 252M samples in approximately 14 h using an low budget RTX A4000 GPU. Figure 6a shows the posterior distributions over 2 variables after conditioning on a single test image. The posterior distribution of the translation components **x** is shown in Fig. 6a. This posterior indicates more uncertainty across the y-axis. This result is seen across most of our samples, and seems logical given that the y-axis provides us less pixel information about the possible position and size of the objects. Moreover, while the point estimate of our translation is off by one centimeter in the y-axis, the posterior distribution captures the direction of the biggest source of error. This result can be relevant for robot manipulation, where we could inform the robot's behavior with the given uncertainty in order to consider it while performing a task. Additional posterior results and point estimates can be observed in the supplementary Sect. 14.

8   Probabilistic Prototypical Programs

In this section we reuse the posterior samples to build a prototypical object representation. Specifically, we perform a Gaussian kernel density estimate using Scott's bandwidth [44] for the posterior samples of the variables in $\psi_S = \{\mathbf{s}, \psi_M, \kappa\}$. Thus, our prototypical representation consists of all our previous posterior samples excluding the pose variables **x** and θ. These posterior

(a) Observation (b) Median point estimate (c) Posterior samples

Fig. 7. Posterior results from conditioning on a single observation: Subfigure 7a shows the observation used for conditioning our PGM. Subfigure 7b shows a single point summary of the estimated posterior distributions of the PGM after conditioning with the observation. We can observe how this point estimate provides an accurate description of the observation. Moreover, we are not only estimating a single point value for each of our variables, but rather full probability distributions. Subfigure 7c shows how our posterior distributions capture similar representations of the concept seen in the observation.

distributions are used to build a new generative model by removing these variables from our previous inverse graphics model 5a. A visualization of this new graphical model is shown in the supplementary Sect. 15. Moreover, we define the functions `distance` and `merge` between two generative models. We define the *distance* between two generative models C_I and C_k as the sum of the Kullback-Leibler divergences across our selected variables ψ_S

$$d(C_I, C_k) = \sum_{\psi_S} \mathrm{KL}(C_k^{\psi_S} \| C_I^{\psi_S}) = \sum_{\psi_S} \sum_x C_k^{\psi_S}(x) \log \frac{C_k^{\psi_S}(x)}{C_I^{\psi_S}(x)}. \tag{11}$$

The `merge` operation ($\otimes$) is defined as performing KDE on the concatenated posterior samples for each variable in both PGMs. We define this conditioned probabilistic generative models with these two additional functions as a protoprogram C. Moreover, protoprograms have the additional functionalities associated to all PGMs; those being the capacity to `sample` and to compute the `probability` of any given sample. Consequently, protoprograms allow us to generate new concepts and images that are similar to our given prototypical observation. Figure 7c shows ordered samples of the protoprogram conditioned on observation 7a. This characteristic was indicated to be a relevant human trait that is not present in most few-shot learning methods [29]. Having defined our protoprograms we proceed to present a classification algorithm. Given N example images (shots) of an object class k, we proceed to build a protoprogram for this class by merging all conditioned programs as $C_k = C_1^k \otimes C_2^k \otimes \ldots C_N^k$. Given a new observation I, we proceed to learn a program C_I following the same structure as before. We then use the program *distance* to compute a probability conditioned on each protoprogram class c by applying softmax on the negative program distances.

$$p(c = k|I) = \frac{\exp(-d(C_I, C_k))}{\sum_k \exp(-d(C_I, C_k))}. \tag{12}$$

9 Results

We present the results of our prototypical probabilistic programs (P3) applied to the datasets FS-CLVR, FS-CLVR-room, FS-CLVR-dark, and YCB-OOD. As previously mentioned, these datasets test generalization in a low sample training regime, as well as in different background, lighting and out-of-distribution shapes. Moreover, we tested two versions of our model.

Table 2. Few-shot accuracy results for multiple shots

(a) Accuracies on the FS-CLVR and FS-CLVR-room test dataset

Model	FS-CLVR test dataset				FS-CLVR-room test dataset			
	5-way		10-way		5-way		10-way	
	1-shot	5-shot	1-shot	5-shot	1-shot	5-shot	1-shot	5-shot
MAML$_{56\times56}$ [9]	76.96%	87.48%	62.82%	69.84%	77.94%	79.18%	47.23%	61.46%
MAML$_{84\times84}$ [9]	70.86%	32.38%	51.77%	64.95%	72.96%	81.72%	32.12%	57.01%
ProtoNets$_{56\times56}$ [46]	60.52%	85.54%	51.22%	79.73%	66.70%	83.04%	54.65%	72.18%
ProtoNets$_{84\times84}$ [46]	51.16%	74.94%	40.13%	67.09%	47.12%	68.32%	33.65%	54.41%
P3 (ours)	95.98%	**98.98%**	92.61%	**97.51%**	91.66%	96.98%	86.01%	93.59%
NP3 (ours)	**97.18%**	98.86%	**94.52%**	97.47%	**94.36%**	**98.96%**	**90.52%**	**97.53%**

(b) Accuracies on the FS-CLVR-dark and YCB-OOD test dataset

Model	FS-CLVR-dark test dataset				YCB-OOD test dataset			
	5-way		10-way		5-way		10-way	
	1-shot	5-shot	1-shot	5-shot	1-shot	5-shot	1-shot	5-shot
MAML$_{56\times56}$ [9]	79.56%	86.22%	60.39%	62.77%	47.22%	32.70%	36.55%	39.16%
MAML$_{84\times84}$ [9]	69.08%	80.36%	49.15%	63.00%	52.22%	37.56%	39.83%	47.56%
ProtoNets$_{56\times56}$ [46]	65.34%	86.66%	52.88%	79.32%	49.80%	67.26%	39.13%	57.37%
ProtoNets$_{84\times84}$ [46]	43.92%	70.58%	32.51%	58.19%	41.26%	62.28%	30.96%	50.33%
P3 (ours)	96.86%	98.04%	93.88%	96.62%	66.42%	67.84%	60.32%	57.31%
NP3 (ours)	**97.30%**	**98.48%**	**94.88%**	**97.31%**	**67.44%**	**71.26%**	**62.09%**	**61.36%**

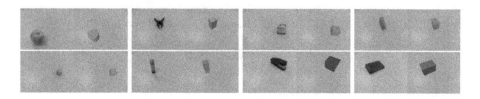

Fig. 8. NP3 applied to real images

These correspond to a generative model which uses both the color and neural likelihood functions (NP3), and the P3 model which only considers the color likelihood. We compared the performance of our model with respect to the standard metric-based, and meta learning neural-only models in Table 2. These are respectively ProtoNets [46], and MAML [9]. We used the same learning rate (1e-3) and the same resolution (84×84) suggested by the original authors. Moreover, we observed that sometimes the resolution of 56×56 was outperforming the 84×84 resolution; thus we include both results. In the supplementary Sect. 16 we show more experiments with different resolutions. Our model outperforms these few-shot neural models while using considerably less parameters. Our probabilistic graphical model P3 has only 13 parameters per class (Ω). That is a 1,738-fold decrease in parameter count when using 5-ways. While the number of parameters should not be taken as a measure of model complexity, this parameter reduction allows us to perform full Bayesian inference and compute the posterior of our parameters to determine the uncertainty of our model. Furthermore, our zero-shot pose estimation evaluation can be found in the supplementary Sect. 17. Finally, as observed in Fig. 8, without any modification to our model we are able to directly apply it to unseen real objects.

10 Conclusion and Future Work

This paper presents a novel Bayesian inverse graphics framework that encodes images as prototypical probabilistic programs. This approach addresses some of the limitations of existing neural algorithms such as high sample and model complexity, and lack of uncertainty quantification. Moreover, we use these probabilistic programs to build a few-shot learning classification algorithm. This algorithm integrates our newly introduced differentiable renderer with probabilistic programming languages, gradient descent optimization libraries, and deep learning frameworks. Our method achieves higher classification accuracy than standard few-shot neural methods, while using considerably less parameters. Furthermore, we demonstrate generalization to different lighting conditions, backgrounds, and unseen complex objects. Additionally, we proposed a neural likelihood function which combines deep learning models with Bayesian inference. In future work we plan to extend our generative models to merge primitive shapes to fit more complex objects.

Acknowledgements. This work was funded by the German Aerospace Center (DLR) with federal funds (Grant 50RA2126A / 50RA2126B) from the German Federal Ministry of Economic Affairs and Climate Action (BMWK) in the project PhysWM.

11 Physics based priors and likelihood parameters

The parameters and visualizations of our prior distributions and likelihood functions are displayed in Fig. 9 and Table 3 shows all our prior and likelihood parameters.

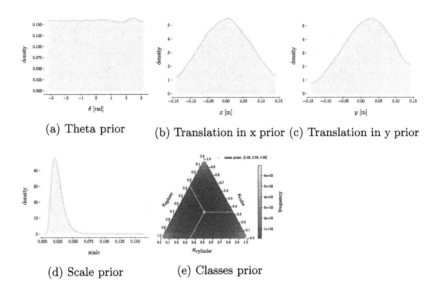

Fig. 9. Prior distributions

12 Training data based priors

In this section we show the data driven priors fitted for the FS-CLVR dataset for the variables color **c**, ambient k^a, diffuse k^d, specular k^s, and shininess α.

13 Bijection results

Reparametrizing probability distributions can increase the number of effective samples without increasing computational costs. We transformed the prior probability distributions to fit Normal distributions using the appropriate bijection functions. Specifically for $\mathbf{x}, \theta, \mathbf{s}, \kappa$ we apply the following bijections parametrized by ω and ϕ:

$$\hat{\mathbf{x}} = \omega_{\mathbf{x}} \mathbf{x} + \phi_{\mathbf{x}} \qquad (13)$$

$$\hat{\theta} = \text{sigmoid}(\frac{\pi}{2}\theta) \qquad (14)$$

$$\hat{\mathbf{s}} = \text{sigmoid}(\omega_{\mathbf{s}} \mathbf{s} + \phi, -\pi, \pi) \qquad (15)$$

$$\hat{\kappa} = \text{softmax}(\omega_{\kappa} \kappa) \qquad (16)$$

Table 3. Prior and likelihood parameters

Parameter	Value
shift mean (μ_t)	[0.0, 0.025]
shift scale (σ_t)	0.08
theta mean (μ_θ)	0.0
theta concentration (α_θ)	0.0
scale mean (μ_s)	0.025
scale scale (σ_s)	0.0001
classes temperature (t)	0.5
class probabilities (σ)	[1/3, 1/3, 1/3]
Neuro likelihood $\propto$ constant	0.05
Color likelihood scale (σ_I)	1.0
Color likelihood scale ($\sigma_I^{\text{FS-CLVR-DARK}}$)	0.35

Moreover, the GMM priors were reparametrized by minimizing the negative log-likelihood with respect to an affine bijector and a Normal distribution:

$$\hat{m} = \omega_k m + \phi_k \tag{17}$$

Visualizations of reparametrizations for all GMM, as well as translation, theta and scale distributions are shown below:

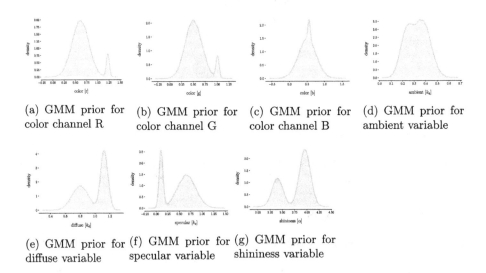

(a) GMM prior for color channel R
(b) GMM prior for color channel G
(c) GMM prior for color channel B
(d) GMM prior for ambient variable
(e) GMM prior for diffuse variable
(f) GMM prior for specular variable
(g) GMM prior for shininess variable

Fig. 10. Data-driven priors.

14 Posterior results

This section contains more posterior results. Specifically, we show the median point estimates of all our predictions in Fig. 12 for the FS-CLVR dataset, in Fig. 13 for FS-CLVR-room, Fig. 14 for FS-CLVR-dark and Fig. 15 for the YCB-OOD dataset.

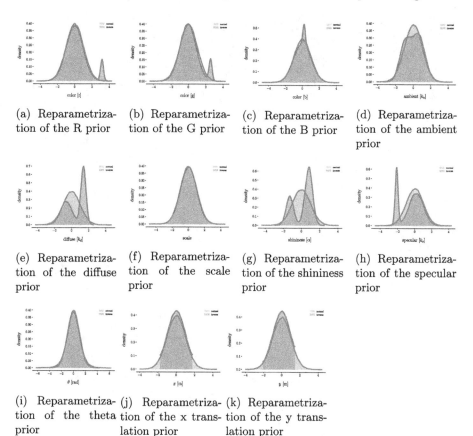

Fig. 11. Reparametrized priors. Red indicates a Normal distribution. Blue the reparametrized prior. (Color figure online)

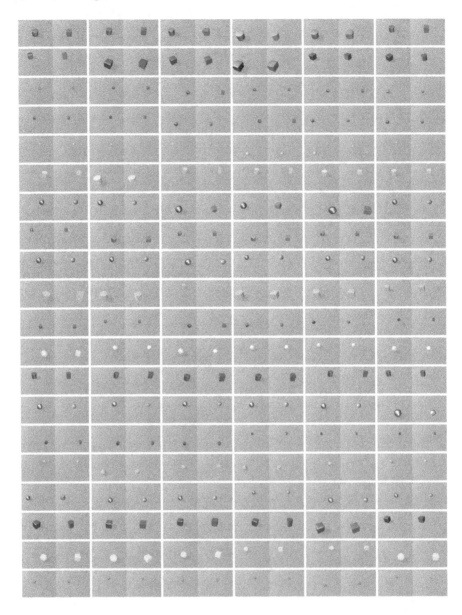

Fig. 12. True image with NP3 median point estimate of the FS-CLVR test split

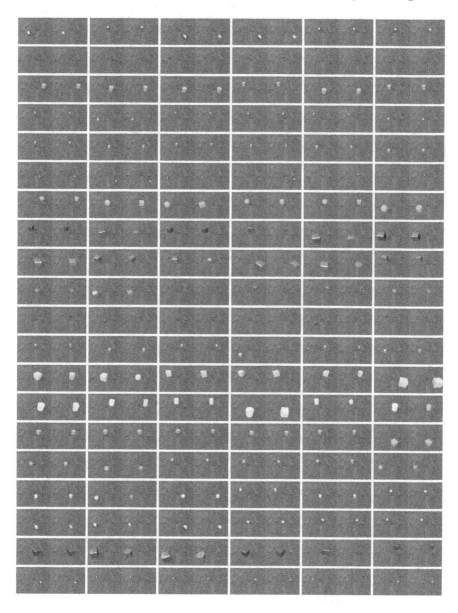

Fig. 13. True image with NP3 median point estimate of the FS-CLVR-room test split

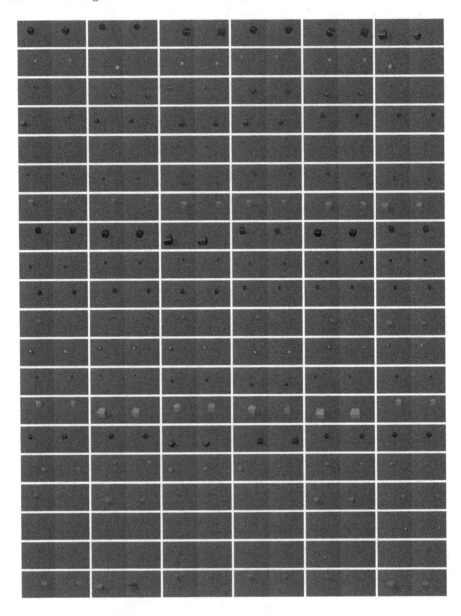

Fig. 14. True image with NP3 median point estimate of the FS-CLVR-dark test split

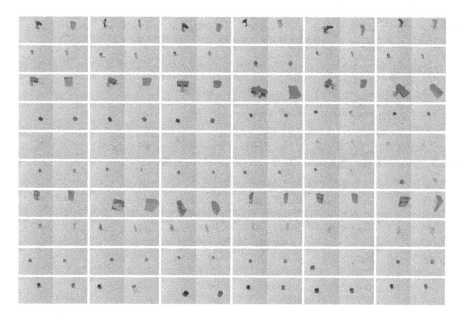

Fig. 15. True image with NP3 median point estimate of the YCB-OOD dataset

15 Prototypical program results

In the image below we show our probabilistic prototypical program (P3) in graphical form. This model is derived from our probabilistic generative model 5a by removing the variables translation $\mathbf{x}$ and rotation θ of our inverse graphics model.

16 MAML and ProtoNets results

We now present the additional experimental results of the CNN models used in MAML and ProtoNets. This CNN model corresponds to the default architecture proposed in both papers. Specifically it consists of 4 blocks, each having in sequence the following layers: Conv2D with 64 3 × 3 filters, BatchNorm, ReLU and MaxPool2D. Initially we did some preliminary experiments for determining the image resolutions. We set the training iteration steps to 20K and the image sizes of the FS-CLVR dataset were downsampled to 28 × 28, 56 × 56, 84 × 84, 112 × 112, 168 × 168. The corresponding test accuracies for these resolutions were respectively 67.9%, 80.5%, 71%, 30.4%, 22.4% under the MAML training framework. From here it could be seen that the lower resolutions could achieve better performance. In all our experiments we trained the models for 60K iterations using the optimizer (ADAM) and learning rates (1e-3) suggested by the original authors.

17 Evaluation of pose estimation

In this section, we present our evaluation results of pose estimation with respect to the ADI metric (Average Distance of Indistinguishable Model Point) [18] for our different version of models on our different test datasets in Table 4. This ADI metric is commonly used for symmetric objects and measures the average deviation of the transformed model points to the closest model point. The values in the Table 4a and 4b represents the mean value of the ADI error for our total 6 shots of each test class in our `FS-CLVR`, `FS-CLVR-room`, `FS-CLVR-dark`, and `YCB-OOD` test dataset.

Table 4. Evaluation of pose estimation with ADI metric on our datasets

(a) Evaluation on the FS-CLVR, FS-CLVR-room, and FS-CLVR-dark test dataset

Test Classes	FS-CLVR		FS-CLVR-room			FS-CLVR-dark
	P3	NP3	P3	NP3	P3	NP3
Class 0	0.0153	0.018	0.0075	0.0086	0.0235	0.0197
Class 1	0.0174	0.0176	0.0369	0.0110	0.0791	0.0798
Class 2	0.0092	0.0059	0.0072	0.0098	0.0694	0.0663
Class 3	0.0136	0.0145	0.0054	0.0090	0.0781	0.0553
Class 4	0.0697	0.0391	0.0072	0.0069	0.086	0.086
Class 5	0.0258	0.0265	0.0215	0.0200	0.0852	0.0856
Class 6	0.0045	0.0058	0.0109	0.0115	0.0509	0.0497
Class 7	0.011	0.0108	0.0154	0.0181	0.0148	0.0126
Class 8	0.0031	0.0054	0.0203	0.0228	0.042	0.0407
Class 9	0.0119	0.0111	0.0211	0.0168	0.0394	0.0364
Class 10	0.0088	0.0104	0.0729	0.0725	0.0515	0.0184
Class 11	0.0115	0.0117	0.0246	0.0225	0.0642	0.0263
Class 12	0.0134	0.0125	0.0169	0.0205	0.075	0.0745
Class 13	0.0059	0.0057	0.018	0.0197	0.0168	0.0146
Class 14	0.007	0.0067	0.0139	0.0111	0.055	0.0454
Class 15	0.0095	0.0088	0.0111	0.0140	0.0697	0.053
Class 16	0.0076	0.0098	0.019	0.0200	0.0552	0.0148
Class 17	0.0139	0.0119	0.013	0.0177	0.0849	0.0857
Class 18	0.0106	0.0095	0.0173	0.0185	0.0772	0.0779
Class 19	0.0344	0.024	0.0095	0.0080	0.024	0.0175

(b) Evaluation on the YCB-OOD test dataset

Test Classes	YCB-OOD	
	P3	NP3
power-drill	0.0274	0.0272
tomato-soup	0.0219	0.0218
airplane-A	0.0212	0.0198
foam-brick	0.0259	0.0274
softball	0.0768	0.0749
apple	0.0466	0.0435
cracker-box	0.0313	0.0326
mustard-bottle	0.0534	0.0494
tuna-fish-can	0.0312	0.0333
mug	0.0242	0.0231

References

1. Babuschkin, I., et al.: The DeepMind JAX Ecosystem (2020). http://github.com/deepmind
2. beejisbrigit, Y.C.: 2018 FGCVx fungi classification challenge (2018). https://kaggle.com/competitions/fungi-challenge-fgvc-2018

3. Bertinetto, L., Henriques, J.F., Torr, P.H., Vedaldi, A.: Meta-learning with differentiable closed-form solvers (2018). arXiv preprint arXiv:1805.08136
4. Bradbury, J., Frostig, R., et al.: JAX: composable transformations of Python+NumPy programs (2018). http://github.com/google/jax
5. Buck, J., Hogan, B.: The Ray Tracer Challenge: A Test-driven Guide to Your First 3D Renderer. Pragmatic programmers, Pragmatic Bookshelf (2019). https://books.google.de/books?id=13OWswEACAAJ
6. Calli, B., Walsman, A., Singh, A., Srinivasa, S., Abbeel, P., Dollar, A.M.: Benchmarking in manipulation research: The YCB object and model set and benchmarking protocols (2015). arXiv preprint arXiv:1502.03143
7. Dillon, J.V., et al.: TensorFlow distributions (2017). arXiv preprint arXiv:1711.10604
8. Dosovitskiy, A., et al.: An image is worth 16 × 16 words: Transformers for image recognition at scale (2020). arXiv preprint arXiv:2010.11929
9. Finn, C., Abbeel, P., Levine, S.: Model-agnostic meta-learning for fast adaptation of deep networks. In: International Conference on Machine Learning, pp. 1126–1135. PMLR (2017)
10. Gelman, A., et al.: Bayesian workflow (2020). arXiv preprint arXiv:2011.01808
11. Ghahramani, Z.: Probabilistic machine learning and artificial intelligence. Nature **521**(7553), 452–459 (2015)
12. Goodman, N.D., Tenenbaum, J.B., Contributors, T.P.: Probabilistic Models of Cognition (2016). http://probmods.org/v2. Accessed 10 Nov 2023
13. Gopnik, A.: Scientific thinking in young children: theoretical advances, empirical research, and policy implications. Science **337**(6102), 1623–1627 (2012)
14. Gothoskar, N., et al.: 3DP3: 3D scene perception via probabilistic programming. Adv. Neural. Inf. Process. Syst. **34**, 9600–9612 (2021)
15. Griffiths, T.L., Chater, N., Kemp, C., Perfors, A., Tenenbaum, J.B.: Probabilistic models of cognition: exploring representations and inductive biases. Trends Cogn. Sci. **14**(8), 357–364 (2010)
16. He, K., Zhang, X., Ren, S., Sun, J.: Deep residual learning for image recognition. In: Proceedings of the IEEE Conference on Computer Vision and Pattern Recognition, pp. 770–778 (2016)
17. He, Y., Wang, Y., Fan, H., Sun, J., Chen, Q.: FS6D: few-shot 6D pose estimation of novel objects. In: Proceedings of the IEEE/CVF Conference on Computer Vision and Pattern Recognition, pp. 6814–6824 (2022)
18. Hinterstoisser, S., et al.: Model based training, detection and pose estimation of texture-less 3D objects in heavily cluttered scenes. In: Lee, K.M., Matsushita, Y., Rehg, J.M., Hu, Z. (eds.) ACCV 2012. LNCS, vol. 7724, pp. 548–562. Springer, Heidelberg (2013). https://doi.org/10.1007/978-3-642-37331-2_42
19. Hooker, S.: The hardware lottery. Commun. ACM **64**(12), 58–65 (2021)
20. Huang, G., Liu, Z., Van Der Maaten, L., Weinberger, K.Q.: Densely connected convolutional networks. In: Proceedings of the IEEE Conference on Computer Vision and Pattern Recognition, pp. 4700–4708 (2017)
21. Jakob, W., et al.: Mitsuba 3 renderer (2022). https://mitsuba-renderer.org
22. Jang, E., Gu, S., Poole, B.: Categorical reparameterization with Gumbel-Softmax (2016). arXiv preprint arXiv:1611.01144
23. Johnson, J., Hariharan, B., Van Der Maaten, L., Fei-Fei, L., Lawrence Zitnick, C., Girshick, R.: CLEVR: a diagnostic dataset for compositional language and elementary visual reasoning. In: Proceedings of the IEEE Conference on Computer Vision and Pattern Recognition, pp. 2901–2910 (2017)

24. Kidger, P., Garcia, C.: Equinox: neural networks in JAX via callable PyTrees and filtered transformations (2021). arXiv preprint arXiv:2111.00254
25. Kirillov, A., et al.: Segment anything (2023). arXiv preprint arXiv:2304.02643
26. Kulkarni, T.D., Whitney, W.F., Kohli, P., Tenenbaum, J.: Deep convolutional inverse graphics network. In: Advances in Neural Information Processing Systems, vol. 28 (2015)
27. Lake, B., Salakhutdinov, R., Gross, J., Tenenbaum, J.: One shot learning of simple visual concepts. In: Proceedings of the Annual Meeting of the Cognitive Science Society. vol. 33 (2011)
28. Lake, B.M., Salakhutdinov, R., Tenenbaum, J.B.: Human-level concept learning through probabilistic program induction. Science **350**(6266), 1332–1338 (2015)
29. Lake, B.M., Salakhutdinov, R., Tenenbaum, J.B.: The Omniglot challenge: a 3-year progress report. Curr. Opin. Behav. Sci. **29**, 97–104 (2019)
30. Lake, B.M., Ullman, T.D., Tenenbaum, J.B., Gershman, S.J.: Building machines that learn and think like people. Behav. Brain Sci. **40**, e253 (2017)
31. Lao, J., Louf, R.: BlackJAX: A sampling library for JAX (2020). http://github.com/blackjax-devs/blackjax
32. LeCun, Y., Bengio, Y., Hinton, G.: Deep learning. Nature **521**(7553), 436–444 (2015)
33. Maji, S., Kannala, J., Rahtu, E., Blaschko, M., Vedaldi, A.: Fine-grained visual classification of aircraft. Tech. rep. (2013)
34. Martin, O.A., Kumar, R., Lao, J.: Bayesian Modeling and Computation in Python. Chapman and Hall/CRC (2022)
35. Nichol, A., Achiam, J., Schulman, J.: On first-order meta-learning algorithms (2018). arXiv preprint arXiv:1803.02999
36. Nimier-David, M., Vicini, D., Zeltner, T., Jakob, W.: Mitsuba 2: a retargetable forward and inverse renderer. ACM Trans. Graph. (TOG) **38**(6), 1–17 (2019)
37. Park, K., Mousavian, A., Xiang, Y., Fox, D.: LatentFusion: end-to-end differentiable reconstruction and rendering for unseen object pose estimation. In: Proceedings of the IEEE/CVF Conference on Computer Vision and Pattern Recognition, pp. 10710–10719 (2020)
38. Peter Shirley, Trevor David Black, S.H.: Ray tracing in one weekend (2024). https://raytracing.github.io/books/RayTracingInOneWeekend.html
39. Pharr, M., Jakob, W., Humphreys, G.: Physically based rendering: From theory to implementation. MIT Press (2023)
40. Phong, B.T.: Illumination for computer generated pictures. Commun. ACM **18**(6), 311–317 (1975)
41. Ramesh, A., et al.: Zero-shot text-to-image generation. In: International Conference on Machine Learning, pp. 8821–8831. PMLR (2021)
42. Ronneberger, O., Fischer, P., Brox, T.: U-Net: convolutional networks for biomedical image segmentation. In: Navab, N., Hornegger, J., Wells, W.M., Frangi, A.F. (eds.) MICCAI 2015. LNCS, vol. 9351, pp. 234–241. Springer, Cham (2015). https://doi.org/10.1007/978-3-319-24574-4_28
43. Rule, J.S., Tenenbaum, J.B., Piantadosi, S.T.: The child as hacker. Trends Cogn. Sci. **24**(11), 900–915 (2020)
44. Scott, D.: Density estimation: Theory, practice and visualization. The curse of dimensionality and dimension reduction, pp. 195–217 (1992)
45. Simonyan, K., Zisserman, A.: Very deep convolutional networks for large-scale image recognition (2014). arXiv preprint arXiv:1409.1556
46. Snell, J., Swersky, K., Zemel, R.: Prototypical networks for few-shot learning. In: Advances in Neural Information Processing Systems, vol. 30 (2017)

47. Spielberg, A., et al.: Differentiable visual computing for inverse problems and machine learning. Nat. Mach. Intell. **5**(11), 1189–1199 (2023)
48. Sun, J., et al.: OnePose: one-shot object pose estimation without cad models. In: Proceedings of the IEEE/CVF Conference on Computer Vision and Pattern Recognition, pp. 6825–6834 (2022)
49. Tenenbaum, J.B., Kemp, C., Griffiths, T.L., Goodman, N.D.: How to grow a mind: statistics, structure, and abstraction. Science **331**(6022), 1279–1285 (2011)
50. Valdenegro-Toro, M.: I find your lack of uncertainty in computer vision disturbing. In: Proceedings of the IEEE/CVF Conference on Computer Vision and Pattern Recognition, pp. 1263–1272 (2021)
51. Vinyals, O., Blundell, C., Lillicrap, T., Wierstra, D., et al.: Matching networks for one shot learning. In: Advances in Neural Information Processing Systems, vol. 29 (2016)
52. Wang, J., et al.: Deep high-resolution representation learning for visual recognition. IEEE Trans. Pattern Anal. Mach. Intell. **43**(10), 3349–3364 (2020)
53. Wang, Y., Yao, Q., Kwok, J.T., Ni, L.M.: Generalizing from a few examples: a survey on few-shot learning. ACM Comput. Surv. (CSUR) **53**(3), 1–34 (2020)
54. Xu, F., Tenenbaum, J.B.: Word learning as bayesian inference. Psychol. Rev. **114**(2), 245 (2007)
55. Zhang, R., Isola, P., Efros, A.A., Shechtman, E., Wang, O.: The unreasonable effectiveness of deep features as a perceptual metric. In: Proceedings of the IEEE Conference on Computer Vision and Pattern Recognition, pp. 586–595 (2018)
56. Zhao, S., Jakob, W., Li, T.M.: Physics-based differentiable rendering: a comprehensive introduction. In: ACM SIGGRAPH 2020 Courses, vol. 14, pp. 1–14 (2020)

Simple and Effective Transfer Learning for Neuro-Symbolic Integration

Alessandro Daniele[1]($\boxtimes$), Tommaso Campari[1], Sagar Malhotra[2], and Luciano Serafini[1]

[1] Fondazione Bruno Kessler, Trento, Italy
{daniele,tcampari,serafini}@fbk.eu
[2] TU Wien, Vienna, Austria
sagar.malhotra@tuwien.ac.at

Abstract. Deep Learning (DL) techniques have achieved remarkable successes in recent years. However, their ability to generalize and execute reasoning tasks remains a challenge. A potential solution to this issue is Neuro-Symbolic Integration (NeSy), where neural approaches are combined with symbolic reasoning. Most of these methods exploit a neural network to map perceptions to symbols and a logical reasoner to predict the output of the downstream task. These methods exhibit superior generalization capacity compared to fully neural architectures. However, they suffer from several issues, including slow convergence, learning difficulties with complex perception tasks, and convergence to local minima. This paper proposes a simple yet effective method to ameliorate these problems. The key idea involves pretraining a neural model on the downstream task. Then, a NeSy model is trained on the same task via transfer learning, where the weights of the perceptual part are injected from the pretrained network. The key observation of our work is that the neural network fails to generalize only at the level of the symbolic part while being perfectly capable of learning the mapping from perceptions to symbols. We have tested our training strategy on various SOTA NeSy methods and datasets, demonstrating consistent improvements in the aforementioned problems.

1 Introduction

Methods based on Neural Networks (NNs) have advanced the state-of-the-art across a wide array of fields like image recognition [32], speech processing [19], and natural language processing [31]. However, even in applications where Deep Learning (DL) excels, it shows minimal reasoning capabilities [20]. This severely restricts the applicability of NNs in scenarios where reasoning over perception inputs is required to guarantee safety and reliability, e.g., in autonomous driving applications [15]. *Neuro-Symbolic* (NeSy) [4,26] systems integrate NNs and symbolic reasoning. Using a reasoning engine, they allow learning of symbolic abstraction for perception inputs and reasoning over these symbolic abstractions. A key feature of NeSy systems is that they support explainability and out-of-distribution generalization for complex tasks. For

---

A. Daniele and T. Campari—Equal contribution.

© The Author(s), under exclusive license to Springer Nature Switzerland AG 2024
T. R. Besold et al. (Eds.): NeSy 2024, LNAI 14979, pp. 166–179, 2024.
https://doi.org/10.1007/978-3-031-71167-1_9

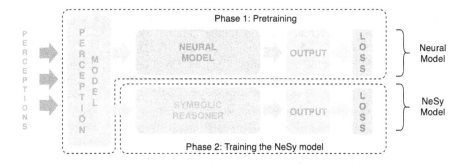

Fig. 1. Training procedure overview: in the first phase, a neural network model is trained on the downstream task; in the second phase, the NeSy method is trained starting from the previously learned perception model.

example, in the MNIST addition task [22], as shown in Fig. 2 (right), a NeSy system can learn the label 3 and 0 for the MNIST images, given only the fact that the MNIST digits sum to 3, and the rule that $3 + 0 = 3$. Since an expert can change the rules in the symbolic reasoner, the same architecture can be utilized for multi-digit addition tasks, where two sequences of MNIST digits must be added. This can be achieved by only providing new expert rules with no additional training required for the perception part. Furthermore, recent lines of NeSy works, such as Deep Symbolic Learning (DSL) [8] and Deep Concept Reasoner (DCR) [3], have also managed to learn both the logical rules and the perception labels simultaneously—showing that NeSy systems have the potential for out-of-distribution generalization even without any expert intervention.

Most NeSy systems comprise a perception part, mapping perception inputs to symbols, and a reasoning engine that gives the final output. The perception part is composed of one or more NNs. A key challenge to NeSy systems is the need to train such NNs through the weak supervision coming from a symbolic reasoning model. This is significantly challenging as the training signal needs to be propagated from discrete symbolic reasoners to continuously parameterized NNs. Consequently, the NeSy model could be affected by slow convergence and difficulties dealing with complex perception inputs. Furthermore, the weak supervision is provided in the form of labels of the downstream task. As an example, the label $x + y = 3$ of the downstream task (see Fig. 2) can be satisfied by multiple labellings, e.g. $1 + 2 = 3, 0 + 3 = 3$ etc. This issue has been formally characterized as *Reasoning Shortcut* (RS) [23] and can lead to stagnation in local minima. More precisely, an RS occurs when some latent concepts learned by a NeSy architecture do not correspond to the intended concept, i.e., the concept expected by the given knowledge. Our strategy could reduce this problem since it reduces the effort of the NeSy model for learning the concepts. One specific instance of this problem has been recognized in [9], where Iterative Local Refinement (ILR) has been trapped in this kind of local minima for the MNISTSum task. For this reason, we tested the pretraining strategy with ILR, obtaining a consistent reduction of local minima.

Previous works show a significant improvement by adopting pre-processing techniques that learn perception labels separately from the reasoning task. [27] uses generative adversarial neural networks (GANs) [16] to obtain MNIST digit clusters. Embed2sym [1] takes a different direction, it trains a fully neural model directly on the downstream task. It then extracts the embeddings for the perception inputs and uses K-Means clustering to cluster the embeddings. The problem of mapping the cluster labels to the intended logical symbols is then solved using answer set programming. A key challenge with both of these methods is that the clustering process requires intervention from an expert for the choice of the clustering algorithm and the distance metric. Furthermore, it is hard to see how these methods can be integrated into or help end-to-end systems where both rules and symbols are learnt simultaneously, e.g., [8,21]. Instead, our framework is easily applicable in these types of methods, like DSL, where the symbolic rules are learned alongside the perceptions.

This paper proposes an adaptive pre-processing step that learns embeddings of the perception inputs based on the downstream task. Unlike the methods proposed in the literature, our framework does not require additional supervision and applies to a vast array of NeSy systems. It constitutes a simple pretraining step that learns informative embeddings for perception inputs, just using the supervision of the downstream task, without any additional clustering or symbolic reasoning. Figure 1 shows a general overview of the method, where two models for the downstream tasks are defined. The neural model continuously approximates the symbolic reasoner and is trained in the first phase. The perception model, which maps input features to embeddings, is then used by the NeSy model in the second learning phase. Then, at inference, only the NeSy architecture is used since the symbolic reasoner perfectly represents the symbolic knowledge rather than approximating it, allowing for better out-of-distribution generalization than the neural architecture.

We empirically demonstrate that these embeddings form a much more tailored input for training the NeSy system than the raw input itself. Our method significantly improves classical NeSy benchmarks and can also scale NeSy systems to previously unattainable, complex tasks.

2 Related Works

Neuro-Symbolic Integration [4,25,26] have evolved in multiple directions. Some of the key differentiating features amongst NeSy systems are the type of logic they use, and the way in which they exploit knowledge.

A large variety of NeSy systems are based on the idea of enforcing logical constraints on the outputs of a NN. In this category, most methods include logical constraints through the addition of a regularization term in the loss, which enforces satisfaction of the logical constraints. Semantic loss [29] aims at guiding the NN training through a logic-based differentiable regularizer based on probabilistic semantics, obtained by compiling logical knowledge into a Sentential Decision Diagram (SDD) [11]. Other methods in this category are Logic Tensor Networks [2] and Semantic-Based Regularization [13], which encode logical knowledge into a differentiable function based on fuzzy logic semantics. This function term is then used as a regularizer in the loss function. Since these methods incorporate symbolic knowledge into the loss function, the knowledge encoded in the logical constraints does not play any role at inference time. Other methods that enforce constraints in NN outputs are Knowledge Enhanced Neural Network (KENN) [10], and Iterative Local Refinement (ILR) [9]. Unlike previously mentioned methods, ILR and KENN extend a basic NN with additional layers that change the predictions to enhance logical knowledge satisfaction. As in LTN and SBR, the satisfaction level of a formula is computed using fuzzy semantics. KENN and ILR exploit background knowledge also at inference time. Note that, unlike the systems based on probabilistic logic, fuzzy logic-based methods have the advantage that the exploration of the symbolic search space can take place without any additional cost of the potentially intractable knowledge compilation and weighted model counting steps. However, these systems tend to stagnate in local minima.

Another strand consists of NeSy methods that are obtained by extending existing symbolic reasoners with neural inputs. DeepProbLog [22] is a neural extension of ProbLog [6]. The key feature of DeepProbLog is that it admits neural predicates i.e., predicates whose associated probability parameters are obtained as an output from a NN. The system utilizes SDD [11] fortified with gradient semirings, to provide an end-to-end differentiable system capable of learning the neural network through the weak supervision coming from the downstream task's labels. Recent advancements have sought to offer similar neural extensions to other symbolic solvers, such as DeepStochLog [28] and NeurASP [30]. DeepStochLog [28] extends Stochastic Definite Clause Grammars [17]—a context-sensitive probabilistic grammar formalism. Similarly, NeurASP [30] extends Answer Set Programming [5]. A key challenge faced by systems extending symbolic reasoners is that they inherit, and potentially worsen, the computational complexity of inference.

More recently, new NeSy approaches have been proposed that enable learning both the symbolic labels for perception inputs and the symbolic rules themselves. Deep Symbolic Learning (DSL) [8] makes use of Reinforcement Learning policies to discretize internal latent symbols and select the underlying symbolic rules. Although it learns also the rules, DSL proved to be more scalable than other NeSy frameworks that exploit the given knowledge. However, training DSL can be challenging due to the slow convergence when the number of internal symbols increases. For instance, to learn the multi-digit version of the sum, it is required to use curriculum learning. Our experimental analysis shows that our pretraining step allows us to highly improve the efficacy of DSL reducing the aforementioned problem, allowing for learning the multi-digit sum without curriculum learning and generally increasing the convergence speed of the method.

A more recent method that learns both rules and perceptions is Deep Concept Reasoner (DCR) [3], which builds syntactic rule structures using concept embeddings. The concept embeddings have vectors of fuzzy truth values associated with them, leading to clear and interpretable semantics for learned rules, and subsequent inference performed on them. However, DCR requires more computational resources as compared to DSL and it has not been considered in our work.

The NeSy approach most relevant to our work is Embed2Sym [1]. It separately trains a NN on the downstream NeSy task and utilizes clustering for extracting symbolic concepts from the learned embeddings. It then uses Answer Set Programming(ASP) to map cluster labels to logical symbols based on the given symbolic knowledge. While similar to our pretraining strategy, the method is specialized on a specific architecture, and can not be applied on other methods. Conversely, our approach can be applied on a variety of NeSy systems, including the ones that learns the logical rules, allowing for solving tasks precluded to Embed2Sym.

3 Method

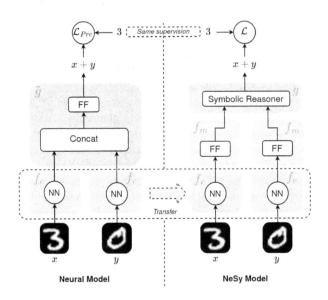

Fig. 2. An example of our learning strategy on the MNISTSum task: on the first phase (left), we train a neural model for the downstream task; on the second phase (right), we use the pretrained weights of the neural network f_e as a starting point for the NeSy architecture, which learns the mapping from embeddings to symbols (f_m) and, in case of DSL, the symbolic function g.

NeSy systems[1] can be seen as a composition of *perception* and *symbolic* functions [8]. In most NeSy systems, the perception function $f : \mathcal{X} \rightarrow \mathcal{S}$ is represented as a NN with learnable parameters, whereas $g : \mathcal{S}^n \rightarrow \mathcal{S}$ represents expert-provided rules which allow to infer the downstream task labels from the internal latent symbols found by f [9,22,28]. In other words, the NeSy system computes a downstream task that consists in the function $g(f(x_1), \ldots, f(x_n))$.

Figure 2 (right) shows the typical architecture of a NeSy system for the MNISTSum task, where two MNIST images x and y are provided as input, and the downstream task consists on calculating the sum of their respective digits. We additionally assume that

---

[1] Here we refer to NeSy systems in the specific context where the symbolic reasoner is employed to infer new facts from the symbolic knowledge. This excludes methods like LTN where the knowledge is merely used to constrain the outputs of the neural network. It should be noted that not all NeSy systems operate in this manner.

Fig. 3. t-SNE applied to embeddings of f_e learned by the neural model on the MNISTSum (left) and CIFARSum (right) tasks. Colours represent different digits.

the perception neural network f is represented as the composition of two functions, f_e (blue box) and f_m (orange box), representing the mapping from perceptions to embeddings and the mapping from embeddings to symbols, respectively. Formally:

$$f(x) = f_m(f_e(x))$$

where $f_e : \mathcal{X}^n \to \mathcal{R}^m$ and $f_m : \mathcal{R}^m \to \mathcal{S}$. The idea is to train a fully neural model (Fig. 2 (left)) for the downstream task. Such a model comprises the f_e function and a continuous approximation $\tilde{g}$ of the symbolic component of the NeSy method:

$$\tilde{g}([z|w]) \approx g(f_m(z), f_m(w))$$

where $[\cdot|\cdot]$ represents the concatenation of two vectors.

Our method consists of two phases: in the first one, we train the neural model; in the second we copy and freeze the learned weights of f_e (blue box in Fig. 2) into the NeSy architecture. In this way, the NeSy method has to learn only f_m (orange box) instead of the entire f. In other words, it has to learn only the mapping from embeddings to symbols. An exception is DSL [8], which learns both f and g (green box). With the pretraining, it has to learn f_m and g, allowing for much faster convergence.

Note that one has to use a neural architecture for pretraining which is task dependent. For instance, for the MNISTSum task, where the inputs are two single images, the concatenated embeddings are parsed by only a Feed Forward layer (Fig. 2 (left)). Instead, in the multi-digit variant of the task, the FF is substituted by a Recurrent Neural Network (RNN).

It is worth mentioning that the RNN has very competitive performance compared to other methods with similar accuracy, but much faster training. However, it generalizes poorly when increasing the number of digits with respect to the training samples. We experimentally observe that its performance does not degrade if the numbers have the same length as compared to the training set. In other words, the RNN struggles with out-of-distribution generalization. This can be seen in Table 4, where the performance of the RNN decrease significantly when passing from 2 digits(accuracy 92.9%) to 4 digit (73.8%) and 15 digit (18.9%) numbers. This behaviour can be explained by errors produced at the symbolic level (i.e., at the level of the function $\tilde{g}$) due to the continuous approximation defined by the neural model. On the contrary, the mapping of the perceptions to the internal symbols (f_e) is generally correct since otherwise, the accuracy would be lower even with length 2 (the training numbers' length). Indeed, when analyzing the learned embeddings with t-SNE (Fig. 3), we can clearly distinguish the various digits, confirming that the learned embeddings contain meaningful information to correctly classify the digits.

4 Experiments

In our experiments, we focus on applying our approach to popular NeSy methods, namely: NeurASP [30], DeepProblog [22], DeepStochLog [28], Iterative Local Refinement [9] and Deep Symbolic Learning [8]. We selected these methods due to their respective challenges:

- NeurASP (NAP), DeepProblog (DPL), and DeepStochLog (DStL) underperform when dealing with complex perception (e.g., CIFAR images);
- Iterative Local Refinement (ILR) often gets trapped in local minima;
- Deep Symbolic Learning (DSL) struggles to converge when dealing with problems with large amounts of latent symbols due to the large hypothesis space it needs to explore.

We test the aforementioned NeSy systems with and without the pretraining technique (PR) proposed in the paper, across a wide range of NeSy tasks. First, we briefly summarise our experimental results, followed by a detailed analysis of each experiment. The key results of our analysis are:

- PR enhances convergence rates, leading to faster convergence across all the tested methods and tasks;
- PR reduces local minima, leading to improved accuracy across most of the tested methods and tasks;
- PR allows the tested NeSy methods to deal with complex perception inputs, where otherwise very poor results are obtained;

Moreover, due to the freezing of f_e parameters, each epoch requires less time and memory for the backward pass of the back-propagation. Consequently, the overhead for the pretraining is negligible compared to the total gains obtained by adding it. For instance, the additional cost for the pretraining phase is 9 s (0.45 s per 20 epochs for the CNN training in Table 1), while the time for training DSL has been reduced from 47.5 to 5.6 s.

Overall, our experiments provide valuable insights into the limitations of the considered methods, showcasing how a pretraining phase overcomes specific challenges and improves their performance across diverse tasks.

Implementation Details. All the experiments were conducted with a machine equipped with an NVIDIA GTX 3070 with 12 GB RAM. For digit classification, we use the same CNN as [22], while for CIFARSum, we used a ResNet18 [18] model, which provides a higher capacity than the CNN used for digit classification. This higher capacity is needed to correctly classify CIFAR images. The embedding e obtained by $f_e(x)$ has size 84. In the MNIST MultiDigitSum model pretrained for DSL^{PR}, the RNN has a hidden size of 80. As optimizer, we used MadGrad [12]. Results are averaged over 10 runs. The t-SNE plots were obtained by applying the reduction technique directly on the embeddings e and by reducing them to size 2.

Evaluation Metrics. The standard metric used for the tackled task is the accuracy applied directly to the predictions of the final output (e.g., the sum value in the MNIST-Sum). This allows us to understand the general behaviour of the entire model. For the MNISTMultiDigitSum we also measured the fine-grained accuracy, that is, the average test accuracy of classifying the individual digits, e.g. if the output of the model is 12344 and the ground truth is 12345, then the fine-grained accuracy will be 0.8, since 4 digits out of 5 in the output are correct. Furthermore, we also measured the number of epochs required for convergence and the epoch time for every model we tested.

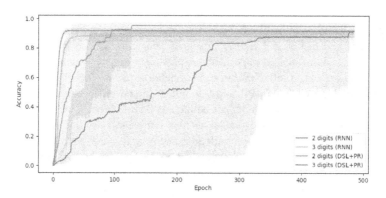

Fig. 4. Minimum and maximum (transparent boundaries) and average accuracies (solid lines) obtained while training the RNN (on 2 or 3 digits) and DSL^{PR}. DSL convergence is slower but can generalize to longer sequences with higher results. The results are obtained across ten runs.

4.1 MNISTSum

In the MNIST sum task, [22], we are given triplets (X, Y, Z), where X and Y are images of hand-written digits, while Z is the result of the sum of the two digits, e.g., (🗷, 🗷, 8). The goal is to learn to recognize MNIST images, using only the sum of the digits they represent as supervision. The results for this task are provided in Table 1.

Table 1. Results on MNISTSum task. Δ_{Acc} is the accuracy difference without and with PR. TE is the time required for each epoch, and #E is the number of epochs.

	Acc.(%)	Δ_{Acc}	TE/#E	$\Delta_{\#E}$
CNN	98.2±0.8	–	0.45s/20	–
NAP	97.3±0.3	–	109s/1	–
NAP^{PR}	98.1±0.5	0.8	74s/1	–
DPL	97.2±0.5	–	367s/1	–
DPL^{PR}	97.6±0.3	0.4	284s/1	–
DStL	97.9±0.1	–	8.2s/2	–
DStL^{PR}	97.4±0.3	-0.5	4.2s/1	-1
ILR	74.0±24.6	–	1.5s/10	
ILR^{PR}	96.2±0.4	22.2	1.7s/1	-9
DSL	98.8±0.3	–	0.95s/50	
DSL^{PR}	98.6±0.1	-0.2	0.56s/10	-40
DSL$_{NB(20)}$	97.9±0.3	–	0.99s/200	
DSL$_{NB(1K)}$	8.7±0.2	–	7.4s/1000	
DSL$_{NB(1K)}^{PR}$	98.2±1.2	89.5	5.2s/30	-970

NeSy methods based on probabilistic semantics, such as DPL, NAP, and DStL, perform both accurately and fast on the MNISTSum task. Hence, DPL^{PR}, NAP^{PR}, and DStL^{PR} show only marginal differences in performance from the non-PR versions, as not much space for improvement is left. Similarly, this phenomenon is also observed for DSL, which performs well with both PR and without it. However, in DSL, the number of symbols is not given apriori and an upper bound can be provided. A larger upper bound on the number of symbols leads to a lesser bias but a larger symbolic search space. We ran DSL on the MNISTSum task with an upper bound of 20 symbols, managing to get good results, even without PR. However, when the upper bound is moved to 1000, DSL does not converge in 1000 epochs (see DSL$_{NB(1K)}$). But when DSL is trained with the proposed pretraining method, i.e., DSL$_{NB(1K)}^{PR}$, it manages to show fast convergence with high accuracy. We see significant improvement with ILR^{PR} compared to ILR, with almost doubling of the accuracy.

4.2 CIFARSum

The CIFARSum task [1] is similar to MNISTSum, but the MNIST digits are replaced by CIFAR10 images, and each class is labelled with a number between 0 and 9. This task allows testing NeSy systems with a more complex perception task while keeping the reasoning complexity the same as the MNISTSum task. The additional complexity in the perception space requires models with higher capacity. To this end, we used a ResNet18 backbone for all the tested NeSy systems. Using a larger model increases the time required for every epoch but provides better perception classification performance. The results obtained on the CIFARSum task are summarized in Table 2. Just like the

Table 2. Results on CIFARSum task. Δ_{Acc} is the accuracy difference without and with PR. TE is the time required for each epoch, and #E is the number of epochs.

	Acc (%)	Δ_{Acc}	TE/#E	$\Delta_{\#E}$
ResNet18	87.1 ±1.4	–	2.2 s/100	–
Embed2Sym	84.4	–	5908 s/–	–
DPL	31.4 ±1.1		699s/20	
DPL^{PR}	75.7 ±1.9	+44.3	473.1s/1	–19
DStL	63.7 ±0.4		10.5s/50	
DStL^{PR}	90.6 ±1.2	+26.9	7.4s/10	–40
DSL	8.4 ±2.7		13.3s/300	
DSL^{PR}	81.6 ±0.9	+73.2	2.7s/30	–270
ILR	32.6 ±16.2		134.0s/30	
ILR^{PR}	69.3 ±0.1	+36.7	133.0s/2	–28
NAP	7.2 ±1.4		1108s/1	
NAP^{PR}	82.0 ±1.7	+74.8	283.0s/1	–

Table 3. Results on MNIST MultiOp task. Δ_{Acc} is the accuracy difference without and with PR. TE is the time required for each epoch, and #E is the number of epochs.

	Acc. (%)	Δ_{Acc}	TE/#E	$\Delta_{\#E}$
CNN	96.6 ±0.8		0.56s/50	
DSL	92.2 ±0.4		0.84s/9000	
DSL^{PR}	93.5 ±0.2	+1.3	0.61s/200	-8800

MNISTSum task, the accuracy is measured over the accuracy of the sum, obtained by adding the digit labels of the CIFAR10 images.

All the tested methods suffered a significant loss of accuracy (in comparison to MNISTSum) when dealing with this task. However, each NeSy method shows significant improvements with the proposed PR method. Furthermore, all the NeSy systems we tested show significant improvements in the number of epochs required for convergence and also in the run time of each epoch. Hence, getting a significant gain in total runtime. Notice that in Table 2, the row with ResNet18, shows the time required for pretraining. Again it can be checked that the overhead for getting the embeddings is marginal in comparison to the total improvement in the run time. Hence, this the CIFARSum task demonstrates that the PR enables both higher accuracy and faster convergence, in presence of complex perception tasks.

4.3 MNISTMultiOp

In this section, we focus on the effect of PR when both perception and symbolic rules need to be learned. To date, very few such NeSy systems exist [21], and in this paper, we choose DSL for this analysis. Already in the MNISTSum task, DSL^{PR} converges faster

Table 4. Results obtained on the MNIST MultiDigitSum task (for 2, 4, 15, 1000 digits). Fine-grained accuracy is the average test digit accuracy. T/O stands for timeout (>14400 s).

Accuracy (%)				
	2	4	15	1000
RNN	92.9 ±0.2	73.8 ±0.4	18.9 ±1.6	0.0 ±0.0
Embed2Sym	97.7	91.6	66.4	–
NAP	93.9 ±0.7	T/O	T/O	T/O
DPL	95.2 ±1.7	T/O	T/O	T/O
DStL	96.4 ±0.1	92.7 ±0.6	T/O	T/O
DSL^{CL}	95.0 ±0.7	88.9 ±0.5	64.1 ±1.5	0.0 ±0.0
DSL^{PR}	95.3 ±0.2	92.2 ±0.2	74.2 ±1.1	0.0 ±0.0

Fine-grained Accuracy (%)				
	2	4	15	1000
RNN	97.5 ±0.1	93.5 ±0.3	89.5 ±0.5	89.3 ±0.5
DSL^{CL}	97.9 ±0.1	97.3 ±0.1	96.7 ±0.1	96.5 ±0.1
DSL^{PR}	98.2 ±0.3	97.9 ±0.2	98.1 ±0.3	97.7 ±0.4

than DSL. We now investigate the effect of PR on DSL, in the much more complex MNISTMultiOp task, as introduced in [8]. This task extends the MNIST Sum task by incorporating additional operators as perception inputs. The perceptions for this task consist of two images from the MNIST dataset and a third symbol representing an operation selected from the set $\{+, -, \times, \div\}$. The images representing the operations are obtained from the EMNIST dataset [7], where we extracted the letter images for A, B, C, and D, corresponding to $+$, $-$, $\times$, and $\div$ respectively. It is important to note that the hypothesis space for this task encompasses a staggering 82^{400} possible symbolic functions. The results obtained with DSL and DSL^{PR} are shown in Table 3. It is worth noticing that DSL required 9000 epochs to solve the task due to the huge exploration phase required to learn the symbolic function. This is majorly due to the wasted exploration that takes place when the underlying perception of symbols mapping learnt by the NN is wrong. Instead, DSL^{PR} converged in 200 epochs, compared to the 9000 epochs required by DSL. DSL^{PR} also gives better accuracy. The key reason to the improvements in DSL^{PR} is that with the embeddings learnt through PR, DSL^{PR} immediately learns to map the MNIST digits to symbols and the EMNIST letters to symbols. This saves significant exploration in the symbolic hypothesis space, which is otherwise done with wrong underlying mappings from the NN.

4.4 MNISTMultiDigitSum

The last task we considered is the MNISTMultiDigitSum. It is a generalization of the MNISTSum, where the goal is to learn to perform the sum of numbers composed of multiple digits. Table 4 shows the results achieved by the SOTA methods[2]. This task is particularly difficult: probabilistic methods like DPL, NAP, and DstL reach good accuracies, but at inference, they can scale to at most to 4 digits. The RNN learns very efficiently (see Fig. 4) and with very high performances, however, it does not generalize to longer sequences. Finally, DSL cannot converge unless trained with Curriculum Learning (DSL^{CL}), i.e., by first learning from examples with one digit numbers, and then learning from more complex numbers of length two. However, when trained with PR, i.e., DSL^{PR} does not require Curriculum Learning.

Notably, DSL^{PR}, as also DSL^{CL}, have an almost perfect Fine-grained accuracy, while the RNN performance degrades when the input digits arity grows. DSL^{PR} is also capable of learning how to solve the task even with a training set composed of 3 digits long numbers, although with a slower convergence compared to the training with 2 digits (see Fig. 4).

Limitations and Future Works. Pretraining on the downstream task greatly helps NeSy systems in faster convergence and mitigation of local minima. However, the extent to which this approach can be extended needs to be investigated, especially in the cases where rules need to be learned from raw perception data. At present, extracting embeddings in settings where the arity of the symbolic function is not known apriori (e.g. autonomous driving) is hard. However, this limitation is fundamental to most NeSy systems, as very few currently manage to learn rules from raw perception inputs. Furthermore, this approach presents some limitations. For example, looking at Fig. 4 shows the slower convergence of DSL when training on three digits sum w.r.t. to the one on two digits. This suggests that when the task becomes harder both in perception and reasoning, the PR alone cannot push to fast convergence. It would be interesting to explore other similar techniques in the future. An example can be to use the model used during the pretraining phase not as a pretraining but as an auxiliary loss to be optimized during the training of the NeSy systems. This should regularize the training pipeline and can be further combined with Self-Supervised tasks such as Rotation [14] or Jigsaw Puzzle [24] to learn complementary signals.

5 Conclusions

The paper introduces a general methodology that allows efficient training and scaling of a vast array of NeSy systems. The key insight of our methodology is that effective embeddings for perception inputs can be obtained with only weak supervision coming from the downstream task, without using any labelled data for the perception inputs or any symbolic reasoning. We investigate the proposed methodology on various state-of-the-art NeSy systems and on multiple NeSy tasks. Our experimental analysis shows that the embeddings generated through the proposed method, form a much more informative input to the NeSy system, than the raw input itself. We observed consistent and significant improvement in both accuracy and run-time on all the tested NeSy methods. Our

---

[2] Note that ILR is not considered since it is propositional. While, in theory, it can be extended to first-order logic through propositionalization, such a change goes beyond the scope of this work.

methodology also enabled tasks with complex perception components (e.g., CIFAR10 images), which were previously unattainable for the tested NeSy systems. Furthermore, the additional computational overhead, required to learn the embeddings is marginal in comparison to the run-time gains obtained by using the embeddings.

Acknowledgments. TC and LS were supported by the PNRR project Future AI Research (FAIR - PE00000013), under the NRRP MUR program funded by the NextGenerationEU.

References

1. Aspis, Y., Broda, K., Lobo, J., Russo, A.: Embed2Sym - scalable neuro-symbolic reasoning via clustered embeddings. In: International Conference on Principles of Knowledge Representation and Reasoning (2022)
2. Badreddine, S., d'Avila Garcez, A., Serafini, L., Spranger, M.: Logic tensor networks. Artif. Intell. (2022)
3. Barbiero, P., et al.: Interpretable neural-symbolic concept reasoning. In: Krause, A., Brunskill, E., Cho, K., Engelhardt, B., Sabato, S., Scarlett, J. (eds.) ICML 2023. Proceedings of Machine Learning Research, vol. 202, pp. 1801–1825. PMLR (2023)
4. Besold, T.R., et al.: Neural-symbolic learning and reasoning: a survey and interpretation. In: Neuro-Symbolic Artificial Intelligence: The State of the Art (2021)
5. Brewka, G., Eiter, T., Truszczyński, M.: Answer set programming at a glance. ACM Commun.(2011)
6. Bruynooghe, M., et al.: Problog technology for inference in a probabilistic first order logic (2010)
7. Cohen, G., Afshar, S., Tapson, J., Van Schaik, A.: Emnist: extending mnist to handwritten letters (2017)
8. Daniele, A., Campari, T., Malhotra, S., Serafini, L.: Deep symbolic learning: discovering symbols and rules from perceptions. In: IJCAI 2023, pp. 3597–3605. ijcai.org (2023)
9. Daniele, A., van Krieken, E., Serafini, L., van Harmelen, F.: Refining neural network predictions using background knowledge. Mach. Learn. 1–39 (2023)
10. Daniele, A., Serafini, L.: Knowledge enhanced neural networks. In: Pacific Rim International Conference on Artificial Intelligence (2019)
11. Darwiche, A.: SDD: a new canonical representation of propositional knowledge bases. In: IJCAI (2011)
12. Defazio, A., Jelassi, S.: Adaptivity without compromise: a momentumized, adaptive, dual averaged gradient method for stochastic optimization. JMLR (2022)
13. Diligenti, M., Gori, M., Saccà, C.: Semantic-based regularization for learning and inference. Artif. Intell. **244**, 143–165 (2017)
14. Feng, Z., Xu, C., Tao, D.: Self-supervised representation learning by rotation feature decoupling. In: CVPR (2019)
15. Giunchiglia, E., Stoian, M.C., Khan, S., Cuzzolin, F., Lukasiewicz, T.: Road-r: the autonomous driving dataset with logical requirements. Mach. Learn. (2023)
16. Goodfellow, I., et al.: Generative adversarial nets. In: NeurIPS (2014)
17. Have, C.T.: Stochastic definite clause grammars. In: Proceedings of the International Conference RANLP-2009 (2009)
18. He, K., Zhang, X., Ren, S., Sun, J.: Deep residual learning for image recognition. In: CVPR (2016)
19. Hinton, G., et al.: Deep neural networks for acoustic modeling in speech recognition: The shared views of four research groups. IEEE Signal Process. Maga. (2012)

20. Liévin, V., Hother, C.E., Motzfeldt, A.G., Winther, O.: Can large language models reason about medical questions? Patterns **5**(3), 100943 (2024)
21. Liu, A., Xu, H., Van den Broeck, G., Liang, Y.: Out-of-distribution generalization by neural-symbolic joint training. In: AAAI (2023)
22. Manhaeve, R., Dumancic, S., Kimmig, A., Demeester, T., De Raedt, L.: Deepproblog: neural probabilistic logic programming. In: NeurIPS (2018)
23. Marconato, E., Teso, S., Passerini, A.: Neuro-symbolic reasoning shortcuts: mitigation strategies and their limitations. In: d'Avila Garcez, A.S., Besold, T.R., Gori, M., Jiménez-Ruiz, E. (eds.) International Workshop on Neural-Symbolic Learning and Reasoning 2023. CEUR Workshop Proceedings, vol. 3432, pp. 162–166. CEUR-WS.org (2023)
24. Noroozi, M., Favaro, P.: Unsupervised learning of visual representations by solving jigsaw puzzles. In: Leibe, B., Matas, J., Sebe, N., Welling, M. (eds.) ECCV 2016. LNCS, vol. 9910, pp. 69–84. Springer, Cham (2016). https://doi.org/10.1007/978-3-319-46466-4_5
25. Raedt, L.D., Dumancic, S., Manhaeve, R., Marra, G.: From statistical relational to neuro-symbolic artificial intelligence. In: Bessiere, C. (ed.) IJCAI 2020, pp. 4943–4950. ijcai.org (2020)
26. Sarker, M.K., Zhou, L., Eberhart, A., Hitzler, P.: Neuro-symbolic artificial intelligence. AI Commun. **34**, 197–209 (2021)
27. Topan, S., Rolnick, D., Si, X.: Techniques for symbol grounding with satnet. In: NeurIPS (2021)
28. Winters, T., Marra, G., Manhaeve, R., De Raedt, L.: Deepstochlog: neural stochastic logic programming. In: AAAI (2022)
29. Xu, J., Zhang, Z., Friedman, T., Liang, Y., den Broeck, G.V.: A semantic loss function for deep learning with symbolic knowledge. In: ICML (2018)
30. Yang, Z., Ishay, A., Lee, J.: Neurasp: embracing neural networks into answer set programming. In: IJCAI (2020)
31. Young, T., Hazarika, D., Poria, S., Cambria, E.: Recent trends in deep learning based natural language processing. CoRR arxiv:1708.02709 (2017)
32. Zhao, Z.Q., Zheng, P., Xu, S.T., Wu, X.: Object detection with deep learning: a review. IEEE Trans. Neural Netw. Learn. Syst. **30**, 3212–3232 (2019)

Ethical Reward Machine

Jessica Ciupa[(✉)] and Vaishak Belle

Informatics Forum, University of Edinburgh, Edinburgh EH8 9AB, UK
{s1810129,vbelle}@ed.ac.uk

Abstract. The Ethical Reward Machine investigates reward design involving ethical constraints with reinforcement learning. Designed to promote good behaviour across specific domains, such as simulated driving and search-and-rescue scenarios, the Ethical Reward Machine explores ethical constraints based on Act Deontology and Utilitarianism. Our contribution to the literature is a novel algorithmic pipeline integrating ethical constraints into reinforcement learning through symbolic language. Our findings indicate ethical principles impact the system significantly if there is a dilemma, and that incorporating ethical principles does not increase runtime. Therefore, our results suggest that ethical considerations do not substantially burden computational resources. Ultimately, the overarching objective is to develop and validate a learning framework that ensures AI alignment with human learning and ethical policies.

Keywords: Knowledge Representation · Interpretable Reinforcement Learning · Ethics

1 Introduction

Ethical Reward Machines (ERM) explore using symbolic language to define ethical constraints in Reinforcement Learning (RL). We integrate ethical constraints into the Reward Machine (RM) framework by Icarte et al. [7]. The Reward Machine was selected for its ability to achieve a human-readable, symbolic, and interpretable reward design for RL systems. This paper addresses the research question: How can we integrate formalised ethical principles into Reward Machines to create interpretable *ethical* decision-making processes in AI? We hypothesise that by constraining the reward design with ethical principles such as Utilitarianism and Act Deontology [9], the Ethical Reward Machine (ERM) can provide human-readable behaviour modelling and justifiable decisions in scenarios like *Autonomous Driving* and *Search and Rescue*. We aim to explore which reward design processes align with each ethical principle, enabling agents to reach optimal policies while adhering to ethical constraints.

Our method involves experimental evaluation in two discrete domains: A Driving World, simulating self-driving car autonomous decisions, and the Dilemma World, simulating autonomous decisions for search and rescue operations. We explore sample efficiency in these contexts through RL methods that leverage the internal reward structure. Specifically, we focus on counterfactual reasoning, problem decomposition, and reward shaping [7]. To ensure optimal ethical policies within these domains, we employ all three methods with each ethical principle, Utilitarianism and Act Deontology [9]. The celebrated Moral Machine Experiment highlights the importance of transparency in the ethical principles guiding AI decision-making [1]. Participants in this experiment faced various moral dilemmas involving autonomous vehicles, revealing significant cultural variations in moral judgments and the complexities of encoding ethical principles into AI algorithms. Transparency in these decisions is crucial, especially when prioritising the safety of passengers versus pedestrians. The Ethical Reward Machine presented in this paper explores which RL methods enable machines to reach optimal policies when constrained by different ethical principles. By understanding how ethical principles guide scenarios via reward design, we can present interpretable decision processes, promote adherence to legal and societal norms, and foster user trust and acceptance [4].

To introduce the Ethical Reward Machine, we explore previous works on reasoning for ethical constraints in automated agents, such as ethical planners [5] and moral machines [15]. The Ethical Reward Machine offers an alternative algorithmic implementation of ethical constraints for RL. Through our experimental evaluation, we aim to identify optimal learning methods for ethical principles, addressing limitations of sample efficiency and observability found in real-world applications, which offer possibilities for complex behavioural constraints, particularly ethical and moral constraints [7]. By incorporating formalised ethical principles [9], such as Act Deontology and Utilitarianism, into the RM framework, this research provides ethical constraints for learning methodologies in RL. This paper adds experimental insights for interpretable AI, insight into learning of moral theory and ethical decision-making in autonomous systems.

2 Background

2.1 Related Works

Previous research has delved into ethical principles guiding autonomous systems in critical scenarios impacting human lives, such as self-driving vehicles [2] and robotic caregivers for vulnerable patients [13]. There is a growing interest in developing interpretable systems that reveal the inner workings of autonomous decision-making to human users, employing various strategies to enhance transparency and trust.

Dennis et al. [5] explored the integration of ethical reasoning within autonomous systems. Their paper significantly contributes to formal methods and logic-based ethical decision-making, mainly through the practical case study of autonomous vehicles. The paper highlights that formal verification, primarily linear temporal logic, is ideal for expressing what should happen at a specific moment, at a point in the future, or all points in the future. Dennis et al.[5] establish a framework for using formal methods to apply ethical principles as soft constraints, thereby enforcing an ethical policy within autonomous systems.

However, they note that future work should refine these methods and address the limitations in capturing the nuanced aspects of human ethics, particularly as their study did not encompass learning, whether in policies or plans.

Our paper aims to address the challenge of capturing the nuances of human ethics by investigating optimal methods for learning ethical principles expressed with symbolic constraints in reinforcement learning. The insights provided by our research into how ethical principles are adopted by learning agents are helpful for understanding the complexities of real-world ethical decision-making.

AI planning systems are used in various complex domains, generating plans to achieve goals from an initial state [10]. Krarup et al. [9] formalised ethical principles of Act-Deontology and Utilitarianism, are similar to the soft constraint algorithms seen in Dennis et al. [5]. However, Dennis et al. [5] allowed an autonomous system to violate an ethical principle only when no ethical option was available, ensuring that the chosen unethical option was the "least of all evils". This approach implies some flexibility in ethical adherence under constrained conditions. For implementing ethical decision-making into a discrete reinforcement learning environment, having a more defined adherence to predefined ethical guidelines is preferable. Thus, the formal methods used by Krarup et al. [9] to embed ethical principles in the planning process inspired the algorithms presented in this paper.

Vanderelst and Winfield [15] have investigated ethical principles in moral decision-making using a consequentialist approach. Their methodology employs a simulation theory of cognition, where robots utilise functional imagination to anticipate and assess potential action outcomes without execution. This concept aligns closely with cognitive theories of mental simulation, enabling predictions and decisions in complex, ethically charged scenarios. Unlike traditional rule-based AI systems that rely on explicit reasoning to dictate behaviour, this approach employs a dynamic form of artificial reasoning, evaluating actions against predefined ethical consequentialist constraints.

Furthermore, Vanderelst and Winfield's [15] research highlighted the significance of mental simulation in ethical robotics, enhancing robots' moral judgment through functional imagination. This research reflects development towards speculative reasoning, following Kahneman's System 2 Rational Reflection [8]. As such, we explore similar concepts in this paper with our learning methodology of Hierarchical Reward Machines (HRM) with ethical constraints. Implementing ethical consideration within the reward function of hierarchical reinforcement learning allows for a similar functional imagination through breaking down the task and evaluating outcomes with an explicit focus on ethical alignment. Additionally, we incorporate alternate learning methodologies beyond task decomposition, with counterfactual reasoning and reward shaping, for further complex evaluations of moral reasoning in an ethical dilemma.

Overall, our paper addresses the identified limitations in previous research by proposing a learning methodology that integrates formalised ethical principles through reward design, providing a more nuanced approach to capturing real-world complexities and enhancing the interpretability of AI decision-making processes in ethical autonomous systems.

2.2 Reward Machines and Reinforcement Learning

Reinforcement Learning (RL) focuses on agents learning sequential decision-making with minimal supervision, adapting through trial and error in dynamic environments to achieve optimal behaviour [14]. RL agents typically operate within a Markov Decision Process (MDP) environment, defined as a tuple $\mathcal{M} = \langle S, A, r, p, \gamma \rangle$, where S is a finite set of *states*, A is a finite set of *actions*, $r : S \times A \times S \rightarrow \mathbb{R}$ represents the *Reward Function*, $p(s_{t+1}|s_t, a_t)$ is the *Transition Probability Distribution*, and $\gamma \in (0, 1]$ denotes the *Discount Factor*. The designated *terminal states* mark the end of the decision-making process.

However, a Reward Machine enhances an RL system by providing an interpretable formal problem description and addresses challenges like sample efficiency and partial observability. It takes abstract descriptions of the environment as inputs and outputs reward functions. A vital advantage of the RM is its ability to integrate various reward functions through concatenation, loops, and conditional rules, offering advantages over traditional black box RL approaches. This versatility facilitates more efficient policy learning through task decomposition, reward shaping, and counterfactual reasoning. We abbreviate Icarte et al.'s work on Reward Machines as IKVM. For more details on the Reward Machines definition, please refer to IKVM [7].

Depending on the state of the RM, the agent receives different reward functions at different times. This flexibility allows the RM to handle temporally extended tasks and behaviours, making it suitable for managing complex scenarios. Additionally, the RM offers flexible planning, allowing dynamic behaviour adjustments based on environmental conditions or task requirements, enhancing adaptability in uncertain environments. These benefits make the RM well-suited for scenarios involving ethical and moral decisions with human life impact, such as self-driving cars or automated search and rescue missions.

2.3 Learning Methodologies for the Reward Machine

The learning methods employed by the Ethical Reward Machine are Counterfactual Reasoning, Reward Shaping and Hierarchical Reasoning. For further details and an in-depth introduction, please refer to IKVM [7].

Counterfactual Reward Machines (CRM): Counterfactual experiences in the RM involve learning policies over the cross product. They utilise counterfactual reasoning to generate synthetic experiences. Off-policy learning methods such as tabular Q-learning, Deep Q-Networks (DQN), or Deep Deterministic Policy Gradients (DDPG) can learn the policy faster. With CRM, we feed one additional set of experiences per RM state after every action rather than just feeding the experience to the RL agent. Adding CRM to the off-policy learning methods adjusts how we use the generated experiences for learning.

Automated Reward Shaping (RS): Automated reward shaping exploits the reward machines based on potential-based reward shaping [12]. This approach involves providing intermediate rewards to the agent as it progresses towards completing the task. This concept is implemented into the reward machine through value iteration over the RM states to compute a potential function. The potential function, facilitates learning optimal policies more efficiently, ensuring policies are optimal concerning the original reward function. Automated RS is used to define a shaped reward function that encourages the agent to progress towards solving the task. This approach is instrumental in scenarios with sparse rewards, as providing intermediate rewards encourages the agent to complete the task more efficiently.

Hierarchical Reward Machines (HRM): Hierarchical reinforcement learning for the reward machine adopts the options framework to exploit the reward structure [14]. This approach decomposes the problem into sub-problems, called options, which are simpler and easier to solve. In the reward machine, agents learn options for the cross-product MDP, focusing on transitioning between RM states. The higher-level policy then learns to select among these options to maximise rewards. The role of the high-level policy is to decide which option to execute in a given state, considering the current environment state. Thus, HRM learns to maximise rewards based on proximity to the agent. HRM is effective in quickly learning policies for RMs. However, due to its myopic approach, it can often converge on sub-optimal solutions. The learned option policies prioritise rapid transitions without considering the long-term impact on performance.

3 Methodology and Approach

The Ethical Reward Machine (ERM) builds upon the existing Reward Machine framework (IKVM) by incorporating constraints from formalised ethical principles of Utilitarianism and Act Deontology adapted from the formal definitions in Krarup et al.[9]. The ERM imposes behavioural constraints that align with specific ethical principles.

We aim to investigate how learning methodologies such as CRM, HRM, and RS within the reward machine framework correspond to different ethical principles. To empirically evaluate the effectiveness of the ERM, we conduct experiments in two distinct domains.

3.1 Experimental Environments

The agent navigates a *Driving World*, adhering to ethical principles to determine the optimal policy. The second environment is the *Dilemma World*, where the agent faces the critical decision of saving one or five individuals while aiming to navigate the environment optimally. In order to navigate the environment optimally, the agent must minimising the number of steps while successfully achieving the goal state. For example, in the context of the *Dilemma World*, to make the choice in accordance to ethical principle while using the available amount of fuel in search and rescue mission.

The reward structures in these environments are represented through Deterministic Finite Automata (DFAs), which facilitate the efficient exploitation of the reward structure to enhance policy learning, as it reveals the reward structure to the agent, enabling interpretable behavior. ERM incorporates moral values (Good, Neutral, Bad) into the state variable by assigning them, such as labelling picking up a passenger as *Good*, parking as *Neutral*, and a minor collision as *Bad*. The agent's task is to navigate the environment while considering the moral implications of its actions.

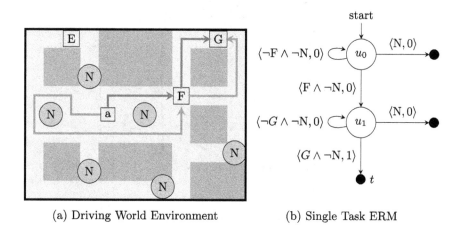

(a) Driving World Environment   (b) Single Task ERM

Fig. 1. An ERM with the Driving World Environment

In Fig. 1a, the blue path illustrates the optimal trajectory for the agent, while the red path depicts one of the possible sub-optimal routes in the *Driving World*. State variables v represent crucial environmental events detectable by the agent. For example, in the *Driving World*, we define v as F (Person 1), E (Person 2), G (Parking), N (Collision). The light grey path signifies a road for the agent to travel on, and the dark grey as buildings to navigate around. Figure 1b provides a graphical representation of the reward machine specific to picking up F. Each node in the graph corresponds to a state within the reward machine, not the environment itself. u_0 denotes the initial state, and terminal states are represented by black circles. In Fig. 1b, the terminal state labeled with t, indicates that progression from u_1 to t is possible only if G becomes true and N remains false $\langle G \wedge \neg N, 1 \rangle$, yielding a reward of 1.

The *Dilemma World*, inspired by the Trolley Problem, introduces events denoted as P and R, akin to the original *Pull* and *Refrain* choices in the moral dilemma scenario. For example, *Pull* alters the trolley's path, opting to sacrifice 1 to save 5 lives, whereas *Refrain* avoids endangering anyone, maintaining a moral stance of not sacrificing a life. It is contextualised in this paper as a search and rescue, as the agent will aim to adhere to the ethical principle while navigating an environment with a restricted amount of fuel. Utilitarianism and Act-Deontology offer divergent ethical perspectives on these decisions. Unlike the *Driving World*, moral values associated with v are absent in the *Dilemma World*; instead, different rewards are assigned to P (5) and R (1), as depicted in Fig. 2. So for example, the agent chooses to save 5 people, it yields a reward of 5. The choice will be dependent on the ethical principle constraint assigned.

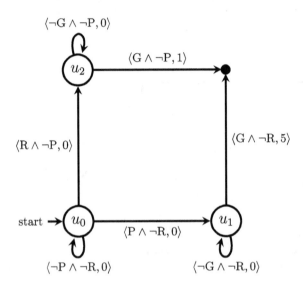

Fig. 2. ERM for the choice in Dilemma World

3.2 Formalised Ethical Principles

The formal ethical principles algorithms are constraints on the Reward Machine, forming the Ethical Reward Machine. A planning model will be constrained by an ethical policy in order to produce an optimal plan, which is the sequence of actions or decisions that the autonomous system follows to reach the goal state while adhering to the specific ethical principles. The planning model, Π, is a formal representation of the environment, actions, states and goals. It outlines the structure of the problem which the agent is faced to solve.

The planning model is a tuple $\Pi = \langle \mathcal{V}, \mathcal{A}, s_0, s_* \rangle$. $\mathcal{V}$ is a finite set of boolean *state variables* v, where each variable can be true or false, defining various aspects of the system's state. In the context of ethical constraints, these variables represent the moral context of the state, indicating whether it is classified as good or bad. A *fact* is either a *state variable* or its negation. $\mathcal{F}$ denotes the set of all facts, and a complete conjunction of facts s is referred to as a *state*. A complete and consistent conjunction of facts is complete because it includes all relevant facts necessary to completely describe a specific state of the system. For example, a conjunction $s = v_1 \wedge \neg v_2 \wedge v_3$ represents a state where v_1 is true, v_2 is false, and v_3 is true, covering all pertinent variables in that context. $\mathcal{S}$ represents the set of states of Π. The set $\mathcal{A}$ consists of *actions*, where each action is defined as a pair $\alpha = \langle pre, eff \rangle$. Here, *pre* denotes the preconditions determining the action's applicability (e.g., if its forbidden), while *eff* specifies the effects on the state variables following execution. $s_0 \in \mathcal{S}$ denotes the *initial state*, and s_* specifies the *goal condition* state that the system aims to achieve.

A constraint is denoted as ϕ, and the planing model by Π. A constraint operator ($\times$) is used to restrict the behaviour of the planning model to adhere to the ethical principles. For a restricted planning model, it is represented by: $\Pi' = \Pi \times \phi$. Therefore, a plan for Π' is a plan for Π which also satisfies the conditions of the ethical constraint operators ϕ.

Act-Deontology Constraint: Moral value is assigned to the states S in the environments seen in Algorithm 1. As Act Deontology is built upon the qualities of the action a and state s, it queries the environment for the moral assignment. The agent can continue if and only if all actions are deemed *Good* from the query. Otherwise, the run will terminate. Incorporating the Act Deontology constraint into the RM environment ensures that in all states, the agent is in alignment with the ethical principle. Act-Deontology, in principle, works very similarly to the original Reward Machine. However, the difference is the moral assignment to the S, is what determines the system to terminate.

Algorithm 1. Reward Machines with Act Deontology

Input: Π, ϕ
Output: Policy for Π' ($\Pi' = \Pi \times \phi$) or Impermissible
$episode\_ended \leftarrow$ **False**
while $\neg episode\_ended$ **do**
    Observe s' from a'
    Check moral result of $\forall s \in S, s' = \{\text{Good}(s) \vee \text{Neutral}(s) \vee \text{Bad}(s)\}$
    if s' is $\text{Good}(s) \vee \text{Neutral}(s)$ **then**
        $episode\_ended \leftarrow$ **False**
        Policy for ERM $\times \Pi'$
    else
        $episode\_ended \leftarrow$ **True**
        Impermissible
    end if
end while

Utilitarian Constraint: The ethical theory aims to maximize overall utility shown in Algorithm 2. In the context of the ERM, it evaluates the consequences of states s and whether they positively or negatively impact the overall rewards

R of the system. If a state s positively impacts the system, resulting in a net positive outcome, the ERM can continue after encountering a *Bad* state, denoted as Bad(s). However, it will end if the state s does not outweigh the overall results R for the ERM. This evaluation is conducted based on the accumulation of *Good* and *Bad* points collected.

The maximum potential of *Good* and *Bad* points achievable in each environment is calculated, the agent's ability to continue is determined by whether the overall utility is greater than or equal zero, $GEq(s_n, s_i)$. If the agent encounters a *Bad* state, if the overall utility is positive, the terminal state will be interrupted, allowing the agent to continue. However, if the overall utility is negative, reaching the terminal state will not trigger an interruption, and the episode will end accordingly. By promoting a utilitarian view of the environment, it permits mistakes to be made as long as they result in a long-term net positive impact in ERM.

Algorithm 2. Reward Machines with Utilitarianism

Input: Π, ϕ
Output: Policy for Π' ($\Pi' = \Pi \times \phi$) or Impermissible
while episode_ended = **False do**
    Observe s' from a'
    Check moral result of $\forall s \in S$, $s' = \{\text{Good}(s) \vee \text{Neutral}(s) \vee \text{Bad}(s)\}$
    if $s' = \text{Good}(s)$ **then**
        Add 100 to Overall Utility
    else if $s' = \text{Neutral}(s)$ **then**
        Add 0 to Overall Utility
    else if $s' = \text{Bad}(s)$ **then**
        Subtract 100 from Overall Utility
    end if
    $s_n \leftarrow \max(S)$ where $\text{GEq}(s_n, s_i)$ $\forall s_i \in S \setminus s_n$
    if Overall Utility $\models \text{GEq}(s_n, s_i)$ **then**
        ERM $\times \Pi'$
        episode_ended $\leftarrow$ **False**
    else
        Impermissible
        episode_ended $\leftarrow$ **True**
    end if
end while

The *max* function seen in Algorithm 2, takes a set of states and aims to return the highest utility set of state variables, i.e. for the set of states S; it returns $s_n \in S$ where $GEq(s_n, s_i)$ $\forall s_i \in S \setminus s_n$.

4 Experimental Evaluation

In this section, we provide the experimental evaluation of the methods in the two environments and with the two ethical principles. The Driving Domain includes multi-task and single-task learning. However, as the Dilemma domain forces a choice on the agent, it is only a single task. The summary of the results is the following:

1. Driving Domain has no difference in policy learning between Ethical Principles. Only slight differences were seen for Multi-Task, but no change to the overall pattern.
2. Dilemma Domain sees convergence to an optimal policy with Act Deontology with all learning methods, with both QL and QL-RS eventually catching up to CRM and HRM learning methods.
3. Utilitarianism shows optimal policy for HRM, CRM-RS and CRM but fail for QL-RS, HRM-RS.
4. There is no runtime difference between the ethical constraints and learning methodologies across both domains.

4.1 Results in Driving Domain

This domain has four tasks. We ran sixty independent trials and recorded the average reward per step across the four tasks. We normalised the average reward per step to be 1 for an optimal policy. Therefore, we can report the median performance across the sixty runs.

As expected, Act-Deontology did not alter the original results from the Reward Machine, as its ethical principle does not alter the decision for the agent. As such, CRM and CRM with RS were the first to optimally solve all tasks, outperforming the cross-product baseline (QL). HRM initially learns faster; however, it converges to sub-optimal policies as expected. HRM with RS has a decreased performance compared to HRM. This is visualised in Fig. 3.

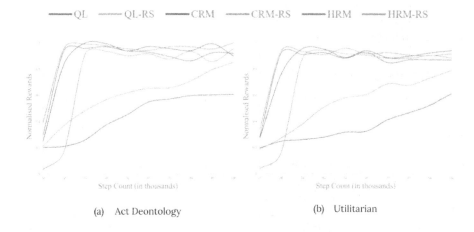

Fig. 3. Results for Driving World for Multi-Taskx

The single-task experiments for Act-Deontology also followed the original results from IKVM. Figure 4 shows CRM outperforming the other methods. However, there is less of a gap between QL and CRM. HRM and HRM with RS converge on sub-optimal policies.

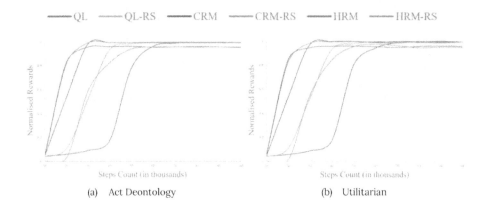

Fig. 4. Results for Driving World for Single-Task

The utilitarian constraint was added to the Driving World, which interrupted the steps of the original reward machine by allowing collisions to occur if the overall utility calculation of the situation was positive. There were no differences made for the reward structure. The results show that the ethical principle does not affect the learning methodologies patterns for optimal policy. Even when the parameters would set the agent never to end the episode, it manages to navigate to the goal state following the same patterns seen in IKVM. As seen in Fig. 1b, the reward structures remained the same for both ethical principles, with the constraint being the only difference.

4.2 Results in Dilemma Domain

The task proposes two options: save 5 people or 1. As as the nature of the environment promotes a moral dilemma, which presents a choice to the agent, there was not a task for saving both as this would negate the moral dilemma. As shown in Fig. 4a, Act Deontology has CRM and HRM with RS to reach optimal, with HRM converging to optimal first. Both QL and QL+RS have significant spikes towards optimal midway through the system.

Figure 4b presents the Utilitarian choice, where the agent reaches optimal policy with HRM, CRM, and CRM-RS; however, HRM-RS and QL-RS perform poorly. QL initially plateaus but then spikes towards the end, converging to a sub optimal policy. In IKVM, the Reward Machine also saw the HRM-RS perform more poorly than expected, as reward shaping usually encourages the agent to obtain an optimal policy (Fig. 5).

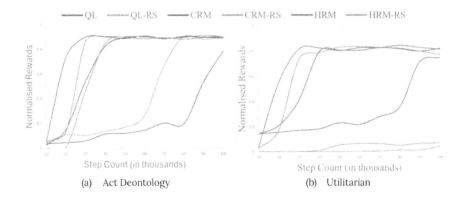

Fig. 5. Results for Dilemma World Choice

4.3 Runtime Comparison

CRM and HRM are more computationally expensive than QL, even though it has a more substantial sample efficiency. IKVM references similar results in [7]. In ERM experimental evaluation, there was no significant difference between the run times between the two ethical principles in both domains.

5 Discussion and Future Work

The results for the Driving World suggest that adding constraints without altering reward specifications does not affect policy learning. However, when comparing this to the Dilemma World results, we observe differences between policy learning and ethical principles due to varying reward specifications, as illustrated in Fig. 2. In the Dilemma World, the results for Act-Deontology may indicate that the ERM is optimal across all learning policies because it aligns both options with the ethical principle. Act-Deontology focuses on the morality of the action itself rather than its outcomes, making the action of saving a life ethically permissible regardless of other options. Conversely, policy learning for Utilitarianism in the Dilemma World is more challenging because it seeks to maximise potential rewards.

Our results correlate with IKVM [7] results for their discrete domain, especially for HRM with RS performing sub-optimally compared to other learning methodologies. As this result is an unexpected pattern, further investigation is required. Lastly, our findings indicate no significant differences in runtime across ethical principles. Therefore, our findings suggest that integrating ethical principles does not significantly add computational burdens beyond those inherent to the base learning algorithms, which is promising for the scalability of ERM frameworks.

We had only explored to simple discrete environments in the paper. Even though we predict with the nature of the changes to the algorithm, functioning as a constraint, even in more complex domains, we expect a minor difference in policy learning and computation time. However, verification of this prediction is necessary, especially in continuous domains. In future work, exploring diverse cultural contexts will be helpful as they can significantly influence the definition of what constitutes good and bad actions, highlighting the need for culturally sensitive specifications through the reward function. Moreover, the RM's capability to accommodate reward functions specified in different languages [3], automatically converting them into RM format, underscores its adaptability and potential for application across diverse cultural contexts [11]. This benefit of the RM can facilitate cross-cultural verification of the interpretability of ethical principles within the decision-making process through its reward structure.

6 Conclusion

In this paper, we introduced the Ethical Reward Machine (ERM), a new framework that integrates ethical principles, specifically Utilitarianism and Act Deontology, into the decision-making processes of autonomous agents. We conducted experimental evaluations in a Driving and Dilemma domain, which provided valuable insights into implementing and enforcing ethical constraints in RL environments. The interpretability of ERM, which is achieved by DFAs to specify the reward functions of the RL agent, is particularly well-suited for ethical decision-making scenarios. We successfully added behavioural constraints based on ethical principles to the specification of arbitrary rewards, sparse rewards, and rewards for temporally extended behaviour.

The Ethical Reward Machine results suggest that the sample efficiency of the Reward Machine is not affected by ethical frameworks, enabling the integration of ethics and guarantee to find solutions faster and with limited interactions with the environment. This suggests that ethical principles should be integrated within the reward structure to significantly constrain the system, as seen in the Dilemma World. Therefore, ethical principles should not be an afterthought in the system but integrated into its reward design.

In conclusion, through empirical evaluations in diverse domains, we have demonstrated the efficacy of integrating ethical principles into reinforcement learning environments without compromising sample efficiency. Our paper adds to the literature for ethical planning models with interpretable reward designs. Ethical AI doesn't operate in a moral vacuum. ERM can work towards System 2 processes, to allow us to consciously consider and embed societal values and ethical principles into AI development [6]. Ultimately, by embedding ethical considerations into the reward structure of autonomous systems, we strive to create AI agents that perform tasks efficiently and are interpretable to the human user, thereby fostering trust and acceptance of AI technologies.

References

1. Awad, E., et al.: The moral machine experiment. Nature **563**(7729), 59–64 (2018). https://doi.org/10.1038/s41586-018-0637-6. https://www.nature.com/articles/s41586-018-0637-6
2. Basich, C., Svegliato, J., Wray, K.H., Witwicki, S., Biswas, J., Zilberstein, S.: Learning to optimize autonomy in competence-aware systems. https://doi.org/10.48550/arXiv.2003.07745. http://arxiv.org/abs/2003.07745
3. Camacho, A., McIlraith, S.A.: Learning interpretable models expressed in linear temporal logic. In: Proceedings of the International Conference on Automated Planning and Scheduling, vol. 29, pp. 621–630 (2019). https://doi.org/10.1609/icaps.v29i1.3529. https://ojs.aaai.org/index.php/ICAPS/article/view/3529
4. Ciupa, M.: Is AI in jeopardy? the need to under promise and over deliver - the case for really useful machine learning. In: Proceedings of the International Conference on Computer Science and Information Technology (CS & IT), pp. 59–70. Academy & Industry Research Collaboration Center (AIRCC) (2017). https://doi.org/10.5121/csit.2017.70407. http://airccj.org/CSCP/vol7/csit76607.pdf
5. Dennis, L., Fisher, M., Slavkovik, M., Webster, M.: Formal verification of ethical choices in autonomous systems. Rob. Auton. Syst. **77**, 1–14 (2016). https://doi.org/10.1016/j.robot.2015.11.012. https://www.sciencedirect.com/science/article/pii/S0921889015003000
6. Francessca Rossi, A.L.: Preferences and ethical priorities: thinking fast and slow in AI. In: International Conference on Autonomous Agents and Multiagent Systems (2019)
7. Icarte, R.T., Klassen, T.Q., Valenzano, R., McIlraith, S.A.: Reward machines: exploiting reward function structure in reinforcement learning. J. Artif. Intell. Res. **73**, 173–208 (2022). https://doi.org/10.1613/jair.1.12440. http://arxiv.org/abs/2010.03950
8. Kahneman, D.: Thinking, Fast and Slow. Farrar, Straus and Giroux, New York (2011)
9. Krarup, B., Lindner, F., Krivic, S., Long, D.: Understanding a robot's guiding ethical principles via automatically generated explanations (2022). https://doi.org/10.48550/arXiv.2206.10038. http://arxiv.org/abs/2206.10038
10. Krivic, S., Ugur, E., Piater, J.: A robust pushing skill for object delivery between obstacles. In: 2016 IEEE International Conference on Automation Science and Engineering (CASE), pp. 1184–1189 (2016). https://doi.org/10.1109/COASE.2016.7743539. https://ieeexplore.ieee.org/document/7743539. ISSN: 2161-8089
11. Middleton, J., Klassen, T.Q., Baier, J., McIlraith, S.A.: FL-AT: a formal language–automaton transmogrifier. In: Proceedings of the 30th International Conference on Automated Planning and Scheduling (ICAPS) (2020)
12. Ng, A.Y., Harada, D., Russell, S.J.: Policy invariance under reward transformations: theory and application to reward shaping. In: Proceedings of the Sixteenth International Conference on Machine Learning, ICML 1999, pp. 278–287. Morgan Kaufmann Publishers Inc. (1999)
13. Shim, J., Arkin, R., Pettinatti, M.: An intervening ethical governor for a robot mediator in patient-caregiver relationship: implementation and evaluation. In: 2017 IEEE International Conference on Robotics and Automation (ICRA), pp. 2936–2942 (2017). https://doi.org/10.1109/ICRA.2017.7989340. https://ieeexplore.ieee.org/document/7989340

14. Sutton, R.S., Precup, D., Singh, S.: Between MDPs and semi-MDPs: a framework for temporal abstraction in reinforcement learning. Artif. Intell. **112**(1), 181–211 (1999). https://doi.org/10.1016/S0004-3702(99)00052-1. https://www.sciencedirect.com/science/article/pii/S0004370299000521
15. Vanderelst, D., Winfield, A.: An architecture for ethical robots inspired by the simulation theory of cognition. Cogn. Syst. Res. **48**, 56–66 (2018). https://doi.org/10.1016/j.cogsys.2017.04.002. https://www.sciencedirect.com/science/article/pii/S1389041716302005

Embed2Rule Scalable Neuro-Symbolic Learning via Latent Space Weak-Labelling

Yaniv Aspis[1]([✉]), Mohammad Albinhassan[1]([✉]), Jorge Lobo[2,3]([✉]), and Alessandra Russo[1]([✉])

[1] Imperial College London, London, UK
{yaniv.aspis17,m.albinhassan23,a.russo}@imperial.ac.uk
[2] ICREA, Barcelona, Spain
[3] Universitat Pompeu Fabra, Barcelona, Spain
jorge.lobo@upf.edu

Abstract. Neuro-symbolic approaches have garnered much interest recently as a path toward endowing neural systems with robust reasoning capabilities. Most proposed end-to-end methods assume knowledge to be given in advance and do not scale up over many latent concepts. The recently proposed Embed2Sym tackles the scalability limitation by performing end-to-end neural training of a visual perception component from downstream labels to generate clusters in the latent space of symbolic concepts. These are later used to perform downstream symbolic reasoning but symbolic knowledge is still engineered. Taking inspiration from Embed2Sym, this paper introduces a novel method for scalable neuro-symbolic learning of first-order logic programs from raw data. The learned clusters are optimally labelled using sampled predictions of a pre-trained vision-language model. A SOTA symbolic learner, robust to noise, uses these labels to learn an answer set program that solves the reasoning task. Our approach, called Embed2Rule, is shown to achieve better accuracy than SOTA neuro-symbolic systems on existing benchmark tasks in most cases while scaling up to tasks that require far more complex reasoning and a large number of latent concepts.

Keywords: Neuro-Symbolic AI · Weak-Labelling · Inductive Logic Programming

1 Introduction

Neuro-symbolic AI seeks to integrate neural approaches with symbolic reasoning capabilities. While neural systems excel at learning from raw data, symbolic AI offers robust and human-interpretable inference with better generalization out-of-distribution. Many approaches separate the neuro-symbolic model into two components: a neural perception component that maps raw inputs (image, text, etc.) to latent symbolic concepts, and a symbolic reasoning component that maps the latent symbolic concepts into downstream predictions. However, learning the symbolic rules jointly with the neural networks is exceedingly difficult, as the reasoning component depends on accurate neural predictions to learn meaningful rules while the neural component relies on accurate rules to receive a useful training signal. Hence, most approaches choose to hand-engineer the rules. Approaches either use approximate symbolic reasoning [3,34], which comes with limitation on the type of reasoning one can perform (for example, no recursion), or else employ a symbolic solver to compute a loss signal [38,42], at the cost of limited scalability. Embed2Sym [1] is another system with hand-engineered knowledge that overcomes the scalability issue while using an answer set solver as its reasoning component. It does so by breaking the training task into multiple stages: end-to-end pre-training of a fully neural model, followed by identification of clusters in latent space, and labelling of the clusters using the symbolic knowledge of the downstream task.

To avoid the need to engineer the symbolic knowledge, methods have recently been proposed for performing Inductive Logic Programming [32] on raw data. MetaABD [8] can learn first-order datalog programs. NSIL [6] and Neural-FastLAS [4] learn the more expressive answer set programs. However, these approaches suffer from the same scalability issues encountered by systems with engineered complete knowledge.

In this paper, we take inspiration from the Embed2Sym approach and introduce a scalable neuro-symbolic learning system that can learn answer set programs from raw data. Our approach, Embed2Rule, does so by splitting the training of the neural network and the rule learning into two steps. After training the network, we discover latent symbolic concepts by clustering the learned latent space and optimally labelling the clusters using weak labels generated by an open-source Vision-Language Model (VLM) [28]. The cluster labels are optimised with respect to these weak labels. Finally, the optimised labels are used by the (noise-robust) symbolic learner ILASP 4 [21] to find optimal rules for solving the downstream task. Our key contributions are as follows:

– We propose Embed2Rule, a neuro-symbolic learning framework that can train neural networks for perception tasks while inducing answer set programs from raw data.
– We leverage a pre-trained VLM in a novel way to ground raw inputs into symbolic latent concepts and overcome scalability issues in learning rules from raw data.
– We evaluate Embed2Rule on existing benchmark tasks, demonstrating it achieves better accuracy than baselines while scaling up to tasks infeasible to other approaches.

In addition, Embed2Rule is modular with respect to both the VLM and the symbolic learner and will benefit from the continued improvement of either.

The paper is structured as follows: Sect. 2 provides a background on topics needed to understand the rest of the paper. Section 3 presents the main methodology of the Embed2Rule approach. Section 4 provides an evaluation of Embed2Rule on existing benchmark tasks and compares it to existing systems. Section 5 discusses related work, and Sect. 6 concludes the paper.

2 Background

In this section, we cover two topics necessary to understand our proposed Embed2Rule method. First, we discuss BLIP-2, which is used to weakly label images to facilitate scalable cluster labelling. We also discuss the Learning from Answer Sets framework, which we use to perform symbolic learning of reasoning tasks.

BLIP-2. [28] is a large VLM designed for text generation with images. The BLIP-2 training process leverages two pre-trained models: a vision encoder and a text encoder (LLM). BLIP-2 supports zero-shot classification of images by leveraging an Image-Text matching head: for a given image and a text prompt, it returns a probability of the text matching the contents of the image. For example, given the input pair < 🖼, "the digit 1"> encoded as a prompt, the Image-Text matching head returns a normalized probability. The digit label which receives the highest probability is then predicted as the classification label. We use the weights of a publicly available pre-trained model of BLIP-2 [27].

Learning from Answer Sets (LAS). [23] is an Inductive Logic Programming [32] paradigm to learn Answer Set Programs (ASP) that support default negation and can solve NP-Hard problems. Given atoms $h, h_1, \ldots, h_k, b_1, \ldots, b_n, c_1, \ldots, c_m$ a normal rule is of the form $h \leftarrow b_1, \ldots, b_n, \text{not } c_1, \ldots, \text{not } c_m$, where not is negation-as-failure. A hard constraint is $\leftarrow b_1, \ldots, b_n, \text{not } c_1, \ldots, \text{not } c_m$. A choice rule is of the form $l \{h_1, \ldots, h_k\} u \leftarrow b_1, \ldots, b_n, c_1, \ldots, c_m$ where l and u are integers. In this paper, an answer set program is a set of normal rules, hard constraints and choice rules.

The Herbrand base is the set of all atoms in the program. An interpretation is a subset of the Herbrand base. Given a program P and a Herbrand interpretation I, the reduct P^I is constructed from the grounding of P in 4 steps. Firstly, removing rules whose bodies contain the negation of an atom in I; secondly, removing all negative literals from the remaining rules; thirdly, replacing every choice rule whose head is not satisfied by I with a hard constraint with the same body; finally, replacing any remaining choice rule $l\{h_1, \ldots, h_m\}u \leftarrow b_1, \ldots, b_n$ with the set of rules $\{h_i \leftarrow b_1, \ldots, b_n \mid h_i \in I \cap \{h_1, \ldots, h_m\}\}$. An interpretation I is an answer set of P if it is the minimal model of P^I.

A LAS task is a tuple $\langle B, S_M, \langle E^+, E^- \rangle \rangle$, where B is an ASP called *background knowledge*, S_M is a set of rules known as a *hypothesis space* and E^+ and E^- are *positive* and *negative examples*, respectively. The hypothesis space is specified through a set of *mode declarations*, describing which predicates can appear in the head or body of a rule. In this work, we use the SOTA LAS system ILASP 4 [21]. Examples in ILASP 4 are referred to as *weighted context-dependent partial interpretations*. Formally, an example is a tuple $\langle e_{id}, e_{pen}, \langle e^{inc}, e^{exc} \rangle, e_{ctx} \rangle$, where e_{id} is an identifier for the example, e_{pen} is a penalty for not covering an example, which can be either a positive integer or infinite[1] and e_{ctx} is an ASP known as *context*, and can be used to provide example-specific information, such as extracted

---
[1] Examples with infinite penalty must be covered by the induced hypothesis.

image features. $\langle e^{inc}, e^{exc} \rangle$ is called a partial interpretation, where both e^{inc} and e^{exc} are disjoint sets of atoms. A hypothesis $H \subseteq S_M$ covers a positive example if there exists an answer set of $B \cup e_{ctx} \cup H$ that contains every atom in e^{inc} and no atom in e^{exc}, while a negative example is covered if there is no such answer set. The score of a hypothesis H is the sum of the length of H (in terms of the number of literals) and the total penalties of uncovered examples. An optimal solution is a hypothesis $H \subset S_M$ with a minimal score.

3 Methodology

We formalise a neuro-symbolic learning task as a tuple $\langle \mathcal{X}, \mathcal{Y}, \mathcal{C}, B, S_M, \mathcal{D} \rangle$. $\mathcal{X}$ is the space of inputs, in this work assumed to be either images or symbolic. Each element $X \in \mathcal{X}$ is a sequence of inputs $X = (x_1, x_2, \ldots, x_n)$. $\mathcal{Y}$ is the space of *downstream labels* or *target labels*. $\mathcal{C}$ is a set of (symbolic) *latent concepts*. A latent concept $C \in \mathcal{C}$ is a tuple (c, S_c) where c is the name of the latent concept and S_c is a set of values associated with C, which is assumed to be finite. For example, for MNIST images, a latent concept C is (digit, $\{0, ..., 9\}$). Each input image x_i is associated with a single latent concept, denoted $C(i) \in \mathcal{C}$. In the case an image needs to be associated with more than one, we define a composite latent concept. For example, if an image x_i should be associated with two latent concepts: $C_1 = (c_1, S_{c_1})$, $C_2 = (c_2, S_{c_2})$, we define the latent concept $C_{1,2} = (c_{1,2}, S_{c_1} \times S_{c_2})$. The *latent space* is the Cartesian product of the latent concept values of each input, i.e. $\mathcal{Z} = S_{C(1)} \times S_{C(2)} \times \cdots \times S_{C(n)}$. B is *background knowledge* and S_M a *hypothesis space* which can be used by the symbolic solver to find a logic program that solves the reasoning task. $\mathcal{D}$ is a dataset of pairs $(X, Y) \in \mathcal{X} \times \mathcal{Y}$. $\mathcal{D}$ does not contain any labels for the latent concepts $z \in \mathcal{Z}$. A solution to the above task is a function $f = h \circ g : \mathcal{X} \to \mathcal{Y}$, where $g : \mathcal{X} \to \mathcal{Z}$ is a sequence of one or more perception functions that can be applied to raw input sequences to map them into latent concept values, as follows:

$$f(X) = h(g_1(x_1), g_2(x_2), \ldots, g_n(x_n)) \qquad (1)$$

Note that g_i may be identical for all i and $h : \mathcal{Z} \to \mathcal{Y}$ is a reasoning function that maps the latent concepts to downstream labels.

In Embed2Rule, we learn the function f in stages (see Fig. 1). In the first stage, we learn a fully neural model, end-to-end from the downstream labels, and apply clustering to the learned latent embedding space. Next, we label the learned clusters by weakly labelling sampled images and optimising the cluster assignments over the space of symbolic concepts. Finally, we apply a symbolic learner to learn the rules of the reasoning task given noisy latent concepts as inputs. In the rest of this section, we discuss each stage in detail.

Fully Neural Model and Clustering. This first stage of Embed2Rule follows the first two stages of the Embed2Sym approach. The fully neural model comprises two parts: a perception component (g) and a reasoning component (h). The perception component is a vision neural network (e.g. CNN) that maps individual raw images to continuous embedding vectors. These vectors are concatenated and

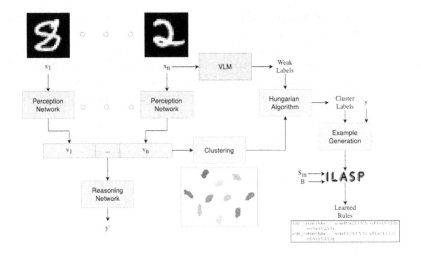

Fig. 1. Architecture of the Embed2Rule system.

fed into the reasoning component, which in this stage is a neural network (*the reasoning network*), such as an MLP. In later stages, the reasoning network will be replaced by a learned symbolic program. The entire architecture is trained using the downstream labels only. After training, embedding vectors associated with the same latent concept values tend to be clustered together in the latent space (see example in Fig. 1) due to the use of a CNN to learn meaningful latent representations. We perform K-Means clustering to discover meaningful clusters to map the outputs of the perception networks to their associated unlabelled clusters.

Weak and Cluster Labelling. After obtaining the clusters, we must learn how each cluster maps to a latent concept value (the cluster labels) before learning the rules for the reasoning task. In theory, this can be jointly learned. For example, we could encode a learning task into ILASP that induces cluster labels as facts in a logic program, in addition to rules for mapping the latent labels to downstream labels. In practice, such an approach has limited scalability: the hypothesis space explodes as the number of latent concepts increases. In addition, ILP systems are not typically designed for inducing facts, as they prefer to learn general rules rather than specific ones.

To design a more practical and scalable system, this stage employs a weak labeller to detect latent concepts in sampled images, such that we can optimally assign latent concepts to clusters later on. In recent years, various VLMs have been publicly released that can be used to interrogate the contents of images [46]. These models are quite general and can be used for various tasks, but their performance tends to lag behind specialised classification models on any given dataset. However, they are suitable for use as weak labellers. In this work, we use the BLIP-2 model, a SOTA among open-source models, in a zero-shot manner.

To find the optimal mapping of clusters to latent concept values, we first sample images from the dataset and assign them weak labels. The idea is to find the assignment that agrees maximally with the weak labeller over the sampled dataset. This is formalised as an optimisation task where the score of the assignment is the number of images that have been mapped to the correct cluster label according to the weak labeller. We employ the Hungarian Algorithm to solve this optimisation task [20].

Symbolic Learning. Having mapped the raw inputs to symbolic labels, this stage symbolically learns the reasoning task (the reasoning network can be disregarded at this stage). To perform symbolic learning, we use ILASP 4 as it is a SOTA ILP method and is robust to noise over the predicted latent concept values, which is critical for our method. Recall ILASP expects a task of the form $\langle B, S_M, \langle E^+, E^- \rangle \rangle$. B and S_M are already given. The set of examples E^+ and E^- can now be constructed from $\mathcal{D}$ in a process that depends on the nature of the task. Most tasks involve the classification of samples into a set number of classes. In this case, positive examples are sufficient and can be constructed as follows. For a sample $(X, Y) \in \mathcal{D}$, Y is encoded into the inclusion and exclusion set as follows:

$$e^{inc} = \{y \in Y\} \qquad e^{exc} = \{y' \in \mathcal{Y} \mid y' \neq y\} \tag{2}$$

and the inputs are encoded into the context using g:

$$e^{ctx} = \{\text{holds}\,(i, g_i(x_i)) \mid x_i \in X\} \tag{3}$$

where holds is a special predicate used to encode the latent concept predictions. If B or S_M expect latent concepts to be encoded in terms of other predicates, this can be easily remedied by adding to B (first-order) rules that map the holds atoms to the expected ones. Some tasks, such as the Hitting Sets (see the evaluation section), do not offer direct symbolic classification into classes but rather classify in terms of the existence or nonexistence of a solution (realised as the existence or nonexistence of an answer set in ASP). In such cases, both positive and negative examples are used, where positive examples encode samples with a solution while negative examples encode those that do not. These samples have the same context as described above, but empty inclusion and exclusion sets (as the nature of the example already encodes the label).

Since the prediction of latent concepts is noisy, it is necessary to give a finite penalty to each example, to allow ILASP to optimise over examples with incorrect context. In this work, we use a uniform penalty for all examples, although it is possible a non-uniform penalty (based on some measure of confidence) would be beneficial. We leave such investigation to future work. We also note that the data-efficient nature of ILP means that in practice, only a small subset of $\mathcal{D}$ is needed to learn the correct hypothesis.

4 Evaluation

We conducted several experiments on existing neuro-symbolic tasks to evaluate the performance and scalability of Embed2Rule[2] In our experiments, we aim to answer the following questions: 1. Can Embed2Rule solve tasks involving both perception and reasoning while inducing missing symbolic knowledge? 2. How does Embed2Rule compare to both neuro-symbolic learning and reasoning systems in terms of accuracy of prediction of latent concepts and downstream labels? 3. Can Embed2Rule solve tasks involving complex reasoning, such as NP-hard problems? 4. How well does Embed2Rule scale up to tasks involving a large number of image inputs, compared to other neuro-symbolic systems? 5. How well does Embed2Rule perform in the presence of a large number of latent concepts, compared to other neuro-symbolic systems?

To address these questions, we chose tasks that involve relatively large-scale complex reasoning:

1. **Hitting Sets** [6]: A visual version of the hitting set problem, which is NP-Hard [17]. The program to be induced involves both choice and constraints and therefore cannot be represented without default negation. We demonstrate that Embed2Rule can indeed solve this task.
2. **Visual Sudoku Classification** [2]: The task is to determine if a given complete Sudoku board is valid or invalid (according to the rules of Sudoku). This requires correctly identifying a large number of images (16 or 81, depending on board size). We show Embed2Rule can successfully scale up to this task while learning the rules of Sudoku.
3. **Follow Suit Winner** [5]: This task involves a card game where the winner is to be determined. As all cards in the deck are used, the number of latent concept values is quite large (namely, 52 for a standard deck of cards). We show Embed2Rule can successfully deal with this large number of cards while inducing the correct rules of the game.

We compare Embed2Rule to two SOTA neuro-symbolic baselines with existing public codebases that can be easily adapted to perform all three tasks. The Neuro-Symbolic Inductive Learner [6], to our knowledge, is the only existing system that can both train a perception component and learn general first-order answer set programs (see related work for discussion on two other systems, MetaABD and NeuralFastLAS, that can learn first-order logic programs). We also tested against a neuro-symbolic reasoning system, SLASH [38], where the symbolic knowledge is fully given. Like Embed2Rule and NSIL, SLASH represents its symbolic knowledge in the form of answer set programs and has been shown to be more scalable than other neuro-symbolic reasoning systems, using its SAME method, in which gradients are computed for only a portion of the answer sets that seem most promising. We also compare against SLASH's exact method, which computes gradients for all answer sets.

---

[2] Implementation/data can be found at https://github.com/YanivAspis/Embed2Rule.

An interesting ablation study would be to use BLIP-2 directly as the perception network and learning rules using the weak labels. We omit this experiment as such an approach was already proposed and evaluated on two of the three tasks we consider, showing worse accuracy than we achieve in Embed2Rule [7].

We report results for downstream accuracy, latent accuracy and training time. We run each method 5 times and report the average to account for random initialization. If a method did not complete any of the runs within 24 h, we report a timeout. See appendices for details on training, dataset generation, and learnt symbolic programs.

Hitting Sets. In the Hitting Sets task, we are given a universe of elements U, and a set of sets S, where for each set $T \in S$, T is a subset of U. A hitting set for S is a set $H \subseteq U$ such that for every $T \in S$, $T \cap H \neq \emptyset$. Given an integer $k \geq 1$, the hitting set task is to determine if there exists a hitting set H with $|H| \leq k$.

Example 1. Consider the universe $U = \{0, 1, 2, 3, 4\}$ and $S = \{\{1\}, \{1, 3\}, \{3\}\}$. For $k \geq 2$ the answer is *yes* as there exists a hitting set $H = \{1, 3\}$. For $k = 1$ the answer is no since there is no hitting set of one element.

The visual version of this task replaces the elements of S with corresponding images, such as MNIST digits [26]. Previously, Cunnington et al. [6] considered a limited case where $|U| = 5$ and $|\bigcup S| = 4$ (that is, 4 images only). Here we relax this restriction and also consider the cases where $|U| = 10$ and $|\bigcup S| = 4, 5$ or 6. As in Cunnington et al., we set $k = 2$. We generated a dataset of 200k samples for all cases and report the results in Tables 1, 2 and 3. When training, we employ an MLP with residual connections as the reasoning network. Note the relatively large dataset size is introduced to account for Embed2Rule's first stage which involves end-to-end differentiable learning without prior knowledge assumed. Later stages of Embed2Rule are data efficient and can be learned using a relatively small sample. While Embed2Rule does not solve the data efficiency issue of neural networks, it does introduce other benefits of neuro-symbolic learning, such as interpretable and generalizable inference, while being scalable.

Table 1. Average downstream test accuracy (%) on the Hitting Sets task. 5-4 means 5 elements in U and 4 images. T/O = "timeout", OOM = "Out of Memory".

Task	5-4	10-4	10-5	10-6
NSIL	99.6 ± 0.25	T/O	T/O	T/O
SLASH (exact)	50.0 ± 0.00	OOM	OOM	OOM
SLASH (SAME)	50.0 ± 0.00	OOM	OOM	OOM
Embed2Rule	99.4 ± 0.20	98.6 ± 1.00	96.8 ± 3.13	92.9 ± 1.18

Both NSIL and Embed2Rule can solve the task in the case of 5 elements in U and 4 images, with comparable accuracy and correctly inducing the rules of the hitting set problem. However, Embed2Rule can solve the task even in the more

Table 2. Average latent test accuracy (%) on the Hitting Sets task.

Task	5-4	10-4	10-5	10-6
NSIL	99.4 ± 0.12	T/O	T/O	T/O
SLASH (exact)	22.1 ± 0.00	OOM	OOM	OOM
SLASH (SAME)	22.1 ± 0.00	OOM	OOM	OOM
Embed2Rule	**99.5 ± 0.12**	**89.0 ± 6.50**	**83.9 ± 10.27**	**69.1 ± 6.63**

Table 3. Average training time (sec) on the Hitting Sets task.

Task	5-4	10-4	10-5	10-6
NSIL	4117.7	T/O	T/O	T/O
SLASH (exact)	642.0	OOM	OOM	OOM
SLASH (SAME)	156.4	OOM	OOM	OOM
Embed2Rule	957.1	3147.4	6867.5	7754.1

challenging cases of 10 elements and 4 or more images, while learning the correct program (note that this program is also general enough to handle any number of raw inputs). NSIL, on the other hand, is unable to complete its bootstrap stage in these cases. The bootstrap stage involves encoding an ILASP task with an example for every possible set S, which is infeasible even for 10 elements and 4 digits. SLASH is not able to solve this task, even in the case of 5 elements, due to its inability to learn from negative samples. The loss function used by SLASH involves a sum over all answer sets that entail the downstream label. However, in the case of negative samples, there are no answer sets. Therefore, only positive samples can be passed to SLASH during training, which are insufficient to learn from, as the network quickly learns to predict the same digit for any given image, resulting in random guess results. Furthermore, SLASH does not scale to the task with 10 elements, as the publicly-available implementation quickly runs out of memory when computing gradients in this case, not completing even a single iteration.

Visual Sudoku Classification. Augustine et al. [2] introduced this version of the visual Sudoku task, inspired by a previous task introduced by Wang et al. [41]. In this task, complete Sudoku boards (all cells filled) are presented in visual form. Specifically, the board is given as a sequence of MNIST digits. The task is to classify these boards as valid (no repeats in rows, columns, or blocks) or invalid. We consider three versions of the task:

1. **4 × 4 Fixed:** Each sample is a 4 × 4 board with the same digits used across all samples, namely 0-3.
2. **4 × 4 Random:** Similar to 4 × 4 fixed, but instead of using the digits 0-3 only, we randomly select 4 digits from 0-9 per puzzle. Hence, the perception task is more challenging than the 4 × 4 Fixed case while the reasoning task remains the same.

Table 4. Average downstream test accuracy (%) on the Visual Sudoku Classification task.

Task	4 × 4 Fixed	4 × 4 Random	9 × 9 Fixed
NSIL	50.0 ± 0.00	50.0 ± 0.00	50.0 ± 0.00
SLASH (exact)	98.1 ± 0.37	OOM	OOM
SLASH (SAME)	98.0 ± 0.40	OOM	OOM
Embed2Rule	**99.1 ± 0.37**	**97.8 ± 0.09**	**78.3 ± 3.37**

Table 5. Average latent test accuracy (%) on the Visual Sudoku Classification task.

Task	4 × 4 Fixed	4 × 4 Random	9 × 9 Fixed
NSIL	23.6 ± 0.00	10.1 ± 0.00	11.2 ± 0.00
SLASH (exact)	99.7 ± 0.04	OOM	OOM
SLASH (SAME)	99.7 ± 0.06	OOM	OOM
Embed2Rule	**99.9 ± 0.07**	**99.2 ± 0.07**	**99.3 ± 0.14**

3. **9 × 9 Fixed:** Similar to 4 × 4 Fixed but on a 9 × 9 board (with digits 0-8). This is by far the most challenging task as it involves 81 inputs that need to be classified correctly.

"Fixed" and "Random" correspond to the "Basic" and "PerPuzzle" cases from Augustine et al.. Note that this task is more challenging than the related task of visual Sudoku solving, as there is only a single binary label per sample, providing very little information on the contents of each cell. We generated datasets of 50K samples for the 4 × 4 cases and 200K samples for the 9 × 9 case and report results in Tables 4, 5 and 6. Note we do not use the original dataset of Augustine et al. as it contains a very small number of samples (200), which is not sufficient to train the fully neural model. For this reason, we do not directly compare to results previously published by other authors on this task.

In this task, we use a small transformer (400K parameters, can be trained on local hardware) as the reasoning network, which is particularly suited to model position-based correlations between a large number of image inputs. Such correlations are integral to determining Sudoku board validity.

Embed2Rule can be successfully trained in all cases to achieve high accuracy, even in the challenging 9 × 9 Fixed case (the downstream accuracy of 78.3% is the result of compounding errors that occur when predicting 81 latent labels with 99.2% accuracy). In the 4 × 4 cases, Embed2Rule learns the constraint on rows and columns of a Sudoku board, but not on blocks. This is due to the small number of cases where the restrictions on rows and columns are insufficient, and ILASP's preference of learning shorter programs. For the 9 × 9 case, ILASP usually learns either the restrictions on rows or columns, as the relatively large number of misclassified board cells means ILASP can cover fewer samples with addi-

Table 6. Average training time (sec) on the Visual Sudoku Classification task.

Task	4×4 Fixed	4×4 Random	9×9 Fixed
NSIL	2887.9	3384.1	45732.8
SLASH (exact)	8067.4	OOM	OOM
SLASH (SAME)	691.0	OOM	OOM
Embed2Rule	3654.4	3794.4	65208.6

tional restrictions, making it less preferable to induce them. Regardless, the downstream accuracy remains relatively high.

NSIL does not succeed in learning in this case. During the bootstrap stage, it learns a "perfectly wrong" hypothesis which assigns board as valid if all digits in a row or column are identical. The perception network then learns to predict all images as the same digits. The corrective examples do not help NSIL in this case, and it proceeds to relearn the same perfectly wrong hypothesis in an endless cycle. We consulted with the author who confirmed this can occur in binary tasks when a perfectly wrong hypothesis is learned. SLASH can solve the 4×4 Fixed case if provided only positive examples (as negative examples yield too many answer sets to be feasible). SLASH then achieves similar accuracy to our system, and the SAME algorithm even allows for faster training than Embed2Rule. However, both NSIL and SLASH cannot solve the 4×4 Random or 9×9 Fixed cases as the number of answer sets becomes too large, and the system runs out of memory. Note that even though SAME is more efficient than the exact method overall, it still requires enumerating all answer sets during the first few iterations, when all answer sets are equally likely, hence confronting the same scalability issues of the exact method.

Follow Suit Winner. In the Follow Suit Winner task, we are asked to predict the winner of a card game. The game consists of 4 players, numbered 1 to 4, each drawing a single card from the same deck (no repeats). The winner is the player with the highest rank card that has the same suit as the first player. For example, if the cards drawn (in order) are: $(3, \heartsuit)$, $(5, \spadesuit)$, $(J, \heartsuit)$, $(8, \heartsuit)$, the winner is player 3, while for the following cards: $(2, \clubsuit)$, $(9, \heartsuit)$, $(Q, \diamondsuit)$, $(10, \spadesuit)$ the winner is player 1 as no other player drew the same suit. Each card corresponds to two latent concepts: rank and suit. Therefore this is an example of a composite latent concept as discussed in Sect. 3. Since all cards of a standard deck are used, there are 52 latent concepts to learn from only a winner label, making this task challenging. We use the same set of card images as Cunnington et al. [5] and generate a dataset of 200K samples. We report results in Table 7.

Embed2Rule was able to solve this task while the baseline methods failed to do so. In addition, it correctly induced the rules of the game. To investigate the source of errors in the model's latent prediction, we inspected the clusters formed in latent space and discovered the model was able to produce 52 distinct clusters, i.e. the perception network learned to discriminate card images correctly. However, BLIP-2 had a high source of errors in its weak labelling, resulting in lower latent accuracy

Table 7. Results for Follow Suit Winner. Training time is in seconds.

	Downstream (%)	Latent (%)	Train time
NSIL	OOM	OOM	OOM
SLASH (exact)	OOM	OOM	OOM
SLASH (SAME)	OOM	OOM	OOM
Embed2Rule	**86.2 ± 2.16**	**81.5 ± 2.53**	13219.1

when labelling the clusters and consequently affecting downstream performance, despite the correctly learned rules. It is quite likely, however, that future work on vision-language models would produce better weak labeller that could perform better at this task.

As for the baselines, the large number of latent concepts results in a large number of answer sets that is infeasible for those systems. SLASH does not complete even a single iteration before running out of memory. NSIL can perform the bootstrap stage (which does not result in the correct hypothesis), but as it relies on NeurASP [45] to train its perception component, it encounters the same scalability issues as SLASH.

5 Related Work

Recently proposed neuro-symbolic work assumes symbolic knowledge is fully given in advance. This knowledge is integrated into the neuro-symbolic system (a scenario we refer to as *neuro-symbolic reasoning*). Most commonly, logic operations are replaced with differentiable approximations, using various forms of fuzzy logic or probabilistic inference [3,10,31,34,35]. Another line of research begins with existing symbolic solvers that are extended to support neural inputs via special predicates [14,30,39,42]. Among these, NeurASP [45] and SLASH [38] extend an Answer Set Solver. NeurASP uses a semantic loss [43] computed over all answer sets of a program to train its perception component. SLASH extends NeurASP by integrating probabilistic circuits into neural predicates, allowing for joint probability estimations. It improves scalability by introducing the SAME method for computing gradients, which subsamples answer sets as the perception component becomes more confident, but still requires the enumeration of answer sets at the beginning of training, which is computationally infeasible in large-scale tasks. Embed2Sym [1] is a neuro-symbolic reasoning system that differs from the above by pre-training the perception network differentiably, avoiding these combinatorial difficulties. A-NESI [19] tackles the combinatorial difficulty by pre-training an inference model using synthetic data generated from the (full) symbolic knowledge, used to train a perception component.

Among neuro-symbolic works that learn interpretable rules (*neuro-symbolic learning*), most either restrict themselves to the propositional case [9,11,29] or pre-train the perception component from latent labels [5]. Recently, Inductive Logic Programming has been realised using differentiable methods [12,36,37,44]. These are always applied to symbolic data or otherwise employ a pre-trained network to extract symbolic facts. These approaches have been claimed to be advantageous over symbolic ILP due to the tolerance of noisy data. However, they are often limited in the expressivity of the learned rules and do not necessarily learn optimal rules. In addition, it has been shown that ILASP can tolerate noise as well as differentiable ILP systems [22] while supporting the learning of more expressive knowledge, making it more suitable for our use case.

There have been few works that jointly train a perception network while inducing first-order logic programs. MetaABD [8,15,16] extends Meta Interpretive Learning [33] to learn datalog programs from raw images using an abduction-induction procedure. It performs a search for an optimal hypothesis together with optimal latent concept values for the current neural network predictions and downstream labels. The abduced latent concept values are used as pseudo-labels to train the network. The expressivity of the datalog rules that can be induced by MetaABD does not permit it to learn tasks that require default negation, such as the Hitting Sets task. In addition, the search phase encounters combinatorial difficulties that prevent its application to large-scale tasks. In contrast, our Embed2Rule approach can learn programs that have the full expressivity of ASP and scales up well.

NSIL [6] learns Answer Set Programs from raw data, using either ILASP or FastLAS [24]. It runs a symbolic bootstrap task to generate an initial hypothesis to begin training the perception network using NeurASP. After every epoch, NSIL generates *corrective examples* for ILASP, based on downstream accuracy and network confidence, enabling ILASP to revise the hypothesis if required before training proceeds. NSIL inherits the combinatorial difficulties of NeurASP as well as potential scalability issues in the bootstrap stage and the construction of corrective examples. Embed2Rule avoids these difficulties by adopting the pre-training strategy of Embed2Sym and exploiting a weak-labeller to learn the latent concept values.

NeuralFastLAS [4] is another neuro-symbolic learning approach that adapts FastLAS2 to support the joint learning of symbolic knowledge and a perception network. However, it inherits the limitations of the FastLAS2 system. Namely, it partially supports non-observational predicate learning and does not support recursive programs or predicate invention. In particular, it cannot learn the Hitting Set rules. As such, we chose not to directly compare to NeuralFastLAS. Embed2Rule uses ILASP, which supports all of these features.

6 Conclusion

This paper introduced Embed2Rule, a neuro-symbolic learning system that supports ILP over raw data in a scalable manner. Our approach makes use of a SOTA vision-language model as a weak-labeller to assign cluster labels efficiently, and a SOTA symbolic learner that can robustly deal with noise. Empirical results show Embed2Rule can solve existing benchmark tasks while learning complex knowledge, and scaling up with respect to the number of raw inputs and latent concepts, infeasible to existing approaches.

Limitations: Embed2Rule suffers from some limitations. The approach is not as data efficient as other neuro-symbolic systems as it relies on the pre-training of a reasoning network, although this can be mitigated with data augmentation and regularization. The weak-labeller may also underperform on tasks that require highly specific domain knowledge, which can only be overcome using a relatively expensive fine-tuning process. Future work will address these limitations.

Acknowledgments. This work was partly supported by UKRI grant EP/X040518/1.

Disclosure of Interests. The authors have no competing interests to declare that are relevant to the content of this article.

A Datasets

In this appendix, we describe the datasets used throughout the experiments described in the main paper.

A.1 Raw Datasets

For raw data (images), we use the standard MNIST [26] dataset as provided by the PyTorch module, and the Cards dataset by Cunnington *et al.* [5]. The Cards dataset is publicly available at: https://github.com/DanCunnington/FFNSL. For both datasets, we split the training images into a training and validation set, while using the test images as the test set.

Hitting Sets. For this task, we generated a dataset of 200K training samples, 1K validation samples, and 1K test samples for each case. The generation process was as follows: We randomly generated collections of sets of a given size (4-6) with a given number of elements (5 or 10) and checked if a hitting set of size 2 or less exists. We split the generated collections into training, validation and test sets with an equal number of positive and negative samples, ensuring there is no overlap between the sets. Then, we assigned each of the elements in a sample to a random image from MNIST with a label corresponding to that element, and from the appropriate split (train/validation/test). Note that MNIST images may repeat across different samples from the same split.

Visual Sudoku Classification. For the 4 × 4 cases (Fixed and Random), we generated 50K training samples, 5K validation samples and 5K test samples. For the 9 × 9 case, we generated 200K training samples, 20K validation and 20K test samples. When generating samples, we followed a process similar to Augustine et al. [2]. We began by generating valid boards and then corrupted half to generate negative samples. There are two types of corruption: 1. Replacement - a cell is randomly chosen and its content is replaced with a different digit. 2. Substitution - two cells are randomly chosen and their contents are swapped. We apply at least one corruption (at random) to each board and then flip a (biased) coin to decide if further corruptions are to be applied. If we get heads, we apply another random corruption and flip again until we get tails. We then checked to see if the multiple corruptions did not accidentally create a valid board. In the 4 × 4 cases, the coin has a bias of 0 (always landing on tails) so the board contains a single corruption. For the 9 × 9 Fixed case, we used a bias of 0.75, so a board contains, on average, 4 corruptions. The generated (valid and invalid) puzzles are then split into a training, validation and test set, with an equal number of positive and negative samples, and ensuring no overlap. Assigning MNIST images to cells followed the same procedure as Hitting Sets.

Follow Suit Winner. We generated 200K training samples, 1K validation and 1K test samples. The generation process is done by continuously simulating games and recording the winner. The process of assigning images to cards is similar to the other tasks.

B Training Details

In this section, we provide further details on the training of the Embed2Rule model and baselines in the various experiments described in the evaluation section of the paper.

B.1 Training Hardware

We trained on a system with an Intel i7-12700K @ 3600 MHz, 32 GB of RAM and a Nvidia GeForce RTX 3090.

B.2 Embed2Rule Hyperparameters

In all tasks, K-Means is trained with 1000 random samples from the training set, and another 1024 random samples are given to BLIP-2 for weak-labelling.

Hitting Sets. We employ LeNet-5 [25] as a perception network with the output layer changed to size 32 with ReLU activation. The output embeddings are concatenated and fed into the reasoning network, an MLP with residual connections. This MLP is comprised of a stack of residual blocks. Each block is a fully connected layer with an output size of 128, followed by a GELU activation, batch norm and finally adding the block input. We use 4 such residual blocks. The network is trained for 100 epochs (50 in the 5-4 case) with a learning rate of 0.0009 and a batch size of 256 using the Adam optimiser [18]. The prompt for BLIP-2 was simply the digit in numerical form. We set a uniform penalty of 100 to the ILASP examples and set a maximum rule length of 10 (to allow learning long choice rules). We provide ILASP with 50 examples from the training set.

Visual Sudoku Classification. We utilise a CNN similar to that used in SATNet [41] for the perception network containing 2 convolutional and max-pooling layers, followed by 2 feed-forward layers with ReLU activations functions. We use a transformer encoder [40] for the reasoning network employing multi-headed self-attention with learnable positional embeddings. We set the number of attention heads to 4, the number of encoder blocks to 1, the feed-forward layer embedding dimensions to 512, the activation functions to GELU, and a dropout value of 0.1. The inputs and outputs of the transformer are embeddings of dimensions $batch \times seq \times emb$, where $batch$ is the batch size fixed to 512, seq is the sequence length set to 16 and 81 for the 4×4 and 9×9 Sudoku boards, respectively, and emb is the dimensions of the individual latent concept embeddings set to 128. We apply a single-layer classification head with a Sigmoid activation function to the layer-normalized outputs of the transformer to obtain the neural predictions. We train the network for 50 epochs using an AdamW optimizer with a linear warm-up phase from 0.0 to a base learning rate of 0.003 for 30% and 20% of the total number of iterations for the 4×4 and 9×9 boards, respectively, followed by a cosine annealing learning rate schedule between the base learning rate and 0.0001. We clip the gradient norm of each layer at 1.0. The prompt for BLIP-2 is again the digit in numerical form. We give ILASP 100 training examples with a uniform penalty of 1.

Follow Suit Winner. We use a ResNet-18 [13] as the perception network, with an output layer of size 128. As a reasoning network, we use a similar MLP architecture to the Hitting Sets task, with 4 residual blocks and a hidden size of 256. We train for 50 epochs with a learning rate of 0.0001 and a batch size of 128. For BLIP-2 we use a prompt of the format "The playing card *rank* of *suit*" where *rank* and *suit* are replaced with their appropriate values. We provide ILASP with 100 examples with a uniform penalty of 1.

B.3 Baseline Hyperparameters

We use the official implementations of NSIL and SLASH in our experiments, using the same perception networks as Embed2Rule. As both NSIL and SLASH are more data efficient than Embed2Rule, we used smaller training sets of 10K samples to avoid artificially increasing training time. We found no gain from using additional data.

NSIL. For Hitting Sets, we follow the same hyperparameters used in the official implementation. NSIL is trained for 20 iterations using the SGD optimiser with a learning rate of 0.0008, momentum of 0.7643 and a batch size of 64. The λ value (that affects the weight of neural network confidence in symbolic learning) is set to 1. For Visual Sudoku Classification and Follow Suit Winner, no set of hyperparameters affects the result, as NSIL could not solve either. For Sudoku, as the number of iterations did not change the performance of NSIL, we reported training time results when using 5 iterations.

SLASH. For Visual Sudoku Classification, we trained for 20 epochs using the Adam optimiser with a learning rate of 0.001 and a batch size of 100 (for 4×4 random and 9×9 we attempted to use batch sizes as small as 8 to overcome the memory issues, but found it did not help. Due to a bug in the implementation, batch sizes smaller than 8 are not possible.). For the Hitting Sets task, we found no set of hyperparameters that would allow SLASH to learn from positive samples alone, and so we report results for 5 epochs of training.

C Symbolic Learning Tasks

We include here the background knowledge and mode declarations given to ILASP in each task.

```
num_elements(5). super_set_size(4). hitting_set_target_size(2).
element(0). element(1). element(2). element(3). element(4).
index(0..N) :- super_set_size(N+1).
set(S) :- index(S).
pow2(0, 1).
pow2(X, R) :- index(X), pow2(X-1, T), R = 2 * T.
value(0..M) :- super_set_size(N), pow2(N-1, M+1).
num_ones(0, 0).
num_ones(1, 1).
num_ones(X, N) :- value(X), num_ones(X / 2, M),
      num_ones(X \ 2, L), N = M+L.
num_ones_until(T, I, N) :- template(T), index(I), pow2(I, R),
      M = T \ R, num_ones(M, N).
set_assignment(I, S) :- index(I), template(T),
      num_ones_until(T, I, S).
template(T) :- holds(input_template, T).
super_set_entry(I, V) :- holds(input_element(I), V).
```

Listing 1.1. Background knowledge of the Hitting Sets 5-4 task.

```
#modeha(hitting_set_element(const(element))).
#constant(element, 0).
#constant(element, 1).
#constant(element, 2).
#constant(element, 3).
#constant(element, 4).
#minhl(5).
#maxhl(5).
#modeh(set_hit(var(set))).
#modeb(1, hitting_set_element(var(element))).
#modeb(1, super_set_entry(var(index), var(element))).
#modeb(1, set_assignment(var(index), var(set))).
#modeb(1, set_hit(var(set))).
#max_penalty(1000).
```

Listing 1.2. Mode declarations for the Hitting Sets 5-4 task.

```
element(0). element(1). element(2). element(3). element(4).
element(5). element(6). element(7). element(8). blockSize(3).
cellIdx(1..M) :- blockSize(N), M = N * N.
blockIdx(1..N) :- blockSize(N).
cell((X, Y)) :- cellIdx(X), cellIdx(Y).
block((BX, BY)) :- blockIdx(BX), blockIdx(BY).
sameRow((X, Y), (X, Z)) :- cell((X, Y)), cell((X, Z)), Y != Z.
sameCol((X, Y), (Z, Y)) :- cell((X, Y)), cell((Z, Y)), X != Z.
inBlock((X, Y), (BX, BY)) :- blockSize(N), cell((X, Y)),
        block((BX, BY)), BX = (X - 1) / N + 1,
        BY = (Y - 1) / N + 1.
sameBlock(C1, C2) :- inBlock(C1, B), inBlock(C2, B),
        C1 != C2.
valid_output(true) :- not valid_output(false).
cellVal((X, Y), V) :- holds(cell(X, Y), V).
```

Listing 1.3. Background knowledge of the Visual Sudoku 9x9 task.

```
#constant(valid, false).
#constant(valid, true).
#modeh(valid_output(const(valid))).
#modeb(1, sameRow(var(cell), var(cell))).
#modeb(1, sameCol(var(cell), var(cell))).
#modeb(1, sameBlock(var(cell), var(cell))).
#modeb(2, cellVal(var(cell), var(element))).
```

Listing 1.4. Mode declarations for the Visual Sudoku 9x9 task.

```
rank(two). rank(three). rank(four). rank(five). rank(six).
rank(seven). rank(eight). rank(nine). rank(ten). rank(jack).
rank(queen). rank(king). rank(ace). rank_value(two,2).
rank_value(three,3). rank_value(four,4). rank_value(five,5).
rank_value(six,6). rank_value(seven,7). rank_value(eight,8).
rank_value(nine,9). rank_value(ten,10). rank_value(jack,11).
rank_value(queen,12). rank_value(king,13). rank_value(ace,14).
suit(diamonds).
suit(spades).
suit(hearts).
suit(clubs).
rank_higher(R1,R2) :- rank_value(R1,V1), rank_value(R2,V2),
      V1 > V2.
player(1..4).
priority_player(P1, P2) :- player(P1), player(P2), P1 < P2.
player_card(P, R, S) :- holds(player_card(P), R, S).
player_suit(P, S) :- player_card(P, _, S).
player_rank_higher(P1, P2) :- player_card(P1, R1, _),
      player_card(P2, R2, _), rank_higher(R1, R2).
maybe_winner(P) :- player(P), not loses(P).
actually_loses(P1) :- maybe_winner(P1), maybe_winner(P2),
      priority_player(P2, P1).
winner(P) :- maybe_winner(P), not actually_loses(P).
```

Listing 1.5. Background knowledge of the Follow Suit Winner task.

```
#constant(player, 1). #constant(player, 2). #constant(player, 3).
#constant(player, 4). #modeh(loses(var(player))).
#modeb(1, var(suit) != var(suit)).
#modeb(2, player_suit(var(player), var(suit)), (positive)).
#modeb(1, player_suit(const(player), var(suit)), (positive)).
#modeb(1, player_rank_higher(var(player), var(player)),
      (positive)).
```

Listing 1.6. Mode declarations for the Follow Suit Winner task.

D Induced Programs

We include here some of the answer set programs induced by Embed2Rule (using ILASP) to solve the reasoning tasks in the paper.

```
:- set_assignment(V1,V2); not set_hit(V2).
set_hit(V1) :- hitting_set_element(V3); super_set_entry(V2,V3);
        set_assignment(V2,V1).
2{hitting_set_element(0); hitting_set_element(1);
        hitting_set_element(2); hitting_set_element(3);
        hitting_set_element(4) }2.
```

Listing 1.7. Induced rules for the Hitting Sets 5-4 task.

```
valid_output(false) :- sameRow(V1,V2); cellVal(V1,V3);
        cellVal(V2,V3).
valid_output(false) :- sameCol(V1,V2); cellVal(V1,V3);
        cellVal(V2,V3).
```

Listing 1.8. Induced rules for the Visual Sudoku 4x4 cases. Only the constraints over rows and columns are learned.

```
valid_output(false) :- sameCol(V1,V2); cellVal(V1,V3);
        cellVal(V2,V3).
```

Listing 1.9. Induced rules for the Visual Sudoku 9x9 case. Only the constraints over columns is learned

```
loses(V1) :- V2 != V3; player_suit(V1,V2); player_suit(1,V3).
loses(V1) :- player_suit(V1,V3); player_suit(V2,V3);
        player_rank_higher(V2,V1).
```

Listing 1.10. Induced rules for the Follow Suit Winner task.

References

1. Aspis, Y., Broda, K., Lobo, J., Russo, A.: Embed2Sym - scalable neuro-symbolic reasoning via clustered embeddings. In: Proceedings of the 19th International Conference on Principles of Knowledge Representation and Reasoning, pp. 421–431, August 2022. https://doi.org/10.24963/kr.2022/44, https://doi.org/10.24963/kr.2022/44
2. Augustine, E., Pryor, C., Dickens, C., Pujara, J., Wang, W.Y., Getoor, L.: Visual sudoku puzzle classification: a suite of collective neuro-symbolic tasks. In: d'Avila Garcez, A.S., Jiménez-Ruiz, E. (eds.) Proceedings of the 16th International Workshop on Neural-Symbolic Learning and Reasoning as part of the 2nd International Joint Conference on Learning & Reasoning (IJCLR 2022), Cumberland Lodge, Windsor Great Park, UK, September 28-30, 2022. CEUR Workshop Proceedings, vol. 3212, pp. 15–29. CEUR-WS.org (2022), https://ceur-ws.org/Vol-3212/paper2.pdf
3. Badreddine, S., d'Avila Garcez, A., Serafini, L., Spranger, M.: Logic tensor networks. Artificial Intelligence **303**, 103649 (2022). https://doi.org/10.1016/j.artint.2021.103649, https://www.sciencedirect.com/science/article/pii/S0004370221002009
4. Charalambous, T., Aspis, Y., Russo, A.: Neuralfastlas: Fast logic-based learning from raw data (2023)
5. Cunnington, D., Law, M., Lobo, J., Russo, A.: Ffnsl: feed-forward neural-symbolic learner. Mach. Learn. **112**(2), 515–569 (2023)
6. Cunnington, D., Law, M., Lobo, J., Russo, A.: Neuro-symbolic learning of answer set programs from raw data. In: Proceedings of the Thirty-Second International Joint Conference on Artificial Intelligence, pp. 3586–3596. International Joint Conferences on Artificial Intelligence Organization (8 2023)
7. Cunnington, D., Law, M., Lobo, J., Russo, A.: The role of foundation models in neuro-symbolic learning and reasoning (2024). https://arxiv.org/abs/2402.01889
8. Dai, W.Z., Muggleton, S.: Abductive knowledge induction from raw data. In: Zhou, Z.H. (ed.) Proceedings of the Thirtieth International Joint Conference on Artificial Intelligence, IJCAI-21. pp. 1845–1851. International Joint Conferences on Artificial Intelligence Organization (8 2021). https://doi.org/10.24963/ijcai.2021/254. https://doi.org/10.24963/ijcai.2021/254, main Track
9. Daniele, A., Campari, T., Malhotra, S., Serafini, L.: Deep symbolic learning: Discovering symbols and rules from perceptions. In: Elkind, E. (ed.) Proceedings of the Thirty-Second International Joint Conference on Artificial Intelligence, IJCAI-23, pp. 3597–3605. International Joint Conferences on Artificial Intelligence Organization (8 2023). https://doi.org/10.24963/ijcai.2023/400. https://doi.org/10.24963/ijcai.2023/400, main Track
10. Dasaratha, S., Puranam, S.A., Phogat, K.S., Tiyyagura, S.R., Duffy, N.P.: Deeppsl: End-to-end perception and reasoning. In: Elkind, E. (ed.) Proceedings of the Thirty-Second International Joint Conference on Artificial Intelligence, IJCAI-23, pp. 3606–3614. International Joint Conferences on Artificial Intelligence Organization, August 2023. https://doi.org/10.24963/ijcai.2023/401, https://doi.org/10.24963/ijcai.2023/401, main Track
11. Defresne, M., Barbe, S., Schiex, T.: Scalable coupling of deep learning with logical reasoning. In: Elkind, E. (ed.) Proceedings of the Thirty-Second International Joint Conference on Artificial Intelligence, IJCAI-23, pp. 3615–3623. International Joint Conferences on Artificial Intelligence Organization (8 2023). https://doi.org/10.24963/ijcai.2023/402, https://doi.org/10.24963/ijcai.2023/402, main Track

12. Evans, R., Grefenstette, E.: Learning explanatory rules from noisy data. J. Artif. Intell. Res. **61**, 1–64 (2018)
13. He, K., Zhang, X., Ren, S., Sun, J.: Deep residual learning for image recognition. In: Proceedings of the IEEE Conference on Computer Vision and Pattern Recognition, pp. 770–778 (2016)
14. Huang, Y.X., Dai, W.Z., Cai, L.W., Muggleton, S.H., Jiang, Y.: Fast abductive learning by similarity-based consistency optimization. Adv. Neural. Inf. Process. Syst. **34**, 26574–26584 (2021)
15. Huang, Y.X., Dai, W.Z., Jiang, Y., Zhou, Z.: Enabling knowledge refinement upon new concepts in abductive learning. In: AAAI Conference on Artificial Intelligence (2023). https://api.semanticscholar.org/CorpusID:259731271
16. Huang, Y.X., Sun, Z., Li, G., Tian, X., Dai, W.Z., Hu, W., Jiang, Y., Zhou, Z.H.: Enabling abductive learning to exploit knowledge graph. In: Elkind, E. (ed.) Proceedings of the Thirty-Second International Joint Conference on Artificial Intelligence, IJCAI-23, pp. 3839–3847. International Joint Conferences on Artificial Intelligence Organization (8 2023). https://doi.org/10.24963/ijcai.2023/427, https://doi.org/10.24963/ijcai.2023/427, main Track
17. Karp, R.M.: Reducibility among Combinatorial Problems, pp. 85–103. Springer US, Boston, MA (1972). https://doi.org/10.1007/978-1-4684-2001-2_9, https://doi.org/10.1007/978-1-4684-2001-2_9
18. Kingma, D.P., Ba, J.: Adam: A method for stochastic optimization (2017)
19. van Krieken, E., Thanapalasingam, T., Tomczak, J.M., van Harmelen, F., Teije, A.T.: A-nesi: A scalable approximate method for probabilistic neurosymbolic inference. arXiv preprint arXiv:2212.12393 (2022)
20. Kuhn, H.W.: The hungarian method for the assignment problem. Naval Res. Logistics Quarterly **2**(1–2), 83–97 (1955)
21. Law, M.: Conflict-driven inductive logic programming. Theory Pract. Logic Program. **23**(2), 387–414 (2023)
22. Law, M., Russo, A., Broda, K.: Inductive learning of answer set programs from noisy examples. arXiv preprint arXiv:1808.08441 (2018)
23. Law, M., Russo, A., Broda, K.: The ilasp system for inductive learning of answer set programs. https://arxiv.org/abs/2005.00904 (2020)
24. Law, M., Russo, A., Broda, K., Bertino, E.: Scalable non-observational predicate learning in asp. In: Zhou, Z.H. (ed.) Proceedings of the Thirtieth International Joint Conference on Artificial Intelligence, IJCAI-21, pp. 1936–1943. International Joint Conferences on Artificial Intelligence Organization, August 2021. https://doi.org/10.24963/ijcai.2021/267, https://doi.org/10.24963/ijcai.2021/267, main Track
25. LeCun, Y., Bottou, L., Bengio, Y., Haffner, P.: Gradient-based learning applied to document recognition. Proc. IEEE **86**(11), 2278–2324 (1998)
26. LeCun, Y., Cortes, C., Burges, C.: Mnist handwritten digit database. ATT Labs. http://yann.lecun.com/exdb/mnist **2** (2010)
27. Li, D., Li, J., Le, H., Wang, G., Savarese, S., Hoi, S.C.: LAVIS: a one-stop library for language-vision intelligence. In: Proceedings of the 61st Annual Meeting of the Association for Computational Linguistics (Volume 3: System Demonstrations), pp. 31–41. Association for Computational Linguistics, Toronto, Canada, July 2023. https://aclanthology.org/2023.acl-demo.3
28. Li, J., Li, D., Savarese, S., Hoi, S.: BLIP-2: bootstrapping language-image pre-training with frozen image encoders and large language models. In: ICML (2023)
29. Li, Z., et al: Neuro-symbolic learning yielding logical constraints. In: Thirty-seventh Conference on Neural Information Processing Systems (2023)

30. Manhaeve, R., Dumančić, S., Kimmig, A., Demeester, T., De Raedt, L.: Neural probabilistic logic programming in deepproblog. Artificial Intelligence **298**, 103504 (2021). https://doi.org/10.1016/j.artint.2021.103504, https://www.sciencedirect.com/science/article/pii/S0004370221000552
31. Manhaeve, R., Marra, G., De Raedt, L.: Approximate Inference for Neural Probabilistic Logic Programming. In: Proceedings of the 18th International Conference on Principles of Knowledge Representation and Reasoning, pp. 475–486, November 2021. https://doi.org/10.24963/kr.2021/45, https://doi.org/10.24963/kr.2021/45
32. Muggleton, S.: Inductive logic programming. New Generation Comput. **8**, 295–318 (1991)
33. Muggleton, S.H., Lin, D., Tamaddoni-Nezhad, A.: Meta-interpretive learning of higher-order dyadic datalog: predicate invention revisited. Mach. Learn. **100**(1), 49–73 (2015)
34. Pryor, C., Dickens, C., Augustine, E., Albalak, A., Wang, W.Y., Getoor, L.: Neupsl: Neural probabilistic soft logic. In: Elkind, E. (ed.) Proceedings of the Thirty-Second International Joint Conference on Artificial Intelligence, IJCAI-23, pp. 4145–4153. International Joint Conferences on Artificial Intelligence Organization, August 2023. https://doi.org/10.24963/ijcai.2023/461, https://doi.org/10.24963/ijcai.2023/461, main Track
35. Riegel, R., et al.: Logical neural networks. arXiv preprint arXiv:2006.13155 (2020)
36. Sen, P., de Carvalho, B.W., Riegel, R., Gray, A.: Neuro-symbolic inductive logic programming with logical neural networks. In: Proceedings of the AAAI Conference on Artificial Intelligence, vol. 36, pp. 8212–8219 (2022)
37. Shindo, H., Pfanschilling, V., Dhami, D.S., Kersting, K.: α ilp: thinking visual scenes as differentiable logic programs. Mach. Learn. **112**(5), 1465–1497 (2023)
38. Skryagin, A., Ochs, D., Dhami, D.S., Kersting, K.: Scalable neural-probabilistic answer set programming. J. Artif. Int. Res. **78** (dec 2023). https://doi.org/10.1613/jair.1.15027, https://doi.org/10.1613/jair.1.15027
39. Tsamoura, E., Hospedales, T., Michael, L.: Neural-symbolic integration: a compositional perspective. In: Proceedings of the AAAI Conference on Artificial Intelligence, vol. 35, pp. 5051–5060 (2021)
40. Vaswani, A., et al.: Attention is all you need. Advances in neural information processing systems **30** (2017)
41. Wang, P.W., Donti, P.L., Wilder, B., Kolter, Z.: Satnet: Bridging deep learning and logical reasoning using a differentiable satisfiability solver. In: International Conference on Machine Learning (2019), https://api.semanticscholar.org/CorpusID:168170169
42. Winters, T., Marra, G., Manhaeve, R., Raedt, L.D.: Deepstochlog: neural stochastic logic programming. In: Proceedings of the AAAI Conference on Artificial Intelligence **36**(9), 10090–10100, June 2022. https://doi.org/10.1609/aaai.v36i9.21248, https://ojs.aaai.org/index.php/AAAI/article/view/21248
43. Xu, J., Zhang, Z., Friedman, T., Liang, Y., Van den Broeck, G.: A semantic loss function for deep learning with symbolic knowledge. In: Dy, J., Krause, A. (eds.) Proceedings of the 35th International Conference on Machine Learning. Proceedings of Machine Learning Research, vol. 80, pp. 5502–5511. PMLR (10–15 Jul 2018). https://proceedings.mlr.press/v80/xu18h.html
44. Yang, Y., Song, L.: Learn to explain efficiently via neural logic inductive learning. In: International Conference on Learning Representations (2020). https://openreview.net/forum?id=SJlh8CEYDB

45. Yang, Z., Ishay, A., Lee, J.: Neurasp: Embracing neural networks into answer set programming. In: Bessiere, C. (ed.) Proceedings of the Twenty-Ninth International Joint Conference on Artificial Intelligence, IJCAI-20, pp. 1755–1762. International Joint Conferences on Artificial Intelligence Organization (7 2020). https://doi.org/10.24963/ijcai.2020/243, https://doi.org/10.24963/ijcai.2020/243, main track
46. Yin, S., et al.: A survey on multimodal large language models (2023)

ULLER: A Unified Language for Learning and Reasoning

Emile van Krieken[1]($\boxtimes$), Samy Badreddine[2]($\boxtimes$), Robin Manhaeve[3], and Eleonora Giunchiglia[4]

[1] University of Edinburgh, Edinburgh, Scotland
van.Krieken@ed.ac.uk
[2] Sony AI, Fondazione Bruno Kessler and UniTrento, Barcelona, Spain
samy.badreddine@sony.com
[3] Department of Computer Science, KU Leuven, Leuven, Belgium
[4] Imperial College London, London, England

Abstract. The field of neuro-symbolic artificial intelligence (NeSy), which combines learning and reasoning, has recently experienced significant growth. There now are a wide variety of NeSy frameworks, each with its own specific language for expressing background knowledge and how to relate it to neural networks. This heterogeneity hinders accessibility for newcomers and makes comparing different NeSy frameworks challenging. We propose a unified language for NeSy, which we call ULLER, a Unified Language for LEarning and Reasoning. ULLER encompasses a wide variety of settings, while ensuring that knowledge described in it can be used in existing NeSy systems. ULLER has a first-order logic syntax specialised for NeSy for which we provide example semantics including classical FOL, fuzzy logic, and probabilistic logic. We believe ULLER is a first step towards making NeSy research more accessible and comparable, paving the way for libraries that streamline training and evaluation across a multitude of semantics, knowledge bases, and NeSy systems.

1 Introduction

Deep learning has driven innovation in many fields for the past decade. Among the many reasons behind its central role is the ease with which it can be applied to a multitude of problems. Recently, neuro-symbolic (NeSy) methods (see, e.g., [4, 21, 24, 30, 35, 50, 57]), which belong to the NeSy subfield *informed machine learning*, [20, 53] have overcome some well-known problems affecting deep learning models by exploiting *background knowledge* available for the problem at hand. For example, knowledge can help to train models with fewer data points and/or incomplete supervisions, to create models that comply by design to a set of requirements, and to be more robust in out-of-distribution prediction tasks.

However, background knowledge makes it more challenging to obtain "frictionless reproducibility" [17] which characterises machine learning (ML). Indeed,

---

E. van Krieken and S. Badreddine—Equal Contribution.

© The Author(s), under exclusive license to Springer Nature Switzerland AG 2024
T. R. Besold et al. (Eds.): NeSy 2024, LNAI 14979, pp. 219–239, 2024.
https://doi.org/10.1007/978-3-031-71167-1_12

shared datasets and clear evaluation metrics allow ML practitioners to quickly get started with evaluating new methods and comparing it to existing work. To achieve this goal for NeSy research, we also need *frictionless sharing of knowledge*. Current NeSy frameworks all have different approaches to encode the background knowledge: some use logical languages, like first-order [4,35] and propositional logic [2,21,56], logic programming [30] or answer set programming [57] - with a wide array of different syntaxes - while other methods use plain Python programs [14]. See Sect. 5 for an overview. To compare the performance of different NeSy systems, a researcher needs to specify the same knowledge in many languages. This is a significant barrier both for researchers new to the field or even for experts, as it is a time-consuming and error-prone task.

ULLER, a Unified Language for LEarning and Reasoning. We take a first step towards frictionless sharing of knowledge in the NeSy field by proposing a *Unified Language for Learning and Reasoning* (ULLER, pronounced "OOHler" like the god of the Norse mythology). ULLER allows us to express the knowledge used in informed machine learning. Our long-term goal is to create a Python library implementing ULLER to be shared among the significant NeSy systems. First, the user expresses the knowledge in ULLER. Then, they load the data, after which they call different NeSy systems with a single line of code to train neural networks, or to use the knowledge at prediction time. This allows the NeSy community (i) to define benchmarks that include both data and knowledge, (ii) to easily compare the available NeSy systems on such benchmarks, and (iii) to lower the entry barrier to NeSy research for the broader machine learning community.

To achieve the above requires us to decouple the *syntax* of the knowledge representation from the *semantics* given by the NeSy system of interest. The syntax of ULLER, defined in Sect. 2, is based on first-order logic (FOL). However, we introduce *statements* for ULLER. Statements simplify the process of writing down function application and composition - and hence dealing with data sampling and processing pipelines. We opt for a FOL syntax because it generalises propositional logic, while being a common language for declaring general constraints. Secondly, FOL with statements is more familiar to ML researchers, who are mostly used to writing procedural statements like in Python, while having a well-defined semantics for logicians. Finally, FOL is highly expressive: We believe that it can express all knowledge currently used in NeSy methods.

The semantics of ULLER (Sect. 3), depends on (i) an *interpretation*, often referred to as a "symbol grounding" [23], which maps symbols to meanings, and (ii) a "NeSy system", which takes knowledge and its interpretation, and computes loss functions and outputs accordingly. We formalise the differences between NeSy systems by what they compute given a program in ULLER and an interpretation. For classical boolean semantics, ULLER is equivalent to standard FOL. However, we also provide example semantics for several common NeSy frameworks of fuzzy logic (such as Logic Tensor Networks [4]) and probabilistic logic (such as Semantic Loss [56] and DeepProbLog [30]). This highlights the flexibility of our language, as it can be used to express knowledge in many formalisms.

2 Syntax of ULLER

Let $\mathcal{V}$ be a set of variable symbols, $\mathcal{C}$ be a set of constant symbols, $\mathcal{D}$ be a set of domain symbols, $\mathcal{P}$ be a set of predicate symbols, $\mathcal{T}$ be a set of property symbols, and $\mathcal{F}$ be a set of function symbols. We then define the syntax of ULLER $\mathcal{L}_{\text{ULLER}}$ as a context-free grammar:

$$\begin{aligned} F &::= \forall x \in D\ (F) \mid \exists x \in D\ (F) \\ F &::= F \wedge F \mid F \vee F \mid F \Rightarrow F \mid \neg F \mid \text{P}(T, ..., T) \mid (F) \\ F &::= x := f(T, ..., T)\ (F) \\ T &::= x \mid c \mid T.\text{prop} \mid T + T \mid T - T \mid ... \end{aligned} \quad (1)$$

where $D \in \mathcal{D}$, $x \in \mathcal{V}$, $c \in \mathcal{C}$, $f, +, - \in \mathcal{F}$, $\text{P} \in \mathcal{P}$ and $\text{prop} \in \mathcal{T}$. The nonterminal symbol F is a *formula* and T is a *term*. We call $x := f(T, ..., T)(F)$ a *statement*, or just *statement*, which we discuss in Sect. 2.1. Notice that, except for basic arithmetic operations $(+, -, ...)$, functions only appear in statements.

The syntax of ULLER does not include a special syntactic construct for neural networks. Instead, we treat them as functions, where the intended meaning is given by the semantics specified by the NeSy system. We therefore hide how the NeSy system uses the neural networks to the user, so the focus is on specifying constraints rather than implementation details.

Syntactic Sugar. We use $\forall x_1 \in D_1, x_2 \in D_2(F)$ as syntactic sugar for $\forall x_1 \in D_2\ (\forall x_2 \in D_2\ (F))$ for the quantifiers. We use $x_1 := f_1(T, ..., T), x_2 := f_2(T, ..., T)\ (F)$ as syntactic sugar for $x_1 := f_1(T, ..., T)\ (x_2 := f_2(T, ..., T)\ (F))$. Finally, we also allow for binary predicates in infix notation, such as $T \leq T$.

Typing. ULLER is a dynamically typed language. We do not guarantee syntactically nor via type checker that functions and predicates only take arguments from the domain defined in their interpretations. This mimics the design of the type system of Python.

2.1 Statements

A key design choice of ULLER is the use of special statements $x := f(T, ..., T)\ (F)$ to declare (possibly random) variables obtained by applying (possibly non-deterministic) functions. The function symbols f appear only in statements, and not in the definition of terms T, like in standard FOL. Statements simplify the composition of functions. They give a syntax that is both familiar to ML researchers who are used to writing Python, and gives a clear separation between the machine learning pipeline that processes data and the constraints on the data given by the logic. We will motivate statements with the two following examples.

Example 1 (Procedural composition of functions). Consider the MNISTAdd example from Appendix A. To emphasise the ease of composing functions in ULLER, consider a scenario where the classifier f expects greyscale images while the data points in the dataset T are RGB images. We can easily apply transformations and formulate the new condition using ULLER statements:

$$\forall x \in T(\\
\quad x_1' := \text{greyscale}(x.\text{im1}), x_1'' := \text{normalise}(x_1'),\\
\quad x_2' := \text{greyscale}(x.\text{im2}), x_2'' := \text{normalise}(x_2'),\\
\quad n_1 := f(x_1''), n_2 := f(x_2'')\\
\quad (n_1 + n_2 = x.\text{sum})\\
) \tag{2}$$

◁

Example 2 (Scoping independence). Another key feature of ULLER statements is that they explicitly delimit the scopes of variables, giving control over the memoisation and independence assumptions. Consider a non-deterministic function dice() which associates a probability to each outcome of a six-sided dice throw. Consider the following program written in ULLER:

$$x := \text{dice}() \ (x = 6 \wedge \text{even}(x)). \tag{3}$$

The formula asks whether a die-throw outcome is both a six and even. For a fair dice, the probability of the formula is $\frac{1}{6}$ under probabilistic semantics.

Now consider the alternative ULLER program:

$$(x := \text{dice}() \ (x = 6)) \wedge (x := \text{dice}() \ (\text{even}(x))). \tag{4}$$

In this program, we throw two independent dice, and check if the first lands on six and the second is even. For fair dice, the probability of this formula is $\frac{1}{6} \cdot \frac{1}{2} = \frac{1}{12}$.

Consider a similar program in regular FOL (which is not allowed in ULLER):

$$(\text{dice}() = 6) \wedge \text{even}(\text{dice}()) \tag{5}$$

Here, it is ambiguous whether the outcomes of the dice are shared like in the ULLER program of (3) or not, like in (4). Many probabilistic NeSy frameworks choose the first option and memoise the outcome of the function. We argue that this behaviour should not be a default assumption from the NeSy system. Instead, dependence and memoisation scopes should be explicitly defined by the program. ULLER statements give researchers control over these scopes. ◁

3 Semantics of ULLER

In this Section, we define the semantics of ULLER. In Sect. 3.1 we discuss how ULLER interprets the symbols in the language, such as the function and domain symbols. Then, in Sect. 3.2, we discuss how some example NeSy systems interpret the formulas in ULLER.

3.1 Interpretation of the Symbols

To assign meaning to ULLER programs, we need to *interpret* the non-logical symbols in $\mathcal{L}_{\text{ULLER}}$, that is, $\mathcal{D}$, $\mathcal{P}$, $\mathcal{F}$, and $\mathcal{C}$, using an interpretation function I.

Definition 1. *An interpretation I is a function assigning a meaning to the symbols in $\mathcal{L}_{\text{ULLER}}$ under the following rules, where $\Omega_1, ..., \Omega_n, \Omega_{n+1}$ are sets.*

1. *The interpretation of a domain $D \in \mathcal{D}$ is a set Ω.*
2. *The interpretation of a predicate P of arity n is a function of n domains to $\{0, 1\}$. That is, $I(\text{P}) : \Omega_1 \times ... \times \Omega_n \rightarrow \{0, 1\}$.*
3. *The interpretation of the predicate true $\in \text{P}$ is the identity function on $\{0, 1\}$, that is, $I(\text{true}) : \{0, 1\} \rightarrow \{0, 1\}$ such that $I(\text{true})(x) = x$.*
4. *The interpretation of a constant c is an element of a domain $I(c) \in \Omega_i$.*
5. *The interpretation of a function f of arity n is a* conditional probability distribution[1] *$I(f) : \Omega_1 \times ... \times \Omega_n \rightarrow (\Omega_{n+1} \rightarrow [0, 1])$. That is, for any set of inputs $x_1 \in \Omega_1, ..., x_n \in \Omega_n$, $I(f)(x_1, ..., x_n)$ is a probability distribution on the domain Ω_{n+1}. If for all $x_1 \in \Omega_1, ..., x_n \in \Omega_n$ the probability distribution $I(f)(x_1, ..., x_n)$ is a deterministic distribution, we say that $I(f)$ is a* deterministic function.

Next, we give a probabilistic interpretation to both domains and functions. In particular, we treat functions, such as neural networks, as a *conditional distribution* given assignments $x_1 \in \Omega_1, ..., x_n \in \Omega_n$ to input variables. This allows us to represent the uncertainty of the neural networks, which NeSy systems using, for example, probabilistic and fuzzy semantics can use to compute probabilities and fuzzy truth values. We will also frequently want to use regular (deterministic) functions $f : \Omega_1 \times ... \times \Omega_n \rightarrow \Omega_{n+1}$. A regular function is a special case of a conditional distribution that we refer to as a deterministic function. We define deterministic functions with a conditional distribution using the Dirac delta distribution at $f(x_1, ..., x_n)$ for continuous distributions, and a distribution that assigns 1 to the output value $f(x_1, ..., x_n)$ for finite domains, and 0 to the other values.

3.2 Semantics of Neuro-Symbolic Systems

We next define the meaning of a formula in $\mathcal{L}_{\text{ULLER}}$, which requires both an interpretation I and a *NeSy system* $[\![\cdot]\!]$. Here, $[\![\cdot]\!]$ is a function that interprets

---

[1] To be precise, our definition is equivalent to a *probability kernel* or *Markov kernel*, which is a formalisation of the concept of a conditional probability distribution in measure theory.

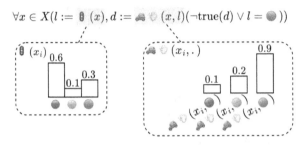

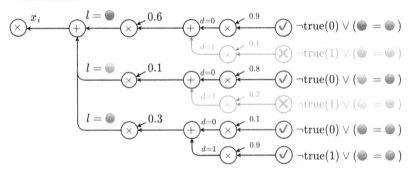

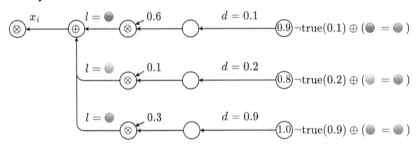

Fig. 1. The meaning of an example ULLER formula under classical, probabilistic and fuzzy semantics. We interpret the function symbols as conditional distributions. θ : $X \to (\{\bullet, \bullet, \bullet\} \to [0, 1])$ detects the concepts for red, orange, and green in the crossing representations. : $(X \times \{\bullet, \bullet, \bullet\}) \to (\{0, 1\} \to [0, 1])$ takes the decision of continuing given an extracted color light concept and the rest of the crossing scene. With abuse of notation, we ignore $I()$ and $[\![\,]\!]$. (Color figure online)

the semantics of the program statements in $\mathcal{L}_{\text{ULLER}}$. We also need a variable assignment $\eta : \mathcal{V} \to \mathcal{O}$ that maps variables $v \in \mathcal{V}$ to an element of a domain $\mathcal{O} = \cup_i \Omega_i$, where $\Omega_i = I(D_i)$ is a set associated to a domain $D_i \in \mathcal{D}$.

Definition 2. *A NeSy structure is a tuple $(I, \eta, \mathcal{B}, [\![\cdot]\!]_{I,\eta})$ where I is an interpretation, $\eta : \mathcal{V} \to \mathcal{O}$ is a variable assignment, $\mathcal{B}$ is a set of outputs and $[\![\cdot]\!]_{I,\eta} : \mathcal{L}_{\text{ULLER}} \to \mathcal{B} \cup \mathcal{O}$ is a neuro-symbolic system which is a function that assigns an output in $\mathcal{B}$ to each formula in $\mathcal{L}_{\text{ULLER}}$ and a domain element in $\mathcal{O}$ for terms T. If the interpretation and variable assignment are clear from the context, we write $[\![\cdot]\!]$ for $[\![\cdot]\!]_{I,\eta}$.*

We discuss several NeSy systems and their semantics for the NeSy language in the following sections, and provide a visual overview in Fig. 1. Each NeSy system is defined over some set of outputs $\mathcal{B}$. For example, classical logic is defined over the output $\{0, 1\}$, while fuzzy logics are defined over the interval $[0, 1]$. A neuro-symbolic system $[\![\cdot]\!]_{I,\eta}$ defines the semantics of a language expression. When a language expression is a term T, $[\![\cdot]\!]_{I,\eta}$ returns an element of the universe $\mathcal{O}$. When the language expression is a formula F, it returns an element in $\mathcal{B}$.

Notation. We use $\eta[x \mapsto a]$ to update a variable assignment η with the assignment of a to x:
$$\begin{aligned} \eta[x \mapsto a](x) &= a \\ \eta[x \mapsto a](x') &= \eta(x') \quad \text{for } x' \neq x \end{aligned} \tag{6}$$

We also define $p_f(a|T_1, ..., T_n) = I(f)([\![T_1]\!], ..., [\![T_n]\!])(a)$, which computes the probability of the element $a \in \Omega_{n+1}$ under the distribution $I(f)$, conditioned on the interpretation of the terms T_1 to T_n. That is, under $[\![T_1]\!], ..., [\![T_n]\!]$. In the coming sections, we will frequently use this shorthand to talk about the semantics of the different NeSy systems.

3.3 Classical Semantics

We first define the semantics of the NeSy language if we "choose" an option deterministically from a conditional distribution. Then, under the classical (boolean) semantics of the logical symbols, ULLER is a regular first-order logic: It becomes exactly as expressive as FOL. In this paper, we will make the deterministic choice from a distribution by taking the mode, that is, the most likely output of the conditional distribution. However, other choices are also possible.

Definition 3. *The classical structure* $(I, \eta, \{0,1\}, [\![\cdot]\!]_{I,\eta}^C)$ *is defined on boolean outputs* $\{0,1\}$ *as:*

$$[\![\forall x \in D \ (F)]\!]_{I,\eta}^C = \min_{a \in I(D)} [\![F]\!]_{I,\eta[x \mapsto a]}^C \tag{7}$$

$$[\![\exists x \in D \ (F)]\!]^C = [\![\neg \forall x \in D \ (\neg F)]\!]^C \tag{8}$$

$$[\![F_1 \wedge F_2]\!]^C = \min([\![F_1]\!]^C, [\![F_2]\!]^C), \ [\![F_1 \vee F_2]\!]^C = [\![\neg(\neg F_1 \wedge \neg F_2)]\!]^C \tag{9}$$

$$[\![\neg F]\!]^C = 1 - [\![F]\!]^C, \ [\![F_1 \Rightarrow F_2]\!]^C = [\![\neg F_1 \vee F_2]\!]^C \tag{10}$$

$$[\![P(T_1, \ldots, T_n)]\!]_{I,\eta}^C = I(P)([\![T_1]\!]^C, \ldots, [\![T_n]\!]^C) \tag{11}$$

$$[\![x]\!]_{I,\eta}^C = \eta(x), \ [\![c]\!]^C = I(c) \tag{12}$$

$$[\![T_1 + T_2]\!]^C = [\![T_1]\!]^C + [\![T_2]\!]^C \tag{13}$$

$$[\![T.\text{prop}]\!]^C = \text{get}([\![T]\!]^C, \text{prop}) \tag{14}$$

$$[\![x := f(T_1, \ldots, T_n)(F)]\!]_{I,\eta}^C = [\![F]\!]_{I,\eta[x \mapsto \arg\max_{a \in \Omega_{n+1}} p_f(a|T_1, \ldots, T_n)]}^C \tag{15}$$

In Eq. 14, $\text{get}([\![T]\!]^C, \text{prop})$ *is a deterministic function that retrieves the value of an object property.*

Equation 15 demands some explanation. The arg max takes the probability distribution given by the interpretation of the function f and chooses a value from the codomain Ω_{n+1}. In the classical structure, this choice is made deterministically by picking the mode of the distribution: the most likely element a. Then we assign this element a to the variable x through the variable assignment $\eta[x \mapsto a]$, and evaluate the rest of the formula F under this new assignment.

Importantly, the classic semantics allows us to prove whether a neuro-symbolic system "is faithful" to classical logic when all functions are deterministic. We formally introduce this notion by noting we can transform any program into a deterministic program by choosing the mode of the distribution like in Eq. 15.

Definition 4. *For some interpretation I, the* mode interpretation *$\hat{I}$ is another interpretation such that for all function symbols $f \in \mathcal{F}$, $\hat{I}(f)$ returns the mode of p_f. That is, $\hat{p}_f(a|T_1, \ldots, T_n) = \delta(a - \arg\max_{a'} p_f(a'|T_1, \ldots, T_n))$, where δ is the Dirac delta distribution. Then a neuro-symbolic system $[\![\cdot]\!]$ is* classical in the limit *if for all language statements $L \in \mathcal{L}_{\text{ULLER}}$, $[\![L]\!]_{\hat{I},\eta} = [\![L]\!]_{I,\eta}^C$.*

3.4 Probabilistic Semantics

Probabilistic semantics, also known as weighted model counting or possible world semantics in the literature, computes the probability that a formula is true. This is done by iterating over all possible assignments to the variables. We give a straightforward implementation of a probabilistic semantics for ULLER in Definition 5, but note that other probabilistic semantics exist which would require different NeSy systems.

In the upcoming definitions, we will not redefine semantics whenever it is equal to the classical semantics, up to domain differences. For instance, we will not repeat constants and variable semantics.

Definition 5. *The probabilistic structure* $(I, \eta, [0,1], \llbracket \rrbracket^P)$ *is defined on probabilities* $[0,1]$ *as:*

$$\llbracket \forall x \in D\ (F) \rrbracket^P = \prod_{a \in I(D)} \llbracket F \rrbracket^P_{I, \eta[x \mapsto a]} \qquad (16)$$

$$\llbracket F_1 \wedge F_2 \rrbracket^P = \llbracket F_1 \rrbracket^P \cdot \llbracket F_2 \rrbracket^P \qquad (17)$$

$$\llbracket x := f(T_1, ..., T_n)\ (F) \rrbracket^P = \mathbb{E}_{a \sim p_f(\cdot | T_1, ..., T_n)} \left[\llbracket F \rrbracket^P_{I, \eta[x \mapsto a]} \right] \qquad (18)$$

In probabilistic semantics, a function $f(x)$ is interpreted as a conditional distribution conditioned on x. In this case, we require computing the *expectation* of the formulas being true under the interpreted functions. This happens in Eq. 18. We also define universal aggregation as a product of independent probabilities in Eq. 16, reflecting the common i.i.d. assumption in Machine Learning. This assumption may not hold [43], in which case users can define more sophisticated NeSy systems to model a different universal aggregation behaviour.

The computation of the expectation depends on whether the output domain Ω_{n+1} is discrete or continuous. For discrete domains, Eq. 18 equals

$$\llbracket x := f(T_1, ..., T_n)\ (F) \rrbracket^P = \sum_{a \in \Omega_{n+1}} p_f(a | T_1, ..., T_n) \cdot \llbracket F \rrbracket^P_{I, \eta[x \mapsto a]}, \qquad (19)$$

while for continuous domains it equals

$$\llbracket x := f(T_1, ..., T_n)\ (F) \rrbracket^P = \int_{a \in \Omega_{n+1}} p_f(a | T_1, ..., T_n) \cdot \llbracket F \rrbracket^P_{I, \eta[x \mapsto a]} \mathrm{d}a. \qquad (20)$$

We should note that probabilistic semantics in most practical cases will be intractable because of the exponential recursion introduced in Eq. 19, not to mention the usually intractable integral in Eq. 20 [5]. We can speed this up with techniques that compile formulas into representations where computing the probability of the formula is tractable [8,11]. The probabilistic semantics is classical in the limit (Appendix C.1), and is connected to the standard weighted model counting semantics used in, for example, Semantic Loss [56], SPL [2] and DeepProbLog [30]. See Appendix D for details.

We can generalise the probabilistic semantics to algebraic model counting [15,25] by considering semirings $\mathcal{B}$ together with a product and a sum operation. This, for example, allows us to compute the most likely assignment to the variables in a formula, or to compute the gradient of the probabilistic semantics using dual numbers.

3.5 Fuzzy Semantics

Our definition for a fuzzy semantics is very similar to that of the probabilistic semantics. The two differences are using t-norms and t-conorms to connect fuzzy truth values, and the interpretation of sampling from boolean distributions.

Definition 6. *The fuzzy structure* $(I_F, \eta, [0,1], [\![ ]\!]^F)$, *where I_F is an interpretation I except that the predicate symbol* true *is interpreted as the identity function on* $[0,1]$, *is defined on fuzzy truth values* $[0,1]$ *as:*

$$[\![\forall x \in D\ (F)]\!]^F_{I_F,\eta} = \bigotimes_{a \in I(D)} [\![F]\!]^F_{I_F,\eta[x \mapsto a]} \tag{21}$$

$$[\![\exists x \in D\ (F)]\!]^F_{I_F,\eta} = \bigoplus_{a \in I(D)} [\![F]\!]^F_{I_F,\eta[x \mapsto a]} \tag{22}$$

$$[\![F_1 \wedge F_2]\!]^F = [\![F_1]\!]^F \otimes [\![F_2]\!]^F, \quad [\![F_1 \vee F_2]\!]^F = [\![F_1]\!]^F \oplus [\![F_2]\!]^F \tag{23}$$

$$[\![\text{true}(x)]\!]^F_{I,\eta} = \eta(x), \quad if\ \eta(x) \in [0,1] \tag{24}$$

$$[\![\text{eval}(x)]\!]^F = x \tag{25}$$

$$[\![x := f(T_1, ..., T_n)(F)]\!]^F = \begin{cases} [\![F]\!]^F_{I_F,\eta[x \mapsto p_f(1|T_1,...,T_n)]} & if\ \Omega_{n+1} = \{0,1\} \\ \bigoplus_{a \in \Omega_{n+1}} \begin{pmatrix} p_f(a|T_1,...,T_n) \\ \otimes [\![F]\!]^F_{I_F,\eta[x \mapsto a]} \end{pmatrix} & if\ \Omega_{n+1}\ is\ finite \end{cases} \tag{26}$$

where $\otimes : [0,1] \times [0,1] \mapsto [0,1]$ is a fuzzy t-norm and $\oplus : [0,1] \times [0,1] \mapsto [0,1]$ is a fuzzy t-conorm [4,49].

In the first case of Eq. 25, fuzzy semantics manipulates distributions over boolean codomains $\Omega_{n+1} = \{0,1\}$ as a single truth value $p_f(1|T_1, ..., T_n)$. The second case is defined for discrete, non boolean codomains. Fuzzy semantics reasons disjointly over all possible outcomes $a \in \Omega_{n+1}$ by interpreting the probability $p_f(a|T_1, \ldots, T_n) \in [0,1]$ as truth degrees. This truth degree is then conjoined with the interpretation of the rest of the formula F. Intuitively, they ask if there "exists a such that $f(T_1, \ldots, T_n)$ maps to a and that a verifies the rest of the formula F". We do not give a semantics for continuous or infinite domains in the fuzzy semantics, as we do not know of a standard definition in the neuro-symbolic literature. The fuzzy semantics is classical in the limit (see Appendix C.2), and is closely related to differentiable fuzzy logics such as Logic Tensor Networks [4,49] (see Appendix E).

In addition to Fuzzy Logics with t-norms and t-conorms for conjunction and disjunction, other NeSy frameworks such as DL2 [18] and STL [52] can also be implemented with this semantics. While fuzzy logic acts on truth values in $[0,1]$, DL2 acts on truth values in $[-\infty, 0]$ and STL in $[-\infty, \infty]$. They choose appropriate differentiable operators to implement the conjunction and disjunction. We refer the reader to [42] for details.

3.6 Sampling Semantics

The sampling semantics $[\![ ]\!]^S$ is a simple modification to the classical semantics. It samples a value from each conditional distribution and uses that value to evaluate the formula. Therefore, the only difference in $[\![ ]\!]^S$ with classical semantics in Definition 3 is in Eq. 15:

$$[\![x := f(T_1, ..., T_n)\ (F)]\!]^S = [\![F]\!]^S_{I,\eta[x \mapsto \text{sample}(p_f(\cdot|T_1, ..., T_n))]} \tag{27}$$

Here, sample is a (random) function that takes a probability distribution and samples a value from the codomain Ω_{n+1} under the distribution $p_f(\cdot|T_1, ..., T_n)$. We can repeat the computation of the sampling semantics $[\![]\!]^S$ to reduce variance, like in standard Monte Carlo methods. This semantics can be combined with gradient estimation methods to learn the parameters of neural networks [39,51]. A recent implementation of gradient estimation in the context of NeSy is the CatLog derivative trick [14], but any type of estimator based on the score function (commonly known as REINFORCE) can be used [26]. See Appendix B for a short discussion.

4 Learning and Reasoning

This section describes how to use ULLER for neuro-symbolic learning and reasoning. For a learning setting, we extend the definition of an interpretation (Definition 1) to a *parameterised interpretation*. A parameterised implementation allows us to implement neural networks with learnable parameters. For instance, a function model() can be interpreted as a neural network $I_\theta(\text{model}) = NN_\theta$.

Definition 7. *A parameterised interpretation is an interpretation I_θ that is uniquely defined by a set of parameters $\boldsymbol{\theta} \in \mathbb{R}^d$.*

Let $F \in \mathcal{L}_{ULLER}$ denote a ULLER formula that has a quantifier ranging over a dataset symbol T (for instance Example 1). Learning a parameterised interpretation typically involves searching for an optimal set of parameters $\boldsymbol{\theta}^* \in \mathbb{R}^d$ maximising the neuro-symbolic system on F over a dataset Ω_T. In most machine learning settings, we are interested in minimising a loss function over a random minibatch $x_1, ..., x_n \sim \Omega_T$. We can define such a loss function $L(\boldsymbol{\theta})$ and corresponding minimisation problem for finding parameters $\boldsymbol{\theta}^*$ with

$$L(\boldsymbol{\theta}) = -[\![F]\!]_{I_\theta \cup \{T \mapsto \{x_1,...,x_n\}\},\{\}}, \quad \boldsymbol{\theta}^* = \arg\max_{\boldsymbol{\theta} \in \mathbb{R}^d} L(\boldsymbol{\theta}). \tag{28}$$

To allow for minibatching, we interpret the domain symbol T as the minibatch $\{x_1, ..., x_n\}$. We can easily implement variations of this loss. For instance, we can combine multiple formulas and give each different weights. Notice that, for probabilistic and fuzzy semantics, $L(\boldsymbol{\theta})$ is differentiable, allowing us to use common optimisers. However, not all NeSy structures can be optimised over: This loss only makes sense when a semantics returns a value in an ordered set $\mathcal{B}$, but we also allow NeSy structures to return other kinds of values.

A different pattern, more related to reasoning, is to find the input x that maximises (or minimises) the neuro-symbolic system:

$$x^* = \arg\max_{x' \in X} [\![F]\!]_{I_\theta \cup \{T \mapsto \{x\}\},\{\}} \tag{29}$$

This strategy can be combined with adversarial learning to first find the input that most violates the background knowledge, and then corrects that input [34].

5 Related Work

The last decade has seen the rise of neuro-symbolic frameworks that allow for specifying knowledge about the behaviour of neural networks symbolically [31]. However, unlike ULLER they are restricted to a single semantics, usually variations of probabilistic (Sect. 3.4) or fuzzy semantics (Sect. 3.5). The majority of current frameworks use the syntactic *neural predicate* construct as discussed in Sect. 3.1. DeepProbLog [30] is a probabilistic logic programming language [12] with neural predicates. Variations of its syntax are used in multiple follow-up works [13,28,54]. Scallop [24] chooses to restrict its language to Datalog to improve scalability, among others [29]. For ULLER, we choose to use an expressive first-order language, leaving scalable inference to the implementation of the NeSy system. Other NeSy frameworks are based on Answer Set Programming [3,41,57], relational languages [9,33,36], temporal logics [46] and description logics [44,45,55], while Logic Tensor Networks [4] is also based on first-order logic, among others [16,32]. Finally, many commonly used NeSy frameworks are restricted to propositional logic [2,10,18,21,27,56].

Logic of Differentiable Logics (LDL) [42] defines a first-order language to compare formal properties of several NeSy frameworks. Compared to ULLER, LDL is strongly typed, while ULLER is weakly typed, and LDL does not model probabilistic semantics. In LDL, uncertainty comes from predicates, rather than functions, and does not have a syntactic construct like ULLERs statement blocks. Pylon [1] is a Python library similar in goal to ULLER. It also allows for expressing propositional logic (CNF) formulas, which can then get compiled into a Semantic Loss or fuzzy loss functions. However, by being restricted to a propositional language, Pylon is limited in expressiveness, and requires the user to manually ground out formulas.

ULLER is also heavily inspired by probabilistic programming languages [22] such as Stan [7] that specify probabilistic models in a high-level language. In particular, ULLER can be considered a first-order probabilistic programming language (FOPPL) [47] defined on boolean outputs. These boolean outputs represent the conditioning (observations) of the probabilistic model. By being first-order, the language is restricted to having a finite number of random variables. Other FOPPL languages centred on neural networks include Pyro [6] and ProbTorch [40]. These languages enforce a probabilistic semantics corresponding to that of ULLER defined in Sect. 3.4. However, ULLER does not enforce this semantics and also supports, for instance, fuzzy semantics. We leave an in-depth analysis of the relations between ULLER and aforementioned probabilistic programming languages for future work.

Other related work attempts to define building blocks for neuro-symbolic AI [48] or to categorise existing approaches [38]. We instead focus on a particular set of informed machine learning approaches, and develop a unifying language to allow communicating with them.

6 Conclusion

We introduced ULLER, a Unified Language for LEarning and Reasoning. ULLER is a first-order logic language designed for neuro-symbolic learning and reasoning, with a special statement syntax for constraining neural networks. We showed how to implement the common fuzzy and probabilistic semantics in ULLER, allowing for easy comparison between different NeSy systems. For future work, we want to implement ULLER as an easy-to-use Python library to increase the "frictionless reproducibility" of NeSy research. In this library, a researcher can easily write and share knowledge, and develop new NeSy benchmarks. We also believe such a library is a good avenue for reducing the barrier of entry into NeSy research.

Acknowledgements. We would like to thank Frank van Harmelen, Tarek Richard Besold, Luciano Serafini, Antonio Vergari, Pasquale Minervini, Thiviyan Thanapalasingam, Guy van den Broeck, Connor Pryor, Patrick Koopmann, and Mihaela Stoian for fruitful discussions during the writing of this paper. We also thank the anonymous reviewers of NeSy 2024 for their valuable feedback. This work was supported by the EU H2020 ICT48 project "TAILOR" under contract #952215. Emile van Krieken was funded by ELIAI (The Edinburgh Laboratory for Integrated Artificial Intelligence), EPSRC (grant no. EP/W002876/1).

A Practical Examples

Example 3 (MNIST Addition). Suppose we want to express the standard (single-digit) MNIST addition program using ULLER. In this setting, we have a domain T that represents a training dataset $I(T)$. In Sect. 4, we discuss how this training dataset can also be a minibatch of examples.

Each data point x consists of a pair of images (which we access with the properties im1 and im2) associated to a label representing the value of their sum (which we can intuitively access via the property sum). Finally, we have a function f that we interpret as a neural network classifying MNIST images. Then, if we want to write that for every input the outputs of the neural network should be equal to the sum of the inputs, we can write:

$$\forall x \in T$$
$$(n1 := f(x.\text{im1}), n2 := f(x.\text{im2})$$
$$(n1 + n2 = x.\text{sum}))$$

Example 4 (Smokes Friends Cancer). In this classical example of Statistical Relational Learning introduced by [37], uncertain facts in a population group are modeled using the neural predicates $\text{Friends}(x, y)$ for friendship, $\text{Smokes}(x)$ for smoking, and $\text{Cancer}(x)$ for cancer. As ULLER relies on functions rather than predicates to model uncertainty, we must use $\text{true}(a)$ to formalise the problem in our language as explained in Sect. 3.1. For simplicity, we use $(A \Leftrightarrow B) \equiv ((A \Rightarrow B) \land (B \Rightarrow A))$ to denote logical equivalences.

Here is an example of a knowledge base for this problem. Friends of friends are friends:

$$\forall x \in \text{People}, y \in \text{People}, z \in \text{People}$$
$$(a_1 := \text{Friends}(x,y), a_2 := \text{Friends}(y,z), a_3 := \text{Friends}(x,z)$$
$$((\text{true}(a_1) \land \text{true}(a_2)) \Rightarrow \text{true}(a_3))))$$

If two people are friends, either both smoke or neither does:

$$\forall x \in \text{People}, y \in \text{People}$$
$$(a_1 := \text{Friends}(x,y), a_2 := \text{Smokes}(x), a_3 := \text{Smokes}(y)$$
$$(\text{true}(a_1) \Rightarrow (\text{true}(a_2) \Leftrightarrow \text{true}(a_3))))$$

Friendless people smoke:

$$\forall x \in \text{People}$$
$$(\neg \exists y \in \text{People} \ (a_1 := \text{Friends}(x,y)(\text{true}(a_1))))$$
$$\Rightarrow a_2 := \text{Smokes}(x)(\text{true}(a_2)))$$

Smoking causes cancer:

$$\forall x \in \text{People}$$
$$(a_1 := \text{Smokes}(x), a_2 := \text{Cancer}(x)$$
$$(\text{true}(a_1) \Rightarrow \text{true}(a_2)))$$

Notice that, according to the definitions of Sect. 3.1, the probabilistic interpretation of the above formula will assume conditional independence between $a_1 \sim p_{\text{Smokes}}(\cdot|x)$ and $a_2 \sim p_{\text{Cancer}}(\cdot|x)$. To model a dependence of cancer on smoking, i.e. $a_2 \sim p_{\text{Cancer}}(\cdot|x, a_1)$, we can make the probability explicitly depend on the previous variable:

$$\forall x \in \text{People}$$
$$(a_1 := \text{Smokes}(x), a_2 := \text{Cancer}(x, a_1)$$
$$(\text{true}(a_1) \Rightarrow \text{true}(a_2)))$$

Next, we have labelled examples for each relationship. For example, for Friends(), drawing examples from a dataset T_{Friends}:

$$\forall t \in T_{\text{Friends}}$$
$$(l := \text{Friends}(t.x, t.y)$$
$$(l = t.\text{label}))$$

B Gradient Estimation

The sampling semantics in Eq. 27 is a simple way to estimate the truth value of a formula. However, since sampling is not a differentiable operation, it is not possible to use this semantics to train the neural networks. Instead, we can use the score function gradient estimation method [39] to estimate the gradient of the truth value of a formula with respect to the parameters of the neural networks. However, this requires adapting the evaluation of the formula to incorporate score function terms.

One way to implement gradient estimation methods for simple ULLER programs is to use the DiCE estimator [19] which introduces the *MagicBox* operator $\boxdot(x) = \exp(x - \bot(x))$, where $\bot$ is the StopGradient operator used in deep learning frameworks. This operator allows us to add a term that only appears when we differentiate it, and equals 1 during the forward pass. To incorporate DiCE for Unified Language for LEarning and Reasoning, we have to modify Eq. 15

$$[\![x := f(T_1, \ldots, T_n)(F)]\!]^S = [\![F]\!]^C_{\hat{I}, \mathcal{A}(\eta, S)} \cdot \sum_{i=1}^{n} \boxdot(\log p_{f_i}(\mathcal{A}(\eta, S)[x_i])) \quad (30)$$

Extensions of the DiCE estimator can be used to implement a wide variety of gradient estimation methods [51].

C Classical in the Limit

C.1 Probabilistic Semantics

The probabilistic semantics is *classical in the limit*. To show this, we note that we require that the domain becomes $\{0, 1\}$ instead of probabilities $[0, 1]$. Under this domain, the product is equal to the min function. We can use this to rewrite all but the interpretation of statements into the classical semantics.

Next, take for a statement $x := f(T_1, ..., T_n)(F)$ the induction assumption that $[\![F]\!]^P_{\hat{I}, \eta} = [\![F]\!]^C_{\hat{I}, \eta}$, where $\hat{I}$ is defined as in Definition 4. Then the interpretation of a statement is:

$$\mathbb{E}_{a \sim p_{\hat{f}}(\cdot | T_1, ..., T_n)}[[\![F]\!]^P_{\hat{I}, \eta[x \mapsto a]}] = [\![F]\!]^P_{\hat{I}, \eta[x \mapsto \arg\max_{a \in \Omega_{n+1}} p_f(a|T_1, ..., T_n)]}$$

Here, we reduce the expectation by noting that since $p_{\hat{f}}(a|T_1, ..., T_n) = \delta(a - \arg\max_{a'} p_f(a'|T_1, ..., T_n))$, exactly one element gets 1 probability (or a single element with non-zero probability, in the case of continuous distributions). This single element is chosen on the right side. Then, we use the induction assumption to find that this is equal to the classical semantics of statements given in Eq. 15.

C.2 Fuzzy Semantics

Using the axioms of t-norms, we find that the fuzzy semantics is also classical in the limit. This again can be proven by induction. For Eqs. 21 and 23, we use the boundary conditions of t-norms, which states that $x \otimes 1 = x$ for $x \in [0, 1]$. Therefore, if $x = 0$, $0 \otimes 1 = 0$ and if $x = 1$, $1 \otimes 1 = 1$, meaning t-norms act as the min operator under the domain $\{0, 1\}$.

Next, consider the program fragment $x := f(T_1, ..., T_n)$ (F) and take the induction assumption $[\![F]\!]^F_{\hat{I},\eta} = [\![F]\!]^C_{I,\eta}$. First, assume the domain $\Omega_{n+1} = \{0, 1\}$ and assume $\arg\max_{a \in \{0,1\}} p_f(a|T_1, ..., T_n) = 1$. Then, the interpretation of the statement is $[\![F]\!]^F_{\hat{I},\eta[x \mapsto p_{\hat{f}}(a=1|T_1,...,T_n)]} = [\![F]\!]^F_{\hat{I},\eta[x \mapsto 1]}$, since the Dirac distribution will put all its mass on the output 1. Similarly, if $\arg\max_{a \in \{0,1\}} p_f(a|T_1, ..., T_n) = 0$, then the interpretation is $[\![F]\!]^F_{\hat{I},\eta[x \mapsto 0]}$. Then we can simply use the induction assumption.

Finally, if $\Omega_{n+1} \neq \{0, 1\}$, then we know there is a unique output $a \in \Omega_{n+1}$ such that $p_{\hat{f}}(a|T_1, ..., T_n) = 1$, while for the other outputs $p_{\hat{f}}(a|T_1, ..., T_n) = 0$. Then, using associativity and commutativity of the t-conorm $\oplus$, the interpretation of the statement is

$$[\![F]\!]^F_{\hat{I},\eta[x \mapsto a]} \otimes p_{\hat{f}}(a|T_1, ..., T_n) \oplus \bigoplus_{a' \in \Omega_{n+1}\setminus\{a\}} [\![F]\!]^F_{\hat{I},\eta[x \mapsto a']} \otimes p_{\hat{f}}(a'|T_1, ..., T_n)$$

$$[\![F]\!]^F_{\hat{I},\eta[x \mapsto a]} \otimes 1 \oplus \bigoplus_{a' \in \Omega_{n+1}\setminus\{a\}} [\![F]\!]^F_{\hat{I},\eta[x \mapsto a']} \otimes 0$$

$$[\![F]\!]^F_{\hat{I},\eta[x \mapsto a]} \oplus \bigoplus_{a' \in \Omega_{n+1}\setminus\{a\}} 0 = [\![F]\!]^F_{\hat{I},\eta[x \mapsto a]}$$

where we again use the boundary conditions of the t-norm $\otimes$ $(1 \otimes x = x)$ and t-conorm $(0 \oplus x = x)$.

D Relation of Probabilistic Semantics to the Semantic Loss

Here, we show why the probabilistic semantics is equivalent to the weighted model counting semantics used in, for instance, the Semantic Loss. Let F be a closed formula without any statements $x := f(T_1, ..., T_n)(F')$ that only involves variables $x_1, ..., x_n$ over finite domains. The *weighted model count (WMC)* is the evaluation of the classical semantics weighted by probabilities of the assignments to variables. These probabilities are often assumed to be independent, although our framework also allows for the probabilities to depend on previous variables. This is illustrated in Example 4. The definition of the WMC is

$$\text{WMC} = \sum_{a_1 \in \Omega_1} \cdots \sum_{a_n \in \Omega_n} \prod_{i=1}^{n} p_{f_i}(a_i) [\![F]\!]^C_{I,\{x_1 \mapsto a_1, ..., x_n \mapsto a_n\}}$$
$$= \sum_{a_1 \in \Omega_1} p_{f_1}(a_1) ... \sum_{a_n \in \Omega_n} p_{f_n}(a_n) [\![F]\!]^C_{I,\{x_1 \mapsto a_1, ..., x_n \mapsto a_n\}}. \tag{31}$$

Next, we rewrite this into a program $x_1 := f_1(), ..., x_n := f_n()$ (F) such that the probabilistic semantics in Definition 5 is equal to the weighted model count. For ease of notation, let us denote S_i each statement $x_i := f_i()$ for $i = 1, ..., n$. Then, we find the probabilistic semantics of the program by sequentially expanding the interpretation of the statements:

$$[\![S_1, ..., S_n(F)]\!]^P_{I,\{\}} = \sum_{a_1 \in \Omega_1} p_{f_1}(a_1) \cdot [\![S_2, ..., S_n(F)]\!]^P_{I,\{x_1 \mapsto a_1\}}$$

$$\cdots$$
$$= \sum_{a_1 \in \Omega_1} p_{f_1}(a_1) ... \sum_{a_n \in \Omega_n} p_{f_n}(a_n) [\![F]\!]^C_{I,\{x_1 \mapsto a_1, ..., x_n \mapsto a_n\}} \quad (32)$$

$$= \text{WMC}$$

where in the last step we use that since the domains are finite and F does not contain statements, the probabilistic semantics of F is equal to the classic one.

E Relation of Fuzzy Semantics to Differentiable Fuzzy Logics

Fuzzy logics are actively used in NeSy [4,10,21,49]. We show how existing NeSy systems using fuzzy logics arise from the fuzzy semantics of ULLER. Existing fuzzy logics systems align with our interpretations of terms and logical operators, but differ in their use of fuzzy predicates, which are interpreted as functions to $[0,1]$, that is, $I_{\text{NeSy}}(P) : \Omega_1 \times \cdots \times \Omega_n \to [0,1]$. Then, the truth value of a formula is computed by evaluating the formula with the fuzzy semantics.

We can emulate this in our fuzzy semantics with the true() predicate and proof by induction. For each neural predicate $I_{\text{NeSy}}(P_i) : \Omega_1^i \times \cdots \times \Omega_{n_i}^i \to [0,1]$, we define a ULLER function $I(f_i) : \Omega_1^i \times \cdots \times \Omega_{n_i}^i \to (\{0,1\} \to [0,1])$ such that:

$$I_{\text{NeSy}}(P_i)(T_1^i, \ldots, T_{n_i}^i) = I(f_i)(T_1^i, \ldots, T_{n_i}^i)(1) \quad (33)$$

Let F be a first-order logic formula with no statements nor functions, and $[\![F]\!]^{\text{NeSy}}$ be its interpretation in a fuzzy NeSy system. Let F contain k neural atoms $P_i(T_1^i, \ldots, T_{n_i}^i)$, $i = 1 \ldots k$. Let $S_1, \ldots, S_k$ (F') be a ULLER program with k statements where S_i defines $x_i := f_i(T_1^i, \ldots, T_{n_i}^i)$, $i = 1, \ldots, k$, and F' is F where we replace every mention of $P_i(T_1^i, \ldots, T_{n_i}^i)$ by $\text{true}(x_i)$. We have:

$$[\![S_1, \ldots, S_k (F')]\!]^F = [\![F']\!]^F_{I, \eta[x_1 \mapsto p_{f_1}(1|T_1^1, \ldots, T_{n_1}^1), \ldots, x_k \mapsto p_{f_k}(1|T_1^k, \ldots, T_{n_k}^k)]} \quad (34)$$

$$= [\![F']\!]^F_{I, \eta[x_1 \mapsto I_{\text{NeSy}}(P_1)(T_1^1, \ldots, T_{n_1}^1), \ldots, x_k \mapsto I_{\text{NeSy}}(P_k)(T_1^k, \ldots, T_{n_k}^k)]} \quad (35)$$

$$= [\![F]\!]^{\text{NeSy}} \quad (36)$$

Equality (35) stems from definition (33). We derive equality (36) by induction. First, note that according to the definition of $I(\text{true})$ and the assignment in (35), we have:

$$[\![\text{true}(x_i)]\!]^F = I_{\text{NeSy}}(P_i)(T_1^i, \ldots, T_{n_i}^i) = [\![P(T_1^i, \ldots, T_{n_i}^i)]\!]^{\text{NeSy}} \quad \text{for } i = 1, \ldots, k \quad (37)$$

If our semantics use the same t-norm operator $\otimes$ as the NeSy system, then:

$$[\![F_1 \wedge F_2]\!]^{\text{F}} = [\![F_1]\!]^{\text{F}} \otimes [\![F_2]\!]^{\text{F}} = [\![F_1']\!]^{\text{NeSy}} \otimes [\![F_2']\!]^{\text{NeSy}} = [\![F_1' \wedge F_2']\!]^{\text{NeSy}} \tag{38}$$

where in the second equality we use the induction hypothesis $[\![F_1]\!]^{\text{F}} = [\![F_1']\!]^{\text{NeSy}}$ and $[\![F_2]\!]^{\text{F}} = [\![F_2']\!]^{\text{NeSy}}$. The same can naturally be derived for other logical connectives. It follows that we can emulate any formula F built with the neural predicates $P(T_1^i, \ldots, T_{n_i}^i)$, by building formula F' with the equivalently interpreted $\text{true}(x_i)$ (see Eq. (35)) and the same logical constructs, such that $[\![F]\!]^{\text{NeSy}} = [\![S_1, \ldots, S_k\ (F')]\!]^{\text{F}}$.

References

1. Ahmed, K., et al.: PYLON: a pytorch framework for learning with constraints. In: Thirty-Sixth AAAI Conference on Artificial Intelligence, AAAI 2022, Thirty-Fourth Conference on Innovative Applications of Artificial Intelligence, IAAI 2022, The Twelveth Symposium on Educational Advances in Artificial Intelligence, EAAI 2022 Virtual Event, 22 February–1 March 2022, pp. 13152–13154. AAAI Press (2022). https://doi.org/10.1609/AAAI.V36I11.21711
2. Ahmed, K., Teso, S., Chang, K., den Broeck, G.V., Vergari, A.: Semantic probabilistic layers for neuro-symbolic learning. In: Koyejo, S., Mohamed, S., Agarwal, A., Belgrave, D., Cho, K., Oh, A. (eds.) Advances in Neural Information Processing Systems 35: Annual Conference on Neural Information Processing Systems 2022, NeurIPS 2022, New Orleans, LA, USA, 28 November–9 December 2022 (2022). http://papers.nips.cc/paper_files/paper/2022/hash/c182ec594f38926b7fcb827635b9a8f4-Abstract-Conference.html
3. Aspis, Y., Broda, K., Lobo, J., Russo, A.: Embed2Sym - scalable neuro-symbolic reasoning via clustered embeddings. In: Proceedings of the Nineteenth International Conference on Principles of Knowledge Representation and Reasoning. International Joint Conferences on Artificial Intelligence Organization, Haifa, Israel, pp. 421–431 (2022). https://doi.org/10.24963/kr.2022/44
4. Badreddine, S., d'Avila Garcez, A., Serafini, L., Spranger, M.: Logic tensor networks. Artif. Intell. **303**, 103649 (2022). https://doi.org/10.1016/j.artint.2021.103649
5. Belle, V., Passerini, A., Van den Broeck, G.: Probabilistic inference in hybrid domains by weighted model integration. In: Proceedings of 24th International Joint Conference on Artificial Intelligence (IJCAI), vol. 2015, pp. 2770–2776 (2015)
6. Bingham, E., et al.: Pyro: deep universal probabilistic programming. J. Mach. Learn. Res. **20**, 28:1–28:6 (2019)
7. Carpenter, B., et al.: Stan: a probabilistic programming language. J. Stat. Softw. **76** (2017)
8. Chavira, M., Darwiche, A.: On probabilistic inference by weighted model counting. Artif. Intell. **172**(6), 772–799 (2008). https://doi.org/10.1016/j.artint.2007.11.002
9. Cohen, W.W.: TensorLog: a differentiable deductive database. arXiv:1605.06523 (2016)
10. Daniele, A., van Krieken, E., Serafini, L., van Harmelen, F.: Refining neural network predictions using background knowledge. Mach. Learn. **112**(9), 3293–3331 (2023). https://doi.org/10.1007/S10994-023-06310-3

11. Darwiche, A.: SDD: a new canonical representation of propositional knowledge bases. In: IJCAI International Joint Conference on Artificial Intelligence, pp. 819–826 (2011). https://doi.org/10.5591/978-1-57735-516-8/IJCAI11-143
12. De Raedt, L., Kimmig, A.: Probabilistic (logic) programming concepts. Mach. Learn. **100**(1), 5–47 (2015). https://doi.org/10.1007/s10994-015-5494-z
13. De Smet, L., et al.: Neural probabilistic logic programming in discrete-continuous domains (2023). https://doi.org/10.48550/arXiv.2303.04660
14. De Smet, L., Sansone, E., Zuidberg Dos Martires, P.: Differentiable sampling of categorical distributions using the catlog-derivative trick. Adv. Neural Inf. Process. Syst. **36** (2024)
15. Derkinderen, V., Manhaeve, R., Dos Martires, P.Z., De Raedt, L.: Semirings for probabilistic and neuro-symbolic logic programming. Int. J. Appro. Reason. 109130 (2024)
16. Diligenti, M., Gori, M., Sacca, C.: Semantic-based regularization for learning and inference. Artif. Intell. **244**, 143–165 (2017)
17. Donoho, D.: Data science at the singularity. arXiv preprint arXiv:2310.00865 (2023)
18. Fischer, M., Balunovic, M., Drachsler-Cohen, D., Gehr, T., Zhang, C., Vechev, M.: Dl2: training and querying neural networks with logic. In: International Conference on Machine Learning, pp. 1931–1941. PMLR (2019)
19. Foerster, J., Farquhar, G., Al-Shedivat, M., Rocktäschel, T., Xing, E., Whiteson, S.: DiCE: the infinitely differentiable Monte Carlo estimator. In: International Conference on Machine Learning, pp. 1529–1538 (2018)
20. Giunchiglia, E., Stoian, M.C., Lukasiewicz, T.: Deep Learning with Logical Constraints. In: Raedt, L.D. (ed.) Proceedings of the Thirty-First International Joint Conference on Artificial Intelligence, IJCAI 2022, Vienna, Austria, 23–29 July 2022, pp. 5478–5485. ijcai.org (2022). https://doi.org/10.24963/ijcai.2022/767
21. Giunchiglia, E., Tatomir, A., Stoian, M.C.ă., Lukasiewicz, T.: CCN+: a neuro-symbolic framework for deep learning with requirements. Int. J. Appro. Reason. 109124 (2024). https://doi.org/10.1016/j.ijar.2024.109124
22. Gordon, A.D., Henzinger, T.A., Nori, A.V., Rajamani, S.K.: Probabilistic programming. In: Future of Software Engineering Proceedings, pp. 167–181 (2014)
23. Harnad, S.: The symbol grounding problem. Physica D **42**(1–3), 335–346 (1990)
24. Huang, J., et al.: Scallop: from probabilistic deductive databases to scalable differentiable reasoning. Adv. Neural Inf. Process. Syst. (2021)
25. Kimmig, A., Van den Broeck, G., De Raedt, L.: Algebraic model counting. J. Appl. Log. **22**, 46–62 (2017)
26. Kool, W., van Hoof, H., Welling, M.: Buy 4 REINFORCE samples, get a baseline for free!, p. 14 (2019)
27. van Krieken, E., et al.: A-nesi: A scalable approximate method for probabilistic neurosymbolic inference. In: Oh, A., Naumann, T., Globerson, A., Saenko, K., Hardt, M., Levine, S. (eds.) Advances in Neural Information Processing Systems 36: Annual Conference on Neural Information Processing Systems 2023, NeurIPS 2023, New Orleans, LA, USA, 10–16 December 2023 (2023). http://papers.nips.cc/paper_files/paper/2023/hash/4d9944ab3330fe6af8efb9260aa9f307-Abstract-Conference.html
28. Maene, J., Raedt, L.D.: Soft-unification in deep probabilistic logic. In: Thirty-Seventh Conference on Neural Information Processing Systems (2023)
29. Magnini, M., Ciatto, G., Omicini, A.: On the design of PSyKI: a platform for symbolic knowledge injection into sub-symbolic predictors. In: Calvaresi, D., Najjar,

A., Winikoff, M., Frä mling, K. (eds.) Explainable and Transparent AI and Multi-Agent Systems, vol. 13283, pp. 90–108. Springer, Cham (2022). https://doi.org/10.1007/978-3-031-15565-9_6
30. Manhaeve, R., Dumancic, S., Kimmig, A., Demeester, T., De Raedt, L.: DeepProbLog: neural probabilistic logic programming. In: Proceedings of NeurIPS (2018)
31. Marra, G., Dumančić, S., Manhaeve, R., De Raedt, L.: From statistical relational to neural symbolic artificial intelligence: a survey. arXiv:2108.11451 (2021)
32. Marra, G., Giannini, F., Diligenti, M., Gori, M.: LYRICS: a general interface layer to integrate logic inference and deep learning. In: Brefeld, U., Fromont, E., Hotho, A., Knobbe, A., Maathuis, M., Robardet, C. (eds.) ECML PKDD 2019. LNCS (LNAI), vol. 11907, pp. 283–298. Springer, Cham (2020). https://doi.org/10.1007/978-3-030-46147-8_17
33. Marra, G., Kuželka, O.: Neural Markov logic networks. In: Uncertainty in Artificial Intelligence, pp. 908–917. PMLR (2021)
34. Minervini, P., Riedel, S.: Adversarially regularising neural NLI models to integrate logical background knowledge. In: Korhonen, A., Titov, I. (eds.) Proceedings of the 22nd Conference on Computational Natural Language Learning, pp. 65–74. Association for Computational Linguistics, Brussels (2018). https://doi.org/10.18653/v1/K18-1007. https://aclanthology.org/K18-1007
35. Pryor, C., Dickens, C., Augustine, E., Albalak, A., Wang, W.Y., Getoor, L.: NeuPSL: neural probabilistic soft logic. In: Proceedings of the Thirty-Second International Joint Conference on Artificial Intelligence, pp. 4145–4153. International Joint Conferences on Artificial Intelligence Organization, Macau (2023). https://doi.org/10.24963/ijcai.2023/461
36. Pryor, C., Dickens, C., Augustine, E., Albalak, A., Wang, W.Y., Getoor, L.: Neupsl: neural probabilistic soft logic. In: Proceedings of the Thirty-Second International Joint Conference on Artificial Intelligence, IJCAI 2023, Macao, SAR, China, 19–25 August 2023, pp. 4145–4153. ijcai.org (2023). https://doi.org/10.24963/IJCAI.2023/461
37. Richardson, M., Domingos, P.: Markov logic networks. Mach. Learn. **62**(1–2), 107–136 (2006). https://doi.org/10.1007/s10994-006-5833-1
38. Sarker, M.K., Zhou, L., Eberhart, A., Hitzler, P.: Neuro-symbolic artificial intelligence. AI Commun. **34**(3), 197–209 (2021). https://doi.org/10.3233/AIC-210084
39. Schulman, J., Heess, N., Weber, T., Abbeel, P.: Gradient estimation using stochastic computation graphs. Adv. Neural Inf. Process. Syst. (2015)
40. Siddharth, N., et al.: Learning disentangled representations with semi-supervised deep generative models. In: Guyon, I., et al. (eds.) Advances in Neural Information Processing Systems, vol. 30, pp. 5927–5937. Curran Associates, Inc. (2017)
41. Skryagin, A., Stammer, W., Ochs, D., Dhami, D.S., Kersting, K.: SLASH: embracing probabilistic circuits into neural answer set programming. arXiv:2110.03395 (2021)
42. Slusarz, N., Komendantskaya, E., Daggitt, M.L., Stewart, R., Stark, K.: Logic of differentiable logics: towards a uniform semantics of dl. In: Proceedings of 24th International Conference on Logic, vol. 94, pp. 473–493 (2023)
43. Stol, M.C., Mileo, A.: Iid relaxation by logical expressivity: a research agenda for fitting logics to neurosymbolic requirements (2024)
44. Tang, Z., Hinnerichs, T., Peng, X., Zhang, X., Hoehndorf, R.: Falcon: faithful neural semantic entailment over alc ontologies. arXiv preprint arXiv:2208.07628 (2022)

45. Tang, Z., Pei, S., Peng, X., Zhuang, F., Zhang, X., Hoehndorf, R.: TAR: neural logical reasoning across TBox and ABox (2022)
46. Umili, E., Capobianco, R., De Giacomo, G.: Grounding ltlf specifications in image sequences. In: Proceedings of the International Conference on Principles of Knowledge Representation and Reasoning, vol. 19, pp. 668–678 (2023)
47. van de Meent, J.W., Paige, B., Yang, H., Wood, F.: An introduction to probabilistic programming (2021). https://doi.org/10.48550/arXiv.1809.10756
48. van Harmelen, F., ten Teije, A.: A boxology of design patterns for hybrid learning and reasoning systems. J. Web Eng. 18(1), 97–124 (2019). https://doi.org/10.13052/jwe1540-9589.18133
49. van Krieken, E., Acar, E., van Harmelen, F.: Analyzing differentiable fuzzy logic operators. Artif. Intell. **302**, 103602 (2022). https://doi.org/10.1016/j.artint.2021.103602
50. van Krieken, E., Thanapalasingam, T., Tomczak, J., van Harmelen, F., Ten Teije, A.: A-NeSI: a scalable approximate method for probabilistic neurosymbolic inference. In: Oh, A., Neumann, T., Globerson, A., Saenko, K., Hardt, M., Levine, S. (eds.) Advances in Neural Information Processing Systems, vol. 36, pp. 24586–24609. Curran Associates, Inc. (2023)
51. van Krieken, E., Tomczak, J., Ten Teije, A.: Storchastic: a framework for general stochastic automatic differentiation. In: Ranzato, M., Beygelzimer, A., Dauphin, Y., Liang, P., Vaughan, J.W. (eds.) Advances in Neural Information Processing Systems, vol. 34, pp. 7574–7587. Curran Associates, Inc. (2021)
52. Varnai, P., Dimarogonas, D.V.: On robustness metrics for learning STL tasks. In: 2020 American Control Conference (ACC), pp. 5394–5399. IEEE (2020)
53. von Rueden, L., et al.: Informed machine learning - a taxonomy and survey of integrating prior knowledge into learning systems. IEEE Trans. Knowl. Data Eng. **35**(1), 614–633 (2023). https://doi.org/10.1109/TKDE.2021.3079836
54. Winters, T., Marra, G., Manhaeve, R., De Raedt, L.: Deepstochlog: neural stochastic logic programming. In: Proceedings of the AAAI Conference on Artificial Intelligence, vol. 36, pp. 10090–10100 (2022)
55. Wu, X., Zhu, X., Zhao, Y., Dai, X.: Differentiable Fuzzy $\mathcal{ALC}$: a neural-symbolic representation language for symbol grounding (2022)
56. Xu, J., Zhang, Z., Friedman, T., Liang, Y., den Broeck, G.V.: A semantic loss function for deep learning with symbolic knowledge. In: Dy, J.G., Krause, A. (eds.) Proceedings of the 35th International Conference on Machine Learning, ICML 2018, Stockholmsmässan, Stockholm, Sweden, 10–15 July 2018. Proceedings of Machine Learning Research, vol. 80, pp. 5498–5507. PMLR (2018). http://proceedings.mlr.press/v80/xu18h.html
57. Yang, Z., Ishay, A., Lee, J.: NeurASP: embracing neural networks into answer set programming. In: Bessiere, C. (ed.) Proceedings of the Twenty-Ninth International Joint Conference on Artificial Intelligence, IJCAI-20, pp. 1755–1762. International Joint Conferences on Artificial Intelligence Organization (2020). https://doi.org/10.24963/ijcai.2020/243

Disentangling Visual Priors: Unsupervised Learning of Scene Interpretations with Compositional Autoencoder

Krzysztof Krawiec[ ] and Antoni Nowinowski[✉][ ]

Institute of Computing Science, Poznan University of Technology, Poznań, Poland
antoni.nowinowski@doctorate.put.poznan.pl

Abstract. Contemporary deep learning architectures lack principled means for capturing and handling fundamental visual concepts, like objects, shapes, geometric transforms, and other higher-level structures. We propose a neurosymbolic architecture that uses a domain-specific language to capture selected priors of image formation, including object shape, appearance, categorization, and geometric transforms. We express template programs in that language and learn their parameterization with features extracted from the scene by a convolutional neural network. When executed, the parameterized program produces geometric primitives which are rendered and assessed for correspondence with the scene content and trained via auto-association with gradient. We confront our approach with a baseline method on a synthetic benchmark and demonstrate its capacity to disentangle selected aspects of the image formation process, learn from small data, correct inference in the presence of noise, and out-of-sample generalization.

Keywords: scene interpretation learning · image understanding · disentanglement

1 Introduction

Computer vision (CV) experiences rapid progress thanks to recent advances in deep learning (DL), which keeps outperforming humans not only on benchmarks but also in demanding real-world applications. Unfortunately, the mainstream DL models still lack the capacity of structural, higher-level interpretation of visual information. Most of their impressive feats concern low-level image processing, where local features and patterns are essential. As a result, DL excels at tasks like denoising, superresolution, style transfer, object detection, and similar. However, as soon as higher-level, structural descriptions become essential, DL models tend to overfit, fail, and – in the generative setting – hallucinate, producing images that are obviously incoherent for humans.

The remedy that is nowadays being proposed to address these issues is to throw more data at the model. While this may indeed bring measurable improvements in some cases, the law of diminishing returns renders this strategy impractical: gaining even a tiny improvement may require vast amounts of data, which often needs to be subject to costly labeling. Moreover, empirical and theoretical works indicate that this policy is fundamentally flawed and will never address the problem of the long tails of distributions and out-of-sample generalization (see, e.g., [5]). Recent works suggest that these limitations affect even the most sophisticated and largest architectures, large language models [21]. It becomes thus evident that contemporary DL still lacks the means for principled capturing and handling of fundamental CV concepts, like objects, shapes, spatial relationships between them, and other higher-level structures.

In this study, we posit that *the promising avenue for making CV systems capable of principled, scalable scene interpretation is to equip them with elements of domain-specific knowledge about the image formation process*. We achieve that by designing a neurosymbolic architecture of Disentangling Visual Priors (DVP) that uses a domain-specific language (DSL) to capture selected priors of image formation, including object compactness, shape, appearance, categorization and geometric transforms. Using this DSL, we can express template programs that explain scene content and learn how to parameterize them using features extracted from the scene by a convolutional neural network (CNN). The execution of the parameterized program produces geometric primitives that are then rendered and assessed for their correspondence with the scene content. As the DSL programs and scene rendering are realized in a differentiable way, DVP forms a *compositional autoencoder* that is trainable with gradient end-to-end. Crucially, it learns from raw visual data, without object labels or other forms of supervision.

In the experimental part of this study, we demonstrate how DVP manages to autonomously learn to *disentangle* several aspects of scene content and image formation: object color from its shape, object shape from its geometric transforms, geometric transforms from each other, and object category from the remaining aspects. As a result, we obtain an interpretable, transparent image formation pipeline, which naturally explains the chain of reasoning, can learn from small data, and conveniently lends itself to further inference (e.g. object classification) and out-of-sample generalization.

This paper is organized as follows. Section 2 presents DVP. Section 3 discusses the related work. Section 4 covers the results of extensive experimenting with DVP and its juxtaposition with several baseline architectures. Section 5 concludes the paper and points to possible future research directions.

2 The Proposed Approach

In DVP, the model attempts to produce a symbolic interpretation of the perceived scene and learns by trying to align the rendering of that interpretation with the actual scene content. In this study, we consider 2D scenes featuring a single object filled with color and placed at the center of a uniform background.

DVP is a neurosymbolic architecture comprising three components (Fig. 1):

1. The **Perception** module, a convolutional neural network (CNN) that transforms the 2D input image of the scene into an image latent z,

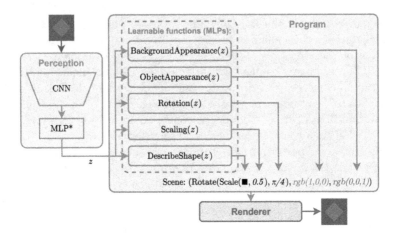

Fig. 1. DVP architecture. Perception encodes an image into a latent vector z. Program maps z to a Scene. Renderer renders the Scene as a raster image.

2. The DSL **Program** that generates and transforms visual primitives parameterized with geometric features derived from z and so produces a *hypothesis* (guess) about the scene content in terms of symbolic representation comprising objects and their visual properties,
3. The **Renderer** that renders that symbolic representation on a raster canvas.

In the following, we describe these modules on the conceptual level; for implementation details and hyperparameter setting, we refer the reader to Sect. 4.

The **Perception** can be an arbitrary neural network mapping the input image to a fixed-dimensional latent vector z, typically a CNN followed by a stack of dense layers (MLP), often referred to as *backbone* in DL jargon. The specific variants of Perception used in this study are covered in Sect. 4.

The **Program** is parameterized with the latent z and expressed in a bespoke DSL that features the following types:

– Latent, the type of z, which is the only input to the program,
– Double, for floating-point scalar values,
– Appearance, a 3-tuple of Doubles encoding color in the RGB format,
– Shape, which stores a closed silhouette of an object (detailed below),
– Scene, a 3-tuple (Shape, Appearance, Appearance) describing respectively the object's shape, its color, and the color of the background.

Programs are composed of *functions*, some of which depend on internal parameters that can change in training. Such **learnable DSL functions** are:

– ObjectAppearance: Latent → Appearance
– BackgroundAppearance: Latent → Appearance
– Scaling: Latent → Double
– Rotation: Latent → (Double, Double)

- DescribeShape: Latent → Shape
- Prototype: Latent → Shape

Each learnable function contains a separate dense neural network (MLP) that determines the outcome of function's calculation in direct or indirect manner. The direct mode is used by all but the last function in the above list. For instance, Rotation is an MLP with the number of inputs equal to the dimensionality of z and two outputs that encode the perceived object's predicted rotation angle ϕ as $(\cos\phi, \sin\phi)$; Scaling is an MLP that returns a single positive scalar to be interpreted as a magnification factor of the object; DescribeShape contains an MLP that learns to retrieve the shape of the input object observed by Perception and conveyed by the latent z, and encode it as a vector of Elliptic Fourier Descriptors (EFD, [15]), detailed in Appendix 5. Technically, the output of the MLP is interpreted as real and imaginary parts of complex coefficients that form the spectrum which is mapped with inverse Fourier Transform to object's contour represented as complex 'time series' (x_t, y_t).

The Prototype function implements the indirect mode. It holds an array A of shape prototypes, represented as a learnable embedding (i.e. the elements of the array are parameters of this operation). It also contains an MLP which, when queried, returns the predicted index of the prototype. Overall, Prototype returns thus $A[\mathrm{MLP}(z)]$; however the indexing operation is implemented in differentiable fashion, which makes it amenable to gradient-based training algorithms.

The **non-learnable DSL functions** are:

- Scale: (Shape, Double) → Shape
- Rotate: (Shape, (Double, Double)) → Shape

where the former scales the input shape according to the scaling factor given by the second argument, and the latter rotates the input shape by ϕ given as $(\cos\phi, \sin\phi)$.

The DSL allows expressing a number of programs. For the purpose of this study, we are interested in programs with the signature Latent → Scene, where the result is passed to the Renderer. One of the programs used in the experiments in Sect. 4 is shown in Fig. 1 and has the form:

$P(z\colon \text{Latent}) \to \text{Scene} = ($
    Rotate(Scale(DescribeShape(z), Scaling(z)), Rotation(z)),
    ObjectAppearance(z),
    BackgroundAppearance(z)
)

where the shape inferred from the latent by DescribeShape is subsequently subject to scaling and rotation, after which the transformed shape is combined with its appearance and the appearance of the background, and returned as a Scene to be rendered. In Sect. 4, we compare a few variants of DVP equipped with such predefined programs.

The **Renderer** is responsible for producing the rasterized and differentiable representation of the scene produced by the Program. In recent years, several approaches to differentiable rendering have been proposed [8,11,16,19]; of those, we chose the rendering facility available in PyTorch3D [19] for our implementation of DVP, which was motivated by its versatility and ease of use.[1] This renderer operates similarly to computer graphics pipelines: the scene is approximated with a mesh, the triangles comprising the mesh are rasterized, and the resulting rasters are merged to form the final image.

Training. We train DVP via autoassociation, like conventional autoencoders. As all its components are differentiable, it can be trained with an arbitrary gradient-based algorithm. In each iteration, a training image x (or a batch thereof) is fed into the model, which responds with the raster canvas $\hat{x} =$ Renderer(Program(Perception(x))) containing the predicted rendering. Then, a loss function L is applied to these images and measures the pixel-wise error between them. Finally, we take the gradient $\nabla_\theta L(x, \hat{x})$ with respect to all parameters of the model θ and use it to update θ, accordingly to the specific variant of stochastic gradient descent. θ collects the parameters of Perception and all learnable DSL instructions in the Program. The Renderer is non-parametric; therefore, its only role is to 'translate' the gradient produced by L into the updates of θ required by the Program and the Perception.

3 Related Work

DVP represents the category of image understanding systems inspired by the *"vision as inverse graphics"* [1], which can be seen as a CV instance of the broader *analysis-by-synthesis* paradigm. While considered in the CV community for decades (see, e.g., [14]), it experienced significant advancement in recent years, thanks to the rapid progress of DL that facilitated end-to-end learning of complex, multi-staged architectures. Below, we review selected representatives of this research thread; for a thorough review of other approaches to compositional scene representation via reconstruction, see [22]; also, [6] contains a compact review of numerous works on related CV topics, including learning object geometry and multi-object scene representations, segmentation, and shape estimation.

The Multi-Object Network (MONet), proposed in [2] and used in the experimental part of this study as a baseline, is a composite unsupervised architecture that combines image segmentation based on an attention mechanism (to delineate image components) with a variational autoencoder (VAE), for rendering individual components in the scene. As such, the approach does not involve geometric aspects of image formation and scene understanding. Also, it does not involve geometric rendering of objects: the subimages of individual components are generated with the VAE and 'inpainted' into the scene using raster masks.

PriSMONet [6] attempts decomposition of 3D scenes based on their 2D views. Similarly to MONet, it parses the scene sequentially, object by object, and

---

[1] Pytorch3D can render several classes of geometric objects using representations such as meshes, point clouds, volumetric grids, and neural-network based representations, also in 3D; while this last capability was not used in this study, we plan to engage it in further works on this topic.

learns to generated objects' views composed from several aspects: shape, textural appearance and 3D extrinsics (position, orientation and scale). The background is handled separately. Object shapes are represented using the Signed Distance Function formalism, well known in CV, and generated using a separate autoencoder submodel (DeepSDF); in this sense, PriSMONet does not involve shape priors. In contrast to [2], the architecture engages differentiable rendering.

Another related research direction concerns part discovery, where the goal is to decompose the objects comprising the scene into constituents, which preferably should have well-defined semantics (i.e., segmentation at the part level, not the object level). The approaches proposed therein usually rely on mask-based representations (see, e.g. [4,10]); some of them involve also geometric transforms (e.g. [10]).

DVP distinguishes itself from the above-cited works in several ways. Firstly, it relies on a physically plausible, inherently differentiable, low-dimensional shape representation (EFD), while most other works use high-dimensional and localized representations, like pixel masks, point clouds, meshes, or signed distance functions (see [6] for review). DVP represents geometric transforms explicitly, rather than as an implicit latent, like e.g. [2]. Last but not least, it expresses the image formation process in a DSL, which facilitates disentanglement of multiple aspects of this process, i.e. object shape, appearance, and pose.

4 Experimental Results

We compare the performance of several variants of DVP to related methods and assess its ability to learn from small data and robustness to noise.

Task Formulation. One of the most popular benchmarks for compositional scene interpretation is Multi-dSprites [2]. In this study, we consider a similar problem but involving a single object. We generated a dataset of 100,000 images, each containing a single shape from one of 3 categories (ellipse, square, heart), randomly scaled and rotated, and rendered using a randomly picked color at the center of a 64×64 raster filled with a different random color. The task of the model is to reproduce this simple scene in a compositional fashion. The dataset was subsequently divided into training, validation, and test subsets of, respectively, 90k, 5k, and 5k examples. While our dataset is similar to dSprites [18], it diverges from it in centering objects in the scene, using color and a larger range of object sizes, and applying anti-aliasing in rendering.

Configurations of DVP and Baselines. We compare DVP architectures that feature two types of DSL programs, those based on *direct* inference of the object shape from the latent (DVP-D), and those based on object *prototypes* (DVP-P). In the former, we employ the program P presented in Sect. 2. In DVP-P, we replace in P the Describe(z) call with Prototype(z).

We consider two categories of Perception modules ('backbones'), i.e. subnetworks that map the raster image to a fixed-dimensional latent vector (Sect. 2): pre-trained and not pre-trained ones (Table 1). Our pre-trained architecture of

Table 1. The configurations of DVP and the baseline models.

Name	Perception (backbone)	Number of parameters		Frozen backbone
		Total	Perception	
DVP-D❄	ConvNeXt-B	107,833,773	87,564,416	yes
DVP-P❄	ConvNeXt-B	107,827,861	87,564,416	yes
DVP-D$_{small}$	CNN1	7,940,907	4,504,320	no
DVP-P$_{small}$	CNN1	7,928,851	4,504,320	no
MONet❄	ConvNeXt-B	88,598,293	87,923,599	yes
MONet	CNN2	896,486	221,792	no

choice is ConvNeXt-B [17], a large modern model that proved very effective at many computer vision tasks [9]. In the non-pretrained case, Perception is trained from scratch alongside the rest of the model. For this variant, Perception is a 6-layer CNN (CNN1) followed by an MLP (see Appendix 5 for details).

Our baseline model is MONet [2], outlined in Sect. 3. To provide for possibly fair comparison, we devise its pre-trained and non-pretrained variant: in the former, we combine it with ConvNeXt-B serving as part of the feature extraction backbone network (the counterpart of Perception in DVP); in the latter it is the original CNN used in MONet (CNN2 in Table 1).

The models were trained using the Adam algorithm [12] with the learning rate 0.0001. The training lasted for 40 epochs, except for DVP$_{small}$ configurations trained on the full dataset, which were trained for 160 epochs. A typical training run lasted 3 to 4 h on a PC with NVIDIA GeForce RTX 3090 GPU.

Data Scalability. We expect the compositional constraints imposed by the DSL to narrow the space of possible scene interpretations and facilitate learning from small data, so we trained DVP and the baseline architectures in three scenarios: on the entire training set (100%, 90k examples) and on the training set reduced (via random sampling) to 5% and 1%, i.e. respectively 4.5k and 900 examples.

In Table 2, we juxtapose the test-set reconstruction accuracy of DVP with the reference configs using commonly used metrics: Mean Square Error (MSE), Structural Similarity Measure (SSIM, [20]), Intersection over Union (IoU), and Adjusted Rand Index (ARI[2]). While MSE is calculated directly from the RGB values of the input image and model's rendering (scaled to the $[0, 1]$ interval), IoU and ARI require the rendered pixels to be unambiguously assigned to objects or the background. We achieve that by forcing the models to render scenes with white objects on a black background, which results in binary masks representing

---

[2] ARI measures the similarity of two clusterings by counting the numbers of pairs of examples that belong to the same/different clusters in them and adjusting those numbers for the odds of chance agreement. Here, the examples are pixels, and there are two clusters: the background and the foreground.

Table 2. Reconstruction accuracy of DVP and the baselines. The best results are highlighted in bold.

Method	Training set size	MSE	SSIM	IoU	ARI
DVP-D❄	100%	0.000305	0.9864	**0.9852**	0.9843
DVP-P❄	100%	0.000606	0.9745	0.9772	0.9754
DVP-D$_{small}$	100%	0.001597	0.9264	0.9115	0.9028
DVP-P$_{small}$	100%	0.002636	0.8960	0.8767	0.8679
MONet	100%	0.000141	0.9889	0.9754	**0.9877**
MONet❄	100%	**0.000137**	0.9897	0.9751	0.9875
DVP-D❄	5%	0.001216	0.9635	0.9744	0.9729
DVP-P❄	5%	0.001204	0.9623	0.9717	0.9699
DVP-D$_{small}$	5%	0.005360	0.8387	0.7965	0.7952
DVP-P$_{small}$	5%	0.006917	0.8150	0.7531	0.7495
MONet	5%	0.000544	0.9761	0.9752	**0.9859**
MONet❄	5%	**0.000324**	**0.9829**	**0.9753**	**0.9859**
DVP-D❄	1%	**0.004970**	**0.8945**	**0.9351**	**0.9334**
DVP-P❄	1%	0.007167	0.8444	0.8608	0.8591
DVP-D$_{small}$	1%	0.008119	0.7910	0.7094	0.7118
DVP-P$_{small}$	1%	0.009051	0.7778	0.6832	0.6788
MONet	1%	0.020961	0.7654	0.6390	0.7764
MONet❄	1%	0.012958	0.8277	0.7640	0.8457

the assignment of pixels[3] (in contrast to complete rendering, where the model controls also the colors).

When training models on the full training set (100%), DVP is clearly worse than MONet on MSE, which can be explained by the latter using raster masks to delineate objects from the background. Nevertheless, the remaining metrics suggest that the gap between the methods is not that big; in particular, when using the pre-trained large perception, DVP in the direct mode manages to perform almost on par on SSIM and beats MONet on the IoU.

When trained on 5% examples from the original training set, all methods observe deterioration on all metrics (though MONet configurations maintain almost unaffected IoU and ARI); this is particularly evident for the MSE, which increases several folds for all configurations. When training on 1% of the original training set, all configurations experience further deterioration on all metrics. However, this time MONet seems to be more affected than DVP, in particular on MSE (almost 2 orders of magnitude compared to the 5% scenario) and on the IoU (over 20% point loss for both pre-trained and non-pretrained variant). In contrast, MSE for DVP increases by a single-digit factor, and other metrics

---

[3] Our implementation reuses object masks produced in the RGB rendering process.

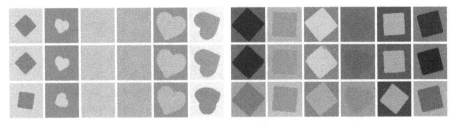

(a) Scene reconstructions produced by models trained on full training dataset.
(b) Scene reconstructions produced by models trained on 5% of the training data.

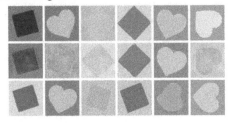

(c) Scene reconstructions produced by models trained on 1% of the training data.

Fig. 2. The reconstructions for 6 test-set examples that DVP fared worst on in terms of MSE, for models trained on 5% (a) and 1% (b) of the training set. Row-wise: the input image; the output of MONet$_*$; the output of DVP-P$_*$.

drop only moderately. This confirms that DVP is capable of learning effectively from small data, also when forced to train the Perception from scratch.

In Fig. 2, we present the rendering of selected test-set examples produced by one of the DVP models (DVP-P$_*$) and compare it with one of the baselines (MONet$_*$). As the best renderings produced by all configurations are virtually indistinguishable from the input image, we focus on the worst cases, i.e. the 6 examples rendered with the largest MSE error by DVP-P$_*$. For the models trained on 5% of data, the differences between the reconstructions produced by DVP and MONet can be traced back to their different operating principles: MONet is better at reproducing colors, but worse at modeling the shape of the objects. On the other hand, DVP can occasionally fail to predict the correct rotation of the object. For the models trained on 1% of data, DVP can mangle the shape, while MONet may struggle with figure-ground separation, producing incorrect masks that blur the object and the background. It is important to note that the examples with the largest MSE error contain large objects, as pixel-wise metrics roughly correlate with object size.

Robustness. Figure 3 presents how the metrics of the models trained on all data (100%) degrade with the increasing standard deviation σ^2 of normally distributed white noise added to pixels of test-set images. While MONet exhibits the best robustness on MSE, DVP is better on the qualitative metrics (IoU, SSIM and ARI), degrading more gracefully.

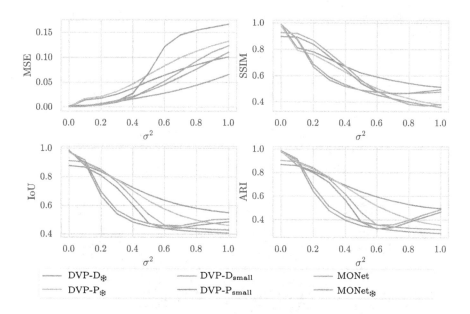

Fig. 3. The impact of introducing noise to the test-set on the metrics. Noise was sampled from normal distribution with mean 0 and standard deviation σ^2.

Explanatory Capacity. Figure 5 shows the visual representation of the prototypes formed by DVP-P$_*$ in its learnable 8-element embedding. The EFDs represent them as closed curves (Sect. 5), which may occasionally coil (e.g. #5 and #6 at the bottom of Fig. 5). All presented models, including the one trained on just 1% of data, learned prototypes that correctly capture shape categories. The remaining embedding slots contain random curves, used sparingly and contributing only marginally to the predicted shape, as evidenced by the normalized sum of embedding weights visualized in color. Models usually allocate a single embedding slot per category, except for hearts, for which they often form two prototypes. Given that these prototypes are rotated in opposite (or almost opposite) directions and used alternatively (notice lower weights), we posit that in the early stages of learning, the hearts' prototype is an equilateral triangle, and Rotation co-adapts to the 120° invariance of this shape by generating a limited range of rotation angles. Once the prototype shape becomes more accurate, that invariance is lost, and it is easier to form a second prototype than to re-learn Rotate.

By assigning labels to the identified categories, we can use a DVP model as a classifier that points to the predicted category with the arg max over the outputs of the MLP in the Prototype function. We determined that all DVP models presented in Table 2, when queried in this mode, achieve classification accuracy of 99.7% or more when queried on the test set.

Table 3. Comparison of models on out-of-sample shape categories. The best results are highlighted in bold.

Method	MSE	SSIM	IoU	ARI
DVP-D$_{\circledast}$	0.009847	0.8031	0.4910	0.5858
DVP-P$_{\circledast}$	0.013051	0.7810	0.4364	0.5297
DVP-D$_{small}$	0.006580	0.8368	0.5373	0.6170
DVP-P$_{small}$	0.006772	0.8303	0.5130	0.5922
MONet	**0.001357**	**0.9554**	0.9026	0.9203
MONet$_{\circledast}$	0.002064	0.9482	**0.9308**	**0.9359**

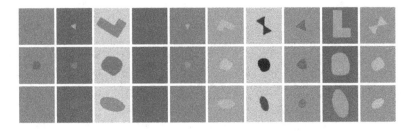

Fig. 4. Reconstructions for out-of-sample objects created by replacing shapes in the first 10 testing examples with hourglass, triangle, and L-shape. Row-wise: input scene; the output of DVP-D$_{\circledast}$; the output of DVP-D$_{small}$.

Out-of-Sample Generalization. To determine if the disentanglement of image formation aspects helps DVP to generalize well beyond the training distribution, we query selected variants of DVP and the baseline configurations on shapes from previously unseen categories: hourglass, triangle, L-shape. Table 3 and Fig. 4 summarize the quality of reconstruction. As expected, the metrics are worse than in Table 2; however, visual inspection of the reconstructed scenes reveals that DVP not only correctly models the background and the foreground colors, but also makes reasonably good predictions about object scale/size and orientation. Shape is the only aspect that is not modeled well enough. Interestingly, while DVP-D$_{small}$ substantially outperforms DVP-D$_{\circledast}$ on metrics, the latter is more faithful at reconstructing shape. Overall, the results confirm that DVP effectively disentangles the visual aspects also when faced with new types of objects.

Discussion. While conventional DL models still maintain the upper hand when compared with DVP on pixel-wise metrics (Table 2), it is important to emphasize that the precise reconstruction of all minutiae of the image content is not the primary goal here. Reconstruction error serves here only as the guidance for the learning process, and in most use cases robust information about scene structure and composition will be of more value than attention to detail. Moreover, having

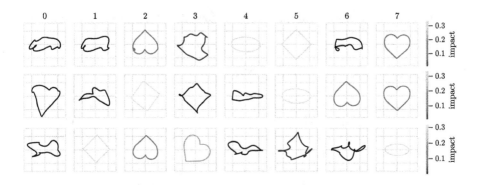

Fig. 5. The prototypes learned by DVP-P$_*$ trained on 100% (top), 5% (middle), and 1% (bottom) of training data. Color represents the overall impact, i.e. the normalized sum of weights assigned to each prototype embedding by the Prototype function, estimated from the test-set. The order of prototypes is irrelevant.

a correctly inferred scene structure significantly facilitates further processing, like precise segmentation of individual objects with conventional techniques.

One of the key advantages of DVP is *transparency* and *explainability*. For the sake of *global explanation*, each component of the model is by construction endowed with an a priori known interpretation. For *local explanation*, the outputs produced by DVP components in response to a concrete image can be inspected and interpreted, as evidenced above by our analysis of the learned prototypes. DVP produces an *'evidence-based', compositional interpretation of the scene* that can be verified and reasoned about.

Thanks to task decomposition provided by DSL programs, DVP can disentangle image formation aspects using a simple pixel-wise loss function, rather than resorting to more sophisticated means. This disentanglement addresses the combinatorial explosion of the number of interactions of shape, size, orientation, and appearance. The DSL program informs the model about the way they interact with each other, and so facilitates learning and generalization, without any need for data labeling, tagging, or other forms of supervision. In particular, even though we endow each DSL function with a specific semantic (e.g. that Rotation controls the orientation), we do not train them via supervision, with concrete output targets—the guidance they receive in training originates in the *interactions* with other DSL functions they are composed with.

Compared to conventional disentangling autoencoders (like the Variational Autoencoder, VAE [13]), the disentanglement in DVP is arguably not *entirely* emergent, as it is guided by a *manually designed* DSL program. In this sense, DVP offers 'explanation by design'. Notice, however, that explanation always requires pre-existing domain knowledge. If, for instance, one strives to determine whether a DL model has learned the concept of object rotation, that concept must be first known *to him/her*. In other words, one can equip the model with snippets of domain knowledge in advance or look for them in the model only once it has been trained. Our approach follows the first route, offering both explanation and efficient learning.

5 Conclusions and Future Work

This study demonstrated our preliminary attempt at developing a compositional and versatile DSL framework for well-founded image interpretation. Our long-term goal is the structural decomposition of complex scenes (prospectively 3D), involving multiple composite objects, alternative object representations, and other aspects of image formation (e.g. texture, object symmetry). In particular, parsing more complex scenes than those considered here will require extending the DSL to allow analysis of multiple objects while resolving the ambiguities that may originate in, among others, occlusion. In general, one may expect different types of scenes to be more amenable to interpretation by different DSL programs. For ambiguous scenes (e.g. due to occlusion), there might be multiple alternative interpretations. For these reasons, we intend to equip DVP with a generative program synthesis module that will produce alternative scene parsing DSL programs in a trial-and-error fashion, guided by feedback obtained from the confrontation of the produced rendering with the input image.

Acknowledgments. This research was supported by TAILOR, a project funded by EU Horizon 2020 research and innovation program under GA No. 952215, by the statutory funds of Poznan University of Technology and the Polish Ministry of Education and Science grant no. 0311/SBAD/0726.

Appendix 1 Technical Details of DVP

Architecture

Perception Module. The perception module is composed of CNN used for feature extraction and a submodule used for mapping those features to latent vector z (Fig. 1).

Both DVP_{small} configurations employ a CNN1 architecture, which consists of repeating the following block: a convolutional layer with a kernel size of 3×3, a GELU[4] activation function, an average pooling layer with a window size of 2×2, and a batch normalization layer. This block is repeated six times, while increasing the number of output channels: 64, 128, 256, 256, 512, 512. This is followed by a single convolutional layer with a kernel size of 1×1 (equivalent to a linear layer applied per pixel) to reduce the number of output channels to 256. The resulting tensor of size $1 \times 1 \times 256$ is flattened, forming a 256-dimensional z vector.

DVP_{*} configurations use ConvNeXt-B as the feature extraction submodule. We use the pretrained instance of this network which was trained on the ImageNet-1K dataset. The feature extractor is frozen, which means its weights

---

[4] Gaussian Error Linear Unit.

are not updated during the optimization process. The feature map produced by the extractor is extended with spatial positional encoding, flattened, and passed to the Transformer submodule, whose task is to transform the feature map into 256-dimensional z vector. This approach is inspired by Detection Transformer (DETR) [3]; our Transformer submodule reuse DETR's hyperparameters.

Learnable Functions. All learnable functions of the DSL use 3-layer MLPs with a hidden layers' size of 256 and GELU activation function. The output layer is designed to match the needs of a given DLS function in terms of the number of units and activation function. For instance, the ObjectAppearance function produces 3-dimensional vectors in the range $[0, 1]$, therefore its MLP has 3 units in the last layer, each equipped with the sigmoid activation function.

Training

Training DVP models in a generic way, i.e. starting from default random initialization of all parameters and using bare MSE as the loss function, leads on average to worse results than those reported in Table 2. To attain the reported level of accuracy, DVP needs additional guidance, particularly in its prototype-based variant DVP-P. While these aspects are usually not critical for progress in training and its convergence, we cover them in this section for completeness.

DVP-D configurations require relatively little guidance. Initially, EFD shape contours produced by the model often appear 'jagged' and contain many intersections and loops. To address this issue, we add to the main MSE loss function an extra component that encourages the model to increase the amplitude of the first component and penalizes the subsequent low-frequency components (i.e., in the absence of MSE error, this component would in the limit cause the model to produce perfect circles). This form of regularization is applied with a weight of 0.001 while processing the first 30 kimg[5] in training.

DVP-P configurations require more supervision and hyperparameter tuning. We apply the following techniques:

- The prototypes are initialized with random hexagons (even though technically speaking, the EFD order used in our configurations (8) is insufficient to precisely model all the corners of these polygons, resulting in rounded shapes).
- The prototypes are frozen for the first 30 kimg of training in case of all DVP-P$_*$ models, and respectively 480 kimg, 240 kimg and 60 kimg in case of DVP-P$_{small}$ models trained on 100%, 5%, and 1% of the training set. Without freezing, the prototypes tended to collapse to a local minimum (a circle), which made it difficult to learn how to rotate them.
- We employed the load balancing loss [7] to encourage the P prototype-weighing MLP in the Prototype DSL function to choose the prototypes uniformly. The balancing loss is turned off after 120 kimg for DVP-P$_*$ models, and respectively after 960 kimg, 480 kimg and 240 kimg in case of DVP-P$_{small}$ models trained on 100%, 5%, and 1% of the training set.

---
[5] 1 kimg = 1024 images.

- As illustrated in Fig. 5, the models occasionally reconstruct the shapes as mixtures of multiple prototypes. In order to address this issue, we apply *distribution sharpening* to the distribution produced by the prototype-weighing MLP. The sharpening starts at the 5th epoch for DVP-P$_*$ models, the 10th epoch for DVP-P$_{\text{small}}$ trained on 5% and 1% of the training set, and the 20th epoch for DVP-P$_{\text{small}}$ trained on the full training set.
- We apply gradient clipping by norm to the prototypes with the maximum norm of 0.01 in order to stabilize the training.

Appendix 2 Representing Shapes with Elliptic Fourier Descriptors

The elliptic Fourier Transform [15] is a method of encoding a closed contour with Fourier coefficients. The method can be viewed as an extension of the discrete-time Fourier Transform from the time domain to the spatial domain. We assume the contour to be encoded with the transform to be represented as a sequence of K contour points (x_p, y_p) such that $x_1 = x_K$ and $y_1 = y_K$. The elliptic Fourier transform of order N is defined as:

$$A_n = \frac{T}{2n^2\pi^2} \sum_{p=1}^{K} \frac{\Delta x_p}{\Delta t_p} \left(\cos \frac{2n\pi t_p}{T} - \cos \frac{2n\pi t_{p-1}}{T} \right)$$

$$B_n = \frac{T}{2n^2\pi^2} \sum_{p=1}^{K} \frac{\Delta x_p}{\Delta t_p} \left(\sin \frac{2n\pi t_p}{T} - \sin \frac{2n\pi t_{p-1}}{T} \right)$$

$$C_n = \frac{T}{2n^2\pi^2} \sum_{p=1}^{K} \frac{\Delta y_p}{\Delta t_p} \left(\cos \frac{2n\pi t_p}{T} - \cos \frac{2n\pi t_{p-1}}{T} \right)$$

$$D_n = \frac{T}{2n^2\pi^2} \sum_{p=1}^{K} \frac{\Delta y_p}{\Delta t_p} \left(\sin \frac{2n\pi t_p}{T} - \sin \frac{2n\pi t_{p-1}}{T} \right)$$

for $n = 1, 2, ..., N$ \quad (1)

where $\Delta x_p \equiv x_p - x_{p-1}$, $\Delta y_p \equiv y_p - y_{p-1}$, $\Delta t_p = \sqrt{\Delta x_p^2 + \Delta y_p^2}$ and $T = \sum_{p=1}^{K} \Delta t_p$.

The Elliptic Fourier Descriptors (EFD) are the coefficients A_n, B_n, C_n, and D_n. They are translation invariant by design and can be further normalized to be invariant w.r.t. rotation and scale.

The original contour can be reconstructed using the inverse transform given by the following equations:

$$x_p = \sum_{n=1}^{N} \left(A_n \cos \frac{2n\pi t_p}{T} + B_n \sin \frac{2n\pi t_p}{T} \right)$$

$$y_p = \sum_{n=1}^{N} \left(C_n \cos \frac{2n\pi t_p}{T} + D_n \sin \frac{2n\pi t_p}{T} \right)$$

for $p = 1, 2, ..., K$ \quad (2)

References

1. Barrow, H., Tenenbaum, J., Hanson, A., Riseman, E.: Recovering intrinsic scene characteristics. Comput. Vis. Syst. **2**(3–26), 2 (1978)
2. Burgess, C.P., et al.: Monet: unsupervised scene decomposition and representation arXiv:1901.11390 (2019). https://doi.org/10.48550/arXiv.1901.11390
3. Carion, N., Massa, F., Synnaeve, G., Usunier, N., Kirillov, A., Zagoruyko, S.: End-to-end object detection with transformers. In: Vedaldi, A., Bischof, H., Brox, T., Frahm, J.-M. (eds.) ECCV 2020. LNCS, vol. 12346, pp. 213–229. Springer, Cham (2020). https://doi.org/10.1007/978-3-030-58452-8_13
4. Choudhury, S., Laina, I., Rupprecht, C., Vedaldi, A.: Unsupervised part discovery from contrastive reconstruction. In: Ranzato, M., Beygelzimer, A., Dauphin, Y., Liang, P., Vaughan, J.W. (eds.) Advances in Neural Information Processing Systems, vol. 34, pp. 28104–28118. Curran Associates, Inc. (2021)
5. Cremer, C.Z.: Deep limitations? Examining expert disagreement over deep learning. Prog. Artif. Intell. **10**(4), 449–464 (2022). https://doi.org/10.1007/s13748-021-00239-1
6. Elich, C., Oswald, M.R., Pollefeys, M., Stueckler, J.: Weakly supervised learning of multi-object 3D scene decompositions using deep shape priors. Comput. Vis. Image Underst. **220**, 103440 (2022). https://doi.org/10.1016/j.cviu.2022.103440
7. Fedus, W., Zoph, B., Shazeer, N.: Switch transformers: scaling to trillion parameter models with simple and efficient sparsity. J. Mach. Learn. Res. **23**(120), 1–39 (2022). http://jmlr.org/papers/v23/21-0998.html
8. Fuji Tsang, C., et al.: Kaolin: a pytorch library for accelerating 3D deep learning research (2022). https://github.com/NVIDIAGameWorks/kaolin
9. Goldblum, M., et al.: Battle of the backbones: a large-scale comparison of pretrained models across computer vision tasks. In: Advances in Neural Information Processing Systems, vol. 36, pp. 29343–29371 (2023)
10. Hung, W.C., Jampani, V., Liu, S., Molchanov, P., Yang, M.H., Kautz, J.: Scops: self-supervised co-part segmentation. In: 2019 IEEE/CVF Conference on Computer Vision and Pattern Recognition (CVPR), pp. 869–878 (2019). https://doi.org/10.1109/CVPR.2019.00096
11. Jakob, W., et al.: Mitsuba 3 renderer (2022). https://mitsuba-renderer.org
12. Kingma, D.P., Ba, J.: Adam: a method for stochastic optimization. In: Bengio, Y., LeCun, Y. (eds.) 3rd International Conference on Learning Representations, ICLR 2015, San Diego, CA, USA, 7–9 May 2015, Conference Track Proceedings (2015). http://arxiv.org/abs/1412.6980
13. Kingma, D.P., Welling, M.: Auto-encoding variational bayes arXiv:1312.6114 (2013). https://doi.org/10.48550/arXiv.1312.6114
14. Krawiec, K.: Generative learning of visual concepts using multiobjective genetic programming. Pattern Recogn. Lett. **28**(16), 2385–2400 (2007). https://doi.org/10.1016/j.patrec.2007.08.001
15. Kuhl, F.P., Giardina, C.R.: Elliptic fourier features of a closed contour. Comput. Graphics Image Process. **18**(3), 236–258 (1982). https://doi.org/10.1016/0146-664X(82)90034-X
16. Li, T.M., Lukáč, M., Michaël, G., Ragan-Kelley, J.: Differentiable vector graphics rasterization for editing and learning. ACM Trans. Graph. (Proc. SIGGRAPH Asia) **39**(6), 193:1–193:15 (2020)

17. Liu, Z., Mao, H., Wu, C.Y., Feichtenhofer, C., Darrell, T., Xie, S.: A convnet for the 2020s. In: 2022 IEEE/CVF Conference on Computer Vision and Pattern Recognition (CVPR), pp. 11966–11976 (2022). https://doi.org/10.1109/CVPR52688.2022.01167
18. Matthey, L., Higgins, I., Hassabis, D., Lerchner, A.: Dsprites: disentanglement testing sprites dataset (2017). https://github.com/deepmind/dsprites-dataset/
19. Ravi, N., et al.: Accelerating 3D deep learning with pytorch3d arXiv:2007.08501 (2020). https://doi.org/10.48550/arXiv.2007.08501
20. Wang, Z., Bovik, A., Sheikh, H., Simoncelli, E.: Image quality assessment: from error visibility to structural similarity. IEEE Trans. Image Process. **13**(4), 600–612 (2004). https://doi.org/10.1109/TIP.2003.819861
21. Wu, Z., et al.: Reasoning or reciting? Exploring the capabilities and limitations of language models through counterfactual tasks arXiv:2307.02477 (2023). https://doi.org/10.48550/arXiv.2307.02477
22. Yuan, J., Chen, T., Li, B., Xue, X.: Compositional scene representation learning via reconstruction: a survey. IEEE Trans. Pattern Anal. Mach. Intell. **45**(10), 11540–11560 (2023). https://doi.org/10.1109/TPAMI.2023.3286184

Probing LLMs for Logical Reasoning

Francesco Manigrasso[1](✉)[iD], Stefan Schouten[2][iD], Lia Morra[1][iD], and Peter Bloem[2][iD]

[1] Politecnico di Torino, Turin, Italy
{francesco.manigrasso,lia.morra}@polito.it
[2] Vrije Universiteit, Amsterdam, Netherlands
{stefan.schouten,peter.bloem}@vu.nl
https://www.polito.it/ , https://vu.nl/en

Abstract. Recently, the question of what types of computation and cognition large language models (LLMs) are capable of has received increasing attention. With models clearly capable of convincingly faking true reasoning behavior, the question of whether they are also capable of real reasoning—and how the difference should be defined—becomes increasingly vexed. Here we introduce a new tool, Logic Tensor Probes (LTP), that may help to shed light on the problem. Logic Tensor Networks (LTN) serve as a neural symbolic framework designed for differentiable fuzzy logics. Using a pretrained LLM with frozen weights, an LTP uses the LTN framework as a diagnostic tool. This allows for the detection and localization of logical deductions within LLMs, enabling the use of first-order logic as a versatile modeling language for investigating the internal mechanisms of LLMs. The LTP can make deductions from basic assertions, and track if the model makes the same deductions from the natural language equivalent, and if so, where in the model this happens. We validate our approach through proof-of-concept experiments on hand-crafted knowledge bases derived from WordNet and on smaller samples from FrameNet.

Keywords: NeuroSymbolic AI · Logic Tensor Networks · Probing Large Language Models

1 Introduction

With the recent release of ChatGPT and GPT-4 [27], there has been a notable interest regarding the types of reasoning that large language models (LLMs) can exhibit [7,20,30]. It is evident that LLMs have the ability to generate outputs resembling reasoning that may initially appear well-reasoned but lack genuine insight upon closer examination. Nevertheless, within specific domains, LLMs demonstrate the capability to provide accurate and well-reasoned responses [1,4,17,37]. A methodology capable of distinguishing authentic reasoning from "hallucinatory" outputs generated by LLMs can offer the

---

F. Manigrasso and S. Schouten—Equal contribution.

© The Author(s), under exclusive license to Springer Nature Switzerland AG 2024
T. R. Besold et al. (Eds.): NeSy 2024, LNAI 14979, pp. 257–278, 2024.
https://doi.org/10.1007/978-3-031-71167-1_14

advantage of precisely isolating the reasoning behaviors and capabilities of LLMs and developing systems capable of choosing between valid reasoning and superficial or incorrect results. Furthermore, it could be useful during the training phase to promote accurate reasoning behaviors and discourage the production of unreliable results.

In this research, we introduce the *Logic Tensor Probe (LTP)*, tailored specifically for assessing the reasoning capabilities of Large Language Models (LLMs). The LTP analyzes the knowledge acquired by the LLM model and evaluates the validity of statements within a given knowledge base. The fundamental idea is to use the *Logic Tensor Network (LTN)* framework [2,29], which normally functions as an auxiliary loss to promote symbolic reasoning, and to have it function as a *probe* [11,18] instead. A *probe*[1] is a shallow machine learning model that is optimized to predict a target value t, based only on the hidden activations produced by a larger, frozen model m for each instance x. If the probe succeeds in predicting t, it shows that the model's representation of x contains the information necessary to map x to t. This can, for instance, be used to quantify for each layer to what extent m has learned how t relates to x [5].

The LTN framework is a *Neural Symbolic (NeSy)* method that formulates learning as maximizing the satisfiability of a knowledge base $\mathcal{K}$ expressed in Real Logic, a differentiable First Order Logic (FOL) language. Here, the LTP is trained to compute the degree of truthiness of predicates, such as `isOfClass`, that map the properties of specific instances. The LTP predicates are grounded by shallow classifiers thus acting as the probes. At training time, the LTP is trained to encode statements, such as "Gordon is a German Shepherd" and "A German Shepherd is a Dog" by learning to satisfy the corresponding FOL statements. The LTP is then used to probe the LLM for the degree of truthiness of statements that are logically entailed by those used to train it, such as "Gordon is a German Shepherd and Gordon is a Dog". If the FOL formula is satisfied, even though the `isOfClass` predicate was not explicitly trained to map the concept "Gordon" to the concept "Dog", we take it as evidence that the LTP must be able to compute the correct truth value based on information implicitly contained in the LLM embeddings.[2] By observing in which layers the degree of truthiness is maximized, we can investigate whether and which types of logical deductions are in principle possible based on the LLM embeddings. To be consistent with some form of deductive reasoning, we would expect the degree of truthiness of different FOL statements to be maximized by layers at different depths, e.g., `isOfClass`($Gordon, GermanShepherd$) to be optimally satisfied at deeper levels than `isOfClass`($Gordon, Dog$). We evaluate a proof-of-concept of this approach in two settings: first, using a newly constructed knowledge base

---

[1] The phrase *probe* is also used to refer to general inspection methods for neural networks. Here, we use it specifically to refer to shallow classifiers that take hidden activations as features.

[2] Throughout the text we use the word *embedding* to refer to the LLM's representations of its input tokens at *any* stage of the LLM's execution, not just at the initial embedding stage.

retrieved from WordNet [12], modeled on named animals and their habitats, as shown in the running examples. Second, using a subset of FrameNet [3].

Our experiments show that:

1. we can successfully train an LTN probe to use the data contained within the LLM representations
2. we can determine when an LLM deduces information from a given sentence that is not explicitly stated but is implied and captured by logical knowledge.[3]

The remainder of the paper is structured as follows. Section 2 introduces background information on the LTN framework and related work. The Sect. 3 describes the proposed architecture. In Sect. 3.2, we analyze the behavior of the LLM with sentences retrieved from WordNet and FrameNet including in Sect. 4 a description of the LLM models included in our settings. Finally, in Sect. 5 and Sect. 6, we discuss the results and future work. Code and data available at: https://github.com/sfschouten/ltn_probes.

2 Related Work

Probing Previous work has investigated probes for the semantic roles of phrases, which involves predicting what *role* different noun phrases play in the meaning of a sentence [9]. The investigation task would then involve predicting the syntactical or semantic roles of each sentence from the representation of (parts of) a sentence [23,33]. This is a specific case of our investigative task, in which we try to specifically recover that argumentative structure of the predicates that come closest to what is explicitly stated or predicates not explicitly expressed within, but still *implicit* from the sentence.

The probe training is separate from the LLM training, ensuring they measure the LLM's pre-existing knowledge. A key difference among different approaches is how the LLM internal representations are mapped to the probe inputs. Some previous work has used sentence representations [11,21], whereas others take representations specific to the spans of the relevant noun phrases [6,9,19,31,32]. Our probe does not operate only on those representations related to the span of the argument noun phrases, but *learns* to attend to the relevant parts of the sentence as part of its training procedure.

NeSy Architectures. In recent years, a considerable number of researchers have focused their attention on NeSy architectures for post-hoc interpretability [28]. Logic Tensor Networks (LTNs) [2] and Real Logic (RL) are NeSy architectures

---

[3] Possible alternative explanations include a model recalling a stored association rather than reasoning from scratch. LTN probes are *tools* that can be used to investigate such possibilities and, through careful use, eliminate them. We do not claim that a successfully trained LTN probe is always proof that an LLM shows the modelled reasoning.

used in various image tasks such as zero-shot learning and Sudoku puzzle classification, as well as reasoning tasks in combination with NeSy models and curriculum learning [22,25,26]. RL refers to the mapping of a FOL to a differentiable fuzzy logic, and LTNs refer to the neural nets built to implement an RL knowledge base. LTNs are typically incorporated as an additional module, to enhance the reasoning capabilities of the overall architecture. Manigrasso [24] et al. demonstrated that an end-to-end training approach can facilitate knowledge sharing between a feature extractor and the LTN block. Two recent works have applied LTNs in the natural language domain, focusing on Aspect-Term Sentiment Analysis [36] and argument mining [14]. To the best of our knowledge we are the first to use LTNs as a *probe*, with the weights of the main network explicitly frozen.

3 Methodology: Logic Tensor Probe

In this section, we introduce the basic notation to define *LTNs* used as *probes*. We build the concepts to translate a sentence into FOL language showing how the *LTP* training is constructed by substituting the original training set with a grounded knowledge base 𝒦. A *diagnostic* classifier is introduced taking as input the representations (hidden states) produced by an LLM while the original loss is converted into the best satisfiability framework of the LTN.

3.1 Conversion into Real Logic

In LTNs, grounding refers to the assignment of real-valued semantics to logical symbols, where individuals are depicted as vectors in a high-dimensional space and variables are associated with specific entities. Neural networks are used to model predicates, establishing relationships between entities and their truth values. Complex expressions are formed using a combination of logical connectives ($\wedge, \vee, \rightarrow, \neg$) and quantifiers ($\forall, \exists$), grounded through mathematical functions, generally neural networks, into true domain[0,1]. Training LTNs involves constructing a knowledge base with FOL axioms, with the aim of maximizing the satisfaction of these axioms. The loss is quantified by the cumulative degree of truthiness of the axioms. The objective is to determine the optimal parameters that maximize this satisfaction, as described by the formula:

$$\theta^* = \arg\max_{\theta} \left(\text{SatAgg}_{\phi \in \mathcal{K}} \left(\mathcal{G}_\theta(\phi) \right) \right).$$

3.2 From a Sentence to a Probe

Defining the LTP requires a knowledge base comprising natural language sentences paired with corresponding FOL formulas expressing (part of) their semantics. In our experiments, we used two datasets: WordNet and FrameNet.

While LLMs process sentences token-by-token, to compute the LTP we instead need embeddings organized into subject, predicate and object components. Previous work has assumed that we know exactly which tokens represent

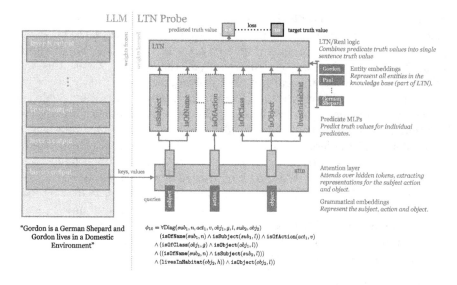

Fig. 1. A diagram of our approach. The LLM weights are frozen and a forward pass is calculated for a simple English sentence. Next, the activations of a chosen layer (in this case the first) are fed to an LTN that logically represents the sentence, along with some known implications that we are interested in. ϕ_{10} (Eq. 29) represents the sentence FOL representation of the sentence "Gordon is a German shepherd and Gordon lives in a domestic environment". Using the LLM model with an appropriate attention mechanism, subject, action and object embeddings are extracted and set as inputs to the predicates of the LTN, which computes the degree of truthiness of the FOL representation of the entire sentence.

which component, and typically use a fixed mapping between them [15,23]. We instead use a scaled dot-product attention mechanism, where each component gets a query vector (the grammatical embedding), and each token a key and value vector. The query vectors are a learned part of the probe and are initialized randomly. The key and value vectors are extracted from the LLM embeddings with a linear transformation. The final representation for each component is constructed with a standard attention operation: as a weighted sum over token representations (the value vectors), where the weights are calculated based on the (scaled) dot product between the query and key vectors. Thus, our LTN probes do not make any a priori assumptions about which tokens represent the subject, predicate, and object. Our goal is to analyze the information learned at each level of the LLM in the context of the selected sentence, identifying syntactic roles that emerge within specific layers. An illustrative example of this process is presented in Fig. 1.

Knowledge Base Construction from WordNet Synsets. Concepts were extracted from the synsets of WordNet [12] (see also Appendix B). This knowledge base $\mathcal{K}$ consists of statements related to various entities and categories within the animal kingdom, as inferred from the synsets. Categories were extracted through a hierarchical process involving two levels (macro class and class), starting from a root synset and traversing the tree formed by the hypernym relation. This methodology allows for the formulation of a knowledge base $\mathcal{K}$ containing a series of statements used to express relationships between the training data and the labels employed to train the probe. Subsequently, a different set of axioms is introduced at test time to assess the consistency of the information present in the LLM model by testing it with the probe.

We extracted 271 animal names, 753 distinct animal classes, 28 distinct habitat types, and 8 macro classes. The training set comprises a total of 6014 statements, evenly distributed between positive and negative statements.

The training set comprises statements that serve as examples for the LTP to learn the predicate grounding. The training set contains sentences such as:

- "Gordon is a German Shepherd" (positive sentence)
- "German Shepherd is a Carnivore" (positive sentence)
- "German Shepherd lives in a Domestic Environment" (positive sentence)
- "German Shepherd is a Gordon" (negative sentence)

A negative sentence is one in which the subject and object are reversed, creating semantically incorrect or logically inconsistent statements.

Conversely, the test set consists of FOL statements, and corresponding natural language sentences, that the LTP has not been exposed to during training. These statements are used to investigate whether LLMs are capable of making logical deductions. Below is a sample of the test set:

- "Kobe is a cheetah" (positive sentence)
- "Kobe is a carnivore" (positive sentence)
- "Lancelot is a saiga" (positive sentence)
- "Lancelot lives in Grassland" (positive sentence)

Through logical deductions enabled by the FOL representation, we obtain more complex sentences to probe the LLM:

- "Kobe is a cheetah and Kobe is a carnivore" (positive sentence)
- "Lancelot is a saiga and Lancelot lives in Grassland" (positive sentence)

Since the LTP must learn to map the extracted embeddings to entities, we include the same entities in both training and test sets, but in different sentences.

LTN Probing with WordNet. Each entity and animal class, along with its corresponding macro class and reference habitat, is formulated in the LTN framework. Below are the axioms used to train the LTP:

$$\phi_1 = \forall \text{Diag}(sub, n)(\text{isOfName}(sub, n)) \tag{1}$$
$$\phi_2 = \forall \text{Diag}(act, v)(\text{isOfAction}(act, v)) \tag{2}$$
$$\phi_3 = \forall \text{Diag}(obj, g)(\text{isOfClass}(obj, g)) \tag{3}$$
$$\phi_4 = \forall \text{Diag}(obj, q)(\text{isOfMacroclass}(obj, q)) \tag{4}$$
$$\phi_5 = \forall \text{Diag}(obj, h)(\text{livesInHabitat}(obj, h)) \tag{5}$$
$$\phi_6 = \forall \text{Diag}(sub, l)(\text{isSubject}(sub, l)) \tag{6}$$
$$\phi_7 = \forall \text{Diag}(obj, l)(\text{isObject}(obj, l)) \tag{7}$$

where the variables g, q, n, a, h, and l represent different class labels, each belonging to a specific set: G (Classes, e.g., animal species), Q (Macroclasses, e.g., macro categories), N (Names, e.g., specific entity names), A (Actions, e.g., verbs describing actions), H (Habitats, e.g., environments where entities live), and L (Labels indicating whether the element is a subject or object in the sentence). One-hot encoding is used for labels (refer to Appendix B.1 for more details on the LTN grounding). In the LTP training, we use labeled examples for each component of a sentence. Specifically, we extract features for the subject (*sub*), action (*act*), and object (*obj*) to train the predicates. For instance, in the sentence "Gordon is a German Shepherd", *sub* denotes "Gordon", *act* indicates "is a" and *obj* refers to "German Shepherd". The extracted *sub* feature is used for predicates such as isOfName and isSubject, the *act* feature for the isOfAction predicate, and the *obj* feature for predicates such as isOfClass, isOfMacroclass, livesInHabitat, and isObject. In sentences like "German Shepherd is a Carnivore" and "German Shepherd lives in a Domestic Environment", the *obj* feature is used for the isOfMacroclass and livesInHabitat predicates, respectively.

The ∀ aggregator is grounded by the generalized mean with respect to the error. More details on the grounding of logical and non-logical symbols can be found in Appendix B.3, while the hyperparameters used during training are provided in Appendix A.1.

During the testing phase, we introduce a series of complex sentences to evaluate the LTP's ability to identify relationships between entities based on its training.

For example, while giving to the LLM as input a sentence like "Gordon is a German Shepherd and Gordon is Carnivorous", we use the LTP to verify the satisfiability of the axioms Eq. 28 and Eq. 29.

The probe handles multiple embeddings ($sub_1, sub_2, act_1, obj_1, obj_2$, etc.) by simultaneously processing the entire sentence and extracting the necessary components in a single pass. This allows us to identify whether the extracted representations are related to the first or second part of the sentence.

$$\phi_8 = \forall \text{Diag}(sub, n, act, v, obj, g, l)$$
$$(\text{isOfName}(sub, n) \land \text{isSubject}(sub, l)) \land \text{isOfAction}(act, v)$$
$$\land\, (\text{isOfClass}(obj, g) \land \text{isObject}(obj, l)) \tag{8}$$
$$\phi_9 = \forall \text{Diag}(sub_1, n, act_1, v, obj_1, g, l, sub_2, act_2, obj_2)$$
$$(\text{isOfName}(sub_1, n) \land \text{isSubject}(sub_1, l)) \land \text{isOfAction}(act_1, v)$$
$$\land\, (\text{isOfClass}(obj_1, g) \land \text{isObject}(obj_1, l))$$
$$\land\, (\text{isOfName}(sub_2, n) \land \text{isSubject}(sub_2, l)) \land$$
$$(\text{isOfMacroclass}(obj_2, q) \land \text{isObject}(obj_2, l)) \tag{9}$$
$$\phi_{10} = \forall \text{Diag}(sub_1, n, act_1, v, obj_1, g, l, sub_2, obj_2)$$
$$(\text{isOfName}(sub_1, n) \land \text{isSubject}(sub_1, l)) \land \text{isOfAction}(act_1, v)$$
$$\land\, (\text{isOfClass}(obj_1, g) \land \text{isObject}(obj_1, l))$$
$$\land\, ((\text{isOfName}(sub_2, n) \land \text{isSubject}(sub_2, l)))$$
$$\land\, (\text{livesInHabitat}(obj_2, h)) \land \text{isObject}(obj_2, l)) \tag{10}$$

Axiom ϕ_8 represent the degree of truthiness of the sentence like "Gordon is a German Shepherd", axiom ϕ_9 of "Gordon is a German Shepard and Gordon is Carnivorous", axiom ϕ_{10} of "Gordon is a German Shepard and Gordon lives in a domestic environment" as showed in Sect. 3.2.

Knowledge Base Construction from FrameNet Synsets. In a second experiment we apply our method to data from FrameNet [3]. FrameNet is a database of manually annotated sentences that provides a mapping from words to semantic frames[4]. Each kind of situation or event is associated with its own frame, such that a sentence like "John lives in Amsterdam" could be annotated as eliciting the frame Residence. Frames have elements which correspond to the entities involved with the situation/event, such as "John" being the Resident and "Amsterdam" the Location.

FrameNet contains information on how frames relate to one another. We use the following set of relations to find a suitable subset of FrameNet:

- inheritance - when frames are more specific/generic versions of each other (e.g. Temporary_stay inherits from Residence);
- using - when frames presuppose the existence of each other (e.g. Colonization presupposes that the Colonists have taken up Residence somewhere);
- subframe - when frames are part of each other (e.g. Arrest and Arraignment are part of Criminal_Process);

---

[4] A frame in FrameNet is a structured representation of a situation, including participants, props, and conceptual roles. Each frame contains a textual description (frame definition), associated elements, lexical units, example sentences, and relations with other frames.

- `perspective_on` - when a frame captures a specific perspective on another (neutral) frame (e.g. `Hiring` and `Get_a_job` are perspectives on `Employment_start`).

To process frames that can be inferred from the presence of other frames even when nothing in the text explicitly alludes to it:

1. count the number of available annotated sentences;
2. create a list of other frames from which this one may be inferred, by finding paths through the directed graph formed by the frame relations listed above; then,
3. discard each frame that cannot be inferred from at least five and at most ten other frames that themselves have at least one hundred annotated sentences.

By requiring there to be at least five frames to infer from, we increase the chances that we are learning to infer this frame rather than some other property that they have in common. We require at most ten to filter out the most generic frames that are inferable from almost any frame. All frames meeting these conditions (*implicit* frames) and the corresponding five to ten frames from which they may be inferred (*explicit* frames) are used to create the labels with which our probes are trained. This process allows us to extract implications like "`Hostile_encounter` $\implies$ `Emotions`" (see also Appendix C).

LTN Probing with FrameNet. Each Frame and Frame Element becomes a predicate in the LTN. The attention mechanism, rather than building representations for subject, action, object, builds one representation for each frame element that could be mentioned.

As in the WordNet-based experiments, axioms are introduced to express the relation between the data and the labels, which are used to train the probe. And similarly, additional statements are used at test time to query the consistency of the probe's predictions with our knowledge. In this case, this consists of the implications which have as their antecedent the presence of an explicit frame, and as their consequent an implicit frame whose presence is inferable. The hyperparameters adopted during training are reported in Appendix A.2.

4 Design of Model and Probe Structures

For our experiments, we used pretrained embeddings from two large language models: BERT-large (uncased) [10] and OpenLLAMA-7b [16]. We use a 4-bit OPTQ [13] quantized version of OpenLLaMA[5]. The embedding dimension is 1024 and 4096 for BERT-large and OpenLLAMA-7b, respectively. We trained LTP on the extracted embeddings separately for each layer of the LLM to determine the optimal layer to satisfy each predicate. The number of layers are 24 and 32 for BERT-large and OpenLLAMA-7b, respectively. We use standard scaled dot-product attention as is also used in the Transformer architecture [35] on

---
[5] hf.co/TheBloke/open-llama-7b-open-instruct-GPTQ

which the LLMs are based. The weights of this mechanism are optimized along with the LTN itself as part of the probe (see Appendix B for more implementation details).

The primary metric used to evaluate the LTP is the satisfiability score, which measures how well the LTN taking as input the LLM's embeddings satisfy the logical statements.

5 Results

Table 1 shows the main experimental results, reporting the average satisfiability of each statement for each dataset. For both LLMs it presents the best-performing layer and the corresponding score. The LTP was compared against two baselines: probes trained with the labels shuffled w.r.t. the features; and a probe trained on completely random features. When the probes outperform these baselines (as they do), it indicates that the representations contain relevant information that the probes are exploiting.

Table 1. Probe performance for WordNet and FrameNet test sets on best-performing layers ℓ, compared to baselines 'shuffled' and 'random'. Mean ± standard deviation (w.r.t. different random initialization of probe weights) of satisfiability (and F1 on rows with '(F1)') for all axioms in the knowledge base are shown. Rows marked with † highlight axioms present only at test time. Scores are also displayed as gradient on cell background color.

Axioms		BERT			OpenLLama		
	ℓ	score	shuffled	ℓ	score	shuffled	random
WordNet							
isOfName	8	.97 ± .03	.00 ± .00	24	.99 ± .00	.00 ± .00	.00 ± .00
isOfAction	8	.99 ± .00	.82 ± .00	24	.99 ± .00	.78 ± .02	.82 ± .03
isOfClass	8	.67 ± .06	.00 ± .00	24	.79 ± .11	.00 ± .00	.00 ± .00
isOfMacroclass	8	.92 ± .04	.19 ± .03	24	.99 ± .00	.17 ± .03	.19 ± .03
livesinHabitat	8	.74 ± .03	.12 ± .00	24	.97 ± .03	.08 ± .01	.08 ± .02
isOfName ∧ isOfAction ∧ isOfClass (ϕ_8)†	8	.66 ± .05	.00 ± .00	24	.74 ± .01	.00 ± .00	.00 ± .00
isOfName ∧ isOfAction ∧ isOfClass ∧ isOfName ∧ isOfMacroclass (ϕ_9)†	8	.65 ± .05	.00 ± .00	24	.74 ± .01	.00 ± .00	.00 ± .00
isOfName ∧ isOfAction ∧ isofClass ∧ isOfName ∧ livesinHabitat (ϕ_{10})†	8	.58 ± .05	.00 ± .00	24	.73 ± .02	.00 ± .00	.00 ± .00
FrameNet							
Explicit							
Frame Elements	8	.77 ± .00	.63 ± .00	4	.75 ± .00	.64 ± .00	.64 ± .00
Frames	8	.82 ± .00	.46 ± .00	4	.80 ± .01	.49 ± .00	.47 ± .00
Frames (F1)	8	.76 ± .12	.06 ± .05	8	.73 ± .15	.07 ± .05	.03 ± .05
Element ⟹ Frame †	12	.98 ± .00	.95 ± .00	12	.98 ± .00	.97 ± .00	.96 ± .00
Implicit							
Frames	8	.72 ± .00	.46 ± .00	8	.71 ± .00	.50 ± .01	.45 ± .00
Frames (F1)	8	.82 ± .04	.41 ± .11	8	.80 ± .05	.42 ± .10	.34 ± .10
Explicit Frame ⟹ Implicit Frame †	12	.96 ± .10	.90 ± .00	8	.96 ± .00	.89 ± .01	.94 ± .01

5.1 WordNet

In Table 1 the first five rows reflect the ability of the probe to correctly predict the presence of named entities (ϕ_1), the action performed (ϕ_2), the class(ϕ_3) and macro class of the animal (ϕ_4), and its habitat (ϕ_5). The representations learnt by the LLM contain information to distinguish the subject, the object and the action mentioned by the sentence, and to determine which concepts can appear as the subject or object of a given action. In this case, the higher performance of the random baseline reflects the lower number of classes; likewise, the lower satisfiability of the isOfClass predicate could be explained by the higher number of classes.

The second part of the table (rows 5 to 10) show to what extent logical consequences of the atomic formulas mentioned above are correctly computed at inference time. For instance, for the sentence of "Gordon is a German Shepherd", not only should the name ("Gordon"), the action ("is") and the class ("German Shepherd") be correctly predicted, but the probe should be able to infer the macro class ("dog") from the LLM internal representations. Hence, the conjunction of all the predicates (indicated as ϕ_9 in Table 1) should evaluate to true, as indeed shown by our results. The satisfiability of these axioms is not enforced during the training of the LTP, and thus is derived by the logical consistency of the predictions of the probe and thus, by extension, of the LLM internal representations.

In Fig. 2f and Fig. 2e the results are analyzed on a layer by layer basis. We focus in particular on axioms evaluated only at test time ($\phi_8 - \phi_{10}$), which support the possibility of deductive reasoning. The two investigated models appear to behave quite differently in this respect. For OpenLLAMA, the satisfiability is higher in deeper layers, with a clear gap between layer 4 and 8, and a peak at layer 24. For BERT, on the other hand, consistency appears to be higher in the earliest layers, with a peak around layer 8, whereas the satisfiability is much lower in the deepest layer. Results in Fig. 2e show that the LLMs internal representations of syntactic roles are distributed differently across layers in each model. Specifically, OpenLLAMA seems to consolidate this information in its deeper layers, while BERT captures it more effectively in its earlier layers. Comparable to [6,19], our findings demonstrate that different layers of models process and interpret syntactic information and complex concepts at varying depths.

5.2 FrameNet

In Table 1 under FrameNet, the first three rows of results show how well the probe is able to correctly predict the explicitly mentioned Frame Elements and Frames. The fourth row shows to what extent the probe is logically consistent with element-frame implications, because for each element mentioned in the input sentence, the frame to which it belongs must also be evaluated true by the LTP. The fifth and sixth lines display the analysis results on implicit frames. The seventh and final row of results shows logical consistency with respect to

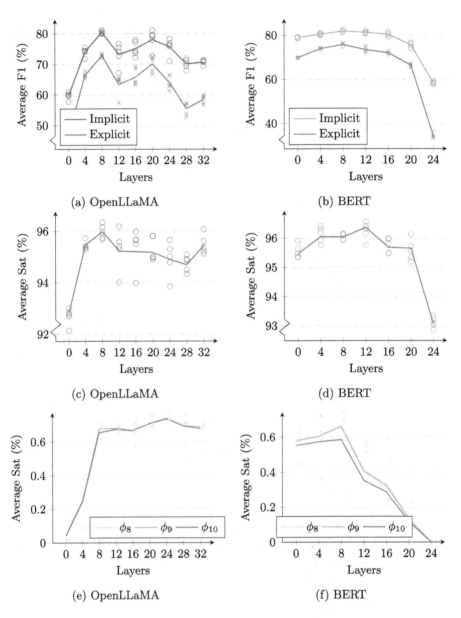

Fig. 2. Probe F1 scores obtained for FrameNet after five runs for each layer on OpenLLaMA (Fig. 2a) and BERT (Fig. 2b). Probe satisfiability of 'Explicit Frame $\implies$ Implicit Frame' rules for FrameNet obtained after five runs for each layer on OpenLLaMA (Fig. 2c) and BERT (Fig. 2d). Probe satisfiability of axioms ϕ_8 through ϕ_{10} obtained for WordNet after five runs for each layer on OpenLLaMA (Fig. 2e) and BERT (Fig. 2f).

frame-to-frame implications. We know for each explicit frame if it implies an implicit frame, and thus when the probe predicts the former it must also predict the presence of the latter. Both the element-frame and frame-frame implications show a modest, but significant difference with the baselines (note that for the implications the random guessing baseline is already .75). In Fig. 2b and Fig. 2a we can see the average F1 scores obtained by the explicit and implicit frames. Both obtain their maximum performance in the same layers for both models. This indicates that on average, the models are not inferring the presence of implicit frames from the presence of explicit frames, as would be the case when reasoning deductively. Rather, it seems that the model reaches the conclusions about both types of frames simultaneously. Figure 2d and Fig. 2c displays the satisfaction of the 'Explicit Frame $\implies$ Implicit Frame' rules by layer. For OpenLLaMA we see consistency with these rules reach its maximum in concert with the frame prediction F1, in layer 8. For BERT the consistency is highest in layer 12, rather than layer 8, which shows the best frame prediction performance.

5.3 Discussion

Table 1 shows that identification of semantic roles(classes, actions) and names entities achieves high scores, while the more complex axioms that introduce logical expressions obtain lower results, in line with [31] findings. In Fig. 2c and Fig. 2d, in line with the findings of [31], we observe that BERT tends to use the lower layers to maximize the satisfiability of the knowledge base. Specifically, in BERT the axioms introduced for WordNet are maximized in layer 8 decreasing significantly in later layers, which is not the case for FrameNet. For OpenLLaMA, satisfiability also sees the largest increase up to layer 8, but does not decrease (as much) after, with WordNet satisfiability peaking in layer 24. The results obtained for WordNet and FrameNet, as supported by [21], may be influenced by the linguistic formalism used in their representation. FrameNet, for example, organizes verbs and their possible interpretations around broader conceptual scenarios called frames, which represent specific situations or events and include the roles that different parts of a sentence can take on. For example, in frame *Arriving*, a sentence like "She arrived at the station", is analyzed by identifying *Theme* (the entity that arrives, "She") and *Goal* (the destination, "the station"). In contrast, WordNet focuses on more specific contexts for individual sentences than these broader frames. The type of information examined can significantly impact the probe's ability to extract relevant information at different layers.

6 Conclusion

We have shown that LTNs can be effectively repurposed to probe large language models. We envision practitioners using this tool to investigate LLMs, and in particular whether they perform certain logical inferences, and how much information needs to be present in its input, before it does so. To accomplish this, they will write a small knowledge base of domain-specific facts and rules for the type of reasoning they are interested in, together with a method for translating a given logical sentence into natural language. Then, a probe may be trained and queried to provide insight into the LLM.

Our WordNet experiments revealed that LLM layers differ in capturing logical predicates, with deeper layers generally performing better on complex predicates. For instance, satisfiability scores of axioms ϕ_8, ϕ_9, and ϕ_{10} showed that deeper layers (e.g., layer 24 in OpenLLAMA) were more effective. This suggests that as the model progresses, it refines abstract representations crucial for complex predicates. In BERT, early to middle layers (e.g., layer 8) perform better, while in OpenLLAMA, deeper layers (e.g., layer 24) are more effective. In FrameNet experiments, it appears that the model simultaneously arrives at conclusions about both types of frames. This may indicate that information relevant to identify semantic roles emerges within these specific layers. This versatility makes LTPs valuable for applications like natural language understanding, automated reasoning, and decision-making systems. Insights from LTPs can guide the development of future LLMs, helping to design models with better logical capabilities, leading to more robust and interpretable AI systems.

We believe that our approach can be further extended in several ways. For example, it is possible to introduce other datasets to investigate other kinds of logical deductions. The knowledge base could also be extended to consider other types of relationships, beyond class hierarchies or geographical location. Finally, several kinds of large language models can be used.

A Hyperparameters

For all experiments, the aggregation function parameter in the knowledge base defined in Eq. 27 is set to $p_\forall = 2$. We implemented the probes in PyTorch, using the LTNtorch library [8] and training was done using the Adam optimizer.

A.1 WordNet

To train the WordNet probes, we adopted a learning rate of 1e-5 and trained our architecture for 100 epochs. The knowledge base during training included batches of 128 randomly chosen sentences, both positive and negative. Experiments were done on a single Nvidia 2080 Ti GPU.

A.2 FrameNet

To train the FrameNet probes, we adopted a learning rate of 1e-3 and trained our architecture for 15 epochs and a batch size of 128. The experiments were performed on a single Nvidia 3090 GPU.

B WordNet LTN

B.1 Variables, Predicates and Axioms

In this subsection, we present the foundations of variables and predicates with the definition of the knowledge base $\mathcal{K}$.

Grounding Variables and their corresponding domains are grounded as follows:

$$\mathcal{G}(n) = \mathbb{N}^N, \ \mathcal{G}(v) = \mathbb{N}^V, \ \mathcal{G}(g) = \mathbb{N}^G, \ \mathcal{G}(q) = \mathbb{N}^Q,$$
$$\mathcal{G}(h) = \mathbb{N}^H, \ \mathcal{G}(l) = \mathbb{N}^L, \ \mathcal{G}(s) = \mathbb{R}^{B \times D},$$
$$\mathcal{G}(sub), \mathcal{G}(act), \mathcal{G}(obj) = \mathbb{R}^{T \times m}$$
(11)

where g, q, n, a, h represent the class labels belonging to a set of classes G, macroclasses Q, names N, actions A, and habitats H sets. Additionally, l represents the label used to distinguish different sections of the sentence, such as subject and object. The variables B and D are used in the definition of s to represent the dimensions of the feature space, where B is the batch size and D is the dimensionality of the features.

On the other hand *sub*, *act* and *obj* retrieved with the attention model of an entire sentence s, are grounded into a feature space. *obj* can be translated into macroclass when the sentence is in the form `isOfName isOfAction isOfMacroclass` instead of `isOfName isOfAction isofObject`. Within the FOL language, different predicates are defined: `isOfName(sub, n)`, `isOfAction(act, a)`, `isOfClass(obj, c)` with the aim of categorizing the sentence components, `livesInHabitat(obj, h)` and `isOfMacroclass(obj, q)` allow classifying objects respect to habitat and macroclass and finally `isSubject(sub, l)` with `isObject(obj, l)` to predict if a sentence is logically true by investigating whether the subject and its complement are inserted in a correct order.

The predicate groundings $\mathcal{G}(\text{isOfName})$, $\mathcal{G}(\text{isOfAction})$, $\mathcal{G}(\text{isOfClass})$ are formed by the similarity between the input features and the corresponding trainable class vectors with an MLP p_1 with softmax activation function, as the classes are mutually exclusive.

$$\mathcal{G}(\text{isOfName}) : sub, n \rightarrow n^T p_1(\mathcal{G}(sub), n) \quad (12)$$

$$\mathcal{G}(\text{isOfAction}) : act, v \rightarrow v^T p_1(\mathcal{G}(act), v) \quad (13)$$

$$\mathcal{G}(\text{isOfClass}) : obj, g \rightarrow g^T p_1(\mathcal{G}(obj), g) \quad (14)$$

Likewise, the $\mathcal{G}(\text{isOfMacroclass})$, $\mathcal{G}(\text{livesInHabitat})$ predicates are grounded with two simple MLP layers with a softmax activation function p_2, p_3:

$$\mathcal{G}(\text{isOfMacroclass}) : obj, q \rightarrow v^T p_2(\mathcal{G}(obj), q) \quad (15)$$

$$\mathcal{G}(\text{isOfMacroclass}) : obj, q \rightarrow v^T p_2(\mathcal{G}(obj), q) \quad (16)$$

$$\mathcal{G}(\text{livesInHabitat}) : obj, h \rightarrow g^T p_3(\mathcal{G}(obj), h) \quad (17)$$

Finally, for the grounding of isSubject and isObject two parametric similarity functions based on two simple MLP layers with softmax activation function p_4, p_5:

$$\mathcal{G}(\text{isSubject}) : \text{sub}, l \to l^T p_4(\mathcal{G}(sub), l) \tag{18}$$

$$\mathcal{G}(\text{isObject}) : \text{obj}, l \to l^T p_5(\mathcal{G}(obj), l) \tag{19}$$

where l allows us to distinguish the different sections (subject, action, object) of the sentence.

B.2 Learning from Labeled Examples

The following is each axiom representing the labeled examples used during training:

$$\phi_1 = \forall \text{Diag}(sub, n)(\text{isOfName}(sub, n)) \tag{20}$$
$$\phi_2 = \forall \text{Diag}(act, v)(\text{isOfAction}(act, v)) \tag{21}$$
$$\phi_3 = \forall \text{Diag}(obj, g)(\text{isOfClass}(obj, g)) \tag{22}$$
$$\phi_4 = \forall \text{Diag}(obj, q)(\text{isOfMacroclass}(obj, q)) \tag{23}$$
$$\phi_5 = \forall \text{Diag}(obj, h)(\text{livesInHabitat}(obj, h)) \tag{24}$$
$$\phi_6 = \forall \text{Diag}(sub, l)(\text{isSubject}(sub, l)) \tag{25}$$
$$\phi_7 = \forall \text{Diag}(obj, l)(\text{isObject}(obj, l)) \tag{26}$$

B.3 Grounding Logical Connectives and Aggregators

The knowledge base $\mathcal{K}$ includes a collection of axioms, with a view to reconstructing logical connectives and aggregators into Real Logic. Gradient descent is adopted to train the probe to maximize the satisfiability of the problem. In this configuration, we make use of the standard negation $\neg$ defined as $N_S(a) = 1 - a$, and the Reichenbach implication $\to$ defined as $I_R(a, b) = 1 - a + ab$, where a and b are both truth values within the range of $[0, 1]$. To approximate the universal quantifier $\forall$, we use the generalized mean with respect to the error, denoted as A_{pME}, as described in [2,34]. Given a set of n truth values $a_1, \ldots, a_n \in [0, 1]$:

$$\forall : A_{pME}(a_1, \ldots, a_n) = 1 - \left(\frac{1}{n}\sum_{i=1}^{n}(1-a_i)^{p_\forall}\right)^{\frac{1}{p_\forall}} \quad p_\forall \geq 1 \tag{27}$$

A_{pME} is a measure of how much, on average, truth values a_i deviate from the true value of 1. Further details on the role of $p_\forall$ can be found in [2].

B.4 Knowledge Base for Inference Time

The knowledge base used at testing time is shown below:

$$\phi_8 = \forall \text{Diag}(sub, n, act, v, obj, g, l)$$
$$(\text{isOfName}(sub, n) \land \text{isSubject}(sub, l)) \land \text{isOfAction}(act, v)$$
$$\land (\text{isOfClass}(obj, g) \land \text{isObject}(obj, l)) \quad (28)$$
$$\phi_9 = \forall \text{Diag}(sub_1, n, act_1, v, obj_1, g, l, sub_2, act_2, obj_2)$$
$$(\text{isOfName}(sub_1, n) \land \text{isSubject}(sub_1, l)) \land \text{isOfAction}(act_1, v)$$
$$\land (\text{isOfClass}(obj_1, g) \land \text{isObject}(obj_1, l))$$
$$\land (\text{isOfName}(sub_2, n) \land \text{isSubject}(sub_2, l)) \land$$
$$(\text{isOfMacroclass}(obj_2, q) \land \text{isObject}(obj_2, l)) \quad (29)$$
$$\phi_{10} = \forall \text{Diag}(sub_1, n, act_1, v, obj_1, g, l, sub_2, obj_2)$$
$$(\text{isOfName}(sub_1, n) \land \text{isSubject}(sub_1, l)) \land \text{isOfAction}(act_1, v)$$
$$\land (\text{isOfClass}(obj_1, g) \land \text{isObject}(obj_1, l))$$
$$\land ((\text{isOfName}(sub_2, n) \land \text{isSubject}(sub_2, l)))$$
$$\land (\text{livesInHabitat}(obj_2, h)) \land \text{isObject}(obj_2, l)) \quad (30)$$

The subscript introduced in the annotation allows us to identify whether the extracted representations come from the previous sentence or the following one. Axiom ϕ_8 represent the degree of truthiness of a sentence like "Gordon is a German Shepherd", axiom ϕ_9 express "Gordon is a German Shepard and Gordon is Carnivorous", axiom ϕ_{10} highlights "Gordon is a German Shepard and Gordon lives in a domestic environment".

C FrameNet Data Details

C.1 Frame-Frame Implications

The following is the complete list of all implications included with the FrameNet experiments. For more information on the meaning of each of the frames, please see https://framenet.icsi.berkeley.edu/frameIndex.

```
                       f_192_Locale_(asserted)->
                f_196_Locale_by_use_(asserted)->
               f_191_Natural_features_(asserted)->
                    f_173_Buildings_(asserted)->
                    f_203_Roadways_(asserted)->
                                        -> f_960_Being_located_(implied)

                       f_192_Locale_(asserted)->
                f_196_Locale_by_use_(asserted)->
                      f_54_Arriving_(asserted)->
f_1178_Interior_profile_relation_(asserted)->
          f_199_Locative_relation_(asserted)->
           f_191_Natural_features_(asserted)->
                    f_173_Buildings_(asserted)->
                    f_203_Roadways_(asserted)->
                                        -> f_660_Existence_(implied)
```

```
                    f_196_Locale_by_use_(asserted)->
         f_191_Natural_features_(asserted)->
                   f_173_Buildings_(asserted)->
                   f_203_Roadways_(asserted)->
                                            -> f_192_Locale_(implied)

                     f_429_Vehicle_(asserted)->
                      f_426_Weapon_(asserted)->
                       f_106_Gizmo_(asserted)->
                   f_173_Buildings_(asserted)->
                    f_421_Artifact_(asserted)->
                        f_298_Text_(asserted)->
                                            -> f_1141_Using_(implied)

                     f_513_Purpose_(asserted)->
                     f_54_Arriving_(asserted)->
                    f_5_Causation_(asserted)->
                    f_1158_Project_(asserted)->
                     f_1346_Supply_(asserted)->
                                     -> f_88_Eventive_affecting_(implied)

                      f_192_Locale_(asserted)->
              f_196_Locale_by_use_(asserted)->
                     f_54_Arriving_(asserted)->
f_1178_Interior_profile_relation_(asserted)->
          f_191_Natural_features_(asserted)->
                   f_173_Buildings_(asserted)->
                   f_203_Roadways_(asserted)->
                                  -> f_199_Locative_relation_(implied)

                     f_513_Purpose_(asserted)->
                      f_424_Attack_(asserted)->
                    f_5_Causation_(asserted)->
          f_93_Hostile_encounter_(asserted)->
                    f_1158_Project_(asserted)->
                              -> f_720_Cognitive_connection_(implied)

                    f_660_Existence_(asserted)->
                      f_192_Locale_(asserted)->
              f_196_Locale_by_use_(asserted)->
                     f_54_Arriving_(asserted)->
f_1178_Interior_profile_relation_(asserted)->
          f_199_Locative_relation_(asserted)->
          f_191_Natural_features_(asserted)->
                   f_173_Buildings_(asserted)->
                   f_203_Roadways_(asserted)->
                       -> f_2100_Cycle_of_existence_scenario_(implied)

                      f_192_Locale_(asserted)->
              f_196_Locale_by_use_(asserted)->
                     f_54_Arriving_(asserted)->
f_1178_Interior_profile_relation_(asserted)->
          f_199_Locative_relation_(asserted)->
          f_191_Natural_features_(asserted)->
                   f_173_Buildings_(asserted)->
                   f_203_Roadways_(asserted)->
                                  -> f_2790_Locative_scenario_(implied)

                     f_513_Purpose_(asserted)->
                     f_54_Arriving_(asserted)->
                    f_5_Causation_(asserted)->
                    f_1158_Project_(asserted)->
                     f_1346_Supply_(asserted)->
                              -> f_2961_Undergoing_scenario_(implied)

                     f_513_Purpose_(asserted)->
                      f_424_Attack_(asserted)->
```

```
              f_5_Causation_(asserted)->
 f_93_Hostile_encounter_(asserted)->
         f_1158_Project_(asserted)->
                           -> f_2902_Conditional_scenario_(implied)

         f_114_Likelihood_(asserted)->
                 f_972_Age_(asserted)->
                f_2282_Size_(asserted)->
         f_1152_Research_(asserted)->
              f_424_Attack_(asserted)->
 f_93_Hostile_encounter_(asserted)->
             f_80_Frequency_(asserted)->
              f_31_Scrutiny_(asserted)->
          f_990_Capability_(asserted)->
        f_354_Desirability_(asserted)->
                           -> f_964_Attributes_(implied)

         f_114_Likelihood_(asserted)->
                 f_972_Age_(asserted)->
                f_2282_Size_(asserted)->
         f_1152_Research_(asserted)->
              f_424_Attack_(asserted)->
 f_93_Hostile_encounter_(asserted)->
             f_80_Frequency_(asserted)->
              f_31_Scrutiny_(asserted)->
          f_990_Capability_(asserted)->
        f_354_Desirability_(asserted)->
                           -> f_1015_Gradable_attributes_(implied)

              f_513_Purpose_(asserted)->
              f_366_Desiring_(asserted)->
               f_424_Attack_(asserted)->
 f_93_Hostile_encounter_(asserted)->
         f_1158_Project_(asserted)->
        f_354_Desirability_(asserted)->
                           -> f_1712_Emotions_(implied)

              f_513_Purpose_(asserted)->
              f_366_Desiring_(asserted)->
               f_424_Attack_(asserted)->
 f_93_Hostile_encounter_(asserted)->
         f_1158_Project_(asserted)->
        f_354_Desirability_(asserted)->
                           -> f_48_Experiencer_focus_(implied)

              f_429_Vehicle_(asserted)->
               f_426_Weapon_(asserted)->
                f_106_Gizmo_(asserted)->
            f_173_Buildings_(asserted)->
                 f_298_Text_(asserted)->
                           -> f_421_Artifact_(implied)

              f_192_Locale_(asserted)->
       f_196_Locale_by_use_(asserted)->
    f_191_Natural_features_(asserted)->
            f_173_Buildings_(asserted)->
             f_203_Roadways_(asserted)->
                           -> f_329_Boundary_(implied)

              f_192_Locale_(asserted)->
       f_196_Locale_by_use_(asserted)->
    f_191_Natural_features_(asserted)->
            f_173_Buildings_(asserted)->
             f_203_Roadways_(asserted)->
                           -> f_237_Bounded_entity_(implied)

           f_1321_Substance_(asserted)->
    f_1322_Active_substance_(asserted)->
```

```
                    f_192_Locale_(asserted)->
           f_196_Locale_by_use_(asserted)->
      f_191_Natural_features_(asserted)->
             f_173_Buildings_(asserted)->
             f_203_Roadways_(asserted)->
                                        -> f_302_Physical_entity_(implied)

                   f_513_Purpose_(asserted)->
                    f_424_Attack_(asserted)->
                  f_5_Causation_(asserted)->
      f_93_Hostile_encounter_(asserted)->
                  f_1158_Project_(asserted)->
                                        -> f_2950_Alternativity_(implied)
```

References

1. Azaria, A., Mitchell, T.: The internal state of an LLM knows when it's lying. In: The 2023 Conference on Empirical Methods in Natural Language Processing (2023)
2. Badreddine, S., Garcez, A.d., Serafini, L., Spranger, M.: Logic tensor networks. Artif. Intell. **303**, 103649 (2022)
3. Baker, C.F., Fillmore, C.J., Lowe, J.B.: The Berkeley FrameNet project. In: 36th Annual Meeting of the Association for Computational Linguistics and 17th International Conference on Computational Linguistics, vol. 1, pp. 86–90. Association for Computational Linguistics, Montreal (1998). https://doi.org/10.3115/980845.980860
4. Bang, Y., et al.: A multitask, multilingual, multimodal evaluation of ChatGPT on reasoning, hallucination, and interactivity. In: Proceedings of the 13th International Joint Conference on Natural Language Processing and the 3rd Conference of the Asia-Pacific Chapter of the Association for Computational Linguistics (Volume 1: Long Papers), pp. 675–718 (2023)
5. Belinkov, Y.: Probing classifiers: promises, shortcomings, and advances. Comput. Linguist. **48**(1), 207–219 (2022)
6. Bronzini, M., Nicolini, C., Lepri, B., Staiano, J., Passerini, A.: Unveiling LLMS: the evolution of latent representations in a temporal knowledge graph. arXiv preprint arXiv:2404.03623 (2024)
7. Bubeck, S., et al.: Sparks of artificial general intelligence: early experiments with GPT-4. arXiv preprint arXiv:2303.12712 (2023)
8. Carraro, T.: LTNtorch: PyTorch Implementation of Logic Tensor Networks (2022). https://doi.org/10.5281/zenodo.6394282
9. Conia, S., Navigli, R.: Probing for predicate argument structures in pretrained language models. In: Proceedings of the 60th Annual Meeting of the Association for Computational Linguistics (Volume 1: Long Papers), pp. 4622–4632. Association for Computational Linguistics, Dublin (2022)https://doi.org/10.18653/v1/2022.acl-long.316
10. Devlin, J., Chang, M.W., Lee, K., Toutanova, K.: Bert: pre-training of deep bidirectional transformers for language understanding. In: North American Chapter of the Association for Computational Linguistics (2019). https://api.semanticscholar.org/CorpusID:52967399
11. Ettinger, A., Elgohary, A., Resnik, P.: Probing for semantic evidence of composition by means of simple classification tasks. In: Proceedings of the 1st Workshop on Evaluating Vector-Space Representations for NLP, pp. 134–139 (2016)

12. Fellbaum, C.: WordNet: An Electronic Lexical Database. Bradford Books (1998). https://mitpress.mit.edu/9780262561167/
13. Frantar, E., Ashkboos, S., Hoefler, T., Alistarh, D.: OPTQ: accurate quantization for generative pre-trained transformers. In: The Eleventh International Conference on Learning Representations (2022)
14. Galassi, A., Lippi, M., Torroni, P.: Investigating Logic Tensor Networks for Neural-Symbolic Argument Mining (2021)
15. Ganesh, P., et al.: Compressing large-scale transformer-based models: a case study on BERT. Trans. Assoc. Comput. Linguist. **9**, 1061–1080 (2020). https://api.semanticscholar.org/CorpusID:211532645
16. Geng, X., Liu, H.: OpenLLaMA: An Open Reproduction of LLaMA (2023). https://github.com/openlm-research/open_llama
17. Huang, J., Chang, K.C.C.: Towards reasoning in large language models: a survey. arXiv preprint arXiv:2212.10403 (2022)
18. Hupkes, D., Veldhoen, S., Zuidema, W.: Visualisation and "diagnostic classifiers" reveal how recurrent and recursive neural networks process hierarchical structure. J. Artif. Intell. Res. **61**, 907–926 (2018)
19. Jin, M., et al.: Exploring concept depth: how large language models acquire knowledge at different layers? arXiv preprint arXiv:2404.07066 (2024)
20. Kosinski, M.: Theory of mind may have spontaneously emerged in large language models. Stanford University, Graduate School of Business, Tech. rep. (2023)
21. Kuznetsov, I., Gurevych, I.: A matter of framing: the impact of linguistic formalism on probing results. In: Proceedings of the 2020 Conference on Empirical Methods in Natural Language Processing (EMNLP), pp. 171–182. Association for Computational Linguistics, Online (2020). https://doi.org/10.18653/v1/2020.emnlp-main.13
22. Kyriakopoulos, S., d'Avila Garcez, A.S.: Continual reasoning: non-monotonic reasoning in neurosymbolic AI using continual learning. In: International Workshop on Neural-Symbolic Learning and Reasoning (2023). https://api.semanticscholar.org/CorpusID:258461140
23. Liu, Y.H., et al.: Understanding LLMS: a comprehensive overview from training to inference. arXiv preprint arXiv:2401.02038 (2024)
24. Manigrasso, F., Miro, F.D., Morra, L., Lamberti, F.: Faster-LTN: a neuro-symbolic, end-to-end object detection architecture. In: Farkaš, I., Masulli, P., Otte, S., Wermter, S. (eds.) ICANN 2021. LNCS, vol. 12892, pp. 40–52. Springer, Cham (2021). https://doi.org/10.1007/978-3-030-86340-1_4
25. Manigrasso, F. Morra, L., Lamberti, F.: Fuzzy Logic Visual Network (FLVN): a neuro-symbolic approach for visual features matching. In: Foresti, G.L., Fusiello, A., Hancock, E. (eds.) ICIAP 2023, Part II, pp. 456–467. Springer, Cham (2023). https://doi.org/10.1007/978-3-031-43153-1_38
26. Morra, L., et al.: Designing logic tensor networks for visual sudoku puzzle classification. In: International Workshop on Neural-Symbolic Learning and Reasoning (2023)
27. OpenAI, R.: GPT-4 technical report. arXiv pp. 2303–08774 (2023)
28. Padalkar, P., Wang, H., Gupta, G.: NeSyFOLD: extracting logic programs from convolutional neural networks. In: ICLP Workshops (2023). https://api.semanticscholar.org/CorpusID:263875519
29. Serafini, L., Garcez, A.D.: Logic tensor networks: deep learning and logical reasoning from data and knowledge. arXiv preprint arXiv:1606.04422 (2016)
30. Shapira, N., et al.: Clever Hans or neural theory of mind? Stress testing social reasoning in large language models. arXiv preprint arXiv:2305.14763 (2023)

31. Tenney, I., Das, D., Pavlick, E.: BERT rediscovers the classical NLP pipeline. In: Annual Meeting of the Association for Computational Linguistics (2019). https://api.semanticscholar.org/CorpusID:155092004
32. Tenney, I., et al.: What do you learn from context? Probing for sentence structure in contextualized word representations (2018). https://openreview.net/forum?id=SJzSgnRcKX
33. Thawani, A., Ghanekar, S., Zhu, X., Pujara, J.: Learn your tokens: word-pooled tokenization for language modeling. In: Findings of the Association for Computational Linguistics: EMNLP 2023, pp. 9883–9893 (2023)
34. Van der Maaten, L., Hinton, G.: Visualizing data using t-SNE. J. Mach. Learn. Res. (11) (2008)
35. Vaswani, A., et al.: Attention is all you need. In: Advances in Neural Information Processing Systems, vol. 30. Curran Associates, Inc. (2017). https://proceedings.neurips.cc/paper/2017/hash/3f5ee243547dee91fbd053c1c4a845aa-Abstract.html
36. Zhang, B., et al.: Sentiment interpretable logic tensor network for aspect-term sentiment analysis. In: Proceedings of the 29th International Conference on Computational Linguistics. pp. 6705–6714. International Committee on Computational Linguistics, Gyeongju (2022). https://aclanthology.org/2022.coling-1.582
37. Zhang, Y., et al.: Siren's song in the AI ocean: a survey on hallucination in large language models. arXiv preprint arXiv:2309.01219 (2023)

Enhancing Machine Learning Predictions Through Knowledge Graph Embeddings

Majlinda Llugiqi[(✉)], Fajar J. Ekaputra, and Marta Sabou

Vienna University of Economics and Business, Vienna, Austria
{majlinda.llugiqi,fajar.ekaputra,marta.sabou}@wu.ac.at

Abstract. Despite their widespread use, machine learning (ML) methods often exhibit sub-optimal performance. The accuracy of these models is primarily hindered by insufficient training data and poor data quality, with particularly severe consequences in critical areas such as medical diagnosis prediction. Our hypothesis is that enhancing ML pipelines with semantic information such as those available in knowledge graphs (KG) can address these challenges and improve ML prediction accuracy. To that end, we extend the state of the art through a novel approach that uses KG embeddings to augment tabular data in various innovative ways within ML pipelines. Concretely, we introduce and examine several integration techniques of KG embeddings and the influence of KG characteristics on model performance, specifically accuracy and F2 scores. We evaluate our approach with four ML algorithms and two embedding techniques, applied to heart and chronic kidney disease prediction. Our results indicate consistent improvements in model performance across various ML models and tasks, thus confirming our hypothesis, e.g. we increased the F2 score for the KNN from 70% to 82.22%, and the F2 score for SVM from 74.53% to 81.71%, for heart disease prediction.

Keywords: Neurosymbolic AI · Knowledge Graph Embeddings · Machine Learning · Data Augmentation

1 Introduction

In the rapidly evolving landscape of Artificial Intelligence (AI), the field of Neurosymbolic AI (NeSy) marks a significant paradigm shift [10,16,31] by combining the strengths of symbolic reasoning and machine learning (ML) to address the limitations of traditional AI techniques. Central to this integration are semantic structures such as taxonomies, ontologies or knowledge graphs (KGs), which provide structured, semantic representations of domain-specific information [3,11,15,37]. These semantic structures play a pivotal role in enhancing data sparsity with rich semantics, thus enabling AI systems to make better informed decisions based on a broader contextual understanding.

Despite these advancements, there are some challenges, particularly in classification tasks within the healthcare domain, such as disease prediction. ML

© The Author(s), under exclusive license to Springer Nature Switzerland AG 2024
T. R. Besold et al. (Eds.): NeSy 2024, LNAI 14979, pp. 279–295, 2024.
https://doi.org/10.1007/978-3-031-71167-1_15

models often suffer from limited accuracy due to sparse training data [26]. In this study, we focus on a setting characterised by a tabular dataset with features that represent patients' medical records and address a binary classification problem, aiming to predict the presence or absence of a specific disease. Addressing the limitations of such settings, our study explores the potential of augmenting standard tabular datasets with semantic information from KG. By enriching these datasets with KG embeddings, we aim to improve the models' performance in terms of accuracy and F2 score. The choice of these metrics is driven by the importance of maximizing true positive identification in disease prediction, as discussed in Sect. 4.2. Our research is guided by the following research questions:

- RQ1: How can we best infuse KGs as input into a ML pipeline in order to enhance its performance, in terms of accuracy and F2 score?
- RQ2: In what ways do the size and structural variations of KGs affect performance gains among various ML algorithms?
- RQ3: How do different ML algorithms perform when information from KGs is infused into the input data?

To address these research questions, we build on our previous work [23], which initially introduced different ways to use KGs to augment the tabular data for heart disease prediction. In this paper we extend and formalize our methodology, proposing also an additional approach to further explore the integration techniques of KG embeddings. Additionally, we expand our empirical evaluation to include not only heart disease prediction but also chronic kidney disease prediction. We develop techniques for integrating KG embeddings, demonstrating the broader applicability of our approach beyond the diagnostic prediction, suggesting its utility in various fields where ontologies can be developed, expanded or extracted.

We continue with an overview of the related work Sect. 2, then discuss the proposed approach in Sect. 3. Then in Sect. 4 we discuss the experimental analysis. We then conclude our findings and discuss the future work in Sect. 5.

2 Related Work

We review related work about (i) the use of ML models in disease prediction and (ii) enhancing ML predictions by incorporating semantic knowledge, and we conclude by discussing the novelty of our approach.

Predicting Diseases with ML Techniques. The application of ML in healthcare, especially in disease prediction, is an area of significant research interest. Notably, the use of ML algorithms to predict conditions such as heart disease [20,28,32,35] and kidney disease [5,27,34,36] using different techniques for preprocessing data, feature selection, and hyper-parameter tuning to enhance prediction accuracy. There has been work on combining different ML approaches for better performance such as (i) [24] that combined random forest and linear methods, to enhance prediction accuracy for heart disease prediction and (ii) [2] introduced a predictive framework for heart failure, using dual SVM (support vector machine) models, the first model was dedicated to identifying relevant features, while the second model focused on the actual prediction task.

Eventhough the papers discussed above show a relatively good performance, they require extensive preprocessing[1], feature selection and hypherparameter tunning, for a better performance. Moreover, the performance of ML models is often hindered by the lack of data or data of sub-optimal quality. In the healthcare domain, there exist ontologies [6,9,18,19,25], that provide a structured and semantically rich layer of information, which could be used to improve the contextual understanding of ML models, as investigated in this paper.

Using Semantic Knowledge in Combination with ML for Prediction.
The paradigm of knowledge-infused learning is a vast and evolving field, as outlined in [21]. Our research focuses on the transformation of input data to ML models [8], a process that falls within the shallow level of infusion as discussed in [21], when the knowledge is injected into the input data. This input transformation represents a step towards tackling the challenge of ML models' heavy reliance on data. Recent research has been successfully exploring the integration of semantic knowledge across various domains. In the field of opinion mining, [1] developed a methodology that merges semantic knowledge bases with ML to enhance data analysis and classification accuracy. They construct a *Semantic Feature Matrix* that captures structured semantic information related to domain features in reviews, and combined it with *Statistical Feature Matrix*, into a hybrid matrix, used in the ML classifiers, to infer review ratings, showing the efficacy of infusing semantics with traditional statistical methods. Furthermore, Szilagyi et al. [33] examine an intelligent system in smart building management that integrates ML with semantic knowledge via of taxonomies, schemas, and logic rules. This hybrid model optimizes building management by synergizing data-driven insights and rule-based knowledge. Huang et al. [17] introduce ABductive Learning with Knowledge Graph (ABL-KG), which automatically mines logic rules from KG using a knowledge forgetting mechanism to filter irrelevant information. These rules are then used to optimize both the ML model and logic inference, and it is shown to improve ML performance even with a limited amount of labeled data.

Ziegler et al. [38] adopt a different approach by enhancing neural networks with semantic knowledge using graph embeddings for credit-card fraud detection. They utilize embeddings created for country nodes in DBpedia [22] and augment the dataset with information about public holidays, demonstrating that the injection of semantic background knowledge into the training dataset can improve classification outcomes. Moreover, Bhatt et al. [3] present four case studies that illustrate how different forms of KGs can enhance ML in applications such as sentiment analysis, personalized news recommendation, machine

---

[1] The importance of preprocessing step for achieveing good performance is shown by Hassler et al. [14].

translation, and recommender systems. Gazzotti et al. [12], on the other hand, address the limitations of electronic medical records (EMRs), which contain sparse patient information, by augmenting features extracted from EMRs with ontological resources before transforming them into vectors for ML algorithms. They extract ontological knowledge from text fields within EMRs to evaluate the benefits in predicting hospitalization.

Ruiz et al. [30] present PLATO, a method designed to enhance ML performance on tabular datasets with high-dimensional features and limited samples. PLATO leverages an auxiliary KG to regularize a multilayer perceptron (MLP), where each input feature is linked to a node in the KG, and the MLP's first layer weights are inferred from these nodes using a trainable message-passing function. This approach was shown to outperform existing methods on six datasets characterized by high dimensionality and low sample sizes.

The papers discussed above underscore the benefits of integrating ML pipeline with semantic data. Building on our previous work [23], we use KGs as supplementary data sources, introducing a novel method of incorporating KG embeddings into ML models, a technique not previously explored in medical prediction or NeSy systems. We also examine how the size and structure of KGs affect ML model performance and outline methods for adding knowledge from KG embeddings. We apply these techniques for heart and chronic kidney disease prediction.

3 Approach: Knowledge Graph Injection for Data Augmentation

ML models are typically trained on datasets that are semantically sparse. To enhance the performance of these models, we have focused on enriching the data and extracting as much semantic information as possible. In order to make use of the semantic knowledge from KGs and infuse it into ML process, we use a two-step approach, as illustrated in Fig. 2: *(i) KG Construction*, which involves using an ontology to enrich tabular data, transforming it into a KG (Sect. 3.1), and *(ii) Knowledge Injection into Data*, which takes this KG and transformers it into vectorial representation, that is then used to augment the training data (Sect. 3.2).

3.1 Knowledge Graph Construction

To incorporate additional knowledge into a ML pipeline, for our approach it is essential to construct the KGs. The top part of Fig. 1 outlines the approach for constructing these KGs, representing the data, initially captured in tabular formats. We provide a formal description of this process in the following steps.

Step 1: Ontology Definition. We define an ontology, denoted as $O = (C, R, H^C)$, which contains a set of concepts C, a set of relations R, and a concept hierarchy H^C. Each relation $r \in R$ signifies an association between concept pairs, such

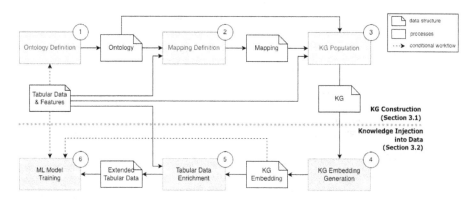

Fig. 1. Overview of the proposed approach including (i) KG construction (top) and (ii) knowledge injection into data (bottom).

that $r \subseteq C \times C$. The concept hierarchy H^C is a subset of $C \times C$, representing the hierarchical structure among concepts. The development of the ontology can involve (i) creating a new ontology from scratch, (ii) reusing and extending existing ontologies to encompass additional domain-specific knowledge, or (iii) extracting only the relevant parts of a larger ontology (see Sect. 4.2).

Step 2: Mapping Definition. Mapping dataset features to ontology concepts is crucial for using tabular data to populate the ontology, thereby creating a KG. A fundamental element of this process is the **mapping function** $\phi : F \to C$, where $F = \{f_1, f_2, \ldots, f_n\}$ represents the set of features in the tabular data T, which data can be defined as a matrix of dimensions $m \times n$. This function involves manually mapping each feature f_i to a concept C in the ontology O.

Step 3: Knowledge Graph Population. We build the knowledge graph KG by using the ontology O and the tabular data T, and applying the mapping function $\phi : F \to C$. The KG is populated automatically using a Python script. We denote it as $KG = (E, R', Tr)$ where:

- E represents the set of entities. Each entity $e_i \in E$ corresponds to an instance in the tabular data, derived from each row m_i in T,
- R' denotes the set of instantiated relations in KG encompassing relations from R through the mapping ϕ, and represent direct relationships between entities or between an entity and a literal value in E,
- Tr consists of triples generated for each feature value in an instance row m_i, based on the mapping ϕ. For example, for a feature f_{age} and an instance e_i with an age value of 23, the corresponding triple would be $(e_i, r_{hasAge}, 23)$, indicating the relation r_{hasAge} between entity e_i and the literal value 23.

This preprocessing ensures a semantic representation of features from the tabular data T into the Knowledge Graph KG, using the ontology O.

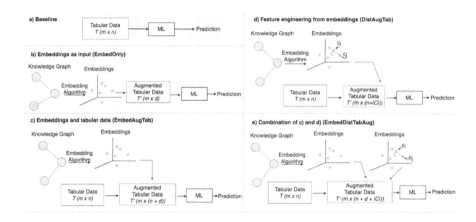

Fig. 2. Different ways of infusing the KG as input into ML pipeline.

3.2 Knowledge Injection into Data

The process of knowledge injection into the data involves various ways to augment an existing datasets with richer semantic content. In the Sect. 3.1, we discussed constructing richer data structures that capture more semantics than just the data. This section will focus on the methods for transforming these enriched data structures into a vectorial space amenable to processing with ML methods, and on how to augment the ML input in the optimal way as shown in the bottom part of Fig. 1.

Step 4: Knowledge Graph Embedding Generation. To be able to use the KGs as readable format by ML algorithms we transform them into embedding vectors. Knowledge graph embeddings (KGE) involve mapping entities E and relations R from a knowledge graph KG to a vector space. This can be represented as two functions: $f_e : E \rightarrow \mathbb{R}^d$ is an embedding function for entities, mapping each entity to a d-dimensional vector. And $f_r : R \rightarrow \mathbb{R}^d$ is an embedding function for relations, mapping each relation to a d-dimensional vector. The goal of the embedding algorithms is to learn these functions such that the geometric relationships in the vector space reflect the semantic relationships in the KG.

Step 5 & 6: Tabular Data Enrichment and ML Model Training. Multiple strategies exist for incorporating KG embeddings into the training process of ML models. We discuss the baseline, traditional ML pipeline using tabular data only, and four methods of enriching the training set with these KG embeddings.

Baseline. This represents training with only tabular data (shown in Fig. 2a), as traditional approach for training ML models with tabular datasets T.

Embeddings as ML Model Inputs (EmbedOnly). We train models using only KG embeddings, without tabular data (Fig. 2b). We specifically focus on the subset

$P \subseteq E$ of KG, where P represents the set of entities corresponding to instances in tabular data. The embedding function for entities, $f_e : E \to \mathbb{R}^d$, is used to map each instance entity $p_i \in P$ to a d-dimensional vector space. Consequently, for both the training and testing phases of our ML models, only the embeddings $\{f_e(p) \mid p \in P\} \subset \mathbb{R}^d$ derived from the instance entities are used. This approach ensures that the models are specifically trained and tested on the vector representations that encapsulate the characteristics and semantic relationships relevant to instances within the KG. These embeddings can be generated with different embedding mechanisms, such as RDF2Vec [29] or Node2Vec [13].

Combining Embeddings with Tabular Data Features (EmbedAugTab). This approach entails training ML algorithms using datasets that combine the original tabular dataset with additional columns from embeddings, (Fig. 2c). Specifically, for each instance p in tabular data T, we augment T with the embedding vector $f_e(p)$ for the same instance $p \in P$, derived from the embedding function $f_e : E \to \mathbb{R}^d$. This results in an augmented tabular matrix T' of dimensions $m \times (n+d)$, where each row i now includes the original features from T concatenated with the d-dimensional embedding vector $f_e(p)$. The augmented matrix T' is then used to train the ML models, leveraging both the original tabular features and the enriched vector representations of the instances.

In the domain of healthcare, each instance p represents a patient, and the embedding vectors are added to enhancing the models' ability to predict the presence or absence of specific diseases (e.g. heart or chronic kidney disease).

Tabular Dataset Enrichment with Distance Measures from Knowledge Graphs (DistAugTab). We enhance the tabular dataset T with embeddings through feature engineering (Fig. 2d). We incorporate additional features to improve the representation of each instance within the dataset. Specifically, for each instance i in the dataset T, we introduced $|C|$ extra columns/features, where C denotes the target classes, in the augmented tabular data T, resulting in an expanded dataset T' with dimensions $m \times (n + |C|)$.

The new columns, compute the Euclidean distance between the embedding vector v_i for instance i and the centroid c_i of a particular target class. These distance features, are designed to more accurately reflect the proximity of each instance's embedding to the known target class centroids, thereby potentially enhancing the classification accuracy for differentiating between the specified target classes or categories. For example, in the domain of healthcare, these target classes could represent the presence or absence of a particular disease $C = \{disease, noDisease\}$.

Embedding and Distance Features Augmented Tabular Data (EmbedDistTabAug). This approach combines DistAugTab and EmbedAugTab, such that the augmented dataset incorporates both the distance measurements and embedding vectors, as seen in Fig. 2e. For each instance $i \in I$ within the dataset, $d+|C|$ extra columns are added, resulting in an augmented tabular data T' with dimensions $m \times (n + d + |C|)$, where d and C are defined as previously discussed.

4 Experimental Analysis

We outline the objectives of our experiments guided by our research questions (Sect. 4.1), then discuss the methodologies, materials, and procedures used, providing clarity on execution and supporting reproducibility (Sect. 4.2). Lastly, Sect. 4.3 presents and analyzes the experiment outcomes.

4.1 Experimental Goals

The aim of our experimental evaluation is to explore the synergistic impact of KGs and ML techniques within our proposed approach. In this approach, ontologies are used to provide essential semantics, while KGE serve as the mechanism to encode these semantics effectively. Accordingly we aim to assess their influence on the overall system performance. The main goals of our experiment are:

Infusion of KGs into ML Pipelines (RQ1): We investigate the optimal ways to incorporate KGs as input into ML pipelines to enhance model performance, specifically focusing on accuracy and F2 score. This involves assessing how KGs can be integrated to maximize the predictive capabilities of ML models.

Impact of KG Size and Structure (RQ2): We aim to determine how the size and structural variations of KGs influence performance gains across different ML algorithms. This question addresses the scalability and adaptability of KG-infused ML systems under varying KG characteristics.

Performance of ML Algorithms with KG Infusion into the Data (RQ3): We explore the comparative performance of various ML algorithms when augmented with information from KGs. This includes evaluating how different algorithms leverage KG semantics to improve prediction outcomes.

4.2 Experiment Setup and Experimental Materials

Datasets. We perform experiments in the medical domain, in two subdomains, namely heart disease and chronic kidney disease and use two public datasets:

- The Heart Disease dataset[2], which includes 14 features related to cardiovascular health, such as chestpain and heart rate for 303 patients, for classifying the presence of heart disease.
- The Chronic Kidney Disease dataset[3] containing 20 features related to kidney function and overall patient health, such as white blood cell count and red blood cell count for 400 patients, for classifying weather the patient suffers chronic kidney disease.

---

[2] https://www.kaggle.com/datasets/johnsmith88/heart-disease-dataset.
[3] https://www.kaggle.com/datasets/mansoordaku/ckdisease?select=kidney_disease.csv.

Ontologies. For the heart disease domain, we have used three ontologies:
- *Small* a handcrafted ontology $O = (C, R, H^C)$ from Trepan Reloaded [7] representing the features from the Heart Disease dataset,
- *Extended* ontology $O = (C', R, H^C)$, is created from an existing ontology[4] $O = (C, R, H^C)$, which we extended with the features from the dataset,
- *Snomed* ontology, is created from the SNOMED-CT ontology[5], with the approach introduced by Chen et al. [4], that extracts ontologies from SNOMED-CT for a specific domain based on an input set of seed-concepts that need to appear in the output ontology. We first identified the necessary concepts in the SNOMED-CT browser[6] that correspond to the features of our dataset. These identified concepts were then used as seed-concepts in the tool to extract an ontology that includes these specific concepts.

For the chronic kidney disease we only used the third approach, extracting a sub-ontology from SNOMED-CT, due to the lack of ontologies available for this domain. The overview of the ontologies for both domains, specifically the number of classes, and properties are shown in Table 3 in Appendix A.

KG Embedding Methods. We used two embedding methods:
- RDF2Vec: RDF2Vec is tailored for processing RDF (Resource Description Framework) graphs within the Semantic Web. It leverages random walks to create sequences from these RDF graphs, which are subsequently transformed into embeddings through Word2Vec models. This approach is adept at capturing the semantic and relational attributes inherent in RDF graphs.
- Node2Vec: Node2Vec offers a more flexible solution, suitable for various types of graphs, whether labeled or unlabeled, directed or undirected. It uses random walks as well, but distinguishes itself with an adjustable bias parameter that enables exploration of both the local neighborhood and global search methodologies. Hence, while both algorithms employ random walks for embedding generation, RDF2Vec focuses specifically on semantic web applications, emphasizing semantic relationships, whereas Node2Vec offers broader applicability, emphasizing structural characteristics.

We generate embeddings using varied parameters tailored to the specific characteristics of the KG, as detailed in Table 4 Appendix A.

Machine Learning Methods. We used four supervised ML models: (i) K-Nearest Neighbors (KNN), (ii) Support Vector Machines (SVM), (iii) eXtreme Gradient Boosting (XGB), and (iv) Feedforward Neural Network (NN). We decided for the first two models due to their usage of distances, aligning with our use of KG embeddings, which we expect to yield improved performance. The latter two models were chosen because they have more complex architectures. During the training phase, we fine-tuned the models' hyperparameters via grid search, with the search spaces detailed in Table 5 Appendix A.

---
[4] https://bioportal.bioontology.org/ontologies/HFO
[5] https://www.snomed.org
[6] https://termbrowser.nhs.ukmar

Evaluation Metrics. We use accuracy and F2 score. The choice of F2 score is particularly relevant in disease prediction, where the goal is to maximize the identification of true positive cases, even if it entails a higher false positive rate, since the cost of missing a true case is higher that of a false alarm.

4.3 Results

We present the results from our experiments structured along the two domains (heart and kidney disease prediction).

Results for Heart Disease Prediction. Table 1 depicts the accuracy and F2 scores of various ML models (KNN, NN, SVM, XGB), comparing the use of tabular data, baseline, against augmented approaches. Training with data represented in KGs consistently improves model performance. Notably, integrating Euclidean distances from patient instances to the target class vector, derived using each of the three different KGs, enhances results. This enhancement is pronounced when these distances are added as extra features (DistAugTab) or combined with patient vector representations (EmbedDistAugTab), marking this method as the most effective for leveraging KG-derived embeddings.

Investigating the Performance of Different ML Models. Among the evaluated models, KNN and SVM showed the most improvements in terms of accuracy and F2 score, when incorporating the information from KG into the tabular data. A possible explanation would be the "distance nature" of these two algorithms, as identified in Sect. 4.2. This improvement is especially present when incorporating Euclidean distances to target classes (DistAugTab) as additional features derived from small, extended, or snomed KGs. For KNN, the F2 Score increases from 70.4% to 77.03%, 79.36%, and 79.48% respectively. Similarly, SVM shows enhancements, with the F2 Score increasing from 74.53% to 78.97%, 80.64%, and 81.71% using small, extended, and snomed KGs respectively.

More complex models such as NN and XGB also experience performance increase when leveraging KG information from small, extended, and snomed KGs. NN shows an enhancement from 78.24% to 79.71%, 82.22%, and 80.95% F2 score, respectively, while for XGB, F2 score increased from 74.18% to 78.23%, 79.40%, and 78.42% respectively.

Furthermore, we can observe that using KG increases the accuracy of the KNN and SVM to the level of NN model, when Snomed KG is being used to augment the data using DistAugTab approach.

Investigating the Impact of KGs. Table 1 shows the impact of differently sized and modeled KGs used in our experiments. For KNN and SVM, when data is augmented with information from snomed KG shows the best performance. On the other hand, NN and XGB performed the best when data is augmented with information from extended KG. Additionally, Fig. 3 (left) shows the average F2 score of different ML models, using small, extended and snomed KG, in different forms to augment the input of the model. On average, the figure shows that when data is augmented with knowledge from extended KG, it performs the best

Table 1. Comparison of accuracy and F2 score across models infusing knowledge from KG in different ways for heart disease prediction using various KG.

Methods	KNN Acc.	KNN F2	NN Acc.	NN F2	SVM Acc.	SVM F2	XGBoost Acc.	XGBoost F2
Baseline	80.52	70.40	82.06	78.24	78.52	74.53	78.83	74.18
Small KG								
EmbedOnly-R2V	78.13	67.31	80.42	77.48	82.01	77.34	77.93	74.15
EmbedOnly-N2V	75.54	61.96	79.01	77.35	81.10	75.39	74.49	69.39
EmbedAugTab-R2V	81.43	71.64	82.50	79.35	83.77	**78.97**	80.14	75.79
EmbedAugTab-N2V	80.51	70.53	81.52	77.82	80.58	76.79	78.86	74.54
DistAugTab-R2V	**81.88**	76.42	82.73	78.22	81.60	76.03	80.81	77.36
DistAugTab-N2V	81.79	**77.03**	78.21	61.00	83.18	78.45	80.86	**78.23**
EmbedDistAugTab-R2V	81.53	71.87	**83.16**	**79.71**	**84.18**	**78.73**	**81.24**	76.66
EmbedDistAugTab-N2V	80.53	70.55	81.96	78.15	82.03	78.26	79.47	75.47
Extended KG								
EmbedOnly-R2V	81.33	73.15	79.65	77.31	82.83	79.07	79.67	76.04
EmbedOnly-N2V	79.70	72.84	79.98	77.14	81.80	76.81	78.00	73.64
EmbedAugTab-R2V	81.72	72.82	82.17	78.71	84.21	79.32	81.25	77.60
EmbedAugTab-N2V	80.78	71.42	81.19	78.41	82.16	78.19	79.82	75.67
DistAugTab-R2V	83.41	78.71	**84.81**	**82.22**	83.74	78.63	**81.98**	**79.40**
DistAugTab-N2V	**83.65**	**79.36**	83.40	75.45	83.89	**80.64**	80.98	77.58
EmbedDistAugTab-R2V	81.82	73.07	81.64	78.90	**85.06**	79.79	80.94	77.67
EmbedDistAugTab-N2V	80.82	71.47	82.29	79.71	82.52	78.43	80.00	75.48
Snomed KG								
EmbedOnly-R2V	79.52	69.02	80.74	79.20	83.04	79.24	78.99	73.81
EmbedOnly-N2V	77.39	67.50	79.97	76.63	80.97	75.63	75.06	68.83
EmbedAugTab-R2V	81.39	71.89	82.50	79.96	84.11	79.61	81.38	76.62
EmbedAugTab-N2V	80.57	70.93	82.18	79.07	80.70	76.74	79.60	74.88
DistAugTab-R2V	83.77	79.10	**84.05**	**80.95**	84.25	79.94	81.30	78.03
DistAugTab-N2V	**84.13**	**79.48**	74.80	52.07	**84.88**	**81.71**	81.30	**78.42**
EmbedDistAugTab-R2V	81.51	72.26	83.26	79.74	84.48	79.30	**81.99**	77.98
EmbedDistAugTab-N2V	80.49	70.87	81.74	78.26	81.88	78.02	79.78	74.93

among the four models that we used, followed by snomed KG. We can argue that this happens because the extended KG is the biggest and it is modeled by experts and only extended by us, compared to the snomed KG where the ontology is being extracted with a tool that could prune the ontology, whereas the small KG is from a small handcrafted ontology by non-medical experts.

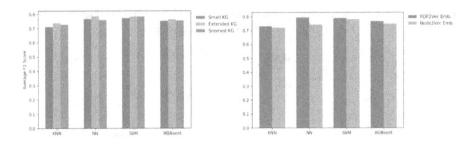

Fig. 3. Comparing ML model performance with (left) different KGs to augment the input of the models and (right) using two different embedding algorithms.

Table 2. Comparison of accuracy and F2 score across models infusing knowledge from KG in different ways for chronic kidney disease prediction.

Methods	KNN		NN		SVM		XGBoost	
	Acc.	F2	Acc.	F2	Acc.	F2	Acc.	F2
Baseline	97.22	98.55	99.92	99.96	100	100	99.75	99.46
EmbedOnly-R2V	97.22	94.44	99.08	99.38	99.40	99.20	93.67	89.54
EmbedOnly-N2V	97.03	95.66	99.25	99.33	99.17	99.01	92.49	87.37
EmbedAugTab-R2V	97.47	98.67	99.75	99.46	100	100	99.75	99.46
EmbedAugTab-N2V	97.17	98.52	**100**	**100**	100	100	99.75	99.46
DistAugTab-R2V	**99.06**	**99.22**	99.25	99.33	99.54	99.54	97.88	96.71
DistAugTab-N2V	98.21	97.85	94.25	86.24	99.39	99.53	97.68	96.36
EmbedDistAugTab-R2V	97.57	98.73	99.75	99.46	100	100	99.75	99.46
EmbedDistAugTab-N2V	97.17	98.52	99.92	99.96	100	100	99.75	99.46

Investigating the Impact of KG Embeddings. When examining two distinct algorithms used for embedding KG), Fig. 3 (right) shows that augmenting the data with embeddings generated by these algorithms yields comparable performance. However, RDF2Vec slightly outperforms the other algorithm in capturing information, due to the tailored nature of RDF2Vec for processing RDF graphs that makes it particularly well-suited for our specific task.

Results for Chronic Kidney Disease Prediction. *Investigating the performance of different ML models.* Table 2 shows the accuracy and F2 score across various ML models, when no extra information is being used in the training process, baseline, and when different ways of integrating information from embeddings from KGs are being used. Although the models already exhibit high performance with tabular data alone, introducing KG embeddings yields improvements. For KNN, adding distances from patient embeddings to target class embeddings when the embeddings are calculated with RDF2Vec algorithm (DistAugTab-RDF), the accuracy is improved from 97.22% to 99.06% and the F2 score is improved from 98.55% to 99.22%. On the other hand, for NN, when data is augmented with vector embeddings from Node2Vec (EmbedAugTab-N2V), it shows the best performance with accuracy and F2 score improvements from 99.92% to 100% and from 99.96% to 100% respectively.

Investigating the Impact of KG Embeddings. Figure 4 shows the average F2 score across various ML models, illustrating the impact of augumenting the data with embeddings from Node2Vec and RDF2Vec in various forms. We can see that in general both embeddings algorithms show comparable performances when used to enhance the data, with a slightly more improvement when RDF2Vec is being used to generate the embeddings, especially for NN and XGB models.

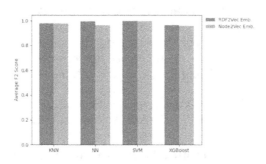

Fig. 4. Comparing ML model performance when two embedding algorithms are being used to augment the input of the models.

5 Conclusion and Future Work

In this paper, we aim to enhance the performance of ML-based predictions by incorporating semantic information and propose four novel methods for utilizing KG embeddings to enrich the tabular data employed in training ML models.

Based on our experiments, addressing RQ1, we discovered that infusing KG Embeddings into ML training process, improves the performance. This improvement is especially when KGEs are used to augment tabular data with additional features, derived by calculating distances from instances to target classes. This approach is notably effective in improving performance metrics such as accuracy and F2 score, even in domains with minimal room for improvement, such as chronic kidney disease. These findings underscore the potential of KGs to refine ML models, especially in data-sparse domains, highlighting the need for more research on efficient integration methods of KGs into ML pipelines.

Regarding RQ2, we observed that the performance enhancements provided by KGs are influenced by their size and structural complexity, with larger and more complex KGs leading to better results. This finding emphasizes the necessity of constructing KGs with specific characteristics tailored to optimize performance in these settings.

In response to RQ3, our comparative analysis of ML algorithms' pipeline augmented with KG information shows a consistent improvement in performance across all models tested. This enhancement is attributed to the richer feature sets provided by RDF2Vec and Node2Vec embeddings. Notably, RDF2Vec captured and utilized knowledge more effectively than Node2Vec, achieving slightly better performance results. This underscores the importance of selecting an ML algorithm that aligns well with the characteristics of KG-infused data to maximize benefits.

Future work will focus on refining the integration of tabular data into KGs by experimenting with alternative mapping techniques to potentially enhance model performance. Additionally, we aim to explore and measure the effectiveness of KGs in various domains, especially those with limited data by augmenting sparse datasets with additional information to tackle data dependency problem of ML models. Moreover, experiments will be conducted to understand the scalability and efficiency of our proposed approach based on the size and structure of the data. We also plan to evaluate embedding algorithms that capture more semantics and analyze their impact on various ML models.

Acknowledgements. This work was supported by the FWF HOnEst project (V 745-N), FFG SENSE project (894802) and FAIR-AI project (904624).

A Appendix: Additional Experimental Analysis

Tables in the appendix depicts the information about the experiment setup.

- Table 3 shows the details of the ontologies used for heart and kidney disease domain where classes (or concepts) represent distinct groups e.g., 'Patient' or 'Disease'; object properties describe the relationships between two classes e.g., 'hasSymptom' connecting 'Patient' to 'Symptom'; and data properties define characteristics or attributes of classes e.g., 'Patient's' age.
- Table 4 shows the embedding algorithms parameters used. The embeddings are generated with vector sizes of 64, 100, and 128, to ensure a better capture of the semantic knowledge from the KG. The reported results represent the average performance across these three vector dimensions.
- Table 5 shows the parameters used for the ML models.

Table 3. Details of the ontologies for heart and kidney disease domain.

Domain	Ontologies	Classes	Object prop.	Data prop.
Heart	Small	29	6	10
	Extended	1664	6	10
	Snomed	80	24	10
Kidney	Snomed	113	27	21

Table 4. Node2Vec and RDF2Vec parameters for different KGs.

Domain	KG	Dimens.	Node2Vec Param.			RDF2Vec Param.		
			Walk length	Walks	Window	Depth	Walks/node	Window
Heart	Small	[64,128,100]	40	200	5	4	100	5
	Extended	[64,128,100]	60	200	10	6	150	10
	Snomed	[64,128,100]	50	200	7	5	100	7
Kidney	Snomed	[64,128,100]	50	200	7	10	100	7

Table 5. Parameter grid for ML methods.

Method	Parameter	(Grid) Values
KNN	N_neighbors	[5, 10, 15, 20, 25, 30, 35, 40, 45, 50]
SVM	C; kernel; probability	[0.1, 0.2, ..., 2.1]; linear; True
XGB	learning_rate	[0.01, 0.02, ..., 0.20]
NN	layers; activation; loss; optimizer	[32, 16, 1]; [relu, relu, sigmoid]; binary crossentropy; adam

References

1. Alfrjani, R., Osman, T., Cosma, G.: A hybrid semantic knowledgebase-machine learning approach for opinion mining. Data Knowl. Eng. **121**, 88–108 (2019)
2. Ali, L., et al.: An optimized stacked support vector machines based expert system for the effective prediction of heart failure. IEEE Access **7**, 54007–54014 (2019)
3. Bhatt, S., Sheth, A., Shalin, V., Zhao, J.: Knowledge graph semantic enhancement of input data for improving AI. IEEE Internet Comput. **24**(2), 66–72 (2020)
4. Chen, J., Alghamdi, G., Schmidt, R.A., Walther, D., Gao, Y.: Ontology extraction for large ontologies via modularity and forgetting. In: Proceedings of the 10th International Conference on Knowledge Capture, pp. 45–52 (2019)
5. Chittora, P., et al.: Prediction of chronic kidney disease-a machine learning perspective. IEEE Access **9**, 17312–17334 (2021)
6. Chute, C.G., Çelik, C.: Overview of ICD-11 architecture and structure. BMC Med. Inform. Decis. Mak. **21**(6), 1–7 (2021)
7. Confalonieri, R., Weyde, T., Besold, T.R., del Prado Martín, F.M.: Using ontologies to enhance human understandability of global post-hoc explanations of black-box models. Artif. Intell. **296**, 103471 (2021)
8. Dash, T., Chitlangia, S., Ahuja, A., Srinivasan, A.: A review of some techniques for inclusion of domain-knowledge into deep neural networks. Sci. Rep. **12**(1), 1040 (2022)
9. El-Sappagh, S., Franda, F., Ali, F., Kwak, K.S.: SNOMED CT standard ontology based on the ontology for general medical science. BMC Med. Inform. Decis. Mak. **18**, 1–19 (2018)
10. Garcez, A.D., Lamb, L.C.: Neurosymbolic AI: the 3rd wave. Artif. Intell. Rev. 1–20 (2023)
11. Gaur, M., et al.: "Let me tell you about your mental health!" contextualized classification of reddit posts to DSM-5 for web-based intervention. In: Proceedings of the

27th ACM International Conference on Information and Knowledge Management, pp. 753–762 (2018)
12. Gazzotti, R., Faron-Zucker, C., Gandon, F., Lacroix-Hugues, V., Darmon, D.: Injecting domain knowledge in electronic medical records to improve hospitalization prediction. In: Hitzler, P., et al. (eds.) ESWC 2019. LNCS, vol. 11503, pp. 116–130. Springer, Cham (2019). https://doi.org/10.1007/978-3-030-21348-0_8
13. Grover, A., Leskovec, J.: node2vec: scalable feature learning for networks. In: Proceedings of the 22nd ACM SIGKDD International Conference on Knowledge Discovery and Data Mining, pp. 855–864 (2016)
14. Hassler, A.P., Menasalvas, E., García-García, F.J., Rodríguez-Mañas, L., Holzinger, A.: Importance of medical data preprocessing in predictive modeling and risk factor discovery for the frailty syndrome. BMC Med. Inform. Decis. Mak. **19**, 1–17 (2019)
15. Herron, D., Jiménez-Ruiz, E., Weyde, T.: On the benefits of OWL-based knowledge graphs for neural-symbolic systems. In: Proceedings of the 17th International Workshop on Neural-Symbolic Learning and Reasoning, vol. 3432, pp. 327–335. CEUR Workshop Proceedings (2023)
16. Hitzler, P., Eberhart, A., Ebrahimi, M., Sarker, M.K., Zhou, L.: Neuro-symbolic approaches in artificial intelligence. Natl. Sci. Rev. **9**(6), nwac035 (2022)
17. Huang, Y.X., et al.: Enabling abductive learning to exploit knowledge graph. In: Proceedings of the Thirty-Second International Joint Conference on Artificial Intelligence, pp. 3839–3847 (2023)
18. Ivanović, M., Budimac, Z.: An overview of ontologies and data resources in medical domains. Expert Syst. Appl. **41**(11), 5158–5166 (2014)
19. Jovic, A., Prcela, M., Gamberger, D.: Ontologies in medical knowledge representation. In: 2007 29th International Conference on Information Technology Interfaces, pp. 535–540. IEEE (2007)
20. Katarya, R., Meena, S.K.: Machine learning techniques for heart disease prediction: a comparative study and analysis. Heal. Technol. **11**, 87–97 (2021)
21. Kursuncu, U., Gaur, M., Sheth, A.: Knowledge infused learning (k-il): towards deep incorporation of knowledge in deep learning. arXiv preprint arXiv:1912.00512 (2019)
22. Lehmann, J., et al.: Dbpedia-a large-scale, multilingual knowledge base extracted from wikipedia. Semant. web **6**(2), 167–195 (2015)
23. Llugiqi, M., Ekaputra, F.J., Sabou, M.: Leveraging knowledge graphs for enhancing machine learning-based heart disease prediction. In: The Knowledge Graphs and Neurosymbolic AI (KG-NeSy) 2024 Workshop co-located with AIRoV – The First Austrian Symposium on AI, Robotics, and Vision (accepted for publication) (2024). https://semantic-systems.org/sites/KG-NeSy/papers/P28.pdf
24. Mohan, S., Thirumalai, C., Srivastava, G.: Effective heart disease prediction using hybrid machine learning techniques. IEEE Access **7**, 81542–81554 (2019)
25. Pisanelli, D.M.: Ontologies in Medicine, vol. 102. IOS press (2004)
26. Poulinakis, K., Drikakis, D., Kokkinakis, I.W., Spottswood, S.M.: Machine-learning methods on noisy and sparse data. Mathematics **11**(1), 236 (2023)
27. Rady, E.H.A., Anwar, A.S.: Prediction of kidney disease stages using data mining algorithms. Inf. Med. Unlocked **15**, 100178 (2019)
28. Rani, P., Kumar, R., Ahmed, N.M.S., Jain, A.: A decision support system for heart disease prediction based upon machine learning. J. Reliable Intell. Environ. **7**(3), 263–275 (2021)

29. Ristoski, P., Paulheim, H.: RDF2Vec: RDF graph embeddings for data mining. In: Groth, P., Simperl, E., Gray, A., Sabou, M., Krötzsch, M., Lecue, F., Flöck, F., Gil, Y. (eds.) ISWC 2016. LNCS, vol. 9981, pp. 498–514. Springer, Cham (2016). https://doi.org/10.1007/978-3-319-46523-4_30
30. Ruiz, C., Ren, H., Huang, K., Leskovec, J.: High dimensional, tabular deep learning with an auxiliary knowledge graph. Adv. Neural Inf. Process. Syst. **36** (2024)
31. Sarker, M.K., Zhou, L., Eberhart, A., Hitzler, P.: Neuro-symbolic artificial intelligence. AI Commun. **34**(3), 197–209 (2021)
32. Shah, D., Patel, S., Bharti, S.K.: Heart disease prediction using machine learning techniques. SN Comput. Sci. **1**, 1–6 (2020)
33. Szilagyi, I., Wira, P.: An intelligent system for smart buildings using machine learning and semantic technologies: a hybrid data-knowledge approach. In: 2018 IEEE Industrial Cyber-Physical Systems (ICPS), pp. 20–25. IEEE (2018)
34. Vijayarani, S., Dhayanand, S., Phil, M.: Kidney disease prediction using SVM and ANN algorithms. Int. J. Comput. Bus. Res. (IJCBR) **6**(2), 1–12 (2015)
35. Yadav, A.L., Soni, K., Khare, S.: Heart diseases prediction using machine learning. In: 2023 14th International Conference on Computing Communication and Networking Technologies (ICCCNT), pp. 1–7. IEEE (2023)
36. Yildirim, P.: Chronic kidney disease prediction on imbalanced data by multilayer perceptron: chronic kidney disease prediction. In: 2017 IEEE 41st Annual Computer Software and Applications Conference (COMPSAC), vol. 2, pp. 193–198 (2017). https://doi.org/10.1109/COMPSAC.2017.84
37. Yin, C., Zhao, R., Qian, B., Lv, X., Zhang, P.: Domain knowledge guided deep learning with electronic health records. In: 2019 IEEE International Conference on Data Mining (ICDM), pp. 738–747. IEEE (2019)
38. Ziegler, K., et al.: Injecting semantic background knowledge into neural networks using graph embeddings. In: 2017 IEEE 26th International Conference on Enabling Technologies: Infrastructure for Collaborative Enterprises (WETICE), pp. 200–205. IEEE (2017)

Terminating Differentiable Tree Experts

Jonathan Thomm[1,2], Michael Hersche[1], Giacomo Camposampiero[1,2], Aleksandar Terzić[1,2], Bernhard Schölkopf[2,3], and Abbas Rahimi[1]

[1] IBM Research – Zurich, Rüschlikon, Switzerland
abr@zurich.ibm.com
[2] ETH Zürich, Zürich, Switzerland
[3] Max Planck Institute for Intelligent Systems, Tübingen, Germany

Abstract. We advance the recently proposed neuro-symbolic Differentiable Tree Machine, which learns tree operations using a combination of transformers and Tensor Product Representations. We investigate the architecture and propose two key components. We first remove a series of different transformer layers that are used in every step by introducing a mixture of experts. This results in a Differentiable Tree Experts model with a constant number of parameters for any arbitrary number of steps in the computation, compared to the previous method in the Differentiable Tree Machine with a linear growth. Given this flexibility in the number of steps, we additionally propose a new termination algorithm to provide the model the power to choose how many steps to make automatically. The resulting Terminating Differentiable Tree Experts model sluggishly learns to predict the number of steps without an oracle. It can do so while maintaining the learning capabilities of the model, converging to the optimal amount of steps.

Keywords: Mixture of Experts · Differentiable Tree Machine · Tensor Product Representations · Structure-to-structure Transformation · Termination

1 Introduction

Neuro-symbolic AI aims to combine the strengths of statistical AI, like machine learning, with the capabilities of symbolic AI, to address the weaknesses of each. Recent neuro-symbolic AI methods exhibit notable benefits from a tight integration of low-level statistical perception and high-level reasoning, e.g., in various tasks demanding out-of-distribution (OOD) generalization [1–7]. However, compared to pure neural approaches, neuro-symbolic AI suffers from the non-differentiability of inherently discrete symbolic operations, unlike real numerical values, which makes them incompatible with gradient-based learning methods. One solution can be reinforcement learning-based learning approaches; however, they suffer from ill-defined gradients [8]. Another solution is to use a fully symbolic search. For instance, DreamCoder [9] builds an increasing library of functions from input-output examples and uses wake, abstraction, and sleep phases to find meaningful algorithm primitives for the library. Another example is the Neural-Symbolic Stack Machine [10] which uses a neural model giving instructions in a fixed language to be executed by a non-deep-learning part. This approach, however, is not differentiable, and therefore, during training, a correct execution trace is searched to obtain the multi-step training target. While such solutions excel at solving surprisingly complex examples, their base language might possess strong inductive biases, and it is unclear how to connect such a system to noisy or continuous signal streams.

One viable option is to integrate Tensor Product Representations (TPR) [11] inside neural networks. TPR is a general schema for mapping symbolic structures to numerical vector representations that allow continuous manipulations. Moreover, TPR can express a general formalization of compositional structure which is defined by an instance of a structure resulting from assigning a set of roles to particular fillers [12]: a role characterizes a position in the structure, and its filler is the substructure that occupies that position. In TPR, such compositional structure is constructed by binding the role vectors with the filler vectors using an outer product between the two vectors, which grows exponentially in dimension with the number of bound vectors. To alleviate this explosion, there are closely related lossy compressed representational schemes [13,14] in which the vectors are closed under binding operations: i.e., all roles, fillers (substructures), and resulting compositional structures themselves can be represented by fixed-dimensional distributed vectors.

The TPR has been integrated into various deep neural network architectures [15–18] (see [19] for an overview). Recently, TPR has been combined with a transformer to construct a Differentiable Tree Machine (DTM) [20] which learns sequences of operations on trees. The DTM represents trees using TPR tensors, defines a set of operations analogous to a subset of the Lisp [21] language on the TPR tree representations, and learns to execute the right Lisp operations to transform trees within multiple steps. A transformer model predicts the operations and arguments, and a TPR interpreter executes them in a differentiable manner. The DTM has shown OOD generalization in several tree transformation tasks, and provides a fairly general idea for learning of sequences of discrete symbolic operations on trees by making transformations and computations differentiable.

The DTM, on which our work is based on, faces several limitations. First, it uses a different parameterization of the transformer layer for each computation step. This means that as the number of steps of computation increases, the total model size increases linearly. Second, due to the first limitation, the DTM model only operates in a fixed number of steps. With that, the DTM also needs an oracle termination mechanism, i.e., one needs to know how many steps to compute for a given task. Further, the operations defined in the DTM have strong inductive biases towards certain tree operations. Therefore, the OOD performance shown in the original paper seems to exist because the model is invariant to those specific OOD cases. In contrast, its true OOD generalization is not as good in general as we demonstrate on a new tree reversal task in Sect. 4.2.

In this work, we enhance the DTM architecture by making the following contributions that address these limitations:

- We introduce a Mixture of Experts [22–24] to the DTM architecture, resulting in a Differentiable Tree Experts (DTE) model. DTE uses the same parameters at every step and soft-chooses different weight combinations from a weight pool. This allows for more general use-cases as the DTE can iterate arbitrarily long without needing more parameters.
- We experiment with halting and introduce a new halting mechanism that adapts delicately enough to work with the slightly unstable training convergence of the DTM. This avoids the need for hyperparameter tuning and theoretically allows the model to learn how much computation is needed for a given task, similar to what has been used in Universal Transformers [25].
- Our DTE and Terminating DTE architectures exhibit similar ID and OOD performances as the DTM. However, the number of parameters of the proposed architectures scales constantly with the number of transformations required to solve the problem, compared to the linear scaling that characterizes the DTM. For example in Table 4, DTM has $47\,M$ parameters compared to $27\,M$ for our DTE, with the difference getting larger with the number of steps. We also observe that sparsifying expert selection, which reduces the computational burden during training and inference, has no significant impact on performance.
- We ablate the DTM and DTE architectures on a novel tree reversal task. We demonstrate that the OOD performance of the DTM architecture is attributable to invariance rather than generalization (see Sect. 4.2).

2 Background

In this section, we briefly introduce Tensor Product Representations (TPRs) and the architecture of DTM.

2.1 Tensor Product Representations

Tensor Product Representation (TPR) provides a general encoding of structured symbolic objects in vector space. A TPR consists of roles and fillers [11]. While fillers describe the data, the roles define its context, and therefore, the TPR allows for a compositional symbolic representation via distributed vectors and tensors.

To represent a symbolic object, one computes the outer product ($\otimes$) of the filler (**f**) and the role (**r**) vectors, resulting in a matrix $\mathbf{M} = \mathbf{f} \otimes \mathbf{r} = \mathbf{fr}^T$. A set of N symbolic objects is represented by the superposition of the role-filler products:

$$\mathbf{T} = \sum_{n=1}^{N} \mathbf{f}_n \otimes \mathbf{r}_n. \tag{1}$$

If all role vectors are orthonormal, the individual fillers can be retrieved from $\mathbf{T}$ using an associative recall, e.g.,

$$\mathbf{f}_i = \mathbf{Tr}_i = \sum_{n=1}^{N} \mathbf{f}_n \mathbf{r}_n^T \mathbf{r}_i.$$

The orthonormality constraint on the roles requires their dimensionality to be $\geq N$.

Equation (1) allows us to encode tree structures as well [20]. Let us consider an example of a binary tree of depth 4, illustrated in Fig. 1. The leaves of the tree can be represented with TPR by $\mathbf{T} = \mathbf{f}_{some} \otimes \mathbf{r}_{00} + \mathbf{f}_{sad} \otimes \mathbf{r}_{100} + \mathbf{f}_{sheep} \otimes \mathbf{r}_{1100}$. Here, the subscript (x) of a role $(\mathbf{r}_x)$ describes the path from the root to the leaf, e.g., $x = 100$ describes the sequence right→left→left.

2.2 Differentiable Tree Machine

The Differentiable Tree Machine (DTM) [20] manipulates TPR-based tree representations using three Lisp operations: CAR, CDR, and CONS. Given a tree ($\mathbf{T}$), Lisp CAR extracts the subtree that is the left child of the root by $\text{CAR}(\mathbf{T}) = \mathbf{D}_0 \mathbf{T}$. Here, $\mathbf{D}_0 = \mathbf{I} \otimes \sum_x \mathbf{r}_x \mathbf{r}_{0x}^T$ is a linear operator that shifts all roles from the left subtree up to the root by one level, and $\mathbf{I}$ corresponds to the identity matrix on the filler space. Applying Lisp CAR to the example tree in Fig. 1 would yield $\mathbf{T}_0 = \text{CAR}(\mathbf{T}) = \mathbf{f}_{some} \otimes \mathbf{r}_0$. Lisp CDR extracts the right child by $\text{CDR}(\mathbf{T}) = \mathbf{D}_1 \mathbf{T}$, where $\mathbf{D}_1 = \mathbf{I} \otimes \sum_x \mathbf{r}_x \mathbf{r}_{1x}^T$ is the linear operator that shifts all roles from the right subtree up to the root. Finally, the CONS operation takes two trees ($\mathbf{T}_0$ and $\mathbf{T}_1$) as arguments plus a new root node ($\mathbf{s}$) and assembles a new tree by $\text{CONS}(\mathbf{T}_0, \mathbf{T}_1, \mathbf{s}) = \mathbf{E}_0 \mathbf{T}_0 + \mathbf{E}_1 \mathbf{T}_1 + \mathbf{s} \otimes \mathbf{r}_{root}$. The linear operators $\mathbf{E}_0 = \mathbf{I} \otimes \sum_x \mathbf{r}_{0x} \mathbf{r}_x^T$ and $\mathbf{E}_1 = \mathbf{I} \otimes \sum_x \mathbf{r}_{1x} \mathbf{r}_x^T$ shift all roles to the left and right subtrees down to the leaves, respectively.

DTM generates a sequence of trees $(\mathbf{T}^{(0)}, \mathbf{T}^{(1)}, ..., \mathbf{T}^{(L)})$, where the initial tree $(\mathbf{T}^{(0)})$ is the source tree, and the final tree $(\mathbf{T}^{(L)})$ is the target tree (i.e., the result of the task). DTM computes the tree at step t as a convex combination of the results provided by the three Lisp operations, which creates a TPR representation of a new tree superposition:

$$\mathbf{T}^{(t+1)} = w_{\text{CAR}}^{(t)} \text{CAR}(\mathbf{T}_{\text{CAR}}^{(t)}) + w_{\text{CDR}}^{(t)} \text{CDR}(\mathbf{T}_{\text{CDR}}^{(t)}) + w_{\text{CONS}}^{(t)} \text{CONS}(\mathbf{T}_{\text{CONS},0}^{(t)}, \mathbf{T}_{\text{CONS},1}^{(t)}, \mathbf{s}^{(t)}).$$

A transformer encoder layer (with the standard quadratic attention) predicts the weights $(w_{\text{CAR}}^{(t)}, w_{\text{CDR}}^{(t)}, w_{\text{CONS}}^{(t)})$ for the three Lisp operations, and their arguments $(\mathbf{T}_{\text{CAR}}^{(t)}, \mathbf{T}_{\text{CDR}}^{(t)}, \mathbf{T}_{\text{CONS},0}^{(t)}, \mathbf{T}_{\text{CONS},1}^{(t)}, \mathbf{s}^{(t)})$. Given a list of previously generated trees plus the input tree, each tree is encoded as one token by encoding the tree TPR representation to a dense vector using a deep learning encoder [26]. Each tree argument for the next Lisp operation is computed as a weighted sum of all past trees, e.g.,

$$\mathbf{T}_{\text{CAR}}^{(t)} = \sum_{i=0}^{t-1} a_{\text{CAR}}^{(i)} \mathbf{T}^{(i)}$$

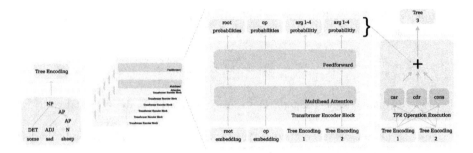

Fig. 1. The DTM architecture. In each step, a new tree superposition is generated (in TPR) using a different transformer encoder layer for each step. The instruction probabilities are predicted by the transformer encoder layer. CAR, CDR, and CONS are the three Lisp operations.

The weight of a tree ($a_{\text{CAR}}^{(i)}$) is predicted by the transformer encoder layer at the position where the corresponding tree ($\mathbf{T}^{(i)}$) was put into the transformer encoder layer. The operation weights and the new root weights for the CONS operation are predicted at two special classification tokens given as input to the transformer encoder layer.

The DTM runs for a predefined number of steps (between 12 and 28, configured as a hyperparameter), each time generating a new tree superposition. Each step however uses a different transformer encoder layer to predict the next action. The output of the last step is taken as the model's answer. See Fig. 1 for an architecture diagram. In the experiments reported in this paper, we use a newer version of the original DTM paper's code which has improved training stability and provided a lower parameter count [26].

3 Terminating Differentiable Tree Experts

3.1 Differentiable Tree Experts

This section presents the main contribution of our paper: Differentiable Tree Experts (DTE). Instead of learning a different transformer encoder in each step for DTM, one could share the weights. However, according to our experiments, using the same transformer encoder layer leads to a non-converging DTM. We, therefore, propose integrating a Mixture of Experts in the DTM architecture, which enables convergence again despite the weight sharing between each step. This means that in every step, the same router in DTE weights several experts (in our experiments, 16 experts) that then give proposals for the operation and the arguments. Those predictions are weighted, and then the DTE execution takes place.

In our router, a transformer encoder layer encodes all current trees. The current step is encoded as a sinusoidal positional encoding [27]. From the concatenation of the tree encoding and the step encoding, the router probabilities are computed with a linear map. See Fig. 2 for an architecture diagram of DTE.

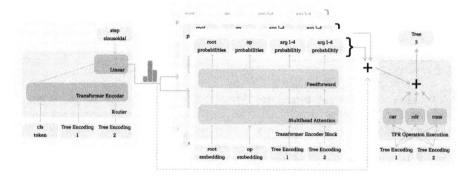

Fig. 2. The architecture of the DTE. In each step, a new tree is generated using the same model. Our transformer encoder layer is now a Mixture of Experts (MoE) with the router itself being a combination of a transformer encoder layer and a linear map. The router chooses the expert weights, which then are used to weigh the outputs of each expert. In our sparse MoE ablations, only the top 4 experts are activated.

This architecture modification scales much better when the number of steps increases. While DTM needs an additional transformer encoder layer for every step, DTE stays constant in size. Together with a termination algorithm, this also allows for deciding the number of steps flexibly, e.g., allowing for a different number of steps during inference (in our experiments between 12 and 28).

3.2 Sluggish Termination

Several termination heuristics have been proposed in the literature [28,29]. For this work, we found termination inspired by speculative execution to work best for our Terminating DTE (TDTE). In general, the training convergence of DTE is brittle, as also observed with the DTM. In particular, changing the termination decision too often caused the model to not converge anymore. We, therefore, use two termination predictors. One predictor follows the other as soon as it is confident. This way, changes in the termination are only made if a certain confidence is reached.

Let us denote $i_\text{damp} := \arg\max_s (p_\text{damp}(s))$, $i_\text{expl} := \arg\max_s (p_\text{expl}(s))$ the predictions of the two predictors, and $p(i_\text{damp}), p(i_\text{expl})$ the probabilities of the predictors at those indices. The probabilities over all steps sum up to 1 for each predictor. We define the loss label (i.e., the target step) of the two termination predictors as:

$$y_\text{damp} = \begin{cases} i_\text{expl} & p(i_\text{expl}) \geq 0.8 \\ i_\text{damp} & \text{otherwise} \end{cases} \quad (2)$$

$$y_\text{expl} = \begin{cases} \arg\max_{s \in S} \left(\text{loss}(s) * 1.05^{\text{idx}(s)}\right) & \text{if } p(i_\text{damp}) \geq 0.8 \wedge i_\text{damp} = i_\text{expl} \\ i_\text{expl} & \text{otherwise} \end{cases} \quad (3)$$

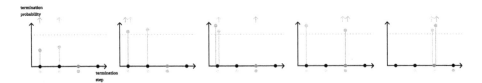

Fig. 3. Cases of the sluggish termination losses. The two arrows indicate the labels of the termination predictors in each case. The cases are given by whether the predictors are below or above the yellow confidence threshold. The orange dots show where the main model loss is and the two (relatively small) residual losses. The purple dot is the best local termination (e.g., best loss with some step penalty). The green predictor is called the "explorer", the blue one the "damper", as it will start to follow the explorer when the explorer becomes confident and otherwise stays where it is. (Color figure online)

As shown in Eqs. (2) and (3), we use a confidence threshold of 0.8 which was determined by a grid search based on the training convergence. S denotes the local set of choices around the current prediction, i.e. $S = \{i_{\text{damp}} - 4, i_{\text{damp}}, i_{\text{damp}} + 5\}$ and $\text{idx}(i_{\text{damp}} - 4) = 0$, $\text{idx}(i_{\text{damp}}) = 1$, $\text{idx}(i_{\text{damp}} + 5) = 2$. The choices in S are hyperparameters that worked well in practice.

We learn one termination for the DTM on each task. Each predictor consists of a series of constant parameters, one for each potential step, which is enough for the datasets investigated here and in the datasets used in [20]. By scaling the termination parameters (and initializing them to small values) by a large factor, one can make sure that the gradient updates are high enough for those single values. The method can also be applied to sample-wise predictors from the main model, which remains to be explored in future work.

Figure 3 visualizes Equations (2) and (3), i.e. which losses are applied to the two termination predictors in which cases. The exploration predictor (blue) will stay where it is until the damping predictor (green) is confident. When this happens, the exploration predictor stays where it is, and the damping predictor follows. As soon as both are at the same place and confident, the exploration predictor starts exploring for better termination options again.

To compute which of the three considered termination steps is the best (see Eq. 3 top case), we calculate the loss at each of the three steps and deduct a small multiplicative factor for later termination. This way the model will choose to terminate earlier if iterating longer does not bring significant improvements. We use cross-entropy loss to train the predictors, which are single numbers for each step and predictor. Our main loss is on the last choice, i.e., after the termination (see Fig. 3), to make sure the model can learn to do intermediate work at the current termination and then decide to terminate later.

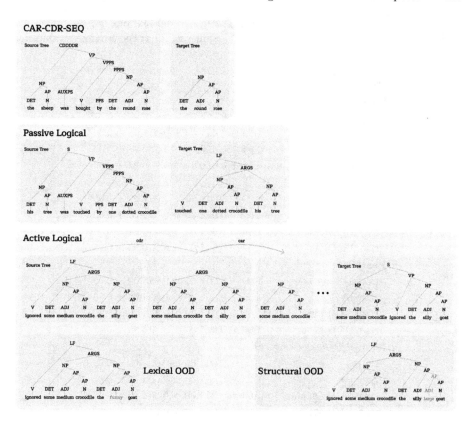

Fig. 4. Examples of the CAR-CDR-SEQ, PASSIVE↔LOGICAL, and ACTIVE↔LOGICAL dataset [20]. The model has to transform a source tree to the target tree. For the PASSIVE↔LOGICAL case we show the intermediate trees that the model could produce to get to the target tree. Moreover, we show an example of lexical generalization that uses unseen adjectives (in this case "funny"), as well as one for the structural generalization test set that adds additional adjectives.

The DTM and DTE architectures use the last tree as the final model output. When the termination changes, a step previously computing the final answer now computes an intermediate result. This could lower training performance; therefore, having a separate read-out transformer layer and choosing the termination over intermediate results only, could be an improvement for future work.

Table 1. Performance of the reproduced DTM (our runs) and our new architectures DTE and Terminating DTE (TDTE) on the same set of tasks used for evaluating DTM [20].

Dataset	DTM	DTE	TDTE
Car-Cdr-Seq			
–TRAIN	0.99 ± 0.00	1.00 ± 0.00	0.99 ± 0.00
–TEST ID	1.00 ± 0.00	1.00 ± 0.00	1.00 ± 0.00
–TEST OOD LEXICAL	0.99 ± 0.01	0.99 ± 0.01	0.98 ± 0.01
–TEST OOD STRUCTURAL	0.96 ± 0.01	0.97 ± 0.01	0.94 ± 0.03
Active↔Logical			
–TRAIN	1.00 ± 0.00	1.00 ± 0.00	1.00 ± 0.00
–TEST ID	1.00 ± 0.00	1.00 ± 0.00	1.00 ± 0.00
–TEST OOD LEXICAL	1.00 ± 0.00	1.00 ± 0.00	0.94 ± 0.06
–TEST OOD STRUCTURAL	1.00 ± 0.00	1.00 ± 0.00	0.96 ± 0.05
Passive↔Logical			
–TRAIN	1.00 ± 0.00	1.00 ± 0.00	1.00 ± 0.00
–TEST ID	1.00 ± 0.00	1.00 ± 0.00	1.00 ± 0.00
–TEST OOD LEXICAL	1.00 ± 0.00	1.00 ± 0.00	1.00 ± 0.00
–TEST OOD STRUCTURAL	1.00 ± 0.00	1.00 ± 0.00	0.99 ± 0.02
Active&Passive→Logical			
–TRAIN	1.00 ± 0.00	1.00 ± 0.00	1.00 ± 0.00
–TEST ID	1.00 ± 0.00	1.00 ± 0.00	1.00 ± 0.00
–TEST OOD LEXICAL	1.00 ± 0.00	1.00 ± 0.00	1.00 ± 0.00
–TEST OOD STRUCTURAL	0.98 ± 0.02	0.99 ± 0.03	0.98 ± 0.02

4 Experiments

We evaluate our Differentiable Tree Experts (DTE) and the Terminating DTE (TDTE) on the same set of four tasks used for the evaluation of DTM [20]. Figure 4 visualizes examples of these tasks. The first task, CAR-CDR-SEQ, encodes left-subtree and right-subtree Lisp operations in the root node of the input tree. Those should be executed, and the resulting sub-tree is the answer. The task ACTIVE↔LOGICAL task contains sentence grammar trees in either active or logical form; the task is to transform the tree into the other grammatical form. The PASSIVE↔LOGICAL task is analogous, having a sentence grammar in passive form instead of active. Finally, the ACTIVE&PASSIVE→LOGICAL task contains either active or passive sentence grammar trees and the target is the logical form. All tasks come with an ID test set and two OOD test sets. The lexical OOD set contains trees with adjectives never seen on the leaves. The structural OOD test set contains trees where additional adjectives are added.

While DTM and DTE use the same hidden dimension in the transformer encoder layers (64), we observe that TDTE requires a larger one (256) in order to obtain performance competitive with DTM and DTE. For the Mixture of Experts router, unlike other works [22], we do not use a load balancing loss for the router as it did not improve performance. In practice, the DTE and TDTE have more operations during training because of the (parallelizable) mixture of experts and the additional router. In more complex settings where the termination is different for different samples, the DTE and TDTE can become more efficient. The mixture of experts models become smaller in the number of parameters than the DTE for high depth.

We used 16 experts for all of our experiments which turned out to work well. This results in 17 transformer layer weights (one additional for the router) compared to 16–28 layers of the DTM for the datasets in Table 1 and up to 56 in Sect. 4.2.

Table 1 shows the comparison results. We use the DTM as the strongest baseline, as it outperformed vanilla Transformers, Tree Transformers, LSTMs, and Tree2Tree LSTMs [20]. Similarly to the original DTM paper, runs that reached validation accuracy less than 90% were excluded because the training is unstable for all models. 5 remaining runs were taken per data point. As shown, both DTE and TDTE perform very similarly compared to DTM. At the same time, our DTE and TDTE require a constant number of parameters with respect to the number of steps, whereas DTM's model size grows linearly with the number of steps. Moreover, TDTE does not access the oracle knowledge of the required number of steps, yet it performs on par with DTM.

4.1 Ablation: Sparse Mixture of Experts

One can further reduce the computational amount required for the DTE during training and inference by introducing sparsity in the selection of experts. To this end, we always select only the top four experts and normalize the corresponding selection weights using the softmax function.

Table 2 shows the results. The performance of DTE is the same as in Table 1 and only repeated for the reader's convenience. Again, we observe very similar performance, with small OOD performance reductions for the Sparse TDTE and an outlier in Test OOD Lexical for the Sparse DTE. This shows that sparse experts, in principle, also work with this model and can provide up to four times faster training and inference speed in the deep learning part.

4.2 New Task: Tree Reversal

This section evaluates DTM and TDTE on a new tree reversal task. The model gets a tree and has to reverse it exactly. This means that every inner node that has two children has to be extracted and reversed. Because the trees sometimes differ and subtrees to a higher depth have to be extracted, this task is more challenging. Especially the structural OOD now requires more and different operations. The input trees are the same as the input trees of the ACTIVE↔LOGICAL task. See Fig. 5 for a visualization with 28 steps.

As shown in Table 3, the models are able to learn tree reversals partially, which is a good sign, since the model needs to choose different Lisp operations for different samples. The structural OOD test set now needs other Lisp instructions and here we see that the model does not generalize to them at all.

Table 2. Performance of the DTE and Terminating DTE with sparse Mixture of Experts (with 4 out of 16 experts being active each time). Except for outliers, the performance of the sparse models is very similar and within the same range as the dense model.

Dataset	DTE	Sparse DTE	Sparse TDTE
Car-Cdr-Seq			
–TRAIN	1.00 ± 0.00	0.99 ± 0.01	0.99 ± 0.01
–TEST ID	1.00 ± 0.00	1.00 ± 0.01	1.00 ± 0.01
–TEST OOD LEXICAL	0.99 ± 0.01	0.99 ± 0.01	0.99 ± 0.01
–TEST OOD STRUCTURAL	0.97 ± 0.01	0.96 ± 0.03	0.93 ± 0.03
Active↔Logical			
–TRAIN	1.00 ± 0.00	1.00 ± 0.00	1.00 ± 0.00
–TEST ID	1.00 ± 0.00	1.00 ± 0.00	1.00 ± 0.00
–TEST OOD LEXICAL	1.00 ± 0.00	0.94 ± 0.14	0.98 ± 0.05
–TEST OOD STRUCTURAL	1.00 ± 0.00	0.98 ± 0.04	0.98 ± 0.04
Passive↔Logical			
–TRAIN	1.00 ± 0.00	1.00 ± 0.00	1.00 ± 0.00
–TEST ID	1.00 ± 0.00	1.00 ± 0.00	1.00 ± 0.00
–TEST OOD LEXICAL	1.00 ± 0.00	1.00 ± 0.00	0.90 ± 0.10
–TEST OOD STRUCTURAL	1.00 ± 0.00	0.95 ± 0.09	0.99 ± 0.02
Active&Passive→Logical			
–TRAIN	1.00 ± 0.00	1.00 ± 0.00	1.00 ± 0.00
–TEST ID	1.00 ± 0.00	1.00 ± 0.00	1.00 ± 0.00
–TEST OOD LEXICAL	1.00 ± 0.00	0.99 ± 0.01	0.96 ± 0.08
–TEST OOD STRUCTURAL	0.99 ± 0.03	0.97 ± 0.07	0.97 ± 0.06

We also train the model on many more steps (56 steps, see Table 4). This should give the model enough room to execute enough Lisp operations to reverse the whole tree. The ID accuracy increases significantly, especially for DTE, which outperforms DTM while having a lower parameter count ($27\,M$ vs $47\,M$). The good ID performance confirms that the model can learn more complicated tree transformations, and its application to more complex datasets looks promising in general. The TDTE does not learn.

Furthermore, it can be observed that the model generalizes to the lexical OOD set, but not structurally. This can be explained because the model can entirely ignore the precise adjectives, and as they are the tree leaves, they are unlikely to be extracted by the Lisp operations. In other words, the models are mostly invariant to OOD samples also for the reverse task. However, this is not the case for the structural OOD (which adds an additional adjective to the tree and therefore requires reversing two or more adjectives), and we see that once the invariance drops, there is no generalization at all anymore for all models in this experiment.

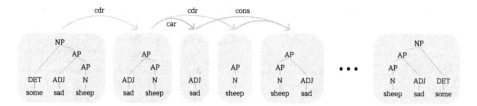

Fig. 5. Visualization of how the DTM and our (T)DTE can solve our novel tree reversal task. As shown, with the three operations CDR, CAR, and CONS, reversing a tree requires several steps and more with growing tree size since every child of a branching node needs to be extracted to assemble the tree in reverse order afterward.

Table 3. Performance of the original DTM architecture and our DTE and TDTE architectures (both dense and sparse) on the tree reversal task. The training performance is highly dependent on the seed. Since these models are not invariant to this structural OOD, we observe 0% performance everywhere on this split.

Dataset	DTM	DTE	TDTE	SDTE	STDTE
Reverse					
–TRAIN	0.25±0.18	0.37±0.34	0.02±0.04	**0.80±0.19**	0.16±0.23
–TEST ID	0.23±0.17	0.37±0.34	0.02±0.04	**0.79±0.20**	0.14±0.22
–OOD LEXICAL	0.02±0.03	0.05±0.06	0.00±0.00	**0.39±0.39**	0.09±0.16
–OOD STRUCTURAL	0.00±0.00	0.00±0.00	0.00±0.00	0.00±0.00	0.00±0.00

5 Discussion

DTM is a neuro-symbolic method for solving tree-to-tree transformation tasks, effectively combining a neural controller (i.e., a transformer) with a symbolic manipulator (TPR). The TPR engine performs symbolic manipulations in a continuous vector space, which allows a convex combination of different discrete operations (i.e., CAR, CDR, and CONS) and their operators (i.e., weighted superposition of past trees). This yields a fully differentiable neuro-symbolic architecture that can be trained end-to-end, without requiring reinforcement learning techniques. We further enhanced DTM by introducing a mixture of experts and a novel automatic termination method, which reduces both the number of parameters and the required knowledge about the number of steps.

Both the DTM and TDTE still face some inherent limitations, which we elaborate on in this section. Future work addressing the following limitations would notably enhance the DTM/TDTE approach.

Table 4. DTM and DTE architectures on the reversal task when given many steps. The DTM and DTE architectures all use a hidden dimension size of 256 here (instead of 64), because it performed better. Only one run is taken per model.

Dataset	DTM	DTE	TDTE
Reverse (56 steps)			
–TRAIN	0.82	**1.00**	0.00
–TEST ID	0.79	**1.00**	0.00
–TEST OOD LEXICAL	0.05	**1.00**	0.00
–TEST OOD STRUCTURAL	0.00	0.00	0.00

5.1 Limited Lisp Operations

DTM and TDTE models focus on binary tree-to-tree transformation tasks that can be solved with a limited subset of Lisp operations (CAR, CDR, and CONS). We have seen that the tasks presented in [20] can be solved with a relatively low number of sequential operations. By introducing the novel tree reversal task, however, we could show that DTE can indeed learn to execute longer sequences of the three operations.

Distributed representations are not restricted to the three Lisp operations. For example, leveraging fractional power encoding (FPE) [13] would allow one to perform arithmetic operations. In fact, FPE has been applied in probabilistic abductive reasoning to solve Raven's progressive tests [6]. Representing both logical and arithmetic rules with distributed representations yielded a differentiable and fast symbolic engine, which can even learn the underlying rules [30]. Using FPE to support arithmetic operations in DTM or TDTE would further enrich the architectures and is an interesting avenue for future work.

5.2 OOD Generalization

Our novel tree reversal task reveals an important limitation of the DTM and TDTE models in OOD generalization, showing that when the data does not fit the strong inductive biases of Lisp operations, the models do not seem to generalize well. The three Lisp operations have strong inductive biases to allow certain tasks to be done in very few steps. However, other tasks, such as tree reversal, require many steps. The fixation on the Lisp operations, therefore, is a limitation for other tree-to-tree tasks than the tasks evaluated in the previous sections.

Further, the tree-to-tree tasks evaluated in the original paper [20] require mostly the same sequence of the three Lisp operations for all samples including the OOD test sets. This allows DTM to generalize very well—the model is invariant to the OOD variants tested, rather than generally having excellent OOD capabilities. For ACTIVE↔LOGICAL and PASSIVE↔LOGICAL, the model only has to detect if the input is a sentence tree in active or in logical form, which is possible by simply looking at the children of the root node. These nodes are not really out of distribution in the OOD splits, where the only trees changed are the ones close to the leaves. See Fig. 4 for a visualized example. In ACTIVE&PASSIVE→LOGICAL the same holds and the task CAR-CDR-SEQ is only about executing the steps encoded in the root node of the tree. Those operations encoded in the root are ID in the OOD split samples (the trees are different only close to the leaves but the model only needs to look at the root).

For example, in the lexical generalization test, new adjective fillers are used at the tree leaves. During execution, these values are never taken into account during execution, as the TPR engine is invariant to the filler values. In the structural generalization test set, additional adjectives are added to the tree, while the operations that the model needs to learn are still the same, i.e., the transformer can ignore the bigger tree and only look at the inner nodes, which are still exactly equal. Such invariance is also the case for the lexical generalization of the tree reversal task but not for the structural OOD. This is because for the tree reversal, the fillers of the leaves do not matter; the model does not need to reverse the leaves and only needs to reverse the tree based on the inner nodes. However, when the structure of the tree contains additional adjectives its shape changes, and with it the inner nodes. Therefore, more different operations are necessary to reverse the tree.

5.3 Training Stability

Although the model combines deep learning and TPR successfully, the brittle training convergence is still a limitation. Removing this issue would be critical to allow the broader applicability of these hybrid models. The dependence on the initialization suggests that the optimization landscape is very non-convex or that the correct gradients are vanishing. Given the nature of the model, which linearly superposes all operations, the latter seems especially plausible. Investigating this problem and potentially finding improved optimizers or in-model solutions would make the applications of deep learning combined with TPR much more attractive to a broader audience. To avoid vanishing gradients, one could also introduce a hybrid optimization including elements to limit the number of superpositions and, therefore, strengthen the remaining ones.

6 Conclusion

We have introduced Terminating Differentiable Tree Experts (TDTE) which enhances the recently proposed DTM architecture. Our improvements allow the model to scale constantly when the depth of computation increases. Based on this, we are further able to introduce a new halting mechanism that changes its decisions slowly and looks ahead multiple steps to be more precise and have less impact on the model performance. This method makes it possible to learn the right termination without having access to an oracle termination information within the training data (which is usually not given).

Acknowledgment. This work is supported by the Swiss National Science foundation (SNF), grant 200800. We thank Paul Soulos for providing the DTM code as well as inputs on the work.

References

1. Manhaeve, R., Dumancic, S., Kimmig, A., Demeester, T., De Raedt, L.: DeepProbLog: neural probabilistic logic programming. Adv. Neural Inf. Process. Syst. (NeurIPS) **31** (2018)
2. Xu, J., Zhang, Z., Friedman, T., Liang, Y., Van den Broeck, G.: A semantic loss function for deep learning with symbolic knowledge. In: Proceedings of the 35th International Conference on Machine Learning (ICML), vol. 80, pp. 5502–5511 (2018)
3. Mao, J., Gan, C., Kohli, P., Tenenbaum, J.B., Wu, J.: The neuro-symbolic concept learner: interpreting scenes, words, and sentences from natural supervision. In: International Conference on Learning Representations (ICLR) (2019)
4. Chen, X., Liang, C., Yu, A.W., Song, D., Zhou, D.: Compositional generalization via neural-symbolic stack machines. Adv. Neural Inf. Process. Syst. (NeurIPS) **33**, 1690–1701 (2020)
5. Zhang, C., Jia, B., Zhu, S.C., Zhu, Y.: Abstract spatial-temporal reasoning via probabilistic abduction and execution. In: Proceedings of the IEEE Conference on Computer Vision and Pattern Recognition (CVPR) (2021)
6. Hersche, M., Zeqiri, M., Benini, L., Sebastian, A., Rahimi, A.: A neuro-vector-symbolic architecture for solving Raven's progressive matrices. Nat. Mach. Intell. **5**(4), 363–375 (2023)
7. Liu, A., Xu, H., Van den Broeck, G., Liang, Y.: Out-of-distribution generalization by neural-symbolic joint training. In: Proceedings of the AAAI Conference on Artificial Intelligence, vol. 37, pp. 12252–12259 (2023)
8. Lorello, L.S., Lippi, M.: The challenge of learning symbolic representations. In: Proceedings of the 17th International Workshop on Neural-Symbolic Learning and Reasoning (NeSy) (2023)
9. Ellis, K., et al.: DreamCoder: growing generalizable, interpretable knowledge with wake-sleep bayesian program learning. Phil. Trans. Royal Soc. A: Math. Phys. Eng. Sci. **381**, 202220050 (2023)
10. Chen, X., Liang, C., Yu, A.W., Song, D., Zhou, D.: Compositional generalization via neural-symbolic stack machines. In: Proceedings of the 34th International Conference on Neural Information Processing Systems (NeurIPS). Curran Associates Inc., Red Hook (2020)
11. Smolensky, P.: Tensor product variable binding and the representation of symbolic structures in connectionist systems. Artif. Intell. **46**, 159–216 (1990)
12. Newell, A.: Physical symbol systems. Cogn. Sci. **4**(2), 135–183 (1980)
13. Plate, T.A.: Holographic reduced representations. IEEE Trans. Neural Netw. **6**(3), 623–641 (1995)
14. Gayler, R.W.: Vector symbolic architectures answer Jackendoff's challenges for cognitive neuroscience. In: Joint International Conference on Cognitive Science (ICCS/ASCS) (2003)
15. Palangi, H., Smolensky, P., He, X., Deng, L.: Question-answering with grammatically-interpretable representations. In: Proceedings of the AAAI Conference on Artificial Intelligence (2018)

16. Schlag, I., Smolensky, P., Fernandez, R., Jojic, N., Schmidhuber, J., Gao, J.: Enhancing the transformer with explicit relational encoding for math problem solving. arXiv preprint arXiv:1910.06611 (2019)
17. Chen, K., Huang, Q., Palangi, H., Smolensky, P., Forbus, K., Gao, J.: Mapping natural-language problems to formal-language solutions using structured neural representations. In: International Conference on Machine Learning (ICML), pp. 1566–1575 (2020)
18. Jiang, Y., et al.: Enriching transformers with structured tensor-product representations for abstractive summarization. In: Proceedings of the 2021 Conference of the North American Chapter of the Association for Computational Linguistics: Human Language Technologies, pp. 4780–4793 (2021)
19. Smolensky, P., McCoy, R.T., Fernandez, R., Goldrick, M., Gao, J.: Neurocompositional computing: from the central paradox of cognition to a new generation of ai systems. AI Mag. **43**(3), 308–322 (2022)
20. Soulos, P., et al.: Differentiable tree operations promote compositional generalization. In: Proceedings of the 40th International Conference on Machine Learning (ICML), vol. 202, pp. 32499–32520 (2023)
21. Steele, G.L.: Common LISP: The Language. Digital Press (1984)
22. Fedus, W., Zoph, B., Shazeer, N.: Switch transformers: scaling to trillion parameter models with simple and efficient sparsity. J. Mach. Learn. Res. **23**(120), 1–39 (2022)
23. Jiang, A.Q., et al.: Mixtral of experts. arXiv preprint arXiv:2401.04088 (2024)
24. Shazeer, N., et al.: Outrageously large neural networks: the sparsely-gated mixture-of-experts layer. arXiv preprint arXiv:1701.06538 (2017)
25. Dehghani, M., Gouws, S., Vinyals, O., Uszkoreit, J., Łukasz Kaiser: Universal transformers. In: International Conference on Learning Representations (ICLR) (2019)
26. Soulos, P., Conklin, H., Opper, M., Smolensky, P., Gao, J, Fernandez, R.: Compositional generalization across distributional shifts with sparse tree operations (2020)
27. Vaswani, A., et al.: Attention is all you need. In: Proceedings of the 31st International Conference on Neural Information Processing Systems (NeurIPS), pp. 6000–6010 (2017)
28. Graves, A.: Adaptive computation time for recurrent neural networks. arXiv preprint arXiv:1603.08983 (2016)
29. Banino, A., Balaguer, J., Blundell, C.: Pondernet: Learning to ponder. In: 8th ICML Workshop on Automated Machine Learning (AutoML) (2021)
30. Hersche, M., di Stefano, F., Sebastian, A., Hofmann, T., Rahimi, A.: Probabilistic abduction for visual abstract reasoning via learning vector-symbolic architecture formulations. In: 3rd Workshop on Mathematical Reasoning and AI at NeurIPS (2023)

Valid Text-to-SQL Generation with Unification-Based DeepStochLog

Ying Jiao[1]($^{\boxtimes}$), Luc De Raedt[1,2], and Giuseppe Marra[1]

[1] KU Leuven, Department of Computer Science, Leuven.AI, 3000 Leuven, Belgium
{ying.jiao,lucde.raedt,giuseppe.marra}@kuleuven.be
[2] AASS, Örebro University, Örebro, Sweden

Abstract. Large language models have been used to translate natural language questions to SQL queries. Without hard constraints on syntax and database schema, they occasionally produce invalid queries that are not executable. These failures limit the usage of these systems in real-life scenarios. We propose a neurosymbolic framework that imposes SQL syntax and schema constraints with unification-based definite clause grammars and thus guarantees the generation of valid queries. Our framework also builds a bi-directional interface to language models to leverage their natural language understanding abilities. The evaluation results on a subset of SQL grammars show that all our output queries are valid. This work is the first step towards extending language models with unification-based grammars. We demonstrate this extension enhances the validity, execution accuracy, and ground truth alignment of the underlying language model by a large margin. Our code is available at https://github.com/ML-KULeuven/deepstochlog-lm.

Keywords: Generative neurosymbolic · Language models · DeepStochLog · Text-to-SQL

1 Introduction

The text-to-SQL task is to map natural language sentences to SQL queries given database schema. It provides a natural language interface to empower users regardless of their technical background to access and derive value from vast relational databases. This task also plays a central role in emerging retrieval-augmented agents [3,11,15] for various applications, such as question answering, personal assistance, and intelligent customer service. While most existing studies focus on the accuracy of queries only, we emphasize the importance of validity, ensuring that they are executable. Invalid queries that fail to execute potentially introduce vulnerabilities to automatic agents.

Deep learning models, from early recurrent ones [14,29] to recent large language models [7,18], have been successful in text-to-SQL. Though often effective, they can produce queries that violate SQL syntax and schema. Therefore, sketch-[4,29,32,33] and grammar-based approaches [8,14,25,31] guided by context-free

Table 1. A comparison of our framework and the existing approaches. Syntax and schema information suggests the guidance of syntax and schema rules. Validity guarantee underscores the assurance that the output SQL queries are always executable. Learning and inference show if the methods can be applied during the learning and inference stages.

	Syntax information	Schema information	Validity guarantee	Learning	Inference
Neural-based : [7,18]				-	-
Sketch-based : [4,29,32,33]	✓			✓	✓
Grammar-based : [8,14,25,31]	✓			✓	✓
Constraint-based : [13,17,20]	✓	✓			✓
Execution-guided : [6,12,22,26]	✓	✓			✓
Ours	✓	✓	✓	✓	✓

grammars have been proposed to avoid syntax errors. This idea is extended by constraint-based [13,17,20] and execution-guided methods [6,12,22,26] by adding schema information. They filter errors at inference time but cannot be used at learning time. These methods cannot ensure the production of valid outputs as they can exit without finding a valid query in their search space. Table 1 summarizes the properties of the studies mentioned above.

We present a neurosymbolic framework for text-to-SQL with a validity guarantee. Our framework uses DeepStochLog [27], a sequence-based neural stochastic logic programming method, as a backbone. DeepStochLog introduces neural definite clause grammars (NDCGs) which integrate stochastic definite clause grammars and neural networks. Unlike grammars employed in previous works, the unification-based, Turing-complete definite clause grammars we use can represent any syntax and schema knowledge. Our generated queries are guaranteed to have no syntax or schema errors and are always valid. To apply DeepStochLog to the text-to-SQL task, we define LM definite clause grammars (LMDCGs), an extension of NDCGs for language models. They help harness the powerful language understanding capabilities of language models and handle dynamic variable domains. In experiments, we demonstrate the effectiveness of our approach in generating valid queries on a subset of SQL grammars. Our framework also substantially improves the alignment with ground truth queries and the execution accuracy of the underlying language model. In summary, our contributions are as follows:

- We propose a neurosymbolic framework for text-to-SQL. To the best of our knowledge, we are the first to guarantee the production of valid queries with neural unification-based grammars.
- We introduce LMDCGs, an extension of DeepStochLog that integrates language models.
- We empirically show that our neurosymbolic framework significantly improves the validity, ground truth alignment, and execution accuracy of the encapsulated language model. We surpass state-of-the-art text-to-SQL approaches in terms of validity.

- We show the text-to-SQL task as a challenge and benchmark for neurosymbolic systems.

2 Problem Formulation

Given a natural language sentence nl and the schema S of a database db, the text-to-SQL task translates nl into an SQL query q. S includes: 1) a set of tables $T = \{t_1, ..., t_N\}$ of size N, and 2) a set of columns $C = \{c_1^1, ..., c_{n_1}^1, ..., c_1^N, ..., c_{n_N}^N\}$ linked to the tables, where n_i represents the number of columns in table t_i.

Figure 1 demonstrates the workflow of our framework. We aim to generate a valid and correct q that can retrieve the right answers to nl from db without runtime errors.

Fig. 1. Illustration of a text-to-SQL instance solved by our framework (basic grammar is used for brevity). Given the inputs, the system maximizes the probability of the ground truth SQL query when it is known and produces the most probable query when the target is unknown. The first LMDCG rule nn_{lm} in the logic program prompts the language model $table\_lm$ and gets a probability distribution over the three tables in the dog_kennels database. Similarly, the second one prompts $column\_lm$ and gets a probability distribution over the columns in a given table. The inference steps are shown in Fig. 2.

3 Preliminaries

This section provides essential background information on grammar and DeepStochLog. We refer to the original DeepStochLog paper [27] for more details.

Context-free grammars (CFGs) define a set of rewriting rules of the form $V \rightarrow W_1, ..., W_n$, where V is a non-terminal and W_i is either a terminal or a non-terminal. **Definite clause grammars (DCGs)** are a popular logic-programming-based extension of CFGs that can be executed as Prolog programs [16]. They are unification-based and can encode context-sensitive languages. DCGs replace the non-terminals in CFGs by logical atoms $a(l_1,..,l_n)$ with a predicate a and n terms l_i. A term is a constant, a logical variable, or a structured term $f(l_1,...,l_k)$ where f is a functor. DCG rules take the format $nt \to g_1,...,g_n$, where nt is an atom, a goal $g_1,...,g_n$ is a sequence and g_i is an atom or a list of terminals and logical variables. **Stochastic definite clause grammars (SDCGs)** formed as $p_i::nt \to g_1,...,g_n$ add probabilities p_i to DCG rules. They define a probability distribution over possible parses of a sequence and allow the most likely parse to be determined. SDCGs require the probabilities of the rules with the same non-terminal predicate to sum to 1.

DeepStochLog extends SDCGs to **neural definite clause grammars (NDCGs)** that integrate neural networks. An NDCG rule is defined as $nn(m, [I_1,...,I_X], [O_1,...,O_Y], [D_1,...,D_Y])::nt \to g_1,...,g_n$. The nn predicate denotes a neural network m that takes input variables $I_1,...,I_X$ and outputs a probability distribution over variables $O_1,...,O_Y$ with domains $D_1,...,D_Y$. For instance, $nn(table\_nn, [\text{"Find...dogs."}], T, [\text{"Dogs"}, \text{"Professionals"}, \text{"Treatments"}])::table(\text{"Find...dogs."}) \to [T]$ represents a neural network $table\_nn$ that takes a natural language sentence "Find the ids of professionals who have ever treated dogs" as input and outputs a probability distribution over the table domain of "Dogs", "Professionals", "Treatments".

Inference in DeepStochLog (see Sect. 4.1) computes the probability of a logical goal given an input sequence and a DCG, using probabilities computed by neural networks. The set of parses of the input sequence is translated first into a logical proof tree (e.g. Fig. 2 (a)), which is then turned into a computational graph (e.g. Fig. 2 (b)) that computes the likelihood of the goal. In particular, the probability $P_G(derives(G,T))$ is computed, where G is a logical goal (e.g. the starting symbol) and T is a sequence to parse. Logical inference uses resolution to find all derivations $d(G\theta)$ that produce T with an answer substitution θ. The resolution process is then translated into an AND-OR circuit. Probability inference calculates $P_G(derives(G,T)) = \sum_{d(G\theta)=T} P((G\theta)) = \sum_{d(G\theta)=T} \prod_{r_i \in d(G\theta)} p_i^{k_i}$, where p_i is the probability of rule r_i used for k_i times in a derivation. This computation equals a bottom-up evaluation of the AND-OR circuit where the logical circuit is compiled to an arithmetic circuit with the $(+, \times)$ semiring [9]. Similarly, the most probable derivation for G can be identified with the $(\max, \times)$ semiring.

Learning in DeepStochLog (see Sect. 4.1) is cast into the maximization of the likelihood of the input sequences. It is defined as

$$\min_p \sum_{(G_i\theta_i, T_i, t_i) \in \mathcal{D}} \mathcal{L}(P_G(derives(G_i\theta_i, T_i); p), t_i) \qquad (1)$$

where p is a vector of rule probabilities, $\mathcal{D}$ is a dataset of triples $\{G_i\theta_i, T_i, t_i\}$, t_i is a target probability and $\mathcal{L}$ is a differentiable loss function. This learning problem is solved with standard gradient descent techniques like the Adam optimizer [10]. The gradients of $\mathcal{L}$ w.r.t p can be computed automatically and backpropagated seamlessly to train the internal parameters of neural networks.

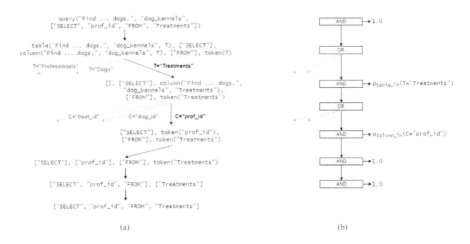

Fig. 2. Inference steps on the text-to-SQL instance in Fig. 1. (a) The SLD tree for *derives*(*query*("Find the ids of professionals who have ever treated dogs.", "dog_kennels", ["SELECT", "prof_id", "FROM", "Treatments"])). Thanks to unification, the branches of the wrong table and column substitutions will fail. Failing branches are in grey. (b) The corresponding AND-OR circuit. The probabilities of failing branches are not considered.

4 Methodology

We propose a neurosymbolic framework for text-to-SQL based on LM definite clause grammars (LMDCGs). LMDCGs are an extension of neural definite clause grammars (NDCGs) that integrate stochastic definite clause grammars (SDCGs) with language models. In Sect. 4.1, we show the workflow of our framework with the text-to-SQL instance in Fig. 1. We define LMDCGs and illustrate the bidirectional interface to language models they provide in Sect. 4.2. Lastly, we demonstrate the advantage of our definite clause grammars (DCGs) over the rules in the previous sketch- and grammar-based approaches in Sect. 4.3.

4.1 Our Workflow

Our logic program has three parts: facts, rules, and a Prolog query.

Facts. The facts represent associations between the database, tables, and columns. They are automatically generated from the database schema to define the domain of possible table and column variable substitutions. For example, in Fig. 1, the fact with *database* predicate describes the three tables in the database "dog_kennels". The *table* predicate describes the columns in each table. The *table_domain* and *column_domain* predicates retrieve the tables in dog_kennels and the columns in a given table respectively.

Rules. The rules encoding DCGs will be used to find answers to $query(nl, db, Q)$, where Q is the ground truth SQL query. Each rule can be assigned a probability. In our task, language models determine probabilities of LMDCG rules using the predicate nn_lm (see Sect. 4.2). Figure 2 (a) shows how the rules are applied to parse the ground truth SQL query ["SELECT", "prof_id", "FROM", "Treatments"] step by step. As in Fig. 2 (b), $table\_lm$ and $column\_lm$ determine the probability of the table and column grammar branches respectively. The *query* and *token* rules are deterministic, i.e. purely logical, with a probability of 1.0.

Prolog Query. The Prolog query[1] $query(nl, db, Q)$ defines the output of our framework. During training, Q is known and the system outputs the probability of producing Q given natural language sentence nl and database db. To this end, DeepStochLog inference with the $(+, \times)$ semiring is used (see Sect. 3). For example, in Fig. 2, given the sentence "Find ... dogs" and the database dog_kennel, the probability of the ground truth SQL query

$P(derives(query(\text{"Find...dogs."}, \text{"dog\_kennels"}, [\text{"SELECT"}, \text{"prof\_id"}},$

$\text{"FROM"}, \text{"Treatments"}]))) = 1.0 \times (0 + 0 + P_{table\_lm}(\text{T} = \text{"Treatments"}) \times$

$(0 + 0 + P_{column\_lm}(\text{C} = \text{"prof\_id"}) \times 1.0 \times 1.0))$

The learning process maximizes the probability of this query. Since DeepStochLog produces end-to-end differentiable inference graphs (i.e. AND/OR circuit in Fig. 2 (b)), this can be easily achieved by standard backpropagation and stochastic gradient descent. During evaluation, the Q is unknown. The system outputs the most likely SQL query given nl and db. To this end, DeepStochLog inference with the $(\max, \times)$ semiring is used.

4.2 LMDCGs

We define an LMDCG rule as:

$$nn_{lm}(lm, [NL], O_Y, D_Y, Prompt) :: nt \rightarrow g_1, ..., g_n$$

where lm is a language model, NL is a natural language sentence, O_Y is an output variable with domain $D_Y = [y_1, ..., y_n]$, and $Prompt$ is a constant sentence.

LMDCGs communicate with the underlying language model bi-directionally: 1) by constructing the input to execute them; and 2) by re-normalizing their output to build probabilities for SDCGs. Since the probabilities produced by language models are used during inference, we can backpropagate gradients seamlessly to language models and fine-tune them.

---

[1] Notice that the Prolog query is the logical goal to be proved, which differs from the SQL query to generate.

Language Model Input Construction. In the text-to-SQL task, the language model input is designed as the concatenation of 1) NL, 2) the possible substitutions of O_Y with their indexes in D_Y, i.e. "Answer i for y_i", and 3) $Prompt$ = "the answer should be Answer". The substitutions of O_Y in D_Y can be tokenized into several parts with language models, for example, the column name "abandoned_yn". We require the language models to output indexes instead of the substitutions to make them treat every substitution as a whole. For example, in Fig. 1, given the natural language sentence "Find ... dogs.", the table domain ["Dogs", "Professionals", "Treatments"], and the rule "$nn_{lm}(table\_lm, [NL], T, table\_domain\ (DB, T), Prompt)$::$table(NL, DB, T) \rightarrow $[].", the input to the $table\_lm$ is "Find ... dogs. Answer 1 for Dogs, Answer 2 for Professionals, Answer 3 for Treatments, the answer should be Answer ". $table\_lm$ takes this input and outputs a logit for every token in its vocabulary.

Language Model Output Normalization. To get the probability distribution over D_Y, for language models with a decoder, we extract the logits for indexes i from the decoder outputs and renormalize them with the softmax function. For the encoder-only language models, we apply a linear layer on top of them. For example, in Fig. 1, the logits for the token "1", "2" and "3" are extracted and the softmax distribution could be 0.2, 0.2, and 0.6. Thus, the LMDCG rule represents a set of grammar branches: 0.2::$table$("Find...dogs.", "dog_kennels", "Dogs") $\rightarrow$ []; 0.2::$table$("Find...dogs.", "dog_kennels", "Professionals") $\rightarrow$ []; 0.6::$table$("Find ...dogs.", "dog_kennels", "Treatments") $\rightarrow$ []. Here, we apply the empty production. The rule produces an empty sequence but provides substitutions of the table variable T, which helps determine the column domain in the column rule through the Prolog unification mechanism. Unlike the autoregressive models, the empty production allows us to deal with tables before columns which better fits human intuitions.

4.3 DCGs v.s. Previous Rules

The rules in previous sketch- [4,29,32,33] and grammar-based approaches [8,14,25,31] do not explicitly represent relationships between tables and columns. When generating basic SQL queries, they are equivalent to CFGs in Example 1 a). Considering the dog_kennels database in Fig. 1, these approaches can overgenerate and lead to invalid queries mismatching tables and columns, for example, "SELECT treat_id FROM Dogs".

The example DCG avoids this error and encodes the associations of tables and columns by bounding the column domain to columns in a specific table. We demonstrate that DCGs can guarantee the correctness of syntax and the faithfulness to schema and thus guarantee the validity of outputs with this basic SQL generation scenario. As DCGs are Turing-complete, they can be generalized to express sophisticated SQL syntax and semantic constraints and produce valid, advanced SQL queries.

Example 1. An equivalent CFG of rules in previous works a) and a DCG b).

a) $T \rightarrow$ "Dogs", "Professionals", "Treatments"
   $C \rightarrow$ "dog_id", "abandoned_yn", "prof_id", "name", "treat_id"
   $Q \rightarrow$ "SELECT" C "FROM" T

b) $table$("Dogs") $\rightarrow$ "Dogs"
   $table$("Professionals") $\rightarrow$ "Professionals"
   $table$("Treatments") $\rightarrow$ "Treatments"
   $column$("Dogs") $\rightarrow$ "dog_id", "abandoned_yn"
   $column$("Professionals") $\rightarrow$ "prof_id", "name"
   $column$("Treatments") $\rightarrow$ "treat_id", "dog_id", "prof_id"
   $Q \rightarrow$ "SELECT" $column(T)$ "FROM" $table(T)$

5 Experiments

5.1 Research Questions

Our experiments aim to address the following questions:

Q1 Which language model produces more correct queries?
Q2 Does our framework ensure validity? How does it compare to other text-to-SQL approaches?
Q3 Does our framework improve exact matching and execution accuracy?

5.2 Tasks

Task 1 (Q1). We explore which language model should we encapsulate to achieve better performance. The language models in our framework can be classified into two types. Type 1 produces probability distributions over table and column grammar branches with dynamic domains. For type 1, we use T5-small models with an encoder-decoder structure. T5 [19] is popular in addressing the text-to-SQL task [20,21]. The vocabulary of its decoder allows us to handle the domains of the table and the column that vary with the database. Type 2 provides probability distributions over grammar branches defined by SQL syntax with fixed output domains. For example, the selection branches between "SELECT" and "FROM" could be "*", "COUNT(*)", a column with an aggregation function, etc.

In task 1, we compare T5-small with Bert-base [5] plus a linear layer for type 2 using a grammar for the SELECT clause (in Appendix A.1). Setting 1 uses two T5-small models and one Bert-base for the table, column, and selection branch respectively. Setting 2 uses three T5-small models. The training and evaluation details for task 1 are in Appendix A.2.

Task 2 (Q2, Q3). We evaluate our system with a recursion-free grammar covering the SELECT, WHERE, GROUP BY, ORDER BY clauses and EXCEPT between two simple SELECT clauses. The recursive cases are left for future studies. The exact inference in Sect. 3 is inefficient for the extended grammar. We use the greedy inference that takes the most likely grammar branch. Appendix B describes more training and evaluation details, the grammar, and the language models employed.

We compare our framework with the following baselines:

- Neural-based:
  - T5-small: fine-tuned T5-small that treats text-to-SQL as sequence-to-sequence generation.
  - DAIL-SQL [7] and DIN-SQL [18]: GPT-4 [1] under few-shot prompting.
- Grammar-based:
  - T5-small + CFGs: an ablation of our framework which does not consider the relations between table and column. It simulates the rules in previous sketch- [4,29,32,33] and grammar-based approaches [8,14,25,31].
- Constraint-based:
  - Graphix-T5 [13]: T5-3B augmented with graph-aware layers and constrained decoding PICARD [20].
- Execution-guided:
  - C3 [6]: zero-shot ChatGPT. The final output is selected based on execution results.

More information on the methodology of baselines is in Sect. 6. Their implementation details are in Appendix C

Following [34], we consider evaluation metrics: exact matching that compares the predicted and the ground truth query, and the execution accuracy that compares their execution results. We also report validity that checks whether the predicated queries are executable.

Data. We extract samples that satisfy the scope of our grammar from Spider [34], a large-scale complex and cross-domain benchmark dataset for text-to-SQL. All models are evaluated on the instances extracted from Spider's development division. In task 1, we employ 384 training samples and 59 evaluation samples. Task 2 uses 2106 training samples and 258 evaluation samples.

5.3 Results

Q1. For task 1 setting 1 that uses Bert-base for the selection branch, the percentage of outputs with correct execution results is limited to 61%. Its results always start with "SELECT COUNT(*)". This is caused by the unbalanced training data shown in Table 2. Setting 2 using T5-small for the selection branch is less affected by the biased data. 93% outputs lead to the right results. Since the training data for grammar branches is often unbalanced, we encapsulate T5-small for all neural components in task 2 experiments.

Table 2. Selection branch statistics of task 1 training data. col. stands for column.

*	COUNT(*)	col.	COUNT(col.)	SUM(col.)	AVG(col.)	MIN(col.)	MAX(col.)
2.1%	55.5%	14.9%	3.7%	7.3%	12.1%	0.5%	3.9%

Q2. Table 3 compares our framework with state-of-the-art text-to-SQL approaches. Our DeepStochLog with LMDCGs is able to guarantee validity in 100% of the test queries. We ensure faithfulness to both SQL syntax and database schema. In comparison, neural-based methods (T5-small, DAIL-SQL, and DIN-SQL) without hard schema constraints can produce non-valid queries by using identifiers not defined in the schema. T5-small + CFGs can mismatch tables and columns due to the lack of constraints on their relations. Graphix with constrained decoding can exit without finding a valid query and output incomplete results. C3 with execution-guided decoding also produces 100% valid queries for the extracted evaluation examples. However, execution is not always feasible in application scenarios. Table 4 shows examples of common errors made by the baselines.

Table 3. Comparison with state-of-the-art models for text-to-SQL on the selected subset of Spider. (*) Execution-based methods are not applicable in real settings as they need to execute the query during generation. Params. means parameters.

		Validity%	Exact Matching %	Execution Accuracy%
Smaller Models (Millions Params.)	T5-small	53.9	41.1	41.1
	T5-small+CFGs	88.8	67.1	70.9
	Ours (T5-small+DCGs)	**100.0**	75.6	77.9
Larger Models (B/Trillions Params.)	DAIL-SQL (GPT-4)	99.2	88.8	89.9
	DIN-SQL (GPT-4)	99.2	78.7	90.7
	Graphix-T5 (T5-3B+PICARD)	99.6	**91.9**	**91.9**
Execution Required	C3 (ChatGPT+Execution)	100.0*	80.6*	85.3*

Table 4. Examples of invalid outputs from baseline models.

	Example	Error
T5-small	SELECT Name FROM country WHERE Independence > 1950	Invent identifiers Independence not in schema
T5-small+CFGs	SELECT COUNT(*) FROM Has_Pet WHERE weight > 10	Mismatch table and column, weight not in Has_Pet
DAIL-SQL	SELECT Paragraph_Details FROM Paragraphs WHERE Paragraph_Text LIKE '%Korea%'	Invent identifiers Paragraph_Details not in schema
DIN-SQL	SELECT T1.first_name, ... ORDER BY T2.rank_points DESC LIMIT 1	Invent identifiers rank_points not in schema
Graphix	select	Incomplete query

Q3. The performance on exact matching and execution accuracy (see Table 3) also suggests the effectiveness of integrating unification-based grammars with language models. Compared to the vanilla T5-small model, our framework that extends T5-small with unification-based grammars improves the exact matching and execution accuracy by a large margin. We also outperform T5-small + CFGs due to the bounding of column domains to corresponding tables. However, T5-small, with 60 million parameters, limits the capability of our framework to produce correct SQL queries. As shown in Table 5, our outputs with incorrect execution results are caused by misunderstanding user intentions and linking the natural language sentences to the wrong SQL components. The results of DAIL-SQL, DIN-SQL, Graphix, and C3 indicate that this problem could be alleviated by accessing larger-scaled models with billions or trillions of parameters and by employing graph-aware layers that model relations better.

Table 5. Examples of incorrect outputs from our framework. Pred. refers to predication.

Mislinking Type	Example	Proportion %
Identifier(s)	Find the number of distinct name of losers.	65.0
	Pred.: SELECT COUNT(DISTINCT first_name) FROM players	
	Gold: SELECT count(DISTINCT loser_name) FROM matches	
Selection branch	Count the number of dogs that went through a treatment.	19.7
	Pred: SELECT COUNT(*) FROM Treatments	
	Gold: SELECT count(DISTINCT dog_id) FROM Treatments	
Clause	Count the number of high schoolers.	12.0
	Pred: SELECT COUNT(*) FROM Highschooler WHERE grade = 1	
	Gold: SELECT count(*) FROM Highschooler	
Operator	Which cities do more than one employee under age 30 come from?	3.3
	Pred: SELECT City FROM employee WHERE Age > 30 GROUP BY City HAVING COUNT(*) > 1	
	Gold: SELECT city FROM employee WHERE age < 30 GROUP BY city HAVING count(*) > 1	

6 Related Work

Neural-Based. The state-of-the-art text-to-SQL approaches are based on large language models (LLMs). They do not employ any hard constraints to guarantee valid outputs. DAIL-SQL [7] designs the few-shot prompt for LLMs. It uses code question representation and selects examples based on both question and query. DIN-SQL [18] decomposes the text-to-SQL task into sub-problems: schema linking, classification and building different prompts from each class, SQL generation, and self-correction. The first three steps are conducted by LLMs under the few-shot setting and the last one by instructing a LLM.

Sketch-Based. Sketch-based methods [4,29,32,33] model text-to-SQL as a sequence-to-set problem considering the possible equivalent serialization of one query. They define a dependency graph of slots filled by independently trained neural components. The query synthesis process is viewed as an inference on the graph. Their sketches agree with SQL syntax but do not encode schema information like table and column relations. Therefore, the produced queries can be non-executable due to violations of schema.

Grammar-Based. Grammar-based methods [8,14,25,31] introduce a sequence-to-action formalism of text-to-SQL that generates a derivation Abstract Syntax Tree [30] or a similar intermediate representation [8]. At each time step, they use context-free grammars to define the possible actions, and a trained neural model to predict the probability distribution over the action set. Similar to sketch-based approaches, these probabilistic grammar models cannot ensure the validity of their outputs as they do not include semantic constraints.

Constraint-Based and Execution-Guided. Constraint-based methods [17,20] accept only tokens that align with defined SQL syntax and semantic constraints during decoding. Graphix-T5 [13] applies constraint-based PICARD [20] to prune erroneous tokens during its beam-search phase. It also enhances T5 with graphix layers to better model the relational structures in text-to-SQL. Execution-guided approaches [12,22,26] execute queries and filter out faulty ones during generation. C3 [6] samples a set of SQL queries from zero-shot ChatGPT and votes for the most consistent one based on their execution results. The methods in these two categories are effective but can fail to generate valid outputs when the underlying models put low probabilities on valid predictions.

7 Conclusion and Future Work

We introduce LM definite clause grammars (LMDCGs), an extension of DeepStochLog [27] that integrates language models with unification-based grammars to provide a validity guarantee to the text-to-SQL task. We evaluate our method on a subset of SQL syntax. The results suggest that this integration eliminates non-executable queries and significantly contributes to the alignment with ground truth queries and execution accuracy.

Several limitations of our framework are interesting to explore in future studies. First, the prompt part of LMDCGs is not yet built dynamically to indicate the parsing states. Second, our system could be further enhanced by employing billion-level open-source large language models like Llama [24], Falcon [2], and Alpaca [23]. Lastly, scaling the current framework to larger grammars is not trivial. An interesting direction for speeding up the inference process would be searching for the k-best derivations.

Acknowledgments. This project has received funding from the European Union's Horizon Europe research and innovation programme under the Marie Skłodowska-Curie grant agreement No 101073307 and the Flemish Government (AI Research Program). Luc De Raedt is also supported by the Wallenberg AI, Autonomous Systems and Software Program (WASP) funded by the Knut and Alice Wallenberg Foundation. We thank Thomas Winters for the helpful discussions. We also thank the anonymous reviewers for their valuable feedback.

A Task 1

A.1 Logic Program

Task 1 grammar is modeled as follows:

```
S_domain(Y) :- member(Y, [0, 1, 2, 3, 4, 5, 6, 7]).
table_domain(DB, T) :- database(DB, Tables), member(T, Tables).
column_domain(DB, T, C) :- table(DB, T, Columns), member(C, Columns).
token(X) --> [X].
selection_branch(_, _, _, 0) --> ['*'].
selection_branch(_, _, _, 1) --> ['COUNT(*)'].
selection_branch(NL, DB, T, 2) --> column(NL, DB, T).
selection_branch(NL, DB, T, 3) --> ['COUNT('], column(NL, DB, T), [')'].
selection_branch(NL, DB, T, 4) --> ['SUM('], column(NL, DB, T), [')'].
selection_branch(NL, DB, T, 5) --> ['AVG('], column(NL, DB, T), [')'].
selection_branch(NL, DB, T, 6) --> ['MIN('], column(NL, DB, T), [')'].
selection_branch(NL, DB, T, 7) --> ['MAX('], column(NL, DB, T), [')'].
nn_lm(selection_lm, [NL], Y, S_domain(Y), Prompt) :: selection(NL, DB, T) --> selection_branch(NL, DB, T, Y).
nn_lm(table_lm, [NL], T, table_domain(DB, T), Prompt) :: table(NL, DB, T) --> [].
nn_lm(column_lm, [NL], C, column_domain(DB, T, C), Prompt) :: column(NL, DB, T) --> token(C).
query(NL, DB) --> table(NL, DB, T), ['SELECT'], selection(NL, DB, T), ['FROM'], token(T).
```

A.2 Training and Evaluation

We train settings 1 and 2 end-to-end for 7 epochs using the Adam optimizer [10] with a batch size of 8 and a learning rate of $1e^{-3}$. For evaluation, we employ DeepStochLog inference with the (max, ×) semiring, i.e. the exact inference. Examples of *column_lm* and *selection_lm* inputs are listed in Table 7. The inputs of *table_lm* have the same format as those of *column_lm*.

Pre- and Post-processing. In pre-processing, we tokenize the ground truth SQL queries to sequences with list format. Table and column identifiers in the sequences are replaced by their semantic names [12]. The semantics names provided in Spider [34] are closer to natural expressions, which facilitate the understanding of language models. This replacement is also conducted for the facts in logic programs. After generation, we restore the identifiers in the output sequence to their original names and join the sequence to get the SQL query. This pre- and post-progressing are also performed in task 2 experiments.

B Task 2

B.1 Logic Program

Task 2 grammar covers two types of queries: 1) single selection and 2) two selections connected by the set operator "EXCEPT". The grammar for single-selection queries covers the "SELECT", "WHERE", "GROUP BY", and "ORDER BY" clauses including "DISTINCT" and aggregation functions in the "SELECT" clause, "HAVING" in the "GROUP BY" clause, and "ASC / DESC" and "LIMIT" in the "ORDER BY" clause. "WHERE" and "HAVING" allow one condition. For type 2), the two selection clauses have the format "SELECT [column] FROM [table]". The columns in the two selection clauses are currently restricted to foreign keys linking the two tables. Task 2 grammar is modeled as follows:

```
selection_domain(Y) :- member(Y, [0, 1, 2, 3, 4, 5, 6, 7, 8, 9]).
boolean_domain(Y) :- member(Y, [0, 1]).
where_operator_domain(Y) :- member(Y, ['=', '>', '<', '>=', '<=', 'LIKE']).
having_operator_domain(Y) :- member(Y, ['=', '>', '<', '>=', '<=']).
except_table_1_domain(DB, T) :- database_foreign_tables(DB, ForeignTables), member(T, ForeignTables).
except_table_2_domain(DB, T1, T) :- table_foreign_relations(DB, T1, ForeignTables), member(T, ForeignTables).
table_domain(DB, T) :- database(DB, Tables), member(T, Tables).
column_domain(DB, T, C) :- table(DB, T, Columns), member(C, Columns).
token(X) --> [X].
nn_lm(table_lm, [NL, State], T, table_domain(DB, T), Prompt) :: table(NL, DB, T, State) --> [].
nn_lm(column_lm, [NL, State], C, column_domain(DB, T, C), Prompt) :: column(NL, DB, T, State) --> token(C).
selection_branch(_, _, _, 0) --> ['*'].
selection_branch(_, _, _, 1) --> ['COUNT(*)'].
selection_branch(NL, DB, T, 2) --> column(NL, DB, T, 0).
selection_branch(NL, DB, T, 3) --> ['DISTINCT'], column(NL, DB, T, 0).
selection_branch(NL, DB, T, 4) --> ['COUNT('], column(NL, DB, T, 0), [')'].
selection_branch(NL, DB, T, 5) --> ['COUNT(', 'DISTINCT'], column(NL, DB, T, 0), [')'].
selection_branch(NL, DB, T, 6) --> ['SUM('], column(NL, DB, T, 0), [')'].
selection_branch(NL, DB, T, 7) --> ['AVG('], column(NL, DB, T, 0), [')'].
selection_branch(NL, DB, T, 8) --> ['MIN('], column(NL, DB, T, 0), [')'].
selection_branch(NL, DB, T, 9) --> ['MAX('], column(NL, DB, T, 0), [')'].
nn_lm(selection_lm, [NL], Y, selection_domain(Y), Prompt) :: selection(NL, DB, T) --> selection_branch(NL, DB, T, Y).
where_branch(_, _, _, 0) --> [].
where_branch(NL, DB, T, 1) --> ['WHERE'], column(NL, DB, T, 1), where_operator(NL, 0), ['WHERE-VALUE'].
nn_lm(where_lm, [NL, State], Y, boolean_domain(Y), Prompt) :: where(NL, DB, T) --> where_branch(NL, DB, T, Y).
nn_lm(operator_lm, [NL, State], Y, having_operator_domain(Y), Prompt) :: having_operator(NL, State) --> token(Y).
having_branch(_, 0) --> [].
having_branch(NL, 1) --> ['HAVING'], ['COUNT(*)'], having_operator(NL, 1), ['HAVING-VALUE'].
nn_lm(having_lm, [NL], Y, boolean_domain(Y), Prompt) :: having(NL) --> having_branch(NL, Y).
groupby_branch(_, _, _, 0) --> [].
groupby_branch(NL, DB, T, 1) --> ['GROUP BY'], column(NL, DB, T, 2), having(NL).
nn_lm(groupby_lm, [NL], Y, boolean_domain(Y), Prompt) :: group_by(NL, DB, T) --> groupby_branch(NL, DB, T, Y).
limit_branch(0) --> [].
limit_branch(1) --> ['LIMIT'], ['LIMIT-VALUE'].
nn_lm(limit_lm, [NL], Y, boolean_domain(Y), Prompt) :: limit(NL) --> limit_branch(Y).
desc_branch(0) --> ['ASC'].
desc_branch(1) --> ['DESC'].
nn_lm(desc_lm, [NL], Y, boolean_domain(Y), Prompt) :: desc(NL) --> desc_branch(Y).
orderby_branch(_, _, _, 0) --> [].
orderby_branch(NL, DB, T, 1) --> ['ORDER BY'], column(NL, DB, T, 3), desc(NL), limit(NL).
nn_lm(orderby_lm, [NL], Y, boolean_domain(Y), Prompt) :: order_by(NL, DB, T) --> orderby_branch(NL, DB, T, Y).
query_type(NL, DB, 0) --> table(NL, DB, T, 0), ['SELECT'], selection(NL, DB, T), ['FROM'], token(T), where(NL, DB, T), group_by(NL, DB, T), order_by(NL, T).
nn_lm(table_lm, [NL, State], T, except_table_1_domain(DB, T), Prompt) :: except_table_1(NL, DB, T, State) --> [].
nn_lm(table_lm, [NL, State], T, except_table_2_domain(DB, T1, T), Prompt) :: except_table_2(NL, DB, T1, T, State) --> [].
query_type(NL, DB, 1) --> except_table_1(NL, DB, T1, 0), except_table_2(NL, DB, T1, T2, 1), {foreign_key(T1, T2, C1, C2)}, ['SELECT'], token(C1), ['FROM'], token(T1), ['EXCEPT'], token(C2), ['FROM'], token(T2).
nn_lm(except_lm, [NL], Y, boolean_domain(Y), Prompt) :: query(NL, DB) --> query_type(NL, DB, Y).
```

B.2 Underlying Language Models

We employ 11 fine-tuned T5-small models. All models used in this work are from Huggingface [28].

table_lm and *column_lm* provide the probability distribution over the given table and column domain respectively. Their output domains vary with the database. The output domain of other language models is fixed. *except_lm*, *where_lm*, *groupby_lm*, *having_lm*, *order_lm*, *desc_lm*, *limit_lm* are used to produce the probability distribution on the existence of the corresponding SQL clause. *selection_lm* provides the probability distribution over 10 possible selection branches. *operator_lm* outputs the probability distribution over possible operators in "WHERE" and "HAVING" conditions. For the queries with two selection clauses connected by "EXCEPT", we call *table_lm* twice to get probability distributions over the possible substitutions for the table in each selection clause. The pair of columns in each selection clause are decided deterministically based on the pair of tables. Our current framework does not predict any value in SQL conditions. We assume the gold values are given. When we predict wrong conditions that cannot be mapped to the gold values, we assign the values to 1.

table_lm, *column_lm*, and *opertor_lm* can be used at different positions. *table_lm* can be called twice for the selection clause before "EXCEPT" and the one after "EXCEPT". *column_lm* is used for the column in the "SELECT", "WHERE", "GROUP BY" and "ORDER BY" clauses. *operator_lm* is used for operators in "WHERE" and "HAVING" conditions. We add states in their inputs to help them distinguish different cases. Examples of *column_lm* inputs are shown in Table 7 to showcase the inputs with states. We also include examples of *where_lm* and *selection_lm* inputs in Table 7. *except_lm*, *where_lm*, *groupby_lm*, *having_lm*, *order_lm*, *desc_lm*, *limit_lm* shares a similar input format as *where_lm*.

B.3 Training and Evaluation

In the text-to-SQL task, the grammar can always be written unambiguously, which leads to only one possible derivation for the ground-truth query Q. With the negative log-likelihood loss function and all positive samples in dataset $\mathcal{D}$ (target probability $t_i = 1.0$),

$$(1) = \min_p \sum_{(G_i \theta_i, Q_i) \in \mathcal{D}} -log(\prod_{r_j \in d(G_i \theta_i) = Q_i} p_j^{k_j})$$

$$= \sum_{(G_i \theta_i, Q_i) \in \mathcal{D}} \sum_{r_j \in d(G_i \theta_i) = Q_i} \min_{p_j} -k_j log p_j$$

As all the intermediate goals are observable given Q, the learning problem collapses to supervised training.

We fine-tune the T5-small models using the Adam optimizer. Table 6 shows the number of fine-tuning epochs, the batch size, and the learning rate for each model. The hyper-parameters are determined with cross-validation.

In evaluation, we perform the greedy inference to speed up the inference process. Instead of considering the re-normalized distributions obtained from the language models, the greedy inference takes the substitution with the largest probability.

Table 6. Fine-tuning hyper-parameters of our T5-small models.

	table	column	except	where	group by	having	order by	desc	limit	selection	operator
Epochs	5	16	3	14	4	2	7	10	3	7	17
Batch size	64	32	64	32	64	64	64	32	64	64	64
Learning rate	$1e^{-3}$	$5e^{-4}$	$5e^{-4}$	$5e^{-4}$	$1e^{-3}$	$5e^{-4}$	$1e^{-3}$	$5e^{-4}$	$5e^{-4}$	$1e^{-3}$	$1e^{-3}$

C Baselines

We fine-tune the vanilla T5-small baseline for 10 epochs using the Adam optimizer, a batch size of 32, and a learning rate $1e^{-3}$. T5-small + CFGs shares the same language models with ours T5-small + DCGs except the *column_lm*. Without table unification, the domain of *column_lm* used in T5-small + CFGs covers all the columns in a given database. We fine-tune a T5-small model for *column_lm* in T5-small + CFGs using the Adam optimizer for 13 epochs with a batch size of 32, and a learning rate $5e^{-4}$. Table 8 shows the example inputs for T5-small and *column_lm* in T5-small + CFGs.

For the state-of-the-art models (DAIL-SQL [7], DIN-SQL [18], Graphix-T5 [13], and C3 [6]), we extract their predictions on the samples in our evaluation set from their official results for the full Spider development set [34].

Table 7. Examples of inputs of our T5-small models.

Task 1	column_lm	On average how large is the population of the counties? Answer 1 for county id, Answer 2 for county name, Answer 3 for population, Answer 4 for zip code, the answer should be Answer
	selection_lm	How many singers do we have? Answer 1 for *, Answer 2 for COUNT(*), Answer 3 for column, Answer 4 for COUNT(column), Answer 5 for SUM(column), Answer 6 for AVG(column), Answer 7 for MIN(column), Answer 8 for MAX(column), the answer should be Answer
Task 2	column_lm	What is the average hours across all projects? SELECT [column], Answer 1 for code, Answer 2 for name, Answer 3 for hours, the answer should be Answer
		Find the ids of all the order items whose product id is 11. WHERE [column], Answer 1 for order item id, Answer 2 for product id, Answer 3 for order id, Answer 4 for order item status, Answer 5 for order item details, the answer should be Answer
		Find the number of followers for each user. GROUP BY [column], Answer 1 for user id, Answer 2 for follower id, the answer should be Answer
		List all pilot names in ascending alphabetical order. ORDER BY [column], Answer 1 for pilot id, Answer 2 for name, Answer 3 for age, the answer should be Answer
	selection_lm	How many singers do we have? Answer 1 for *, Answer 2 for COUNT(*), Answer 3 for column, Answer 4 for DISTINCT column, Answer 5 for COUNT(column), Answer 6 for COUNT(DISTINCT column), Answer 7 for SUM(column), Answer 8 for AVG(column), Answer 9 for MIN(column), Answer 10 for MAX(column), the answer should be Answer
	where_lm	How many king beds are there? Answer 1 for empty, Answer 2 for WHERE, the answer should be Answer

Table 8. Examples of baseline inputs.

T5-small	Please show the categories of the music festivals with count more than 1. database is music_4. tables are artist, volume, music festival. columns in artist are artist id, artist, age, famous title, famous release date. columns in volume are volume id, volume issue, issue date, weeks on top, song, artist id. columns in music festival are id, music festival, date of ceremony, category, volume, result.
T5-small + CFGs (column_lm)	What is the average hours across all projects? SELECT [column], Answer 1 for ssn, Answer 2 for name, ..., Answer 7 for project, the answer should be Answer
	Find the ids of all the order items whose product id is 11. WHERE [column], Answer 1 for customer id, Answer 2 for customer name, ..., Answer 27 for order item id, the answer should be Answer
	Find the number of followers for each user. GROUP BY [column], Answer 1 for user id, Answer 2 for follower id, ..., Answer 11 for followers, the answer should be Answer
	List all pilot names in ascending alphabetical order. ORDER BY [column], Answer 1 for pilot id, Answer 2 for name, ..., Answer 28 for aircraft id, the answer should be Answer

References

1. Achiam, J., et al.: GPT-4 technical report. arXiv preprint arXiv:2303.08774 (2023)
2. Almazrouei, E., et al.: Falcon-40B: an open large language model with state-of-the-art performance (2023)
3. Chase, H.: LangChain (2022). https://github.com/langchain-ai/langchain
4. Choi, D., Shin, M., Kim, E., Shin, D.: RYANSQL: recursively applying sketch-based slot fillings for complex text-to-SQL in cross-domain databases. Comput. Linguist. **47**(2), 309–332 (2021)
5. Devlin, J., Chang, M.W., Lee, K., Toutanova, K.: BERT: pre-training of deep bidirectional transformers for language understanding. In: Proceedings of the 2019 Conference of the North American Chapter of the Association for Computational Linguistics: Human Language Technologies, Volume 1 (Long and Short Papers), pp. 4171–4186 (2019)
6. Dong, X., et al.: C3: Zero-shot text-to-SQL with ChatGpt. arXiv preprint arXiv:2307.07306 (2023)
7. Gao, D., et al.: Text-to-SQL empowered by large language models: a benchmark evaluation. arXiv preprint arXiv:2308.15363 (2023)
8. Guo, J., et al.: towards complex text-to-SQL in cross-domain database with intermediate representation. In: Proceedings of the 57th Annual Meeting of the Association for Computational Linguistics, pp. 4524–4535 (2019)
9. Kimmig, A., Van den Broeck, G., De Raedt, L.: An algebraic prolog for reasoning about possible worlds. In: Proceedings of the AAAI Conference on Artificial Intelligence, vol. 25, pp. 209–214 (2011)

10. Kingma, D.P., Ba, J.: Adam: a method for stochastic optimization. arXiv preprint arXiv:1412.6980 (2014)
11. Lewis, P., et al.: Retrieval-augmented generation for knowledge-intensive NLP tasks. Adv. Neural. Inf. Process. Syst. **33**, 9459–9474 (2020)
12. Li, H., Zhang, J., Li, C., Chen, H.: ResdSQL: decoupling schema linking and skeleton parsing for text-to-SQL. In: Proceedings of the AAAI Conference on Artificial Intelligence, vol. 37, pp. 13067–13075 (2023)
13. Li, J., et al.: Graphix-t5: mixing pre-trained transformers with graph-aware layers for text-to-SQL parsing. In: Proceedings of the AAAI Conference on Artificial Intelligence, p. 13076–13084 (2023)
14. Lin, K., Bogin, B., Neumann, M., Berant, J., Gardner, M.: Grammar-based neural text-to-SQL generation. arXiv preprint arXiv:1905.13326 (2019)
15. Liu, J.: LlamaIndex (2022). https://doi.org/10.5281/zenodo.1234, https://github.com/jerryjliu/llama_index
16. Pereira, F.C., Warren, D.H.: Definite clause grammars for language analysis-a survey of the formalism and a comparison with augmented transition networks. Artif. Intell. **13**(3), 231–278 (1980)
17. Poesia, G., et al.: Synchromesh: reliable code generation from pre-trained language models. arXiv preprint arXiv:2201.11227 (2022)
18. Pourreza, M., Rafiei, D.: DIN-SQL: decomposed in-context learning of text-to-SQL with self-correction. In: Advances in Neural Information Processing Systems, vol. 36 (2024)
19. Raffel, C., et al.: Exploring the limits of transfer learning with a unified text-to-text transformer. J. Mach. Learn. Res. **21**(140), 1–67 (2020)
20. Scholak, T., Schucher, N., Bahdanau, D.: Picard: parsing incrementally for constrained auto-regressive decoding from language models. In: Proceedings of the 2021 Conference on Empirical Methods in Natural Language Processing, pp. 9895–9901 (2021)
21. Shaw, P., Chang, M.W., Pasupat, P., Toutanova, K.: Compositional generalization and natural language variation: can a semantic parsing approach handle both? In: Proceedings of the 59th Annual Meeting of the Association for Computational Linguistics and the 11th International Joint Conference on Natural Language Processing (Volume 1: Long Papers), pp. 922–938 (2021)
22. Suhr, A., Chang, M.W., Shaw, P., Lee, K.: Exploring unexplored generalization challenges for cross-database semantic parsing. In: Proceedings of the 58th Annual Meeting of the Association for Computational Linguistics, pp. 8372–8388 (2020)
23. Taori, R., et al.: Stanford alpaca: an instruction-following llama model (2023). https://github.com/tatsu-lab/stanford_alpaca
24. Touvron, H., et al.: LLaMA: open and efficient foundation language models. arXiv preprint arXiv:2302.13971 (2023)
25. Wang, B., Shin, R., Liu, X., Polozov, O., Richardson, M.: RAT-SQL: relation-aware schema encoding and linking for text-to-SQL parsers. In: Proceedings of the 58th Annual Meeting of the Association for Computational Linguistics, pp. 7567–7578 (2020)
26. Wang, C., et al.: Robust text-to-SQL generation with execution-guided decoding. arXiv preprint arXiv:1807.03100 (2018)
27. Winters, T., Marra, G., Manhaeve, R., De Raedt, L.: DeepStochLog: neural stochastic logic programming. In: Proceedings of the AAAI Conference on Artificial Intelligence, vol. 36, pp. 10090–10100 (2022)

28. Wolf, T., et al.: Transformers: state-of-the-art natural language processing. In: Proceedings of the 2020 Conference on Empirical Methods in Natural Language Processing: System Demonstrations, pp. 38–45 (2020)
29. Xu, X., Liu, C., Song, D.: SQLnet: generating structured queries from natural language without reinforcement learning. arXiv preprint arXiv:1711.04436 (2017)
30. Yin, P., Neubig, G.: A syntactic neural model for general-purpose code generation. In: Proceedings of the 55th Annual Meeting of the Association for Computational Linguistics (Volume 1: Long Papers), pp. 440–450 (2017)
31. Yin, P., Neubig, G.: TRANX: a transition-based neural abstract syntax parser for semantic parsing and code generation. In: Proceedings of the Conference on Empirical Methods in Natural Language Processing (Demo Track) (2018)
32. Yu, T., Li, Z., Zhang, Z., Zhang, R., Radev, D.: TypeSQL: knowledge-based type-aware neural text-to-sql generation. In: Proceedings of the 2018 Conference of the North American Chapter of the Association for Computational Linguistics: Human Language Technologies, Volume 2 (Short Papers) (2018)
33. Yu, T., et al.: Syntaxsqlnet: Syntax tree networks for complex and cross-domain text-to-sql task. In: Proceedings of the 2018 Conference on Empirical Methods in Natural Language Processing, pp. 1653–1663 (2018)
34. Yu, T., et al.: Spider: a large-scale human-labeled dataset for complex and cross-domain semantic parsing and text-to-sql task. In: Proceedings of the 2018 Conference on Empirical Methods in Natural Language Processing, pp. 3911–3921 (2018)

Enhancing Geometric Ontology Embeddings for $\mathcal{EL}^{++}$ with Negative Sampling and Deductive Closure Filtering

Olga Mashkova(✉)🆔, Fernando Zhapa-Camacho🆔, and Robert Hoehndorf🆔

Computer Science Program, Computer, Electrical, and Mathematical Sciences and Engineering Division, King Abdullah University of Science and Technology, Thuwal 23955, Saudi Arabia
{olga.mashkova,fernando.zhapacamacho,robert.hoehndorf}@kaust.edu.sa

Abstract. Ontology embeddings map classes, relations, and individuals in ontologies into $\mathbb{R}^n$, and within $\mathbb{R}^n$ similarity between entities can be computed or new axioms inferred. For ontologies in the Description Logic $\mathcal{EL}^{++}$, several embedding methods have been developed that explicitly generate models of an ontology. However, these methods suffer from some limitations; they do not distinguish between statements that are unprovable and provably false, and therefore they may use entailed statements as negatives. Furthermore, they do not utilize the deductive closure of an ontology to identify statements that are inferred but not asserted. We evaluated a set of embedding methods for $\mathcal{EL}^{++}$ ontologies based on high-dimensional ball representation of concept descriptions, incorporating several modifications that aim to make use of the ontology deductive closure. In particular, we designed novel negative losses that account both for the deductive closure and different types of negatives. We demonstrate that our embedding methods improve over the baseline ontology embedding in the task of knowledge base or ontology completion.

Keywords: Ontology Embedding · Knowledge Base Completion · Description Logic $\mathcal{EL}^{++}$

1 Introduction

Several methods have been developed to embed Description Logic theories or ontologies in vector spaces [6,7,13,18,24–26,31]. These embedding methods preserve some aspects of the semantics in the vector space, and may enable the computation of semantic similarity, inferring axioms that are entailed, and predicting axioms that are not entailed but may be added to the theory. For the lightweight Description Logic $\mathcal{EL}^{++}$, several geometric embedding methods have been developed [13,18,24,25,31]. They can be proven to "faithfully" approximate a model in the sense that, if a certain optimization objective is reached (usually, a loss function reduced to 0), the embedding method has constructed a model of the

$\mathcal{EL}^{++}$theory. Geometric model construction enables the execution of various tasks. These tasks include knowledge base completion and subsumption prediction via either testing the truth of a statement under consideration in a single (approximate) model or aggregating truth values over multiple models.

Advances on different geometric embedding methods have usually focused on the expressiveness of the embedding methods; originally, hyperballs [18] where used to represent the interpretation of concept symbols, yet hyperballs are not closed under intersection. Therefore, axis-aligned boxes were introduced [13,26,31]. Furthermore, $\mathcal{EL}^{++}$allows for axioms pertaining to relations, and several methods have extended the way in which relations are modeled [13,18,31]. However, there are several aspects of geometric embeddings that have not yet been investigated. In particular, for $\mathcal{EL}^{++}$, there are sound and complete reasoners with efficient implementations that scale to very large knowledge bases [16]; it may therefore be possible to utilize a deductive reasoner together with the embedding process to improve generation of embeddings that represent geometric models.

We evaluate geometric embedding methods and incorporate deductive inference into the training process. We use the *ELEmbeddings* [18] model for our experiments due to its simplicity; however, our results also apply to other geometric embedding methods for $\mathcal{EL}^{++}$.

Our main contributions are as follows:

- We investigate and reveal biases in some evaluation datasets that are related to how the task of knowledge base completion is formulated, and demonstrate that, due to these biases, even when models collapse, predictive performance can be high.
- We introduce loss functions that avoid zero gradients and improve the task of knowledge base completion.
- We introduce a fast approximate algorithm for computing the deductive closure of an $\mathcal{EL}^{++}$theory and use it to improve negative sampling during model training.
- We propose loss functions that incorporate negative samples in most normal forms.

2 Preliminaries

2.1 Description Logic $\mathcal{EL}^{++}$

Let $\Sigma = (\mathbf{C}, \mathbf{R}, \mathbf{I})$ be a signature with set $\mathbf{C}$ of concept names, $\mathbf{R}$ of role names, and $\mathbf{I}$ of individual names. Given $A, B \in \mathbf{C}$, $r \in \mathbf{R}$, and $a, b \in \mathbf{I}$, $\mathcal{EL}^{++}$concept descriptions are constructed with the grammar $\bot \mid \top \mid A \sqcap B \mid \exists r.A \mid \{a\}$. ABox axioms are of the form $A(a)$ and $r(a,b)$, TBox axioms are of the form $A \sqsubseteq B$, and RBox axioms are of the form $r_1 \circ r_2 \circ \cdots \circ r_n \sqsubseteq r$. $\mathcal{EL}^{++}$*generalized concept inclusions* (GCIs) and *role inclusions* (RIs) can be normalized to follow one of these forms [2]: $C \sqsubseteq D$ (GCI0), $C \sqcap D \sqsubseteq E$ (GCI1), $C \sqsubseteq \exists R.D$ (GCI2),

$\exists R.C \sqsubseteq D$ (GCI3), $C \sqsubseteq \bot$ (GCI0-BOT), $C \sqcap D \sqsubseteq \bot$ (GCI1-BOT), $\exists R.C \sqsubseteq \bot$ (GCI3-BOT) and $r \sqsubseteq s$ (RI0), $r_1 \circ r_2 \sqsubseteq s$ (RI1), respectively.

To define the semantics of an $\mathcal{EL}^{++}$ theory, we use [2] an *interpretation domain* $\Delta^{\mathcal{I}}$ and an *interpretation function* $\cdot^{\mathcal{I}}$. For every concept $A \in \mathbf{C}$, $A^{\mathcal{I}} \subseteq \Delta^{\mathcal{I}}$; individual $a \in \mathbf{I}$, $a^{\mathcal{I}} \in \Delta^{\mathcal{I}}$; role $r \in \mathbf{R}$, $r^{\mathcal{I}} \in \Delta^{\mathcal{I}} \times \Delta^{\mathcal{I}}$. Furthermore, the semantics for other $\mathcal{EL}^{++}$ constructs are the following (omitting concrete domains and role inclusions):

$$\bot^{\mathcal{I}} = \emptyset$$
$$\top^{\mathcal{I}} = \Delta^{\mathcal{I}},$$
$$(A \sqcap B)^{\mathcal{I}} = A^{\mathcal{I}} \cap B^{\mathcal{I}},$$
$$(\exists r.A)^{\mathcal{I}} = \{a \in \Delta^{\mathcal{I}} \mid \exists b : ((a,b) \in r^{\mathcal{I}} \land b \in A^{\mathcal{I}})\},$$
$$(a)^{\mathcal{I}} = \{a\}$$

An interpretation $\mathcal{I}$ is a model for an axiom $C \sqsubseteq D$ if and only if $C^{\mathcal{I}} \subseteq D^{\mathcal{I}}$, for an axiom $B(a)$ if and only if $a^{\mathcal{I}} \in B^{\mathcal{I}}$; and for an axiom $r(a,b)$ if and only if $(a^{\mathcal{I}}, b^{\mathcal{I}}) \in r^{\mathcal{I}}$ [3].

2.2 Knowledge Base Completion

The task of knowledge base completion is the addition (or prediction) of axioms to a knowledge base that are not explicitly represented. We call the task "ontology completion" when exclusively TBox axioms are predicted. The task of knowledge base completion may encompass both deductive [15,28] and inductive [4,10] inference processes and give rise to two subtly different tasks: adding only "novel" axioms to a knowledge base that are *not* in the deductive closure of the knowledge base, and adding axioms that are in the deductive closure as well as some "novel" axioms that are not deductively inferred; both tasks are related but differ in how they are evaluated.

Inductive inference, analogously to knowledge graph completion [8], predicts axioms based on patterns and regularities within the knowledge base. Knowledge base completion, or ontology completion, can be further distinguished based on the information that is used to predict "novel" axioms. We distinguish between two approaches to knowledge base completion: (1) knowledge base completion which relies solely on (formalized) information within the knowledge base to predict new axioms, and (2) knowledge base completion which incorporates side information, such as text, to enhance the prediction of new axioms. Here, we mainly consider the first case.

3 Related Work

3.1 Graph-Based Ontology Embeddings

Graph-based ontology embeddings rely on a construction (projection) of graphs from ontology axioms mapping ontology classes, individuals and roles to nodes and labeled edges [32]. Embeddings for nodes and edge labels are optimized using Knowledge Graph Embedding (KGE) methods [30]. These type of methods have been shown effective on knowledge base and ontology completion [6] and have been applied to domain-specific tasks such as protein–protein interaction prediction [6] or gene–disease association prediction [7]. Graph-based methods rely on adjacency information of the ontology structure but cannot easily handle logical operators and do not approximate ontology models. Therefore, graph-based methods are not "faithful", i.e., do not approximate models, do not allow determining whether statements are "true" in these models, and therefore cannot be used to perform semantic entailment.

3.2 Geometric-Based Ontology Embeddings

Multiple methods have been developed for the geometric construction of models for the $\mathcal{EL}^{++}$ language. ELEmbeddings [18] constructs an interpretation of concept names as sets of points lying within an open n-dimensional ball and generates an interpretation of role names as the set of pairs of points that are separated by a vector in $\mathbb{R}^n$, i.e., by the embedding of the role name. EmEL++ [24] extends ELEmbeddings with more expressive constructs such as role chains and role inclusions. ELBE [26] and BoxEL [31] use n-dimensional axis-aligned boxes to represent concepts, which has an advantage over balls because the intersection of two axis-aligned boxes is a box whereas the intersection of two n-balls is not an n-ball. BoxEL additionally preserves ABox facilitating a more accurate representation of knowledge base's logical structure by ensuring, e.g., that an entity has the minimal volume. Box^{2}EL [13] represents ontology roles more expressively with two boxes encoding the semantics of the domain and codomain of roles. Box^{2}EL enables the expression of one-to-many relations as opposed to other methods. Axis-aligned cone-shaped geometric model introduced in [25] deals with $\mathcal{ALC}$ ontologies and allows for full negation of concepts and existential quantification by construction of convex sets in $\mathbb{R}^n$. This work has not yet been implemented or evaluated in an application.

3.3 Knowledge Base Completion Task

Several recent advancements in the knowledge base completion rely on side information as included in Large Language Models (LLMs). [14] explores how pretrained language models can be utilized for incorporating one ontology into another, with the main focus on inconsistency handling and ontology coherence. HalTon [5] addresses the task of event ontology completion via simultaneous event clustering, hierarchy expansion and type naming utilizing BERT [9] for instance encoding. [19] formulates knowledge base completion task as a Natural Language Inference (NLI) problem and examines how this approach may be combined with concept embeddings for identifying missing knowledge in ontologies. As for other approaches, [23] proposes a method that converts an ontology into a graph to recommend missing edges using structure-only link analysis methods, [29] constructs matrix-based ontology embeddings which capture the global and local information for subsumption prediction. All these methods use side information from LLMs and would not be applicable, for example, in the case where a knowledge base is private or consists of only identifiers; we do not consider methods based on pre-trained LLMs here as baselines.

4 Methods

4.1 Datasets

Following previous works [13,18,26] we use common benchmarks for the prediction of protein–protein interactions (PPIs). We also reorganize the same data for the task of protein function prediction. For our experiments we use four datasets; each of them consists of the Gene Ontology [1] with all its axioms, protein–protein interactions (PPIs) and protein function axioms extracted from the STRING database [22]; we use one dataset focusing on only yeast and another dataset focusing on only human proteins. GO is formalized using OWL 2 EL [11].

For PPI yeast network we use the built-in dataset `PPIYeastDataset` available in the mOWL [33] Python library (release 0.2.1) where axioms of interest are split randomly into train, validation and test datasets in ratio 90:5:5 keeping pairs of symmetric PPI axioms within the same dataset, and other axioms are placed into the training part; validation and test sets are made up of TBox axioms of type $\{P_1\} \sqsubseteq \exists interacts\_with.\{P_2\}$ where P_1, P_2 are protein names. In case of yeast proteins, the GO version released on 2021-10-20 and the STRING database version 11.5 were used. Alongside with the yeast *interacts_with* dataset we collected the yeast *has_function* dataset organized in the same manner with validation and test parts containing TBox axioms of type $\{P\} \sqsubseteq \exists has\_function.\{GO\}$. The human *interacts_with* and *has_function* datasets were built from STRING PPI human network (version 10.5) and GO released on 2018-12-28. Based on the information in the STRING database, in PPI yeast, the *interacts_with* relation is symmetric and the dataset is closed against symmetric interactions; the PPI human dataset does not always contain the inverse of interactions and is not closed against symmetry. We normalize all ontology axioms using the implementation of the jcel [21] reasoner, accessed through the mOWL library [33]. Role inclusion axioms are ignored since we experiment with modifications of the *ELEmbeddings* method where role inclusion axioms are omitted as well. The number of GCIs of each type in the datasets can be found in [20].

4.2 Objective Functions

ELEmbeddings use a single loss for "negatives", i.e., axioms that are not included in the knowledge base; the loss is used only for axioms of the form $C \sqsubseteq \exists R.D$ which are randomly sampled, and negatives are not considered for other normal forms. We add three more "negative" losses: $C \sqsubseteq D$, $C \sqcap D \sqsubseteq E$, and $\exists R.C \sqsubseteq D$:

$$loss_{C \not\sqsubseteq D}(c,d) =$$
$$= l(r_\eta(c) + r_\eta(d) - \|f_\eta(c) - f_\eta(d)\| + \gamma) + \qquad (1)$$
$$+ |\|f_\eta(c)\| - 1| + |\|f_\eta(d)\| - 1|$$

$$loss_{C \sqcap D \not\sqsubseteq E}(c,d,e) =$$
$$= l(-r_\eta(c) - r_\eta(d) + \|f_\eta(c) - f_\eta(d)\| - \gamma) +$$
$$+ l(r_\eta(c) - \|f_\eta(c) - f_\eta(e)\| + \gamma) + \qquad (2)$$
$$+ l(r_\eta(d) - \|f_\eta(d) - f_\eta(e)\| + \gamma) +$$
$$+ |\|f_\eta(c)\| - 1| + |\|f_\eta(d)\| - 1| + |\|f_\eta(e)\| - 1|$$

$$loss_{\exists R.C \not\sqsubseteq D}(r,c,d) =$$
$$= l(r_\eta(c) + r_\eta(d) - \|f_\eta(c) - f_\eta(r) - f_\eta(d)\| + \gamma) + \qquad (3)$$
$$+ |\|f_\eta(c)\| - 1| + |\|f_\eta(d)\| - 1|$$

Here, l denotes a function that determines the behavior of the loss when the axiom is true (for positive cases) or not true (for negative cases); in our case, we consider ReLU and LeakyReLU; γ stands for a margin parameter. We employ notations from the *ELEmbeddings* method: $r_\eta(c)$, $r_\eta(d)$, $r_\eta(e)$ and $f_\eta(c)$, $f_\eta(d)$, $f_\eta(e)$ denote the radius and the ball center associated with classes c, d, e, respectively, $f_\eta(r)$ denotes the embedding vector associated with relation r. There is a geometrical part as well as a regularization part for each new negative loss forcing class centers to lie on a unit ℓ_2-sphere. Negative loss 3 is constructed similarly to $C \sqcap D \sqsubseteq E$ loss: the first part penalizes non-overlap of C and D classes (we do not consider disjointness case since for every class X we have $\bot \sqsubseteq X$); the second and the third part force the center corresponding to E not to lie in the intersection of balls associated with C and D. Here we do not consider constraints on radius of the ball for E class and focus only on relative positions of C, D and E class centers and overlapping of n-balls representing C and D. In our experiments, we also use a relaxed regularization where $\|f_\eta(c)\| = R$ is replaced with $\|f_\eta(c)\| \leq R$ on n-ball centers representing concepts forcing them to lie inside the corresponding closed ball of radius R centered at 0. Relaxed version of regularization may allow for more accurate representation of a knowledge base since it is not forcing all ball centers corresponding to concept names to lie on a unit sphere.

4.3 Deductive Closure: Negatives Filtration

The *deductive closure* of a theory T refers to the smallest set containing all statements which can be inferred by deductive reasoning over T; for a given deductive relation $\vdash$, we call $T^\vdash = \{\phi \mid T \vdash \phi\}$ the deductive closure of T. In knowledge bases, the deductive closure is usually not identical to the asserted axioms in the knowledge base, and will contain axioms that are non-trivial; it is also usually infinite.

Representing the deductive closure is challenging since it is infinite, but in $\mathcal{EL}^{++}$ any knowledge base can be normalized to one of the seven normal forms; therefore, we can compute the deductive closure with respect to these normal forms. However, existing $\mathcal{EL}^{++}$ reasoners such as ELK [16] compute all axioms of the form $C \sqsubseteq D$ in the deductive closure but not the other normal forms. We use the inferences computed by ELK (of the form $C \sqsubseteq D$) to design an algorithm that computes the deductive closure with respect to the $\mathcal{EL}^{++}$ normal forms; the algorithm implements sound but incomplete inference rules (see Algorithm 1 for further details); specifically, it computes entailed axioms for all normal forms based on the concept hierarchy pre-computed by ELK.

4.4 Training Procedure

To address the issue of data imbalance (see [20]), i.e., the imbalance between the number of axioms of different normal forms represented in a knowledge base which may have an impact on how well certain types of axioms are represented in the embedding space, we weigh individual GCI losses based on frequency of the axiom types sampled during one epoch. All models are optimized with respect to the weighted sum of individual GCI losses (here we define the loss in most general case using all positive and all negative losses):

$$\begin{aligned}\mathcal{L} = {} & w_{C \sqsubseteq D} \cdot l_{C \sqsubseteq D} + w_{C \sqcap D \sqsubseteq E} \cdot l_{C \sqcap D \sqsubseteq E} + w_{C \sqsubseteq \exists R.D} \cdot l_{C \sqsubseteq \exists R.D} + \\ & + w_{\exists R.C \sqsubseteq D} \cdot l_{\exists R.C \sqsubseteq D} + w_{C \sqsubseteq \bot} \cdot l_{C \sqsubseteq \bot} + w_{\exists R.C \sqsubseteq \bot} \cdot l_{\exists R.C \sqsubseteq \bot} + \\ & + w_{C \not\sqsubseteq D} \cdot l_{C \not\sqsubseteq D} + w_{C \sqcap D \not\sqsubseteq E} \cdot l_{C \sqcap D \not\sqsubseteq E} + w_{C \not\sqsubseteq \exists R.D} \cdot l_{C \not\sqsubseteq \exists R.D} + \\ & + w_{\exists R.C \not\sqsubseteq D} \cdot l_{\exists R.C \not\sqsubseteq D}\end{aligned} \quad (4)$$

To study the phenomenon of biases in data affecting model training and performance, we build a 'naive' model which predicts only based on the frequency with which a class appears in an axiom. Intuitively, it is designed to resemble predictions based on node degree in knowledge graphs:

$$score_{C \sqsubseteq \exists R.D}(c, r, d) = \frac{\sum_{c'} M_r(c', d)}{\sum_{k,l} M_r(k, l)} \quad (5)$$

All model architectures are built using mOWL [33] library on top of mOWL's base models. All models were trained using the same fixed random seed. Training code for all experiments and models is available on https://github.com/bio-ontology-research-group/geometric_embeddings.

All models are trained for 400 epochs with batch size of 32,768. Training and optimization is performed using Pytorch with Adam optimizer [17] and ReduceLROnPlateau scheduler with patience parameter 10. We apply early stopping if validation loss does not improve for 20 epochs. Hyperparameters are tuned using grid search over the following set: margin $\gamma \in \{-0.1, -0.01, 0, 0.01, 0.1\}$, embedding dimension $\{50, 100, 200, 400\}$, regularization radius $R \in \{1, 2\}$, learning rate

{0.01, 0.001, 0.0001}. For *ELEmbeddings*, the strict version of regularization $\|f_\eta(c)\| = R$ was used with $R = 1$; see [20] for details on optimal hyperparameters used.

4.5 Evaluation Score and Metrics

We predict GCI2 axioms of type $\{P_1\} \sqsubseteq \exists interacts\_with.\{P_2\}$ or $\{P\} \sqsubseteq \exists has\_function.\{GO\}$ depending on the dataset. As the core evaluation score we use the scoring function introduced in *ELEmbeddings*:

$$score_{C \sqsubseteq \exists R.D}(c, r, d) = \\ = -l(-r_\eta(c) - r_\eta(d) + \|f_\eta(c) + f_\eta(r) - f_\eta(d)\| - \gamma) \quad (6)$$

The predictive performance is measured by Hits@n metrics for $n = 10, 100$, macro and micro mean rank and area under ROC curve (AUC ROC). For rank-based metrics, we calculate the score of $C \sqsubseteq \exists R.D$ for every class C from the test set and for every D from the set **C** of all classes (or subclasses of a certain type, such as proteins or functions) and determine the rank of a test axiom $C \sqsubseteq \exists R.D$. For macro mean rank and AUC ROC we consider all axioms from the test set whereas for micro metrics we compute corresponding class-specific metrics averaging them over all classes in the signature:

$$micro\_MR = Mean(MR_C(\{C \sqsubseteq \exists R.D, D \in \mathbf{C}\})) \quad (7)$$

$$micro\_AUC\_ROC = Mean(AUC\_ROC_C(\{C \sqsubseteq \exists R.D, D \in \mathbf{C}\})) \quad (8)$$

Additionally, we remove axioms represented in the train set and obtain corresponding filtered metrics (FHits@n, FMR, FAUC).

5 Results

Geometric methods such as *ELEmbeddings* address the task of knowledge base completion by constructing a single (approximate) model for a knowledge base and determining the truth of statements in this model based on geometric scoring functions. However, a single model does not suffice to compute entailments, or approximate entailments. In first order logic or more expressive Description Logics, it is possible to reduce entailment to the task of finding a single model, but since $\mathcal{EL}^{++}$ does not allow for explicit negation, this approach does not work; furthermore, reducing entailment to consistency (i.e., not having a model) relies on solving an optimization problem ("finding a model") to compute each entailment. Therefore, geometric methods only construct a single model; the assumption is that any entailed statement has to be true in this model, and some non-entailed statements will also be true. The success of this approach relies on the model being sufficiently expressive, and not constructing "trivial" models of knowledge bases.

Table 1. *ELEmbeddings* experiments: the first column corresponds to the original model, the second one – to LeakyReLU replacement and soft regularization, the third – to GCI0-GCI3 losses added, and, finally, the last one – to negatives filtering. *iw* refers to *interacts_with* dataset, *hf* – to *has_function* dataset.

		ReLU	Leaky+Reg	Losses	Neg. filter
Yeast iw	FHits@10	0.00	0.26	0.25	**0.29**
	FHits@100	0.15	0.74	0.74	**0.78**
	macro_FMR	287.06	182.93	185.81	**172.80**
	macro_FAUC	0.95	**0.97**	**0.97**	**0.97**
Yeast hf	FHits@10	0.00	**0.25**	0.23	0.24
	FHits@100	0.00	**0.55**	0.54	0.54
	macro_FMR	5183.01	3211.80	**2869.43**	2875.67
	macro_FAUC	0.90	**0.94**	**0.94**	**0.94**
Human iw	FHits@10	0.00	**0.02**	0.00	0.00
	FHits@100	0.03	0.24	0.50	**0.63**
	macro_FMR	490.09	1361.12	258.17	**196.76**
	macro_FAUC	0.97	0.93	**0.99**	**0.99**
Human hf	FHits@10	0.00	**0.14**	0.06	0.06
	FHits@100	0.00	**0.35**	0.28	0.28
	macro_FMR	7642.15	4059.81	2270.35	**2261.06**
	macro_FAUC	0.85	0.92	**0.95**	**0.95**

Table 2. Naive approach vs *ELEmbeddings* with LeakyReLU, soft regularization constraints, GCI0-GCI3 negative losses and filtered negatives. *iw* refers to *interacts_with* dataset, *hf* – to *has_function* dataset. For Human iw dataset we report here metrics for M'_{iw}, *sym* here corresponds to the symmetric Human iw dataset (for further details see Appendix (Sect. A)).

		Naive	ELEm
Yeast iw	FHits@10	0.05	**0.29**
	FHits@100	0.23	**0.78**
	macro_FMR	1174.33	**172.80**
	macro_FAUC	0.81	**0.97**
Yeast hf	FHits@10	0.21	**0.24**
	FHits@100	0.41	**0.54**
	macro_FMR	**2690.58**	2875.67
	macro_FAUC	**0.95**	0.94
Human iw (sym)	FHits@10	**0.02**	0.00
	FHits@100	0.08	**0.63**
	macro_FMR	2299.09	**196.76**
	macro_FAUC	0.88	**0.99**
Human hf	FHits@10	**0.18**	0.06
	FHits@100	**0.39**	0.28
	macro_FMR	**1967.45**	2261.06
	macro_FAUC	**0.96**	0.95

We use the *ELEmbeddings* method to perform knowledge base completion in two applications which are used widely to benchmark geometric ontology embedding methods, predicting protein–protein interactions and predicting protein functions (see Table 1; Appendix Fig. 5 shows the resulting ROC curves). To evaluate learned embeddings under different modifications we run the original *ELEmbeddings* model and use the obtained results instead of extracting metrics from the original paper [18]. This is also motivated by the utilization of different versions of GO and STRING database in our work compared to the original paper [18]. We additionally perform an ablation study to evaluate the effect of individual modifications (see [20]). We observe that *ELEmbeddings* ranks thousands of axioms at the same rank (i.e., scores them as "true"), and mainly achieves its performance (measured in AUC) by ranking rare protein functions, or proteins that interact rarely, at lower ranks. To further substantiate this hypothesis, we developed a "naive" classifier that predicts solely based on the number of times a class appears as part of an axiom during training; Table 2 shows the results and demonstrates that only based on frequency of a class, a predictive performance close to the actual performance of *ELEmbeddings* can be achieved.

We first investigate whether a relaxation of the loss functions to ensure nonzero gradients at all times can improve performance in the knowledge base completion task. The loss functions are designed to construct a model, and once an axiom from the knowledge base is true in the constructed model, their losses remain zero; however, it may be useful to provide a small gradient even once axioms are true in the constructed model. For this purpose, we change the ReLU function used in constructing losses to a LeakyReLU function. First, we study the effect of replacing ReLU function with LeakyReLU together with relaxed version of regularization (see Table 1; Appendix [20] for full results). Since LeakyReLU prevents gradients from being stuck at zero, we expect the improvement of model's performance. Likewise, not forcing the centers of n-balls representing concepts increases the expressiveness of the model. We demonstrate that, in general, incorporating LeakyReLU and relaxing regularization improves the performance of the initial model allowing learnable concepts to receive gradients at all times and, as a consequence, construct a better approximate model. Furthermore, a LeakyReLU adds the potential for optimization beyond "truth" (i.e., where statements are true in the constructed model and receive no further updates that improve the task of knowledge base completion).

While the LeakyReLU improves the predictive performance of *ELEmbeddings* in the task of knowledge base completion, it does not prevent models from collapsing, i.e., generating trivial models (see Appendix C). The original *ELEmbeddings* model and other geometric models only use negative losses (i.e., losses for the case that an axiom does not hold) for a single normal form (GCI2, $C \sqsubseteq \exists R.D$, which is also used for prediction). We evaluate whether adding negative losses for other normal forms will prevent the model from collapsing and improve the performance in the task of knowledge base completion. We formulate and add GCI0-GCI3 negative losses given by Eqs. 1–3, either separately or with LeakyReLU and soft regularization from the previous experiment. We find that just adding the additional losses improves the performance and seems to prevent models from collapsing (Appendix Fig. 7). In terms of mean rank and AUC ROC, the model with the negative losses generally exhibits improved performance relative to using only negative losses for GCI2.

Similarly to how negative sampling works in knowledge graph completion, geometric ontology embedding methods select negatives by corrupting an axiom by replacing one of the classes with a randomly chosen one; in the case of knowledge base completion where the deductive closure contains potentially many non-trivial entailed axioms, this approach may lead to suboptimal learning since some of axioms treated as negatives are entailed (and will therefore be true in any model, in particular the one constructed by the geometric embedding method). We suggest to filter selected negatives based on the deductive closure of the knowledge base: for each randomly generated axiom to be used as negative, we check whether it is present in the deductive closure and if it is, we delete it. To compute the deductive closure, we use an approximate algorithm (see Appendix D). Table 1 shows results in the tasks we evaluate. We find that excluding axioms in the deductive closure for negative selection improves the results in the task of predicting PPIs, and yields similar results in function prediction tasks. One possible reason is that a randomly chosen axiom is very unlikely to be entailed since very few axioms are entailed compared to all possible axioms to choose from.

Because the chance of selecting an entailed axiom as a negative depends on the knowledge base on which the embedding method is applied, we perform additional experiments where we bias the selection of negatives; we chose between 100% negatives to 0% negatives from the entailed axioms. We find that reducing the number of entailed axioms from the negatives has an effect to improve performance and the effect increases the more axioms would be chosen from the entailed ones (Appendix Fig. 9).

The deductive closure can also be used to modify the evaluation metrics. So far, ontology embedding methods that have been applied to the task of knowledge base completion have used evaluation measures that are taken from the task of knowledge graph completion; in particular, they only evaluate knowledge base completion using axioms that are "novel" and not entailed. However, any entailed axiom will be true in all models of the knowledge base, and therefore also in the geometric model that is constructed by the embedding method. These entailed axioms should therefore be considered in the evaluation. We show the difference in performance, and the corresponding ROC curves, in Appendix Fig. 6. We find that methods that explicitly construct models generally predict entailed axioms first, even when the models make some trivial predictions (such as in the original *ELEmbeddings* model); model-generating embedding first predict the entailed axioms, and then predict "novel" axioms that are not entailed. However, when replacing the ReLU with the LeakyReLU in *ELEmbeddings*, "novel", non-entailed axioms are predicted first, before entailed axioms are predicted (see Appendix Fig. 8). We evaluate a more recent ontology embedding method Box^2EL [13] and find that this model predicts primarily "novel" axioms but does not predict entailed axioms (see Appendix Fig. 10).

6 Discussion

We evaluated properties of *ELEmbeddings*, an ontology embedding method that aims to generate a model of an $\mathcal{EL}^{++}$ theory; the properties we evaluate hold similarly for other ontology embedding methods that construct models of $\mathcal{EL}^{++}$ theories. While we demonstrate several improvements over the original model, we can also draw some general conclusions about ontology embedding methods and their evaluation. Knowledge base completion is the task of predicting axioms that should be added to a knowledge base; this task is adapted from knowledge graph completion where triples are added to a knowledge graph. The way both tasks are evaluated is by removing some statements (axioms or triples) from the knowledge base, and evaluating whether these axioms or triples can be recovered by the embedding method. This evaluation approach is adequate for knowledge graphs which do not give rise to many entailments. However, knowledge bases give rise to potentially many non-trivial entailments that need to be considered in the evaluation. In particular embedding methods that aim to generate a model of a knowledge base will first generate entailed axioms (because entailed axioms are true in all models); these methods perform knowledge base completion as a generalization of generating the model where either other statements may be true, or they may be approximately true in the generated structure. This has two consequences: the evaluation procedure needs to account for this; and the model needs to be sufficiently rich to allow useful predictions.

We have introduced a method to compute the deductive closure of $\mathcal{EL}^{++}$ knowledge bases; this method relies on an automated reasoner and is sound but not complete. We use all the axioms in the deductive closure as positive axioms to be predicted when evaluating knowledge base completion, to account for methods that treat knowledge base completion as a generalization of constructing a model and testing for truth in this model. We find that some models (e.g., the original ELEmbedding model) can predict entailed axioms well, some (a modified model using a LeakyReLU function as part of the loss instead of the ReLU) preferentially predict "novel", non-entailed axioms, and others (e.g., the *Box2EL* model) are tailored to predict primarily "novel" knowledge and do not predict entailed axioms; these methods solve subtly different problems (either generalizing construction of a model, or specifically predicting novel non-entailed axioms). We also modify the evaluation procedure to account for the inclusion of entailed axioms as positives; however, the evaluation measures are still based on ranking individual axioms and do not account for semantic similarity. For example, if during testing, the correct axiom to predict is $C \sqsubseteq \exists R.D$ but the predicted axiom is $C \sqsubseteq \exists R.E$, the prediction may be considered to be "more correct" if $D \sqsubseteq E$ was in the knowledge base than if $D \sqcap E \sqsubseteq \bot$ was in the knowledge base. Novel evaluation metrics need to be designed to account for this phenomenon, similarly to ontology-based evaluation measures used in life sciences [27]. It is also important to expand the set of benchmark sets for knowledge base completion.

Use of the deductive closure is not only useful in evaluation but also when selecting negatives. In formal knowledge bases, there are at least two ways in which negatives for axioms can be chosen: they are either non-entailed axioms, or they are axioms whose negation is entailed. However, in no case should entailed axioms be considered as negatives; we demonstrate that filtering entailed axioms from selected negatives during training improves the performance of the embedding method consistently in knowledge base completion (and, obviously, more so when entailed axioms are considered as positives during evaluation).

While we only report our experiments with *ELEmbeddings*, our findings, in particular about the evaluation and use of deductive closure, are applicable to other geometric ontology embedding methods. As ontology embedding methods are increasingly applied in knowledge-enhanced learning and other tasks that utilize some form of approximate computation of entailments, our results can also serve to improve the applications of ontology embeddings.

Appendix

A Naive Model Construction

Similarly to [12] we construct $n \times n$ PPI and $n \times m$ function prediction matrices M_{iw} and M_{hf} respectively: $M_{iw}(P_1, P_2) = 1$ if $\{P_1\} \sqsubseteq \exists interacts\_with.\{P_2\}$ is in the train set for PPI and 0 otherwise, and $M_{hf}(P, GO) = 1$ if $\{P\} \sqsubseteq \exists has\_function.\{GO\}$ is in the train set for function prediction (0 otherwise). Assuming that *interacts_with* relation is symmetric we additionally design matrix M'_{iw} for human data where $M'_{iw}(P_1, P_2) = M'_{iw}(P_2, P_1) = 1$ when $\{P_1\} \sqsubseteq \exists interacts\_with.\{P_2\}$ or $\{P_2\} \sqsubseteq \exists interacts\_with.\{P_1\}$ can be found in the train part of the dataset. Scoring function used for rank-based predictions is described in Sect. 4.4.

B Detailed Results of Comparison with the "Naive" Classifier

Naive approach vs *ELEmbeddings* with LeakyReLU, soft regularization constraints, GCI0-GCI3 negative losses and filtered negatives. *iw* refers to *interacts_with* dataset, *hf* – to *has_function* dataset. For Human iw dataset we report here metrics both for M'_{iw} and M_{iw}, *sym* here corresponds to the symmetric Human iw dataset (for further details see Appendix (Sect. A).

		Naive	ELEm
Yeast iw	Hits@10	0.01	**0.09**
	FHits@10	0.05	**0.29**
	Hits@100	0.12	**0.55**
	FHits@100	0.23	**0.78**
	macro_MR	1228.68	**231.70**
	micro_MR	1845.96	**296.12**
	macro_FMR	1174.33	**172.80**
	micro_FMR	1819.47	**266.51**
	macro_AUC	0.80	**0.96**
	micro_AUC	0.72	**0.96**
	macro_FAUC	0.81	**0.97**
	micro_FAUC	0.72	**0.96**

		Naive	ELEm
Yeast hf	Hits@10	0.20	**0.21**
	FHits@10	0.21	**0.24**
	Hits@100	0.40	**0.53**
	FHits@100	0.41	**0.54**
	macro_MR	**2694.33**	2879.59
	micro_MR	**2658.51**	2858.37
	macro_FMR	**2690.58**	2875.67
	micro_FMR	**2654.98**	2854.69
	macro_AUC	**0.97**	0.94
	micro_AUC	0.95	0.95
	macro_FAUC	**0.95**	0.94
	micro_FAUC	0.95	0.95

		Naive	ELEm
Human iw (sym)	Hits@10	**0.01**	0.00
	FHits@10	**0.02**	0.00
	Hits@100	0.07	**0.32**
	FHits@100	0.08	**0.63**
	macro_MR	2377.39	**277.22**
	micro_MR	3313.50	**283.61**
	macro_FMR	2299.09	**196.76**
	micro_FMR	3276.97	**245.83**
	macro_AUC	0.88	**0.99**
	micro_AUC	0.84	**0.99**
	macro_FAUC	0.88	**0.99**
	micro_FAUC	0.85	**0.99**

Note that by definition filtered metrics should be less than or equal to corresponding non-filtered metrics, yet here filtered naive AUC ROC is less than non-filtered one. The reason is trapezoidal rule for numerical integration used

		Naive	ELEm
Human iw (non-sym)	Hits@10	**0.01**	0.00
	FHits@10	**0.02**	0.00
	Hits@100	0.07	**0.32**
	FHits@100	0.08	**0.63**
	macro_MR	2433.80	**277.22**
	micro_MR	3412.09	**283.61**
	macro_FMR	2353.87	**196.76**
	micro_FMR	3374.88	**245.83**
	macro_AUC	0.88	**0.99**
	micro_AUC	0.84	**0.99**
	macro_FAUC	0.88	**0.99**
	micro_FAUC	0.84	**0.99**

		Naive	ELEm
Human hf	Hits@10	**0.16**	0.06
	FHits@10	**0.18**	0.06
	Hits@100	**0.39**	0.28
	FHits@100	**0.39**	0.28
	macro_MR	**1978.53**	2272.33
	micro_MR	**1785.81**	1963.87
	macro_FMR	**1967.45**	2261.06
	micro_FMR	**1777.73**	1955.62
	macro_AUC	0.97	**0.95**
	micro_AUC	0.97	**0.97**
	macro_FAUC	**0.96**	0.95
	micro_FAUC	0.97	**0.97**

to calculate AUC ROC based on FPR and TPR points: due to the facts that the number of different rank values is relatively small compared to the number of GO classes and that the score relies exclusively on the number of proteins having the function, it provides the grid not accurate enough, and the same non-filtered rank converts into multiple lower ranks while filtered forming more well-suited computational grid (Figs. 1, 2, 3, 4).

C ROC Curves for LeakyReLU Function

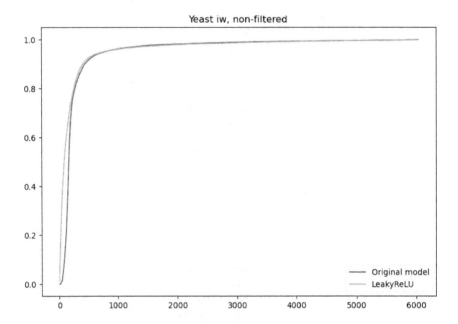

Fig. 1. ROC curves, Yeast iw dataset

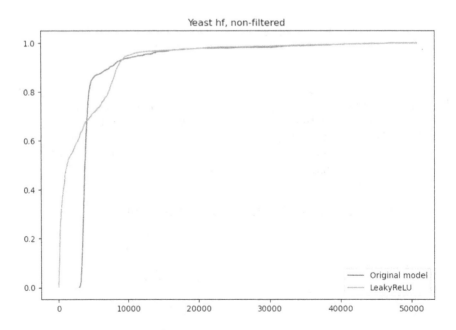

Fig. 2. ROC curves, Yeast hf dataset

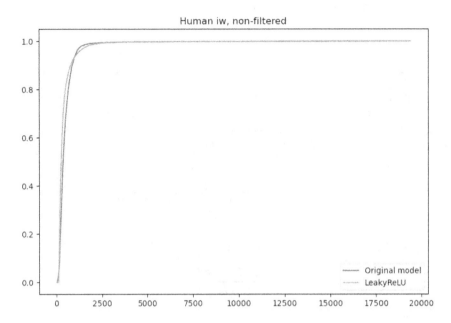

Fig. 3. ROC curves, Human iw dataset

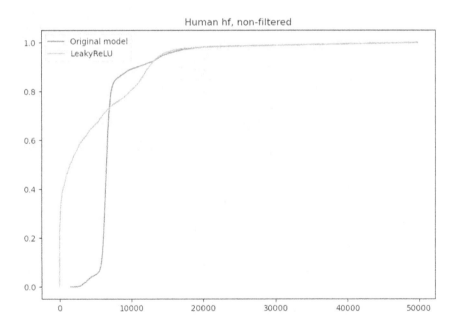

Fig. 4. ROC curves, Human hf dataset

D Approximate Deductive Closure

Algorithm 1

An algorithm for approximate computation of the deductive closure using inference rules; axioms in bold correspond to subclass/superclass axioms derived using ELK reasoner (here we use the transitive closure of the ELK inferences); plain axioms come from the knowledge base.

---

for all $C \sqsubseteq D$ in the knowledge base **do**

$$\frac{C \sqsubseteq D \quad \boldsymbol{D \sqsubseteq D'}}{C \sqsubseteq D'} \qquad \frac{C \sqsubseteq D \quad \boldsymbol{C' \sqsubseteq C}}{C' \sqsubseteq D}$$

end for

for all $C \sqcap D \sqsubseteq E$ in the knowledge base **do**

$$\frac{C \sqcap D \sqsubseteq E \quad \boldsymbol{C' \sqsubseteq C}}{C' \sqcap D \sqsubseteq E}$$

end for

for all $C \sqsubseteq \exists R.D$ in the knowledge base **do**

$$\frac{C \sqsubseteq \exists R.D \quad \boldsymbol{D \sqsubseteq D'}}{C \sqsubseteq \exists R.D'} \qquad \frac{C \sqsubseteq \exists R.D \quad \boldsymbol{C' \sqsubseteq C}}{C' \sqsubseteq \exists R.D}$$

end for

for all $\exists R.C \sqsubseteq D$ in the knowledge base **do**

$$\frac{\exists R.C \sqsubseteq D \quad \boldsymbol{D \sqsubseteq D'}}{\exists R.C \sqsubseteq D'} \qquad \frac{\exists R.C \sqsubseteq D \quad \boldsymbol{C' \sqsubseteq C}}{\exists R.C' \sqsubseteq D}$$

end for

for all $C \sqsubseteq \bot$ in the knowledge base **do**

$$\frac{C \sqsubseteq \bot \quad \boldsymbol{C' \sqsubseteq C}}{C' \sqsubseteq \bot}$$

end for

for all $\exists R.C \sqsubseteq \bot$ in the knowledge base **do**

$$\frac{\exists R.C \sqsubseteq \bot \quad \boldsymbol{C' \sqsubseteq C}}{\exists R.C' \sqsubseteq \bot}$$

end for

E Additional Figures

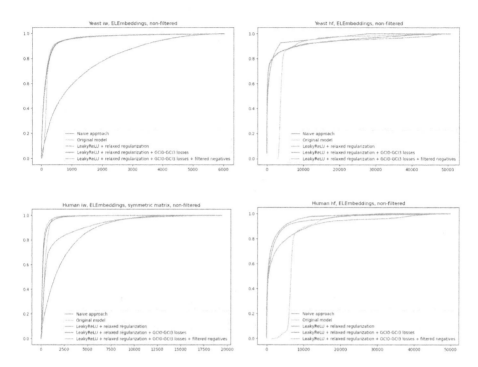

Fig. 5. ROC curves across different models

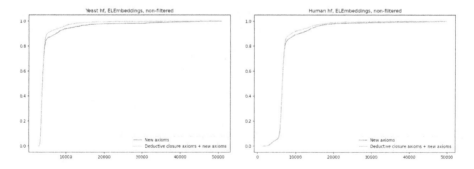

Fig. 6. *ELEmbeddings*, ReLU, ROC curves for entailed axioms and novel axioms

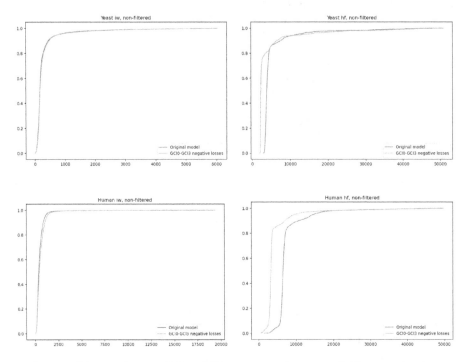

Fig. 7. *ELEmbeddings*, GCI0-GCI3 negative losses vs GCI2 negative loss

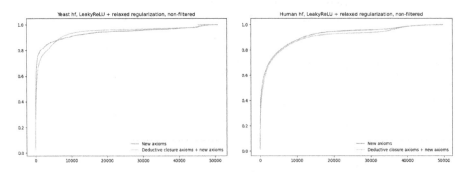

Fig. 8. *ELEmbeddings*, LeakyReLU, ROC curves for entailed axioms and novel axioms

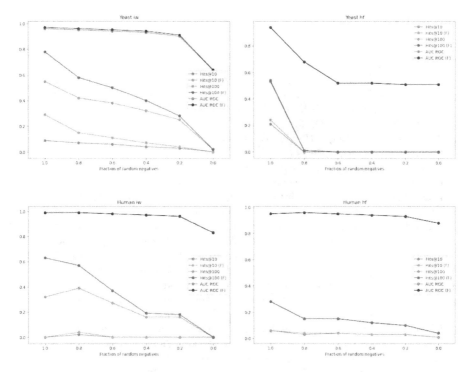

Fig. 9. Random negatives sampling

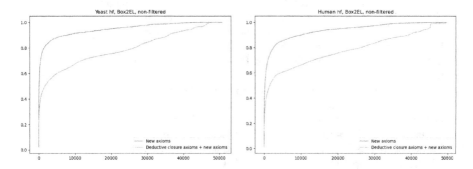

Fig. 10. Box^2EL, ROC curves for entailed axioms and novel axioms

References

1. Gene ontology consortium: going forward. Nucleic Acids Res. **43**(D1), D1049–D1056 (2014). https://doi.org/10.1093/nar/gku1179
2. Baader, F., Brandt, S., Lutz, C.: Pushing the $\mathcal{EL}$ envelope. In: Proceedings of the Nineteenth International Joint Conference on Artificial Intelligence IJCAI-05. Morgan-Kaufmann Publishers, Edinburgh, UK (2005)
3. Baader, F., Calvanese, D., McGuinness, D., Nardi, D., Patel-Schneider, P.F. (eds.): The Description Logic Handbook: Theory, Implementation, and Applications. Cambridge University Press (2003)
4. Bouraoui, Z., Jameel, S., Schockaert, S.: Inductive reasoning about ontologies using conceptual spaces. In: Proceedings of the AAAI Conference on Artificial Intelligence, vol. 31, no. 1 (2017). https://doi.org/10.1609/aaai.v31i1.11162
5. Cao, P., et al.: Event ontology completion with hierarchical structure evolution networks. In: Bouamor, H., Pino, J., Bali, K. (eds.) Proceedings of the 2023 Conference on Empirical Methods in Natural Language Processing, pp. 306–320. Association for Computational Linguistics, Singapore (2023). https://doi.org/10.18653/v1/2023.emnlp-main.21, https://aclanthology.org/2023.emnlp-main.21
6. Chen, J., Hu, P., Jimenez-Ruiz, E., Holter, O.M., Antonyrajah, D., Horrocks, I.: OWL2Vec*: embedding of OWL ontologies. Mach. Learn. (2021). https://doi.org/10.1007/s10994-021-05997-6
7. Chen, J., Althagafi, A., Hoehndorf, R.: Predicting candidate genes from phenotypes, functions and anatomical site of expression. Bioinformatics **37**(6), 853–860 (2020). https://doi.org/10.1093/bioinformatics/btaa879
8. Chen, Z., Wang, Y., Zhao, B., Cheng, J., Zhao, X., Duan, Z.: Knowledge graph completion: a review. Ieee Access **8**, 192435–192456 (2020)
9. Devlin, J., Chang, M., Lee, K., Toutanova, K.: BERT: pre-training of deep bidirectional transformers for language understanding. In: Burstein, J., Doran, C., Solorio, T. (eds.) Proceedings of the 2019 Conference of the North American Chapter of the Association for Computational Linguistics: Human Language Technologies, NAACL-HLT 2019, Minneapolis, MN, USA, 2-7 June 2019, Volume 1 (Long and Short Papers), pp. 4171–4186. Association for Computational Linguistics (2019). https://doi.org/10.18653/V1/N19-1423, https://doi.org/10.18653/v1/n19-1423
10. d'Amato, C., Fanizzi, N., Fazzinga, B., Gottlob, G., Lukasiewicz, T.: Ontology-based semantic search on the web and its combination with the power of inductive reasoning. Ann. Math. Artif. Intell. **65**(2–3), 83–121 (2012). https://doi.org/10.1007/s10472-012-9309-7
11. Golbreich, C., Horrocks, I.: The OBO to OWL mapping, GO to OWL 1.1! In: Golbreich, C., Kalyanpur, A., Parsia, B. (eds.) Proceedings of the OWLED 2007 Workshop on OWL: Experiences and Directions, Innsbruck, Austria, 6-7 June 2007. CEUR Workshop Proceedings, vol. 258. CEUR-WS.org (2007). https://ceur-ws.org/Vol-258/paper35.pdf
12. Hinnerichs, T., Hoehndorf, R.: DTI-Voodoo: machine learning over interaction networks and ontology-based background knowledge predicts drug-target interactions. Bioinformatics **37**(24), 4835–4843 (2021). https://doi.org/10.1093/bioinformatics/btab548
13. Jackermeier, M., Chen, J., Horrocks, I.: Dual box embeddings for the description logic EL++. In: Proceedings of the ACM Web Conference 2024. WWW 2024 (2024). https://doi.org/10.1145/3589334.3645648
14. Ji, Q., et al.: Ontology revision based on pre-trained language models (2023)

15. Jiang, X., Huang, Y., Nickel, M., Tresp, V.: Combining information extraction, deductive reasoning and machine learning for relation prediction. In: Simperl, E., Cimiano, P., Polleres, A., Corcho, O., Presutti, V. (eds.) ESWC 2012. LNCS, vol. 7295, pp. 164–178. Springer, Heidelberg (2012). https://doi.org/10.1007/978-3-642-30284-8_18
16. Kazakov, Y., Krötzsch, M., Simančík, F.: The Incredible ELK. J. Autom. Reasoning **53**(1), 1–61 (2013). https://doi.org/10.1007/s10817-013-9296-3
17. Kingma, D.P., Ba, J.: Adam: a method for stochastic optimization. In: Bengio, Y., LeCun, Y. (eds.) 3rd International Conference on Learning Representations, ICLR 2015, San Diego, CA, USA, 7-9 May 2015, Conference Track Proceedings (2015)
18. Kulmanov, M., Liu-Wei, W., Yan, Y., Hoehndorf, R.: El embeddings: geometric construction of models for the description logic EL ++. In: International Joint Conference on Artificial Intelligence (2019)
19. Li, N., Bailleux, T., Bouraoui, Z., Schockaert, S.: Ontology completion with natural language inference and concept embeddings: an analysis (2024)
20. Mashkova, O., Zhapa-Camacho, F., Hoehndorf, R.: Enhancing geometric ontology embeddings for $\mathcal{EL}^{++}$ with negative sampling and deductive closure filtering. arXiv preprint arXiv:2405.04868 (2024)
21. Mendez, J.: jcel: a modular rule-based reasoner. In: Horrocks, I., Yatskevich, M., Jiménez-Ruiz, E. (eds.) Proceedings of the 1st International Workshop on OWL Reasoner Evaluation (ORE-2012), Manchester, UK, July 1st, 2012. CEUR Workshop Proceedings, vol. 858. CEUR-WS.org (2012). https://ceur-ws.org/Vol-858/ore2012_paper12.pdf
22. Mering, C.v.: STRING: a database of predicted functional associations between proteins. Nucleic Acids Res. **31**(1), 258–261 (2003). https://doi.org/10.1093/nar/gkg034
23. Mežnar, S., Bevec, M., Lavrač, N., Škrlj, B.: Ontology completion with graph-based machine learning: a comprehensive evaluation. Mach. Learn. Knowl. Extr. **4**(4), 1107–1123 (2022). https://doi.org/10.3390/make4040056
24. Mondal, S., Bhatia, S., Mutharaju, R.: EmEL++: embeddings for EL++ description logic. In: Martin, A., et al. (eds.) Proceedings of the AAAI 2021 Spring Symposium on Combining Machine Learning and Knowledge Engineering (AAAI-MAKE 2021), Stanford University, Palo Alto, California, USA, 22-24 March, 2021. CEUR Workshop Proceedings, vol. 2846. CEUR-WS.org (2021)
25. Özcep, O.L., Leemhuis, M., Wolter, D.: Embedding ontologies in the description logic ALC by axis-aligned cones. J. Artif. Intell. Res. **78**, 217–267 (2023). https://doi.org/10.1613/jair.1.13939
26. Peng, X., Tang, Z., Kulmanov, M., Niu, K., Hoehndorf, R.: Description logic EL++ embeddings with intersectional closure (2022)
27. Radivojac, P., Clark, W.T.: Information-theoretic evaluation of predicted ontological annotations. Bioinformatics **29**(13), i53–i61 (2013). https://doi.org/10.1093/bioinformatics/btt228
28. Sato, Y., Stapleton, G., Jamnik, M., Shams, Z.: Deductive reasoning about expressive statements using external graphical representations. In: Proceedings of the 40th Annual Conference of the Cognitive Science Society, pp. 0–0. Cognitive Science Society (2018). cogSci 2018 ; Conference date: 25-07-2018 Through 28-07-2018
29. Shiraishi, Y., Kaneiwa, K.: A self-matching training method with annotation embedding models for ontology subsumption prediction (2024)
30. Wang, Q., Mao, Z., Wang, B., Guo, L.: Knowledge graph embedding: a survey of approaches and applications. IEEE Trans. Knowl. Data Eng. **29**(12), 2724–2743 (2017)

31. Xiong, B., Potyka, N., Tran, T.K., Nayyeri, M., Staab, S.: Faithful embeddings for EL++ knowledge bases. In: Proceedings of the 21st International Semantic Web Conference (ISWC2022), pp. 1–18 (2022)
32. Zhapa-Camacho, F., Hoehndorf, R.: From axioms over graphs to vectors, and back again: evaluating the properties of graph-based ontology embeddings (2023)
33. Zhapa-Camacho, F., Kulmanov, M., Hoehndorf, R.: mOWL: Python library for machine learning with biomedical ontologies. Bioinformatics (2022). https://doi.org/10.1093/bioinformatics/btac811

Lattice-Preserving $\mathcal{ALC}$ Ontology Embeddings

Fernando Zhapa-Camacho[1,2] and Robert Hoehndorf[1,2,3]

[1] Computational Bioscience Research Center (CBRC), King Abdullah University of Science and Technology, Thuwal, Saudi Arabia
[2] Computer, Electrical and Mathematical Sciences and Engineering Division (CEMSE), King Abdullah University of Science and Technology, 4700 King Abdullah University of Science and Technology (KAUST), 23955–6900 Thuwal, Saudi Arabia
{fernando.zhapacamacho,robert.hoehndorf}@kaust.edu.sa
[3] SDAIA-KAUST Center of Excellence in Data Science and Artificial Intelligence, King Abdullah University of Science and Technology, 4700 King Abdullah University of Science and Technology, Thuwal, Saudi Arabia

Abstract. Generating vector representations (embeddings) of OWL ontologies is a growing task due to its applications in predicting missing facts and knowledge-enhanced learning in fields such as bioinformatics. The underlying semantics of OWL ontologies is expressed using Description Logics (DLs). Initial approaches to generate embeddings relied on constructing a graph out of ontologies, neglecting the semantics of the logic therein. Recent semantic-preserving embedding methods often target lightweight DL languages like $\mathcal{EL}^{++}$, ignoring more expressive information in ontologies. Although some approaches aim to embed more descriptive DLs like $\mathcal{ALC}$, those methods require the existence of individuals, while many real-world ontologies are devoid of them. We propose an ontology embedding method for the $\mathcal{ALC}$ DL language that considers the lattice structure of concept descriptions. We use connections between DL and Category Theory to materialize the lattice structure and embed it using an order-preserving embedding method. We show that our method outperforms state-of-the-art methods in several knowledge base completion tasks. We make our code and data available at https://github.com/bio-ontology-research-group/catE.

Keywords: Ontology embedding · Knowledge Base Completion · Neuro-symbolic AI

1 Introduction

Ontologies are usually developed and maintained by manual curation of experts and therefore the knowledge therein can be inconsistent or incomplete. Traditionally, symbolic reasoners are used to test for consistency of the knowledge within ontologies and to infer new statements. However, they are designed to infer statements that are logically entailed from the ontology or knowledge base;

in some cases, it is useful to also suggest axioms that are probably true but not entailed, leading to the task of "ontology completion" or "knowledge base completion".

From the viewpoint of knowledge graph completion [10], we can initially define knowledge base completion as the task of predicting "missing" or "novel" axioms in a knowledge base (or ontology). "Novel" may be understood temporally as axioms that are added at a later time to a knowledge base, or, more commonly, with respect to existing axioms in the knowledge base. However, unlike knowledge graphs, a knowledge base (ontology) has an infinitely large deductive closure with deductively entailed statements. Those statements can be considered "novel" because they do not exist in the knowledge base but can effectively be generated by a deductive reasoner. Therefore, knowledge base completion can have a two-fold presentation: (1) knowledge base completion as approximate entailment, where the completion system first generates the deductively entailed statements, and then, with potentially lower confidence, the system generates the non-entailed but probable statements, and (2) the completion system generates only non-entailed statements and, optionally, has access to information to the deductive closure.

Transversally, knowledge base completion methods can be evaluated based on the type of axioms to complete. We distinguish between two sub-tasks: "TBox completion", when the axioms to generate are terminological and are of the form $C \sqsubseteq D$, and "ABox completion", when the axioms to generate are assertional and are of the form $C(a)$ or $r(a,b)$. TBox completion systems have been proposed as supporting tools to assist or automate ontology curation procedures [6,8] or to match concepts between ontologies [8]. ABox completion systems are evaluated alongside neuro-symbolic reasoners in challenges like SemREC [6]. Furthermore, ABox completion can be regarded as knowledge graph completion enhanced with ontological knowledge [14].

Several neuro-symbolic approaches have been developed to perform the knowledge base completion tasks [8,9,15,18], and most are based on generating embeddings that preserve some logical properties of a knowledge base. Methods which perform knowledge base completion follow different strategies. One type of methods corresponds to transforming ontology axioms into graphs. Under this approach, axioms in a DL knowledge base are transformed into a graph and then knowledge graph completion methods are applied [9]. Although this strategy has proved to be useful, this set of methods does not capture *all* information in axioms and the embedding process is usually not invertible [29]; therefore, these methods do not allow exact inference of axioms and are often used for similarity-based tasks.

Another type of methods for embedding DL knowledge bases constructs an approximate model of the knowledge base. ELEmbeddings [18] represent concepts as $n-$dimensional balls and roles are represented as geometric translations of concepts. By modifying the geometric structure from balls to boxes, methods such as BoxEL [28] guarantee intersectional closure of concepts (i.e., the intersection of two boxes is a box). However, representing roles as translations can only encode one-to-one relations. Therefore, Box^{2}EL [15] represents roles as two boxes, representing the domain and the codomain of the role, respectively. This representation enables encoding many-to-many relations. However, all these methods target the $\mathcal{EL}^{++}$ language, which is a lightweight language that does not support the construction of axioms involving full negation or universal restrictions, therefore they cannot leverage more expressive statements in DL knowledge bases. In this regard, methods such as FALCON [24], which is a method similar to Logic Tensor Networks [5], can construct an approximate model for $\mathcal{ALC}$ knowledge based. FALCON represents concepts as fuzzy sets and treats logical connectives as fuzzy operators [25]. However, FALCON requires the existence of individuals to populate the fuzzy sets, which is a limiting factor in cases involving knowledge bases without individuals such as GO. Other approaches for modeling the $\mathcal{ALC}$ language is found in [21] with a theoretical analysis on the use of axis-aligned cones to represent ontology concepts.

To overcome limitations of current ontology embedding approaches, we propose CatE, a lattice-preserving embedding method for the $\mathcal{ALC}$ language. Our approach relies on the fact that the concept descriptions in a DL knowledge base can be arranged in a lattice structure. The lattice construction of DL concepts can be formulated in the context of Formal Concept Analysis [4], using connections between DL and Modal Logic [3,22,27] or using connections between DL and Category Theory [7,13]. We use the category-theoretical formulation and construct a lattice out of all concept descriptions that are sub-concepts of any concept description in the knowledge base.

After materializing the lattice we represent its elements as vectors in an ordered-vector space. To enforce the ordered structure of the vector space, we use an *order-embedding method*. We apply CatE and show that it can outperform state-of-the-art methods in the different forms of the knowledge base completion task. Our contributions are the following:

- We propose an embedding method for $\mathcal{ALC}$ knowledge bases that preserves the lattice structure of the semantics of concept descriptions.
- We show that our method can perform competitively on generating statements in the deductive closure and generating probable statements.
- We show that our method can perform competitively in both TBox and ABox completion tasks.

2 Preliminaries

2.1 Description Logics

A Description Logic signature $\Sigma = (\mathbf{C}, \mathbf{R}, \mathbf{I})$ consists of a set of concept names $\mathbf{C}$, a set of role names $\mathbf{R}$, and a set of individual names $\mathbf{I}$. In the Description Logic $\mathcal{ALC}$, all concept names are concept descriptions; if A and B are concept descriptions, r a role name, and a, b are individual names, then $A \sqcap B$, $A \sqcup B$, $\neg A$, $\exists r.A$, and $\forall r.A$ are concept descriptions; $A \sqsubseteq B$, $A(a)$ and $r(a, b)$ are axioms. A set of axioms is an $\mathcal{ALC}$ theory [2].

An interpretation $\mathcal{I}$ of an $\mathcal{ALC}$ theory consists of an interpretation domain $\Delta^{\mathcal{I}}$ and an interpretation function $\cdot^{\mathcal{I}}$ such that for every concept name $C \in \mathbf{C}$, $C^{\mathcal{I}} \subseteq \Delta^{\mathcal{I}}$; for every individual name $a \in \mathbf{I}$, $a^{\mathcal{I}} \in \Delta^{\mathcal{I}}$; and every role name $r \in \mathbf{R}$, $r^{\mathcal{I}} \in \Delta^{\mathcal{I}} \times \Delta^{\mathcal{I}}$; and, inductively:

$$\bot^{\mathcal{I}} = \emptyset$$
$$\top^{\mathcal{I}} = \Delta^{\mathcal{I}}$$
$$(\neg A)^{\mathcal{I}} = \Delta^{\mathcal{I}} \backslash A^{\mathcal{I}},$$
$$(C \sqcap D)^{\mathcal{I}} = C^{\mathcal{I}} \cap D^{\mathcal{I}}$$
$$(C \sqcup D)^{\mathcal{I}} = C^{\mathcal{I}} \cup D^{\mathcal{I}},$$
$$(\exists r.C)^{\mathcal{I}} = \{a \in \Delta^{\mathcal{I}} \mid \exists b.((a,b) \in r^{\mathcal{I}} \wedge b \in C^{\mathcal{I}})\}$$
$$(\forall r.C)^{\mathcal{I}} = \{a \in \Delta^{\mathcal{I}} \mid \forall b.((a,b) \in r^{\mathcal{I}} \rightarrow b \in C^{\mathcal{I}})\}$$

An interpretation $\mathcal{I}$ is a model for an axiom $C \sqsubseteq D$ iff $C^{\mathcal{I}} \subseteq D^{\mathcal{I}}$, for an axiom $B(a)$ iff $a^{\mathcal{I}} \in B^{\mathcal{I}}$, and for an axiom $r(a,b)$ if and only if $(a^{\mathcal{I}}, b^{\mathcal{I}}) \in r^{\mathcal{I}}$ [2]. Given an $\mathcal{ALC}$ theory $\mathcal{T}$, an axiom is entailed from $\mathcal{T}$ if it is true in all models of $\mathcal{T}$.

3 Construction of the Lattice Structure

A *preorder* $(P, \leq)$ contains a set P equipped with a reflexive and transitive binary relation $\leq$. A partial order is a preorder that is also antisymmetric. A lattice is a partially ordered set where each two-element subset has a least upper bound and greatest lower bound. If a lattice has a greatest element, it is denoted $\top$, and if it has a least element it is denoted $\bot$ [11].

In a $\mathcal{ALC}$ theory $\mathcal{T}$, the set $\mathbf{C}$ of concept names can be used to create arbitrarily complex and infinitely many concept descriptions. We consider only the concept descriptions in the knowledge base with their sub-expressions and call this set $\tilde{\mathbf{C}}$. We furthermore denote $\tilde{\mathbf{C}}^{\mathcal{I}} = \{C^{\mathcal{I}} \mid C \in \tilde{\mathbf{C}}\}$.

The pair $(\tilde{\mathbf{C}}^{\mathcal{I}}, \subseteq)$ can form a lattice where concept descriptions $C^{\mathcal{I}}, D^{\mathcal{I}} \in \tilde{\mathbf{C}}^{\mathcal{I}}$ stand in a relationship if $C^{\mathcal{I}} \subseteq D^{\mathcal{I}}$. Within models of $\mathcal{ALC}$ theories, the relation $\subseteq$ is reflexive and transitive. For a pair of concepts descriptions $A^{\mathcal{I}}, B^{\mathcal{I}} \in \tilde{\mathbf{C}}^{\mathcal{I}}$, the least upper bound is denoted as $(A \cup B)^{\mathcal{I}}$ and the greatest lower bound is denoted using $(A \cap B)^{\mathcal{I}}$. Additionally, for any concept description X it holds $\bot^{\mathcal{I}} \subseteq X^{\mathcal{I}} \subseteq \top^{\mathcal{I}}$.

To represent the lattice $(\tilde{\mathbf{C}}^{\mathcal{I}}, \subseteq)$, we use the syntactic representation of the axioms (where the operator is $\sqsubseteq$ and not $\subseteq$) and denote it as $(\tilde{\mathbf{C}}, \sqsubseteq)$ (Fig. 1). The representation based on $\sqsubseteq$ does not hold all the properties of lattices; however, it is used as an intermediate structure between the lattice $(\tilde{\mathbf{C}}^{\mathcal{I}}, \subseteq)$ and the embedding space which will be introduced later (Sect. 3.1).

The concepts in $\tilde{\mathbf{C}}$ are materialized following a recursive process and, depending on the type of concept descriptions, $\tilde{\mathbf{C}}$ can be extended with new elements. We rely on connections between DL and Category Theory described in [13].

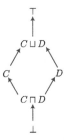

Fig. 1. Lattice representation. $\bot$ is the bottom element and $\top$ is to top element. Arrows represent the $\sqsubseteq$ operator.

Intersection of Concepts: Given a concept description $A \sqcap B$ in the theory, we add the following relationships to $(\tilde{\mathbf{C}}, \sqsubseteq)$: $A \sqcap B \sqsubseteq A$ and $A \sqcap B \sqsubseteq B$. Additionally, for any X, if relationships $X \sqsubseteq A \sqcap B$ are found in $(\tilde{\mathbf{C}}, \sqsubseteq)$, we add the relationships $X \sqsubseteq A$ and $X \sqsubseteq B$ (Fig. 2a). Concepts A, B are processed recursively.

Union of Concepts: Given a concept description $A \sqcup B$ in the theory, we add the following relationships to $(\tilde{\mathbf{C}}, \sqsubseteq)$: $A \sqsubseteq A \sqcup B$ and $B \sqsubseteq A \sqcup B$. Additionally, for any X, if relationships $A \sqcup B \sqsubseteq X$ are found in $(\tilde{\mathbf{C}}, \sqsubseteq)$, we add the relationships $A \sqsubseteq X$ ad $B \sqsubseteq X$ (Fig. 2c). Concepts A, B are processed recursively.

Negation of Concepts: Given a concept $\neg C$, elements $C \sqcap \neg C$ and $C \sqcup \neg C$ are added to $\tilde{\mathbf{C}}$. The relationships $C \sqcap \neg C \sqsubseteq \bot$, $\top \sqsubseteq C \sqcup \neg C$ are added to $(\tilde{\mathbf{C}}, \sqsubseteq)$. Additionally, for any X, if the relationship $C \sqcap X \sqsubseteq \bot$ is found in $(\tilde{\mathbf{C}}, \sqsubseteq)$, we add the relationship $X \sqsubseteq \neg C$, and if the relationship $\top \sqsubseteq C \sqcup X$ is found in $(\tilde{\mathbf{C}}, \sqsubseteq)$, we add the relationship $\neg C \sqsubseteq X$ (Fig. 2c). The concept C is processed recursively.

Existential Restriction of Concepts: First, an auxiliary preorder is constructed for DL roles, denoted as $(\tilde{\mathbf{R}}, \sqsubseteq)$. In this preorder, elements r, s stand in a relationship $r \sqsubseteq s$ if $r^{\mathcal{I}} \subseteq s^{\mathcal{I}}$ or if $r \sqsubseteq s$ is entailed. $\tilde{\mathbf{R}}$ is extended from $\mathbf{R}$ during the lattice construction process. For any role r represented in $\tilde{\mathbf{R}}$, elements $domain(r)$ and $codomain(r)$ are added to $\tilde{\mathbf{C}}$. Given a concept description $\exists r.C$, the relationship $r_{\exists r.C} \sqsubseteq r$ is added to $(\tilde{\mathbf{R}}, \sqsubseteq)$. Relationships $codomain(r_{\exists r.C}) \sqsubseteq C$, $domain(r_{\exists r.C}) \sqsubseteq \exists r.C$ and $\exists r.C \sqsubseteq domain(r_{\exists r.C})$ are added to $(\tilde{\mathbf{C}}, \sqsubseteq)$. Additionally, if there are roles $s \in \tilde{\mathbf{R}}$ with relationships $s \sqsubseteq r$ and $codomain(r) \sqsubseteq C$, the relationship $domain(s) \sqsubseteq domain(r_{\exists r.C})$ is added to $(\tilde{\mathbf{C}}, \sqsubseteq)$. The concept C is processed recursively.

Universal Restriction of Concepts: Given a concept description $\forall r.C$, the element $\neg \exists r.\neg C$ is added to $\tilde{\mathbf{C}}$ with relationships $\forall r.C \sqsubseteq \neg \exists r.\neg C$ and $\neg \exists r.\neg C \sqsubseteq \forall r.C$. Furthermore, if there are roles $s \in \tilde{\mathbf{R}}$ with relationships $s \sqsubseteq r$ and $domain(s) \sqsubseteq \forall r.C$, the relationship $codomain(r) \sqsubseteq C$ is added to $(\tilde{\mathbf{C}}, \sqsubseteq)$. Concepts $\neg \exists r.\neg C$, $\neg C$ and C are processed recursively.

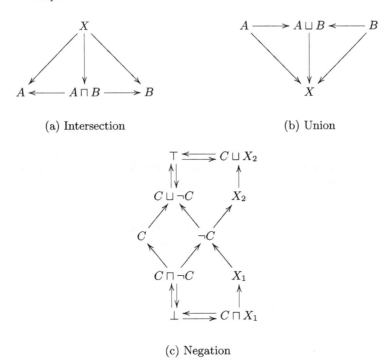

Fig. 2. Lattice representations of complex concept descriptions.

Subsumption Axioms: Axioms $C \sqsubseteq D$ are incorporated directly to the lattice. Additionally, relationships $\top \sqsubseteq \neg C \sqcup D$ are added to $(\tilde{\mathbf{C}}, \sqsubseteq)$. Concepts C and D are processed recursively.

Class assertion Axioms: Given an axiom $C(a)$, we construct the element $\{a\}$ in $\tilde{\mathbf{C}}$ with the following relationships: $\bot \sqsubseteq \{a\}$, $\{a\} \sqsubseteq C$ and $\{a\} \sqsubseteq \top$.

Role assertion axioms: Given an axiom $r(a,b)$, we construct elements $\{a\}, \{b\}$ in $\tilde{\mathbf{C}}$ with the following relationships: $\bot \sqsubseteq \{a\}$, $\{a\} \sqsubseteq \top$, $\bot \sqsubseteq \{b\}$, $\{b\} \sqsubseteq \top$ and $\{a\} \sqsubseteq \exists r.\{b\}$.

Every operator $(\sqcap \mid \sqcup \mid \neg \mid \exists \mid \forall \mid \sqsubseteq)$ introduces a constant number of elements into $\tilde{\mathbf{C}}$ and a constant number of relationships in $(\tilde{\mathbf{C}}, \sqsubseteq)$. Therefore, for a formula in the knowledge base with n operators the space and time complexity to process it is $O(n)$. The lattice construction process is not complete since we consider a subset $\tilde{\mathbf{C}}$ from the infinite set $\mathbf{C}$ of possible concept descriptions.

3.1 Embedding Into an Ordered-Vector Space

With the structure $(\tilde{\mathbf{C}}, \sqsubseteq)$ in place, we proceed to embed it into an ordered-vector space. This step is crucial for preserving the hierarchical relationships within the lattice, ensuring that our embeddings reflect the inherent ordering of concepts descriptions. We use an ordered-vector space $(X, \preceq)$ over $\mathbb{R}^n$ where, for elements in $a, b \in X$ with $a = (a_1, ..., a_n)$ and $b = (b_1, ..., b_n)$, $a \preceq b$ if and only if $a_1 \leq b_1, ..., a_n \leq b_n$.

Theorem 1. $((X, \preceq)$ **is a partial order**). *The pair $(X, \preceq)$ over $\mathbb{R}^n$, where for elements $a, b \in X$ with $a = (a_1, ..., a_n)$ and $b = (b_1, ..., b_n)$, $a \preceq b$ if and only if $a_1 \leq b_1, ..., a_n \leq b_n$, is a partial order.*

Proof. We demonstrate for each property of a partial order:

1. Reflexivity ($\Rightarrow$): Let $a \in X$ with $a \preceq a$. By definition, we have $a_i \leq a_i$ for any i. ($\Leftarrow$): Let $a \in X$. Since $a_i \leq a_i$ for any i, then $a \preceq a$.
2. Transitivity ($\Rightarrow$): Let $a, b, c \in X$. If $a \preceq b$ and $b \preceq c$, we have that $a_i \leq b_i$ and $b_i \leq c_i$; therefore, $a_i \leq c_i$ for any i. ($\Leftarrow$): Let $a, b, c \in X$ with $a_i \leq b_i$ and $b_i \leq c_i$ for any i. It follows that $a_i \leq c_i$, which implies $a \preceq c$.
3. Antisymmetry ($\Rightarrow$): Let $a, b \in X$. If $a \preceq b$ and $b \preceq a$, it follows that $a_i \leq b_i$ and $b_i \leq a_i$. Therefore, $a_i = b_i$ and $a = b$. ($\Leftarrow$): Let $a, b \in X$ with $a_i = b_i$ for any i. It implies that $a_i \leq b_i$ and $b_i \leq a_i$, therefore, $a \preceq b$ and $b \preceq a$.

□

Consequently, we introduce a parameterized function f_θ which maps objects in $(\tilde{\mathbf{C}}, \sqsubseteq)$ to the ordered-vector space $(X, \preceq)$ over $\mathbb{R}^n$. In this way, we intend f_θ to be a lattice-preserving function of $(\tilde{\mathbf{C}}, \sqsubseteq)$. Since f_θ is unknown, our task is to find the set of parameters $\theta \in \Theta$ that accommodates to the intended structure of the space X. We optimize f_θ using gradient descent. We use the following order-preserving scoring function [26]:

$$s(A, B) = \| \max(0, f_\theta(A) - f_\theta(B)) \|_2 \tag{1}$$

for elements $A, B \in \tilde{\mathbf{C}}$ with a relationship $A \sqsubseteq B$. If $f_\theta(A) \preceq f_\theta(B)$, then $s(A, B) = 0$, and otherwise $s(A, B) > 0$. We apply the following loss function to all relationships $A \sqsubseteq B \in (\tilde{\mathbf{C}}, \sqsubseteq)$:

$$\mathcal{L} = \sum_{A \sqsubseteq B \in (\tilde{\mathbf{C}}, \sqsubseteq)} \sum_{A \sqsubseteq B' \notin (\tilde{\mathbf{C}}, \sqsubseteq)} s(A, B) + \max(0, \gamma - s(A, B')) \tag{2}$$

Relationships $A \sqsubseteq B' \notin (\tilde{\mathbf{C}}, \sqsubseteq)$ are called negative samples and are generated by replacing B in an existing relationship $A \sqsubseteq B$ by a corrupted entity B' obtained by random sampling in a uniform distribution. The parameter γ is a margin parameter enforcing a minimum score value of the negative samples.

We show that the space X gets a partial order structure whenever the loss function $\mathcal{L} = 0$.

Theorem 2. (**Lattice-preserving embeddings**). *Let $\mathcal{O}$ be a $\mathcal{ALC}$ theory with signature $\Sigma = (\mathbf{C}, \mathbf{R}, \mathbf{I})$ and $(\tilde{\mathbf{C}}, \sqsubseteq)$ the lattice of concepts descriptions generated from $\mathcal{O}$. Let $(X, \preceq)$ be an ordered-vector space where for elements $a, b \in X$ with $a = (a_1, ..., a_n)$ and $b = (b_1, ..., b_n)$, $a \preceq b$ if and only if $a_1 \leq b_1, ..., a_n \leq b_n$. Let f_θ be a function mapping objects from $\tilde{\mathbf{C}}$ to X. If $\mathcal{L} = 0$, then f_θ is a lattice preserving function of $(\tilde{\mathbf{C}}, \sqsubseteq)$ into $(X, \preceq)$.*

Proof. Let us assume that $\mathcal{L} = 0$ and there exist a relationship $A \sqsubseteq B$ in the lattice such that $f_\theta(A) \npreceq f_\theta(B)$, meaning that the order is not preserved in the vector space X. Reordering the definition of L in Eq. 2, we have that $\mathcal{L} = s(A, B) + K$, where K is a non-negative number. Therefore, since $\mathcal{L} = 0$, it follows that $s(A, B) = \|\max 0, f_\theta(A) - f_\theta(B)\| = 0$. Consequently, we have that $f_\theta(A) \preceq f_\theta(B)$, which leads to a contradiction.

Now that we have shown that any relationship $A \sqsubseteq B$ in the lattice $(\tilde{\mathbf{C}}, \sqsubseteq)$ is preserved as $f_\theta(A) \preceq f_\theta(B)$ in $(X, \preceq)$, we now verify that f_θ preserves partial-order properties:

1. Reflexivity: Let $A \sqsubseteq A$ be a relationship in $(\tilde{\mathbf{C}}, \sqsubseteq)$. Since $\mathcal{L} = 0$, it implies that $f_\theta(A) \preceq f_\theta(A)$.
2. Transitivity: Let $A \sqsubseteq B$ and $B \sqsubseteq C$ be relationships in $(\tilde{\mathbf{C}}, \sqsubseteq)$. Since $\mathcal{L} = 0$, it follows that $f_\theta(A) \preceq f_\theta(B)$ and $f_\theta(B) \preceq f_\theta(C)$ and, by the transitive property of $\preceq$ (Theorem 1), $f_\theta(A) \preceq f_\theta(C)$.
3. Antisymmetry: Let $A \sqsubseteq B$ and $B \sqsubseteq A$ be relationships in $(\tilde{\mathbf{C}}, \sqsubseteq)$. Since $\mathcal{L} = 0$, it follows that $f_\theta(A) \preceq f_\theta(B)$ and $f_\theta(B) \preceq f_\theta(A)$ and, by the antisymmetry property of $\preceq$ (Theorem 1), $f_\theta(A) = f_\theta(B)$.

□

4 Evaluation

To show the effectiveness of our method, we evaluate on the following tasks: (1) generation of entailed axioms and (2) generation of probable axioms. In the task of generating entailed axioms, we use the ORE1 dataset from SemREC [6] and generate axioms of the form $C(a)$, where C is a concept name and a is an individual. In the case of generating probable axioms, we constructed datasets using GO [1] and FoodOn [12] to generate axioms of the form $C \sqsubseteq D$, where C, D are concept names. Additionally, we applied our method to the biomedical task of predicting protein–protein interactions. This task is a form of generation of probable statements of the form $r(a, b)$, where r is a role and a, b are individuals. We show information about datasets in Table 1.

4.1 Experimental Setup

To find the optimal hyperparameters for our method, we performed a grid search over parameters: embedding dimension $\in [50, 100, 200]$, margin $(\gamma) \in [0, 0.01, 0.1, 1]$, negative samples $\in [1, 2, 4]$, batch size $\in [8192, 16384, 32768]$, and learning rate $\in [1e^{-5}, 1e^{-4}, 1e^{-3}, 1e^{-2}]$. We used the Adam optimizer [17] with a Cyclic Learning Rate scheduler [23].

Table 1. Number of axioms in training, validation and testing ontologies and number of relationships in the corresponding training lattices.

Dataset	Training	Validation	Testing	Lattice
ORE1	61245	7578	15157	364849
FoodOn	34224	2977	5957	631423
GO	81844	7260	14521	1257443
PPI	351435	12038	12040	4479085

Table 2. Prediction of axioms $C(a)$ where C is a concept and a is an individual. We selected the ORE1 dataset proposed in [6].

Method	MR	MRR	Hits@3	Hits@10	Hits@100	AUC
ELEmbeddings	105	0.12	0.08	0.22	0.87	0.99
Box^{2}EL	122	0.10	0.08	0.18	0.70	0.98
FALCON	603	0.02	0.00	0.02	0.34	0.92
CatE	**37**	**0.18**	**0.10**	**0.51**	**0.96**	**0.99**

As baseline methods we selected those approaches that use only the ontology axioms, without any external knowledge such as text [8,9]. Therefore, we selected ELEmbeddings [18] and Box^{2}EL [15]. We used the implementations provided in the mOWL library [30]. To obtain optimal parameters for baseline methods, we performed a grid search over embedding dimension $\in [50, 100, 200]$, margin $\in [0, 0.01, 0.1]$ batch size $\in [5000, 10000, 20000]$ and learning rate $\in [1e^{-5}, 1e^{-4}, 1e^{-3}]$. Additionally, we compared with FALCON [24]; however, due to high memory and time requirements, we were unable to test different hyperparameters for this method. All selected hyperparameters are provided in the Appendix A (Table 5).

We report a variety of rank-based metrics such as Mean Rank (MR), Mean Reciprocal Rank (MRR), Hits@3, Hits@10, Hits@100 and ROC AUC. In all tasks we report filtered metrics only and filter statements from the training set. In the task of generating axioms $C(a)$, we additionally filter statements from the deductive closure of the training set.

4.2 Generating Entailed Axioms $C(a)$

The SemREC challenge [6], which evaluates neuro-symbolic reasoners, provides a number of benchmark datasets. We selected a representative data set called ORE1. We used the ORE1 dataset to test our method on the task of predicting axioms $C(a)$, where C is a concept description and a is an individual. We perform a ranking-based evaluation, where we rank every testing statement $C(a)$ against every $C'(a)$ where C' is a named concept. We show results in Table 2, where we can see CatE performs better than baseline methods across all metrics.

Table 3. TBox completion task over axioms $C \sqsubseteq D$ in GO and FoodOn.

Method	GO				FoodOn			
	MR	H@10	H@100	AUC	MR	H@10	H@100	AUC
ELEmbeddings	<u>3562</u>	<u>0.19</u>	0.37	<u>0.92</u>	3336	<u>0.25</u>	0.38	0.88
Box²EL	6621	0.01	0.07	0.85	**2763**	0.06	0.19	**0.90**
FALCON (5 models)	8982	0.02	0.08	0.79	3815	0.02	0.12	0.86
CatE	**2968**	**0.22**	**0.58**	**0.93**	<u>2764</u>	**0.30**	**0.47**	**0.90**

4.3 Generating Probable Axioms $C \sqsubseteq D$

To evaluate on the task of generating probable axioms, we generate two benchmark sets following procedures designed in previous methods [9,20]. We create two datasets using the Gene Ontology [1] and the Food Ontology [12]. In each ontology we remove 30% of the axioms $C \sqsubseteq D$ uniformly at random and distribute 10% for validation and 20% for testing. The training set contains the 70% of the subsumption axioms together with the other axioms existing in the ontology.

We focus on the prediction of subsumption axioms $C \sqsubseteq D$ and perform a rank-based evaluation ranking scores of axioms of interest $C \sqsubseteq D$ over all axioms $C \sqsubseteq D'$ where D' are named concepts. Table 3 shows the results. We can see that CatE consistently outperforms baselines in all metrics.

4.4 Protein–Protein Interaction Prediction

Protein-protein interactions (PPIs) are direct or indirect interactions between proteins, and information about PPIs is useful in systems biology and network-based bioinformatics methods. While PPIs can be investigated experimentally, several strategies have been developed to predict them using a variety of information, including the predicted or experimentally determined functions of proteins. The functions of proteins can be represented using the GO, and if X is a class from the GO, the axiom $p_1 \sqsubseteq \exists hasFunction.X$ asserts that the class of proteins p_1 has function X. PPIs can be encoded in axioms $interacts(p_1, p_2)$ where p_1, p_2 are proteins. In order to apply our method, we need to ensure that elements $\exists interacts.p_i$ exists in the lattice for any class of proteins p_i. Therefore, we added the relationships $\bot \sqsubseteq \exists interacts.p_i$ and $\exists interacts.p_i \sqsubseteq \top$ to the lattice structure for all classes of proteins p_i. We used the PPI dataset provided in [30]. We compare our method against state-of-the-art methods such as ELEmbeddings and Box²EL. [19,28], We show the results in Table 4, where we can see that CatE is not able to outperform over baselines. The PPI benchmark relies on the assumption that the information GO acts as background knowledge to predict protein–protein interactions. To further investigate on this task, we evaluate how well the methods capture the hierarchy of GO functions, which are axioms of the type $C \sqsubseteq D$. We compute the deductive closure of axioms $C \sqsubseteq D$

Table 4. Protein-protein interaction prediction on Yeast. Left-side shows the results on PPI axioms. Right side shows the results on axioms $C \sqsubseteq D$ that are learned during training.

Method	PPI axioms $r(a,b)$						Axioms $C \sqsubseteq D$		
	MR	MRR	H@3	H@10	H@100	AUC	MR	H@100	AUC
ELEmbeddings	289	0.10	0.09	0.25	0.73	0.95	23812	0.00	0.53
Box^{2}EL	188	**0.17**	**0.19**	**0.43**	**0.81**	**0.97**	23234	0.00	0.54
CatE	223	0.08	0.07	0.18	0.69	0.96	**8936**	**0.28**	**0.82**

using the ELK reasoner [16], and evaluate the capability of each method to generate the axioms in this new set. We find that ELEmbeddings and Box^{2}EL do not capture the semantics of GO axioms at all, yet they can perform PPI predictions. Originally, ELEmbeddings and Box^{2}EL are trained with negative samples just for PPI axioms, which can cause the other axioms types to converge to a trivial solution. Since CatE uses negative samples for all relationships in the lattice, it can predict PPIs while capturing other type of information in GO. Our analysis shows that predicting PPIs on its own is not sufficient to show that a particular embedding method is utilizing the background knowledge. Further analysis on embedding methods should be required, which is out of the scope of this work.

4.5 Effect of Hyperparameters

The time and space complexity of CatE increases linearly with the number of operators. However, the number of operators can be arbitrarily large for axioms in $\mathcal{ALC}$. Furthermore, hyperparameters such as embedding size and number of negative samples can have an impact on training and/or inference time as well as on memory consumption. In Fig. 3, we analyze how these hyperparameters impact on performance. We chose Hits@100 and ROC AUC metrics and show that while the embedding dimension has a direct impact performance (the higher the dimension the better the performance), the number of negative samples does not have a large effect (either positive or negative).

5 Discussion

We have developed a method that generates embeddings for the $\mathcal{ALC}$ language. Our method materializes a lattice structure using concept descriptions found in a $\mathcal{ALC}$ knowledge base. Furthermore, we use an order-preserving loss function to optimize the embedding space, and we show that when our loss function is minimized, the embedding space preserves partial order properties. We have applied our method to different forms of knowledge base completion tasks, and we showed that our method can outperform several state-of-the-art methods.

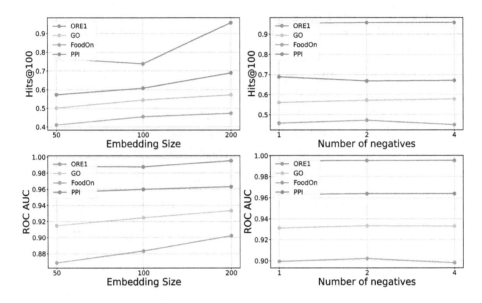

Fig. 3. Impact of embedding size and number of negatives on the Hits@100 and ROC AUC over different datasets.

Current graph-based methods to embed DL knowledge bases (ontologies) construct graphs relying on syntactic information therein and the embedding process is not guaranteed to be invertible. On the other hand, methods such as ELEmbeddings, Box^{2}EL and FALCON are able to generate approximate models for DL knowledge bases. We state that CatE stands in a midpoint between both types of methods. CatE looks into the syntactical information in the knowledge base to construct a lattice and, consequently, an embedding space that is consistent to the semantics.

However, as in graph-based embeddings, CatE cannot make inferences over concepts that are not explicitly stated in the lattice. This is a limitation that was exposed in the protein–protein interaction task, where we had to add concept descriptions a priori in order to be able to make inferences over them. To mitigate this issue, future work can focus on solutions based on inductive learning over knowledge graphs, which can be applicable in the context of lattices.

6 Conclusion

We developed an embedding method for the $\mathcal{ALC}$ that preserves the lattice structure of concept descriptions. Our method materializes the lattice structure following connections between Description Logics and Category Theory. The lattice in place is embedded into an ordered-vector space. We provide empirical results that our method can perform effectively across different tasks involving knowledge base completion.

A Hyperparameters Selection

Table 5. Selection of hyperparameters for the different methods with respect to the dataset used. E.S.: Embedding size, L.R.: learning rate, M: margin, B.S.: batch size, N.N.: number of negative samples. '–' means that the batch size is the whole dataset.

Method	E.S.	L.R.	M	B.S.	N.N.
GO					
ELEmbeddings	200	0.0001	0.1	20000	1
Box^{2}EL	200	0.00001	0.1	20000	1
CatE	200	0.00001	1	32768	4
FoodOn					
ELEmbeddings	50	0.001	0.1	20000	1
Box^{2}EL	200	0.0001	0.1	40000	1
CatE	200	0.0001	1	8192	2
ORE1					
ELEmbeddings	200	0.00001	0.01	4096	1
Box^{2}EL	200	0.0001	0	8192	1
CatE	200	0.0001	1	32768	4
PPI					
ELEmbeddings	200	0.01	0.01	–	1
Box^{2}EL	200	0.0001	1	–	1
CatE	200	0.00001	0.1	65536	1

References

1. Ashburner, M., et al.: Gene ontology: tool for the unification of biology. Nat. Genet. **25**(1), 25–29 (2000). https://doi.org/10.1038/75556
2. Baader, F., Calvanese, D., McGuinness, D., Nardi, D., Patel-Schneider, P.F. (eds.): The Description Logic Handbook: Theory, Implementation, and Applications. Cambridge University Press (2003)
3. Baader, F., Lutz, C.: 13 description logic. In: Blackburn, P., Van Benthem, J., Wolter, F. (eds.) Handbook of Modal Logic, Studies in Logic and Practical Reasoning, vol. 3, pp. 757–819. Elsevier (2007). https://doi.org/10.1016/S1570-2464(07)80016-4, https://www.sciencedirect.com/science/article/pii/S1570246407800164
4. Baader, F., Sertkaya, B.: Applying formal concept analysis to description logics. In: Eklund, P. (ed.) ICFCA 2004. LNCS (LNAI), vol. 2961, pp. 261–286. Springer, Heidelberg (2004). https://doi.org/10.1007/978-3-540-24651-0_24
5. Badreddine, S., d'Avila Garcez, A., Serafini, L., Spranger, M.: Logic tensor networks. Artif. Intell. **303**, 103649 (2022). https://doi.org/10.1016/j.artint.2021.103649. https://www.sciencedirect.com/science/article/pii/S0004370221002009

6. Banerjee, D., Usbeck, R., Mihindukulasooriya, N., Singh, G., Mutharaju, R., Kapanipathi, P. (eds.): Joint Proceedings of Scholarly QALD 2023 and SemREC 2023 co-located with 22nd International Semantic Web Conference ISWC 2023, Athens, Greece, November 6-10, 2023, CEUR Workshop Proceedings, vol. 3592. CEUR-WS.org (2023). https://ceur-ws.org/Vol-3592
7. Brieulle, L., Duc, C.L., Vaillant, P.: Reasoning in the description logic ALC under category semantics (extended abstract). In: Arieli, O., Homola, M., Jung, J.C., Mugnier, M. (eds.) Proceedings of the 35th International Workshop on Description Logics (DL 2022) co-located with Federated Logic Conference (FLoC 2022), Haifa, Israel, August 7th to 10th, 2022. CEUR Workshop Proceedings, vol. 3263. CEUR-WS.org (2022). https://ceur-ws.org/Vol-3263/abstract-7.pdf
8. Chen, J., He, Y., Geng, Y., Jiménez-Ruiz, E., Dong, H., Horrocks, I.: Contextual semantic embeddings for ontology subsumption prediction. World Wide Web **26**(5), 2569–2591 (2023). https://doi.org/10.1007/s11280-023-01169-9
9. Chen, J., Hu, P., Jimenez-Ruiz, E., Holter, O.M., Antonyrajah, D., Horrocks, I.: OWL2Vec*: embedding of OWL ontologies. Mach. Learn. (2021). https://doi.org/10.1007/s10994-021-05997-6
10. Chen, Z., Wang, Y., Zhao, B., Cheng, J., Zhao, X., Duan, Z.: Knowledge graph completion: A review. IEEE Access **8**, 192435–192456 (2020). https://doi.org/10.1109/access.2020.3030076
11. Davey, B.A., Priestley, H.A.: Ordered sets, p. 1-32. Cambridge University Press, 2 edn. (2002). https://doi.org/10.1017/CBO9780511809088.003
12. Dooley, D.M., et al.: FoodOn: a harmonized food ontology to increase global food traceability, quality control and data integration. npj Science of Food **2**(1) (Dec 2018). https://doi.org/10.1038/s41538-018-0032-6
13. Duc, C.L.: Category-theoretical semantics of the description logic ALC. In: Homola, M., Ryzhikov, V., Schmidt, R.A. (eds.) Proceedings of the 34th International Workshop on Description Logics (DL 2021) part of Bratislava Knowledge September (BAKS 2021), Bratislava, Slovakia, September 19th to 22nd, 2021. CEUR Workshop Proceedings, vol. 2954. CEUR-WS.org (2021). https://ceur-ws.org/Vol-2954/paper-22.pdf
14. Hao, J., Chen, M., Yu, W., Sun, Y., Wang, W.: Universal representation learning of knowledge bases by jointly embedding instances and ontological concepts. In: Proceedings of the 25th ACM SIGKDD International Conference on Knowledge Discovery &; Data Mining. KDD '19, ACM (Jul 2019). https://doi.org/10.1145/3292500.3330838
15. Jackermeier, M., Chen, J., Horrocks, I.: Box^{2}el: Concept and role box embeddings for the description logic el++ (2023)
16. Kazakov, Y., Krötzsch, M., Simančík, F.: The incredible ELK. J. Autom. Reason. **53**(1), 1–61 (2013). https://doi.org/10.1007/s10817-013-9296-3
17. Kingma, D.P., Ba, J.: Adam: A method for stochastic optimization. In: Bengio, Y., LeCun, Y. (eds.) 3rd International Conference on Learning Representations, ICLR 2015, San Diego, CA, USA, May 7-9, 2015, Conference Track Proceedings (2015)
18. Kulmanov, M., Liu-Wei, W., Yan, Y., Hoehndorf, R.: El embeddings: geometric construction of models for the description logic el ++. In: International Joint Conference on Artificial Intelligence (2019)
19. Kulmanov, M., Smaili, F.Z., Gao, X., Hoehndorf, R.: Semantic similarity and machine learning with ontologies. Briefings Bioinform. **22**(4) (10 2020). https://doi.org/10.1093/bib/bbaa199, bbaa199

20. Mondal, S., Bhatia, S., Mutharaju, R.: Emel++: Embeddings for EL++ description logic. In: Martin, A., Hinkelmann, K., Fill, H., Gerber, A., Lenat, D., Stolle, R., van Harmelen, F. (eds.) Proceedings of the AAAI 2021 Spring Symposium on Combining Machine Learning and Knowledge Engineering (AAAI-MAKE 2021), Stanford University, Palo Alto, California, USA, March 22-24, 2021. CEUR Workshop Proceedings, vol. 2846. CEUR-WS.org (2021)
21. Özcep, Ö.L., Leemhuis, M., Wolter, D.: Embedding ontologies in the description logic ALC by axis-aligned cones. J. Artif. Intell. Res. **78**, 217–267 (2023)
22. Schild, K.: A correspondence theory for terminological logics: preliminary report. In: Mylopoulos, J., Reiter, R. (eds.) Proceedings of the 12th International Joint Conference on Artificial Intelligence. Sydney, Australia, August 24-30, 1991. pp. 466–471. Morgan Kaufmann (1991). http://ijcai.org/Proceedings/91-1/Papers/072.pdf
23. Smith, L.N.: Cyclical learning rates for training neural networks (2017)
24. Tang, Z., Hinnerichs, T., Peng, X., Zhang, X., Hoehndorf, R.: FALCON: faithful neural semantic entailment over ALC ontologies (2023)
25. van Krieken, E., Acar, E., van Harmelen, F.: Analyzing differentiable fuzzy logic operators. Artif. Intell. **302**, 103602 (2022) https://doi.org/10.1016/j.artint.2021.103602. https://www.sciencedirect.com/science/article/pii/S0004370221001533
26. Vendrov, I., Kiros, R., Fidler, S., Urtasun, R.: Order-embeddings of images and language. In: Bengio, Y., LeCun, Y. (eds.) 4th International Conference on Learning Representations, ICLR 2016, San Juan, Puerto Rico, May 2-4, 2016, Conference Track Proceedings (2016)
27. Venema, Y.: 6 algebras and coalgebras. In: Blackburn, P., Van Benthem, J., Wolter, F. (eds.) Handbook of Modal Logic, Studies in Logic and Practical Reasoning, vol. 3, pp. 331–426. Elsevier (2007). https://doi.org/10.1016/S1570-2464(07)80009-7, https://www.sciencedirect.com/science/article/pii/S1570246407800097
28. Xiong, B., Potyka, N., Tran, T.K., Nayyeri, M., Staab, S.: Faithful embeddings for EL++ knowledge bases. In: Proceedings of the 21st International Semantic Web Conference (ISWC2022), pp. 1–18 (2022)
29. Zhapa-Camacho, F., Hoehndorf, R.: From axioms over graphs to vectors, and back again: evaluating the properties of graph-based ontology embeddings (2023)
30. Zhapa-Camacho, F., Kulmanov, M., Hoehndorf, R.: mOWL: Python library for machine learning with biomedical ontologies. Bioinformatics (12 2022). https://doi.org/10.1093/bioinformatics/btac811, btac811

Towards Learning Abductive Reasoning Using VSA Distributed Representations

Giacomo Camposampiero[1,2](✉)[iD], Michael Hersche[1][iD], Aleksandar Terzić[1,2][iD], Roger Wattenhofer[2][iD], Abu Sebastian[1][iD], and Abbas Rahimi[1][iD]

[1] IBM Research – Zurich, Rüschlikon, Switzerland
[2] ETH Zürich, Zürich, Switzerland
giacomo.camposampiero1@ibm.com

Abstract. We introduce the Abductive Rule Learner with Context-awareness (ARLC), a model that solves abstract reasoning tasks based on Learn-VRF. ARLC features a novel and more broadly applicable training objective for abductive reasoning, resulting in better interpretability and higher accuracy when solving Raven's progressive matrices (RPM). ARLC allows both programming domain knowledge and learning the rules underlying a data distribution. We evaluate ARLC on the I-RAVEN dataset, showcasing state-of-the-art accuracy across both in-distribution and out-of-distribution (unseen attribute-rule pairs) tests. ARLC surpasses neuro-symbolic and connectionist baselines, including large language models, despite having orders of magnitude fewer parameters. We show ARLC's robustness to post-programming training by incrementally learning from examples on top of programmed knowledge, which only improves its performance and does not result in catastrophic forgetting of the programmed solution. We validate ARLC's seamless transfer learning from a 2×2 RPM constellation to unseen constellations. Our code is available at https://github.com/IBM/abductive-rule-learner-with-context-awareness.

1 Introduction

Abstract reasoning can be defined as the ability to induce rules or patterns from a limited source of experience and generalize their application to similar but unseen situations. It is widely acknowledged as a hallmark of human intelligence, and great efforts have been poured into the challenge of endowing artificial intelligence (AI) models with such capability.

As a result, a wide range of benchmarks to assess human-like fluid intelligence and abstract reasoning in AI models has been proposed in the past decade [1–4]. In this work, we focus on Raven's progressive matrices (RPM) test [1,5,6]. RPM is a visual task that involves perceiving pattern continuation and elemental abstraction as well as deducing relations based on a restricted set of underlying rules, in a process that mirrors the attributes of advanced human intelligence [7,8]. Recently, RPM has become a widely used benchmark for effectively testing AI capabilities in abstract reasoning, making analogies, and dealing with out-of-distribution (OOD) data [9–13].

With the advent of large language models, it was suggested that the attainment of abstract reasoning abilities required to solve this kind of task may hinge upon the scale of the model. To support this claim, it was shown that adequately large pre-trained language models can exhibit emergent abilities for logical [14] and analogical [15,16] reasoning. Nevertheless, the internal mechanisms underlying the emergence of these abilities are still not well understood. In addition, recent works provided evidence on the acute brittleness of these abilities [17,18], while others showed that language models fail to attain levels of general abstract reasoning comparable to humans [19–22].

An alternative and promising direction is neuro-symbolic AI. Neuro-symbolic approaches combine sub-symbolic perception with various forms of symbolic reasoning, resulting in cutting-edge performance across a spectrum of domains, including visual [23–26], natural language [27], causal [28], mathematical [29], and analogical [30–34] reasoning tasks. In the context of RPM, recent neuro-symbolic architectures focused on abductive reasoning [33,34]. Abductive reasoning allows to selectively infer propositions based on prior knowledge represented in a symbolic form to explain the perceptual observations in the best possible way [35]. The appeal of the abductive approach lies in its accommodation of perceptual uncertainties within symbolic reasoning. Abductive reasoning can be implemented in systems that leverage distributed vector-symbolic architectures (VSAs) [36–38] representations and operators, such as the Neuro-Vector Symbolic Architecture (NVSA) [34]. However, these neuro-symbolic architectures [33,34] necessitate complete knowledge over the application domain (which might not be available) to program the right inductive bias into the model.

Learn-VRF [39] overcomes this limitation by introducing a probabilistic abduction reasoning approach that learns a subset of the rules underlying RPM from data. Learn-VRF transparently operates in the rule space, learning them through a soft-assignment of VSA attribute representations to a fixed rule template. During inference, it generates the answer panel by executing all the learned rules and applying a soft-selection mechanism to their outputs. Nevertheless, Learn-VRF comes with several limitations, including a sub-optimal selection mechanism, poor performance on the RPM constellations involving multiple objects, and a constraint on the expressiveness of the RPM rules it can learn.

To make progress towards learning-to-reason, we propose the Abductive Rule Learner with Context-awareness (ARLC) to tackle the main limitations of Learn-VRF [39]. We advance a novel context-augmented formulation of the optimization problem and a more expressive rule template, which allows sharing rules with the same parameters in both execution and selection steps and offers better interpretability. An overview of ARLC is depicted in Fig. 1. ARLC features programmability and can further learn from data on top of programmed knowledge. We evaluate ARLC on in-distribution (ID) and out-of-distribution (OOD) tests of the I-RAVEN dataset, and demonstrate that ARLC significantly outperforms neuro-symbolic and connectionist baselines, including large language models. Further, the number of trainable parameters is reduced by two orders of magnitude compared to Learn-VRF. We experimentally validate the programmability of ARLC by encoding domain knowledge, and discover that post-programming training, contrary to other studies [40], does not compromise the validity of the solution, but rather improves it. Finally, training the model on a single constellation and evaluating it on all the others, we show that, unlike previous baselines [34,39], the learned rules can seamlessly be transferred across constellations of the I-RAVEN dataset.

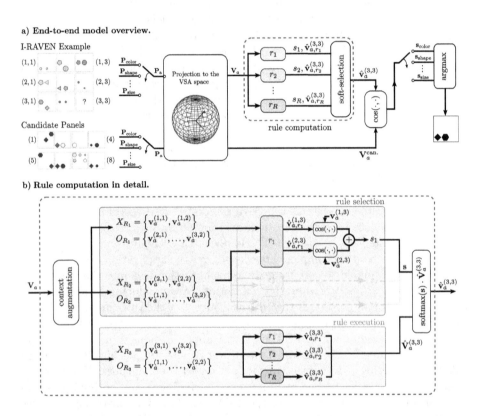

Fig. 1. Proposed ARLC architecture. **a)** Overview of the end-to-end inference pipeline. **b)** Detailed rule computation block, exploded from (a), which highlights the difference between the two steps of the rule computation: rule selection and rule execution. We also illustrate the proposed context-augmentation abstraction (that translates VSA vectors into different sets X_{R_i} and O_{R_i} depending on the row R_i), and the parameter sharing between rules ($r_1, \ldots, r_R$) across the selection and execution steps (rule blocks with the same color share the same parameters $\mathbf{w}, \mathbf{u}, \mathbf{v}$).

2 Background

2.1 Vector Symbolic Architectures

Vector-symbolic architectures (VSAs) [36–38] are a family of computational models that rely on the mathematical properties of high-dimensional vector spaces. VSAs make use of high-dimensional distributed representations for structured (symbolic) representation of data while maintaining the advantages of connectionist distributed vector representations (see [41] for a survey). Here is a formal definition of VSAs:

Definition 1 (VSA). *A vector-symbolic architecture (VSA) consists of a 4-tuple $\mathbb{V} = (\mathbb{C}, \oplus, \otimes, \odot)$, where $\mathbb{C}$ is a set of high-dimensional distributed vectors equipped with two main operations, $\oplus$ (bundling) and $\otimes$ (binding), and on which it is possible to define a similarity measure $\odot$.*

Bundling is a similarity-preserving operation that creates a superposition of the operands, that is, the resulting vector will have a high similarity with the two operands. Binding, on the other hand, is an operation that allows to bind a vector (value) to another vector (key) and does not preserve similarities; it usually allows an inverse operation, called unbinding. The specific realization of the bundling, binding, and vector space constitutes the main difference between members of the VSA family.

2.2 Raven's Progressive Matrices

In this work, we focus on the I-RAVEN dataset [10], a benchmark that provides RPM tests sampled from unbiased candidate sets to avoid short-cut solutions that were possible in the original RAVEN dataset [13]. Each RPM test is an analogy problem presented as a 3 × 3 pictorial matrix of context panels. Every panel in the matrix is filled with several geometric objects based on a certain rule, except the bottom-right panel, which is left blank. Figure 1 includes an I-RAVEN example test. The task is to complete the missing panel by picking the correct answer from a set of (eight) candidate answer panels that matches the implicit generation rule on every attribute. The object's attributes (color, size, shape, number, position) are governed by individual underlying rules:

- *constant*, the attribute value does not change per row;
- *arithmetic*, the attribute value of the third panel corresponds to either the sum or the difference of the first two panels of the row;
- *progression*, the attribute value monotonically increases or decreases in a row by 1 or 2;
- *distribute three*, the set of the three different values remains constant across rows, but the individual attribute values get shifted to the left or to the right by one position at every row; it also holds column-wise.

Each panel contains a variable number of objects (minimum one, maximum nine) arranged according to one of seven different constellations (center, distribute-four, distribute-nine, left-right, up-down, in-out-center, and in-out-four).

2.3 Learning to Reason with Distributed Representations

In this section, we discuss how vector-symbolic architectures can be used to solve tasks which require analogical and relational reasoning such as RPM. In particular, we focus on Learn-VRF [39], a simple yet powerful approach that enables to solve RPM tests by learning the underlying relations between visual attributes in the VSA representational space.

The key observation behind this approach is that the formulation of every RPM rule in the VSA algebra is a particular instance of a general rule template, which is shared among all the rules and consists of a series of binding and unbinding operations between VSA vectors. Hence, the problem of learning RPM rules can be framed as an assignment problem between vectors representing visual attributes and terms in this general rule template. This alternative formulation allows to tackle one of the main limitations of neuro-symbolic approaches, differentiability, and therefore enables the use of data-driven learning algorithms based on gradient optimization.

Learn-VRF includes several sequential steps, ranging from the translation of visual attributes into the VSA high-dimensional space to the computation of final results, that are detailed in the following paragraphs.

From Visual Attributes to VSA. Following the same procedure of previous works which assume a perfect perception [16, 42], the panel's attribute labels are provided directly by the I-RAVEN metadata. For every attribute a, each panel's label is translated to a probability mass function (PMF) $\mathbf{p}_a^{(i,j)}$, where i is the row index and j is the column index of the panel. The panel's PMF is then projected into the VSA space as

$$\mathbf{v}_a^{(i,j)} = \sum_{k=1}^{N} \mathbf{p}_a^{(i,j)}[k] \cdot \mathbf{b}[k],$$

where N is the number of possible values that the attribute a can assume.

The VSA vectors are drawn from a dictionary of binary generalized sparse block codes (GSBCs) [43] $\mathbb{C} = \{\mathbf{b}_i\}_{i=1}^{512}$. In binary GSBCs, the D-dimensional vectors are divided into B blocks of equal length, $L = D/B$, where only one (randomly selected) element per block is set to 1 ($D = 1024$ and $B = 4$).

The algebraic operations on binary GSBCs are defined in Table 1. Combining GSBCs with fractional power encoding (FPE) [44] allows the representation of continuous attributes (e.g., color or size) and simple algebraic operations, as addition and subtractions, in the corresponding vector space. In other words, the FPE initialization allows to establish a semantic equivalence between high-dimensional vectors and real numbers. This property is consistently exploited in the framework, as it allows to solve the analogies in the puzzles as simple algebraic operations in the domain of real numbers. Finally, we observe that the binding operation for binary GSBCs has properties analogous to addition in the real number domain, including commutativity, associativity, and the existence of a neutral element ($\mathbf{e} \in \mathbb{C}$, s.t. $\mathbf{a} \circledast \mathbf{e} = \mathbf{a} \; \forall \mathbf{a} \in \mathbb{C}$).

Table 1. Supported VSA operations and their equivalent in $\mathbb{R}$.

Operation	Binary GSBCs	Equivalent in $\mathbb{R}$
Binding ($\otimes$)	Block-wise circular convolution ($\circledast$)	Addition $+$
Unbinding ($\oslash$)	Block-wise circular correlation ($\odot$)	Subtraction $-$
Bundling ($\oplus$)	Sum & normalization	—
Similarity ($\odot$)	Cosine similarity ($\cos(\cdot,\cdot)$)	—

Learning RPM Rules as an Assignment Problem. The core idea introduced in Learn-VRF is that the rules used in RPM can be framed in a fixed template which encompasses a series of binding and unbinding operations,

$$r = (\mathbf{c}_1 \circledast \mathbf{c}_2 \circledast \mathbf{c}_3) \odot (\mathbf{c}_4 \circledast \mathbf{c}_5 \circledast \mathbf{c}_6), \qquad (1)$$

where $\mathbf{c}_i$ represents a context panel $\mathbf{v}_a^{(i,j)}$ or the identity $\mathbf{e}$. In this setting, learning the rules of RPM can hence be interpreted as an assignment problem between VSA vectors and terms of Eq. 1. To make it differentiable, Learn-VRF frames every term $\mathbf{c}_i$ as a convex combination over the VSA vectors of the context panels' attributes, augmented with the neutral element

$$\mathbf{c}_k = \sum_{\text{panels } (i,j)} w_k^{(i,j)} \cdot \mathbf{v}_a^{(i,j)} + v_k \cdot \mathbf{e}, \qquad (2)$$

where the following constraints apply to the weights

$$\sum_{\text{panels } (i,j)} w_k^{(i,j)} + v_k = 1, \qquad 0 \le w_k^{(i,j)} \le 1 \, \forall i,j, \qquad 0 \le v_k \le 1, \forall k.$$

Executing and Selecting the Learned Rules. Inference with the learned rule set is a two-step process: an execution step (where all the rules are applied in parallel to the input) and a selection step (where a prediction for the missing panel is generated). The application of each rule r to an RPM example generates a tuple of three VSA vectors $(\hat{\mathbf{v}}_{a,r}^{(i,3)})_{i=1}^{3}$, which corresponds to the result of the rule execution on the three rows of the RPM matrix, together with a rule confidence value s_r. The confidence value is computed as the sum of the cosine similarities between the predicted VSA vectors and their respective ground-truth vector,

$$s_r = \sum_{i=1}^{3} \cos\left(\mathbf{v}_a^{(i,3)}, \hat{\mathbf{v}}_{a,r}^{(i,3)}\right). \qquad (3)$$

During inference, the last term of the sum ($i = 3$) is omitted, as the ground-truth for the third row is unknown.

The answer is finally produced by taking a linear combination of the VSA vectors generated by executing all the rules, weighted by their respective confidence scores (normalized to a valid probability distribution using a softmax function). More formally, if we define $\mathbf{s} = [s_1, \ldots, s_R]$ to be the concatenation of all rules' confidence score and $\hat{\mathbf{V}}_a^{(3,3)} = [\hat{\mathbf{v}}_{a,1}^{(3,3)}, \ldots, \hat{\mathbf{v}}_{a,R}^{(3,3)}]$ to be the concatenation of all rules' predictions for the missing panel, the final VSA vector predicted by the model for the attribute a becomes

$$\hat{\mathbf{v}}_a^{(3,3)} = \text{softmax}(\mathbf{s}) \cdot \hat{\mathbf{V}}_a^{(3,3)}. \tag{4}$$

The use of the weighted combination can be understood as a *soft selection* mechanism between rules, and was found to be more effective compared to the *hard selection* mechanism provided by sampling [39].

3 Methods

In this section, we present our Abductive Rule Learner with Context-awareness (ARLC) system. An overview of ARLC is depicted in Fig. 1. The framework aligns with the original Learn-VRF at a conceptual level, albeit with key adjustments that allow to improve its expressiveness and boost its downstream performance on the I-RAVEN dataset.

3.1 Learning Context-Augmented RPM Rules

The soft-assignment problem presented in Eq. 2 is designed to assign each term $\mathbf{c}_i$ in Eq. 1 with a fixed, absolute position in the 3×3 RPM matrix. For instance, the rule for arithmetic subtraction could be learned with one-hot assignment weights as $\hat{\mathbf{v}}_a^{(3,3)} = \mathbf{v}_a^{3,1} \oslash \mathbf{v}_a^{3,2}$. A major limitation of this approach is that *the rules cannot be shared across rows of the RPM matrix*. For example, the aforementioned arithmetic subtraction rule is valid only for the third row, but not for the first and second rows.

To overcome this limitation, Learn-VRF instantiates and learns three different rule sets (one per row) simultaneously. During inference, the model leverages the first two sets to produce confidence values (Eq. 3), which are then used to perform a soft-selection of the output panels produced by the third rule set (Eq. 4). While it was empirically shown to be effective, this implementation leaves the door open to different criticalities. For instance, the model has no constraint on the functional equivalence between the three learned rule sets. This renders the interpretability of the model sensibly harder and increases the likelihood of learning spurious correlations in the rule selection mechanism. Furthermore, this formulation diminishes the model's versatility, as its design, tailored to the RPM context, cannot seamlessly transfer to other abstract reasoning tasks without a reconfiguration of its primary components.

Motivated by these issues and by related works in cognitive sciences and psychology that argue for the importance of context in the solution of analogies for humans [45,46] we propose a more general formulation of the soft-assignment problem which abstracts away the positional assignment and instead relies on the notion of *context*. We propose to rewrite Eq. 2 as

$$\mathbf{c}_k = \sum_{i=1}^{I} w_k^i \cdot \mathbf{x}_i + \sum_{j=1}^{J} u_k^j \cdot \mathbf{o}_j + v_k \cdot \mathbf{e}. \tag{5}$$

Here, $\mathbf{X} = \{\mathbf{x}_1, \ldots, \mathbf{x}_I\}$ is the set of attributes that define the current sample, that is, the description of the problem for which we infer a solution. $\mathbf{O} = \{\mathbf{o}_1, \ldots, \mathbf{o}_J\}$ is the set of attributes that define the context for that sample, that could be interpreted as a working memory from which additional information to infer the answer can be retrieved. In Eq. 5, $\mathbf{w}, \mathbf{u}, \mathbf{v}$ are the learned parameters and, as in Eq. 2, they are subject to the following constraints:

$$\sum_{i=0}^{I} w_k^i + \sum_{j=0}^{J} w_k^j + v_k = 1, \qquad 0 \le w_k^i \le 1 \,\forall i, \qquad 0 \le u_k^j \le 1 \,\forall j, \qquad 0 \le v_k \le 1, \,\forall k.$$

Note that the notion of the current sample X and its context O depends on the row chosen for inference, as shown in Fig. 2.

The new formulation does not lose expressiveness compared to Eq. 2. While its terms are no longer tied to fixed positions in the RPM matrix, relative position information can still be preserved by keeping the order of the current and context samples consistent during training. Both row-wise and column-wise relations can be correctly represented by the model.

Most importantly, the new context-aware formulation for the soft-selection allows to have a single set of rules shared across all the rows of the RPM. Contrary to Learn-VRF, the model can now enforce functional equivalence between the rules used for selection and execution *by construction*. Additionally, the number of trainable parameters is reduced by 66% compared to Learn-VRF.

In RPM, the number of current and context examples is equal to $I = 2$ and $J = 5$, respectively. We do not consider $J = 6$ context examples to ensure that the same rules can be shared across rows. Otherwise, the model would fail when used to predict R_1 and R_2, since the panel in position $(3,3)$ is unknown.

3.2 Improving Rule Selection Through Template Generalization

Compared to Learn-VRF, we increase the number of terms in the general rule template (Eq. 1) as

$$r = (\mathbf{c}_1 \circledast \mathbf{c}_2 \circledast \mathbf{c}_3 \circledast \mathbf{c}_4 \circledast \mathbf{c}_5 \circledast \mathbf{c}_6) \odot (\mathbf{c}_7 \circledast \mathbf{c}_8 \circledast \mathbf{c}_9 \circledast \mathbf{c}_{10} \circledast \mathbf{c}_{11} \circledast \mathbf{c}_{12}). \tag{6}$$

Increasing the representational power of the rule template opens up the possibility to learn more general—yet functionally equivalent— formulations of the RPM rules, by also including "validation" terms in their structure, necessary in specific edge cases of the I-RAVEN dataset, such as Example 1. This bridges the gap between Learn-VRF, which could learn a set of rules that are perfect for execution but sub-optimal for selection, and other neuro-symbolic approaches [33,34], which hard-coded an optimal rule set for selection and an optimal rule set for execution. We define the *optimality* of a rule set as follows.

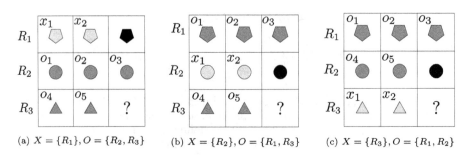

Fig. 2. Visualization of current samples ($X = \{x_1, x_2\}$, in yellow) and context ($O = \{o_1, \ldots, o_5\}$, in green) panels when predicting the third panel for different rows, namely the first row (left), second row (center) and third row (right). Black objects represent panels which are not used for the computation, while the question mark represents the unknown test panel, which is unavailable during inference. (Color figure online)

Definition 2 (Rule Set Optimality). *Consider a rule set $\mathcal{R} = \{r_i\}_{i=1}^R$ and an arbitrary RPM test $\mathbf{V}_a = (\mathbf{v}_a^{(1,1)}, \ldots, \mathbf{v}_a^{(3,2)})$. $\mathcal{R}$ is defined to be optimal for* **execution** *if $\exists r \in \mathcal{R}$ s.t. $\mathbf{v}_a^{(3,3)} = r(\mathbf{V}_a)$, and optimal for* **selection** *if the probability distribution over $\mathcal{R}$ induced by the selection mechanism (through confidence values s_r) concentrates all the probability on the correct rule.*

The importance of this distinction can be understood in the following example.

Example 1 Consider the following RPM test example V, where different numbers correspond to different color attribute values,

$$V = \begin{bmatrix} 9 & 0 & 9 \\ 6 & 3 & 9 \\ 3 & 2 & ? \end{bmatrix}, \text{ with } \begin{cases} x_1 = 9, x_2 = 0, o_1 = 6, o_2 = 3, o_3 = 9 \text{ when } X = R_1 \\ x_1 = 6, x_2 = 3, o_1 = 9, o_2 = 0, o_3 = 9 \text{ when } X = R_2 \\ x_1 = 3, x_2 = 2, o_1 = 9, o_2 = 0, o_3 = 9 \text{ when } X = R_3 \end{cases}$$

and a rule set $\mathcal{R}$ including the two rules that were proposed in Learn-VRF [39] to solve *arithmetic plus* (+) and *distribute three* (d3), rewritten accordingly to our context-augmented formulation

$$\mathbf{v}^+ = \mathbf{x}_1 \circledast \mathbf{x}_2 \equiv x_1 + x_2 = v^+$$
$$\mathbf{v}^{d3} = (\mathbf{o}_1 \circledast \mathbf{o}_2 \circledast \mathbf{o}_3) \odot \mathbf{x}_1 \odot \mathbf{x}_2 \equiv (o_1 + o_2 + o_3) - x_1 - x_2 = v^{d3}$$

where the equivalence between vector space and $\mathbb{R}$ is given by FPE.

Performing the selection using $\mathcal{R}$ can potentially result in a failure of the model for this RPM test. In fact, we can see that both v^+ and v^{d3} will produce the correct answer on the first two rows, and the confidence values (cosine similarity between the output and the true attribute) will be 1 for both. As a result, the model will assign equal probabilities to both rules (even if only one of them is valid), rendering the probability of choosing the correct one equal to a coin toss.

Incorporating a validation term in the rule definition for *distribute three* can, in this case, solve the issue. Consider the functionally equivalent rule

$$v^{d3++} = \underbrace{(o_1 + o_2 + o_3) - x_1 - x_2}_{\text{execution}} + \underbrace{(o_1 + o_2 + o_3) - (o_1 + o_4 + x_1)}_{\text{validation}}.$$

The last two additional terms only cancel out when the sum of the elements of the first context row is equal to the sum of the elements of the first column, which is a property that is always verified for *distribute three* but not for the other RPM rules. Hence, using v^{d3++} instead of v^{d3} the model will be able to rule it out from the list of valid rules, correctly putting all the probability mass into the *arithmetic plus* rule instead. Note that learning v^{d3++} would not have been possible only with the 6 terms available in Eq. 1.

Therefore, we claim that Eq. 6, even if still not optimal for selection, will increase the robustness of the model to RPM edge cases. However, the increase in expressiveness also comes at a cost in terms of the number of trainable parameters, which scales linearly with the number of terms of Eqs. 6.

3.3 Training Loss and Other Implementation Aspects

We follow the training recipe provided by Learn-VRF [39]. The training loss is defined as the inverse cosine similarity between the three predicted panels and their corresponding ground-truth

$$\mathcal{L} = 1 - \sum_{i=1}^{3} \cos\left(\mathbf{v}_a^{(i,3)}, \hat{\mathbf{v}}_a^{(i,3)}\right). \quad (7)$$

As in Learn-VRF, we set the number of rules to $R = 5$. A single set of rules is instantiated and shared between all RPM attributes. In previous works [39], the execution of the rules on the position and number attributes is performed in superposition, since either the number or the position attribute contributes to the generation of the answer. However, the superposition requires a preliminary binding operation with (trainable) key vectors to avoid the binding problem [47]. As a result, vector arithmetic is no longer supported on these attributes. We disentangle the two attributes, speculating that the trade-off between the additional noise introduced by the "unused" attribute, for which no rule is formally defined, and the increased computing accuracy will be significantly in favor of the latter. Removing the superposition also allows us to remove the keys used by the binding, which were *trainable parameters* in Learn-VRF and constituted the majority of parameters of the model (81%).

4 Results

4.1 In-Distribution (ID) Results

Table 2 shows the ARLC's in-distribution downstream accuracy on I-RAVEN compared to a range of neuro-symbolic and connectionist baselines. We present results for three different versions of ARLC: $ARLC_{progr}$, where the model's weights are manually programmed with RPM rules ($R = 4$, since *constant* can be considered as a special case of *progression*), $ARLC_{p\mapsto l}$, where the model is initialized with the programmed rules and then trained with gradient descent, and $ARLC_{learn}$, where the rules are learned from scratch from data.

ARLC achieves the best average accuracy on the in-distribution I-RAVEN dataset, improving the second-best result (NVSA [34], where the rules are hardwired into the model) by almost 5%, while having orders of magnitude fewer parameters than any other baseline model. ARLC also shows lower variance compared to the other baselines on almost every constellation.

Contrary to all the other methods (with the exception of PrAE [33]), ARLC is exclusively trained on the 2×2 constellation, effectively reducing the number of trained parameters and training samples by 85% (6/7). Its seamless adaptation to unseen constellations demonstrates the generality of the learned rules but prevents the model from outperforming the baselines in each single constellation.

Table 2. In-distribution accuracy (%) on the I-RAVEN dataset. The results for PrAE and ARLC are obtained training only on the 2×2 constellation and testing on all the others. Among the baselines, we replicate Learn-VRF; the other results are taken from [34]. The standard deviations are reported over 10 random seeds.

Method	Approach	Param.	Avg.	C	2×2	3×3	L-R	U-D	O-IC	O-IG
GPT-3 [48]	Selective	175b	86.5	86.4	83.2	**81.8**	83.4	84.6	92.8	**93.0**
MLP [39]	Predictive	300k	87.1	97.6	87.1	61.8	99.4	99.4	98.7	65.6
SCL [49]	Selective	961k	$84.3^{\pm 1.1}$	$99.9^{\pm 0.0}$	$68.9^{\pm 1.9}$	$43.0^{\pm 6.2}$	$98.5^{\pm 2.9}$	$99.1^{\pm 1.5}$	$97.7^{\pm 1.3}$	$82.6^{\pm 2.5}$
PrAE [33]	Predictive	n.a.	$71.1^{\pm 2.1}$	$83.8^{\pm 3.4}$	$82.9^{\pm 3.3}$	$47.4^{\pm 3.2}$	$94.8^{\pm 2.1}$	$94.8^{\pm 2.1}$	$56.6^{\pm 3.0}$	$37.4^{\pm 1.7}$
NVSA [34]	Predictive	n.a.	$88.1^{\pm 0.4}$	$99.8^{\pm 0.2}$	$96.2^{\pm 0.8}$	$54.3^{\pm 3.2}$	$100^{\pm 0.1}$	$99.9^{\pm 0.1}$	$99.6^{\pm 0.5}$	$67.1^{\pm 0.4}$
Learn-VRF [39]	Predictive	20k	$79.5^{\pm 4.3}$	$97.7^{\pm 4.1}$	$56.3^{\pm 7.3}$	$49.9^{\pm 2.8}$	$94.0^{\pm 5.0}$	$95.6^{\pm 5.0}$	$98.3^{\pm 2.5}$	$64.8^{\pm 3.4}$
$ARLC_{progr}$	Predictive	n.a.	$92.4^{\pm 0.0}$	$97.2^{\pm 0.0}$	$84.9^{\pm 0.0}$	$81.7^{\pm 0.0}$	$97.8^{\pm 0.0}$	$96.8^{\pm 0.0}$	$98.2^{\pm 0.0}$	$90.0^{\pm 0.0}$
$ARLC_{p\mapsto l}$	Predictive	480	$\mathbf{92.6^{\pm 0.2}}$	$97.6^{\pm 0.0}$	$84.7^{\pm 0.4}$	$80.7^{\pm 0.4}$	$98.5^{\pm 0.0}$	$97.9^{\pm 0.0}$	$98.5^{\pm 0.0}$	$90.3^{\pm 0.3}$
$ARLC_{learn}$	Predictive	480	$92.4^{\pm 1.5}$	$98.4^{\pm 1.5}$	$83.4^{\pm 1.6}$	$80.0^{\pm 2.1}$	$98.7^{\pm 1.2}$	$98.4^{\pm 1.4}$	$98.8^{\pm 1.2}$	$89.4^{\pm 1.6}$

Table 3. Ablation on the proposed improvements, as in-distribution accuracy (%) on the I-RAVEN dataset. The ablations are row-wise incremental.

Method	C	2×2	3×3	L-R	U-D	O-IC	O-IG	Avg.	Δ
Learn-VRF [39]	$97.7^{\pm 4.1}$	$56.3^{\pm 7.3}$	$49.9^{\pm 2.8}$	$94.0^{\pm 5.0}$	$95.6^{\pm 5.0}$	$98.3^{\pm 2.5}$	$64.8^{\pm 3.4}$	$79.5^{\pm 4.3}$	–
p/n sup, 2×2 train	$92.1^{\pm 6.5}$	$78.5^{\pm 5.4}$	$76.1^{\pm 5.3}$	$92.4^{\pm 6.8}$	$92.3^{\pm 6.6}$	$95.1^{\pm 4.2}$	$86.6^{\pm 3.4}$	$87.6^{\pm 5.5}$	+8.1
context-awareness	$95.2^{\pm 4.2}$	$81.9^{\pm 3.4}$	$78.9^{\pm 3.6}$	$95.1^{\pm 4.4}$	$94.9^{\pm 4.5}$	$96.6^{\pm 2.7}$	$88.8^{\pm 2.1}$	$90.2^{\pm 3.6}$	+2.6
12 terms (ARLC)	$\mathbf{98.4^{\pm 1.5}}$	$\mathbf{83.4^{\pm 1.6}}$	$\mathbf{80.0^{\pm 2.1}}$	$\mathbf{98.7^{\pm 1.2}}$	$\mathbf{98.4^{\pm 1.4}}$	$\mathbf{98.8^{\pm 1.2}}$	$\mathbf{89.4^{\pm 1.6}}$	$\mathbf{92.4^{\pm 1.5}}$	+2.2

ARLC produces close to perfect results on all the constellations without the position/number attribute (that is, C, L-R, U-C, and O-IC), strongly outperforming GPT-3 and PrAE. On the other hand, its accuracy degrades for the constellations that include the position/number attribute (that is, 2×2, 3×3, and O-IG). This degradation arises because of three specific rules on the position attribute: progression (corresponding to a circular bit-shifting operation), arithmetic plus (corresponding to the logical operation $a \vee b$), and arithmetic minus (corresponding to the logical operation $a \wedge \neg b$). These rules, which operate at the granularity of *objects*, cannot be easily captured by the model, which operates at the granularity of *panels*.

Finally, comparing the three proposed versions of ARLC, it is interesting to observe that ARLC$_{p \mapsto l}$ outperforms both its fully-learned and fully-programmed equivalents. The post-programming training allows to extend the knowledge of the model, rather than completely erasing it as shown in other settings [40], resulting in a monotonic increase in downstream accuracy.

Table 3 reports a thorough ablation on the novelties introduced in our framework. We can observe that the biggest contribution comes from removing the position/number superposition (+8.1%), which consistently increases the performance on the constellations involving these attributes. However, in all the other constellations we observe a consistent drop in accuracy, due to the evaluation of the model in the "transfer" setting (trained on 2×2, evaluated on all the others). This drop is compensated by the two novel components of the model, the context-awareness and the generalized rule template, which allow ARLC to match and outperform Learn-VRF on every constellation. Interestingly, they also contribute to reduce the variance of the results, suggesting that the two improvements might be increasing the model invariance to weight initialization.

4.2 Out-of-Distribution (OOD) Results

We validate ARLC's out-of-distribution generalization capabilities by following the same recipe proposed by Learn-VRF [39]: the model is trained on a subset of the rule-attributes pairs of the center constellation, and evaluated on its complement. As shown in Table 4, ARLC matches the OOD performance previously showed by Learn-VRF, attaining perfect accuracy on almost every unseen rule-attribute pair in the center constellation.

Table 4. OOD accuracy (%) on unseen rule-attribute pairs on I-RAVEN.

	Type			Size				Color			
	Const.	Progr.	Dist.3	Const.	Progr.	Dist.3	Arith.	Const.	Progr.	Dist.3	Arith.
GPT-3 [39]	88.5	86.0	88.6	93.6	93.2	92.6	71.6	94.2	94.7	94.3	65.8
MLP baseline [39]	14.8	14.9	30.2	22.8	75.0	47.0	46.6	56.3	60.5	44.4	48.9
Learn-VRF [39]	100	100	99.7	100	100	99.8	99.8	100	98.8	100	100
ARLC	100	98.6	99.7	100	100	99.6	99.6	100	100	100	99.8

5 Conclusions and Future Work

In this work, we proposed the Abductive Rule Learner with Context-awareness (ARLC), a model built on top of Learn-VRF [39] to enhance its downstream accuracy, interpretability, model size, and coherence. We conducted evaluations on the I-RAVEN dataset, demonstrating significant performance improvements compared to a diverse array of neuro-symbolic and connectionist baselines, including large language models, across both ID and OOD data. Furthermore, we presented empirical results on the programmability of the model and the generalization across different constellations of the I-RAVEN dataset.

A potential avenue for future research involves addressing the remaining challenge posed by this dataset, specifically, the development of suitable representations to allow the learnability of arithmetic and progression rules on the position attributes. These rules are currently impossible to learn for the model and would allow it to attain perfect accuracy on I-RAVEN. Additionally, extending the evaluation of ARLC to include other reasoning benchmarks, such as ARC [3], also represents a promising direction for further investigation. In fact, while the scope of this work was mostly focused on developing and studying a prototype that could solve RPM, the proposed general formulation of the problem could transfer to other settings that require relations and analogies data-driven learning. Furthermore, as our experiments on learning of top programmed knowledge show, our framework holds potential for application in scenarios where only a partial knowledge on the dynamics is available, and it is necessary to discover and build new knowledge on top of it.

Acknowledgments. This work is supported by the Swiss National Science foundation (SNF), grant 200800.

References

1. Bilker, W.B., Hansen, J.A., Brensinger, C.M., Richard, J., Gur, R.E., Gur, R.C.: Development of abbreviated nine-item forms of the Raven's standard progressive matrices test. Assessment (2012)
2. Cherian, A., Peng, K., Lohit, S., Smith, K.A., Tenenbaum, J.B.: Are deep neural networks smarter than second graders? In: 2023 IEEE/CVF Conference on Computer Vision and Pattern Recognition (CVPR), pp. 10834–10844. IEEE Computer Society, Los Alamitos, CA, USA (2023)
3. Chollet, F.: On the measure of intelligence. arXiv preprint arXiv:1911.01547 (2019)
4. Niedermayr, Y., Lanzendörfer, L.A., Estermann, B., Wattenhofer, R.: RLP: A reinforcement learning benchmark for neural algorithmic reasoning. OpenReview (2023)
5. Carpenter, P.A., Just, M.A., Shell, P.: What one intelligence test measures: a theoretical account of the processing in the Raven progressive matrices test. Psychol. Rev. (1990)
6. Raven, J., Court, J., Raven, J.: Raven's progressive matrices. Oxford Psychologists Press (1938)

7. Snow, R.E., Kyllonen, P.C., Marshalek, B., et al.: The topography of ability and learning correlations. Adv. Psychol. Human Intell. **2**(S 47), 103 (1984)
8. Snow, R.E., Lohman, D.F.: Toward a theory of cognitive aptitude for learning from instruction. J. Educ. Psychol. **76**(3), 347 (1984)
9. Benny, Y., Pekar, N., Wolf, L.: Scale-localized abstract reasoning. In: Proceedings of the IEEE/CVF Conference on Computer Vision and Pattern Recognition (CVPR) (2021)
10. Hu, S., Ma, Y., Liu, X., Wei, Y., Bai, S.: Stratified rule-aware network for abstract visual reasoning. In: Proceedings of the AAAI Conference on Artificial Intelligence (AAAI) (2021)
11. Małkiński, M., Mańdziuk, J.: Deep learning methods for abstract visual reasoning: A survey on Raven's progressive matrices. arXiv preprint arXiv:2201.12382 (2022)
12. Mitchell, M.: Abstraction and analogy-making in artificial intelligence. Ann. N. Y. Acad. Sci. **1505**(1), 79–101 (2021)
13. Zhang, C., Gao, F., Jia, B., Zhu, Y., Zhu, S.C.: Raven: a dataset for relational and analogical visual reasoning. In: Proceedings of the IEEE Conference on Computer Vision and Pattern Recognition (CVPR) (2019)
14. Wei, J., et al.: Emergent abilities of large language models. Trans. Mach. Learn. Res. (2022)
15. Hu, X., Storks, S., Lewis, R., Chai, J.: In-context analogical reasoning with pretrained language models. In: Proceedings of the 61st Annual Meeting of the Association for Computational Linguistics (Volume 1: Long Papers), pp. 1953–1969. Association for Computational Linguistics, Toronto, Canada (2023)
16. Webb, T., Holyoak, K.J., Lu, H.: Emergent analogical reasoning in large language models. Nat. Hum. Behav. **7**(9), 1526–1541 (2023)
17. Gendron, G., Bao, Q., Witbrock, M., Dobbie, G.: Large language models are not strong abstract reasoners (2024)
18. Wu, Z., et al.: Reasoning or reciting? exploring the capabilities and limitations of language models through counterfactual tasks (2024)
19. Camposampiero, G., Houmard, L., Estermann, B., Mathys, J., Wattenhofer, R.: Abstract visual reasoning enabled by language. In: 2023 IEEE/CVF Conference on Computer Vision and Pattern Recognition Workshops (CVPRW), pp. 2643–2647. IEEE Computer Society, Los Alamitos, CA, USA (2023)
20. Lewis, M., Mitchell, M.: Using counterfactual tasks to evaluate the generality of analogical reasoning in large language models. arXiv preprint arXiv:2402.08955 (2024)
21. Odouard, V.V., Mitchell, M.: Evaluating understanding on conceptual abstraction benchmarks. arXiv preprint arXiv:2206.14187 (2022)
22. Thomm, J., Terzic, A., Karunaratne, G., Camposampiero, G., Schölkopf, B., Rahimi, A.: Limits of transformer language models on algorithmic learning. arXiv preprint arXiv:2402.05785 (2024)
23. Han, C., Mao, J., Gan, C., Tenenbaum, J., Wu, J.: Visual concept-metaconcept learning. In: Advances in Neural Information Processing Systems (NeurIPS) (2019)
24. Mao, J., Gan, C., Kohli, P., Tenenbaum, J.B., Wu, J.: The neuro-symbolic concept learner: Interpreting scenes, words, and sentences from natural supervision. In: International Conference on Learning Representations (ICLR) (2019)
25. Mei, L., Mao, J., Wang, Z., Gan, C., Tenenbaum, J.B.: FALCON: fast visual concept learning by integrating images, linguistic descriptions, and conceptual relations. In: International Conference on Learning Representations (ICLR) (2022)

26. Yi, K., Wu, J., Gan, C., Torralba, A., Kohli, P., Tenenbaum, J.: Neural-symbolic VQA: Disentangling reasoning from vision and language understanding. In: Advances in Neural Information Processing Systems (NeurIPS) (2018)
27. Schlag, I., Schmidhuber, J.: Learning to reason with third-order tensor products. In: Advances in Neural Information Processing Systems (NeurIPS) (2018)
28. Yi, K., Gan, C., Li, Y., Kohli, P., Wu, J., Torralba, A., Tenenbaum, J.B.: CLEVRER: collision events for video representation and reasoning. In: International Conference on Learning Representations (ICLR) (2020)
29. Schlag, I., Smolensky, P., Fernandez, R., Jojic, N., Schmidhuber, J., Gao, J.: Enhancing the transformer with explicit relational encoding for math problem solving. arXiv preprint arXiv:1910.06611 (2019)
30. Yang, Y., Sanyal, D., Michelson, J., Ainooson, J., Kunda, M.: A conceptual chronicle of solving raven's progressive matrices computationally. In: Proceedings of the 8th International Workshop on Artificial Intelligence and Cognition (2022)
31. Shah, V., Sharma, A., Shroff, G., Vig, L., Dash, T., Srinivasan, A.: Knowledge-based analogical reasoning in neuro-symbolic latent spaces. In: Proceedings of the 16th International Workshop on Neural-Symbolic Learning and Reasoning (NeSy) (2022)
32. Zhao, S., et al.: An interpretable neuro-symbolic model for raven's progressive matrices reasoning. Cogn. Comput. **15**(5), 1703–1724 (2023)
33. Zhang, C., Jia, B., Zhu, S.C., Zhu, Y.: Abstract spatial-temporal reasoning via probabilistic abduction and execution. In: Proceedings of the IEEE Conference on Computer Vision and Pattern Recognition (CVPR) (2021)
34. Hersche, M., Zeqiri, M., Benini, L., Sebastian, A., Rahimi, A.: A neuro-vector-symbolic architecture for solving raven's progressive matrices. Nat. Mach. Intell. **5**(4), 363–375 (2023)
35. Magnani, L.: Abductive Cognition: The Epistemological and Eco-Cognitive Dimensions of Hypothetical Reasoning. Springer, Berlin, Heidelberg (2009)
36. Gayler, R.W.: Vector symbolic architectures answer Jackendoff's challenges for cognitive neuroscience. In: Joint International Conference on Cognitive Science (ICCS/ASCS) (2003)
37. Kanerva, P.: Hyperdimensional computing: an introduction to computing in distributed representation with high-dimensional random vectors. Cogn. Comput. **1**(2), 139–159 (2009)
38. Plate, T.A.: Holographic reduced representations. IEEE Trans. Neural Netw. **6**(3), 623–641 (1995)
39. Hersche, M., di Stefano, F., Hofmann, T., Sebastian, A., Rahimi, A.: Probabilistic abduction for visual abstract reasoning via learning rules in vector-symbolic architectures. In: The 3rd Workshop on Mathematical Reasoning and AI at NeurIPS 2023 (2023)
40. Wu, X., Zhang, X., Shu, X.: Cognitive deficit of deep learning in numerosity. In: Proceedings of the Thirty-Third AAAI Conference on Artificial Intelligence. AAAI Press (2019)
41. Kleyko, D., Rachkovskij, D.A., Osipov, E., Rahimi, A.: A survey on hyperdimensional computing aka vector symbolic architectures, part I: models and data transformations. ACM Comput. Surv. (2022)
42. Hu, X., Storks, S., Lewis, R.L., Chai, J.: In-context analogical reasoning with pre-trained language models. In: Proceedings of the 61st Annual Meeting of the Association for Computational Linguistics (Long Paper) (2023)
43. Hersche, M., et al.: Factorizers for distributed sparse block codes. arXiv preprint arXiv:2303.13957 (2023)

44. Plate, T.A.: Holographic Reduced Representations: Distributed Representation for Cognitive Structures. Center for the Study of Language and Information, Stanford (2003)
45. Chalmers, D.J., French, R.M., Hofstadter, D.R.: High-level perception, representation, and analogy: a critique of artificial intelligence methodology. J. Exper. Theoret. Artifi. Intell. **4**(3), 185–211 (1992)
46. Cheng, Y.: Context-dependent similarity. In: Proceedings of the Sixth Annual Conference on Uncertainty in Artificial Intelligence, UAI 1990, pp. 41-50. Elsevier Science Inc., USA (1990)
47. Greff, K., Van Steenkiste, S., Schmidhuber, J.: On the binding problem in artificial neural networks. arXiv preprint arXiv:2012.05208 (2020)
48. Brown, T., et al.: Language models are few-shot learners. In: Advances in Neural Information Processing Systems (NeurIPS), vol. 33, pp. 1877–1901 (2020)
49. Wu, Y., Dong, H., Grosse, R., Ba, J.: The scattering compositional learner: Discovering objects, attributes, relationships in analogical reasoning. arXiv preprint arXiv:2007.04212 (2020)

Learning to Solve Abstract Reasoning Problems with Neurosymbolic Program Synthesis and Task Generation

Jakub Bednarek[(✉)] and Krzysztof Krawiec

Institute of Computing Science, Poznan University of Technology, Poznan, Poland
jakub.bednarek@put.poznan.pl,
krzysztof.krawiec@cs.put.poznan.pl

Abstract. The ability to think abstractly and reason by analogy is a prerequisite to rapidly adapt to new conditions, tackle newly encountered problems by decomposing them, and synthesize knowledge to solve problems comprehensively. We present TransCoder, a method for solving abstract problems based on neural program synthesis, and conduct a comprehensive analysis of decisions made by the generative module of the proposed architecture. At the core of TransCoder is a typed domain-specific language, designed to facilitate feature engineering and abstract reasoning. In training, we use the programs that failed to solve tasks to generate new tasks and gather them in a synthetic dataset. As each synthetic task created in this way has a known associated program (solution), the model is trained on them in supervised mode. Solutions are represented in a transparent programmatic form, which can be inspected and verified. We demonstrate TransCoder's performance using the Abstract Reasoning Corpus dataset, for which our framework generates tens of thousands of synthetic problems with corresponding solutions and facilitates systematic progress in learning.

Keywords: Neurosymbolic systems · Program synthesis · Abstract reasoning

1 Introduction

Abstract reasoning tasks have a long-standing tradition in AI (e.g. Bongard problems [2], Hofstadter's analogies [6]). In the past, they have been most often approached with algorithms relying exclusively on symbolic representations and typically involving some form of principled logic-based inference. While this can be successful for problems posed 'natively' in symbolic terms (e.g. [6]), challenges start to mount up when a symbolic representation needs to be inferred from a low-level, e.g. visual, representation [2]. The recent advances in deep learning and increasing possibilities of their hybridization with symbolic reasoning (see Sect. 4) opened the door to architectures that combine 'subsymbolic' processing required to perceive the task with sound symbolic inference.

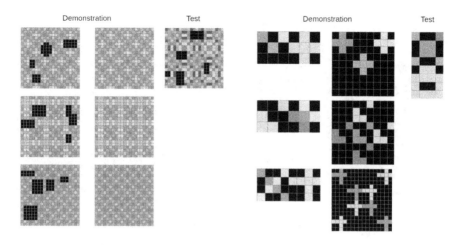

Fig. 1. Examples from the Abstract Reasoning Corpus Dataset.

This study introduces TransCoder, a neurosymbolic architecture that relies on programmatic representations to detect and capture relevant patterns in low-level representation of the task, infer higher-order structures from them, and encode the transformations required to solve the task. TransCoder is designed to handle the tasks from the Abstract Reasoning Corpus (ARC, [4]), a popular benchmark that epitomizes the above-mentioned challenges. Our main contributions include (i) the original neural architecture that synthesizes programs that are syntactically correct by construction, (ii) the 'learning from mistakes' paradigm to provide itself with a learning gradient by synthesizing tasks of adequate difficulty, (iii) an advanced perception mechanism to reason about small-size rasters of variable size, and (iv) empirical assessment on the ARC suite.

2 Abstract Reasoning Corpus

Abstract Reasoning Corpus (ARC) [4] is a collection of 800 visual tasks, partitioned into 400 training tasks and 400 testing tasks.[1] Each task comprises a few (usually 3, maximally 6) *demonstrations* and a *test* (Fig. 1). A demonstration is a pair of raster images, an input image and an output image. Images are usually small (at most 30 by 30 pixels) and each pixel can assume one of 10 color values, represented as a categorical variable (there is no implicit ordering of colors). The test is also a raster image, meant to be interpreted as yet another input for which the corresponding output is unknown to the solver.

For each ARC task, there exists a unique processing rule (unknown to the solver) that maps the input raster of each demonstration to the corresponding output raster. The solver is expected to infer[2] that rule from the demonstrations

---

[1] https://github.com/fchollet/ARC.
[2] Or, more accurately, *induce*, as the demonstrations never exhaust all possible inputs and outputs.

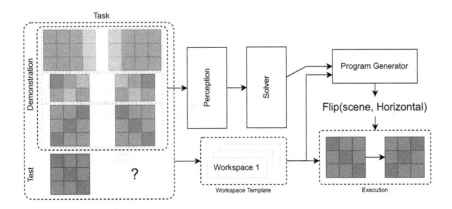

Fig. 2. The overall architecture of TransCoder.

and apply it to the test raster to produce the corresponding output. The output is then submitted to the oracle which returns a binary response informing about the correctness/incorrectness of this solution.

The ARC collection is very heterogeneous in difficulty and nature, featuring tasks that range from simple pixel-wise image processing, re-coloring of objects, to mirroring of the parts of the image, to combinatorial aspects (e.g. counting objects), to intuitive physics (e.g. an input raster to be interpreted as a snapshot of moving objects and the corresponding output presenting the next state). In quite many tasks, the black color should be interpreted as the background on which objects are presented; however, there are also tasks with rasters filled with 'mosaics' of pixels, with no clear foreground-background separation (see e.g. the left example in Fig. 1). Raster sizes can vary between demonstrations, and between the inputs and outputs; in some tasks, it is the *size* of the output raster that conveys the response to the input. Because of these and other characteristics, ARC is widely considered extremely hard: in the Kaggle contest accompanying the publication of this benchmark[3], which closed on the 28th of May 2020, the best contestant entry algorithm achieved an error rate of 0.794, i.e. solved approximately 20% of the tasks from the (unpublished) evaluation set, and most entries relied on a computationally intensive search of possible input-output mappings.

3 The Proposed Approach

The broad scope of visual features, object properties, alternative interpretations of images, and inference mechanisms required to solve ARC tasks suggest that devising a successful solver requires at least some degree of symbolic processing. It is also clear that reasoning needs to be *compositional*; e.g. in some tasks objects must be first delineated from the background and then counted, while in

---

[3] https://www.kaggle.com/c/abstraction-and-reasoning-challenge.

others objects need to be first counted, and only then the foreground-background distinction becomes possible. It is thus essential to equip the solver with the capacity to rearrange the inference steps in an (almost) arbitrary fashion.

The above observation is a strong argument for representing the candidate solutions as *programs* and forms our main motivation for founding TransCoder on *program synthesis*, where the solver can express a candidate solution to the task as a program in a *Domain-Specific Language* (DSL), a bespoke programming language designed to handle the relevant entities. Because (i) the candidate programs are to be generated in response to the content of the (highly visual) task, and (ii) it is desirable to make our architecture efficiently trainable with gradient to the greatest degree possible, it becomes natural to control the synthesis using a neural model. Based on these premises, TransCoder is a *neurosymbolic system* that comprises (Fig. 2):

- **Perception module**, a neural network that maps demonstrations to a latent vector z of fixed dimensionality,
- **Solver**, a (stochastic) network that maps the latent representation of the task z to the latent representation z' of the to-be-synthesized program,
- **Program generator**, (**Generator** for short) a recurrent network that maps z' to the program p represented as an Abstract Syntax Tree,
- **Program interpreter**, (**Interpreter** for short) which executes p, i.e. applies it to rasters.

In training, the Interpreter applies p independently to each of the input rasters of demonstrations and returns the predicted output rasters, which are then confronted with the true output rasters using a loss function. In testing, p is applied to the test raster and the resulting raster is submitted to the oracle that determines its correctness.

We detail the components of TransCoder in the following sections. For technical details, see Appendix A.

3.1 The Perception Module

The perception module comprises the *raster encoder* and the *demonstration encoder*.

The **raster encoder** is based on an attention module that allows processing rasters of different sizes, which is required when solving ARC tasks (see, e.g., the task shown in Fig. 2). However, raster sizes need to be taken into account, as they often convey crucial information about the task. To convey it to the model, we tag each pixel with the color *and* its (x, y) coordinates, the latter acting as a *positional embedding*. The image is flattened to a tagged sequence of tokens representing pixels (see the left part of Fig. 3). The tensor resulting from the Reduce block forms the fixed-length representation of the raster, subsequently fed into the demonstration encoder.

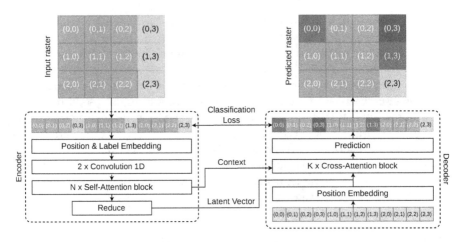

Fig. 3. The autoencoder architecture used to pre-train the raster encoder in Perception. Left: the encoder (used in TransCoder after pre-training). Right: the decoder (used only in pre-training and then discarded).

The raster encoder is pre-trained within an autoencoder framework, where the raster encoder is combined with a compatible decoder that can reproduce varying-length sequences of pixels (and thus the input raster) from a fixed-dimensionality latent (the right part of Fig. 3). The pre-training is intended to make feature extraction invariant to permutations of colors, while accounting for the black color serving the special role of background in a large share of tasks. To this end, the rasters derived from the ARC are treated as dynamic templates colored on the fly during training while preserving the distinctions of colors. As a result of pre-training, the raster encoder achieves the per-pixel reconstruction accuracy of 99.98% and the per-raster accuracy of 96.36% on the testing part of the original ARC.

The **demonstration encoder** concatenates the latent vectors obtained from the raster encoder for the input and output raster of a demonstration and passes them through a two-layer MLP. This is repeated for all demonstrations, and the output vectors produced by the MLP are chained into a sequence, which is then subject to processing with four consecutive self-attention blocks. The sequence of vectors produced in this process is averaged, resulting in a fixed-dimensionality (independent of the number of demonstrations) vector z representing a task.

3.2 Solver

The latent z produced by Perception forms a compressed representation of raster images in an ARC task. As it has been almost perfectly pre-trained via auto-association (see previous section), we expect it to contain the entirety of information about the *content* of the input raster. However, this does not mean that it conveys the knowledge sufficient for *solving* the task. The role of the Solver is to map z to a latent representation z' of the program to be generated. Technically, Solver is implemented as a two-layer MLP.

However, as in most programming languages, the relationship between the programs written in our DSL and their input-output behaviors is many-to-one, i.e. the same mapping from the input to output raster can be implemented with more than one program. As a result, the relationship between DSL programs and ARC *tasks* is many-to-many, i.e. a given task can be solved with more than one DSL program, and this very program can be a solution to more than one ARC task.

To account for this absence of one-to-one correspondence, we make the Solver stochastic by following the blueprint of the Variational Autoencoder (VAE, [8]): the last layer of the Solver does not directly produce z', but parameterizes the normal distribution with two vectors z_μ and z_σ and then calculates $z' = z_\mu + z_\sigma N(0,1)$ where $N(0,1)$ is generated by the random number generator. The intent is to allow z_μ to represent the centroid of the set of programs that solve a given task, while z_σ to model the extent of that set in the latent space.

3.3 Workspace

As many ARC tasks involve qualitative and combinatorial concepts (e.g. counting objects), we supplement the information provided by Perception with selected symbolic percepts inferred from the task independently from Perception, via direct 'procedural parsing' of images. We provide two data structures for that purpose:

- *Workspace Template* that contains the abstract placeholders for entities that appear in *all* demonstrations of a given task,
- *Workspaces* that 'instantiate' that template with concrete values derived from particular demonstrations.

The entries in a Workspace Template act as *keys* that index specific *values* (realizations) in the Workspace of a specific demonstration. For instance, the *Scene* symbol in the Workspace Template may have a different value in each Workspace. For the task shown in Fig. 2, the Workspace Template contains the *Scene* symbol, and its values in the first two Workspaces are different:

```
scene_0 = Region(   # first demonstration
    positions=[[0,0], [0,1], [0,2], ...],
    colors=[Green, Green, Blue, ...]
)
scene_1 = Region(   # second demonstration
    positions=[[0,0], [0,1], [0,2], ...],
    colors=[Brown, Green, Orange, ...]
)
```

The list of workspace keys is predefined and includes constants (universal symbols shared between all tasks), local invariants (values that repeat within a given task, e.g. in each input raster), and local symbols (information specific to a single demonstration pair, e.g. an input *Region*). For a complete list of available keys, see Appendix.

The workspaces require appropriate 'neural presentation' for the Generator of DSL programs. For a given task, all symbols available in the Workspace Template are first embedded in a Cartesian space, using a learnable embedding similar to those used in conventional DL. This representation is *context-free*, i.e. each symbol is processed independently. We then enrich this embedding with the information in the latent z' produced by the Solver (Sect. 3.2) by concatenating both vectors and processing them with a two-layer MLP, resulting in a *contextual embedding* of the symbol.

Moreover, the DSL's operations are also included in the Workspace; each of them is also embedded in the same Cartesian space so that the Generator can choose from them alongside the symbols from the workspace. In this way, the elements of the DSL are presented to the Generator (on the neural level) in the context of the given task, and symbols (such as 'red') may have a different embedding depending on the perception result. This is expected to facilitate alternative interpretations of the roles of particular percepts; for instance, while the black pixels should often be interpreted as the background, some tasks are exceptions to this rule.

3.4 The Domain-Specific Language

The DSL we devised for TransCoder is a typed, functional programming language, with leaves of AST trees fetching input data and constants, and the root of the tree producing the return value. Each operation (an inner AST node) is a function with a typed signature and implementation. The DSL features concrete (e.g. *Int*, *Bool*, or *Region*) and generic (e.g. *List[T]*) data types.

A complete DSL program has the signature *Region* → *Region*, i.e. it can be applied to the input of an ARC demonstration (or the query) and produce the corresponding output.

The current version of the DSL contains 40 operations, which can be divided into data-composing operations (form a more complex data structure from constituents, e.g. *Pair*, *Rect*), property-retrieving operations (fetch elements or extract simple characteristics from data structures, e.g. *Width*, *Area* or *Length*), data structure manipulations (e.g. *Head* of the list, *First* of a *Pair*, etc.), arithmetics (*Add*, *Sub*, etc.), and region-specific operations (high-level transformations of drawable objects, e.g. *Shift*, *Paint*, *FloodFill*). Our DSL features also higher-order functions known from functional programming, for example, *Map* and *Filter* which apply an argument in the form of a subprogram to elements of a compound data structure like a *List*. The complete definition of the DSL can be found in Appendix.

3.5 Program Generator

The Program Generator (Generator for short) is a bespoke architecture based on the blueprint of the doubly-recurrent neural network (see [1] for a simple variant of DRNN). The latent z' obtained from the Solver becomes the initial state of this network, which then iterates over the nodes of the Abstract Syntax Tree (AST) of the program being generated in the breadth-first order. For the root node of the AST, the return type is *Region* for the root node; for other nodes, it is determined recursively by the types of arguments required by DSL functions picked in previous iterations.

In each iteration, the Generator receives the data on the current context of AST generation, including the current size (the number of already generated nodes in the AST) and depth of the node in the AST, the parent of the current node, and the return type of the node. It is also fed with the set of symbols available in the workspaces (including the elements of the DSL), via the embedding described in the previous section. From this set, the Generator selects the symbols that meet the requirements regarding the type and the maximum depth of the tree. Then, it applies an attention mechanism to the embedded representations of the selected symbols. The outcome of attention is the symbol to be 'plugged' into the AST at the current location.

The Generator also determines the hidden state of the DRNN to be passed to each of the child nodes. This is achieved by merging the current state with a learnable embedding indexed with children's indices, so that generation in deeper layers of the AST tree is informed about node's position in the sequence of parent's children. The generation process iterates recursively until the current node requests no children, which terminates the current branch of the AST (but not the others). It is also possible to enforce termination by narrowing down the set of available symbols.

3.6 Training

TransCoder can be trained with reinforcement learning (RL) or supervised learning (SL). The RL mode is most natural for handling ARC tasks: the program p synthesized by the Generator is applied to the query raster and returns an output raster, which is then sent to the oracle. The oracle deems it correct or not and that response determines the value of the reward (1 or 0, respectively), which is then used to update the Generator. In this mode, we rely on the REINFORCE algorithm [10,11].

Unfortunately, the a priori odds for a generated program to solve the given task are minuscule. As a result, training TransCoder only with RL is usually inefficient, especially in the early stages, when the generated programs are almost entirely random: most episodes lead to no reward and, consequently, no updates of TransCoder's parameters. This motivates considering the SL mode, in which we assume that the correct program (target) is known. This allows us to directly confront the actions of the Generator (i.e. the AST nodes it produces) with the target program node-by-node, and apply a loss function that rewards choosing the right symbols at individual nodes and penalizes the incorrect choices. In SL, every training episode produces non-zero updates for the model's parameters (unless the target program has been perfectly generated).

In general, the specific program used as the target in this scenario will be *one of* many programs that implement the input-output mapping required by the demonstrations of the presented task (see Sect. 2). Deterministic models are fundamentally incapable of realizing one-to-many mappings, and the variational layer described in Sect. 3.2 is meant to address this limitation. Upon the (unlikely in practice) perfect convergence of TransCoder's training, we expect the *deterministic* output of the Solver (corresponding to z_μ) to abstractly represent the common semantic of all programs that solve the presented task, and the *variational* layer to sample the latents that cause the Generator to produce concrete programs *with that very semantics*.

The prerequisite for the SL mode is the availability of target programs; as those are not given in the ARC benchmark, we devise a method for producing them online during training, presented in the next section.

3.7 Learning from Mistakes

The programs produced by the Generator are *syntactically correct by construction*. Barring occasional run-time errors (e.g., applying a function to an empty list), a generated program will thus always produce *some* output raster for a given input raster; we refer to it as *response*. By applying such a program p (and arguably *any* syntactically correct program with the Region → Region signature) to the list I of input rasters of some task T, we obtain the corresponding list of responses O. We observe that the resulting raster pairs made of the elements of I and O can be considered as another ARC task T', to which p is the solution (usually *one of* possible solutions, to be precise). The resulting pair (T', p) forms thus a complete example that can be used to train TransCoder in SL mode, as explained in the previous section, where T' is presented to TransCoder and p is the target program.

This observation allows us to *learn from mistakes*: whenever the Generator produces a program p that fails the presented training task T, we pair it with the task T' created in the above way, add the *synthetic task* (T', p) formed in this way to the working collection S of *solved tasks*, and subsequently use them for supervised learning. Crucially, we expect T' to be on average easier than T, and thus provide the training process with a valuable 'learning gradient'. By doing so, we intend to help the model make progress in the early stages of training, when its capabilities fall far behind the difficulty of the ARC tasks.

To model the many-to-many relation between tasks and programs, we implement S as a relational database to facilitate the retrieval of all programs (known to date) that solve a given task, and vice versa—of all tasks solved by a given program. We disallow duplicates in S.

We start with $S = \emptyset$ and L filled with the original ARC tasks, and stage learning into cycles of *Exploration*, *Training*, and *Reduction* phases (Fig. 4).

Exploration. The purpose of this phase is to provide synthetic training examples needed in subsequent phases. A random task T is drawn from L and the Generator is queried on it. If the generated program p solves T, the pair (T, p) is added to S. Otherwise, it is checked whether the responses produced by p meet

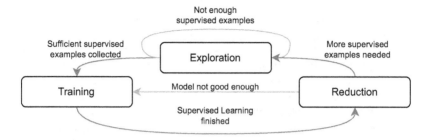

Fig. 4. The state diagram of TransCoder's training, including learning from mistakes.

basic criteria of nontriviality, i.e. are non-empty and depend on the input rasters (i.e. responses vary by demonstration). If T' passes this test, (T', p) is added to the S and L. This continues until enough new tasks have been added to S.

Training consists in applying SL to a random subset of tasks drawn from S. The execution of this phase ends after iterating through all training examples in the drawn subset.

Reduction starts with selecting a subset with known solutions (programs). Then, those tasks are grouped by solutions; a group of tasks with the same solution forms a *category*. Next, n categories are drawn at random. Finally, k tasks are drawn for each category. The tasks selected in this way form a working subset $L' \subset L$.

In the next step, TransCoder is evaluated on L'. If the program produced by the Generator solves a given task from L', the task is marked as *learned* and is removed from S (if present in S). Otherwise, the task is marked as *not learned* and is added to S (if not present in S)[4]. Finally, the results are grouped according to the category from which the tasks come and the average of solved tasks within each of them is calculated. If TransCoder reaches the average value of solved categories above the set threshold in the last iterations and stagnation occurs, we switch to the Exploration phase; otherwise, to the Training phase.

4 Related Work

TransCoder engages programs to process and interpret the input data, and thus bears similarity to several past works on neurosymbolic systems, of which we review only the most prominent ones. In synthesizing programs in response to input (here: task), TransCoder resembles the Neuro-Symbolic Concept Learner (NSCL, [9]). NSCL was designed to solve Visual Query Answering tasks [7] and learned to parameterize a semantic parser that translated a natural language query about scene content to a DSL program which, once executed, produced the answer to the question. The system was trained with RL. Interestingly,

---

[4] In this way, we allow for re-evaluation of tasks marked previously as *learned* and removed from S.

NSCL's DSL was implemented in a differentiable fashion, which allowed it to inform its perception subnetwork in training.

In using a program synthesizer to produce new tasks, rather than only to solve the presented tasks, TransCoder bears some similarity to the Dream-Coder [5]. DreamCoder's training proceeds in cycles comprising *wake*, *dreaming*, and *abstraction* phases which realize respectively solving the original problems, training the model on 'replays' of the original problems and on 'fantasies' (synthetic problems), and refactorization of the body of synthesized programs. The last phase involves identification of the often-occurring and useful snippets of programs, followed by encapsulating them as new functions in the DSL, which is meant to facilitate 'climbing the abstraction ladder'. The DreamCoder was shown to achieve impressive capabilities on a wide corpus of problems, ranging from typical program synthesis to symbolic regression to interpretation of visual scenes. For a thorough review of other systems of this type, the reader is referred to [3].

Table 1. RateSynth and RateARC in consecutive training cycles.

Cycle	1	2	3	4	5
RateSynth	1.72%	4.23%	9.81%	13.95%	21.66%
RateARC	1.00%	0.25%	0.75%	1.50%	2.00%

5 Experimental Evaluation

In the following experiment, we examine TransCoder's capacity to provide itself with a 'reflexive learning gradient', meant as continuous supply of synthetic tasks at the level of difficulty that facilitates further improvement. Therefore, we focus on the dynamics of the learning process.

Setup. To ensure a sufficiently large pool of training examples, each Exploration phase lasts until the set S contains at least 8192 tasks and 32 unique solutions. For the Reduction phase, we set the number of categories to be drawn for L' to $n = 64$, the number k of tasks to be drawn from each category to 32, the solving threshold of 30%, and the number of stagnation iterations to 10. Moreover, generated programs are limited to a maximum number of nodes of 64, a maximum depth of 8 and at most of 2 nestings of higher-order functions (each nesting is considered as a separate program and is also required to meet the above limits).

Metrics. The primary metric is the percentage of tasks solved from the testing subset of the original ARC (**RateARC**). However, because of the difficulty of this corpus, this metric is very coarse. To assess the progress in a more fine-grained way, we prepare a collection of 183,282 synthetic tasks by collecting them from several past runs of the method. This collection is fixed; the percentage of tasks solved from that collection will be referred to as **RateSynth**.

Results. Table 1 presents the metrics at the completion of consecutive training cycles (cf. Fig. 4). RateSynth monotonously increases over time, indicating steady progress of TransCoder's capacity of solving tasks. This positively impacts the RateARC, which achieves the all-high value of 2% at the end of the run, suggesting that the skills learned from the synthetic, easier tasks translate into more effective solving of the harder original ARC tasks.

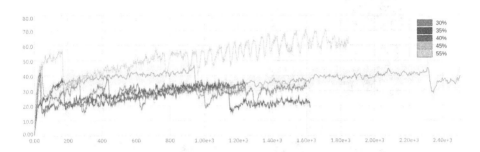

Fig. 5. Solving rate after each Reduction phase for TransCoder runs with different exploration and reduction parameters. The graph shows runs with different thresholds of the solved problem rate that trigger the transition from Reduction to Exploration.

Table 2. Performance of the snapshot of the model from a given cycle (row) on the synthetic examples collected in a given cycle (column). For instance, the model preserved in cycle 2 solves 0.47% of synthetic tasks created in cycle 3.

	Synthetic task set S from cycle				
TransCoder's snapshot from cycle	1	2	3	4	5
1	35.08%	0.56%	0.05%	0.00%	0.01%
2	33.35%	29.68%	0.47%	0.11%	0.11%
3	43.06%	30.44%	34.18%	1.35%	0.65%
4	43.53%	28.11%	30.33%	24.33%	1.84%
5	49.03%	31.22%	31.40%	30.74%	24.74%

Figure 5 shows the percentage of tasks solved estimated from a random sample drawn from the current S. Because S varies dynamically along training, this quantity is not objective, yet illustrates the dynamics of training. The sudden drops in performance occur right after the completion of the Exploration phase, which augments S with new tasks that the method cannot yet solve. Figure 6 shows examples of generated tasks with solutions, i.e. the (T, p) pairs added to S during training.

Table 2 provides yet another perspective: the performance of the snapshots of TransCoder trained for a given number of cycles (in rows) on Ss collected in

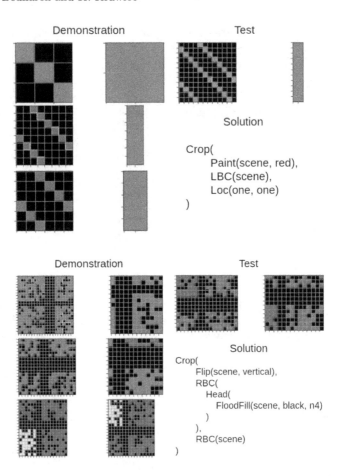

Fig. 6. Examples of (task, program) pairs synthesized by the model.

particular cycles (in columns).[5] Similarly to previous results, the table demonstrates overall consistent improvement of the model's performance. Furthermore, the metric decreases only twice within columns, which suggests that losing the capacity to solve tasks that were solved in the past occurs only occasionally.

6 Conclusions and Future Work

This study summarized our preliminary findings on TransCoder and illustrated its overall capacity to provide itself with a learning gradient. Crucially, the generative aspect of this architecture, combined with expressing candidate solutions in a DSL, allows the method to obtain concrete target DSL programs and so gradually transform an unsupervised learning problem into a supervised one. As

---

[5] Calculated off-line, after the completion of the run.

evidenced by the experiment, supervised learning facilitated in this way provides more informative learning guidance than reinforcement learning.

The modularity of the proposed architecture allows the model to be adapted for other types of data. In particular, the Solver and Generator modules are independent of the input data type, while the only type-specific module is Perception. Future work will include applying the approach to other benchmarks in different domains, developing alternative interchangeable DSLs, transferring abstraction and reasoning knowledge between datasets, and prioritizing the search in the solution space to solve the original ARC tasks.

Acknowledgments. This research was supported by TAILOR, a project funded by EU Horizon 2020 research and innovation program under GA No. 952215, by the statutory funds of Poznan University of Technology and the Polish Ministry of Education and Science grant no. 0311/SBAD/0726.

Appendix

Specification of the DSL

Tables 3, 4, and 5 present the complete definition of a DSL: available types, predefined symbols, and operations.

Table 3. The list of types available in the DSL.

Name	Description
Arithmetic	An abstract type that implements basic arithmetic operations such as addition and subtraction
Bool	Logical type; accepts True/False values
Color	Refers to the categorical value of pixels. It can take one of ten values
Comparable	An abstract type that implements basic operations that allow objects to be compared with each other
Int	Simple integer type
Loc	A location consisting of two integers
Connectivity	The type of neighborhood used by the FloodFill operation; possible values are n4 and n8
Direction	The type of direction used by the Rotate operation; possible values are cw (clockwise) and cww (counterclockwise)
Orientation	The type of direction used by the Flip operation; possible values are vertical and horizontal
Region	An object representing any list of pixels and their colors
List[T]	A generic type representing a list of objects of a compatible type
Pair[T, L]	A generic type representing a pair of objects of a compatible type

Table 4. The list of predefined symbol keys available in the DSL. The keys *Zero*, *One*, *Horizontal*, *Vertical*, *N4*, *N8*, *Cw*, and *Ccw* represent constant values and are always present in a Workspace. *Colors* are only available if they appear within a given task. *Scene* is a key relative to a specific pair of demonstrations. *FunctionalInput* is a special key used by higher-order functions.

Name	Type	Description
Zero	Int	A constant '0'
One	Int	A constant '1'
Horizontal	Orientation	A categorical value used for the Flip operation
Vertical	Orientation	A categorical value used for the Flip operation
N4	Connectivity	A categorical value used for the FloodFill operation
N8	Connectivity	A categorical value used for the FloodFill operation
Cw	Direction	A categorical value used for the Rotate operation
Ccw	Direction	A categorical value used for the Rotate operation
Black	Color	A categorical value of color from ARC
Blue	Color	A categorical value of color from ARC
Red	Color	A categorical value of color from ARC
Green	Color	A categorical value of color from ARC
Yellow	Color	A categorical value of color from ARC
Grey	Color	A categorical value of color from ARC
Fuchsia	Color	A categorical value of color from ARC
Orange	Color	A categorical value of color from ARC
Teal	Color	A categorical value of color from ARC
Brown	Color	A categorical value of color from ARC
Scene	Region	A Region representing input raster from an input-output demonstration pair
Functional Input	–	A special key available only during execution/generation of functional operation subprogram

Table 5. Definitions of the operations available in the DSL.

Name	Signature	Description
Add	(A: Arithmetic, A: Arithmetic) -> A: Arithmetic	Adds two objects of the same type inheriting from Arithmetic
Area	(Region) -> Int	Calculates the surface area of a region
Crop	(Region, Loc, Loc) -> Region	Cuts a subregion based on the top left and bottom right vertices
Deduplicate	(List[A]) -> List[A]	Removes duplicates from the list
Diff	(List[A], List[A]) -> List[A]	Performs a difference operation on two lists
Draw	(Region, Union[Region, List[Region]]) -> Region	Overlays a Region or list of Regions on the given input region
Equals	(A, A) -> Bool	Compares two objects of the same type
Filter	(List[A], (A->Bool)) -> List[A]	Filters the list of input objects based on the result of the subroutine run on each input element
First	(Pair[A, Type]) -> A	Gets the first element of the input pair

(*continued*)

Table 5. (*continued*)

Name	Signature	Description
Flip	(Region, Orientation) -> Region	Performs a vertical or horizontal flip of the input region
FloodFill	(Region, Color, Connectivity) -> List[Region]	Performs segmentation of the input Region using the Flood Fill algorithm and the background color and neighborhood type (n4 or n8)
GroupBy	(List[A], (A->B)) -> List[Pair[B, List[A]]]	Groups objects from the input list based on the results of the subroutine
Head	(List[A]) -> A	Gets the first element of the input list
Height	(Region) -> Int	Returns the height of the region
Intersection	(List[A], List[A]) -> List[A]	Returns the intersection of two lists
LBC	(Region) -> Loc	Returns the location of the left bottom corner
LTC	(Region) -> Loc	Returns the location of the left top corner
Len	(List[Type]) -> Int	Returns the length of the input list
Line	(Loc, Loc, Color) -> Region	Creates a single-color Region that represents a line between two points
Loc	(Int, Int) -> Loc	Location object constructor
Map	(List[A], (A->B)) -> List[B]	Performs the transformation operation of each element of the input list using a subroutine
MostCommon	(List[A], (A->B)) -> B	Returns the most frequently occurring object from the input list based on the value returned by the subroutine applied to the list elements
Neg	(Union[A, B: Bool]) -> Union[A, B: Bool]	Performs a negation operation on the input object
Paint	(Region, Color) -> Region	Colors the input region a solid color
Pair	(A, B) -> Pair[A, B]	The constructor of an object of type Pair
Pixels	(Region) -> List[Region]	Returns a list of pixels of the input region
RBC	(Region) -> Loc	Returns the location of the right bottom corner
RTC	(Region) -> Loc	Returns the location of the right top corner
Rect	(Loc, Loc, Color) -> Region	Creates a single-color Region representing a rectangle bounded by the input locations
Reverse	(List[A]) -> List[A]	Reverses the input list
Rotate	(Region, Direction) -> Region	Rotates the Input Region clockwise or counterclockwise
Scale	(Region, Union[Int, Pair[Int, Int]]) -> Region	Scales the input Region according to the integer argument
Second	(Pair[Type, A]) -> A	Returns the second element of the input pair
Shift	(Region, Union[Loc, Pair[Int, Int]]) -> Region	Shifts the input Region by an integer argument
Sort	(List[A], (A->Comparable) -> List[A]	Sorts the input list based on the result of the subroutine applied to the list
Sub	(A: Arithmetic, A: Arithmetic) -> A: Arithmetic	Subtracts two objects of the same type inheriting from Arithmetic
Tail	(List[A]) -> A	Gets the last element of the input list
Union	(List[A], List[A]) -> List[A]	Returns the sum of two input lists
Width	(Region) -> Int	Returns the width of the region
Zip	(List[A], List[B]) -> List[Pair[A, B]]	Creates a list of pairs of corresponding elements in the input lists

References

1. Alvarez-Melis, D., Jaakkola, T.S.: Tree-structured decoding with doubly-recurrent neural networks. In: International Conference on Learning Representations (2017). https://openreview.net/forum?id=HkYhZDqxg

2. Bongard, M.M.: The problem of recognition. M.: Nauka (1967)
3. Chaudhuri, S., Ellis, K., Polozov, O., Singh, R., Solar-Lezama, A., Yue, Y.: Neurosymbolic programming. Found. Trends® Program. Lang. **7**(3), 158–243 (2021). https://doi.org/10.1561/2500000049
4. Chollet, F.: On the measure of intelligence. arXiv preprint arXiv:1911.01547 (2019)
5. Ellis, K., et al.: Dreamcoder: bootstrapping inductive program synthesis with wake-sleep library learning. In: Proceedings of the 42nd ACM SIGPLAN International Conference on Programming Language Design and Implementation (PLDI 2021), pp. 835–850. Association for Computing Machinery, New York (2021). https://doi.org/10.1145/3453483.3454080
6. Hofstadter, D.R.: Fluid Concepts and Creative Analogies: Computer Models of the Fundamental Mechanisms of Thought. Basic Books, New York (1995)
7. Johnson, J., Hariharan, B., van der Maaten, L., Fei-Fei, L., Zitnick, C.L., Girshick, R.B.: CLEVR: a diagnostic dataset for compositional language and elementary visual reasoning. arXiv preprint arXiv:1612.06890 (2016)
8. Kingma, D.P., Welling, M.: Auto-encoding Variational Bayes (2022)
9. Mao, J., Gan, C., Kohli, P., Tenenbaum, J.B., Wu, J.: The neuro-symbolic concept learner: interpreting scenes, words, and sentences from natural supervision. arXiv preprint arXiv:1904.12584 [cs] (2019)
10. Sutton, R.S., Mcallester, D., Singh, S., Mansour, Y.: Policy gradient methods for reinforcement learning with function approximation. In: Advances in Neural Information Processing Systems. vol. 12, pp. 1057–1063. MIT Press (2000)
11. Williams, R.J.: Simple statistical gradient-following algorithms for connectionist reinforcement learning. Mach. Learn. **8**, 229–256 (1992)

Leveraging Neurosymbolic AI for Slice Discovery

Michele Collevati(✉)[id], Thomas Eiter[id], and Nelson Higuera[id]

Institute of Logic and Computation, Technische Universität Wien, Favoritenstraße 9-11, 1040 Vienna, Austria
{michele.collevati,thomas.eiter,nelson.ruiz}@tuwien.ac.at

Abstract. While remarkable recent developments in deep neural networks have significantly contributed to advancing the state-of-the-art in Computer Vision (CV), several studies have also shown their limitations and defects. In particular, CV models often make systematic errors on important subsets of data called *slices*, which are groups of data sharing a set of attributes. The *slice discovery problem* involves detecting semantically meaningful slices on which the model performs poorly, called *rare* slices. We propose a modular Neurosymbolic AI approach whose distinct advantage is the extraction of human-readable logical rules that describe rare slices, and thus enhances explainability of CV models. To this end, we present a methodology to induce rare slice occurrences in a model. Experiments on datasets from our data generator leveraging on Super-CLEVR show that the approach can correctly identify rare slices and produce logical rules describing them. The rules can be fruitfully used to generate new training data to mend model behavior or may be integrated into the model to enhance its inference capabilities. (The code for reproducing our experiments is available as an online repository: https://gitlab.tuwien.ac.at/kbs/nesy-ai/ilp4sd).

Keywords: Neurosymbolic AI · Slice Discovery · Inductive Logic Programming

1 Introduction

Computer Vision is a field of AI that enables computer systems to extract valuable information from digital images and videos. Following the remarkable recent developments of deep neural networks, significant achievements have been made in advancing state-of-the-art performance in various tasks [11], among which it is crucial to mention safety-critical applications, such as autonomous driving [24].

However, empirical studies, e.g. [20], show that CV models struggle to generalise to new data slightly different from those on which they were initially trained and tested. A related problem is the presence of important subsets of data, called *slices*, for which deep learning models often make systematic errors [7]. A slice is defined as a group of data sharing a set of attributes. For instance, regarding the task of identifying collapsed lungs in chest X-rays, it was observed in [19] that CV models base predictions on the presence of chest drains, which is a device used in treatment. Consequently, such models often make prediction errors on crucial slices where chest drains are absent, posing a significant risk of life-threatening false negatives.

Accurately detecting underperforming slices, called *rare* slices, allows one to carefully analyse such prediction errors and subsequently improve the model. However, identifying rare slices is a complex task, especially for high-dimensional data, e.g. images, where slices are very difficult to spot and extract; furthermore, it is non-trivial to understand what makes slices rare. In view of this, the *slice discovery problem* [7] has been described as mining unstructured input data for semantically meaningful slices on which the model performs poorly.

We propose to tackle the slice discovery problem with a Neurosymbolic (NeSy) AI framework [9], given the capabilities of Machine Learning (ML), and in particular Deep Learning (DL), for unstructured data classification and of Knowledge Representation and Reasoning (KRR) methods for transparent logical inference and explainability. In particular, we aim at a framework that allows one to experiment with different datasets and to study the efficacy of rule-based *slice discovery methods* (SDMs), both in terms of the semantic quality of the description of rare slices, and of the effect in reducing misclassifications. To this end, we leverage on Super-CLEVR [15], which is a well-known synthetic dataset that comes with a data generator for images with objects organised in hierarchical classes.

The main contributions of our work are summarised as follows:

1. We present our modular NeSy framework for slice discovery, in which the generation of training data, the classification of images, the generation of scene graphs describing the semantic contents of images, the learning of rules to detect rare slices, and the mending of the neural network model form a closed loop. To achieve these tasks, we provide a generator for datasets with rare slices that leverages on Super-CLEVR, which we use to train YOLOv5 [21]. We then translated YOLOv5's classifications into scene graphs in the language of Inductive Logic Programming (ILP) [4], which, depending on the ground truth, constitute positive and negative examples, i.e., where the neural network incorrectly resp. correctly classified the image. We then use an ILP system, ILASP [13], to obtain succinct logical rules that reveal which images are hard for the model to classify. Finally, the neural model is trained on its checkpoint with data generated using these rules.
2. While the detection of rare slices has been widely studied, the generation of datasets with rare slices has received less attention. Closest to our work, Eyuboglu et al. [7] considered the generation of rare slices in the context of object hierarchies, but did not take semantic relationships into account; this makes their method inapplicable to scenarios that we are considering. In contrast, we pursue a taxonomy-based approach and present a methodology for building datasets with rare slices.
3. We provide an implementation and experimental results for datasets that we generate to test for the efficacy of the rare slice generation, the rule extraction on the neural network's classification results, and the mending of the network model. The results show that our approach could reliably generate rare slices, and that rule learning delivered meaningful rules describing rare slices. Furthermore, feeding training data generated by using such rules to the network resulted in significant performance improvement, as misclassifications were almost eliminated.

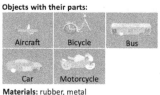

Fig. 1. The figure on the left shows images from Super-CLEVR [15] of vehicles made up of their parts characterised by various attributes, e.g. material, colour, and size. The middle and right figures show examples of Super-CLEVR renderings with generated questions.

Our framework allows one to automatically mine rules that pinpoint the deficiencies of a classifier neural network. Apart from generating training data, we emphasise that these rules could be integrated directly into the neural network [17]. The transparent nature of logical rules makes them highly interpretable and provides a basis for finding explanations from possible background information.

2 Related Work

Several studies [1, 19, 23] have shown that neural models often make systematic errors on critical data slices. Consequently, recent research has proposed automated SDMs aimed at identifying semantically meaningful slices in which the model exhibits prediction errors. An optimal SDM should automatically detect data slices containing *coherent* instances that closely correspond to a concept understandable by humans, and in which the model *underperforms*.

Previous work on the slice discovery problem has focused on datasets with tabular data. Slices are defined there using predicates, such as gender = Male. E.g., in [2] the *Slice Finder* system is proposed, which employs two different automated data slicing methods, viz. decision tree training and lattice searching. In [22], the authors present *SliceLine*, an exact enumeration algorithm that exploits effective pruning techniques to find problematic data slices.

Addressing the slice discovery problem becomes particularly challenging for unstructured input data, such as images. Recent studies have proposed methods for identifying slices in this context, and several of them rely on generative models. The *Domino* SDM [7] exploits cross-modal embeddings and an error-aware Gaussian mixture model to discover and describe coherent slices, while the *Spotlight* method [6] for finding systematic errors is based on the idea that similar inputs tend to have similar representations in the final hidden layer of a neural network. The method exploits this similarity by focusing on such representation space, aiming to identify contiguous regions where the model underperforms. In [8], pattern mining is used to identify frequent recurrent patterns in sentences on which a Natural Language Processing model fails.

From the above review, it appears that research on rare slices has been focusing on their detection but has paid less attention to generating them. In contrast to the SDMs above, our approach has the advantage we can generate controlled rare slices in datasets to then test model behavior on them.

3 Preliminaries

In this section, we give a short overview of Super-CLEVR and our modified dataset generator, and a short introduction to Inductive Logic Programming.

3.1 Super-CLEVR

Inspired by the original CLEVR [10], the Super-CLEVR dataset was designed to test the visual reasoning capabilities of AI systems. It comprises images, each featuring classes of vehicles such as motorcycles, cars, and aeroplanes. The classes are further divided into subclasses, which makes the dataset *hierarchical*, a characteristic crucial for the realisation of our SDM. For example, the motorcycle class contains subclasses chopper, cruiser, dirtbike, and scooter. The vehicles have a range of parts with different attributes like colour, size, and material. Each image is accompanied by a set of questions designed to test various aspects of visual reasoning, including types such as counting, existence, comparison, attribute identification, and spatial relationships as shown in Fig. 1. Super-CLEVR contains $\approx 30k$ images and 10 question-answer pairs for each of them.

The Super-CLEVR dataset generator employs an algorithm that uses Blender [3] to create a diverse set of images and corresponding questions. Each image is generated by randomly placing the vehicles in a three-dimensional *scene*. The properties of these objects are also randomly assigned within predefined categories. Spatial relationships are managed to ensure objects do not overlap unrealistically. Once an image is composed, the generator creates questions based on different types of reasoning tasks. The questions are formulated by randomly selecting objects and attributes in the image and constructing queries that require an understanding of the objects and their relations. This procedural generation ensures a wide variety of questions and scenes, overcoming possible human biases when creating datasets.

3.2 Inductive Logic Programming

Inductive Logic Programming (ILP) [18] is a subfield in the intersection of ML and KRR that focuses on learning logical descriptions from examples, utilising background knowledge (B) and sets of positive (E^+) and negative (E^-) examples. The learning process in ILP aims to find a hypothesis h from the hypothesis space H, such that $B \cup h \models E^+$, and $B \cup h \not\models E^-$, i.e., the background B plus the hypothesis h entails each positive example while it does not entail any negative example. It typically involves, starting from the known facts and relations contained in B, generating hypotheses consistent with E^+, testing them against E^- to ensure that no negative example is entailed, and refining them based on their fitness. A number of approaches and tools are available; for a comprehensive survey on ILP, we refer to [5].

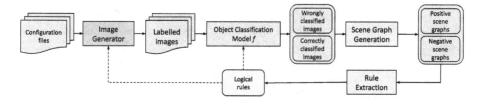

Fig. 2. Overview of the proposed neurosymbolic SDM architecture. The solid arrows show the data flow, while the dashed arrows symbolise the application of the extracted logical rules to improve classification performance, either by using them to generate specific training datasets or by incorporating them into the neural model.

Inductive Learning of Answer Set Programs (ILASP) [12] is a system designed to perform learning tasks in the context of Answer Set Programming (ASP). A key feature of ILASP is its ability to handle noisy data by introducing a penalty mechanism. This mechanism assigns a penalty to each example, which is a cost for not covering that example. The penalties are defined by a user-specified weight, denoted by the variable $\lambda > 0, \lambda \in \mathbb{N}$, which adjusts the importance of different examples. Higher penalties may discourage the system from including certain complex rules if simpler alternatives exist, thus balancing accuracy against simplicity in the learned model.

4 Neurosymbolic Framework for Slice Discovery

In order to realise a neurosymbolic SDM approach, we propose an architecture of a system as shown in Fig. 2. The system comprises several modules, shown as boxes, which process inputs in a pipeline such that from configuration data, synthetic datasets containing rare slices can be generated on which a neural model is trained and evaluated. A semantic description of the images is produced, from which rules for detecting rare slices are extracted. The rules can then be used to mend the neural model by providing suitable training data, closing the loop of model learning. In the following, we describe the tasks in the processing pipeline in more detail.

4.1 Data Generation

The first step in the pipeline is concerned with data generation, i.e., producing datasets that contain rare slices. As discussed above, this is a non-trivial problem that needs careful attention. To address this problem, we provide a methodology for generating datasets with rare slices, which will be detailed in Sect. 5.

At an abstract level, the task consists of creating a labelled dataset D, where elements are labelled with their properties. In our Super-CLEVR setting, D consists of pairs (I, L), where I is an image and $L = \{(b_1, h_1), \ldots, (b_n, h_n)\}$ is its label, where each b_i is a bounding box, i.e., a tuple (x^-, y^-, x^+, y^+) where $(x^-, y^-), (x^+, y^+)$ are the corners of the bounding box of some object o_i in the image, and h_i is in the underlying hierarchy $\mathcal{H}$ the parent class of o_i's class (e.g., motorcycle for dirtbike), $1 \leq i \leq n$. Objects are identified by their bounding boxes, i.e., we can view b_i as an object id.

To generate such datasets, we modified the data generator of Super-CLEVR that renders images, such that we can control the distribution of objects depending on their class membership in $\mathcal{H}$ to create datasets that contain controlled rare slices. Each dataset is split into a training, a validation, and a test part. The respective information is provided in configuration files. Our generator produces then a labelled dataset $D = \{(I_1, L_1), \ldots, (I_{N_s}, L_{N_s})\}$ with $N_s \approx n_s/\beta$ samples per split s, where β is a parameter for the average number of objects per image and n_s corresponds to the total number of objects per split.

The Super-CLEVR generator produces further attributes for the images, such as questions about them (which we disregard, as not needed), attributes of objects (e.g., colour, positioning), and relationships between objects (e.g., behind). This enriched description is the ground truth of the images, which can be used for synthetic scene graph generation and efficacy assessment. For simplicity, we have left out the relationships between objects and considered only their attributes. However, the approach should also work by considering relationships, which would allow for characterising rare slices with further precision but at the expense of higher computational cost. This extension is an interesting development to our work that we consider for the future.

Notably, the modified generator offers the user flexibility to generate datasets with controlled slices and custom hierarchies, which allows one to study how the model reacts and the efficacy of rule extraction.

4.2 Object Detection and Classification

The dataset generated in the previous step is fed into the neural model, and the classification results are collected. Specifically, the neural model is supposed to solve an object detection and classification problem: given an image I, it returns a set $f(I)$ of pairs $(\mathcal{B}, c)$, called *predictions*, where $\mathcal{B}$ is a bounding box, which is identified with an object o, and c is a class from the uppermost classes of the hierarchy $\mathcal{H}$; in case of YOLOv5, we get for each object o also the confidence cf in the class detection.

The function f is obtained by training the neural model on a dataset. For our aim, we use the training split of dataset D featuring rare slices from above, where we expect the model to underperform. After training, the model is run on the validation split of D and the images I in D are divided by the output $f(I)$ of the model into the sets E^+ and E^- of images that were incorrectly and correctly classified by f, respectively.

4.3 Scene Graph Generation

Scene Graph Generation (SGG) deals with generating a *scene graph* from an input image, which is a (labelled) directed graph $G = (V, E)$ with three types of nodes: object nodes, attribute nodes, and relation nodes. Objects in an image are located inside bounding boxes, and each object can have several attributes. Furthermore, different types of relations between pairs of objects, e.g. spatial relations like behind, may exist. Scene graphs provide a powerful semantic representation of images that can be exploited to understand visual data and spot their misclassification patterns. Different SGG methods and tools are available, mainly based on deep neural networks (see [14] for an overview).

```
#pos(s42@5, {hard(s42)}, {}, {
    contains(s42, o0).              % Config
    direction(o0, northwest).       #maxv(2). % Max. vars per rule
    shape(o0, chopper).             ...
    size(o0, small).                % Rule heads
    ...                             #modeh(hard(var(sce_id))).
}).                                 % Rule bodies
#neg(s41@5, {hard(s41)}, {}, {      #modeb(1, contains(var(sce_id),
    contains(s41, o0).                        var(obj_id)), (positive)).
    direction(o0, southeast).       ...
    shape(o0, truck).               % Constants
    size(o0, large).                #constant(shape, airliner).
    ...                             ...
}).
```

Fig. 3. The left side of the figure shows excerpts of two examples (positive and negative) with their background knowledge B in the language of ILASP. The right side of the figure shows an excerpt of the related mode bias. The complete file defining the mode bias can be found in the online repository.

In the realm of the Super-CLEVR setting, we can readily transform the sets E^+ and E^- of incorrectly resp. correctly classified images into suitable scene graphs G_{E^+} resp. G_{E^-}, by taking the bounding boxes (i.e., objects) along with the classes detected for them and supplementing their attributes. In that, we replace detected classes with appropriate subclasses. The latter are not taken from the neural model as it is not trained for such classification, but from the ground truth found in the dataset. Similarly, other attributes of the objects such as colour, size, material, and orientation. This allows us to construct correct scene graphs that are on the positive, negative set when the neural network correctly, incorrectly classifies them, respectively.

4.4 Rule Extraction via Inductive Logic Programming

We specify a *rule extraction problem* instance by translating each scene graph G_{E^+} resp. G_{E^-} into a logical representation ILP(G_{E^+}) resp. ILP(G_{E^-}), and then assembling with them the sets E_{ILP}^+ and E_{ILP}^- of positive and negative examples, respectively, and the background knowledge B describing semantic information about objects in the images. This is complemented with optional domain knowledge and auxiliary control information. Then, E_{ILP}^+, E_{ILP}^-, and B are fed into a rule extraction system. Notably, the positive examples E_{ILP}^+ are the input images for which the model made an incorrect classification, as we look for an explanation of why the model fails. The rule extraction system, for which we envisage using an ILP system, then outputs a set of rules as a hypothesis for rare slice detection.

Figure 3 shows excerpts of positive and negative examples and part of the related mode bias used. The representation is in the language of ILASP, a state-of-the-art ILP system. Its expressive language allows for the description of data and the specification of parameters and mode declarations to shape the search space. Specifically, ILASP allows for a penalty that can be set for each example, by coding sX@Y, where X

is a scene ID and Y is the cost for not covering that example. The positive example, denoted by #pos, is entailed by its background knowledge B, which is the third set {contains(s42, o0)...} listed, combined with the hypothesis h if there is at least one answer set that includes the ground atom hard(s42). The negative example, denoted by #neg, is not entailed if there is no answer set of its background knowledge B (again, the third set) combined with h that includes the hard(s41) atom. Background knowledge B for each example is derived from the ground truth of the images. While the hard/1 predicate was explicitly introduced in the ILASP encoding as a rule head to represent in which case a scene is difficult for the classifier, i.e. contains rare slices, depending on its composition of objects and attributes.

The mode bias in Fig. 3 specifies that the hard(sX) predicate must appear only as a rule head, and that the contains(sX, oZ) predicate, where X is a scene ID and Z is an object ID, can only appear in the rule bodies as a positive literal.

Given the complete input in Fig. 3, ILASP produces the following hypothesis h:

```
hard(V1) :- contains(V1,V2); shape(V2, dirtbike);
            direction(V2,southwest).
```

Informally, this rule expresses that a scene is considered difficult to classify for the model if it contains a dirtbike facing southwest.

4.5 Model Mending

The extracted rules can be used to mitigate the influence of rare slices on model performance, leading to a more robust model. This improvement can be achieved by augmenting the training data with additional samples generated from the rules. To this end, rules may be selected by the user to meet preferences or desiderata; this may, to some degree, already be injected in the rule learning stage, depending on the expressiveness of the rule extraction system.

5 Rare Slice Generation Methodology

Motivated by the drawbacks of existing methods for generating rare slices and the need for a reliable source of data to test our SDM, we present a taxonomy-based methodology to induce the occurrence of rare controlled slices in a model. For the application of this methodology, it is still necessary to have a hierarchical dataset in which each class consists of a set of subclasses. Compared to related work [7], the novelty is that we propose a heuristic that bases its intuition on the fact that a CV model is more likely to confound visually similar objects that belong to different subclasses. Based on this hypothesis, we define a taxonomy that separates similar subclasses into different classes for the classification task.

To generate rare slices, we construct a dataset D such that for a given class Y, the elements of one of its subclasses C occur with a very low probability α, where $0.01 \leq \alpha \leq 0.1$, similar to [7]. We use the following methodology we describe for the Super-CLEVR setting; applying it in similar application settings is suggestive.

Super-CLEVR already defines a class hierarchy, but in our approach, the generator accepts as input also custom hierarchies. For simplicity, we only consider two-level hierarchies $\mathcal{H} = \{h_1 : \bar{s}_1, \ldots, h_m : \bar{s}_m\}$, where each h_i defines a parent class and $\bar{s}_i$ is a list of subclasses for that parent class.

1. We create a slice configuration file containing a list $L = [c_1, \ldots, c_n], n \geq 1$, of class names, where each c_i, $1 \leq i \leq n$, is a subclass of one of the upper classes h_j (in Super-CLEVR, vehicle classes, e.g. motorcycle), i.e., c_i is in $\bar{s}_j$, e.g., dirtbike, according to the hierarchy $\mathcal{H}$. The subclasses may have further attributes that make the slices more specific. The subclasses in list L are defined as rare, while any other subclass is non-rare.
2. We associate with each rare subclass c_i a constant α drawn uniformly at random from $[\alpha_{\min}, \alpha_{\max}]$, where $0.01 \leq \alpha_{\min} \leq \alpha_{\max} \leq 0.1$ are manually defined. Higher α means a higher probability of creating a rare object.
3. A split configuration file is created defining the total number n_s of objects per split $s \in \{train, val, test\}$ (training, validation, or test) and whether the split should contain rare slices. We usually create rare slices in the training split but validate and test on splits without rare slices, i.e., with a uniform distribution of objects.
4. A configuration file is set up that contains the class hierarchy $\mathcal{H}$ together with all possible objects to be rendered including their attributes.
5. The configuration files are passed to the modified image generator, which calculates for each c_i and s the total number $n_{c_i,s} = \alpha \cdot n_s$ of rare objects to be generated, rounded to an integer. If $n_{c_i,s} = 0$, the process stops with an error that no rare objects can be generated with the given n_s and asks the user to increase it. Otherwise, $n_{c_i,s}$ (≥ 1) many rare objects are randomly distributed among the rendered images, where $n_s - n_s \cdot \alpha$ is the number of random non-rare objects to be generated.

Following the above steps, specific rare slices can be generated depending on the taxonomy under consideration. Furthermore, for each generated image, the Super-CLEVR generator produces the corresponding description consisting of the objects in the scene, their attributes, and the relationships between them. From these descriptions, scene graphs can be readily derived that can then be encoded in ILP examples (Fig. 3).

6 Experiments

We have evaluated our SDM approach in a series of experiments, which aimed to assess various aspects. We first describe the experimental setup and then present an overview of the results; all data and details are available in the online repository.

6.1 Experimental Setup

The evaluation platform is a workstation laptop with an Intel Core i7-12800H CPU, 32GB of RAM, and an NVIDIA RTX A2000 Laptop GPU with 8GB of dedicated memory. For the ILASP experiments, we set a timeout of 60 secs.

 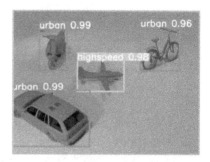

Fig. 4. The left figure shows a scene, based on the *Primary Purpose* taxonomy, in which vehicles corresponding to the "utility bicycle" and "pickup" rare slices are misclassified by YOLOv5 into the "offroad" and "urban" classes, respectively. In contrast, the right figure shows a different scene in which the "utility bicycle" is correctly classified into its "urban" class.

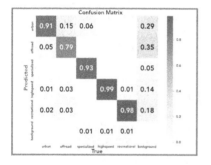 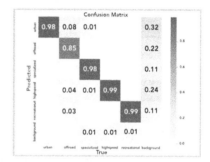

Fig. 5. Both figures refer to the *Primary Purpose* taxonomy. The left figure shows the confusion matrix from model validation after training on the dataset for the rare slices. The right figure shows the improvement after model mending for those classes where ILASP detected rare slices.

Taxonomies. In addition to the original Super-CLEVR taxonomy, we defined two other taxonomies based on heuristics separating similar subclasses into different classes to induce rare slice generation for testing our SDM implementation. The three taxonomies are listed below:

1. **Primary Purpose (PP)** is based on the classification of vehicles according to their primary usage. For example, "scooter" is in the "urban" class, which contains vehicles intended for urban transportation, while "dirtbike" is in the "offroad" class.
2. **Vehicle Type (VT)** classifies vehicles by their type. For example, "private jet" and "airliner" belong to the "aircraft" class, "suv" and "minivan" belong to the "car" class, etc. Note that this is the original taxonomy used in Super-CLEVR.
3. **Refined Primary Purpose (RPP)** is similar to **PP** but further refined by new classes such as "adventure", "family", and "heavyduty", while removing the class "specialized".

Datasets. We generated a training set of 3,000 vehicles for the three taxonomies. For that set, we selected four subclasses, "dirtbike", "articulated", "utility", and "pickup", and set their occurrence probability α in the dataset at 0.1. According to the taxonomy employed, these subclasses are the candidate rare slices; the remaining subclasses are uniformly distributed. We created validation and test sets of 1,250 vehicles each, where all subclasses are uniformly distributed to evaluate the model's behavior.

Neural Network. For each taxonomy, we trained YOLOv5 models on the training set running 80, 160, and 320 epochs. We then evaluated each model on the validation set and inspected the results.

Rule Extraction. We employed ILASP version 4 on the problem classes of each taxonomy to extract the rules that identify their rare slices. For using ILASP in the mode that supports noisy examples, we specified for each example its *penalty*, which is the cost of violating it. To narrow down the hypothesis space for meeting the time limit, we specified to omit constraints and negation as failure of predicates. We ran ILASP for different sampling sizes of the examples (25%, 50%, 75%, and 100%) to study the limits of scalability and precision as the amount of available data varies. Furthermore, we tested with different penalty values for the positive examples (2, 5, and 10) to observe how they affect the quality of the output result, and with different maximum numbers ml of literals (3 and 4) in rule bodies. All the previous values were chosen experimentally to test the capabilities and limitations of ILASP.

```
[24] hard(V1) :- contains(V1,V2); shape(V2,utility).
[4]  hard(V1) :- contains(V1,V2); shape(V2,sedan);
                 color(V2,red); direction(V2,southwest).
[1]  hard(V1) :- contains(V1,V2); shape(V2,sedan);
                 direction(V2,southwest).
```

Fig. 6. Rules extracted by ILASP for the "urban" class in the *Primary Purpose* taxonomy ranked by number of occurrences. Topmost is the rule correctly detecting the "utility bicycle" rare slice.

Rule Selection. For each experimental configuration based on the taxonomy, class, and parameter values considered, we obtained a set of rules. We filtered them, keeping only the rule with the highest number of occurrences. The rationale behind this strategy is supported by the fact that if most ILASP solutions for different experimental configurations agree on the choice of a rule, it means that such a rule is more likely to be the most appropriate in characterizing positive examples, i.e. rare slices, with respect to negative ones.

Model Mending. To assess the selected rules, we generated new datasets in which we restored the probabilities of those subclasses from the four selected ones that were detected by the extracted rules. We further trained the YOLOv5 models for each taxonomy with these new datasets, again for 80, 160, and 320 epochs. Last, we re-evaluate each model on the same validation set to see how the model's performance changes.

6.2 Slice Generation

Rare slices were successfully generated for all three taxonomies using our method, but not for all subclasses (as we wanted to see). Moreover, they impacted the inference capabilities of the YOLOv5 models. From the confusion matrices obtained after model validation, it can be seen that our taxonomy-based method was effective in inducing the presence of rare slices in the neural models. Specifically, three rare slices, "utility", "pickup", and "articulated" were created for the **PP** taxonomy for the classes "urban", "offroad", and "specialized", respectively. In contrast, for the **VT** taxonomy, only the "dirtbike" subclass was found to be a rare slice for the "motorcycle" class, thus showing that the other subclasses with low probability did not affect model performance such that they were considered rare slices. Finally, for the **RPP** taxonomy, "utility" was found to be a rare slice for the "urban" class, "dirtbike" for the "adventure" class, and "articulated" and "pickup" for the "heavyduty" class.

6.3 Results

Due to space restrictions, we focus on providing an overview of the results and pointing out interesting observations. We structure the presentation for slice discovery along the three taxonomies and then report on model mending. Tables 1, 2, 3 show the results for 160 training epochs; the other results can be found in the online repository. In the tables, ✓ stands for the successful production of slice rules, × stands for wrong or no rules obtained, and T for timeout.

Primary Purpose. For the "offroad" class, a sample of 25% every experiment yielded results quickly ($\approx$ 5 secs) for ml of 3 and $\approx$ 30 secs for ml of 4, delivering correct logical rules that increase in number with higher values of varied penalties. All experiments for sample sizes greater than 25% ran into timeout. For the "specialized" class, no rules were produced for penalty 2, while for penalties 5 and 10 runs concluded successfully. For all sample sizes, they terminated within timeout apart for sample size 100% and $ml = 4$. The class "urban" worked best, as seen from the confusion matrix and the extracted rules, see Figs. 5, 6. All 24 ILASP runs terminated within timeout.

Vehicle Type. Our experiments on **VT** show that we can mainly retrieve logical rules when the sampling range is between 50%-75%. When the sample size is 25%, we generally do not obtain rules, while with a sample of 100%, timeouts are predominant.

Refined Primary Purpose. For the "heavyduty" and "urban" classes, our SDM consistently gave positive results across all settings. The "adventure" class is mostly marked with crosses except for some parameters in the 75% and 100% sample sizes with penalties 5 and 10, where timeouts occur; the reasons behind this need further investigation. However, since the hypothesis space H is always defined the same, we can speculate that the reason for timeouts depends on the positive and negative examples considered for the different classes and taxonomies, making finding a solution more or less challenging.

Model Mending. For each taxonomy, from the confusion matrix we observed that the related YOLOv5 model has already been corrected after 80 epochs, i.e., no substantial improvement is gained by further training on data from the selected rules, meaning that the next level of epochs did not lead to further improvement. In particular, for the **PP** taxonomy the model mending worked really well as can be seen from the confusion matrix in Fig. 5, where the confidence values for classes "urban", "offroad", and "specialized" increased by an average of 6%; "urban" and "specialized" are now well-detected, while for "offroad" it significantly improved. For the **VT** taxonomy, model correction increased the confidence value of the "motorcycle" class from 91% to 99%. Finally, for the **RPP** taxonomy, significant improvements are observed for the "urban" and "heavyduty" classes. The former increased from 75% to 96%, the latter from being completely misclassified to 98%.

Table 1. Summary of results for the **PP** taxonomy.

Sample Size (%)	25						50						75						100					
Positive Penalty	2		5		10		2		5		10		2		5		10		2		5		10	
Max. Literals	3	4	3	4	3	4	3	4	3	4	3	4	3	4	3	4	3	4	3	4	3	4	3	4
Offroad	✓	✓	✓	✓	✓	✓	T	T	T	T	T	T	T	T	T	T	T	T	T	T	T	T	T	T
Specialized	×	×	✓	✓	✓	✓	×	×	✓	✓	✓	✓	✓	✓	✓	✓	✓	✓	×	T	✓	T	✓	T
Urban	✓	✓	✓	✓	✓	✓	✓	✓	✓	✓	✓	✓	✓	✓	✓	✓	✓	✓	✓	✓	✓	✓	✓	✓

Table 2. Summary of results for the **VT** taxonomy.

Sample Size (%)	25						50						75						100					
Positive Penalty	2		5		10		2		5		10		2		5		10		2		5		10	
Max. Literals	3	4	3	4	3	4	3	4	3	4	3	4	3	4	3	4	3	4	3	4	3	4	3	4
Motorcycle	×	×	×	×	✓	×	×	×	✓	✓	✓	✓	✓	T	✓	T	✓	T	T	T	T	T	✓	T

Table 3. Summary of results for the **RPP** taxonomy.

Sample Size (%)	25						50						75						100					
Positive Penalty	2		5		10		2		5		10		2		5		10		2		5		10	
Max. Literals	3	4	3	4	3	4	3	4	3	4	3	4	3	4	3	4	3	4	3	4	3	4	3	4
Adventure	×	×	×	×	×	×	×	×	×	×	×	×	T	×	T	×	T	×	T	T	T	T	T	T
Heavyduty	✓	✓	✓	✓	✓	✓	✓	✓	✓	✓	✓	✓	✓	✓	✓	✓	✓	✓	✓	✓	✓	✓	✓	✓
Urban	✓	✓	✓	✓	✓	✓	✓	✓	✓	✓	✓	✓	✓	✓	✓	✓	✓	✓	✓	✓	✓	✓	✓	✓

7 Conclusion and Future Work

We present a NeSy AI approach to address the slice discovery problem, providing a modular architecture and an implementation that leverages on the Super-CLEVR dataset and its synthetic data generator. The architecture connects data generation, a neural model for classification, and symbolic reasoning components for extracting rules from scene graphs, which are semantic representations of images, to detect rare slices that are misclassified. Furthermore, we have described a methodology for generating datasets in which rare slices occur, using a taxonomy-based approach. Our experiments showed that the datasets with rare slices could be generated reliably, and that the rule extraction approach using ILP could produce useful rules describing rare slices. Further training the neural model with data generated from these rules resulted in significant performance improvement.

The results we obtained are encouraging and demonstrate the potential of exploiting DL and KRR methods simultaneously for slice discovery. In this way, compact and human-readable logical rules can be obtained that improve the interpretability and explainability of a CV model under examination, also paving the way to advanced concepts such as causal and contrastive explanations.

Our ongoing and future work aims in different directions. A direction is to improve the current implementation and make it more user-friendly and accessible. Another option is the generation of native scene graphs, for which tools and methods, as mentioned in Sect. 4, will have to be examined and assessed; generating well-suited scene graphs by them is an interesting research issue. Then, as already mentioned, we plan to extend our work to consider relationships between objects, which would be an important added value in identifying rare slices. Furthermore, exploring besides ILASP further ILP systems as well as other rule learning approaches and systems, such as those provided by Statistical Relational Learning, e.g., LERND [16], is on our agenda.

Acknowledgments. The project leading to this research has received funding from the European Union's Horizon 2020 research and innovation programme under grant agreement No 101034440. Additionally, this work was supported by funding from the Bosch Center for AI (BCAI) in Renningen, Germany.

Disclosure of Interests. The authors have no competing interests to declare that are relevant to the content of this article.

References

1. Badgeley, M.A., et al.: Deep learning predicts hip fracture using confounding patient and healthcare variables. NPJ Digit. Med. **2**, 31 (2019). https://doi.org/10.1038/S41746-019-0105-1
2. Chung, Y., Kraska, T., Polyzotis, N., Tae, K.H., Whang, S.E.: Slice finder: automated data slicing for model validation. In: 35th IEEE International Conference on Data Engineering, ICDE 2019, Macao, China, April 8-11, 2019, pp. 1550–1553. IEEE (2019). https://doi.org/10.1109/ICDE.2019.00139
3. Community, B.O.: Blender - a 3D modelling and rendering package. Blender Foundation, Stichting Blender Foundation, Amsterdam (2018). https://www.blender.org/
4. Cropper, A., Dumancic, S.: Inductive logic programming at 30: a new introduction. J. Artif. Intell. Res. **74**, 765–850 (2022). https://doi.org/10.1613/JAIR.1.13507
5. Cropper, A., Dumancic, S., Evans, R., Muggleton, S.H.: Inductive logic programming at 30. Mach. Learn. **111**(1), 147–172 (2022). https://doi.org/10.1007/S10994-021-06089-1
6. d'Eon, G., d'Eon, J., Wright, J.R., Leyton-Brown, K.: The spotlight: a general method for discovering systematic errors in deep learning models. In: FAccT '22: 2022 ACM Conference on Fairness, Accountability, and Transparency, Seoul, Republic of Korea, June 21 - 24, pp. 1962–1981 (2022). ACM (2022). https://doi.org/10.1145/3531146.3533240
7. Eyuboglu, S., et al.: Domino: discovering systematic errors with cross modal embeddings. In: The Tenth International Conference on Learning Representations, ICLR 2022, Virtual Event, April 25-29, 2022. OpenReview.net (2022). https://openreview.net/forum?id=FPCMqjI0jXN
8. Hedderich, M.A., Fischer, J., Klakow, D., Vreeken, J.: Label-descriptive patterns and their application to characterizing classification errors. In: Chaudhuri, K., Jegelka, S., Song, L., Szepesvári, C., Niu, G., Sabato, S. (eds.) International Conference on Machine Learning, ICML 2022, 17-23 July 2022, Baltimore, Maryland, USA. Proceedings of Machine Learning Research, vol. 162, pp. 8691–8707. PMLR (2022). https://proceedings.mlr.press/v162/hedderich22a.html
9. Hitzler, P., Sarker, M.K. (eds.): Neuro-Symbolic Artificial Intelligence: The State of the Art, Frontiers in Artificial Intelligence and Applications, vol. 342. IOS Press (2021). https://doi.org/10.3233/FAIA342
10. Johnson, J., Hariharan, B., van der Maaten, L., Fei-Fei, L., Zitnick, C.L., Girshick, R.B.: CLEVR: a diagnostic dataset for compositional language and elementary visual reasoning. In: 2017 IEEE Conference on Computer Vision and Pattern Recognition, CVPR 2017, Honolulu, HI, USA, July 21-26, 2017, pp. 1988–1997. IEEE Computer Society (2017). https://doi.org/10.1109/CVPR.2017.215
11. Krizhevsky, A., Sutskever, I., Hinton, G.E.: ImageNet classification with deep convolutional neural networks. Commun. ACM **60**(6), 84–90 (2017). https://doi.org/10.1145/3065386
12. Law, M., Russo, A., Broda, K.: The ILASP system for learning Answer Set Programs (2015). www.ilasp.com
13. Law, M., Russo, A., Broda, K.: The ILASP system for inductive learning of answer set programs (2020). CoRR abs/2005.00904. https://arxiv.org/abs/2005.00904
14. Li, H., et al.: Scene graph generation: a comprehensive survey. Neurocomputing **566**, 127052 (2024). https://doi.org/10.1016/J.NEUCOM.2023.127052
15. Li, Z., et al.: Super-CLEVR: a virtual benchmark to diagnose domain robustness in visual reasoning. In: IEEE/CVF Conference on Computer Vision and Pattern Recognition, CVPR 2023, Vancouver, BC, Canada, June 17-24, 2023, pp. 14963–14973. IEEE (2023). https://doi.org/10.1109/CVPR52729.2023.01437
16. Merkys, I.: crunchiness/lernd: Lernd - implementation of ∂ilp (2020). https://doi.org/10.5281/zenodo.4294059, https://github.com/crunchiness/lernd

17. Moriyama, S., Watanabe, K., Inoue, K., Takemura, A.: MOD-CL: multi-label object detection with constrained loss (2024). CoRR abs/2403.07885. https://doi.org/10.48550/ARXIV.2403.07885
18. Muggleton, S.H.: Inductive logic programming. New Gener. Comput. **8**(4), 295–318 (1991). https://doi.org/10.1007/BF03037089
19. Oakden-Rayner, L., Dunnmon, J., Carneiro, G., Ré, C.: Hidden stratification causes clinically meaningful failures in machine learning for medical imaging. In: Ghassemi, M. (ed.) ACM CHIL '20: ACM Conference on Health, Inference, and Learning, Toronto, Ontario, Canada, April 2-4, 2020 [delayed], pp. 151–159. ACM (2020). https://doi.org/10.1145/3368555.3384468
20. Recht, B., Roelofs, R., Schmidt, L., Shankar, V.: Do ImageNet classifiers generalize to ImageNet? In: Chaudhuri, K., Salakhutdinov, R. (eds.) Proceedings of the 36th International Conference on Machine Learning, ICML 2019, 9-15 June 2019, Long Beach, California, USA. Proceedings of Machine Learning Research, vol. 97, pp. 5389–5400. PMLR (2019). http://proceedings.mlr.press/v97/recht19a.html
21. Redmon, J., Divvala, S.K., Girshick, R.B., Farhadi, A.: You only look once: unified, real-time object detection. In: 2016 IEEE Conference on Computer Vision and Pattern Recognition, CVPR 2016, Las Vegas, NV, USA, June 27-30, pp. 779–788 (2016). IEEE Computer Society (2016). https://doi.org/10.1109/CVPR.2016.91
22. Sagadeeva, S., Boehm, M.: SliceLine: fast, Linear-Algebra-based Slice Finding for ML Model Debugging. In: Li, G., Li, Z., Idreos, S., Srivastava, D. (eds.) SIGMOD '21: International Conference on Management of Data, Virtual Event, China, June 20-25, 2021, pp. 2290–2299. ACM (2021). https://doi.org/10.1145/3448016.3457323
23. Winkler, J.K., et al.: Association between surgical skin markings in dermoscopic images and diagnostic performance of a deep learning convolutional neural network for melanoma recognition. JAMA Dermatol. **155**(10), 1135–1141 (2019). https://pubmed.ncbi.nlm.nih.gov/31411641/
24. Zhang, M., Zhang, Y., Zhang, L., Liu, C., Khurshid, S.: DeepRoad: GAN-based metamorphic testing and input validation framework for autonomous driving systems. In: Huchard, M., Kästner, C., Fraser, G. (eds.) Proceedings of the 33rd ACM/IEEE International Conference on Automated Software Engineering, ASE 2018, Montpellier, France, September 3-7, 2018, pp. 132–142. ACM (2018). https://doi.org/10.1145/3238147.3238187

Author Index

A
Adam, Rebecca I-141
Agarwal, Sudhir II-222
Albinhassan, Mohammad I-195
Apriceno, Gianluca II-68
Arriaga, Octavio I-141
Aspis, Yaniv I-195

B
Badreddine, Samy I-219
Barua, Adrita II-109, II-132
Bednarek, Jakub I-386
Belle, Vaishak I-180, II-245, II-258
Bikakis, Antonis I-3
Bloem, Peter I-257
Bortolussi, Luca II-175
Brandão, Anarosa A. F. I-29

C
Campari, Tommaso I-166
Camposampiero, Giacomo I-296, I-370
Christou, Antrea II-41
Ciupa, Jessica I-180
Collevati, Michele I-403
Costa, Vicent II-165
Cozman, Fabio G. I-29
Cunnington, Daniel I-84

D
Dalal, Abhilekha II-109, II-149
Daniele, Alessandro I-166
Dave, Brandon II-41, II-51
de Campos Souza, Paulo Vitor II-68
De Raedt, Luc I-312
de Tarso P. Filho, Paulo I-29
Dellunde, Pilar II-165
Dickens, Luke I-3
Dierckx, Lucile II-80

Domingues, Antoine II-192
Dragoni, Mauro II-68
Draheim, Dirk II-305
Draper, Bruce II-60
Dubray, Alexandre II-80
Duppe, Benjamin II-32

E
Eckhoff, Magnus Wiik I-119
Eells, Andrew II-51
Eian, Martin I-119
Eiter, Thomas I-403
Ekaputra, Fajar J. I-279
Enström, Daniel II-207

F
Faghihi, Hossein Rajaby II-315
Ferfoglia, Irene II-175
Flügel, Simon I-101
Fraile-Parra, Diego II-165

G
Gawrysiak, Zuzanna II-24
Gerevini, Alfonso Emilio II-328
Ghunaim, Yasir II-89
Gilpin, Leilani H. II-291
Giunchiglia, Eleonora I-219
Glauer, Martin I-101
Grov, Gudmund I-119
Guo, Jichen I-141

H
Halvorsen, Jonas I-119
Hansen, Bjørn Jervell I-119
Hersche, Michael I-296, I-370
Higuera, Nelson I-403
Hitzler, Pascal II-51, II-109, II-132, II-149
Hoehndorf, Robert I-331, I-355, II-89

Houben, Sebastian I-141
Huber, Marco F. I-62

I
Iga, Vasile Ionut Remus II-277
Inoue, Katsumi I-47

J
Jain, Nitisha II-192
Järv, Priit II-305
Jiao, Ying I-312
Johansson, Moa II-207
José, Marcos M. I-29

K
Karimian, Hamid II-315
Kirchner, Frank I-141
Kjellberg, Viktor II-207
Kordjamshidi, Parisa II-315
Krawiec, Krzysztof I-240, I-386
Krishnaswamy, Nikhil II-60
Kufeldt, Abigail II-291

L
Lane, Ian II-291
Law, Mark I-84
Ławrynowicz, Agnieszka II-24
Lebiere, Christian II-60
Llugiqi, Majlinda I-279
Lobo, Jorge I-84, I-195

M
Malhotra, Sagar I-166
Manhaeve, Robin I-219
Manigrasso, Francesco I-257, II-14
Marra, Giuseppe I-312
Mashkova, Olga I-331
Maucher, Johannes I-62
Mavroeidis, Vasileios I-119
Meyers, Max II-291
Mileo, Alessandra II-3, II-98
Morra, Lia I-257, II-14
Mossakowski, Till I-101

N
Nafar, Aliakbar II-315
Nenzi, Laura II-175

Neuhaus, Fabian I-101
Nijssen, Siegfried II-80
Nirenburg, Sergei II-60
Nowinowski, Antoni I-240

O
Olivato, Matteo II-328
Onah, Daniel I-3

P
Panas, Dagmara II-258
Peñuela, Albert Meroño II-192
Phua, Yin Jun I-47
Piano, Luca II-14
Pirozelli, Paulo I-29
Putelli, Luca II-328

R
Rahimi, Abbas I-296, I-370
Raj, Kislay II-98
Rayan, Rushrukh II-109, II-149
Rossetti, Nicholas II-328
Russo, Alessandra I-84, I-195
Russo, Alessandro II-14

S
Sabou, Marta I-279
Sarker, Md Kamruzzaman II-109
Saveri, Gaia II-175
Schölkopf, Bernhard I-296
Schouten, Stefan I-257
Sebastian, Abu I-370
Serafini, Luciano I-166
Serina, Ivan II-328
Seth, Sohan II-258
Shakarian, Paulo II-60
Shimizu, Cogan II-41, II-51
Silaghi, Gheorghe Cosmin II-277
Simperl, Elena II-192
Sreepathy, Anu II-222
Stol, Maarten C. II-3

T
Takenaka, Patrick I-62
Tammet, Tanel II-305
Tang, Weizhi II-245
Terzić, Aleksandar I-296, I-370

Author Index

Thomm, Jonathan   I-296
Tummolo, Massimiliano   II-328

U
Uszok, Andrzej   II-315

V
Vakharia, Priyesh   II-291
van Krieken, Emile   I-219
Vasserman, Eugene Y.   II-109
Verrev, Martin   II-305
Vlachidis, Andreas   I-3

W
Wattenhofer, Roger   I-370
Wei, Hua   II-60
Widmer, Cara   II-132

X
Xu, Binxia   I-3

Z
Zhapa-Camacho, Fernando   I-331, I-355
Żywot, Agata   II-24

Printed in the USA
CPSIA information can be obtained
at www.ICGtesting.com
CBHW070533180924
14625CB00007B/161